THE BEST OF THE MUSIC MAKERS

Other Books by George T. Simon:

THE BIG BANDS

SIMON SAYS: THE SIGHTS AND SOUNDS OF THE SWING ERA

GLENN MILLER AND HIS ORCHESTRA

THE BIG BANDS SONGBOOK

THE FEELING OF JAZZ

THE BANDLEADER

DON WATSON STARTS HIS BAND

From Acuff to Ellington to Presley to Sinatra
to Zappa and 279 more of the most popular
performers of the last fifty years

The Best of the Music Makers

by **George T. Simon** and Friends

Foreword by Dinah Shore

DOUBLEDAY & COMPANY, INC., GARDEN CITY, NEW YORK

1979

ACKNOWLEDGEMENTS

Grateful acknowledgement is made for permission to include excerpts from the following copyrighted material:

"By Myself," by Howard Dietz and Arthur Schwartz, copyright © 1937 by DeSilva, Brown & Henderson, Inc. Copyright renewed, assigned to Chappell & Co. Inc. International Copyright secured. All rights reserved. Used by permission.

"Body & Soul," copyright © 1933 Warner Bros. Inc. Copyright renewed. All rights reserved. Used by permission.

"Bridge Over Troubled Water," © 1969, 1970 by Paul Simon. Used by permission. "This Land Is Your Land," words and music by Woody Guthrie. TRO - © Copyright 1956, 1958 & 1970 LUDLOW MUSIC, INC., New York, N.Y. Used by permission.

"Early 1970," words and music by Ringo Starr, copyright © 1970 by Startling Music Ltd. Used by permission.

Library of Congress Cataloging in Publication Data

Simon, George Thomas.
    The best of the music makers.

    1. Musicians—Biography. 2. Music, Popular (Songs, etc.)—History and criticism. I. Title.
ML385.S587   780'.92'2   [B]
ISBN: 0-385-14380- x
Library of Congress Catalog Card Number 78–22358

PICTURE-CREDITS

The photos that appear throughout this book are reproduced through the courtesy of the following:

P. 2, 3, Country Music Foundation. P. 5, Capitol Records. P. 7, *Crawdaddy.* P. 9, A&M Records. P. 11, CBS Records. P. 13, George T. Simon. P. 14, MCA Records. P. 15, *Crawdaddy.* P. 17, courtesy of Lucille Armstrong. P. 19, NBC. P. 21, RCA Records. P. 23, from the Frank Driggs collection. P. 25, Country Music Foundation. P. 26, RCA Records. P. 29, CBS Records. P. 30, Bill Hickock. P. 33, Fred Plaut. P. 35, 37, *Down Beat.* P. 40, from the Frank Driggs collection. P. 43, *Down Beat.* P. 44, Charles Stewart. P. 44, George T. Simon. P. 47, 49, Capitol Records. P. 50, Apple Records. P. 50, Capitol Records. P. 53, Apple Records. P. 55, *Down Beat.* P. 59, RSO Records. P. 61, Dick Sudhalter. P. 63, George T. Simon. P. 64, CBS Records. P. 67, *Crawdaddy.* P. 69, Rogers & Cowan. P. 71, Otto F. Hess. P. 72, *Crawdaddy.* P. 72, Chess Records. P. 75, 77, 78, CBS Records. P. 79, Charles Stewart. P. 81, MCA Records. P. 83, RCA Records. P. 85, the Lymans. P. 87, Charles Stewart. P. 89, George T. Simon. P. 91, 93, CBS Records. P. 95, Capitol Records. P. 97, from the Frank Driggs collection. P. 99, *Down Beat.* P. 101, NARAS*, photo by William Estabrook. P. 103, *Down Beat.* P. 105, CBS Records. P. 108, *Down Beat.* P. 108, RCA Records. P. 110, *Crawdaddy.* P. 112, RCA Records. P. 112, 115, CBS Records. P. 117, from the Frank Driggs collection. P. 119, 121, *Crawdaddy.* P. 122, *Down Beat.* P. 122, RCA Records. P. 125, from the Stanley Green collection. P. 128, Capitol Records. P. 131, *Crawdaddy.* P. 133, from the Frank Driggs collection. P. 135, RCA Records. P. 137, *Down Beat.* P. 139, RCA Records. P. 141, Paul Wilson. P. 142, NBC. P. 142, 147, *Down Beat.* P. 149, *Rock Magazine.* P. 151, CBS Records. P. 153, Atlantic Records. P. 155, CBS Records. P. 157, Reprise Records. P. 159, CBS Records. P. 163, RCA Records. P. 165, CBS Records. P. 166, *Crawdaddy.* P. 169, *Downbeat.* P. 171, RCA Records. P. 173, *Metronome.* P. 175, from the Frank Driggs collection. P. 177, Peter Simon. P. 179, Solters & Roskin. P. 181, *Metronome.* P. 183, *Down Beat.* P. 185, 187, from the Frank Driggs collection. P. 189, George T. Simon. P. 191, RCA Records. P. 193, Sam Shaw. P. 195, CBS Records. P. 197, courtesy of Helen Keane. P. 199, *Crawdaddy*—RCA photo. P. 203, RCA Records, photo by Katsuji Abe. P. 205, from the Frank Driggs collection, photo by Gene Kornman for 20th Century-Fox. P. 207, courtesy NARAS, photo by William Estabrook. P. 209, RCA Records. P. 211, *Down Beat.* P. 213, *Metronome.* P. 215, Peter Simon. P. 217, CBS Records. P. 220, *Crawdaddy,* photo by Sam Emerson. P. 221, Capitol Records. P. 223, *Down Beat.* P. 225, courtesy of Rogers & Cowan, photo by Robin Platzer. P. 227, 228, *Crawdaddy,* Atlantic Records photo. P. 231, CBS Records. P. 233, from the Martha Glaser collection. P. 235, George T. Simon. P. 237, Charles Stewart. P. 239, courtesy of Irving Ruskin. P. 241, CBS Records. P. 243, George T. Simon. P. 245, 247, CBS Records. P. 251, George T. Simon. P. 253, Country Music Foundation. P. 255, *Crawdaddy,* Columbia Pictures photo. P. 257, courtesy Lionel Hampton Enterprises. P. 259, courtesy of Fred Plaut. P. 261, courtesy of NARAS, Enterprise Records photo. P. 263, *Metronome.* P. 265, *Down Beat.* P. 267, from the Frank Driggs collection. P. 269, *Crawdaddy.* P. 271, *Metronome,* photo by William Kahn. P. 272, *Down Beat.* P. 272, RCA Records. P. 275, George T. Simon. P. 279, *Metronome.* P. 279, courtesy of NARAS, MCA Records photo. P. 281, from the Frank Driggs collection. P. 283, Charles Stewart. P. 285, MCA Records. P. 287, 289, CBS Records. P. 291, Jane Buchanan. P. 292, George T. Simon. P. 295, RCA Records. P. 297, MCA Records. P. 299, from the Frank Driggs collection. P. 301, courtesy of NARAS, A&M Records photo. P. 303, *Metronome.* P. 305, London Records. P. 307, CBS Records. P. 309, *Down Beat.* P. 311, CBS Records. P. 313, *Metronome.* P. 314, Capitol Records. P. 317, courtesy of *Crawdaddy,* ABC Records photo. P. 319, *Rock Magazine.* P. 321, Trigger Alpert. P. 323, Capitol Records. P. 325, *Crawdaddy.* P. 327, Fred Plaut. P. 329, CBS Records. P. 331, Charles Stewart. P. 331, *Metronome.* P. 334, CBS Records. P. 337, Charles Stewart. P. 338, courtesy of Photo Files. P. 341, RCA Records. P. 343, Courtesy of NARAS. P. 345, *Crawdaddy,* Playboy Records photo. P. 347, Peter Simon. P. 350, Bill Hickock. P. 353, Nat Shapiro, photo by George Brackman. P. 354, Mercury Records. P. 357, *Down Beat.* P. 359, Columbia Records. P. 361, *Crawdaddy.* P. 363, Saul Richman. P. 365, CBS Records. P. 367, 368, MCA Records. P. 371, courtesy of Marian McPartland. P. 373, Charles Stewart. P. 375, courtesy of NARAS, Dunhill Records photo. P.

*National Academy of Recording Arts and Sciences

379, RCA Records. P. 380, Charles Stewart. P. 383, courtesy Arista Records, photo by John Ruggero. P. 385, London Records. P. 387, 389, CBS Records. P. 391, Capitol Records. P. 393, courtesy of Lucille Armstrong, photo by Studio and Art. P. 395, from the Frank Driggs collection. P. 397, Atlantic Records. P. 399, 401, George T. Simon. P. 403, 405, CBS Records. P. 407, *Down Beat*. P. 409, 411, CBS Records. P. 413, Peter Simon. P. 415, Atlantic Records. P. 417, CBS Records. P. 419, Country Music Foundation. P. 422, George T. Simon. P. 423, RCA Records, photo by Leo Friedman. P. 425, Charles Stewart. P. 427, from the Frank Driggs collection. P. 429, RCA Records. P. 431, F. Rota. P. 433, Solters & Roskin. P. 435, from the Frank Driggs collection. P. 438, RCA Records. P. 441, *Metronome*. P. 443, *Down Beat*. P. 445, from the Frank Driggs collection. P. 447, *Down Beat*. P. 449, Capitol Records. P. 451, Jack Rael, photo by David Workman. P. 453, *Down Beat*. P. 455, RCA Records. P. 457, Capitol Records, photo by Rothschild. P. 461, courtesy of Mary Travers. P. 463, MGM Studios, photo for Verve Records. P. 465, Fred Plaut. P. 467, *Crawdaddy*. P. 469, from the Frank Driggs collection. P. 471, 473, 475, RCA Records. P. 477, from the Frank Driggs collection. P. 479, CBS Records. P. 481, *Crawdaddy*, Atlantic Records photo. P. 483, Capitol Records. P. 485, RCA Records. P. 487, from the Frank Driggs collection. P. 490, RCA Records. P. 493, CBS Records. P. 495, Capitol Records. P. 497, Fred Plaut. P. 499, RCA Records. P. 500, Peter Simon. P. 501, ABKCO Industries. P. 505, *Crawdaddy*. P. 507, courtesy of NARAS, Motown Records photo. P. 509, CBS Records. P. 510, George T. Simon. P. 510, George T. Simon, photo by Otto F. Hess. P. 513, CBS Records. P. 515, RCA Records. P. 517, MCA Records. P. 519, CBS Records. P. 521, *Metronome*, photo by G. Maillard Kesslere. P. 523, *Down Beat*. P. 525, George T. Simon. P. 527, Capitol Records. P. 529, NARAS. P. 531, Peter Simon. P. 534, Timothy White collection. P. 535, CBS Records. P. 537, 538, RCA Records. P. 538, courtesy of NARAS, NBC photo. P. 543, *Crawdaddy*. P. 545, 547, CBS Records. P. 549, RCA Records. P. 551, RCA Records, photo by Leo Friedman. P. 553, Columbia Records. P. 555, *Crawdaddy*, Warner/Reprise Records photo. P. 557, Capitol Records, Rothschild photo. P. 559, CBS Records. P. 563, *Down Beat*. P. 565, Peter Simon. P. 567, George T. Simon, photo by Otto F. Hess. P. 569, *Crawdaddy*. P. 571, Charles Stewart. P. 572, George T. Simon. P. 575, *Down Beat*. P. 577, from the Frank Driggs collection. P. 579, courtesy of NARAS, ABC Records photo. P. 580, *Metronome*. P. 583, RCA Records. P. 585, Charles Stewart. P. 587, *Down Beat*. P. 589, CBS Records. P. 591, *Metronome*. P. 593, Warner Brothers. P. 595, Charles Stewart. P. 597, from the Frank Driggs collection. P. 599, Peter Simon. P. 601, *Metronome*. P. 603, CBS Records. P. 605, Paul Hutcoe. P. 609, Capitol Records, photo by Robert Perkins. P. 611, MCA Records. P. 613, from the Frank Driggs collection. P. 614, CBS Records. P. 617, Country Music Foundation. P. 619, 621, Charles Stewart. P. 623, Country Music Foundation. P. 625, CBS Records. P. 628, *Crawdaddy*, Motown Records photo. P. 631, courtesy of NARAS, Epic Records photo. P. 633, from the Frank Driggs collection. P. 635, Warner/Reprise Records.

CONTENTS

(Articles with no author's credit were written by George T. Simon, who edited all the articles and co-authored some of those contributed by his friends.)

Foreword *by Dinah Shore*	xi
Introduction *by George T. Simon*	xiii
Roy Acuff	3
Julian "Cannonball" Adderley–*Dan Morgenstern*	5
The Allman Brothers–*Mary Campbell*	7
Herb Alpert–*Harvey Siders*	9
Julie Andrews–*Amy Lee*	11
The Andrews Sisters	13
Paul Anka–*Kristin White*	15
Louis Armstrong	17
Eddy Arnold–*Patty Hall*	20
Fred Astaire–*Carol Easton*	22
Chet Atkins–*Bill Ivey*	24
Gene Austin	26
Gene Autry–*Bill Ivey*	28
Charles Aznavour	31
Joan Baez–*Kristin White*	33
Mildred Bailey	35
Pearl Bailey–*John S. Wilson*	37
Josephine Baker–*John S. Wilson*	39
Charlie Barnet	42
Count Basie	45
The Beach Boys–*Kristin White*	47
The Beatles–*Joel Vance*	51
Sidney Bechet–*Dan Morgenstern*	55
The Bee Gees	57
Bix Beiderbecke–*Dan Morgenstern*	60
Harry Belafonte	62
Tony Bennett	65
George Benson	67
Bunny Berigan	70
Chuck Berry–*Mary Campbell*	73
Eubie Blake–*Amy Lee*	75
Blood, Sweat and Tears–*Dan Morgenstern*	77
Pat Boone	79
Connee Boswell and the Boswell Sisters	81
Al Bowlly	83
Fanny Brice–*Amy Lee*	85
James Brown–*Joel Vance*	87
Les Brown	89
Dave Brubeck	91
Cab Calloway	93
Glen Campbell	95
Eddie Cantor–*Amy Lee*	97
Hoagy Carmichael	99
The Carpenters–*Harvey Siders*	101
Benny Carter–*Dan Morgenstern*	103
Johnny Cash–*Patty Hall*	105
Ray Charles–*Mary Campbell*	107
Chubby Checker–*Joel Vance*	110
Maurice Chevalier–*Amy Lee*	113
Chicago–*Mary Campbell*	115
Charlie Christian–*Dan Morgenstern*	117
Eric Clapton–*Timothy White*	119
Rosemary Clooney	123
George M. Cohan–*Amy Lee*	125
Nat "King" Cole	127
Judy Collins–*Joel Vance*	130
Russ Columbo–*Amy Lee*	132
Perry Como	134
Eddie Condon–*John S. Wilson*	136
Sam Cooke–*Kristin White*	138
Jim Croce–*Mary Campbell*	140
Bing Crosby	143
Bob Crosby	147
Crosby, Stills, Nash (and Young)–*Mary Campbell*	149
Xavier Cugat–*John S. Wilson*	151
Bobby Darin–*Joel Vance*	153
Miles Davis–*Dan Morgenstern*	155
Sammy Davis, Jr.	157
Doris Day	159
John Denver	162
Neil Diamond–*Mary Campbell*	164
Fats Domino–*Joel Vance*	167
Jimmy Dorsey	168

Tommy Dorsey   170
Eddy Duchin   172
Jimmy Durante–*Kristin White*   174
Bob Dylan–*Carol Easton*   176
The Eagles–*Barbara Pepe*   179
Bob Eberly and Helen O'Connell   181
Billy Eckstine–*Dan Morgenstern*   183
Nelson Eddy and Jeanette
    MacDonald–*Amy Lee*   185
Cliff "Ukulele Ike" Edwards–*Joel
    Vance*   187
Roy Eldridge–*Dan Morgenstern*   189
Duke Ellington   191
Ruth Etting–*Amy Lee*   195
Bill Evans–*Dan Morgenstern*   197
The Everly Brothers–*Joel Vance*   199
Percy Faith–*Harvey Siders*   201
Arthur Fiedler   203
Gracie Fields–*Richard Sudhalter*   205
The 5th Dimension–*Carol Easton*   207
Eddie Fisher   209
Ella Fitzgerald   211
Roberta Flack   215
Lester Flatt and Earl Scruggs–
    Douglas Green   217
Fleetwood Mac–*Barbara Pepe*   219
Tennessee Ernie Ford–*Joel Vance*   221
Helen Forrest   223
Peter Frampton   225
Aretha Franklin–*Mary Campbell*   227
Judy Garland–*Carol Easton*   231
Errol Garner–*John S. Wilson*   233
Stan Getz–*Dan Morgenstern*   235
Dizzy Gillespie   237
Jean Goldkette–*Amy Lee*   239
Benny Goodman   241
Glen Gray   245
Woody Guthrie–*John S. Wilson*   247
Bobby Hackett   250
Merle Haggard–*Patty Hall*   252
Bill Haley–*Joel Vance*   254
Lionel Hampton   257
Coleman Hawkins–*Dan Morgenstern*   258
Isaac Hayes–*Carol Easton*   260
Dick Haymes   262
Ted Heath–*John S. Wilson*   264

Fletcher Henderson–*Dan
    Morgenstern*   266
Jimi Hendrix–*Dave Marsh*   268
Woody Herman   270
Earl Hines–*John S. Wilson*   271
Billie Holiday–*Dan Morgenstern*   275
Buddy Holly–*Joel Vance*   279
Libby Holman–*Richard Sudhalter*   281
Lena Horne   283
The Ink Spots   285
Burl Ives–*Carol Easton*   287
Mahalia Jackson   289
Harry James   291
Jefferson (Airplane) Starship–
    Mary Campbell   294
Elton John–*Mary Campbell*   296
Al Jolson   298
Quincy Jones   300
Spike Jones–*Kristin White*   303
Tom Jones–*Sy Johnson*   305
Janis Joplin–*Joel Vance*   307
Louis Jordan–*Dan Morgenstern*   309
Sammy Kaye   311
Stan Kenton   313
B. B. King–*John S. Wilson*   316
Carole King–*Carol Easton*   318
Wayne King   320
The Kingston Trio–*Joel Vance*   322
Gladys Knight and the Pips–*Joel
    Vance*   324
Andre Kostelanetz–*Richard
    Sudhalter*   326
Kris Kristofferson–*Joel Vance*   328
Gene Krupa   330
Kay Kyser   332
Frankie Laine   334
Lambert, Hendricks and Ross–*Dan
    Morgenstern*   336
Eddie Lang–*Amy Lee*   338
Mario Lanza–*Amy Lee*   340
Steve Lawrence and Eydie Gorme   343
Leadbelly–*Carol Easton*   345
Led Zeppelin–*Jim Jerome*   347
Peggy Lee   349
Michel Legrand   352
Jerry Lee Lewis –*Douglas Green*   354
Ted Lewis–*Amy Lee*   356

Liberace–*John S. Wilson*   358
Little Richard–*Joel Vance*   360
Guy Lombardo–*John S. Wilson*   362
Jimmie Lunceford   365
Loretta Lynn–*Douglas Green*   367
The Mamas and the Papas–*Harvey
    Siders*   370
Henry Mancini   373
Barry Manilow   375
Herbie Mann   378
Mantovani–*John S. Wilson*   380
Mary Martin–*Richard Sudhalter*   382
Johnny Mathis   384
Marian McPartland   386
Carmen McRae–*Carol Easton*   388
Johnny Mercer   390
Mabel Mercer–*John S. Wilson*   392
Ethel Merman–*Alfred E. Simon*   394
Bette Midler–*Sy Johnson*   397
Glenn Miller   399
Mitch Miller   403
Roger Miller–*Patty Hall*   405
The Mills Brothers   407
Charles Mingus–*Dan Morgenstern*   409
Liza Minnelli–*Kristin White*   411
Joni Mitchell–*Carol Easton*   413
Modern Jazz Quartet–*John S.
    Wilson*   415
Thelonious Monk–*Dan Morgenstern*   417
Bill Monroe–*Douglas Green*   419
Vaughn Monroe   423
Wes Montgomery–*Amy Lee*   425
Helen Morgan–*Sy Johnson*   427
Jelly Roll Morton–*Amy Lee*   429
Gerry Mulligan   431
Anthony Newley–*Amy Lee*   433
Red Nichols–*Dan Morgenstern*   435
Ray Noble   437
Red Norvo   440
Anita O'Day–*Dan Morgenstern*   442
Joe "King" Oliver–*Amy Lee*   444
Sy Oliver   446
Buck Owens–*Patty Hall*   448
Patti Page   450
Charlie Parker–*Dan Morgenstern*   452
Dolly Parton   454

Les Paul and Mary Ford   457
Peter, Paul and Mary   460
Oscar Peterson–*Amy Lee*   463
Edith Piaf–*John S. Wilson*   465
The Platters–*Joel Vance*   467
Ben Pollack   469
Elvis Presley–*Joel Vance*   471
Charley Pride–*Douglas Green*   475
Ma Rainey–*Dan Morgenstern*   477
Johnnie Ray   479
Otis Redding–*Joel Vance*   481
Helen Reddy–*Carol Easton*   483
Jim Reeves–*Patty Hall*   485
Django Reinhardt–*John S. Wilson*   487
Buddy Rich   489
Charlie Rich–*Douglas Green*   492
Tex Ritter–*Douglas Green*   494
Paul Robeson–*Amy Lee*   496
Jimmie Rodgers–*Patty Hall*   498
The Rolling Stones–*Joel Vance*   501
Linda Ronstadt–*Barbara Pepe*   504
Diana Ross and the Supremes–*Mary
    Campbell and Carol Easton*   506
Jimmy Rushing–*John S. Wilson*   508
Pee Wee Russell–*Amy Lee*   511
Santana   513
Sauter-Finegan   515
Neil Sedaka   517
Pete Seeger–*Joel Vance*   519
Ben Selvin–*Amy Lee*   521
Artie Shaw   523
George Shearing–*Carol Easton*   526
Dinah Shore   529
Carly Simon–*Loraine Alterman*   531
Simon and Garfunkel–*Timothy
    White*   533
Nina Simone–*John S. Wilson*   536
Frank Sinatra   539
Sly and the Family Stone–*Joel
    Vance*   543
Bessie Smith–*Dan Morgenstern*   545
Kate Smith–*Joel Vance*   547
Willie (the Lion) Smith–*Richard
    Sudhalter*   549
Hank Snow–*Douglas Green*   551
Jo Stafford   553
The Staple Singers–*Joel Vance*   555

Kay Starr–*Carol Easton* 557
Barbara Streisand–*Richard Sudhalter* 559
Art Tatum–*Amy Lee* 562
James Taylor–*Loraine Alterman* 564
Jack Teagarden 566
The Temptations–*Harvey Siders* 568
Sister Rosetta Tharpe–*John S. Wilson* 570
Claude Thornhill 572
Mel Torme 574
Sophie Tucker–*Amy Lee* 576
Ike and Tina Turner–*Joel Vance* 578
Joe Turner–*Amy Lee* 580
Rudy Vallee 582
Sarah Vaughan–*Carol Easton* 585
Joe Venuti–*Richard Sudhalter* 587
"Fats" Waller–*Joel Vance* 589
Fred Waring–*Amy Lee* 591
Dionne Warwicke–*Joel Vance* 593

Dinah Washington–*Dan Morgenstern* 595
Ethel Waters–*Amy Lee* 597
Muddy Waters–*Joel Vance* 599
Lawrence Welk 601
Paul Weston 603
Paul Whiteman 605
Margaret Whiting 608
The Who–*Joel Vance* 610
Lee Wiley–*John S. Wilson* 612
Andy Williams–*Sy Johnson* 614
Hank Williams–*Douglas Green* 616
Joe Williams–*Amy Lee* 619
Mary Lou Williams–*John S. Wilson* 621
Bob Wills–*Douglas Green* 623
Teddy Wilson 625
Stevie Wonder–*Carol Easton* 627
Tammy Wynette–*Douglas Green* 630
Lester Young–*Dan Morgenstern* 632
Frank Zappa 634

This is a fine and fascinating book. For shows like mine, where there is a constant demand for Music Makers and little-known facts about their careers and personalities, it is a treasure. There are large numbers of musical encyclopedias teeming with or, as I feel, drowning in data and dates and numbers. This lovely book is different because this one deals with the human aspects of the performer *and* it is written and edited by George Simon. To George Simon no one has ever been just a sound, although he is one of the most skilled in his field at recognizing and classifying an approach that is new and inventive— but the performer behind the music has always been his real bag. This singer knows as well as anyone the thrill of picking up *Metronome* magazine more years ago than I care to remember to find a big headline reading, "New Warbler Thrilling!" As simple as that—but of what great significance! A whole article about *me!* The me nobody knew—well, there really wasn't any reason for them to—I was an hour and a half out of Nashville and on my way back there if I didn't make it in the big town soon. They knew a little about me and my voice and my hopes and dreams after that. It was more than a beginning.

Writers and critics like George give us the confidence and courage to be ourselves and a performer must have the courage to be true to himself. The performer is his style, his sound and his experience and naturally it follows that if he is none of these things, he is a pale carbon copy of somebody else or someone too inhibited to have the confidence to express himself—a clone.

(Throughout this little piece you will notice that I'm using the generic "he" when all the world knows an enlightened person uses he or she—but I am too enlightened to fear for a moment someone may be confused about who I am and my feelings about my sisters *and* brothers *and* persons *and* inequities, etc., etc., etc. Music is the denominator—the great leveler—the equalizer—this touches us all in so many wonderful, exquisite ways—whatever your sex or side of the microphone.)

There is as wide a variety of individuals here as you will find on this continent. As George Simon puts it, from Acuff to Zappa, they were selected by experts who were invited to suggest entries for the book.

In all these personality pieces you will find a common factor. The artist who has survived is the one who has grown, not only in developing and pursuing his own style, but who is also capable of recognizing other performers' artistry and accomplishments and reveled in them. Perhaps, knowingly or unknowingly, some of those qualities that pleased him most became a part of his total musical experience and interpretation. This bit of selective "borrowing" only enhanced the original rather than diluted it.

The music today is so exciting—the rhythmic patterns, the lyric patterns— the forms are varied and infinite. As a performer who was raised in the 12 bar blues-jazz-gospel tradition and the 8 bar times 4 (or 16 times 2 bar) phrases of pop music, I am thrilled with the freedom of it all today.

It's an incurable romance. I am in love with music. I am in love with what it does for me and to me as a performer and as a fan. I am sure those of you who will be reading this book will be enjoying it for the same reason.

INTRODUCTION
by George T. Simon

"There have been all sorts of books about movie and sports stars, but there has never been one that covers all the biggest stars of popular music," the late Albert Leventhal, one of book publishing's giants and president of Vineyard Books, pointed out to me one day, "so how about doing one?"

What a great idea! "The biggest stars of popular music." That meant not merely jazz and swing and big bands, all of which I'd written about in some of my previous books, but also rock and country and folk music, rhythm and blues, gospel and nightclub and musical comedy and movie performers—in fact, all of popular music, including those that I'd never written about.

Whom to include? Immediately we began reeling off loads of names of our favorites. On and on we went. But it wasn't long before we realized that if we included them all, we'd run into the thousands, and that within one reasonably sized book we couldn't possibly do each of them justice. All we could possibly create would be a curt, cold encyclopedic reference work, which wasn't what either of us wanted. What we'd much prefer would be a book with a more personal approach, with some warmth and some depth, a book that, in addition to supplying the usual basic data, would delineate each subject's musical motivations, achievements and influences, as well as his or her personal feelings and ambitions. And that meant becoming much more selective in our choices about whom to include. It meant thinking in terms of hundreds, rather than thousands.

And so we agreed to limit our selections to the most important popular music performers of the past fifty years. And to help us choose these, we decided to form an advisory board of outstanding journalists in the pop music field. To each of them we sent a long list of well-known, outstanding performers and asked them to check off about three hundred of those they felt had "contributed most to popular music during the past fifty years. Creativity should of course be an important factor," we wrote them. "But so also should be *deserved* popularity, because this book is intended to interest, inform, and appeal to a large portion of the public." We also asked them to add any important names that we might have missed.

Fourteen of our "advisers" responded: Mary Campbell, who writes music features for the Associated Press; Charles Champlin, entertainment editor of the Los Angeles *Times;* Robert Christgau, popular music editor of the *Village Voice;* verteran musicologist and historian John Hammond; rhythm and blues and gospel critic and author Tony Heilbut; Michele Hush, a former editor of *Rock* magazine; Bill Ivey, executive director of the Country Music Foundation and Hall of Fame; Irv Lichtman, former editor of *Cash Box,* and more recently with *Billboard;* Neil McCaffrey, jazz commentator and former president of the Nostalgia Book Club; well-known rock critic and writer Josh Mills; jazz critic, author, and former *Down Beat* editor Dan Morgenstern; Nat Shapiro, author of numerous pop music anthologies; *Down Beat* publisher Charles Suber, and the New York *Times*'s veteran jazz critic, John S. Wilson.

Their responses were fabulous, for each had obviously done his or her homework. Some appended additional notations. "Impossible, but grand fun," wrote Champlin. "I found 250 'naturals.' Once beyond 'em, you might really pick them all." And Christgau noted, "I didn't check off as many names as you'd hoped. You can chalk that off to excessive conscience."

On the other hand, Wilson felt the list wasn't complete enough. So he added over a hundred more suggested entries, some of which found their way into the book. Suber also added more entries, sixty of them, adding a comment which I wish I'd included in my letter to the board: "Probably my personal prejudice is to creativity and to those persons who have contributed to the music we hear today—in other words, staying power."

"Staying power"—how important that is in determining the most important performers of the past fifty years! As it turned out, with the possible exception of some of the most recent artists who really haven't been around long enough to determine whether or not they will last, the majority of the committee members' selections display a great deal of staying power. This is especially true for some of the jazz artists, some of whom never did gain tremendous commercial success but who, through their uniquely creative talents, did make important contributions to and lasting impressions upon the course of popular music—in other words, helped to give the music itself "staying power."

Except for a few times, when I exercised my privilege as author and editor to add a few performers I felt just should not be overlooked, the entries in this book were selected by at least half the members of the advisory board. And to those fourteen board members, I would once more like to extend my deepest thanks for a difficult job well done, and to take them officially off the hook regarding any complaints that may well come in from those who feel so-and-so should or shouldn't have been included.

I would also like to thank another group, the outstanding authors, critics, and journalists whom I asked to contribute specific pieces that I felt they were especially qualified to write. Their contributions make up somewhat more than half of the book (I wrote the rest and also edited each of their pieces), and you can see exactly who wrote what if you will turn to the table of contents. My thanks go, alphabetically, to Loraine Alterman, who has contributed articles on contemporary pop music to the New York *Times* and other publications; Mary Campbell, music feature writer for the Associated Press; Carol Easton, a West Coast writer best known for *Straight Ahead,* her biography of Stan Kenton; three Nashvilleans, Doug Green, author of *Country Roots,* and Country Music Foundation executive Bill Ivey and his wife, free-lance writer Patty Hall; Jim Jerome, associate editor and popular music specialist on *People* magazine; Sy Johnson, musician, musical arranger, and contributor to various music magazines; Amy Lee, who worked with me for years on *Metronome* magazine and has been the *Christian Science Monitor*'s jazz and pop music critic for an even longer time; the prolific Dan Morgenstern, former editor of *Down Beat,* author of *Jazz People* and director of the Jazz Music Studies Institute at Rutgers University; Dave Marsh, a *Rolling Stone* editor; Barbara Pepe, a free-lance rock writer; Harvey Siders, who writes about pop music and jazz for the Los Angeles *Examiner;* Dick Sudhalter, former UPI correspondent, topnotch jazz musician, author of *Bix: Man and Legend,* and jazz critic of the New York *Post;* Joel Vance, a contributing editor to *Stereo Review* and author of *Fats Waller: His Life and Times;* popular music free-lance writer Kristin White; Timothy White, former senior editor of *Crawdaddy,* and now with *Rolling Stone,* and John S. Wilson, a regular pop music and jazz critic for the New York *Times.* And, of course a special thanks to my good friend of so many years, Dinah Shore, for her splendid foreword.

So much for the words in this book. Now for the pictures. I feel especially indebted to Roy Kohara of Capitol Records, Tim White then with *Crawdaddy* magazine, John Berg and Josephine Mangiaracina of Columbia Records, Chuck Suber and John Maher of *Down Beat,* George Osaki of MCA Records, oft-honored photographer Fred Plaut, who also engineered so many great recordings for Columbia, and Herb Helman and Marguerite Renz of RCA Records, all of whom opened their vast files to me and said, "Here, take anything you want!" Also of tremendous help were Bill Ivey and his compatriots at the Country Music Foundation, Frank Driggs, who specializes in those hard-to-get photos of early performers, Lou Gaudiosi of *Rock* magazine, my supertalented nephew, photographer Peter Simon, Allan Steckler of Apple Records, who came through with large selections of specific artists, and veteran jazz musician photographer Chuck Stewart. And there are others too: Mrs. Louis Armstrong, Jane Buchanan, Bill Hickock, Paul Hutcoe, Helen Keane, Walt Maguire of London Records, Robin McBride of Mercury Records, Bob Asen of *Metronome* magazine, Gerry Mulligan, the National Academy of Recording Arts and Sciences, Sy Oliver, Bill Levy of Polydor Records, Jack Rael and his associate, Corinne Shayne,

Saul Richman, Nat Shapiro, Dick Sudhalter, and Bob Defrin of Atlantic Records, all of whom graciously supplied me with photos.

Earlier, I mentioned the role of Albert Leventhal of Vineyard Books, whose Regina Hersey contributed so much fine editorial assistance, and where, after Albert died, Lucille Ogle and Albert's son, J. P. Leventhal, cooperated so wonderfully to make sure that the book would find just the right publisher. Fortunately along came Ray Roberts, with whom I had worked at Macmillan on *The Big Bands.* He had just joined Doubleday and he enthusiastically recommended *The Best of the Music Makers* as his first contribution to his new alliance. Ray's encouragement and expertise have proved invaluable, as have those of his assistant, Marie Comas, and of my copy editor, Glenn Rounds.

I would also like to thank the various performers who so willingly gave of their time when I suggested updating interviews. And once again, I'd like to thank my wife, Beverly, who not only gave me so much moral support throughout what proved to be a much more complicated venture than I had envisioned, but who also once again served as my "interpretive typist," as she followed all those arrows and cross-outs and scribbled notations to make sense out of many of my original pages of manuscript as well as my edited pages of some of the other contributors.

It's been quite a long time coming, this book has, and, as you can see, it took a lot of work by a lot of people to turn it out. I certainly hope the results will be as satisfying to you, the reader, as working with all those kind and talented people has been for me.

Geog. T. Sim

P.S.   To those music makers whose staying power (see page xiv) became apparent after this book was finished, my regrets that you were not included and my hope and desire that you will be included in subsequent editions.—G.T.S.

THE BEST OF THE MUSIC MAKERS

Fiddler Acuff

Executive Acuff

Roy Acuff

"The music is full of Christianity, sympathy and understanding."

"I'm just a country boy," multimillionaire Roy Acuff kept insisting to TV interviewer Dick Cavett in mid-January 1978. To which the slightly built, smooth-talking "King of Country Music" could have appended "and a singer, fiddler, songwriter, bandleader, music publisher, record executive, world traveler, onetime gubernatorial candidate, and probably the most successful businessman among the many country performers who have made themselves a mint of money from the homespun sounds that have turned Nashville, Tennessee, into thriving Music City, U.S.A."

At the age of seventy-five, the spry, spirited, vigorous Acuff was still driving himself regularly in his sporty Mercedes 450 SL to Nashville's spanking, new, ultra-modern Opryland, where he recently completed forty years of appearances on the top-rated "Grand Ole Opry" Saturday night radio show. Now country music's senior statesman and chief spokesman, he has been performing regularly on "Grand Ole Opry" since his February 1938 audition, when, instead of playing his fiddle, as scheduled, he "just reared back and sang it," and became the program's first singing star and, ever since, its most consistent performer.

Unlike other early country singers who sang mostly through their noses, Acuff learned to "sing from the pit of my stomach" by aping a sister who had been taking operatic singing lessons. His mother, who played piano and guitar, and his father, who played fiddle when not delivering sermons at the Maynard Missionary Baptist Church in East Tennessee, encouraged their five children to dabble in music. Roy started on Jew's harp, then went on to harmonica and eventually to a corny fiddle—it was actually made out of cornstalks! He also played numerous sports and was a thirteen-letter man in high school.

During a tryout in the New York Yankees rookie training camp, he suffered a paralyzing sunstroke, not while shagging flies but instead while catching fish! Forbidden to exercise in the hot sun, he turned in 1932 to fiddling and singing on cool nights with Doc Hauer's Medicine Show. The following year, he and some friends formed the Tennessee Crackerjacks, later called the Crazy Tennesseans, who gained a great deal of attention via a series of successful radio shows on a couple of Knoxville stations. One of the songs Roy sang, "The Great Speckled Bird," attracted executives of the American Record Company, soon to be bought by Columbia Records. On his first session for the company, Acuff recorded two of his all-time hits, "The Great Speckled Bird," which he sang, and "Wabash Cannonball," on which he whistled, and which he re-recorded as a singer nine years later.

In 1938, Roy moved to Nashville, already the heart of country music, where he began his forty-year affiliation with the "Grand Ole Opry." During those two full generations, his style has remained basically the same. His music still features unamplified sounds with a whining guitar, a fiddle, and of course his spirited, easily identifiable "country boy" voice. His attitude toward life hasn't changed much either. Staunchly conservative he has continued to promote old-fashioned American values ("I have no respect for hippies because I don't think they have respect for anything") and pure country music, which, he told author Melvin Shestack, "is down to earth, for the home—not to get all hepped up and smoke a lot of marijuana and go wild about. The music is full of Christianity and sympathy and understanding. It helps make people better." And in his case, thanks to his partnership with Nashville music mogul Wesley Rose in their Acuff-Rose music publishing and recording empire, "much richer."

For years, Acuff has spread the sound of country music all over the world. During World War II, his popularity had grown so big that, according to war correspondent Ernie Pyle, a Japanese battle cry consisted of "To hell with Roose-velt, to hell with Babe Ruth, to hell with Roy Acuff!" He was one of the first to be voted into the Country Music Hall of Fame. Still, according to country music historian Elizabeth Schlappi, he tends to deprecate his singing. "I'm a seller, not a singer. I don't claim to be a musician or a singer, but I like to think I'm an entertainer, a showman." And, of course, just a plain, old-fashioned, millionaire country boy!

(1903–   )

Julian "Cannonball" Adderley

"A brilliant player, with a big, bold sound."

His nickname, a corruption of "cannibal," referred to his huge appetite for food, but also conjured up the very accurate image of a rotund man, large in spirit and size, who moved through life with whirlwind force. Alto saxophonist, bandleader and catalyst, Julian "Cannonball" Adderley was one of the great popularizers of jazz in the post-bebop era, a vital force in the music from his sudden appearance on the national scene in 1955 until his untimely death from a stroke twenty years later.

He was a relatively late bloomer. He had led his own bands in high school in his native Florida, and while serving in the Army, he had opted for a teaching career and was employed as a high school band director in Florida. Then at the age of twenty-seven, he sat in with Oscar Pettiford's group at a New York nightclub in the summer of 1955 and made such an impression on his peers that he was promptly signed to a recording contract.

He soon formed a group with his younger brother, cornetist Nat Adderley,

Cannonball

and was publicized as the heir apparent to Charlie Parker, who had died a few months earlier. Though this was hyperbole and was distasteful to Cannonball himself, he was, nevertheless, a brilliant player, with a big, bold sound, great facility, expressive delivery, and a special gift for the blues. He matured further as a musician while playing with Miles Davis' popular and influential 1957–59 sextet. Then, after leaving the trumpeter, he quickly found the formula that was to bring him great success by way of a hit record, "This Here": a combination of "funk" (that is to say, earthy and basic blues flavor), modified bebop, and melodic lyricism. This hit was soon followed by his best-selling, Grammy award winner "Mercy, Mercy."

Unlike some of his contemporaries, Cannonball never attempted to disguise the enjoyment he found in making music. He was a great communicator, not only through his horn, but also through actions and words. At work in a club or on the concert stage, he was in constant motion, snapping his fingers in time to the music and introducing the musicians and numbers with lengthy but seldom boring monologues (his background as a teacher was evident in his desire to educate and inform his audiences and in his articulate speech). He never forgot that the essence of jazz is a strong, swinging rhythmic pulse. And, according to his associate, Laurie Goldstein, "he never lost his enthusiasm for music and people. He was the kindest man I've ever known."

Playing and writing music and leading a band was not enough to satisfy Cannonball's drive. He was active as a talent scout and record producer (among those he helped bring to prominence was guitarist Wes Montgomery), involved himself in civic affairs (he served enthusiastically on the jazz panel of the National Endowment for the Arts), worked effectively with young musicians as a clinician and lecturer, was seen in acting roles on TV, and, near the end of his life, composed and produced for records a musical drama, *Big Man*. His longtime producer and friend, Orrin Keepnews, aptly summarized Cannonball's personality: he was "one of the most completely alive human beings I had ever encountered."

(1928–1975)

The Allman Brothers

"One of the most musically exciting but personally disastrous of all rock groups."

The rock and roll era saw several successful individual musicians emerge from the South. But the first successful Southern rock band, one that blazed trails with its hard-driving, assertive, at times even pugnacious style, didn't appear until 1969. This was the Allman Brothers Band, one of the most musically exciting but personally disastrous of all rock groups.

From the start the band struggled. Buoyed by a strong belief in its music, it survived a grueling two-year schedule of five-hundred one-nighters, mostly opening shows for other, more important acts. Six band members and five roadies, traveling in a van with two mattresses in the back and some red pills to help them sleep, they just barely managed to make ends meet. Once, early in their

The Allman Brothers with Duane front center and Gregg to his right.

career on their way to play a date at the Fillmore, the eleven of them couldn't muster enough change to pay the toll on the Golden Gate Bridge. They were forced to park their van and beg for the needed coins.

But, unlike a lot of other successful bands, who later could look back and laugh at such a fiasco, the Allman Brothers were to suffer even greater and more personal tragedy.

Duane Allman had founded the group in Florida. After what drummer Butch Truchs called "the legendary Jacksonville Jam" of March 23, 1969—three hours of nonstop playing by Truchs, guitarist Dicky Betts, bass guitarist Berry Oakley, and drummer Jai Johanny Johanson—Duane exclaimed, "Man, this is it!" and phoned his younger brother Gregg. The Allman Brothers Band had been born.

The new band was closer to traditional, rural blues than most blues-based rock groups. Its most unusual qualities as a rock group were two guitarists playing lead (Duane and Dicky Betts) and two drummers. The band signed with manager Phil Walden, who started Capricorn Records in Macon, Georgia, just to record them, and they all moved to Macon.

In October 1971 they took their first vacation. On October 29, Duane Allman, twenty-four, swerved his motorcycle to miss a truck, lost control and was killed. The band, in grief, ended the vacation and, turning its loyalty from an individual leader to the band as a unit, started putting together new five-piece arrangements. They also finished their fourth album, *Eat a Peach,* the first one to receive national attention and acclaim.

When the band took another vacation the following August, rumors flew that it had broken up. Not so. Pianist Chuck Leavell was added and a fifth album was started. Then a year and thirteen days after Duane's death, twenty-four-year-old Berry Oakley's motorcycle collided with a Macon city bus and he died. To fight depression, the band quickly held auditions for a bass guitarist and hired Lamar Williams.

The new unit flourished—for a time at least. A star attraction, it played top rock concerts and arenas throughout the country. Despite the fact that it concentrated more on musicianship than showmanship, that it was a racially integrated group, that its emphasis was as much upon instrumental as vocal sounds, and that it had lost two of its most important members, it held on to its own fans and won new ones. But then came Gregg's much-publicized trouble with drugs, his marriage to Cher, and one-year sabbatical for the group. When the band did get together again, Gregg was optimistic. "People shouldn't listen to rumor," he said. "Rumor had us broken up more often than it had the Beatles back together."

But in 1976 the rumors proved to be right. After a trial involving the use of drugs, during which Gregg testified against one of the group's associates, the band members became to incensed with Allman that they departed en masse, and the most successful of all southern rock bands was no more.

Herb Alpert

"We're four salamis, two bagels, and one American cheese."

In 1962, inside a small garage turned into a recording studio, a twenty-seven-year-old Los Angeles trumpeter named Herb Alpert, who had been working as a studio musician and occasionally with jazz-oriented groups, was struggling with his new group to find a new sound for a tune called "Twinkle Star." With the tall, handsome, rather shy producer/musician was his personal partner, Jerry Moss. Each had put up $100 to form A&M Records (the "A" for Alpert, the "M" for Moss) with the idea of selling masters to established labels.

Alpert

Unable to find just the sound they wanted, they took a break and headed south for Tijuana, Mexico, where they went to a bull fight. In the midst of the excitement, Herb got his inspiration: "Ameriachi"—an Americanization of mariachi, the infectious sound of strolling Mexican bands.

Back in Los Angeles, Herb transformed "Twinkle Star" into "Lonely Bull" by combining Americanized pop sounds with Mexican rhythms. He added some pre-recorded, authentic bull-ring crowd noises and created an instant hit. The best-selling record also created a demand for the group's personal appearances. But even though it was not authentically Mexican (Herb quipped, "We're four salamis, two bagels, and one American cheese."), the Tijuana Brass's Latin appeal captivated so many audiences on both sides of the border that the septet became a pop dynasty that soon embraced not only recordings, but also TV specials and worldwide tours.

Seven years and forty-five million albums later (a figure that only the Beatles and Elvis Presley exceeded in the 1960s), Alpert suddenly called it quits—not only to the TJB, but also to his marriage and even his trumpet. His A&M company, with a roster of fifty artists, had made him a millionaire. But as for his musical life, "It wasn't fun anymore. I was tired, blown out, repeating myself. The music stopped meaning anything. For months at a time, I would just look at my horn, hardly able to play."

For the next five years, Herb kept looking for "the perfect trumpet technique," undergoing analysis, and partaking of his favorite pastime, surfing. Then he met Lani Hall, former lead singer of Brasil '66, "the lady in my life," who helped him find the road back. But perhaps the biggest inspiration came from an uncompromising recording by a younger trumpeter, Chuck Mangione, whose fresh approach proved once more that jazz could swing and still reach the masses. According to Herb, Mangione's "Ballad of the One-Eyed Sailor" was "the performance that made me want to get back into playing the horn again." In Mangione's performance a doubting Alpert found a reaffirmation of his own jazz-pop credo.

By the spring of 1974 Alpert had unveiled a new edition of his Tijuana Brass, still pleasing to his loyal old fans while attracting a host of new converts to his happy brand of pop jazz. The accent was less on the mariachi and more on the swing; less on written notes and more on suggestions to his musicians like "blow your tail off here!"

Looking back at the restrictions imposed upon his original musicians by strict adherence to the Ameriachi style, Alpert recently emphasized: "I want the band to be individually freer; I want more extended solos. I don't want anyone in the new Brass to hate the idea of playing." And none of them ever have, including the very emancipated, much happier, and decidedly more swinging Herb Alpert.

(1935–   )

> **"I have to be very careful about singing contemporary songs."**

In 1965 she was reported to be the top female box-office draw in both the United States and Britain. That was the year her career peaked with the smashing success of _The Sound of Music_, the film that challenged _Gone With the Wind_'s position as biggest money-maker of all time.

As the film's blithe convent-bred heroine, who sang to children on a Tyrolean mountainside, married an Austrian officer and mothered the Trapp Family Singers, Julie Andrews scaled her highest Alps of popularity.

Though famous for her dramatic and comedic abilities, Julie Andrews has also distinguished herself by her rich, full voice with its freak four-octave range. Beginning voice study at age ten, she built up a repertoire of arias and at age twelve stopped the show, _Starlight Roof Revue_, at the London Hippodrome with high F above high C in Titania's aria from _Mignon_. Julie soon joined

Julie

her parents' vaudeville act and there, in her mother's words, got "toughened up" for show business.

That toughening served this plucky, good-humored actress in good stead, for after her Broadway debut, at age nineteen, in the 1920s musical spoof, *The Boy Friend,* Julie worked relentlessly, creating one hit after another. Two years after her debut she began a three-and-a-half-year stint in London and on Broadway as Eliza in *My Fair Lady* and shortly after leaving *Lady* starred in the Broadway musical hit *Camelot,* with Richard Burton.

She made her film debut in 1964 as the nanny in *Mary Poppins,* a film that, among its other charms, set the country trying to spell "supercalifragi . . ." (or how did that go?). For that role she won the Academy Award as Best Actress, an award that helped assuage her disappointment at being bypassed for the film role of Eliza, which had gone to Audrey Hepburn.

Following *Poppins* she took a crack at a nonsinging dramatic role in *The Americanization of Emily.* After that came *Music,* and then big-budget musicals with girl-next-door heroines like Julie lost favor to films of the *Dirty Harry* genre. The year after her 1967 *Thoroughly Modern Millie,* a moderate success, she played Gertrude Lawrence in *Star!* Audiences didn't like Julie as the sophisticated Miss Lawrence and this coolness persisted toward her next films, *Darling Lili* (1970) and *The Tamarind Seed.*

"I can't knock *The Sound of Music* or *Mary Poppins,* "she told Charles Higham of the New York *Times,* "because they gave such an awful lot of pleasure to such an awful lot of people. But that kind of exposure does put one into the greatest danger."

In the mid-1970s she exposed her talents in Las Vegas and at the London Palladium and wisely refrained from appearing too hip. "Yes, I have to be very careful about singing contemporary songs. I'm told I have clear diction and, unless the lyrics are very interesting, it sounds quite wrong," she explained to Higham. "I can't sing 'oh-wo-wo-wo,' now can I? It's *absurd.* Lovely when other people do it, but when I do it, it's just awful."

In the early 1970s, she had her own TV series, which never set the Nielsen soaring, though her occasional specials were well received. But she seemed to be more interested in spending time with her husband, movie director Blake Edwards, and four children, two of them adopted Vietnamese, in their Swiss chalet. There she began developing another talent: writing children's books. *Mandy* and *The Last of the Great Whangdoodles* brought her new acclaim. But she still couldn't seem to lose her lust for playing nonvirginic roles. "I want to do a picture Blake has written and will direct called *S.O.B.,* "she admitted to Higham. "It's a wild comedy about a woman who won an Oscar for *Peter Pan* years ago and then did utterly different parts and is now trying to find her way back. Wouldn't that be loverly?"

(1935–   )

The Andrews Sisters

"They had led a very sheltered life and they always wanted to break loose."

They never blended especially well, either personally or musically, and yet the Andrews Sisters became the most successful female singing trio in the history of popular music. They had started working early in their native Minneapolis. Vivacious Patti was twelve; serious Maxene was fourteen; stately LaVerne, the only sister with any musical training, was seventeen. Their showmanship easily transcended their lack of musicianship, and they developed into engaging entertainers and produced an easily identifiable sound. "We couldn't read music, Maxene once explained. "But when we heard a song, we heard it in harmony."

Their success was meteoric. Dave Kapp, one of the heads of Decca Records, heard them on a 1937 broadcast with Billy Swanson's band and wanted to record them immediately. But they felt confident of only one tune, "Nice Work If You Can Get It," and couldn't decide what else to record. A song-publishing friend of Kapp's, Lou Levy, who was to become their personal manager and Maxene's husband, suggested a song he had just signed up, "Bei Mir Bist du Schoen." On their first record date they had a huge hit.

Their longtime arranger and director, Vic Schoen, (no relation of "Bei Mir Bist du") recently admitted that he "never could understand their phenomenal success. And I don't think they did either. Certainly they didn't handle it too

The Andrews Sisters, Maxene, Patti, and LaVerne, with Glenn Miller

Maxene, Patti, and LaVerne

well. They had led a very sheltered life and they always wanted to break loose. And when they did, after their parents died, it seemed to me that they were so filled with guilt that they began taking it out on each other. They were always squabbling."

Larry Bruff, announcer for many of Glenn Miller's commercial radio shows on which the sisters appeared, for thirteen weeks, recalls that "the girls weren't even talking to each other, so we were having a helluva time trying to figure out what they wanted to sing."

But neither the differences among the fun-loving Patti, the calculating, aggressive Maxene, and the seemingly sober LaVerne, nor their musical liabilities, hindered their flow of hit records. Theirs was strictly a straight-ahead, middle-of-the-road, no-frills approach that may have driven some musicians up the wall. (Schoen: "I hated 'Beer Barrel Polka' and arranged it as badly as I could, but it turned out to be their biggest hit. So I gave up trying to do anything musically worthwhile.") But it was an approach that mesmerized millions of Americans, who gobbled up recordings like "Don't Sit Under the Apple Tree," "Hold Tight, Hold Tight," "Boogie Woogie Bugle Boy" (revived by Bette Midler in 1973), and "In Apple Blossom Time," which evoked roars of approval when Patti and Maxene themselves revived it in *Over Here!,* their 1974 Broadway musical comedy hit.

Casting the two remaining sisters (LaVerne had died in 1967) in a show set during World War II when the girls had achieved such immense popularity turned out to be a masterful stroke. It also afforded both Patti and Maxene, who had appeared in several Grade B movies, the opportunity to really display their skills as comediennes for the first time and to spread a final luster on two of the most successful of all popular singing careers.

Paul Anka

"Cuddly appeal, polished showmanship, and a schoolboy voice."

His life reads like the favorite fantasy of every insecure teenager. Ottawa-born-and-raised Paul Anka was a pudgy, short, dark-complexioned kid and a poor student except in English. He retreated into dreams of show-biz success, encouraged by the entertainers who hung around the restaurant owned by his Syrian-born parents. He formed a rock trio, the Bobbysoxers, which won a week's nightclub engagement in a contest. Anka did a few local television shots, made a recording and, realizing that Ottawa wasn't the best place to market it, took off for Los Angeles. No dice. He had to take a job as a movie usher to get the fare back home in time to start tenth grade.

Undaunted, he kept plugging, absorbing techniques from older performers, reworking Arabic melodies from the records his parents listened to, borrowing

Anka

rhyme schemes from poetry he read in school. The other kids laughed at him. Hid girlfriend, Diana Ayoub, an eighteen-year-old sophisticate, ditched him. Out of adolescent despair, Anka wrote yet another song, "Diana," and borrowed one hundred dollars from his father to go to New York. There he met his destiny in the person of Don Costa, head of ABC-Paramount. At last count, "Diana" had sold over eight and a half million copies.

Anka could have been just another one-shot teenage record artist, a numerous breed in the late 1950s, had he not signed with manager Irvin Feld, who gave the lad a contract for a cross-country tour just after "Diana" hit the charts. "Fix your image," Feld said, persuading Anka to have his hair barbered becomingly, hounding him to lose weight, and talking him into having his Syrian nose restyled. Feld released Anka's recordings overseas, sent the newly glamorized young star to follow up with personal appearances, and parlayed the hysterical response by fans into more publicity at home. Anka was an international star before he could vote.

Realizing shrewdly that it couldn't last forever, Feld and Anka set about transforming the teenage wonder into an act that would appeal to the older, richer audiences in the nightclubs of Las Vegas, New York, and Los Angeles. The transition didn't bother Paul, who hadn't really liked being identified as a rock-and-roller. "I do pop music," he insisted. "I sing ballads. It all has a beat, but you can't classify it as rock and roll."

His cuddly appeal, polished showmanship, and a schoolboy voice—heavily influenced by his idol, Frank Sinatra—kept him riding high among the traditional nightclub set, at a time when his contemporaries were cashing in on the generation gap, directing their songs to the young, ignoring the older audience.

Though many of Anka's songs have served as vehicles for furthering his career as a performer, some of his best works have been written for other artists—"My Way" for Sinatra, "She's a Lady," for Tom Jones, and the theme for the Johnny Carson show.

In the mid-1970s Paul re-entered the mass music market with a couple of new hit singles, "I Don't Like to Sleep Alone" and "(You're) Having My Baby." His innate gift for melody and for simple expression of real feelings remained undiminished. Show-business writers, knowing that comeback stories make good copy, hailed Anka's "return," but his colleagues in pop music, who had respected his writing and performing talents for nearly twenty years, knew that Paul Anka had never really gone away.

(1941–   )

Louis Armstrong

"I don't need words; it's all in the phrasing."

"He loved his music most of all. And he was always appreciative of audiences that responded to what he liked to call his 'small efforts to please people.' You see, he was definitely a people-pleaser. He lived for that."

That's how Lucille Armstrong described what her late husband had been doing almost all his life. For the man whom Duke Ellington once called "an American standard, an American original, the epitome of jazz" pleased not only jazz musicians, almost all of whom were influenced in one way or another by his musical creativity, but also the millions of other listeners whom he serenaded and entertained all over the world.

From the time he was seven, when he was singing for pennies on the streets of his native New Orleans, Louis Armstrong lived the life of the loving entertainer

Satchmo

who needed to be loved. During his stay in a waif's home he learned to play the trumpet, and, once on his own, he put his accomplishment to good use, proudly blowing his horn in marching bands while doubling at night in jazz groups. In the early 1920s he joined the band of his idol, Joe "King" Oliver, in Chicago, then played in Fletcher Henderson's larger band before forming his own, "Louis Armstrong and His Hot Five," which produced a series of recordings that firmly established its leader as one of the all-time jazz greats.

In 1932 Armstrong's recordings had created such a furor, especially in Europe, that he was asked to play in London's prestigious Palladium. It was the first of many appearances in foreign lands where enthusiastic audiences convinced him that music offered the surest way of comunicating among all people. "In foreign countries we play with their musicians, and we look at each other, but we never say a word. But we understand each other all right," he once explained. "It's like me listening to *Rigoletto*. I like it, but I don't understand a word of it. They don't understand my language either. So I sing them riffs. I don't need words; it's all in the phrasing. They understand that everywhere!"

And everywhere they knew him as "America's Goodwill Ambassador," "Ambassador Satch," or just plain "Satch" (short for his descriptive nickname, "Satchelmouth"). Louis himself was a big man, not always in girth, because he dieted and kept himself in good condition much of the time, but always as a human being. Probably no other famous person ever had so few enemies and so many friends. According to Lucille Armstrong, "Louis's greatest personality traits were humility and his generosity. He was a soft touch, but he was no fool. He just loved people. And he always tried to understand them, too. He could spot a phony in a minute. It took just two words. But if a person was for real, Louis would do almost anything for him."

Certainly Louis's extroversion resulted in his acceptance by a large part of the nonjazz world which might otherwise have never noticed him. He appeared as himself in many movies which helped make him famous but which never even hinted at his true character. He played all of them with abounding enthusiasm, so that his face, his personality, and his music glowed through films like the 1936 *Pennies from Heaven,* which he shared with Bing Crosby; the 1943 *Cabin in the Sky* with Lena Horne, Ethel Waters, and Duke Ellington; the 1947 *New Orleans* with Billie Holiday; and the 1956 *High Society* with Crosby, Frank Sinatra, and Grace Kelly. He also made an appearance in *Hello, Dolly!*

On some of his recordings he shared the spotlight with Crosby and Ellington, as well as with Ella Fitzgerald, the Mills Brothers, and other singers. But his most memorable records focused primarily on Louis himself, beginning with his early Hot Five classics, which included the 1928 "West End Blues," one of the first five sides to be elected into the Recording Academy's Hall of Fame, and continuing through a whole slew of late 1920s and early 1930s pop tunes like "Star Dust," "The Peanut Vendor," and "You're Driving Me Crazy," his famous theme song, "When It's Sleepy Time Down South," and more recent songs like "Blueberry Hill," "Mack the Knife," and "Hello, Dolly!"

All those entertaining renditions of pop songs will long be remembered. And yet their impact on American music pales next to that of Louis Armstrong the emotion-charged trumpeter, who remains to thousands of jazz musicians the greatest single force in their music's history. Dizzy Gillespie has often stated that if it weren't for Armstrong there would have been no Dizzy Gillespie. Once, when Harry James was told he had just won an important jazz poll, he reacted with: "It just doesn't make any sense. How could I win that poll when Louis is around?"

Long after Louis had gone, musicians were still feeling the same way about what he had given to them. And how did Louis feel about what he had received in return? Lucille, who shared the last twenty years of his life with him, remembers him as "extremely grateful and happy and content." She noted, however, that "Louis had everything and more in life than he wanted—everything except one thing, something for which he had been rehearsing for a long, long time, waiting until he'd be asked. But nobody ever did invite him to sing our national anthem over there a few blocks away from our house, Shea Stadium, the home of his beloved Mets."

(1900–1971)

"O-h-h-h . . . Y-e-e-e-s-s!"

Eddy Arnold

"I'm a Heinz 57 singer."

"This may make the purists mad," Eddy Arnold once remarked in an interview with a leading newspaper, "but I figure for every purist I lose, I gain five other fans who like country music the modern way." Like other country artists who have "crossed over" into performing pop material, Arnold accurately anticipated the potential problems inherent in performing both pop and country music; i.e., split stylistic loyalties and possible accusations from both audiences about his not being "pure" anything. But Arnold is philosophical about it and describes his musical variety with: "I'm a Heinz 57 singer—I sing many different kinds of songs which mean something to many different kinds of people."

His repertoire runs the gamut from hard-core country to smooth easy-listening. His record sales of over sixty million and his standing-room-only audiences prove that "crossing-over" hasn't diminished his appeal. From his silken-smooth, flowing cowboy yodels on "Cattle Call" to his heart-rending pop stylistics on "I Really Don't Want to Know," Eddy covers all bases. And he has produced some other big hits like "Bouquet of Roses," "Anytime," and "Make the World Go Away."

Steve Sholes, legendary producer, once summed up Eddy's versatile voice by saying, "He just naturally sings right. It's an unusual quality. Caruso had it, and so has Bing Crosby, but they're the only ones I can think of besides Eddy."

Arnold spent his childhood picking up guitar on an old Sears model procured from a cousin, playing chords learned from his mother. "I'd sing in the cotton fields and the cornfields. I'd sing at the plow—and, Mister, I did plenty of plowing," Eddy recalls. And about his nickname, "The Tennessee Plowboy": "I earned that name the hard way."

Like his singing contemporaries who had rural Depression beginnings, Eddy was resourceful, talented, and driven by a tremendous energy. He held numerous jobs, among them driving a hearse for a funeral home. He continued improving his musical act, and in 1940 went to work for the Grand Ole Opry as a member of Pee Wee King's Golden West Cowboys.

In 1944 Arnold signed a long-term contract with RCA Records and soon attempted to shed his country-boy image and make a conscious move toward a pop image. According to many critics, his voice had always been suited to popular music; it was simply a matter of adding horns, strings, and a tuxedo

Eddy

to the act. And yet, despite all his leanings toward popular music, Arnold continued to maintain a high visibility in Nashville among his fellow performers, appearing at nearly all country-music social events, moving through them in his strong-yet-easy-mannered way, renewing old friendships and kindling new ones. Pop music may have won him over in some ways, but there has always remained a definite place for Nashville in Eddy Arnold's heart. And the feeling has been mutual.

Speaking for his surroundings, but alluding also to his roots and career, Eddy mused in an article he wrote a few years back: "I love to walk around and see and smell those wonderful fresh country smells. I guess it's like they say . . . you can take the man out of the country but you just can't take the country out of the man."

(1918–   )

Fred Astaire

Elegant, graceful, debonair, and charming.

"I'll go my way by myself/I'll teach my heart how to sing/I'll go my way by myself/Like a bird on the wing." © The year was 1953, the movie *The Band Wagon,* and the singer a man whose name is synonymous with everything that is elegant, graceful, debonair, and charming. But to Fred Astaire—the entertainer who added a whole new dimension to the term "song-and-dance man"—it's all in a day's work. "Getting paid very well," as he puts it, "for something I love doing."

His ability to make the difficult look simple developed early. Born Frederic Austerlitz in Omaha, Nebraska, he and his older sister Adele were enrolled in dancing school at ages four and five. Soon they were playing two-a-day in vaudeville, near the top of the bill.

They bowled over Broadway audiences in 1917 with their appearance in a revue called *Over the Top,* and subsequently sang and danced their way into the hearts of New Yorkers and Londoners in such hits as *Lady Be Good* (1924), *Funny Face* (1927), and their super smash *The Band Wagon* (1931), by Dietz and Schwartz, in which Fred immortalized "Dancing in the Dark."

After sister Adele married a titled Englishman and retired forever from the act, Fred teamed with Claire Luce in Cole Porter's *Gay Divorcé,* in which Fred introduced "Night and Day." Always the perfectionist, the internationally famous dancer was sure that his voice was terrible, that he would ruin Porter's beautiful new song. But the audience loved his relaxed, sincere rendition. A few years later, Irving Berlin said he would rather have Fred Astaire sing his songs than anyone else. "He's as good as any of them—as good as Jolson or Crosby or Sinatra," Berlin recently insisted to John S. Wilson of the New York *Times.* "He's just as good a singer as he is a dancer—not necessarily because of his voice, but by his conception of projecting a song." Astaire's renditions of three of Berlin's mid-1930s songs, "Cheek to Cheek," "Let's Face the Music and Dance" and "Top Hat, White Tie and Tails," have become classics.

Astaire's completely unpretentious way of singing has of course also charmed an adoring public who loved the way he crooned along with Crosby in *Holiday Inn,* romanced Rita Hayworth with Jerome Kern's "You Were Never Lovelier" in the movie of the same name, serenaded Leslie Caron with "Something's Gotta Give" in *Daddy Long Legs,* and lent his special singing style to "Cheek to Cheek," "The Way You Look Tonight" and "They Can't Take That Away

Forever-dancing
Fred

From Me," sung to Ginger Rogers in *Top Hat, Swingtime,* and *Shall We Dance,* three of their nine costarring pictures.

In 1959 Astaire played his first dramatic role in *On the Beach,* a performance that was highly praised. At sixty, he tackled TV for the first time; his *An Evening with Fred Astaire* won nine Emmys!

Whatever this phenomenal performer has attempted he has done beautifully. In 1976, during a promotional stint for *That's Entertainment II* (which he conarrated with Gene Kelly), he told a reporter, "I can still do a lot of things. But I'm afraid to; I don't want to throw myself out of gear." If he did, one could be sure he would do it with grace and style.

(1899–   )

Chet Atkins

"I'm a little square, but it helps to be that way."

Chet Atkins is square. He knows and admits it and so do his fans and critics. He once told an interviewer, "Music, to be commercial, should have a melodic line somewhere that is appealing, and I try to keep this in mind in all my recordings. I'm a little square, but it helps to be that way." It is, in fact, this instinctive ability to satisfy the average man's musical taste that enabled Atkins to become one of the best-known guitarists in the world.

Atkins was born in Luttrell, Tennessee, into the grinding poverty that characterized much of the rural South between the world wars. Although his life was sometimes unhappy and frequently unstable, Chet's early musical surroundings were rich. He drew inspiration from musical parents and a talented older half brother, and by the age of eighteen Chet was working as a guitarist and fiddler at radio station WNOX in Knoxville, Tennessee. He remained in country radio for many years, though his desire for personal stardom and his intolerance for musical mediocrity cost him some jobs.

By the time Nashville had begun to emerge as a recording center in the early 1950s, Chet Atkins, who had drifted from job to job as a radio sideman, seemed an unlikely candidate for stardom. But talent and circumstance combined to give him a major role in the growth of the Nashville music scene.

Atkins had associated himself with the Grand Ole Opry in the late 1940s and had begun to record as a soloist for RCA. When big-city recording executives like RCA's Steve Sholes and Decca's Paul Cohen wanted to cut records in Nashville, they asked Chet to serve as the go-between, linking New York companies with Nashville studios, sidemen and publishers. When Sholes eventually committed RCA to the development of a Nashville office in the late 1950s, it was only natural that Chet would be put in charge. Thus, first as studio manager and then as RCA's vice-president in charge of Nashville operations, Atkins influenced the careers of such diverse performers as Hank Snow, Elvis Presley, Eddy Arnold, Waylon Jennings, Al Hirt, and Perry Como. In his work as a record producer, Chet introduced string and horn sections into country sessions. His drive to modernize the sound of country records, a drive that peaked with the popularization of the "Nashville Sound" concept in the early 1960s, later attracted some criticism from traditionalists. Granted, he did alter the sound of country records, but at the same time he helped attract a broad national audience.

Chet

Though one of the most successful record producers, Atkins reserves his greatest enthusiasm for the guitar. His recording pace is extraordinary: He has cut well over six hundred titles during the past twenty-five years, and he often comes out with four or five albums a year. He has recorded country material, pop hits, classical selections, and has flirted with jazz. His unique personal style on the guitar—the use of thumb and fingers to produce simultaneously a bass line and melody—has influenced two generations of guitarists.

Chet Atkins has wealth, power, and artistic recognition. Yet he is still, in many ways, a shy country boy. He remains a man who is simultaneously powerful and modest, very demanding but very, very shy.

(1924–   )

Gene Austin

Traveling, drinking, gambling—happy in his own "Blue Heaven."

He was a millionaire, yet he lived in a trailer. He had a very masculine physique, but his voice was pitched like a girl's. Though he was music's romantic idol of the mid-1920s, what he really liked to do was "to travel and drink and gamble." And what he didn't like to do was "to nest anywhere. Two of my wives were nesters, and that's why we didn't get along."

"My Bl-o-o-o Heaven!"

Still, Gene Austin, the original pop crooner, did nest somewhere—right at the top of the recording heap. And he stayed there, from 1925 to 1928, until he was replaced by two other crooners, Rudy Vallee and Bing Crosby.

What caused him to croon in the first place? "Everybody was trying to sing like Al Jolson. They were all loud and raucous." Austin, with a thin, high-pitched voice, obviously couldn't compete on Jolson's blustery, baritone level. So he decided to emote softly with feeling, never attacking notes, but caressing them gently and holding them languidly, not deep in his throat but seemingly somewhere near the top of his head.

The new gentle approach, interspersed now and then with some light yodeling and whistling, caught on. Austin produced hit after hit record: "My Melancholy Baby," "Ramona," "Sleepy Time Gal," "Ain't She Sweet," and his biggest hit of all, "My Blue Heaven," which sold five million copies.

Austin's attitude toward life belied his gentle, almost demure musical style. Born in Gainsville, Texas, and bred in Louisiana, he ran away from home at fifteen to join a circus, where he learned to play the calliope. A year later he enlisted in the Army to fight in Mexico, but when his parents objected, he was released. The following year, on the day America became embroiled in World War I, he re-enlisted, serving as a bugler. Later he attended the University of Baltimore, leading and playing piano in a dance band.

In 1923 he went into vaudeville, became a song-plugger for a while, and then, in 1924, he made his first recordings, all duets with male and female singing partners. Shortly thereafter he began his fabulously successful career as a soloist and soon after began writing hit songs, such as "The Lonesome Road," "When My Sugar Walks Down the Street," and "How Come You Do Me Like You Do?"

Though he kept recording after Vallee and Crosby had succeeded him, Austin didn't bother to linger long. He had made his money and he could do whatever *he* wanted to do. "Besides," he noted, "once you get to the top, everybody starts telling *you* what to do. You're not living when that happens." So Gene stopped singing and began living the way he wanted to—traveling, drinking, gambling—happy and content in his version of his own "Blue Heaven."

(1900–1972)

The first glimpse of a hillbilly singer as a hero.

Gene Autry glided so easily from country singer to cowboy movie star to wealthy businessman that people are inclined to forget that during the late 1920s and throughout the 1930s he played a leading role in the emergence and establishment of America's country music, as well as in the popularization of other types of songs.

Mention Gene Autry's name and most folks will recall Gene with his horse Champion tracking down criminals; Gene with a guitar serenading a daughter of the West; Gene defending her honor with his fists. But before, during, and after his film career Gene Autry recorded songs like "That Silver-Haired Daddy of Mine," "South of the Border," "Have I Told You Lately That I Love You?" and "Rudolph the Red-Nosed Reindeer." During the thirty years of recording sessions, the artist had hits with country, pop, and children's material. In each genre his simple voice conveyed sincerity and honesty to millions of listeners and earned him election to the Country Music Hall of Fame.

While working for the St. Louis and Frisco Railroad, Autry pursued music as a hobby. Then in 1928 he made a stab at a New York recording career, making several sides, always sounding like his idol, the great country singer Jimmie Rodgers. In 1931 he moved to Chicago, joined radio station's WLS "Barn Dance" and signed with the American Record Company to provide competition for Rodgers on Victor. But he came up with a hit, "That Silver-Haired Daddy of Mine," more in the urban crooning style of Gene Austin that in Rodgers' country tradition. In another shift of musical style Gene began to perform on WLS as "Oklahoma's Singing Cowboy" in the type of role he would play throughout his performing career.

Hollywood heard about him, and he was soon starred in a singing role in a Ken Maynard picture, *Tunbling Tumbleweeds*. By 1937, only two years after the release of his first feature, Gene Autry had become Hollywood's number one western star.

Gene proved a success in many media. Beginning in 1939, he hosted the long-running CBS radio program "Melody Ranch," and at about the same time he began both a live stage show that frequently toured with his films and a spectacular rodeo that played to sellout crowds in the nation's largest auditoriums.

Autry interrupted his entertainment career to serve in World War II and later returned to Hollywood to find the scene passing him by. Though a television series and reruns of his films on TV kept Gene and Champion before the public into the mid-1950s, he never regained the title of number one cowboy. So Autry began to embark on the diverse investments that would insure his continued wealth and would ultimately draw him away from performing. He invested in real estate, established his own film company—Flying A Productions—formed two record companies, purchased radio and television stations, and even acquired the California Angels baseball franchise. His success as a financier has doubtless increased the distance between Autry and his former fans, but he must be given his due. He was, after all, a fine country singer before he was an actor, and once established in film, he provided a mass audience with its first glimpse of a hillbilly singer as a hero—a positive image, which today benefits an entire industry.

(1907–   )

Gene with Dinah Shore

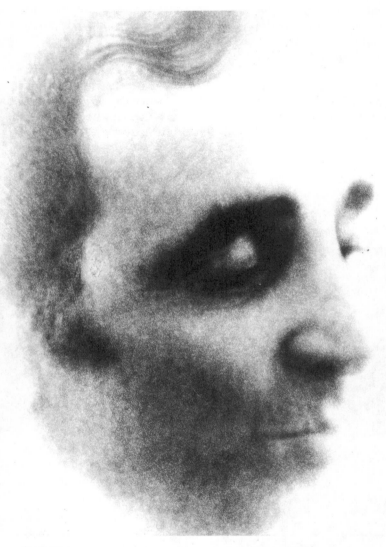

Aznavour

Charles Aznavour

More concerned with telling a story than with making musical waves.

"He is small, thin as a straw, with hugh, vulnerable eyes in a forlorn angular face," wrote John S. Wilson describing Charles Aznavour in the New York *Times.* "But once he starts to sing, producing a voice that may be conversationally casual or billowing with romantic melody, he is in complete command. And not so much through his voice as through those eyes, that face, that slim, wiry body that can project more meaning with an offhand shrug than the whole verse of a song."

No doubt about it, singer, composer, lyricist, and actor Charles Aznavour must be recognized as one of the great interpreters of songs, especially his own and especially those about love. Through a voice as unimposing as his five-foot-three, one-hundred-twelve-pound physique (he has been called "The Charlie Chaplin of Popular Music"), Aznavour unabashedly projects pure romanticism. Recognized by most as a performer, he nevertheless prefers to think of himself as "a writer who sings his own songs. I write for people about people, about human problems, and the first is love. But I don't always make it sweet. I leave it just as it is, with all the good or bad parts of it." Whether his songs are good or bad, he has composed over seven hundred of them and recorded at least a hundred and fifty albums.

Born in Paris of Armenian parents, Aznavour began his singing career in 1933 when he was nine years old, then danced in nightclubs and even hawked newspapers before meeting his greatest influence, Edith Piaf, for whom he was once chauffeur. She encouraged his career, first by featuring him in one of her shows, then by introducing him to American audiences. By the mid-1940s he was appearing regularly in French nightclubs, specializing in songs deemed too risqué for publication in America. For a while his intensely personal style seemed to embarrass audiences, but then in 1956 he scored a tremendous success in Casablanca, and the Aznavour mystique was born. From then on he began to be accepted as a major attraction in the world's most sophisticated nightclubs and concert halls. He made many recordings, scored a huge triumph during the 1950s in Carnegie Hall, later returning to America in 1974 for a TV special with Liza Minnelli and a highly successful 1975 concert tour that tied in with his new RCA record album.

And yet, despite his acceptance as a singer, Aznavour considers himself as much an actor as a singer, and there are those, not too impressed with his "talking-singing" style, who readily agree. Certainly the acclaim for his roles in numerous French movies substantiates his opinion of his talents. What's more, when he performs as a singer, he is, by his own admission, more concerned with telling a story and the dramatics involved than with making musical waves.

Underlining everything he does—singing, acting and writing songs—Aznavour, like so many romantic Frenchmen, appears to be most deeply concerned with just one subject: l-o-v-e (or a-m-o-u-r)—sentimental, passionate, lost, found, requited, unrequited, or any other kind whose mood he can share with audiences all over the world, either by singing-acting or acting-singing, both of which he does so extraordinarily well.

(1924–   )

Joan Baez

She's never studied voice and she'd be afraid to try.

At the beginning and at the end of any discussion of Joan Baez, you've got to talk about her voice. For years she probably preferred to be considered primarily a political person, and certainly there's plenty to say about her steadfast, nonviolent activism during the protest years. You should mention her three-year marriage to resistance leader David Harris and their son, Gabriel. And you could hardly ignore Baez's astonishing beauty, the delicately drawn face with the crack-of-dawn smile that no camera has captured accurately. But all this could pass unnoticed if it weren't for the voice.

Joan

Baez came by it naturally; she's never studied voice and has said that she'd be afraid to try. As a teenager in Palo Alto, California, where her Mexican-born father taught at Stanford University, she learned to play a cheap guitar (Sears, Roebuck, so the legend goes) and forced a vibrato to develop by fluttering her hand against her throat. Miraculously her crystalline soprano emerged—one of the great voices of the century.

That's not to say that Baez had no critics or that she did not, in part, deserve them. When she left Boston University after one month to begin singing in Boston and Cambridge coffeehouses, listeners were mesmerized by her songs but alienated by the abrasive, go-to-hell manner masking her shyness. After her stunning impact at the Newport Folk Festival of 1960, purists attacked her for her eclectic choice of material, for not having gone "into the field" to collect folk songs for herself and even for singing too prettily. If she was going to sing folk music, they said, she should imitate the rough-and-raspy traditional singers. Later when she popularized the songs of Bob Dylan, her close friend and companion, she was taken to task for not writing her own.

Baez has been criticized for relying too completely on the sheer glory of her voice, treating the words as mere sounds. Especially at first, she sang love songs, political songs, and Christmas carols with the same deadpan disregard for their content as if she were singing the Congressional Record. But they always sounded lovely.

A Quaker by upbringing, Baez has never fudged about her convictions. At first she voiced them through topical songs, then she spoke out directly. Early in the battle against racial discrimination she marched in civil-rights demonstrations. She took a year off in 1965 to found her Institute for the Study of Non-Violence in Carmel, California, and she was one of the first public figures to oppose the war in Vietnam. Baez was fined for refusing to pay taxes to support the war, vilified for going to Hanoi to give a Christmas concert, and called a traitor by the hawks and a political innocent by left-wing, violence-approving radicals. But nobody ever called her insincere, except for Al Capp, who satirized her heavyhandedly as "Joanie Phoanie" in the Li'l Abner comic strip. (Baez sued Capp and won.)

Returning to public performing in 1966, Baez has been mellowing musically ever since. By the 1970s she was ranging freely from full-blown country music to ladylike rock to the thoughtful, musically sophisticated songs she began writing when she was thirty. Politically she remains outspoken and committed to her beliefs, centering her attention most recently on the relief of political prisoners.

Divorced from Harris and settled with her son, she shows no signs of losing interest in either her politics or her music, wherever they may lead. The matchless voice flows on.

(1941–   )

Mildred Bailey

A great, uncompromising artist . . . a sometimes joyous, sometimes miserable woman.

Bing Crosby called her "a genuine artist with a heart as big as Yankee Stadium." Musicians and many of the most discerning music buffs of the 1930s and 1940s were knocked out by the warmth and vitality of Mildred Bailey's thin, high-pitched, emotion-charged voice, putting her in a class with Bessie Smith and Billie Holiday as one of the few truly original female singers. And those who knew the plump, high-spirited singer personally recall her not only as a great, uncompromising artist but also as a sometimes joyous, sometimes miserable

"Ol' Rockin' Chair's got me . . ."

woman with temperamental outbursts that could surpass even the intense emotion she projected through her songs.

A one-eighth Indian native of Tekoa, Washington, Mildred had begun to establish herself as a singer during the late 1920s in Los Angeles, when her brother, Al Rinker, and his singing partner, Harry Lillis (Bing) Crosby, arrived in town. Mildred housed them, fed them, and helped them find jobs, and a grateful Crosby always told people, "Mildred gave me my start." Later, when Bing and Rinker and Harry Barris had established themselves as the Rhythm Boys with Paul Whiteman's orchestra, they returned the favor by persuading their leader to hire Mildred as his first featured girl singer. Her exposure with Whiteman eventually led to her own recording sessions and featured roles on several radio series, where, in recognition of her theme song, she became known as "The Rocking Chair Lady."

During her stay with Whiteman, Mildred had met and fallen in love with his young, shy xylophonist, Red Norvo, and soon after they had left Whiteman they were married. In the mid-1930s, when Norvo organized his own big band, Mildred tried first staying at home, then became a band wife, and finally joined the band as Red's vocalist and partner. Billed as "Mr. and Mrs. Swing," they produced some of the most subtly swinging sounds of the big-band era. But by 1938 the strain of continual traveling and bickering with the musicians, plus offers to return to radio as a soloist, had enticed Mildred back to New York. There she was starred on several CBS shows, including Benny Goodman's "Camel Caravan" series. A divorce from Norvo made her split a final one.

Life from then on was not too happy for Mildred. Continually frustrated by her inability to lose weight (she claimed a glandular deficiency rather than overeating as the cause), she seemed incapable of controlling her emotions, which alternated between towering rages (she felt special bitterness toward less musical but more successful, and especially better-looking, girl singers) and tender displays of deep affection that she showered on close friends and her constant companions, her two dachshunds, who along with those friends, must have been thoroughly confused by the way she spiced her baby-talk with profanities.

During the 1940s she continued to record and play occasional clubs, but ill health gradually forced her into retirement on her New York State farm. Sadly neglected by many of her friends, she was discovered one morning near death in the ward of a local hospital by a few of the more faithful who had driven up to visit her. Two of her greatest admirers, Bing Crosby and Frank Sinatra, made arrangements for her care, and she returned to New York and even made a few brief appearances. But neither the heart, nor the voice, nor the great spirit could be completely revived, and in 1951 one of the most musical of all singers succumbed to a series of illnesses that were almost as complicated and complex as her own personality.

(1907–1951)

Pearl Bailey

"If I just sang a song, it would mean nothing."

Pearl Bailey's daddy was a preacher. And when her brother Bill, one of the great tap dancers of the 1930s and 1940s, hung up his dancing shoes, he became a preacher too. Pearlie Mae herself never had a church or a pulpit, but she takes the preacher's instinct with her wherever she goes.

"You don't have to go in a building to find God," she once said.

Her favorite subject is love for humanity—all humanity. When she first starred in *Hello, Dolly!* in 1967, there were complaints about the show's all-black cast, primarily from blacks who were pushing for integration. "All this talk about integration," said Pearlie Mae. "What are they mixin'? Love and hate? If you work together and you're different races and you don't like each other, darlin', you haven't mixed a thing. But wherever I stand, I call it hallowed ground and whenever anybody stands in love, *that* is integration.

"People ask me, why don't I march. And I say, I march every day in my

Pearlie Mae

heart. When I walk in the street with humanity I am marching, and you know"—
with a Pearlie Mae pause—"my feet are killin' me all the way."

For thirty-five years, until she announced her retirement from the stage in
1976 to serve as a member of the U.S. delegation to the United Nations ("my
gig on the East Side"), Pearl Bailey sang, danced, and philosophized in
nightclubs, theaters, in movies and on television with a relaxed, lazily informal
style accented with expressive gestures of the hands and eyes. (The retirement
as well as her East Side gig turned out to be short-lived.) Those gestures came
from her mother: "Mama could say more with a flick of the wrist, a gesture
here and there, than any words." But the warm, mischievous light in her eyes
was instinctive.

"Knew that from the beginning, honey," she declared, twinkling those eyes.
"You can exude more sex out of your eyes than anywhere else. With things
slow all over, you got to use your eyes."

She tends to deprecate her singing ability. "What I do is more like telling a
story to music," she explained, "more like talking. I do songs that people know
and then add my twist. If I just sang a song, it would mean nothing."

Born in Newport News, Virginia, Pearl Mae Bailey was fifteen when she
first appeared on a stage at the Pearl Theater in Philadelphia. She sang and
danced in small clubs in Pennsylvania and Washington, D.C., before she made
her New York debut at the Village Vanguard in 1941. She was a band singer
for the next three years (with the Sunset Royal Orchestra, Count Basie, and
Cootie Williams) and had her first big record hit, "Tired," which she had introduced while working at the Blue Angel in New York. She made her Broadway
debut in 1946 in *St. Louis Woman* and later appeared in film versions of *Carmen
Jones* and *Porgy and Bess.*

She was married in 1952 to Louie Bellson, the white jazz drummer, despite
her father's objections. But the marriage has worn well, and they have raised
two adopted children. This was Pearlie Mae's fourth try at marriage.

"Let's forget about the others, honey," she once remarked. "Wouldn't it be
kinder all around?"

(1918–   )

Josephine Baker

The epitome of the titillating, hedonistic life of Paris.

"I wanted to find freedom." That was Josephine Baker's explanation for leaving the United States at the age of eighteen to settle in France. At the time, she was thinking primarily of freedom from the racial prejudice with which she grew up in St. Louis. But she also found a freedom of expression that made her the sensation of Paris in the 1920s. Later she devoted herself to freedom for people of all races and colors. This devotion was exemplified by the dozen orphans of varying nationalities, religions, and races whom she adopted and raised.

She was born in a St. Louis slum; by the time she was fifteen years old she was already dancing in chorus lines in nightclubs and theaters. At sixteen she left home for New York City, where she got into the chorus of *Shuffle Along,* the precedent-setting black revue. Her energy and talent for clowning so entranced audiences that she was costarred with Ethel Waters at the Plantation Club in Harlem, and in 1925, when Miss Waters turned down an invitation to appear in *La Revue Nègre* in Paris, Josephine Baker went instead. Her subsequent appearance at the Folies Bergére was the start of her career as a flamboyant international entertainer who seemed the epitome of the titillating, hedonistic life of Paris. Her notoriety and fame stemmed so much from her display and use of her slim, long-legged body (she is remembered most vividly for her appearance in the Folies Bergère wearing nothing but a string of bananas around her hips) that her other talents—particularly her seductive singing—were likely to be overlooked. But she was a first-rate chanteuse, with a sultry voice that oozed through love songs like her unforgettable theme, "Two Loves Have I."

As she starred year after year at the Folies Bergère and the Casino de Paris, "La Bakhair" became a familiar and exotic figure on the boulevards, surrounded by an astounding array of pets—cheetah, monkeys, swans, even perfumed pigs. Having first called attention to herself wearing no clothes, she then became one of the most fabulously dressed women of her time.

She became a French citizen in 1937 and, during World War II, was an ambulance driver and underground agent for the Free French. When she was awarded the Croix de Guerre and the Legion of Honor, she acknowledged her debt to the French people. "They gave me their hearts," she said. "Surely I can give them my life."

She had returned to America once before the war—in 1936 for a ten-month

"Two loves have I . . ."

run in *Ziegfeld Follies*—and she came back again several times and in 1951 made a cross-country tour. It was after her return from that tour that she began adopting orphans—a Korean, a Finn, an Israeli, a Venezuelan, a Japanese, a Colombian, among others. She lived with her "rainbow tribe" in a château on a three-hundred-acre estate until her expenses became unmanageable. The château was sold at auction in 1969 while Miss Baker, ejected from the building, sat defiantly on the steps in the rain. With the help of her friends, she bought a villa in Monaco, where she lived with eleven of her twelve adopted children until she died of a stroke four days after opening in a Paris revue celebrating her fifty years as a French performer.

(1906–1975)

Charlie Barnet

One big ball, both on and off the bandstand.

He has always been a playboy who could play with uninhibited passion and power—personally as well as musically. And both his spirit and his musicianship were contagious, so that good jazz musicians were drawn to Charlie Barnet, knowing that life could be one big ball, both on and off the bandstand.

And yet, despite a life built around kicks, Barnet has always taken his music seriously, and his became one of the country's more popular bands during the late 1930s and early 1940s. However, unlike many other successful leaders, he has never sacrificed the fun in life and music for his career, which is probably why his music has always sounded so fresh and spontaneous and his commercial appeal has never challenged that of bandleading superstars like Goodman, Shaw, Miller, or the Dorseys.

Charlie was handsome, virile, personable, high-spirited, attractive enough to be featured as a leading man in a couple of movies. Women have loved him, and he has loved women, many of whom (the last count was around a dozen) he married and divorced. Fortunately, Charlie could afford such a pastime. His father had been the first vice-president of the New York Central Railroad and had enrolled his son in the best schools, including Yale University, from which he ran away to play in a jazz band. Barnet never wanted for money, even late in life, when he could answer a friend's request for his phone number by listing four of them: at his home, his swimming pool, his country club, and his yacht.

So much ready cash permitted Charlie to play whatever kind of music pleased him most and to hire and encourage fresh young talent on whom other bandleaders might not dare to take chances. Thus he employed and encouraged such future stars as arrangers/leaders Neal Hefti, Billy May, and Eddie Sauter and trumpeters/leaders Maynard Ferguson, Doc Severinsen, and Clark Terry, as well as his most famous graduate, a young singer just beginning to reach her potential, Miss Lena Horne.

Again, it was Barnet's financial independence that made it possible for him to hire black singers and musicians, even if bridging the racial gap meant his band was overlooked for some of the best engagements, including the choice commercial radio shows. He also spent a good deal of his spare time in Harlem, where he made a host of friends, and many of his arrangements were patterned after those of the man he idolized, the great Duke Ellington. And yet, peculiarly

"Four phone numbers have I!"

enough, his theme song, "Cherokee," which was also his biggest hit, was written by Ray Noble, a white bandleader from England. It featured Barnet's tenor sax, blown hard and wild and driving and yet with a pixieish sense of humor—reflecting perfectly both Charlie Barnet the dedicated musician and Charlie Barnet the eternal playboy.

(1913–   )

The Count then.

The Count now.

It's no sin for a man to try to bridge the generation gap.

He'll sit there at the piano in front of his big band—quiet, relaxed, self-assured, a slightly quizzical smile on his face. Then he'll start noodling lightly on the keys—just a couple of swinging notes—and suddenly up goes his right hand; he points, and—*pow!*—the great Count Basie band begins roaring on through another of the thousands of swing numbers that have kept it at the top of the big-band heap for the past forty years.

The Count, or "Bill," as his friends call him, has never been a roarer himself. Off the stand, in fact, he projects as much enthusiasm as a motorist who's just been given a speeding ticket. But in front of his band he's strictly the main man-in-charge—firm, self-assured, knowing just the right thing to do and how to do it. Few leaders have ever deserved and received more respect from their men.

Born in Red Bank, New Jersey, he played jazz piano in New York's Harlem nightclubs, along with jazz stars like Fats Waller, Duke Ellington, and James P. Johnson, before touring the country as part of a vaudeville show. In 1927, while stranded in Kansas City, he joined the band of Walter Page, which featured a rotund blues shouter named Jimmy Rushing. Two years later, after having joined Bennie Moten's well-known band, Basie became its leader (Moten had suddenly died) and hired his ex-boss, Page, as his bassist and Rushing as his singer. He also took on several other future jazz greats like tenor saxophonists Lester Young and Herschel Evans, trumpeter Buck Clayton and drummer Jo Jones.

Wealthy jazz buff John Hammond heard the band in Kansas City and arranged for a New York engagement. Its early 1937 debut at Roseland Ballroom was unimpressive, but personnel changes, including the temporary addition of Billie Holiday as girl singer, resulted in vastly improved performances and eventual gigs at top spots throughout the land. By 1943 the band had become so popular that it was featured in five movies in one year!

Basie has been one of the few leaders working nonstop, except for a few months off following a 1977 heart attack, since the swing era ended in the mid-1940s. He has traveled throughout the world, appeared on numerous TV shows and at just about every important jazz festival, and he had also toured with his band in full concert with Frank Sinatra and Tony Bennett. Regularly stocked with some of his best players in jazz, performing scores by some of the music's finest arrangers, the band has retained a remarkably consistent musicianship, its amazing ability to please all types of audiences. Its basic style has remained the same: thrilling ensembles, spaced by brilliant solos, all supported by a rocking rhythm section. And yet Basie has managed to slip in a few innovations, for the Count remains enough of a realist to recognize that tastes and times do change and that it's no sin for a man, even if he is in his seventies, to try to bridge the generation gap.

"If there's going to be hope for the big bands," he recently commented, "they're going to have to play a little different music and meet the kids halfway and give it a little of *their* flavor. I have been watching the kids of today, and some of them are trying to step back a little toward us. So who are we not to step up a little bit toward them?"

(1904–   )

The Beach Boys

"We sang about sixteen-year-old girls in bikinis."

Just because the Beach Boys sold a lot of records and had an immense following, some people thought their music couldn't possibly be any good. True, their lyrics dealt with ephemera like cars and girls and surfin', but if you *really* listened, you realized that the five blond youths from Hawthorne, California, had a lot more to offer than good, slick musicianship and sunny, mindless little songs.

The Boys claim to have started singing as kids in the back seat of their father's car. In 1961, while still in high school, they made their first record, "Surfin'," on the small Candix label. They were all trained to read and write

The Boys on the Beach

music, and they had always listened to all sorts of records, from Chuck Berry to the classics. Cousin Mike Love and pianist/bassist Brian Wilson, the Beach Boys' principal writers, created incredibly sophisticted music, set to an insistent, movin'-right-along beat, propelled by brother Dennis' Gene Krupa-inspired drumming and aided by guitarists Carl Wilson and Alan Jardine. Above their attractive songs they created effortless-sounding descanted counter-melodies, sung in sweet falsetto, with Brian Wilson's bass line moving sensitively underneath it all.

They seemed on the surface to project the hang-loose pose of California's easy-living surfdom. But in reality they were serious, well-trained musicians whose surfing image was by no means accurate. Only Dennis surfed regularly. Brian, who created so many of their songs, admitted he was too frightened to go into the water. "Dennis told me stories and said it was great, and I made up songs," he later confessed to Timothy White in *Crawdaddy.*

The Boys drove themselves ruthlessly for the first few years, recording many sides for Capitol and concertizing everywhere. While on tour in 1964, Brian experienced a nervous breakdown and swore he'd never travel or perform again. He hid away for three years (Bruce Johnston replaced him) in their half-million-dollar recording studio. At first he composed and recorded quantities of tapes, only to destroy them all. But slowly recovery set in and one day "I looked at the guys and they looked kinda sad." And so he began to expand creatively with bigger, more thoughtful and complex arrangements, which managed to preserve the inventive harmonies and hypnotically interwoven vocals. Many consider the resulting 1966 album, *Pet Sounds,* the Beach Boys' finest. But their pinnacle was "Good Vibrations," a long single surrounded by throw-away tunes in their 1967 album, *Smiley Smile.* Brian's production was a revelation of how to use the modern recording studio to build a record instead of just preserving a performance. The remarkably original orchestration and the usual impeccable Beach Boys' skill applied to this free-form composition set a new standard of recording artistry.

After what was clearly a tough act to follow, the Beach Boys became increasingly experimental but proportionately less interesting. There seemed to be something a bit tired about them, as though they were trying too hard. But they persisted. Long periods overseas helped to restore their perspective, and by the mid-1970s they had returned as active performers, sounding much as they had before but looking quite a bit different, less like boys and, especially Brian and his paunch, more like uncles.

With the help of TM they claimed to have found greater serenity and had learned to accept their past and settle for their present. "We resisted our own history. Now we've learned to embrace the past," explained Carl. To Digby Diehl of *TV Guide* Mike Love was more pragmatic: "We sing songs about our experiences growing up in California . . . We're inseparable from middle-

Beach Boys:
Early Days

class Karma. Other groups were perhaps singing more complex and profound lyrics. But we sang about sixteen-year-old girls in bikinis." Meanwhile, Brian, still the most far-out member of the group, and whom brother Carl called "guileless and vulnerable," in a recent television interview, described the Beach Boys in a manner that probably only their millions of followers could understand: "We are a subliminal, plugged-in group with coded messages of love."

John, Ringo, Paul, and George

Ringo, John, George, and Paul

The Beatles

They gave a sense of community to youth everywhere.

John Lennon, Paul McCartney, George Harrison, and Richard Starkey (Ringo Starr) transformed rock from a popular music of occasional merit to a demonstrable art form. Though they were not exceptional musicians (Lennon once described the group as "average, just average"), their brilliant and audacious powers of musical conception were fortified by their talents for strong melodies and evocative lyrics, as well as by the force of their personalities.

Though the Beatles amazed and delighted the world from 1962 to 1970, they were not universally accepted, at least at first, by music's establishment. "The Beatles," said Mitch Miller scornfully, "that's the British sending us reverse lend-lease with a vengeance." Added Stan Kenton, "If the Beatles can be credited with one thing, it is that they came along and they made fans out of six- and seven-year-old kids. They took it down that low."

But of course the Beatles survived all disparagement. They gave a sense of community to youth everywhere; their personal candor and often bitter wit offered refreshing contrast to the false "aw-shucks" role often projected by many of the early 1960's rock idols. "Beatlemania"—the mass, global, and ecstatic frenzy for their music and their persons—is a happy memory to those who experienced it, and in 1976 there was a revival of "Beatlemania" in America and England in a surge of demands for their original recordings and even for their reunion.

The alchemy of the Beatles was based on their disparate talents and personalities. Lennon was cynical, verbally and physically violent, boiling with rage and passion. Paul McCartney was witty and smooth and shrewd. George Harrison was more withdrawn and was devoted to the delights and disciplines of the guitar, and Ringo Starr, gifted with loyalty and common sense, provided musical personality ballast for the group as its drummer.

All four were from class-obsessed England's lower middle class whose members usually become government clerks or factory workers, and all four were determined, if possible, to avoid such a future. As teenage rock fans, it occurred to them individually that a career in music might be, as per the title of one of their future songs, "A Ticket to Ride."

While in high school, Lennon had organized a folkish "skiffle" group, the Quarrymen. McCartney became a member and the two began a words-and-music collaboration that eventually was to rank them with the Gershwins and

Kurt Weill-Bertolt Brecht in artistic ambition and achievement. Teenaged George Harrison was the next to join the Quarrymen, which changed its sound from "skiffle" to rock and changed its name to the Beatles. Lennon jokingly related how "an angel on a flaming pie" appeared to him with the new name, but it was actually a variation inspired by black American "bird groups"— the Crows, the Flamingos, the Ravens. Lennon decided to rechristen the combo after an insect, but he devised the spelling of the name to reflect the kind of music the band played. In 1960 after using several fill-in drummers, the group auditioned and accepted Peter Best, a shy, good-looking lad. Best was fired, under controversial circumstances, in 1962, and replaced by Ringo Starr.

The Lennon-McCartney collaborations were always distinguished by appealing melodies that made use of minor chords or unexpected chord progressions, coupled with literate and fanciful lyrics. As the career of the Beatles grew, Lennon absorbed some of McCartney's melodic savvy and romantic charm, while McCartney learned from Lennon's aggressiveness and satiric bite.

As lead guitarist, Harrison seldom showed emotion, yet he displayed an exciting and tasteful sense of construction. His solos were thoughtful statements specifically tailored to the sense and meaning of the song being performed. Ringo Starr was, by temperament and technique, a traditionalist drummer who believed (quite rightly) that his function was to keep the beat, hold the band together, and not allow his rhythmic inserts to overpower or distract the front-line men.

The Beatles' first hit recording, "Love Me Do" in 1962, sparked "Beatlemania" in England, as "I Want to Hold Your Hand" commenced the worldwide phenomenon, starting with America, in 1964. Beatle songs became famous—"Yesterday," "Michelle," "And I Love Her," "A Hard Day's Night," "Yellow Submarine"—and so did their outlandish quips:

John Lennon, on the female species: "Women should be obscene and not heard."

McCartney, during a command performance at the Royal Variety Programme:

"This next number's something of a rouser, so you in the cheap seats clap your hands and you in the balcony rattle your jewelry."

George Harrison to a reporter who asked what he called his hair style: "Arthur."

Ringo, explaining why he wore so many rings on his fingers: "Because I can't fit them all through my nose."

By 1966, with the release of the *Rubber Soul* album, the Beatles had gone beyond the normal patterns on pop music to mold a form of their own, and when, in 1967, *Sgt. Pepper's Lonely Hearts Club Band* was issued, it was received as a major artistic event. Brilliantly conceived, composed, written, arranged, and performed, it was a dark and eerie statement on the human animal (all

George

John

Paul

Ringo

the songs dealt with fools, recluses, and the emotionally alienated), delivered with punch and a deceptive charm and was eagerly accepted by America's disillusioned young as symbolic of their own state of mind.

For the next three years the Beatles continued to release albums that contained accomplished songs of hilarity, horror, and tenderness. And they also produced and acted in several successful movies. But personal and professional pressures among the foursome resulted in McCartney's leaving the group in 1970. There followed an embarrassing and dismaying series of interviews and lawsuits of the type which only old mates who have fallen out are capable of—bitter, wasteful, and cruel.

All four embarked on solo careers, of which McCartney's was the most commercially successful. Harrison, increasingly removed from the world by his studies of Indian music and religious philosophy, became a predictable guitarist and songwriter of rigid form and little content. Lennon's old rage over the early death of his mother and his father's desertion of the family exploded in a series of raw, frantic, and clawing performances, some of which appeared in a series of comparatively insipid, self-indulgent albums that he made with his second wife, Yoko Ono. McCartney's efforts with his new group, Wings, were slick and ingratiating, but with none of the fire and sophistication of his Beatle contributions and he went to some lengths to make the public forget he ever was a Beatle.

Only Ringo, faithful and affectionate to the last, continued to respect the memory of the group, and he has had success as a singer and writer of "my little songs." He expressed his own, and the public's, sentiments in a simple but poignant tune titled "Early 1970," in which he expressed the love the world had for the Beatles and the love the Beatles could not keep for themselves:

I play guitar, A, D, E [chords—Harrison]
I don't play bass, 'cause that's too hard
    for me [McCartney]
I play piano if it's in C [Lennon, as
    occasional pianist]
And when I go to town, I wanna see all three
And when I go to town, I wanna see all three.©

Sidney Bechet

> **"The music, it's something you can give only to those who love it."**

"I wish to set down the name of this artist of genius," wrote the Swiss conductor Ernest Ansermet in 1919, in what is considered the first intelligent appraisal of the budding art of jazz. "As for myself, I shall never forget it. It is Sidney Bechet . . . What a moving thing it is to meet this very black, fat boy . . . who is very glad one likes what he does but can say nothing of his art save that he follows his 'own way,' [which] is perhaps the highway the whole world will swing along tomorrow."

Bechet with star pupil Bob Wilber (far right)

Ansermet, who heard Bechet with Will Marion Cook's Southern Syncopated Orchestry, with which the New Orleans-born clarinetist was touring Europe, was right: Bechet was the first great jazz soloist. Duke Ellington, who first encountered him in 1921, also found the experience unforgettable: "I had never heard anything like it. It was a completely new sound and conception to me."

By then, Bechet was concentrating on the soprano saxophone, an instrument better suited to convey his commanding, volatile, and romantic musical personality. A self-taught prodigy, he was a profesional at twelve, worked with the best musicians in his home town, came North early, and spent much of the 1920s in Europe. But he was in the United States long enough to appear in a musical with Bessie Smith, with whom he had a brief, stormy affair; operate his own nightclub (Club Basha) in Harlem; and teach a youngster named Johnny Hodges the secrets of the soprano sax.

He toured Russia in 1927, billed as "The Talking Saxophone," and was deported from France after a shooting incident in Montmartre in 1929. (A fellow musician had taken a shot at him; Bechet retaliated.)

During most of the 1930s, hard times for his kind of music, Bechet worked with Noble Sissle's society band and for a while even operated a tailor shop in Harlem. In 1938 he was rediscovered, in the following year made his famous recording of "Summertime," was reunited on records with his boyhood chum Louis Armstrong (with whom he had made some brilliant recordings in 1924), signed a contract with RCA Victor, and established himself as one of the leading figures in traditional jazz, though his music could never be circumscribed by any narrow categories. In the late 1940s he took up teaching. His most gifted pupil was Bob Wilber, who had done much to keep Bechet's legacy alive.

In 1951 Bechet settled permanently in France. His third marriage in Antibes that year was celebrated with a parade à la New Orleans that was the biggest social event on the Riviera since Aly Khan's wedding to Rita Hayworth. Bechet became a national figure in France, his popularity comparable to that of Chevalier and Piaf; his records sold over one million copies in France alone.

He was a master of the blues but also a great admirer of romantic melodies (one of his favorite artists was the Viennese tenor Richard Tauber). His autobiography, *Treat It Gentle,* was published posthumously; it is a high point in jazz literature and one of the most meaningful documents by an American artist. He wrote: "Oh, I can be mean—I know that. But not to the music. That's a thing you've got to trust . . . The music, it's something you can give only to those who love it . . . It's for giving. But there has to be somebody ready to take it."

When Sidney Bechet gave, there was no shortage of takers.

(1897–1959)

From "New York Mining Disaster" to *Saturday Night Fever*

"Bonded by genetic glue, the voices of the Gibb brothers kiss notes like three suitors seeking the same set of lips," wrote *Crawdaddy's* Greg Mitchell in describing the Bee Gees' superb vocal blend. And Arif Mardin, the record producer credited with having resurrected the trio, points out that "when they sing, their throat vibratos move the same way. That's because they are brothers. They have the same advantage that the Mills Brothers have had."

Hugh Gibb, father of the three brothers who became the late 1970s' most popular recording artists, must have liked that comparison, because for years his favorite singing group had been 'those same Mills Brothers.

In the mid-1950s, the former dance band leader had moved his family from Manchester, England—the boys had been born on the Isle of Man—to Australia, and when Barry, the oldest, was nine, he had given him a guitar for Christmas. The instrument fascinated the youngster, and after Robin and Maurice, the non-identical twins almost three years younger, also showed musical interest, their father began coaching them and got them jobs singing at local Speedways. Soon two gents with Bee Gee initials helped some more: Speedway organizer Bill Good heard a tape they'd made and suggested that his friend, Bill Gates, an Australian disc jockey, play it on the air. The resultant exposure led first to an eighteen-month gig as the resident band in a Queensland club, then to the group's own television show, and eventually to a Festival Records session from which one single, "Spicks and Specks," emerged as number one on Australia's record charts. Hugh Gibb, convinced that his sons, who by then were writing their own material and even selling songs to other artists, had a greater future elsewhere, decided in November 1966 to return his family to England.

Before boarding the boat for the long journey, he had sent a copy of the trio's record, along with a well-written, enthusiastic letter, to EMS, the company that had launched the Beatles. The recording and the letter deeply impressed EMS executive Robert Stigwood, who later admitted to "a frustrating two-week wait, waiting for the boat to arrive." Though he had no idea where they would be staying, Stigwood, who later was to become the most successful of all rock producers, "managed to track them down twenty-four hours after they arrived. And I signed them to a contract that very day."

Success came quickly—almost too quickly for three boys still in their teens. First came a hit single, "New York Mining Disaster," and then a hit album,

Bee Gees First, followed by a glamorous concert in London's famed Royal Albert Hall, with a sixty-piece orchestra, a huge choir, and the Royal Air Force Brass Band as backup artists.

Unprepared for such sudden success, the young lads almost suffocated from the ensuing personal and financial pressures. Fans, journalists, promoters, even financiers and tax men, kept hounding them. "It got to be where we were in danger of being physically injured," later reported Barry, who for a time slept with a gun by his side. His brothers appeared to be equally disturbed. They took to pills, and Maurice reportedly developed a serious drinking problem. They fought among themselves and finally decided to break up their act. They tried separate solo careers that turned out to be separate disasters. By the early 1970s they had hit rock bottom.

But Stigwood continued to believe in them. He urged them to reorganize, and he encouraged them to open their ears wider to more contemporary sounds. Atlantic Records, which had rejected their last album, assigned Arif Mardin, a fine musician with a great ear for the teenage record market, as their producer. Out came "Jive Talkin'," one of the first disc hits, followed by *Main Course,* a hugely successful album, and the Bee Gees were back on the track again.

Some years later, Mardin generously credited the brothers for their own comeback, noting that "they're all extremely hard-working. They've paid their dues. Barry," he went on, "still has that 'older brother' attitude. He protects everybody. He's warm and he's very shy. Robin is also shy. He's very witty with that dry, English humor. And Maurice is the clown, the funny one. He's more outgoing than the others."

Barry, consistently the hardest worker, has continued to play the leading role, as brother, as spokesman, and as singer, with his high falsetto recognized as one of the group's most distinguishable sounds. Robin, more interested in business aspects, constantly watches the record charts to see how the group is doing. Maurice, apparently the least involved of the three, sometimes contributes only marginally. Greg Mitchell's recent descriptions seem quite apt: "As Robin closes his eyes to reach an emotional epiphany, Barry strikes a sympathetic chord—and Maurice pulls up his sleeve and looks at his wristwatch."

After *Main Course* came two more hit albums, *Children of the World* and *Here at Last . . . Bee Gees . . . Live.* Then in 1977 came an urgent call from Stigwood for four or five songs, in a hurry, for his *Saturday Night Fever* movie: "Give me eight minutes of three moods: frenzy, passion, and w-i-i-l-d frenzy!" In two weeks, they had completed the assignment. "How Deep Is Your Love," "Stayin' Alive," and "Night Fever" became successive number one hits on the charts. In the late 1970s the Bee Gees had four of the five most-played songs on the popularity charts. And the *Saturday Night Fever* album, which in 1979 won four Grammys and helped to make disco music more than a mere fad, became such a monster seller that Al Coury, president of Stigwood's

RSO label, predicted that it would earn the trio from fifteen to twenty million dollars.

Such figures and fame still seem to frighten the brothers. Barry, always working (he contributed immensely to the late 1970s successful solo career of Andy Gibb, youngest of the brothers), has surrounded his Miami home with huge, protective fences, and has even installed electric gates and scanning cameras. "We're scared of whatever we do," he confessed to Greg Mitchell. He admitted to fright even about the trio's next album. "We're the same desperate, worried, insecure songwriters we've always been."

And what about their future? "My greatest fear is that we'll always be the Bee Gees—that we'll end up being an old group. You can't go on past forty. I don't want to end up in Vegas." Like the Mills Brothers, perhaps? That mightn't be so bad after all. And Hugh Gibb could still be a very proud father.

The Bee Gees: Maurice, Robin and Barry

"He never was satisfied with his work."

To Hoagy Carmichael, the sound of Bix Beiderbecke's cornet was "like a mallet hitting a chime." To Eddie Condon, it "came out like a girl saying yes."

At six, little Bix could pick out on the piano any tune he'd heard once, though he'd had no music lessons. At fifteen he taught himself to play cornet on a borrowed horn to the tune of his older brother's records by the Original Dixieland Jazz Band. At sixteen he heard and met Louis Armstrong on one of the riverboats that sometimes came up the Mississippi as far as Bix's native Davenport, Iowa, with bands from New Orleans aboard. At seventeen he played his first professional job. At twenty he made his first records with the Wolverines, a band he made famous. At twenty-four he was a featured member of Paul Whiteman's orchestra. At twenty-eight he was dead from lobar penumonia, edema of the brain, and acute alcoholism.

A true child of his times, a classic case of the artist's fate in America, Bix Beiderbecke became a lasting legend in jazz. More has been written about him than about almost any other jazzman, including a great deal of nonsense as well as a definitive, meticulously researched biography, *Bix: Man and Legend* by Richard Sudhalter and Philip Evans. His life and music inspired Dorothy Baker's novel *Young Man with a Horn,* from which an even more fanciful film of the same name was made.

All this attention would no doubt have embarrassed the gentle and rather shy young musician who had been born into a comfortable middle-class family of German ancestry and whose fatal flaw was too much kindness. "He couldn't say no. He couldn't say no to anybody," recalled Pee Wee Russell, one of Bix's true friends.

"I think that everybody he ran with jived him," said Louis Armstrong. "They claimed they thought a lot of Bix, but every time you look around they kept him out for three or four days; no sleep, wouldn't eat half the time . . . They wouldn't say, 'Well, Pops, why don't you come on and get a little rest there; you look beat,' they didn't do nothing but pour him in. So it kept him depressed all the time; he never was satisfied with his work."

One of the most lyrical and original improvisers in early jazz and a gifted composer as well (his impressionistic piano solo, "In a Mist," has become a jazz classic), Bix never found what he was looking for in music—if indeed he knew what it was. Influenced by such diverse strains as authentic black American

Bix (seated center) surrounded by Goldkette bandsmen, (l. to r.) arranger Bill Challis, banjoist Howdy Quicksell, trumpeter Fred Farrar, pianist Irving Riskin, clarinetist Don Murray, bassist Steve Brown, trumpeter Ray Ludwig, trombonist Spiegel Wilcox, saxist Frankie Trumbauer, plus the local zoo's snake charmer

music ("Even in the hands of white composers, [jazz] involuntarily reflects the half-forgotten suffering of the Negro," he said in the only published interview of his life), the works of both great and lesser modern classical composers (Debussy, Delius, Stravinsky, Holst, Eastwood Lane), and the happy pandemonium of the Original Dixieland Jazz Band, he had little time for study or reflection in the hectic atmosphere of Prohibition night life. The two hundred dollars a week Whiteman paid him was a fortune for a single man in that day, another reason for the many "friends." And despite all the company, he was too private a person to permit his real friends to help.

But the music Bix left behind, the product of six brief years of recording activity, much of it circumscribed by commercial considerations, transcends the personal tragedy. Even when the period settings do not stand the test of time, Bix's lovely solo and lead passages survive unimpaired on recordings like "Singin' the Blues," "I'm Coming Virginia," "Riverboat Shuffle," and "Way Down Yonder in New Orleans." "I've heard many trumpeters since then, but I haven't heard another like Bix," said Jimmy McPartland, one of his chief disciples. "Let's call him the master and leave it at that."

(1903–1931)

"The Pied Piper for the civil-rights movement."

"I'm not a great singer; I'm an interpreter of songs—more of an actor and a performer—and lucky enough to have a voice that would be accepted musically."

Harry Belafonte's self-assessment is unduly modest. But then he no longer needs to prove his worth to people; his accomplishments speak for him. As an "interpreter" of folk songs, especially those of the West Indies, he has been successful on recordings, in nightclubs and concerts the world over and in movies and on television, where he was one of the first black performers to star in his own series. And he has also scored as a straight dramatic actor in movies and on the stage.

Acting was the original ambition of this tall, extremely handsome New Yorker. Following a stint in the Navy, he enrolled in the New York Dramatic Workshop and was struggling financially when fellow student and friend Monte Kay invited him to sing during intermissions at the Royal Roost, a Broadway jazz club with which Kay was associated. Except for a few jazz aficionados, Belafonte impressed almost no one, including himself. "I couldn't sing jazz like Dinah Washington or pop like Dinah Shore, so I figured if I couldn't be great, what was the sense in staying in the business."

So he quit. He pushed carts in the garment district; he ran a small Greenwich Village restaurant, and then he hit upon the idea of singing folk songs. "It was the only art form that gave me the possibility of earning a living, because I could use both my dramatic training and my singing, the way I'd seen Big Bill Broonzy and Leadbelly and Josh White do. You've got to remember that in those days no black actors, with the possible exception of Paul Robeson, were making it.

"Folk music was highly contained then; it was performed mostly in small places. So you see I didn't set out to become a star; in fact I was damn glad to get a chance to sing for Max Gordon at the Village Vanguard."

Harry was hired for two weeks at that small Greenwich Village club. He stayed for twenty-two. Then Gordon, a part owner of the fancier Blue Angel uptown, moved Belafonte there. "At last I was in the focus of the mainstream."

He soon graduated to the larger supper rooms at a time when few blacks were permitted to play those swankier spots. Life for him became "a series of breaking down racial as well as musical barriers." On his opening night at a major hotel, he was refused entrance into the room in which he was to perform

Harry

by a headwaiter who saw only his open shirt and the color of his skin. So he sat nonchalantly on a sofa outside as the band kept repeating his entrance music until a frantic official spotted him and rushed him in past the bewildered "Color Guard."

Later, by his admission, he became "the Pied Piper for the civil-rights movement." Asked if he'd rather be remembered for that role, or for hit records like "Matilda" or "Jamaican Farewell" or his million-selling LP *An Evening with Belafonte* or for such starring roles in movies like *Carmen Jones* and *Island in the Sun,* he said: "You know, I'd like to be recognized, I think, for using my platform to enhance the human commitment."

(1927–   )

Tony

Tony Bennett

"The greatest singer I ever heard."—Bing Crosby

"I think of the pop music business today as dealing in lead," Tony Bennett opined in the mid-1970s, "and I'm in the silver business."

More than any other top "middle-of-the-road" singer, the New York born and bred Bennett (born Anthony Dominick Benedetto) criticized the mélange of mechanized devices that so many rock-and-roll artists and producers intruded into the music scene. "Much of what they're doing," he insisted, "doesn't have a note of real feeling. It's just a mechanical exercise."

On the surface, Bennett seems very easygoing and mild-mannered, and most of the time he's just that—until aroused by his almost fanatical devotion to what he considers quality music, like the songs of Irving Berlin, George and Ira Gershwin, Cole Porter, Johnny Mercer, Harold Arlen, and others. He is also constantly fighting the battle for recognition of great jazz artists, often surrounding himself on TV, in concert and recording appearances with soloists like Bobby Hackett or even with the entire Count Basie band. "They make you feel like singing. They almost always come up with something new and fresh, so even if you have to sing the same requests night after night, what they do makes those songs come alive all over again."

Tony has been receiving those requests to sing his hits ever since 1950, when, after being introduced for the first time as "Tony Bennett" on the stage of New York's Paramount Theater by Bob Hope ("He decided that was a better name for me than 'Joe Bari,' which I'd been using in clubs around town."), he launched his fabulously successful recording career with schmaltzy hits like "Because of You" and "Cold, Cold Heart," not at all the type of songs he prefers to sing. But once well established enough to call his own tunes, he began recording great standards like Irving Berlin's "Always," Duke Ellington's "Solitude," Vernon Duke's "April in Paris," and Mercer and Arlen's "One for My Baby."

However, rock and roll soon took over the record market, and Tony's tasteful recordings became instant non-best sellers. A less dedicated, courageous, or perhaps less stubborn idealist might have compromised for some of those "mechanical exercises" in an attempt to create another hit. "But," as Tony recently explained, "what has always kept my sanity is *not* compromising." So he kept doing things his way, and, fortunately for him, in 1962 the record-buying public responded: His moody, tasteful version of "I Left My Heart in San Francisco" sold one and a half million copies and won him two Grammys. More quality hits followed—"I Wanna Be Around," "This Is All I Ask," and "The Good Life"—and they made Bennett more popular than ever. He starred on numerous TV specials and was feted all over the world, wherever he gave concerts. In a 1976 interview, Bing Crosby called Bennett "the greatest singer I ever heard." Other stars, including Sinatra, have handed him similar accolades.

The good life came to Tony Bennett in more than just the lyrics of a hit song. Bennett moved with his wife, Sandy, and two of their four children (his two older boys remained in the East with their own contemporary pop group) into a Beverly Hills mansion, where he enjoys sketching and painting, at which he is impressively proficient, and playing tennis, at which he *hopes* to become proficient. In the mid-1970s he was taking special delight in furthering the careeers of singers and musicians whom he especially admired by recording them, as he did himself, on his own Improv label, devoted, of course, to the "silver" rather than the "lead" in popular music.

(1926–   )

"Sometimes a little compromise can make all the difference in the way a man lives."

"I told George Benson that if anyone has to be number one, I'm glad it's someone who can play," said Dizzy Gillespie in the late 1970s after the singing guitarist's single "This Masquerade" and his album *Breezin'* had won Grammys and topped the popularity charts in the same year.

Gillespie's feelings reflected those of other musicians who didn't seem to resent the commercial success of a performer who had been known primarily as a jazz guitarist. Maybe it's because he still remained such a modest, nice guy. And maybe because they continued to admire his talent. "In all my life

George today

in jazz," notes jazz record producer John Hammond, "I've never known anyone with more technique on his instrument."

Hammond first heard Benson after an anonymous tipster "with an illiterate scrawl told me the greatest guitarist since Charlie Christian was playing at the Palm Tavern on 125th Street. I went up there and heard the George Benson Trio. George was playing up a storm so I decided right then and there to sign him."

On his first Hammond date for Columbia, Benson continued to play up a storm. He also sang "Foggy Day" and "Summertime." But company executives saw nothing unusual and so, despite Hammond's objections, he was dropped from the label.

Benson had recorded previously for Prestige with Jack McDuff, whose band he had joined at nineteen. "Jack used to cuss me out on the bandstand. 'You can't play no guitar and you never will,' he kept telling me." So George kept practicing and thus developed his prodigious technique.

His professional career began at age five when he won a singing contest. Two years later he was strumming his ukelele on the streets of his native Pittsburgh. When he was nine, his mother gave him a guitar, and at ten he was playing in his first nightclub. Mostly he played and sang rhythm and blues numbers. Then, at seventeen, he heard jazz guitarist Hank Garland, "and I decided that I'd like to play like him, fiery and hot." In 1965 he formed his own band and during the next ten years recorded fifteen albums, most of which delighted and even inspired other musicians more than they did record buyers. "I got so sick and tired of young rock musicians telling the world they learned to play listening to my records when they were millionaires and I was scuffling to meet next month's mortgage payment," he once told writer Lisa Robinson.

So he decided to do something about it. With the help of producer Creed Taylor of CTI Records, George found a more commercial formula, less jazz-oriented and more lush. But he never sang on those records and the formulated approach began to pall. So he moved over to Warner Brothers and hooked up with a talented and sympathetic producer in Tommy LiPuma, who encouraged him to sing more and play some jazz. Often he has sung and played the same musical lines simultaneously. The device brought renewed attention, though Benson insisted to writer Leonard Feather it's not a gimmick. "I can't play anything that I can't hum, because it's the same brain that's creating the singing line that's creating the musical line for the guitar."

Like other fine jazz musicians who have made it commercially, Benson has been criticized by purists, just the way the musician/singer he has been most compared with, Nat Cole, also was. But Benson insists, "Playing for people doesn't mean being less of a musician. It just means changing your direction. Sometimes a little compromise can make all the difference in the way a man lives."

"When I hear critics," he told George Goodman, Jr., in the New York *Times,* "I think about the days when I was out on the road playing the segregated ghetto clubs, where all you heard was tinkling glasses after a set. I saw some great fights. I once thought of designing a guitar made out of iron to stop the bullets. It's a good experience, but I don't want to go back to that."

What he does want to and does go back to most of all is his sumptuous New Jersey home, which he shares with his wife and two sons, to whom he is intensely devoted. A deeply religious man, he feels a great responsibility to his family, his fans, and his music. Independently wealthy and owner of three Mercedes cars and three publishing companies, he told Leonard Feather he still "wouldn't stop playing for two reasons. First, it would be like a man who has hooked people on a certain thing and made them happy with it and got them used to it, then suddenly took it away from them. Second, I've devoted twenty-six years of my life to the guitar, cultivating it and bringing people along with my musical ideas, and they responded and said, 'Hey, man, give us more!' " And to put it even more simply: "Playing jazz is what I like to do best!"

(1943–   )

George and dad yesterday

Bunny Berigan

He lived spontaneously, ad-libbing his way through life.

"I Can't Get Started" was Bunny Berigan's theme song and his big hit record. It was also an apt description of his career as a bandleader. For Berigan, one of the greatest jazz trumpeters of all time (he was Louis Armstrong's favorite), lacked entirely the temperament and the self-discipline needed to become a successful leader.

He was easygoing, convivial, irresponsible, out to have a ball, even at the expense of his band's welfare. Like many a jazz musician, he lived spontaneously, ad-libbing his way through life just the way he ad-libbed his way through the fabulous trumpet solos for which he will long be remembered—his glorious, fat-toned horn ringing through Benny Goodman's "Sometimes I'm Happy" and "King Porter Stomp," Tommy Dorsey's recordings of "Marie" and "Song of India," and finally the sides he made with his own band.

Berigan began his musical career in his native Wisconsin as a child violinist. One day his grandfather, a local musician, came home with a trumpet, handed it to young Bernard and said, "Here, this is you. Play you!" And Bunny did— so well, in fact, that one of the top orchestra leaders of the late 1920s and early 1930s, Hal Kemp, hired him. He also played with Paul Whiteman's band for a time. During most of the early 1930s Berigan, who often looked but never acted like a high-school principal, blew his potent horn inside New York's radio and recording studios, alongside such close friends and admirers as Benny Goodman, Artie Shaw, Glenn Miller, and Jimmy and Tommy Dorsey. He developed into such a standout that CBS selected him to head an all-star studio jazz band called "Bunny's Blue Boys" that was featured regularly on the network's "Saturday Night Swing Session" series.

When the big bands began to bloom in the mid-1930s, both Goodman and Tommy Dorsey featured him. Often the results were glorious, though because of Bunny's erratic behavior they could now and then border more on the disastrous. Nevertheless, Dorsey, a gambling businessman, recognizing the reputation Berigan was building with the public, decided to back him as a leader. Because of its first (and only) hit record, "I Can't Get Started," the band, which included several up-and-coming musicians, such as drummer Buddy Rich and arranger/ trombonist Ray Conniff, achieved some initial success. But its greatest asset, Berigan himself, gradually developed into its major debit. His exciting, fat-toned trumpet could and did thrill many audiences as well as his many admiring

Bunny with Tommy Dorsey

fellow musicians. Unfortunately, that kind of performance occurred less and less frequently, for like another great trumpeter, Bix Beiderbecke, Bunny's initials also stood for "Bad Boozer." Promoters and friends began giving up on him, but Bunny never gave up on himself. He organized and dissolved several bands, winding up with a third-rate crew that could never match the quality of musicianship that he could occasionally project. In June 1942 a combination of penumonia and alcoholism ended Bunny's misery and the career of one of the truly great jazz musicians of all time.

(1908–1942)

Chuck

He never achieved the superstar status his music helped others who used his material to attain.

The Beatles said Chuck Berry was the most influential and creative innovator in modern popular music and that listening to—and learning from—his recordings had a profound influence on their music. They sang his "Roll Over Beethoven" and "Rock and Roll Music" in their early albums—in an unnatural twangy American accent.

It seems that at some point or other every rock musician has had a Chuck Berry song in his repertoire. The Rolling Stones performed his "Come On" and "Carol," then did "Bye Bye Johnny," "Nadine," and "Little Queenie." Elvis Presley sang "Johnny B. Goode," Johnny Rivers sang "Memphis" and "The Promised Land." The Beach Boys, after making a name for themselves with "Surfin' U.S.A.," followed their hit with a surfing version of Berry's "Sweet Little Sixteen."

Berry's performing and song-writing style emerged from a variety of influences—the country-western music he listened to on the radio in his native St. Louis; the songs he sang from the age of six onward with his parents in the choir of the Antioch Baptist Church; the ballads of Nat Cole, the musician he most admired; the jazz of guitarist Charlie Christian, and the light, comic touch of Louis Jordan, the musician he most identified with and whom he cited on a 1978 "Today Show" interview, along with Benny Goodman and Glenn Miller, among his inspirations; and of course from his most natural musical expression, the blues. His melodies were infectious, backed with strong, surging rhythms. His lyrics were aimed at teenagers, seldom deep or complicated, zestily good-humored, often wry, sometimes saying "get off my back" to parents and others in authority.

But Charles Edward Berry, as a performer, though nearly always reviewed glowingly for his musicianship and urgent showmanship, never achieved the superstar status his music helped others who used his material to attain. For when rock and roll began to be listened to by the general public, the white rather then the original black performers' versions were played more often on the radio and became hits, so that the white performers were the ones whom teenagers knew about and bought tickets to hear in concert. And since Berry was already well past his teens when he recorded some of his most important works during the 1950s, the younger generation had difficulty identifying with him. And some troubles with the law at an important time in his career didn't help either. From 1961 through 1963 no new Chuck Berry records came on the market.

Berry's recording career had begun when, in 1955, he went on vacation from a routine of studying hair-styling in the daytime and fronting the Chuck Berry Trio nightly for twenty-one dollars a week at clubs in the St. Louis area. He went to Chicago to hear and meet bluesman Muddy Waters. Berry recalled: "I drove up there in a 1937 Olds. We must have had thirteen flats along the way. I played three songs for him during his break. When he was getting back on stage, I asked him how to go about making records and he suggested I go see Leonard Chess." He did and the head of Chess Records asked whether he had any songs of his own. "It surprised me," Berry said. "It was the first time I had thought about creating my own material. I went home and began writing." Two weeks later he showed up again at Chess Records with four new songs. The first release, "Maybelline," became a hit. However, it wasn't until seventeen years later that Berry cut a record, "My Ding-a-Ling," that sold a million copies. But by that time, even without a million-selling record, the spirited, highly creative Chuck Berry didn't need a hit to gain recognition. Thanks to admirers like Presley, the Beatles, and the Stones, he had already become established as one of the pioneer giants and greatest influences in the entire history of rock and roll.

(1926–   )

Song, chatter, and that mighty left hand.

Mama didn't 'low no ragtime playin' at the Blake home, but her son found a lot of other places around Baltimore that did: sporting houses, saloons, dance-halls, where ragtime pianists had to develop that mighty left hand to keep the beat going and "cut" the competition.

It took some doing, and James Hubert Blake started early. As a preschooler in the 1880s he tried out an organ in a downtown store, and the awed manager put one in the Blake home for twenty-five cents a week. The unchurchlike sounds the boy wonder produced on it brought no peace to his mother's religious conscience. The organ went out and piano lessons came in.

Less formal "on the job" training followed for Eubie. An eighth-grade dropout, he had become a skilled second-story man, in this case breaking *out* of his

The eternal Eubie

bedroom window at night to pursue ragtime "studies" downtown. He got his first job when he was still in short pants at Aggie Shelton's sporting house and wrote his first rag, "Charleston Rag," in 1899 when he was sixteen.

Soon he was well on the way to proving he could knock out rags with the best and knock out customers with his finger-busting technique and style, with his running adulatory or cautionary comments to himself, to the piano, and to everyone within earshot. And that's just what he was still doing more than three quarters of a century later. By then the pianos had become grands on concert stages, but the music remained the same, and so did the show-stopping, scene-stealing performances by ex-vaudeville trouper, composer, ragtime pianist Eubie Blake.

Some of Blake's pieces, now classics, he turned out decades ago, among them "I'm Just Wild About Harry," which he wrote with his partner Noble Sissle for their 1921 landmark musical, *Shuffle Along,* and "Memories of You," which he wrote with Andy Razaf for another Broadway show, *Blackbirds of 1930.* He has published over three hundred other songs, ballads, rags. His latter-day "Blue Rag in 12 Keys" was written to prove he could play in all keys, but concert and TV audiences have had no doubt about that. And his continuing awards further confirmed their confidence. In 1970, when he was eighty-seven, Eubie was given the first annual James P. Johnson Memorial Award. At age eighty-nine he won an Ellington Medal from Yale University.

There were long intermissions in Eubie's performing life when ragtime was underground. He decided to retire in his sixties, then remembered another long intermission—the one in his formal schooling after he left eighth grade because "math got me." He enrolled at New York University and studied the tough mathematical Schillinger system of arranging. That time he "got" math. He began writing new arrangements, rags, waltzes.

In 1969 Columbia Records' John Hammond recruited Eubie to make a two-disc album—a joyous smörgåsbord titled *The Eighty-six Years of Eubie Blake,* wherein Eubie hit highlights of his ever-recurring heyday with song, chatter, and that mighty left hand. And ten years later, Broadway theater lights heralded a smash musical revue titled *Eubie* that featured his songs and which at the age of ninety-six he helped publicize with regular television appearances during which he played the piano with the spirit and facility rare in many musicians just half his age.

(1883–   )

Blood, Sweat and Tears

Opening the ears of the rock generation to the charms of jazz.

"Jazz is jazz and rock is rock and never the twain shall meet" was the refrain sung by most spokesmen for both branches of music until the arrival, in 1968, of Blood, Sweat and Tears. "In essence," said drummer Bobby Colomby when the first dew of success was still fresh on the group's young faces, "our band is trying to get the best out of all music and combine it with rock and roll."

By 1969, BS&T was riding high on no less than three monster hits, *Spinning Wheel, And When I Die,* and *You've Made Me So Very Happy,* each of which reached number two positions on the popularity charts. Seven years later, there was still a BS&T, with Colomby the only remaining charter member. But there was never another year to even remotely approach 1969. Nevertheless, few rock bands can boast of similar longevity, and BS&T does belong to the world of rock though it has been called a jazz band *manqué.* The concept of jazz/rock, in fact, was born with BS&T, the first successful rock band to feature brass and reed instruments prominently, employ a number of big band jazz devices, and present jazz-inspired solo excursions by the horns.

Blood, Sweat and Tears with David Clayton-Thomas fifth from left

Blood, Sweat and Tears with David Clayton-Thomas second from left

Like so many rock groups, BS&T was created specifically for recording purposes, and on the strength of the success of the first album, five of the participants decided to stay together as a group. They recruited accomplished musicians willing to go on the road, took on Canadian singer David Clayton-Thomas, and set about to create an eclectic amalgam of rock, jazz, soul, and even classical music.

The real key to their popularity, however, was the singing of Clayton-Thomas, tinged with the sound of Ray Charles and aptly described by Mike Bourne as "reminiscent of beer in quarts and lengthy arm-wrestling matches." The second album, *Blood, Sweat and Tears,* containing the group's three biggest hits, also included a wide variety of numbers: Billie Holiday's "God Bless the Child," an instrumental blues; a hit by the rock group Traffic; and a set of variations on a theme by the pioneer modern French composer Erik Satie. Such range clearly was beyond the grasp of most rock bands; as Colomby said, "Everyone in this band is very bright." But many rock critics considered the band's music "too perfect," and indeed the striving for polish at the expense of passion almost became BS&T's downfall. In 1972, after the departure of Clayton-Thomas and other key members, the revised edition went into a six-month hibernation period, during which it did little else except rehearse and change vocalists several times. Eventually it recorded, still bent on perfection: One of the numbers on its fourth LP required sixty-nine takes in the studio before an acceptable version was made. In the mid-1970s, Clayton-Thomas, whose solo career didn't pan out, returned to the fold, and the band's sagging popularity was revived, not because of anything creatively new and different but rather because it could once more perform its established hits.

Though the BS&T amalgam of musical styles proved less than earth-shaking, there can be no doubt that it contributed strongly to opening the ears of the rock generation to the charms of jazz and of superior musicianship.

Pat Boone

The first teenage idol that Grandma can dig too.

"Elvis Presley was my opening act in Cleveland—but only once," Pat Boone revealed during a TV interview show that featured him, his wife, and his daughter Debbie, who at the time had the country's number one hit record, "You Light Up My Life."

Soon after that Cleveland engagement, which starred Boone above Presley, their paths separated. Elvis became the younger generation's new sex symbol, while parents saw Pat as the answer to Presley's "lewd" mannerisms. *International Celebrity Register* described the clean-cut-looking, smiling, forever-polite Boone as "the first teenage idol that Grandma can dig too . . . He sings in an easy-mannered way, projecting his educated hillbilly sincerity from the soles of his white buck shoes through the relaxed vocal cords topping his Ivy League buttoned-down collar."

Charles Eugene Pat Boone, born in Jacksonville, Florida, a direct descendant of Danial Boone, sure came across as the All-American Boy: president of the student body, most popular boy in his class, and a member of his high school's

All-American
Pat

baseball, basketball, and track teams. He attended David Lipscomb College in Nashville, to which his family had migrated when Pat was only two, sang in a quartet there, then moved on to North Texas State College and sang solo on station WBAP in nearby Fort Worth. Upon his return to Nashville, after having won three Ted Mack Amateur Hours, he recorded several sides for Republic Records, none of which meant much; then in 1954 he went on to New York where he won the Arthur Godfrey Talent Scout Show.

In the following years he was signed by Dot Records, and one of his first sides, "Ain't That a Shame," a white man's version of a black man's (Fats Domino's) earlier recording, became his first hit. That year he sold four million records; the next year ten million more, including two more "vanilla" versions of rhythm and blues songs, Little Richard's "Long Tall Sally" and "Tutti Frutti." To prove that he could record other kinds of hits, he scored a huge success the next year reviving one of Tin Pan Alley's more corny pop tunes, "Love Letters in the Sand."

During the latter 1950s, he attended Columbia University to complete his studies, scoring high honors as an English major and graduating cum laude. "I planned to be a country preacher or an English professor," he once revealed. "I just sang to get through schools; but then the singing took over."

Boone took over his own TV series in 1958 and it ran successfully for several seasons. Meanwhile, he had signed a million-dollar, seven-year movie contract with 20th Century-Fox. Apparently, though, he was not prepared for Hollywood's life-style, and soon his 1954 marriage to Shirley Foley, daughter of country singing star Red Foley, began to founder. And so did some of his deeply rooted religious and social beliefs. He found himself starting to live the typical Hollywood party life, and to question precepts in which he had always believed. But in the end, "I came out of it." Adds Shirley Boone, "Except for God, we could have become another Hollywood statistic."

Though he continued to record with moderate success, from the 1960s on Pat became more and more immersed in other phases of living: in religion (he even baptized people in his swimming pool); in writing helpful books like his successful *'Twixt Twelve and Twenty* and *A New Song;* and above all in his family. With Shirley and his four daughters, he formed a family singing group that specialized in religious songs and which toured all over the world.

In 1977 the vocal focus shifted to daughter Debbie when her recording of "You Light Up My Life" became the year's number one hit. During an appearance with Shirley and Debbie on "The Phil Donahue Show," Pat, in his best paternalistic manner, admitted that he still offers his daughter advice, "but I try not to confuse things," and referring to one of his most successful recordings, he added, "I just use Friendly Persuasion."

With goodwill and cheer and serenity seeming to ooze out of all their pores, Pat beamed and said, "Our happiness I hope is contagious."

(1934–   )

Connee Boswell and the Boswell Sisters

"I also tried singing like Caruso . . . and I did it, too."

They started off in their native New Orleans as a classical instrumental trio with Helvetia, better known as Vet, on violin, Martha on piano, and Connee, also known as "The Little Genius," on cello. But it was as the best of all the female vocal trios that the Boswell sisters achieved international fame.

Sister Connee, who carried on a long and successful solo career after Martha and Vet married and left the trio in 1935, recalled: "At first we played classical selections and sang pop tunes on our local radio station, but then we switched to singing only and we began to get pretty big in the South. A man from

Connee

Victor Records heard about us and came down and recorded us on portable equipment—just the three of us singing, with Martha playing piano—and after that Tom Rockwell of Brunswick Records, who later became our manager, took us into the studios and we made a whole batch of sides."

Those 1931–33 recording sessions, often highlighted by such jazz stars as the Dorsey Brothers, Bunny Berigan, Joe Venuti, and many others, led to frequent radio appearances. But it was a regular gig on Bing Crosby's 1934–35 series that really put them on top.

"You know what we did? We revolutionized trio and group singing!" said the brave and irrepressible Connee, who, because of a bout with polio at the age of three, was forced to sing from a wheelchair. "We didn't sing everything straight, the way other groups did. After the first chorus, we'd start singing the tune a little different—you know, with a beat, the way jazz musicians would."

Connee sketched most of the trio's arrangements, some of which turned out to be too wild for conservative recording executives' tastes. "We'd sing them in clubs. It's a shame, though, they wouldn't let us record them."

The jazz that seemed to fill the air of their hometown certainly influenced the Boswells. Vet, the quietest of the three, was also a tap dancer. Martha, as outgoing and enthusiastic as Connee, played jazz piano with a powerful, rocking left hand. And Connee also played guitar and a barrelhouse piano. "And I tried to sing like Mamie Smith. She was a great blues singer, better even, I thought, than Bessie Smith. When I was a kid, my mama took me to a theater for blacks—they'd let us whites in only on Friday nights—and there I heard Mamie, and after that I always tried to sing like her. And you know what? I also tried to sing like Caruso—holding on to those notes the way he did. And I did it, too, and I can still do it today."

In 1976, a recently widowed Connee Boswell was sitting in her large apartment overlooking New York's Central Park reminiscing with undiminished enthusiasm about the way she and her sisters influenced popular singing—she with her strong, assertive style of blues shouting, once unheard of from white girls (later to become the chief inspiration of a young black girl, Ella Fitzgerald)—and the three of them together with their rhythmic, pulsating harmonies and mellow blend that set such high standards for all future vocal groups. But by the end of that year, courageous little Connee was no longer sitting in that chair, for cancer had done what polio could never do: still forever the sound and spirit of one of popular music's most enthusiastic and creative and most admired performers.

(Connee Boswell: 1912–1976)

He was known to walk off a bandstand with tears streaming down his face.

He was one of the most sensitive, sentimental, and sensuous of all singers. From 1927 to 1941 he recorded approximately eleven hundred selections, hundreds more than the world's most popular crooner, Bing Crosby, made during the same period. The English, and especially the women, idolized him as their top recording star. Yet on the other side of the Atlantic he is remembered only as the boy singer in Ray Noble's orchestra by all except a few deeply

Al

dedicated Al Bowlly fans. In the 1970s it was the undying enthusiasm of these fans that brought about the issuance by Monmouth/Evergreen Records of more than a hundred Bowlly performances spread over seven long-playing records.

Bowlly himself was an incurable romantic. A powerfully built, swarthy man with a shock of black hair, bushy eyebrows, and deep-set, piercing eyes, he was known to walk off a bandstand after a particularly sentimental rendition with tears streaming down his face. According to trumpeter Pee Wee Erwin, who worked with him in the Noble band, Bowlly was also "a real ladies' man"— and an incurable gambler. He won more than sixty thousand pounds in two Irish Sweepstakes, so he bought himself a barbershop. (Like Perry Como, Bowlly had once been a barber.)

Bowlly began his career as a banjo player and guitarist. After leaving his native South Africa in the early 1920s, he wandered throughout Asia and Europe as a singing troubadour, eventually settling in London, where in 1928 he joined Fred Elizalde's outstanding orchestra. He also worked with Roy Fox and Lew Stone, made hundreds of records with those bands and on his own, then achieved international recognition via recordings with first Ray Noble's English and then his American orchestra, an all-star outfit that included Glenn Miller, Charlie Spivak, Claude Thornhill, Will Bradley, and Erwin, who also recalls that "Al used to love to show off the dent in the gold watch that saved his life. A bullet had hit it and glanced off." Unfortunately, Bowlly's luck eventually deserted him. In 1938 he returned to England to continue his highly successful nightclub and recording career which, three years later, was terminated dramatically when a German buzz bomb zeroed in on his London flat.

(1898–1941)

Fanny Brice

"One of the goose-flesh specialists."

Ambitious. Earthy. Able to control an audience like a lion tamer his big cat. That's in part how relatives and friends saw this consummate performer who, on the one hand, could stop a show with a song and, on the other, some thirty years later, crack up a nationwide radio audience with baby talk and bawling as the *enfant terrible,* Baby Snooks. Weeping, in fact, was one of her surefire weapons for melting resistance, one that started her on her ascent from Brooklyn tenement to Beverly Hills mansion, from amateur-night prize winner to *Ziegfeld Follies* star.

Fanny

It rained pennies when she sang affectingly on neighborhood stoops. Later the tears she applied to songs drew audience tears and cheers and big box-office returns. Alternately she drove fans into paroxysms of laughter with her comedy routines, her Jewish dialect songs (which were never offensive or degrading), and her burlesques of dying swans, vamps, tragic heroines. Her third husband, showman-songwriter Billy Rose, called her "one of the goose-flesh specialists," possessing a magic that couldn't be explained but had to be seen.

Plenty of people saw and heard Fanny Brice during her explosive career in more than a dozen shows—in the *Ziegfeld Follies,* in *Music Box Revues,* in vaudeville and on radio. Few perhaps could quite picture the demands of that success. They came into focus for post-Brice theatergoers who saw Barbra Streisand as Fanny in *Funny Girl* on Broadway and in the subsequent film version. Producer Ray Stark, Fanny's son-in-law, wrote in the New York *Times:* "She [Fanny] once said she might be played by Judy Garland . . . apparently she did think of herself as a singer first and a comedienne second, but people now forget that she was, like Helen Morgan, one of the greatest ballad singers of her time . . . Both [Brice and Streisand] have 'soul,' though in Fanny's day the only—and inadequate—word for it was spirit."

Spirit she had, this second daughter and fourth child of saloon-owner Charlie Borach and his Hungarian-born wife, Rosie, who managed the business while he played pinochle in the back rooms. Fanny, who borrowed the name Brice from a neighbor, was addicted to hard work, to devouring know-how about everything from dancing to interior decorating. And she was not above using any generally accepted means to her ends. In exchange for one of her mother's famous dinners cooked especially for him, she got from songwriter Joe Jordan his blues lament, "Lovey Joe." With it she stopped the *1910 Follies* cold. She made history—and three thousand dollars a week—with her now classic torch song, "My Man," in the *1921 Follies.* Its thudding tear-stained message became her personal love song to Nick Arnstein, the father of her two children and the real love of her life. Their eight-year marriage, which survived his prison term for bond theft but not his romantic wanderings, ended in divorce in 1927. In 1928 Fanny sang, "My Man" in her first film, called . . . *My Man.* Divorce terminated her other marriages also. The first, to a barber, was very shortlived. The last, to Rose, ended in 1938 after nine years. Her film, *Ziegfeld Follies,* in 1946 was a reprise of her theatrical career.

In the late 1930s and well into the '40s Baby Snooks turned Fanny's mature performing years into a round of child's play on the air. Off the air she was decorating one performer's lavish home after another and dispensing hospitality to friends, breezily addressing them all, young or old, highborn or low, as "kid."

(1891–1951)

James Brown

"I was so poor my underwear was made out of flour sacks."

The curtains part: electric lights wink on the placard proclaiming: JAMES IS NO. 1. The most disciplined band in rhythm and blues, the J. B.'s, snap into their perfectly executed riffs. Suddenly a chunky, muscular man speeds onto the stage, propelling himself in a one-foot dance shuffle to the microphone. He is James Brown, the most dynamic performer in soul music.

Brown has been a star and hero to black communities for two decades, and his fame and stage appeal are such that during a summer of racial tensions in the 1960s a riot was averted in a large city when a local TV station wisely

James

broadcast Brown and his revue in a live performance. The potential rioters stayed home to watch brother James work out.

Though he became a millionaire through his tours, record sales, ownership of a string of radio stations and other investments, his financial prospects were bleak at birth. His parents were near-destitute. Brown's father, a frustrated entertainer, worked in a filling station in Augusta, Georgia. In his bitter early years, the boy Brown "picked cotton, worked on a farm, worked in a coal yard. I had to walk home along the railroad tracks and pick up pieces of coke that fell off the trains. I'd take that home and we'd use it to keep warm. I was so poor my underwear was made out of flour sacks. But I always intended to be my own man. Being poor makes you very determined. Now I'm number one. Nobody owns me."

Brown's parents separated when he was quite young; he moved to Macon, Georgia, where he was raised by an aunt. Even before his teens he was a notable dancer and a street businessman, charging his friends a dime to see him spin, hop, and wiggle, and wangling "bookings" at a local army base where the GI's threw larger coins.

In 1955 he formed a vocal group, the Famous Flames, and decided that a record was the group's best means of advertisement. Pooling their meager resources, the Flames cut an *a cappella* version of "Please, Please, Please" at a local radio station, Brown persuaded a disc jockey to play it. Response was immediate and in two weeks the Flames had a recording contract and a hit. Not long after, the embryonic version of *The James Brown Show* hit the road. The revue was eventually to have a cast of nearly fifty—orchestra, comedians, bus drivers, and valets.

For ten years, on a grueling schedule, Brown played the black theater circuit around the country. During this time he—like W. C. Fields forty years before—developed the habit of opening accounts in local banks wherever he played, so as never to be stranded. "I always intended to be my own man wherever I went, and if I had my own money anyplace then I was my own man. Nobody was going to own me."

In 1965 his recording of "Pappa's Got a Brand New Bag" was a national smash, bringing him to the mass white audience. His many subsequent hits—"It's a Man's Man's World," "Say It Loud, I'm Black and I'm Proud," and such dance ditties as "Let a Man Come In and Do the Popcorn"—all featuring his brazen, coarse-grain singing and the smooth funk of the J. B.'s, have confirmed his reputation as "Number One."

James Brown is royalty, a constitutional monarch elected by his audience. His fear and hatred of his early poverty often prompt him to say, "Nobody owns me"; but the ownership of James Brown is really a cooperative venture between his blazing talent and the people.

(1936–   )

"The Malted Milk Band."

When he was a starry-eyed Duke University undergraduate in the mid-1930s, fronting a band known as the Duke Blue Devils, Les Brown probably never dreamed that one day he'd become a solid member of the establishment, firmly ensconced in a beautiful home in California's Pacific Palisades, playing bridge and golf with the elite of the entertainment and political worlds and living a life totally foreign to that of a dedicated jazz musician.

But that's exactly what happened, and if these days a relaxed, warm, and ingratiating Les Brown seems more interested in making a seven-spade contract or a hole-in-one, who can blame him, for he has already paid his dues as one of the most devoted, hardest-working of all bandleaders.

Les and his discovery, band singer Doris Day

Of course, all this might not have happened if Les hadn't latched on to Bob Hope in 1947 and vice versa. And how did that happen? Let Les tell it:

"There was an agent on the West Coast named Jimmy Saphier who was trying to sell Doris Day to Hope for his radio show, and so he brought him the records she had made with us. When Hope heard them he asked Jimmy, 'How about that band?' And right after that he hired us. But he didn't hire Doris until two years later, and by then she'd become so famous that he had to pay her a lot more."

The Hope-Brown association lasted for more than twenty years. It brought Les not merely a type of annuity enjoyed by few bandleaders, but Hope's trips to entertain the troops gave Brown the chance, as Les put it, "to see the world and get paid for it too!"

The earlier Brown career had been much less glamorous. After graduating from Duke, Les and his Blue Devils struggled into oblivion, and he became an arranger for other bands. In 1938 he organized a noncollegiate band whose members seemed so cleancut that it was alternately tabbed "The Malted Milk Band" and "The Ice Cream Soda Band." In 1940 "Miss Peaches and Whipped Cream" arrived in the person of Doris Day, and the following year the band recorded its first hit, "Joltin' Joe DiMaggio."

The band's big breakthrough came in 1944 with its recording of "Sentimental Journey," a song it almost left out of its library because it impressed practically no one the first time the band played it during a rehearsal. But a few broadcasts of the tune drew such enthusiastic responses that Les recorded it, and he and Doris were on their ways to becoming established artists. In 1948 the band's popularity received another forward jolt via its recording of "I've Got My Love to Keep Me Warm," and from then on Les's band had the right to the title "Band of Renown."

Like many East Coasters (he was born in Reinertown, Pennsylvania) Les had fallen in love with California. "I wanted to stay there and the Hope thing made that possible." There Les, a devotee of symphonic music, perfected his conducting talents, so that following the Hope radio series he was invited to conduct for the Steve Allen, Dean Martin, and the "Hollywood Palace" television series. In addition to his TV appearances, he was able to keep his band together, so that when he isn't playing bridge or golf or just sitting at home with Claire, his especially attractive wife of more than forty years, he could go out with the boys and produce some of the swinging sounds he loves so much to keep himself warm.

(1912–   )

The results have either delighted or bewildered many of his jazz brethren.

One of the first musicians to intellectualize jazz—and to make a mint of money doing so—pianist-composer Dave Brubeck with his quartet built up a tremendous following among college kids during the early 1950s, then spread their reputation worldwide via personal appearances and a slew of hit recordings, including their most famous, "Take Five."

"We opened up the whole college market for jazz," the tall, soft-spoken, yet eternally enthusiastic Brubeck recalled. "And back in 1958, we also led the way for jazz groups playing with symphonies when we recorded 'Dialogue

Dave and close friend and longtime compatriot, saxist Paul Desmond

for Jazz Combo and Symphony' with Leonard Bernstein and the New York Philharmonic."

Brubeck's musical roots began to sprout at the age of four, nurtured directly by his piano-teacher mother and encouraged by his two older brothers, both music educators. During the early 1930s, when he was only thirteen, he began playing professionally in local jazz groups in or near his Concord, California, home. Later, he attended the College of the Pacific and Mills College, where he studied under Darius Milhaud and then under Arnold Schoenberg. "But I was still basically a jazz musician who wanted to learn composition. I couldn't even read music then."

His relationship with those classical modernists influenced much of his jazz writing and playing. His compositions have utilized numerous current and avant-garde techniques, such as polyrhythms ("Rhythmic experimentation is the way jzzz has to go," he once noted. "After all, the classical composers have already done everything there is to do melodically and harmonically!"), as well as poly- and atonalities, and the results have either delighted or bewildered many of his jazz brethern. And while his classically influenced piano style has left some followers tapping their feet, others have been scratching their heads, wondering why he persists in pounding so ponderously.

Brubeck, honest and sensitive, has never denied that criticism of his playing has bothered him. However, social injustices have riled him even more. In 1958, when his quartet, featuring alto saxophonist Paul Desmond, was winning polls everywhere, he canceled more than twenty concerts on a southern tour rather than replace his black bassist. His cantata, *Truth Is Fallen,* sang out against events at Kent State and Jackson State colleges; another cantata, *The Gates of Justice,* based on teachings of the Old Testament and Martin Luther King, attempted "to bring the Jewish and black communities together." And a major oratorio, *The Light in the Wilderness,* was focused on the temptations and the teachings of Christ.

The lyricist of all these works has been Dave's wife, Iola. They work out of their modern home in Wilton, Connecticut, where, in conjunction with three of their six children, they succeeded in solving another social problem, the generation gap. Their solution became "Two Generations of Brubeck," which, with father Dave at the piano and sons Darius at various keyboards, Chris on trombone and sometimes bass, and Danny at the drums, fused jazz with rock. Highly successful, the group toured for several years through five continents, until 1979, when Dave gave his sons their wings and organized another strictly jazz group that drew immediate raves.

(1920–   )

"I was always terrible at remembering lyrics and so I'd just shout 'Heigh-de-ho.'"

"I guess it was the way I was able to bridge the gap between music and entertainment," Cab Calloway recently replied when asked what he thought had been his major contribution to music. No doubt about it, the "High Prince of Heigh-de-ho" did attract a large segment of the public to music with his sexy, rhythmic dancing, his swiveling hips, and his uninhibited shouting and singing. But he

"Heigh-de-ho!"

was also a man of instinctively good musical taste who could sing a ballad splendidly and whose various bands, filled with top musicians, maintained very high levels of good musicianship.

Born in Rochester, New York, reared in Baltimore, Maryland, Calloway was attending Crane College in Chicago, working toward a law degree, "when I got tied up with Louis Armstrong and Earl Hines and walked right out of school and into music." With their encouragement he organized a band called the Alabamians, brought it to the famed Savoy Ballroom in New York's Harlem, "where we bombed," and eventually fronted another band called the Missourians. "We were working at a place at Forty-eighth Street and Broadway called the Krazy Kat when the people who ran the Cotton Club came in and saw me. Duke Ellington was going to Hollywood to do a movie and they needed a replacement, and I was it!"

His 1931–32 engagement at the Cotton Club, which catered almost exclusively to whites visiting Harlem and from which he broadcast songs like "Minnie the Moocher," "St. James Infirmary," and "Kickin' the Gong Around," established Calloway as a major attraction. His shouting of "Heigh-de-ho" ("I was always terrible at remembering lyrics and so I'd just shout 'Heigh-de-ho' in place of some words. Then, when I saw how people reacted, I just kept 'heigh-de-ho-ing.' "), along with his top hat and sleek tails, became his identifying features, eventually to be heard and seen by millions via his series of movies.

Calloway considers the highlights of his career his engagement at the Cotton Club, his appearance in the 1943 movie *Stormy Weather,* and his starring role in the early 1950s as Sportin' Life in a successful revival of George Gershwin's famous opera *Porgy and Bess.* "Gershwin used to come up regularly to the Cotton Club to see and hear us, and he even offered me the role in the original production. But I had my first chance to go to Europe at that time, so that's where I went."

Seventeen years later, long after disbanding one of the swing era's best bands (Dizzy Gillespie got his start in that band), Calloway toured the world with tremendous success as the compleat Sportin' Life. Now living comfortably with his wife of many years in their White Plains, New York, home, from which he still occasionally roams to fulfill engagements, a somewhat subdued, refreshingly candid Calloway attributes success not just to his major roles and talents but also to an honest, astute manager ("Irving Mills really did things right for me!") and to the musicians at whom he used to wave his long baton ("I was up there doing my act, but it was the guys themselves who were making the band what it was").

(1907–   )

Glen Campbell

He marched defiantly into Capitol's famed Tower and blew his stack.

In one year he claims to have played on 586 recording sessions and of all those performances only three turned out to be hits. And that was because, Glen Campbell figured out, only those three "had lyrics that meant something! The main thing that makes for a hit song is that it tells a story."

The cherub-faced guitar-playing singer from Delight, Arkansas (population 280 down to 279 when Glen dropped out of the tenth grade), has emerged as probably the best cross-over artist extant between straight pop and country music. For the first twenty years of his musical life that began at age four when he got his Sears Roebuck guitar, he played primarily country music. At the same time, though, he was listening to records by guitarists Django

Glen

Reinhardt and Tal Farlow, pianist George Shearing and singers Nat Cole and Frank Sinatra.

He learned his trade well by playing all sorts of dances in Uncle Dick Bills's band for four or five years. He quit in 1958, formed his own band, Glen Campbell and the Western Wranglers, then finally moved his new wife and their trailer into Los Angeles for a job for which he never got paid. Finally, though, he managed to crack the semiclosed studio musicians' ring. His talent, enthusiasm, and engaging personality brought a refreshing approach to many an arid session, and soon he was playing guitar behind Cole and Sinatra as well as Presley, Bobby Darin, Dean Martin, Merle Haggard, and many others. For six months during 1965 he left the studios to tour with the Beach Boys, his blond hair and bright smile fitting in perfectly.

He'd had a small hit record "Turn Around, Look at Me," on a little label in 1961 which drew Capitol's attention. They released just one record that meant anything at all, then forgot about him for the next few years. "Patience," they kept telling him, an attribute he clung to tenaciously for as long as he could. Finally, unable to hold on any longer, he marched defiantly into Capitol's famed Tower in Hollywood and blew his stack. Through he had never depended solely upon the company for a livelihood—he was making seventy-five thousand dollars a year as a studio musician—he'd learned enough about making records and had enough faith in himself to be able to force the situation.

His attack worked. Capitol started rethinking its Glen Campbell approach, and, sure enough, in 1967 out came his first Grammy-winning selection, "Gentle on My Mind," penned by his friend John Hartford. Four months later came "Wichita Lineman," then "Hey, Little One" and "Galveston," followed by a series of hit sides with Bobbie Gentry.

His hits gave him entree to other fields. He appeared at the White House and before Queen Elizabeth II. And his relaxed, infectious personality attracted the TV moguls. His "Glen Campbell Show" series ran for four and a half years on CBS-TV. He made a host of guest appearances and was featured in nightclubs all over the country. He was starred in several movies: *True Grit, Norwood,* and *Strange Homecoming,* and his annual Glen Campbell golf tourney became one of TV's top sports items.

His blending of the simplicity of the country singer and the glamour of the Hollywood star is reflected in the lyrics of his big 1975 hit "Rhinestone Cowboy." Though he still can project the "aw shucks" self-deprecating approach of a cowpoke, he also knows how to move about effectively in the "business" portion of the music business, which is why he is now several Los Angeles apartment buildings and many valuable San Diego acres richer than he was that day when he suddenly discovered why only three records in 586 sessions had lyrics that meant something, and then proceeded to do something about it.

(1936–   )

Eddie Cantor

. . . mingled bounce, cheer, and Lower East Side overtones.

From his Grandma Ester's imitation of a crazy woman (staged in court to avoid sentencing for her illegal cigar-making) Little Orphan Edward "Izzy" Iskowitz, long before he became Big-Time Entertainer Eddie Cantor, got his ideas about mimicry. He first perpetrated his art in school and on the streets of New York's Lower East Side, where he grew up. He also worked hard at

Mr. Banjo Eyes

clowning, possibly to impress a certain girl basketball player named Ida Tobias, on whom he was hooked. But fortunately no producer's "hook" yanked him off the stage when he performed on Amateur Night at Miner's Bowery Theater. Instead, he won ten dollars, soon moved to a spot as weekend singer in a Coney Island saloon, then advanced to singing waiter, assisted by a sixteen-year-old pianist named Jimmy Durante.

To the stock of "characters" he later developed in small-time vaudeville houses, the nonstop comedian-singer added a winner: a high-toned, black-faced minstrel sporting white-rimmed glasses. Audiences loved the character and called for encores. The exuberant young Cantor gradually developed his own identity, running up and down, clapping his hands, and rolling his large, round eyes, which gained him the nickname of "Banjo Eyes."

He projected this happy "I-am-delighted-with-myself-and-hope-you-are-too!" image throughout his career—in a Gus Edwards vaudeville troupe that included Georgie Jessel, and then at the famed Palace Theater, in numerous editions of the *Ziegfeld Follies,* the first in 1917, the last in 1927, and as star of two Broadway shows, *Kid Boots* and *Whoopee.* Later he also appeared in numerous movies, including a celluloid version of *Whoopee, Roman Scandals, Kid Millions,* and *Strike Me Pink.*

His joyous, zestful delivery of the songs he made famous—"If You Knew Susie," "Margie," "Now's the Time to Fall in Love," his theme song "One Hour with You," and of course "Makin' Whoopee"—mingled bounce, cheer, and Lower East Side overtones. His renditions almost always ended with the familiar razz-ma-tazz climax, which sent audiences into gales of applause. Perhaps the song that meant most to him was "Ida," dedicated to that former girl basketball player whom he later married and who bore him five daughters.

Eddie kept his daughters, as well as his announcers and stooges, in the limelight, first by frequently referring to them on his various radio series and then on his TV shows. He liked to encourage young talent and gave singing space on his programs to Bobby Breen, Deanna Durbin, Dinah Shore, and Eddie Fisher when they were still in their formative years. He was not averse to milking nostalgia, and in the 1950s he played on colleage campuses with his one-man show, *My 40 Years in Show Business.* In 1953 his whole show business career was recapped in a movie, *The Eddie Cantor Story,* starring Keefe Brasselle.

In addition to his performing, Eddie was famous for his philanthropies. One of his favorite charities was Surprise Lake Camp where, as a child, he had spent a magic two weeks away from the city's steaming streets. He learned philanthropy, as he had mimcry, from Grandma Esther, who constantly gave, he reports in his book, *Take My Life,* "out of nothing" to those "with less than nothing."

(1892–1964)

Hoagy Carmichael

"Everytime we played something he liked especially, he'd hit his head on the floor."

He has grown famous and rich as the composer of dozens of big hit songs, including the perennial "Star Dust," which one wag insisted should have been renamed "Gold Dust." But Hoagy Carmichael is also, as *Time* magazine described him, "an extraordinarily tasteful, idiomatic singer."

He performed even before he composed, learning the piano by sitting next to his mother as she improvised playing for the silent movies in the local theater in Bloomington, Indiana. But the jazz improvisations of a black pianist named Reggy Duval attracted and influenced him even more, and in 1923, as an undergraduate at Indiana University, he organized his own jazz band, the Collegians. In the following year he booked the still-to-be-famous Bix Beiderbecke and the Wolverines for a fraternity dance. According to a friend, "When Hoagy heard Bix, he went nuts." Because of the cornetist, he rehired the band for

Hoagy

ten consecutive weeks and eventually became Bix's biggest booster and closest friend. When Beiderbecke appeared at a dance with Paul Whiteman's orchestra, Hoagy, according to Whiteman, "would stand in front of our band all night long. Everytime we played something he liked especially, he'd hit his head on the floor."

Hoagy's enthusiasm for jazz also extended to his performing. Never an outstanding pianist, he managed to impart some of the music's spontaneous, free-feeling spirit through his singing. Technically limited, he described himself as "a vocal stylist. I sing 'flatsy' through the nose."

However, his first recording of his own tune, "Washboard Blues," on the Gennett label featured him as pianist, rather than vocalist, of a group called "Hitch's Happy Harmonists." It wasn't until years later, when he had become established as a composer, that he started to sing in public and on records.

In the meantime, he had been studying law. In 1926 he received his degree and for a while he forsook music and practiced law in Florida, New York, and then back home in Indiana. But apparently he preferred practicing piano and composing and so he quit the bar. One evening in 1928, while feeling depressed, he started whistling a haunting strain. Fascinated, he hied himself to the rear of a Greek candy store off the Indiana University campus where there was a piano. There he completed "Star Dust," probably the most popular song of all time.

Instantaneous success did not follow. Armed with a briefcase of songs, he set out for Hollywood, where he was totally rebuffed. Next he traveled to New York where Mitchell Parish added lyrics to "Star Dust." Then, three years after the memorable night in the Greek candy store, the first of hundreds of versions of the song was recorded by Isham Jones and his orchestra.

Hoagy signed a publishing contract with Mills Music, which began promoting his songs. The reactions from singers and from Carmichael's revered jazz performers was tremendous, as Louis Armstrong, Mildred Bailey, Bing Crosby, and others featured songs like "Rockin' Chair," "Georgia on My Mind," "Lazy Bones," and "Lazy River," which Hoagy later also sang on records. Hollywood, which had spurned him, now beckoned, then gobbled up tunes like "Two Sleepy People," "Small Fry," "Ole Buttermilk Sky," and "In the Cool, Cool, Cool of the Evening." It also started featuring him in movies, assigning him parts that fitted his naturally relaxed, down-home personality. His performances were a thespian expression of the feeling of jazz that had first influenced Hoagy, and to which, for more than half a century, he was to contribute his immensely musical and very popular songs.

(1899–   )

The Carpenters

A bubblegum alternative to hard rock.

Ask Richard Carpenter what "the three B's" mean to him and he is likely to respond "the Beach Boys, the Beatles, and Burt Bacharach." Ask Karen Carpenter for her preferences, and she'll admit "my taste naturally evolved from what Richard liked. I am totally into whatever he listens to."

Karen's response provides some insight into the tightness of the Carpenters' brother-sister act. Extremely close, musically and philosophically, their oneness of purpose has been rewarded by such reliable show biz criteria as their consistently high record sales, their growing collection of Grammy Awards, and their many SRO concerts throughout the world.

If they are a pop music phenomenon, they are also an entertainment enigma: adored and despised; emulated and ridiculed. Critic Tom Nolan managed to cut through the smog of press-agent hyperbole in a recent appraisal: "Here are these neatly dressed kids, a polite-seeming brother and sister team, materializing like a weird hallucination in the midst of acid rock."

Of course the Carpenters didn't just materialize whole cloth. They were born and lived their early teen years in New Haven, Connecticut, and in 1963 their family moved to Southern California. By that time, Richard had studied piano at Yale and continued those studies at Cal State University, Long Beach. Karen

The happy Carpenters

taught herself the rudiments of drumming while in high school, where she joined the marching band to get out of gym, and by 1966 the Carpenters (then two thirds of a jazz trio) won a Los Angeles County-sponsored competition, "Battle of the Bands," at the Hollywood Bowl, and the sibling combo was launched, both singing, with Richard playing the piano and Karen at the drums. Three years later, Herb Alpert had the foresight to sign Richard and Karen, by then reduced to a duo, to A&M Records, and the Carpenters have been an institution ever since.

What *kind* of institution is a matter of debate. To those weary of rock's electronic pressures, their unamplified, relaxed, and relatively simple style offered a welcome relief. But some critics complained that the "squeaky clean vitamin swallowers" were little more than a "bubblegum alternative" to hard rock. Still others assumed that little was required to achieve their seemingly simple "seamless sound," causing Richard to protest that "they should be there when we're putting it together. It's anything but simple. There is a hell of a lot going on."

Indeed there is, and Richard has developed into the dominant musical intelligence behind the Carpenters. It's his choice of material (often his own songs), his arrangements, his tasteful, jazz-tinged piano playing, his production of the recording. And, in addition, he usually contributes his voice to the final mix.

Of course the dominant voice has been Karen's. She has become one of the most poised and confident singers on the pop scene. Her rich, lower register has blossomed with maturity, and her poignant phrasing reveals the debt she owes to Kay Starr.

Offstage, Richard seldom reads books and has remained apathetic about politics, admitting, "I'm not into much besides my music and cars and investing money." And there has been considerable to invest. By the mid-1970s Richard and Karen had become millionaires, with their royalties and $30,000-per-night concert fees soundly invested in shopping centers and apartment complexes, two of them named for their biggest hits, "Close to You" and "We've Only Just Begun."

Karen has been described as childlike, having missed out on the normal stages of maturing because of her early acceptance as a star. According to *Rolling Stone,* "she has been sheltered, pampered, and behaves accordingly." Explained Richard to *People's* Richard Windeler: "The problem is we were growing professionally during the years most people were concentrating on being a person."

Personal traits aside, the Carpenters are a solid, chart-busting musical entity, and it is only the product of their combined talents that has been any concern to their adoring fans. And that product reveals an eternal youthfulness that consistently seems to say, "We've Only Just Begun."

(Richard Carpenter: 1947–   )
(Karen Carpenter: 1950–   )

Benny Carter

He has molded musical tastes here and abroad.

"Carter's countenance is deceptively mild. His ready wit, his smile, his soft, quick speech also give slight indication of the iron will encased in his brilliant mind," wrote trumpeter Rex Stewart.

Alto saxophonist, arranger, composer, sometime trumpeter and clarinetist and gentleman to the core, Bennett Lester Carter brings to each of his accomplishments rare gifts.

New York-born and mainly self-taught, Carter began on trumpet, traded it in for a C-melody sax (his first inspiration was Frank Trumbauer, a white saxophonist once featured with Paul Whiteman), turned pro at seventeen, then went to Wilberforce College intending to study theology but soon found himself on the road again with Horace Henderson's Collegians.

Benny

"The greater number of the fellows in the band had graduated," Carter remembered, "but those of us who hadn't decided to forget the university just to keep the band together."

In late 1928, after a stint in the band of Horace's older brother, Fletcher (then the graduate academy for jazzmen), Carter formed his first own big band.

He was a band leader intermittently until 1955, yet he never achieved great commercial success at it, though few bands were so well respected by their peers. "Having worked under Benny's baton is a real recommendation anywhere in the music world," said a Carter alumnus.

Until the advent of Charlie Parker (whom he much admired), Carter and Johnny Hodges had been the pace setters on alto sax. Carter's arranging talents were also much in demand. Bands for which he wrote included those of Duke Ellington, Benny Goodman, Henderson, Don Redman, even Glenn Miller. "Nobody writes for saxophones with such skill and flair," said critic Stanley Dance.

In the spring of 1935 Carter began a three-year stay in Europe with work in Paris. By the following March he was in London as staff arranger for Henry Hall's BBC Dance Band, turning out an average of six scores a week. "I could still do it," he told Dance thirty years later. "An arrangement a day, and two if it were just a matter of vocal backgrounds."

Back home again, Carter led the best bands of his career in the early 1940s, but by 1945 he had settled in Los Angeles and begun the second phase of his professional life—that of a successful and highly proficient motion-picture and television arranger-composer. At first he "ghosted" scores but soon got his own screen credits and has scored dozens of feature films, in some of which he also appears as a player *(The Snows of Kilimanjaro, The View from Pompey's Head)*. The series *M Squad* and *Ironside* are among his TV credits.

Carter was still taking time out for appearances as a player in the 1960s and '70s, most often for Norman Granz of Jazz at the Philharmonic fame.

In 1974 Princeton University (where he has been a visiting lecturer) awarded Carter an honorary Doctor of Humanities degree, citing him as a "musician's musician" whose "modesty and sincerity have become one with his creative abilities so that he has molded musical tastes here and abroad and assumed throughout the world his role of ambassador-at-large in this most indigenous of American arts."

(1907–   )

Johnny Cash

"Maybe people just became ready for me."

The towering man strides onstage, dressed in frock-coat black. His guitar is slung across his back, and running along his chin is a scar. Most folks sitting in the darkened auditorium know that this man had done some "time" in jail and the image is fraught with overtones of dark night knife fights and drug charges. It is inconsequential, of course, that the scar is from the removal of a mole, and the jail time in question was but a couple of nights spent locked up to "sleep it off" in a small town. After all, an image is an image.

He tosses his mane of over-the-collar hair and leans back over his shoulder to mutter something to his bass player. The familiar bass run of "Folsom Prison Blues" rings out. Then, "Hello, I'm Johnny Cash . . ."

Despite all the legends and the imagery that surround him, Johnny Cash is unquestionably real, a man of experience and magnetism who, for years, has conveyed to millions the truth and emotion of country music.

"I've been very successful, but I don't ever try to analyze the reasons for it," said Cash at one point very early in his career. "I just feel that folks will enjoy my brand of country music and that this is not 'here today and gone tomorrow' success."

Johnny

Ultimately he was correct, but the road has been paved with real ups and downs. His childhood and teen years were spent in the grinding poverty which characterized the rural South during the Depression and post-Depression years. He recalls: "We were poor, but we always had enough to eat, even if sometimes it was nothin' but fatback and turnip greens." But he adds, "We didn't know we was poor until we went in to town."

Cash gained some experience as a performer, working as a country singer while in the Air Force between 1951 and 1954 and then began his climb to fame on the legendary Memphis-based Sun Records. Having already spawned Elvis Presley, Sun launched Johnny Cash in 1955 with two songs penned by John himself, "Hey Porter" and "Cry, Cry, Cry."

"Cry, Cry, Cry" was a regional hit and within a year Johnny found himself with a recording contract, road dates, and another contract with the Grand Ole Opry. Two singles, "I Walk the Line" and "Folsom Prison Blues," followed and provided Cash with access to the pop music market.

To look at Johnny Cash in the 1970s it's hard to imagine his being anything but vigorous and very, very together during any period in his career. But times had grown difficult for Johnny during the 1960s. Following his signing with Columbia Records in 1958, Cash left the comfort of the Grand Ole Opry and began touring constantly to keep his name before the public. Soon stories of missed appearances, of sleepless pill-popping nights and murky days began to surround Cash.

Finally one night in 1967 in a small Georgia town, he experienced a brush with death from an overdose that scared him sufficiently to stop popping pills. Divorced from his first wife, he returned to Nashville and married singer June Carter. It turned out to be the kind of marriage, according to Joyce Maynard of the New York *Times,* "that people in Nashville write love songs about when they aren't writing songs about heartbreak." June helped him put his life back in order. "The hard times, the torture and misery I put myself through," he later related, "made me know pain and gave me tolerance and compassion for other people's problems."

By the mid-1970s, thanks to a series of hit records, including his delightful and witty "A Boy Named Sue," plus many outstandingly successful appearances in concerts and on TV, including a memorable collaboration with Bob Dylan, he had become firmly established as one of country music's most respected citizens. A born-again Christian, he has taken his religion seriously enough to travel to Jerusalem, perform on Billy Graham's crusades, produce a film about the life of Jesus and compose country songs drawn from stories in the Bible.

Looking over his acres of Tennessee land he mused recently, "I can't explain it. I haven't changed the way I've been singing over the past fourteen years. Maybe people just became ready for me. Maybe they just started listening."

(1932–   )

"Soul is when you take a song and make it a part of you."

They bring out the superlatives when they talk about Ray Charles. Frank Sinatra has said that he's the only genius in the business. Jerry Wexler of Atlantic Records says, "He's an originator." Aretha Franklin calls him the "Right Reverend."

He's the father of soul. Wexler explains, "He took the melodies and rhythm patterns of gospel music and wrote love lyrics to them and sang them and created this whole thing."

"I wasn't trying to take the church music and make the blues out of it or vice versa," Charles says. "I was raised in the church. So singing in the church and also hearing the blues, I guess this was the only way I could sing. Anything I do, good or bad, is very, very natural."

Charles's definition of soul music focuses on performance. "Soul is when you can take a song and make it part of you—a part that's so true, so real, people think it must have happened to you. I'm not satisfied unless I can make them feel what I feel.

"It's like electricity; it's a force than can light a room. Soul is a power."

Charles projects that power through his voice and his piano. Grunts and groans combine with passionate coos and moans, often climaxed by throbbing shouts that seem to emanate from the very core of his being. He interprets all of his songs with equal fervor, whether they be basic blues, pop ballads, jazz, or even country songs. The soul sound envelops them all.

Part of his total sound includes his own piano accompaniments—forceful, jazz-tinged, rhythmic—blending perfectly with the mood of his voice.

The piano, especially boogie-woogie piano, fascinated him when he was just a kid. He credits Wiley Pittman, a neighbor in Greensville, Florida, for steering him toward music.

"Every time he started playing boogie-woogie on his piano I'd go over to his house and jump on his lap and bang at the keys. I couldn't possibly have been playing anything, but he sensed that a child who loves music enough to give up his playing time has a genuine interest in music. He'd never shoo me away."

That was when Ray could still see, before he contracted glaucoma at age six and went blind. At seven he went to a school for the blind and deaf in Orlando, Florida. There, because of his love for the piano, he was given music

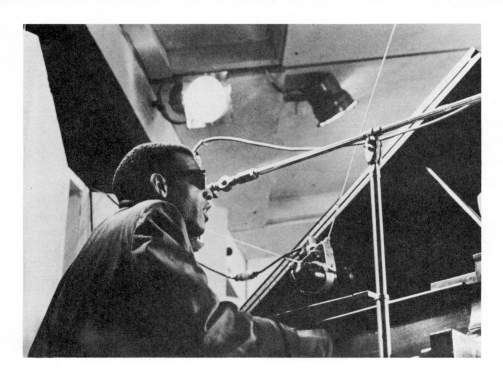

Ray plays . . .

. . . and reads the lyrics (with Cleo Laine)

lessons. After learning the chords, he taught himself to write arrangements for band instruments, a talent that qualified him for jobs with local bands when, at fifteen, he was orphaned and left the school. He shortened his name, dropping the family name, Robinson, so he wouldn't be confused with fighter Sugar Ray Robinson. He tried to live by the philosophy his mother had taught him: "You've got your brain. Use it. Just because you've lost your eyesight you're not stupid."

In his later, more affluent years, when he could have coasted through performances doing his hits by rote, he kept in mind another of his mother's injunctions: "Once you tackle something, do it right. Don't cheat yourself. You're going to have enough people out there doing all the cheating for you you're ever going to need." He says, "I come first. I refuse to let me go out and do a get-by job. I owe it to myself to do it right."

In 1948 he left Florida, going to Seattle by bus. There he got work, trying to sound like Nat Cole, and signed a recording contract with Swingtime in Los Angeles. In the early 1950s Atlantic Records bought the contract. Charles recorded "I Got a Woman" and immediately made a breakthrough to a wider audience. Hit followed hit—"Hallelujah, I Love Her So," "What'd I Say?" and then for ABC Records "Georgia on My Mind," "I Can't Stop Loving You," "Busted," "That Lucky Old Sun."

But life was by no means serene, for Ray had become addicted to drugs, a habit that began, he says, in 1948 because he didn't want to be the "baby" of a band, left out of whatever the other musicians were into. Arrested in Boston in 1963 on a drug charge, he quit cold, after a sudden mental image of his three sons scarred by having a jailbird father. He took a year off from performing, checked into a hospital and met with a psychiatrist, but he insists those things were to prove to the courts he was clean. He says he simply stopped taking drugs. Returning to his career, he cut "Crying Time," the first of a new series of hits, which for the years that followed he performed not only on records but in concerts throughout a world where audiences welcomed Ray Charles as the epitome of soul.

Asked once whether he had desired fame, Charles said no. "Frankly, this may sound egotistical, but I never wanted to be a famous person. But I always wanted to be great. Always."

(1930–   )

Chubby Checker

Ernest Evans, with his powerhouse baritone and whirling dervish dancing.

"When I go on stage, I like to conquer. It's just me, those people and my music. There are no barriers."

Whether in a small club, a posh hotel, or an arena, the tall and broad Ernest Evans, with his powerhouse baritone vocals and whirling dervish dancing, has invariably lived up to his good-time reputation as Chubby Checker, "King of the Twist." His recording of the "The Twist," which inspired a national dance craze in the 1960s, was, according to a 1976 computation by *Billboard* magazine, the most popular single record of the last twenty years.

Born in South Carolina, where his father worked on a tobacco farm, Evans

Chubby the Twister

was four years old when he was taken by his mother to hear a pianist and entertainer named Sugarchild Robinson. After the show the lad told his mother: "Mom, that's what I want to be, a singer."

The family moved to Philadelphia when he was seven, and by his early teens he had already developed into a talented amateur performer.

When he was seventeen he landed a nonpaying assignment recording his imitations of Elvis Presley and Fats Domino for a "talking Christmas card" sent out by popular disc jockey Dick Clark, host of the TV dance program "American Bandstand." Clark's wife was in the studio during the session and, noting the teenager's girth and his nickname of "Chubby" and hearing his mimicry of Fats Domino, suggested he tie up with another game name and bill himself as "Chubby Checker." (In later years he was falsely rumored to be Domino's nephew.)

Checker finally recorded his imitations for commercial release in a single called "The Class," his first hit. The top side for his second single was a novelty item called "Toot," and for the flip side his manager chose "The Twist," which had been written and recorded sometime earlier by Hank Ballard and the Midnighters. Checker remembered: "I didn't want to do that song after Ballard but my manager said it fit my voice, so I did it anyway. It turned out he was right; a couple of months later it was number one."

Originally released in 1960, "The Twist" was reissued late in 1961, when it again went to the top. Meanwhile, Checker was turning out other dance novelty hits—"Pony Time," "The Fly," "Limbo Rock," "Let's Twist Again," and "Hooka Tooka."

The 1964 entrance of the British groups, which so upset the *status quo* of the American pop scene, mauled Checker's career. Beatlemania transformed him almost overnight from a king to a pawn. "After that, Checker did *nothing*. I was scrounging for jobs wherever I could find them. I was in exile."

From 1964 to 1970 he eked out a living on the road. His fortunes revived with the rock nostalgia boom that began at the turn of the decade. In 1971 he appeared before an audience of twenty thousand in Madison Square Garden and wowed them with his lungpower, fancy footwork, and sheer energy.

From that time on he made a rapid comeback. Television and personal appearances confirmed him to be a master entertainer, and he continued to maintain rigid standards of performance. "When I'm out there it has to be great," he insisted. "I knew that people would come round again someday, and I kept working so I'd be ready. I knew the right time would come for me again."

(1941–   )

M. Chevalier

"Every little breeze seems to whisper Louise!"

Maurice Chevalier

"I'm glad I'm not young anymore."

Around the world in his eightieth year he went, visiting sixty cities with his one-man show, gathering new fans. His way with a song—and with audiences— still charmed. Not one wink, one tilt of the straw boater, one deliciously French-accented English syllable did he ever leave to chance. His artistic calculation delighted his audiences but not some of his partners, who found his ego stifling. "All he cared about was his career and his mother," Jeanette MacDonald, the object of his affections in three Hollywood musicals, was quoted as saying.

Maurice Chevalier had two passions: work and love. The price of success he learned early. As a twelve-year-old, Chevalier debuted at a local café in Menilmontant, a workers' suburb of Paris where he was born. He sang in a different key from the piano and was laughed off the stage. But neither this humiliation—not his last or worst—nor the poverty of his childhood and obligations as sole support of his mother, nor a World War I prison camp and World War II dangers, could keep him from his appointed destiny: entertaining.

The clown costumes of his early music-hall years evolved into the white suits and tuxedos of his later years. Comedy routines and revues developed into film roles and one-man shows; his modest voice into a captivating half-talking, half-singing style; the Parisian favorite into the world's beloved quintessential French boulevardier.

Chevalier's performing life was a succession of unfolding careers. At age twenty-one, he "arrived" at the Folies Bergères as dancing partner to famed singer-dancer Mistinguett, with whom he formed a liaison deeper than all his others but which professional rivalry eventually ended. He "arrived" in Hollywood almost twenty years later to evoke sighs from female moviegoers as he protested love—with outthrust lower lip, in French-accented words of American popular songs—in films dominated, in title and/or theme, with the grand passion: *Love Me Tonight, The Love Parade, One Hour with You.* The first of his seven 1928-35 films, *Innocents in Paris,* linked him forever with song-girl "Louise," who, with "Mimi," proved more faithful than his reel- or real-life girls.

In the late-1930s he said *au revoir* to Hollywood and returned home. Through the war and post-war years in France, Chevalier starred in revues, organized entertainment for soldiers, and created his one-man show, dazzling audiences in Paris, London, and eventually America.

In 1947 he resumed his film career in a prize-winning French movie, *Silence*

Est d'Or. Returning to the United States in 1954, Chevalier renewed his love affair with American audiences on Broadway, in supper clubs, and with a "live" TV spectacular. He took up his long-interrupted Hollywood screen career with two films that, ironically, were shot in Paris: *Love in the Afternoon* and the musical *Gigi,* in which he sang one Lerner-Loewe song that seemed specially tailored to his mellowing years and philosophy: "I'm Glad I'm Not Young Anymore." Character roles in four more films and numerous personal appearances followed. At age seventy-eight he received standing ovations for his show at New York's Waldorf-Astoria and at eighty enthusiastic acclaim on his world tour. These triumphs must have fulfilled the expressed wish of this perennially debonair song-and-dance man that "my old age . . . be my best performance."

(1888–1972)

Chicago

"Our roots are basically rock, but we can and do play jazz."

The seven original members of Chicago got the idea in 1967—just about the time that Blood, Sweat and Tears decided to marry jazz and rock—that they could add horn arrangements and freer percussion to rock's electric guitars and get a new, bigger, more interesting sound. And the group did just that and, with remarkable consistency and hard work, kept doing it and turning out hit album after hit album for the next ten years.

Its consistency extended to its personnel as well as to its music. "We were friends before any of this [success] started happening," woodwind-player Walter Parazaider pointed out to Lou O'Neill, Jr., of the New York *Post* in late 1977,

Chicago

who described the group as "one of the most down to earth, unaffected bands it's ever been our pleasure to know. Strength through unity—it's an old strategy but one that still works."

Singer-pianist Robert Lamm, the only member of the septet not born and raised in Chicago, explained to Harvey Siders of *Down Beat,* "Our roots are basically rock, but we can and do play jazz. Blood, Sweat and Tears"—with whom the group is constantly being compared—"is basically a jazz-oriented combo that can play a lot of rock."

But while Blood, Sweat and Tears' personnel changed over the years, Chicago's remained remarkably consistent, with Parazaider, Lamm, trombonist James Pankow, drummer Daniel Seraphine, trumpeter Lee Loughnane, guitarist Terry Kath, and bassist Peter Cetera. Brazilian percussionist Laudir de Oliveira joined the group, and in 1978, after the death in England of Kath, who had sometimes been lead singer, Donnie Dacus became the guitarist.

But perhaps the most important member of the group, almost all of whom had had considerable musical training, has been one who plays no instrument at all: producer James William Guercio, who had known some of the group when they were fellow undergraduates at DePaul University in Chicago. He had left "to make his bucks" as a talent manager, producer, and songwriter in Los Angeles, but came back to listen to the Chicago Transit Authority, as it was called in the mid-1960s, when it was appearing in midwestern clubs and colleges. Guercio took charge. He moved the group to Los Angeles, paid the rent for all, provided rehearsal space, found jobs, brought record companies around to hear them, shortened their name, signed them to Columbia in 1969, and produced all their records. Though they had their share of hits, such as their early "Does Anybody Know What Time It Is" and "Make Me Smile," their biggest recognition and income came from the series of albums released from 1970 on, all identified merely by Roman numerals from I to XI.

Some of their selections were long and quite advanced for immature rock listeners. Yet they were accepted by the public, though at times faulted by critics for not continuing to make stylistic innovations and in fact even accused of sounding stale. Its members, however, never stopped taking their music seriously, concentrating on keeping it fresh, giving each member a chance to improvise at every concert, and, after the *Chicago VI* album, devoting four months out of each year to rehearsing, recording, writing music, and generally trying to improve their commercially oriented, rock-based sound.

At the same time they worked hard at keeping their long-standing personal relationships going. Chicago was able to do that, according to Lamm, because its members had grown as close as brothers, who, after marrying and raising families, had become uncles to each other's children. "Personally and musically," he said, "we're a family." And, he might have added, a family of very wealthy individuals, each of whom could retire, but all of whom seem to want to continue to perform, create, and add higher and higher Roman numerals to their list of best-selling *Chicago* albums.

Charlie Christian

The entire concept of the guitar as a jazz instrument was changed.

On a late-summer evening in 1939, the intrepid talent spotter John Hammond, assisted by Benny Goodman bassist Artie Bernstein, lugged a strange contraption onto the bandstand of the Los Angeles nightclub where the Goodman band was appearing. It was an electric guitar amplifier belonging to twenty-three-year-old, Texas-born and Oklahoma-bred Charlie Christian. Musicians who had heard Christian play had been speaking of him with awe, and this scuttlebut had intrigued Hammond, who ventured to Oklahoma City to hear for himself and promptly brought Christian to audition for Goodman. But the famous bandleader had no intention of expanding his organization and received the young man—resplendent in ten-gallon hat, yellow shoes, green suit, and purple shirt with string bow tie—rather coolly, barely listening to him play a chorus

Charlie

of "Tea for Two." Still, Hammond would not be denied, and when Benny returned from intermission to find the apparition and his apparatus ensconced on the stand, he could not make a scene and resignedly gave the guitarist the nod to take a solo on "Rose Room." Charlie's virtuoso performance, which combined his raw rhythmic drive with the more sophisticated harmonic changes he had picked up from his early idols, like tenor saxist Lester Young, lasted well over half an hour, and the rest is jazz history. Goodman formed a sextet that featured Christian and brought his guitar wizardry to the attention of fans and, even more importantly, of other musicians. So dynamic was Charlie's creativity that the entire concept of the guitar as a jazz instrument was changed, and by the time Christian's life had come to an end on March 2, 1942, the acoustic guitar was on its way out of jazz, and the electric guitar was definitely in.

Charlie was one of five sons who performed with their blind, singer-guitarist father. He started on trumpet, took up guitar in earnest at twelve, and also mastered bass and piano. He turned pro at fifteen, gigged for several years in the South and Midwest and was playing in Bismarck, North Dakota, when guitarist Mary Osborn heard him. She thought at first that she was listening to a tenor sax oddly distorted by amplification until she realized that the sounds came from Charlie's electric guitar, playing single-note line solos and voiced like a horn in the ensembles. "I remember some of the figures he played in his solos," she said. "They were exactly the same things Benny recorded later on as 'Flying Home,' 'Seven Come Eleven,' and all the others."

Featured with Goodman and earning more money than he had ever dreamed of, Charlie was catapulted into fame overnight. But it didn't change the shy, gentle young man, whose two great loves in life were music and girls. He could have plenty of the latter now, and as for the former, he got his kicks playing after regular working hours in jam sessions, particularly at Minton's Playhouse in Harlem, where such young experimenters as Dizzy Gillespie, Kenny Clarke, and Thelonious Monk gathered nightly. The club's manager, ex-band leader Teddy Hill, bought Charlie a second amplifier so he wouldn't have to carry one uptown, and Charlie blissfully spun out the swinging, blues-inflected, catchy lines that would help revolutionize jazz and bring about the phenomenon to be known as bop.

By the time bop became fully visible in 1945, Charlie had been dead for three years, a victim of tuberculosis, then still a major scourge of impoverished blacks. He had been with Goodman for just some twenty months, until June 1941, and spent the rest of his brief life in a sanatorium on Staten Island.

Charlie Christian flashed like a comet across the jazz sky, but the musical stardust trail he left still provides glittering inspiration for young guitarists everywhere.

(1916–1942)

Eric Clapton

"I'd love to knock an audience cold with one note."

One of rock's living legends, the slight, shy Englishman has never been very comfortable with his formidable talents. Although Eric Clapton's blues-based guitar wizardry drew critical acclaim and an audience so adoring that the slogan "Clapton Is God" became a staple of late 1960s graffiti, he remained a troubled, brooding figure, given to long periods of gloomy seclusion. His dissatisfaction

Eric

with his music eventually drove him into a three-year heroin addiction that nearly resulted in self-destruction.

Clapton's strangely sad eyes reflect what must have been a painful childhood. Brought up in Surrey, England, by grandparents, "because my mother went away when I was very young and got married to someone," he attended local schools and then Kingston Art College. Lonely and frequently unhappy, he has described himself as "underprivileged. I was always the seven-stone [ninety-eight-pound] weakling. I used to hang out with three or four other kids who were all in the same kind of predicament. They used to call us the loonies." They formed a tight clique that relished the latest Chuck Berry and Buddy Holly records. "I'd read things on the backs of album covers like 'rock 'n' roll has its roots in the blues,' and stuff like that. And so I thought, 'What's that all about? I'll have to find out.'"

He found out while in art school, where the blues really took over the young introvert and moved him to take up the guitar. He began his professional career busking around Kingston and Richmond, occasionally standing in for a skinny teenager named Mick Jagger. The turning point in Clapton's career came in 1963 when he signed on with the Yardbirds, a pop blues unit whose raw vocals, aggressively amplified guitar textures, and thuddingly heavy percussion laid the groundwork for a new form of rock, later dubbed "heavy metal."

Soon word began to spread about the intense solos of the group's new lead guitarist, Eric "Slowhand" Clapton. But Eric left the Yardbirds in 1965 when they elected to record commercial pop and did a six-month stint with John Mayall's Blues Breakers. And then in 1966 came Cream, an epic synthesis of ashcan power percussion and bare-wire British blues, featuring Clapton, bassist Jack Bruce, and wiry, red-eyed/haired drummer Ginger Baker. Whenever the three squared off onstage to erupt in their self-described "neocontrapuntal" frenzies, the total effect sounded like mountains falling.

By now, Clapton had forged a uniquely elegant guitar style whose leaping attack and fluid phrasing was a deft marriage of his Yardbird roots and his rustic blues conceits. But though Cream's onslaught created audience reactions that nearly drowned out the furor onstage, Clapton, who insisted that the group "was originally meant to be a blues trio," complained that it had become "a jazz-rock group." So he cut out and, after appearing briefly with Blind Faith and Derek and the Dominoes, took the most crucial step of all: admitting that he was finally on his own. Released in 1970, his *Eric Clapton* solo album featured his vocals and his most deferential playing up to that time. More critical and commercial acclaim followed, but Clapton, plagued by heroin addiction, soon disappeared from the music scene, surfacing only to appear at the Concert for Bangladesh and the 1973 Rainbow Concert in London.

After kicking the heroin habit with the help of electro-acupuncture, he managed a triumphant return in 1974 with his sedate *461 Ocean Boulevard* album, followed by a live, blues-heavy *E. C. Was Here* and the unhappy, up-tempo "No Reason to Cry." Still restless and intransigent, his melancholia and private demons seemed to prevent him from finding any lasting serenity from his music. "I'd love to knock an audience cold with one note," he once confided, "but what would I do for the rest of the evening?"

(1945–   )

Eric

Rosie with manager Joe Shribman and producer Mitch Miller

"Come on-a My House!"

Rosemary Clooney

"What's a key?"

She had a delightful shyness about her, both in her singing and in her personality, and she seemed so very real and honest that when she sang "Come on-a My House" on her first hit record in 1951, everyone was ready and willing to accept her invitation.

Rosemary Clooney's was a unique voice, low and relaxed, and the slight lisp that would occasionally slip out only made her seem more vulnerable. Career-wise she seemed to have led a happy life, but her stormy marriage with Jose Ferrer ended in a divorce and left Rosey with five children and a weight problem that took her out of public circulation for several years. In the 1970s, however, she seemed to have put it all together again, and, judged by her appearances on several television shows, her singing was as lovely as ever.

She had never been blessed with overconfidence. When she was only three years old, she sang at her grandfather's political rallies in Kentucky trying to win votes with tunes like "Sweethearts on Parade," "Home on the Range," and "When Your Hair Has Turned to Silver." Convinced that she had bombed, she later related that she had developed "some sort of complex that I couldn't sing. Besides, I wasn't very pretty, so I didn't do any more singing until my junior year in high school." Then she and her younger sister, Betty, decided to audition for their hometown Cincinnati radio station, WLW, as a sister team. As Rosemary later recalled, "We had no music and when somebody asked us, 'What key?' we just looked wide-eyed and asked, 'What's a key?' " But they got the job, and when bandleader Tony Pastor, traveling through town some years later, heard them, he offered them a chance to sing with his band, and they accepted.

They performed as a sister team, with Rosey also featured as a soloist. Betty finally tired of the road and left to get married and soon thereafter, Pastor, convinced that Rosey was ready for her own career, encouraged her to leave.

The folks at Columbia Records had already heard her on the sides she had cut for them with Pastor and were willing to take a chance on her. And CBS radio was enough impressed to spot her on its "Songs for Sale" series. And Duke Ellington became so impressed that he invited her to record an entire album of his songs with his band. Rosey was a nice, quite, polite person, and everyone was rooting for her, but there was little cause for rejoicing until Mitch Miller dug up the unusual "Come on-a My House," a distinct departure from the warm ballads she preferred singing. "But," she said at the time, "if that's what they want me to sing, that's what I'll sing." Fortunately for her and her admirers, who preferred her emoting tender love songs, "House" established her strongly enough so that she could have more say in the choice of her songs. And so she selected and recorded some lovely tunes, like "Hey, There," "Tenderly," "Blues in the Night," "This Ole House," and the unfortunately prophetic "Love, You Didn't Do Right by Me."

After her marriage to Ferrer in 1953, she settled down in a sumptuous home in Beverly Hills. She appeared in several movies and during the mid-1950s presided for a while over "The Rosemary Clooney Show" on television. But domestic responsibilities demanded most of her time and energies. And so she dropped from public sight and sound. However, during all those years, her voice and inherent charm never deserted her, and when she was ready to return to public singing in the 1970s, having found emotional serenity and her svelte figure again, she still imparted the same musical warmth and captivating shyness that a quarter of a century earlier had made her one of popular music's most attractive singers.

(1928–   )

George M. Cohan

Aflutter with American flags and permeated with bright-tempoed, patriotic songs.

He did his thing, long before that became a criterion for happiness. He did it more completely and triumphantly than almost any other performer in show business. He sang, danced, acted, produced, directed, and built and owned theaters. He wrote songs, sketches, musicals, and dramas and wrote them fast: how else could he have turned out seventy-eight plays (only seven of them with collaborators), acted in most of them, and in the same forty-year period (1901–40) put on eighty Broadway productions, either by himself or with his longtime partner, Sam H. Harris?

That was the time of course when George M. Cohan was not part of Nostalgia, when "Yankee Doodle Dandy," "Over There," "Give My Regards to Broadway," and "You're a Grand Old Flag" rang out from Broadway stages and stages around the country, with a "now" pow that bedazzled audiences, a time when George M. was king of the Great White Way.

The Yankee Doodle Dandy

Like all self-respecting performers, he was practically born in the proverbial trunk, and when he was four months old his mother Nellie took him on stage for his debut. She and his father Jerry were then trouping as Two Cohans. The troupe became Four Cohans when seven-year-old George and his eight-and-a half-year-old sister Josephine joined as regulars. George began his career as a fiddle player, and, at thirteen, had a try at acting as the title character in *Peck's Bad Boy.* Meanwhile he was learning from his father about writing comedy sketches and experimenting with rhymes and tunes. It was not too long before Cohan found the sure-fire formula that lifted operaetta and vaudeville skit entertainments into breezy new landscapes, aflutter with American flags and permeated with bright-tempoed, patriotic songs, contemporary slang, punning gags, and good-natured humor. In the preteen and teen years of the century American audiences marched, mentally, to the rousing Cohan measures. And vast numbers of them were to march, physically, to them when World War I involved American forces in Europe and Cohan sent them off with "Over There." It, and "You're a Grand Old Flag," won for him a Congressional Medal of Honor.

In the postwar years, however, the man who had reigned over Broadway with those all-American songs, delivered in a somewhat nasal voice, left corner of his mouth drawn down, with his affable dancing and gags, with his old-fashioned gallantry to women, and preference for male social turfs of baseball and theatrical clubs, that rare entertainer was out of step with the changing times. Though he continued to write plays, produce and act in them, they were already becoming part of the nostalgia of a disappearing era. But in 1933 a role embodying values compatible with his was offered him—the small-town editor in Eugene O'Neill's *Ah, Wilderness!* In this role he hit new heights as a dramatic actor. But he soon put on dancing shoes again: literally as the song-and-dance President in *I'd Rather Be Right;* and psychologically, as consultant for the Walter Kerr–Leo Brady play about his life, *Yankee Doodle Boy* (in 1942 to become the smash film *Yankee Doodle Dandy* starring James Cagney as Cohan). And George M. himself, though ill, was even then writing a new show for the "real" Yankee Doodle Boy, called *The Musical Comedy Man,* when death canceled it. Had Cohan lived to see his "return" to Broadway via Joel Gray in *George M!* in 1969, he might well have again made his famous curtain speech: "My father thanks you, my mother thanks you, my sister thanks you, and I thank you."

(1878–1942)

Nat "King" Cole

"It's a shame when you're told you can't do something just because it's 'too good.'"

"Nat Cole was not so much a singer as a whisperer or a confider. As a fondler of words he was in a class by himself." That's how musicologist Henry Pleasants (in his book *The Great American Popular Singers*) portrays one of the nicest, warmest, most respected entertainers ever to enter (and to depart much too prematurely) the world of popular music. But as Pleasants and other experts and admirers have recognized, Cole was more than a confidential pop singer; he was also an exceptional jazz pianist whose sparkling, swinging style strongly influenced two other major jazz pianists, Oscar Peterson and Bill Evans.

Cole himself admitted to two major influences in his life: his father (on his character) and pianist Earl Hines (on his music). He credited the senior Cole for the presence in him of what he liked to call "moral fiber. My old man, being a minister, always stressed its importance. I guess it rubbed off on me."

When Nat was four years old the Coles moved from his native Montgomery, Alabama, to Chicago. There he played organ and sang in his father's church choir, which was directed by his mother. Also in Chicago he heard Earl Hines play his strong, swinging piano, and Nat became hooked on jazz. He organized his own band, the Rogues of Rhythm, subbed for Hines in his club, played some of his arrangements, and reportedly bested his idol when their outfits locked horns in a Battle of the Bands.

In 1939 Nat left Chicago to tour with the road company of the musical *Shuffle Along*. One big reason: a very pretty dancer named Nadine Robinson, whom he soon married. After the show folded in Los Angeles, he formed a jazz trio and played the smaller clubs. Once, in danger of losing a choice engagement, he turned to friend and arranger Phil Moore for advice. "The man likes my playing, but he wants a singer," he explained. "So sing!" Moore replied. And that's how Nat Cole's singing career began.

From 1940 through 1943 the King Cole Trio sang and played in California clubs and made some jazz-tinged records, including sixteen sides for Decca, that sold poorly. Then in 1943 Cole signed with Capitol Records, which tried a different approach: It began to promote the tall, dark-skinned pianist with the shy, sly smile as a ballad singer. Commercially, the move was brilliant. Hit sides followed hit sides: "Sweet Lorraine," "It's Only a Paper Moon," "For Sentimental Reasons," "The Christmas Song," "Nature Boy," "Mona Lisa,"

"M-o-n-a L-i-s-a!"

"Too Young," and "Unforgettable"—all featuring Nat Cole the crooner and none Nat Cole the great jazz artist.

Though some jazz fans deeply resented the muting of Nat's pulsating piano, many millions more non-jazz fans welcomed him as their favorite crooner. He became a big star, played all the major nightclubs and theaters, appeared regularly on his own radio series and in several movies, headed his own film production company, and eventually starred on his own TV series, which he abandoned in protest when, because of his race, he could garner no national sponsor.

Seemingly as gentle as his singing sounds, Nat often warred vigorously for causes in which he believed. Integration was one of them, and he and his second wife, the former Maria Ellington, a fine singer herself, battled with forceful grace and dignity to gain a home in the Los Angeles neighborhood of their choice for themselves and their children, including young Natalie, who in 1975 was to blossom as one of America's most popular singers.

Quiet dignity was also the way he handled his success in general. "You have to grow up to be able to handle success," he once pointed out. But he also warned against smugness and complacency. "If you're a truly creative person, you'll fight that feeling all the way," he insisted. "And you'll never stop trying to create something new."

On the other hand, he never felt any desire to create some of the simplistic rock sounds that became so fashionable during the 1950s. Instead he persisted in maintaining his high musical standards. He spoke out vigorously against the diminishing opportunities for superior musicians who refused to compromise their professionalism. "It's a shame," he said, "when you're told you can't do something just because it's 'too good.'"

His love of good music was matched only by his love of his family. "After all the glamour is over," he once noted, "it's nice to be able to come home to people who like you for what you are."

In addition to music and family, Nat, in his later years, became ever more aware of the need for another kind of love: the love of oneself. "My ambition," he philosophized not long before lung cancer stilled his voice forever, "is to be able to sit back and appreciate myself as a person as well as a performer," two roles in which he proved himself most "unforgettable."

(1917–1965)

A gentle sadness, a resigned awareness

She broke away from the doctrinaire confines of "folk music" to broaden her repertoire and artistic range, and in so doing Judy Collins became a rare American example of the *chanteuse,* the melancholy balladeer. Her pure, cool alto voice and careful, crafted phrasing channeled her strong expressive powers. In nearly all Judy Collins' performances there has been a gentle sadness, a resigned awareness that something irreplaceable in life has long ago been lost.

She was born in Denver, Colorado, where her blind father was a popular radio personality. Her childhood was emotionally clouded by family tensions, and at an early age she also had bouts with tuberculosis and polio. Yet even in her preteens, she had developed into a child prodigy at the piano. She was the prize pupil of the now famous woman conductor Antonia Brico, and she appeared as a soloist in several classical concerts with the Denver Businessmen's Symphony.

Entering high school in the 1950s, she was introduced to folk music. "Folk" at that time was considered by purists to mean classic English-Irish-Scots ballads, nineteenth-century American songs from the Ozark and Appalachian regions and—for a touch of "modernism"—the populist ditties of Woody Guthrie.

But if the "folk" of that time was elitist, it was also one of the few exciting alternatives to the generally dreary pop music of the day and melodically much more rewarding than early rock and roll. By the time she entered McMasters College in Illinois, Judy Collins was so attracted to folk that she abruptly gave up the piano, took up the guitar and, with no formal vocal training, began to evolve her personal singing technique and style.

She appeared at folk clubs, touring the "coffeehouse circuit," and was one of the first folk artists to perform regularly at colleges. After an engagement at the Gate of Horn club in Chicago, she was signed to a recording contract. She released several albums to critical acclaim and popular response, but her growing independence in choosing nonfolk material, because she felt she was being confined by the limits of folk, caused her to be criticized by purists. She ignored them and followed her sense of artistic adventure.

Her 1966 Christmas concert at Carnegie Hall was notable for her use of supporting musicians to produce a chamber-music effect. She was the first American artist to sing the poignant and searching songs of Jacques Brel, and she offered a moving version of "In My Life," John Lennon's unusually sentimental look at his boyhood.

Judy

In the early 1970s, after the death of her father, she suddenly resumed playing the piano and began to write original material, much of it autobiographical. She became part of the "women's liberation" movement and returned to Denver to write and direct a film documentary on her childhood patron and teacher Antonia Brico.

As the 1970s progressed she continued to record and tour at chosen intervals. Her private life seemed to be happy. "I have always thought I'd reach my prime in my fifties, not my twenties," she told Joyce Maynard of the New York *Times* in late 1976. "The 1960s were not the be-all and end-all of my career. They were just part of the process." And yet the sad longing in her performances and original songs remained. Physically striking because of her large blue eyes, she personified the lyric line from the little-known poet Jules Baurimoeur: "Elle porte dans ses yeux un soif d'amour"—"She carries in her eyes a thirst of love."

(1938–   )

Russ Columbo

Every song he recorded was a love ballad, sung as a violinist would play it.

In three years, 1931–34, he had become a top radio singer, Bing Crosby's only serious challenger, a major recording star who wrote three of his own hits, "You Call It Madness But I Call It Love" (his theme song), "Too Beautiful for Words," and "Prisoner of Love," an emerging film actor, and a bandleader who at one point had such jazz talents in his ranks as Gene Krupa, Joe Sullivan, and Benny Goodman.

The last of twelve children, he was christened Ruggiero Eugenio de Rudolpho Columbo and early in his life showed great talent for Italian opera as well as popular love songs. As a violinist in Gus Arnheim's band, he was influenced by its boy singer, Bing Crosby, and he succeeded him in that spot after Bing left. Within a year, Columbo had also started his solo career, and the two became embroiled in a mythical "Battle of the Baritones," Bing on CBS and Russ on NBC.

But whereas Crosby was sometimes lighthearted and at other times romantic, Columbo concentrated entirely on romance. Every song he recorded was a love ballad, sung as a violinist would play it, with tender feeling and an easy flow of sound.

In early 1932 he described his singing to a Detroit *News* reporter: "I'm not a crooner or a blues singer or a straight baritone. I've tried to make my phrasing different, and I take a lot of liberty with the music. One of the things they seem to like best is the voice obbligato on repeat choruses—very much as I used to do them on the violin." Others described the romantic-voiced performer as "[the] crooning troubadour of the screen and radio," "the Romeo of song," "tall, broad-shouldered, shining black hair, fierce Latin eyes," "[having] more than a faint resemblance to Valentino." In spite of the fact that one director told him he was "too Latin" to get beyond movie bit parts, Russ Columbo made three films, *Broadway Through a Keyhole, Moulin Rouge,* and *Wake Up and Dream* and was the star of the last. Two screen actresses, Carole Lombard and Sally Blane, reportedly were in love with him. Fan letters from other adoring but unknown women poured in every week. One estimate put the number at two thousand, another as high as fifteen thousand. At one point his weekly take-home pay was estimated variously at ten thousand dollars, seven thousand dollars, and just plain "astronomical."

But a gun ended it all, an antique dueling pistol that went off accidentally while a close friend, a leading Hollywood photographer, was showing it to Russ. It killed him. He was twenty-six. For his funeral crowds estimated at three thousand filled the church and sidewalks outside. Bing Crosby was one of the pallbearers.

Though this tragic accident ended Columbo's real career, it started a mythical one that lasted ten years. Seriously ill at the time of the shooting and later blind, Columbo's mother was never told of her son's death. The family read "letters" from Russ in London, Paris, where an ever more demanding career kept him from coming home to visit her. Every month a check arrived—actually payment from his insurance policy. She died in 1944, happy for her son's "success."

(1908–1934)

Russ

Perry Como

"The Walking Miltown."

"I'm convinced it doesn't matter what you do or even how you sing," Perry Como once said. "People have to like you as a person first. If they like you, you're in. When they stop liking you as a person, you're gone."

Perry Como has been "in" for many years for two reasons: he's a whale of a singer, and everyone likes him. As Patrice Munsel remarked after appearing on his TV show: "Perry is heaven, just heaven. He is completely and totally secure."

This feeling of security and of liking and believing in himself have helped to make Como the relaxed, imperturbable, outgoing person that so many of his confreres have found a joy to work with. But of course just that alone might have left him the best-liked barber in his hometown of Canonsburg, Pennsylvania, had he not displayed a talent for singing that eventually carried him to the top of his profession.

That singing career began with Freddy Carlone's local band back in 1933, the same year that he wed Roselle Belline, still his wife almost half a century later. In 1936 Ted Weems, an important bandleader, heard him. "We were playing a gambling casino," Perry recalls, "and Ted came in and played the 'double oh' in roulette, and it came in. He was feeling good by then, so he offered me a job."

Como stayed with Weems until 1942, when, with his leader's blessings, he left to begin a career as a soloist. His idol then, and forever after, was Bing Crosby. "What he would do, I would do," he recently admitted. He not only copied Crosby's singing style, but he carried the Groaner's relaxed approach so far that in later years Perry became known as "The Walking Miltown."

His easygoing, "you-do-your-thing-and-I'll-do-mine" manner has captivated not only audiences but also his fellow performers. Musicians everywhere love to work with him because Perry understands them. "On record dates, I usually managed to do something extra so we'd go overtime and they'd get something extra—you know, like stopping to eat a sandwich or blow my nose."

His first record in 1943, "Goodbye Sue," became a best seller. So did "And I Love You So," recorded more than thirty years later. In between came such hits as "Till the End of Time" (the song he claims "started me on whatever I'm on"), "Prisoner of Love," "Temptation" (which became his first million-seller), "Catch a Falling Star," and "It's Impossible." Meanwhile, he was also

"You do your thing and I'll do mine."

appearing regularly on radio and later on television, beginning in 1943 with a CBS sustaining series, moving on the next year to the "Chesterfield Supper Club," which eventually shifted to television. In 1955 he switched his longtime CBS allegiance to NBC, where he sang on and hosted the successful series "The Perry Como Show," followed four years later by starring on "The Kraft Music Hall."

An inveterate golfer, he forsook the TV grind during the 1960s and moved to Florida. "Down here I don't see anybody except an occasional fish," he recently quipped over the phone. However, he does leave once in a while for TV and personal appearances and to fly to Nashville, Las Vegas, and Rome to make more records. He already has a dozen million-sellers to his credit, some of which he'd like to redo in a modern vein. "Just think how they'd sound with the arrangements they write these days," he exclaims. "They're so wild and wonderful that sometimes I almost feel like an interruption!"

Few arrangements have ever been interrupted by the voice of a nicer or more talented guy.

(1912–   )

Eddie Condon

"We don't flat our fifths. We drink them." ◄

Eddie Condon, who had one of the fastest mouths in jazz, shot from the lip. "He's a game guy," he once said of Hugues Panassie, the French jazz critic, "coming over here and telling us how to play jazz. We don't go over to France and tell them how to jump on a grape, do we?" When bebop, which was anathema to Condon, brought the flatted fifth to prominence, he scornfully remarked, "We don't flat our fifths. We drink them."

Drinking was a subject on which he had lifelong personal authority. "For a bad hangover," he once advised, "take the juice of two quarts of whiskey."

Condon was a short, dapper man who never quite lost the appearance of an unfrocked choirboy. He was known as "Slick" when he was part of the booming Chicago jazz scene in the late 1920s. At seventeen he had started on banjo with Homer Peavey's Jazz Bandits but later switched to rhythm guitar, never taking a solo throughout his career.

His constant concern was the support of unscored small-band jazz. He disdained big bands with their written arrangements. One day in 1927 he expressed contempt for the records of Red Nichols and His Five Pennies because their music was planned. This statement, coming from a brash young squirt who happened at the time to be playing scored banjo parts in Louis Panico's highly commercial band, so irritated Red McKenzie, the jazz vocalist, that he challenged Condon to name anybody half as good as Nichols. Condon said he had a dozen friends who were twice as good. The next day his friends—who included Bud Freeman, Gene Krupa, Jimmy McPartland, and Joe Sullivan—played for McKenzie, who got them a record date. It was the first important step in the careers of all of them and launched Condon as a continuing catalyst and proselytizer for small-band jazz.

When he (and most of his Chicago friends) moved to New York in the 1930s, he rescued them from diets of "transparent hamburgers" by talking his way into recording dates, jobs at society functions, gigs on Fifty-second Street and even with Red Nichols!

He was a jazz gypsy until 1938, when he became its figurehead in New York. That year he made the first recordings for the first label devoted to jazz, Commodore Records. For his second Commodore session Condon, through friends he had made at *Life* magazine, got *Life* to take pictures, which grew into a spread on jazz that presented Condon and his friends as the major

Eddie

contemporary movers in jazz. In the same year he started an eight-year relationship with Nick's in Greenwich Village that ended only when he opened his own club in 1946. And in 1942, in Town Hall, he began the series of jazz concerts that grew into a successful radio and television series during and after World War II.

In keeping with his newfound solidity, he married Phyllis Smith, an advertising copywriter, had two daughters, and settled down in a big apartment facing fashionable Washington Square. Despite this change in life-style, his acerbic wit never left him, although by the time he was fifty-eight he had mellowed enough to admit that "jazz music has become more refined and polished," adding hastily and with emphasis, "but without desecrating the creativity of it."

(1904?–1973)

Sam Cooke

"I got scared and went into the handclapping and shouting bit."

He was the son of a minister, a handsome, studious boy who sang tenor in the Wendell Phillips High School glee club in Chicago. His one solo came when he was a junior, singing "The First Noel" at a Christmas concert.

Sam Cooke's formidable talent was shaped by two forces. He started as an ensemble singer, so that even as a solo superstar he saw himself as part of a larger musical picture. Furthermore, as he said at the height of his success, "All my training and early experience was in spiritual music." Even at his most exuberant, rocking, shouting best, he was still the kid who'd sung hymns and gospel songs with his brother and sisters in a quartet at their father's church.

While in high school he was "discovered" by a local quartet, the Highway QC's, as they walked past Sam's home one day while he was practicing. They liked what they heard, rang the doorbell and, within half an hour, talked themselves into becoming a quintet with Sam as the lead singer.

A couple of years later, as a member of the Soul Stirrers, a Chicago-based spiritual group, Sam sang in a concert at the Los Angeles Shrine Auditorium and was approached by a record company executive. "Why don't you go into popular music?" he asked. Sam said he'd think it over and six months later signed a contract.

But the head of the record company wandered into Sam's first recording session and decided, in one of those moments that are the stuff of legends and nightmares, that the handsome tenor wasn't enough of a rock-and-roller. The session was scrapped. One of the offending cuts was "You Send Me," a classic that made Sam, and a rival label, a lot richer a year or two later.

Never a screamer or a snarler, Sam Cooke kept a hint of sweetness in his voice even when he was singing fast and hard. Maybe this was one reason why he was one of the first uncompromising black artists to reach a wide audience of white rock-and-rollers. His first big hit, "You and Me," in 1957 was followed by the poignant "Chain Gang," the infectious "Twistin' the Night Away," and dozens of other hits. "On singles," he once said, "I'll record anything I think will be a hit, but for the albums I do mostly ballads."

In 1960 after "You Send Me" sold over two million copies, Sam was invited to perform at New York's fabled Copacabana. On opening night he was told the management wanted a sedate, toned-down performance, with no unseemly shouting or handclapping. Unprepared, Cooke tried to wing it with a standard arrangement of "Begin the Beguine."

"About halfway through, the orchestra was going that way and I was going over this way, and I thought we'd never find each other," Sam recalled. "I got scared and went into the handclapping and shouting bit. Jules Podell told me to cut out that stuff or get out." Cooke complied and gamely played the rest of the engagement the way the boss wanted but later recalled, "I wasn't a smash." For the next four years he kept to the studios and to concert dates in the boondocks, quietly getting richer while he rebuilt his confidence. "Next time, I want to be sure they're ready for me," he said.

In 1964 his last, greatest single swept the country. A slow, musing blues with spiritual and social overtones, "A Change Is A-Gonna Come" could have been a testament of Sam's own faith. He'd paid some tough dues—an auto accident in 1963 that killed a close friend and nearly blinded him and the drowning death of his infant son. The song mixed the intensity of his R & B hits with the mellow warmth of his ballads and seemed to foretell new growth for Sam as an artist and changes for the better in his life.

A change came, but it was stark and tragic. He died in a shooting incident at a Los Angeles motel, killed just before his thirtieth birthday.

(1935–1964)

Sam

Jim Croce

More than "just folkies."

His warm, personal, "laid-back," yet assertive style of singing evoked a young, working-class middle America at a time when nobody else was doing that. And the songs he wrote and sang appealed even to those beyond that group; for instance, Frank Sinatra featured "Bad, Bad Leroy Brown" in his stage performances throughout the mid-1970s.

Unlike Janis Joplin and Jimi Hendrix, who died at the peak of their careers, thirty-year-old Jim Croce was just blossoming into a star at the time of his death. One of his two record producers, Terry Cashman, says, "We knew a week before he died that Jim was going to be a gigantic star." Four months after the private plane carrying Croce from a September 20, 1973, performance at Northwestern Louisiana University crashed on takeoff, his first solo LP, "You Don't Mess Around with Jim," had risen to number one on the best-selling charts. "I Got a Name," recorded a week before his death, was number two, and "Life and Times," released in January 1973, was number twenty-two.

Jim Croce was making it in the music business on his second try. In 1966, after having been graduated from Villanova University and teaching emotionally disturbed high-schoolers, Jim had married Ingrid Jacobsen. Together they sang in New York coffeehouses, struggling for a style that would make them more than "just folkies." In 1969 he and Ingrid made an album, *Croce,* for Capitol. It didn't sell. So, the introspective Croce, unsure of his talents, withdrew to a farm in Pennsylvania. "He just lost his will to work" recalls co-producer Tommy West, a friend of Croce's since they had met at a student glee club practice at Villanova.

Jim, no farmer, turned to laboring jobs. He drove gravel trucks, hauling rock, worked on telephone lines, went from heavy excavation, such as putting in pipelines, to construction work and installing roofs. He operated a jackhammer. Later, when he was back on stage, he found that jackhammer-impared hearing made it hard for him to tune his guitar. He would have to arrive for a concert early, let his guitar take on the temperature of the hall and tune it slowly and carefully in a silent dressing room. If it went out of tune during a concert, he pointed out, he couldn't hear to tune it on stage.

When he had moved to the farm Croce felt he was leaving music forever. But his creative juices continued to flow. For their outlet, he decided to carry a cassette recorder in his truck to record the songs that came to him when he was driving. Cashman and West kept encouraging him to resume his career and in 1970 they introduced him to guitarist Maury Muehleisen. Croce went on a tour playing guitar behind Muehleisen and in February 1971 he sent Cashman and West a tape of some of his newly written songs. It included "Operator" and "Time in a Bottle." "We both knew when we heard the tapes that Jimmy had discovered how to make himself sound unique," says Cashman. "Working with Maury he found new chords and began writing about what he was."

Cashman and West took the tape to numerous record companies. All turned them down: They thought Croce sounded too much like James Taylor. But finally ABC signed him. The first single, "You Don't Mess Around with Jim," a humorous approach to the traditional big-bad-guy blues, put Croce in the top ten. Another catchy narrative, Jim's "Bad, Bad Leroy Brown," had just sold a million copies at the time of his death. "I Got a Name," a posthumous hit, showed Croce's other side, the sensitive, introspective balladeer.

Cashman and West remain brokenhearted over the death of their friend. "People were just beginning to see what Jim was all about," West says. "We were at the point where the fight was almost over. We were at the point where we could enjoy the success and the friendship."

(1943–1973)

Warm, personal, laid-back

Der Bingle

The Rhythm Boys: Harry Barris, Bing Crosby, Al Rinker

Bing Crosby

"The personification of the whole jazz movement—the relaxed, casual, natural, uninhibited approach to art."

"As a kid, I had all the good phonograph records in town. I was strictly a follower of good jazz groups, like the Memphis Five and the Mound City Blue Blowers. My ambition was to be around those guys. I never wanted anything more than that."

Of course Harry Lillis "Bing" Crosby (the "Bing" came from "Bingo," a character in a comic strip, *The Bingville Bugle,* which young Crosby loved to read) did get a lot more than that: He became one of the great superstars of all time. But he even stood out in that elite group, for he never acted like a superstar. No entourages. No flunkies. No "prima-donnastics." He even answered his own telephone. He possessed probably the most underswollen head in the business. He thought about and cared about others. "The first time I met him," Peggy Lee once noted, "he knew all the little things about me, about my house, even about Dave's health, which wasn't so good at the time. Bing wants to know about people, all about them. I think that's why he's so happy." Financially independent and perhaps, even more importantly, emotionally secure, he felt no need to focus solely on himself or to trumpet his talents. Once, asked whether his continuing singing wouldn't injure his voice, he replied, "Oh, the kind of singing I do, you can't hurt your voice."

His brand of homey, informal, always musical singing earned him millions of dollars and instant recognition. Still, he never forgot his debt to "the musicians who helped me develop good taste—the Dorsey Brothers and Bix Beiderbecke and Glenn Miller and Bunny Berigan and Joe Venuti and Eddie Lang and Mannie Klein—and all those guys I recorded with the and hung around with in my early days. I was having a helluva good time with them, but I really had no idea then that I was actually learning anything. But I certainly was!"

Bing's earlier learning had taken place in his native Tacoma, Washington, where, after a short stint at playing drums in a local high school band, he began to sing at dances. He went on to study law at Gonzaga University. "But I can't do it," he finally wrote his mother. "Oh, I can study law and get fair marks and graduate and maybe make the bar. But I don't feel right about it. I'd rather sing than eat." So he kept on singing, inspired by recordings by such idols as John McCormack and Al Jolson and Red McKenzie of the Mound City Blue Blowers, as well as those by the various jazz groups he admired. Finally, he and fellow classman Al Rinker, also a singer, left college and migrated to Los Angeles. Paul Whiteman heard and hired them, and eventually took on Harry Barris to form the Rhythm Boys, whose up-tempoed scatting of pop tunes set the standard for many other future vocal groups.

Bing also sang some ballads, though his informal approach failed to impress the manager of New York's Paramount Theater, who hired Whiteman with the stipulation that Crosby not sing a solo. When West Coast bandleader Gus Arnheim showed more appreciation, Bing and the Rhythm Boys joined him. "William Paley heard me while we were playing with Arnheim at the Cocoanut Grove," Crosby recalled. "And he offered me my own fifteen-minute show on CBS." Bing made his network debut on September 2, 1931, singing "Just One More Chance." He never needed another one; he stayed on for years and years.

Paley, one of early radio's master showmen, who later became CBS board chairman, had perceived the appeal of what Henry Pleasants describes in his book *The Great American Popular Singers* as "the mellow richness of the voice, the elegance of the phrasing, the easy, buoyant rhythm, the fastidiousness of the diction." Jack Kapp, then producing records for Brunswick, heard the CBS broadcasts, signed Crosby, and for years thereafter served, to quote Bing, "as a benevolent mogul." His faith in Crosby seemed limitless. "He had me doing things I thought insane, like singing Victor Herbert and Rudolf Friml and Viennese waltzes, and combining me with the Boswell Sisters and the Mills Brothers and a big variety of other outlets."

But Kapp kept Bing happy by letting him also sing what he liked to sing most of all: jazz. "There's nothing like singing jazz with good musicians," Bing was still insisting in the mid-1970s. "And we had the best of them on those dates." Swinging along easily, never forcing the beat, he projected what writer Ralph Gleason later described as "the personification of the whole jazz movement—the relaxed, casual, natural, uninhibited approach to art."

He made hundreds upon hundreds of records, including the very first coupling on the Decca label which Kapp founded in 1934—"I Love You Truly" and "Just A-Wearyin' for You." Bing's favorite of all his records? "I guess it is 'My Isle of Golden Dreams,' " he recently revealed, referring to a simple, dreamy, 1919 ballad he revived in 1939 with Dick McIntyre and His Harmony Hawaiians. "I like the sound of my voice on that best of all."

His love of recording never abated. "You're constantly creating. It's fun, especially when you're working with great musicians. Also, when you're finished with a recording, you've got something that's really your own. I like making records even more than making movies."

His number of movies is as impressive as his number of recordings—a star in more than sixty, beginning with *The Big Broadcast of 1932* and including the famous "Road" series *(Singapore, Zanzibar, Bali, Utopia)* with his pal Bob Hope. Late in 1976 he was talking with Mel Gussow of The New York *Times* about filming another in that series, *The Road to Lamour,* hoping "they could inject more Mel Brooks, Monty Python lunacy into it." Even though he won an Oscar in 1944 for his role as the priest in *Going My Way,* he always tended to deprecate his acting talents. "I never believe myself when I see me on screen," he told Gussow. "I think Sinatra is a better actor than I am."

Great actor or not, his singing in his movies created many hit tunes—"Learn to Croon," "Love in Bloom," "Love Thy Neighbor," "Temptation," "June in January," "It's Easy to Remember," "I'm an Old Cowhand," "Pennies from Heaven," "Sweet Leilani," "Small Fry," and his eternally popular "White Christmas," one of the first five recordings to be voted into the Recording Academy's Hall of Fame.

In his autobiography, *Call Me Lucky,* Bing attributed some of his popularity to his own assumption that "every man who sees one of my movies, or who listens to my records, or who hears me on the radio, believes firmly that he sings as well as I do, especially when he's in the bathroom shower." Others, like Sinatra and Perry Como and Dick Haymes and Bob Eberly, obviously influenced by Crosby, tried in one way or another also to sing as well as Bing did. They seldom succeeded, by their own admissions, either in or out of their showers.

Through the years his singing maintained the same, semi-effortless quality. In the mid-1970s, perhaps as a relief from the many nonmusical interests that were filling his life—owning a baseball club, running golf tournaments, selling orange juice on television—he returned to a heavy performing schedule, starring on his own TV shows and guesting on others, appearing in concerts with his family here and abroad, and recording half a dozen new albums. But, unlike many contemporary singers who labor for months through session after session to produce a single album, Bing easily completed each of his in nine hours. A true pro, he had prepared himself thoroughly for each session, studying his songs and arrangements in advance and knowing exactly what he was going to do and how he was going to do it. "I vocalized before each date. I never did that for some of those early recordings," which to him, he recently confessed, now sound "tired. My voice was bad and had a lot of frogs in it." Many reviewers of his latest albums agree he never sounded better.

Sloppy singing of any sort, his own or that of others, distressed him. "What bothers me about some of today's singers," he said in 1976, "is that I can't understand the words. I wish they would enunciate more clearly."

Nevertheless, he lists some current singers among his all-time favorite, putting Neil Diamond and Neil Sedaka in a class with Sinatra, Como, Andy Williams, Nat Cole, and John Gary. "But," he told Mel Gussow, "the greatest singer I ever heard is Tony Bennett."

A young singer who impressed Crosby greatly and in whom he had much faith was his son Harry, Jr., the youngest of his seven children (four sons by his first wife, Dixie Lee Crosby, and three more, including a girl, by his second wife, actress-singer Kathryn Crosby). Bing was predicting a brilliant future for young Harry, either as a singer or possibly as a classical musician. But his plans for popping his paternal pride ended suddenly while enjoying one of his favorite pastimes, playing golf, during a vacation in Spain, when he suffered a fatal heart attack.

At a private burial, witnessed by just his family and a few close friends, his widow, Kathryn, mirrored her husband's light, informal approach to both life and death when she remarked, "He hated funerals. I'm sure he didn't plan to come to this one at all." His good friend, Phil Harris, however, could summon up none of Bing's lightness. "When God took Bing," said Harris, "he made his *first* mistake."

(1904–1977)

Bob Crosby

"I'm the only guy in the business who made it without talent."

His baritone voice was once described by a critic as having "a tremolo wide enough to drive a Mack truck through." Nevertheless, Bob Crosby also had a warm, expansive personality that compensated for such technical drawbacks and let him succeed as a very attractive bandleader and, later on, as a radio and television showman.

Of course, being Bing's younger brother didn't hinder his career one bit, especially its beginnings. In the early 1930s it helped him get a job with Anson Weeks's West Coast band, then with an orchestra led by the Dorsey Brothers, two of Bing's closest musical compatriots. Finally, when the remnants of Ben Pollack's great band began looking around for a new front man in 1935, he became their leader.

The Bob Crosby band with vocalist Doris Day

The band—a cooperative venture with Gil Rodin as president, six other Pollack alumni plus Bob as corporate partners—was rightfully billed as "The Best Dixieland Band in the Land," for it was its hard-driving, swinging instrumental performances (rather than Bob's singing) that brought it into top hotel rooms, ballrooms, and theaters and the "Camel Caravan" radio series. It starred great jazz musicians, like tenor saxist Eddie Miller, trumpeters Yank Lawson and Billy Butterfield, pianist Joe Sullivan, drummer Ray Bauduc, and bassist Bob Haggart, all of whom at times overawed their young leader. "I'm the only guy in the business," he once commented modestly but inaccurately, "who made it without talent." However, he did mature into a suave leader whose charm and wit bridged many a gap between bandstands and audiences. And his unstinting admiration of the musicians' talents, plus his lack of pretension, endeared him to many of the band's members who could easily have resented a baton being waved at them—not always in good time—by "Bing's kid brother."

The career of the Crosby band, which included a jazz octet called "The Bob Cats" and, from time to time, vocalists like Doris Day, Gloria DeHaven, and Kay Starr, lasted until 1942. Then many of its members were drafted, so Bob began his unmemorable movie-acting career, blurred by appearances in such nonclassics as *The Singing Sheriff,* which, he recalls, "we did in exactly ten days. It set back western movies exactly three years!" A quick Crosby captaincy commission in the Marines, however, saved westerns from any further damage.

After the war Bob tried keeping up with the changing musical times by organizing a band of bop-oriented musicians. It didn't work. So he switched from leading a band to heading a daytime radio series. This did work. "Club 15," produced in Hollywood by Bob's old pal Gil Rodin, ran on CBS for several years and was followed by an equally successful daytime series on television. Crosby yearned for a more prestigious nighttime show, and when sponsors and networks didn't respond, an embittered Crosby withdrew to Hawaii and then Australia for a more secluded life as a disc jockey and part-time writer. In the 1970s he returned to the States, sometimes leading his Bob Cats, sometimes touring with a bigger band, often railing resentfully at the changes in music (son Chris, one of his five children, had become a folk-rock singer) but more often projecting the self-deprecatory charm and wit that had turned him into one of the most likable of all bandleaders.

(1913–   )

Crosby, Stills, Nash (and Young)

There was one thing wrong: superegos.

A super group sounded like a super idea. What could be wrong with taking the best individual talent from the rock groups and putting them together into a second-generation, all-star rock group?

Cream had done it in England, and Crosby, Stills, Nash, and Young were the biggest stars to do it in the United States. The music was good, and the audiences loved it. There was one thing wrong with it, though—superegos.

Each had been a star of his own group, each a guitar player, singer, songwriter. David Crosby was in the Byrds, where folk rock was born. Graham Nash, an Englishman, played rhythm guitar in the Hollies, whose clean rock sound earned it the title of a "band's band." Stephen Stills and Neil Young, the latter a Canadian, were from Buffalo Springfield, a group beginning to be appreciated

Nash, Crosby, Young, and Stills

just as it broke up and revered after its demise. After Crosby left the Byrds and Stills's Springfield group had disbanded, the two got together with Nash and played some music. Conditions were so felicitous that Nash left the Hollies and joined the other two for an album. They maintained that they weren't a group but three individuals recording together. But adding Young turned the "no group" into a super group. When a drummer and bass guitarist were also included, the group's names sounded like those of a law firm—Crosby, Stills, Nash, Young, Taylor, and Reeves.

The harmonies were soft, tight, and sweet, the delivery a likable mixture of grace and wallop. Only the players weren't harmonious. And so Crosby, Stills, Nash, and Young lasted for only fifteen months, through parts of 1969 and 1970. Their subsequent solo careers and solo albums received only so-so acceptance (with the exception of Young, who had two big sellers), and in 1974, with exclamations of how much they had missed each other, they reorganized for a highly publicized tour of the United States. They set off traveling in motor homes—Young, the loner, parking his in different locations from the rest—each with his own sound man and crew, creating an entourage that numbered eighty-four. They performed together with Nash generally banging on a tambourine while the other three played guitar. They all sang, and each had a solo spot at the concerts. There were conflicts about the arrangement of the solos and of course jealousy about the comparisons made by reviewers, some of whom were enthusiastic about the group's ensemble performing, saying, typically, "CSN&Y reaffirmed its position at the top of the hierarchy of smooth, soulfully mellow California folk-rock bands."

When the four ended the tour, dividing four and a half million dollars, they said they were going to rest a month before making a "tour album." Actually, they were so angry and fed up with one another that they didn't even want to meet again, and when they did they never completed an album. Young, the last to join, became the first to leave and in the latter 1970s Crosby, Stills, and Nash were again a trio whose harmonizing New York *Times* critic Robert Palmer found "pretty and sometimes uplifting, in the way that barbershop quartets and church choirs can be pretty and sometimes uplifting." At their 1978 sellout three-hour concert in New York's Madison Square Garden they still sounded to Palmer like "acoustic folkies at heart." Noting that they have been described as "old men trying to rock out," he found "no reason why Crosby, Stills, and Nash cannot go on for another twenty years . . . Nothing they would do would seem inherently ridiculous if they did it at age forty or fifty."

His beret, his chihuahuas, and his beautiful women.

"I would rather play 'Chiquita Banana' and have my swimming pool," Xavier Cugat once said, "than play Bach and starve."

Cugie has displayed an unerring faculty for satisfying a variety of appetites—and never starved, physically or emotionally. Instead of playing Bach, he played popular songs, parlaying his talents as a violinist with an eye for beautiful women and a basic sense of showmanship to carve a niche for himself as the epitome of Latin music in the United States.

Born in Barcelona, Spain, he was trained as a violinist. But as a youngster he seemed more interested in drawing caricatures, and it was this interest that served as the springboard for his friendship with Enrico Caruso, whom he

Cugie

met at the age of eleven, while playing first violin in the Teatro Nacional Symphony Orchestra in Havana.

When his efforts as a violinist—in the Teatro Nacional Orchestra, as a recitalist at Carnegie Hall, and as a sideman in Vincent Lopez's orchestra—gave no indication of producing swimming pools, he became a caricaturist for the Los Angeles *Times*. On the side, he led the Latin relief band at the Cocoanut Grove. In 1932 the manager of the Waldorf-Astoria in New York wanted to book Cugie's fifteen-year-old niece, a dancer who later became famous as the actress, Margo. Margo told the Waldorf manager to talk to her uncle about booking her. He did—and wound up booking Cugat too.

In sixteen years Cugat rose from relief band to the Waldorf's highest paid orchestra. His Latin band came in with the rumba and rose higher with the conga. Meanwhile, Cugat's sense of showmanship was at work, dressing his musicians in exotic Latin-American garb, using sinuous dancers and sensuous singers: Lina Romay, Miguelito Valdes, and three singers whom he married— Carmen Castillo, Abbe Lane, and Charo.

Cugat's luck reached a high point in 1941 when ASCAP (the American Society of Composers, Authors and Publishers) could not agree with the radio networks on performance fees and banned all its music from the air. While Glenn Miller, Benny Goodman, and Harry James were grabbing desperately at public domain material, like the constantly played "Jeannie with the Light Brown Hair," Cugat utilized a library of hundreds of Latin-American songs that had never been assigned to ASCAP. Camel cigarettes saw him as a salvation for the "Camel Caravan" radio program. Soon the colorful Cugie became a household name, and it was not long before Hollywood seized him, his beret, his chihuahuas, and his beautiful women, making him a regular adjunct to Esther Williams' outsize swimming pools.

In the 1950s and 1960s, while other bands played far more authentic Latin music and more exciting blends of Latin and American styles, Cugie remained in the public eye helped by bedroom raids in which a succession of his wives attempted to catch him *in flagrante* with various successors. But by the 1970s, when Cugie was in his seventies, he had settled into a relatively serene (and practically anonymous) existence with Charo, a young singer from Spain who was more than forty years his junior, a serenity that dissolved late in 1977 when Charo, following his previous wives scripts, sued Cugie for divorce, and ill health curtailed almost completely his musical career.

(1900–   )

Bobby Darin

Walden Robert Cassotto of the Bronx, New York, wanted to be a legend.

Walden Robert Cassotto was an aggressive and ambitious entertainer whose youthful proclaimed goal was "to be a legend before I'm thirty." Though never a legend, he became a versatile, well-known, and respected singer, actor, and songwriter.

Giving himself the professional name of Bobby Darin, he set out his traps for stardom in the character of a long-haired Presley-type teen idol. His 1956 televised appearances on the Dorsey Brothers' "Stage Show" programs (Presley had also guested on the variety series) brought him immediate recognition, and his abilities as a commercial songwriter resulted in two pseudo-rock hit records, "Splish, Splash" and "Queen of the Hop."

But the restless and intelligent Darin found the teen-idol persona restrictive, so in the early 1960s he presented himself as a swinging, sometimes cocky, adult song stylist much in the manner of Frank Sinatra. Darin's top-selling,

Bobby

Grammy-winning recording of "Mack the Knife," featuring a jazzy big-band arrangement, was so successful that it became his signature song. It also facilitated his entry to the Las Vegas and New York nightclub circuits, where he was to find a lucrative living and the respect of his performing peers.

Darin's film appearances began in the early 1960s and continued through most of the decade. The quality of his movie vehicles differed, but he proved himself a talented actor; he was nominated for an Academy Award for his supporting role as a distraught soldier in *Captain Newman, M.D.* His two other notable film roles were those of the egocentric jazz musician who finds moral character in *Too Late Blues* and a psychopath in *Pressure Point*.

As the decade continued Darin recorded frequently, showing himself adaptable to different kinds of material; his vocals displayed craftsmanship, technique, and an understanding of his audience. He scored with his own composition, the sentimental "Eighteen Yellow Roses," and with Tim Hardin's contemporary folk ballad, "If I Were a Carpenter," in which Darin gave a masterful demonstration of how to "underphrase" a lyric to create a powerful emotional effect.

Then in 1969, in what was to prove an embarrassingly unsuccessful venture, he announced he was forsaking the nightclub circuit and would only play colleges in order to reach the young. He put together a combo of youthful rock-oriented musicians, dressed himself in blue jean outfits, doffed his toupee, formed his own recording company ("Direction—the label with something to say"), tried to write songs of social commentary, and identified himself as "Bob" Darin in imitation of Bob Dylan. Neither the college kids nor his established audience was interested.

He returned to the nightclub circuit, still a superior entertainer. Then in 1973 he entered a hospital for corrective heart surgery; complications developed, and he died on the operating table. Walden Robert Cassotto of the Bronx, New York, wanted to be a legend. Denied that status, he had comforted himself with being Bobby Darin, the star.

(1936–1973)

Miles Davis

A generous, kind man whose true self is not revealed by his flamboyant, provocative behavior.

"What a lot of people don't understand about Miles," said Dizzy Gillespie, the trumpeter's old friend and onetime idol, "is that he really is a very shy person." That claim may come as a surprise to those who have seen in Davis the archetype of the surly, imperious modern jazzman, who refuses to compromise his art with show-business bonhomie. Before the present-day climate of

Miles

libertarianism, interviews with him were full of elipses to indicate the four-letter epithets with which his speech was richly punctuated. Thousands of words have been written about his flashy clothes, expensive sports cars, stylishly furnished Manhattan townhouse, scrapes with the underworld and with the police and his intransigent manner. Those who know him at all well have found him a generous, kind man whose true self is not revealed by his flamboyant, provocative behavior, but rather by the introspective, complex, often shifting style of his music.

Miles Davis is in fact a brilliantly creative trumpeter of immense emotional warmth and harmonic inventiveness who has established himself as one of the most influential jazz artists of all time. His professional career was launched when his father, a dentist in a suburb of St. Louis, reluctantly agreed to let the eighteen-year-old go to New York to study at the Juilliard School of Music, giving him a liberal allowance, which permitted him not only to live comfortably but also to attract the less affluent Charlie Parker with whom Miles shared a lasting personal and musical friendship. Davis first made a name for himself in Parker's 1947–48 quintet and then presided over an influential series of recordings known as the "Birth of Cool" sessions. In 1955 he began his ascent to great popularity at the helm of a group that included saxophonist John Coltrane, and then through his collaborations with arranger Gil Evans. As key members of the group left, Miles replaced them with brilliant younger players. His record as a spotter and developer of talent is astounding. Among those he brought to the limelight were Ron Carter, Chick Corea, Herbie Hancock, Keith Jarrett, Wayne Shorter, and Tony Williams.

Though he had often been scathing in his comments on the jazz avant-garde (he characterized one famous exponent's playing as sounding as if someone were standing on the man's foot), Miles's own music became increasingly experimental in nature and by the late 1960s could be fully identified with the aims of that movement. Subsequently, he electrically amplified his trumpet and surrounded himself with electronic and percussive instruments, thereby alienating many old fans but gathering a large following among the young.

Plagued by illness in recent years (he lost most of his voice following surgery on his vocal cords, later underwent several painful hip operations, and has suffered from other ailments) Miles continued to contribute fresh and often astounding sounds as he held on determinedly to his commanding position in the world of jazz.

(1926–   )

Sammy Davis, Jr.

"I had to get bigger, that's all. I just had to get bigger."

The first three words of Sammy Davis's autobiography, *Yes I Can,* are "They liked me," and that's not surprising. For all through his life Sammy yearned for approbation, as a person as well as an entertainer. And, as he developed into one of the greatest all-around performers of all time, he got it.

It hadn't always been thus. Rejection was a part of his life. His mother left him when he was two years old. He was very small; he was hardly handsome; and he was black. By his own admission he has "never had a day of formal education. I won't write letters because I can't spell." He had a lot of strikes against him. But he also had a lot of balls. His courage made it possible for him to face vaudeville audiences when he was only three, working as part of the Will Mastin Trio, which included his Uncle Will and his father. With his innate talent as dancer and mugger, he won over audiences easily. Protected

Sammy

by his elders, he knew little of the real life that existed outside the vaudeville circuit.

Then he was drafted into the Army, and unexpectedly bigotry assailed him. Courageously, he literally struck back, flattening red necks twice his size. But he could not overcome their hatred, and he certainly couldn't get them to like him. He was miserable. But then came an opportunity to entertain his fellow soldiers, and what he couldn't accomplish with his fists he could with his talent.

In his autobiography he points out, "My talent was the weapon, the power, the way for me to fight . . . the only thing that made me a little different from everybody else."

And what talent he has displayed during almost half a century of entertaining! Everything he has done, he has done superbly—dance, sing, act, play drums, and render imitations.

It was his ability to mimic that ended a disastrous postwar period for Davis (when the Mastin Trio found bookings hard to come by) and led him toward the glory road. At a party, attended by Frank Sinatra, he was asked to imitate the crooner. Delightfully impressed, Sinatra encouraged Sammy to concentrate on singing and Sammy did, combining much of Sinatra's musicianly phrasing with his own bell-like projection for some tender and also some dramatic renditions.

In a subsequent appearance at Slapsie Maxie's in Hollywood, Sammy was a smash, then an even bigger smash at the more prestigious Ciro's, where an opening-night audience refused to let him get off the stage. After that came New York's Copa Cabana, a club to which he had once been refused admission because of his color. Top nightclubs throughout the country began clamoring for his services. He was a star!

He behaved like a star, too, sometimes well, sometimes poorly. Like Sinatra, he remained intensely loyal to friends, and though associates insisted that he be billed as "Sammy Davis," for years he stood by his father and uncle and persisted in the "Will Mastin Trio" heading, followed by "Featuring Sammy Davis, Jr." He was also extremely generous, buying expensive gifts for friends, even for hangers-on, conceivably, at times, as insurance that he would still be liked by them.

His talent won him his desired approbation everywhere for hit recordings like "Hey There," "What Kind of Fool Am I," "I've Got to Be Me," and "Candy Man," lead roles in Broadway musicals like *Mr. Wonderful, Golden Boy,* and *Stop the World—I Want to Get Off,* and numerous appearances in movies and on television. But it still wasn't enough to reassure this talented and very lovable little man, who was always running, always driven, spending too much, smoking too much, drinking too much, plunging on and on.

At the height of his success he exclaimed, "I had to get bigger, that's all. I just had to get bigger." Sammy Davis could never settle for anything less than the top. And didn't.

(1925–   )

Doris Day

"It must be wonderful to have that freedom—throwing your head back and closing your eyes and just going!"

From among all the performers with whom he has worked, Bob Hope cites Judy Garland and Doris Day as the two ladies with the most natural talent. And bandleader Les Brown, who gave Doris her biggest boost, calls her "one of the most eloquently expressive singers of all time. When she joined us, she just sang the notes. But then she began paying more attention to the lyrics, and, of course, by the time we recorded 'Sentimental Journey,' she had discovered how to really sell a song."

Doris joined the Brown band in 1940, left less than a year later to have a baby, and rejoined Les in 1943. In 1944 she recorded "Sentimental Journey" with him, and her soft, sexy, "you're-the-only-one-who-really-matters" intimate way of cooing made her and the song an instant favorite with lonely GIs all over the world. Two years later she left Brown to launch her career as a single.

During her first big-time solo stint at Billy Reed's Little Club in New York she exclaimed, "Working as a single is just wonderful, but I just can't wait

Doris sings and conductor Frank Devol looks on

to go to Hollywood. I hope I'll be able to get into radio and movies out there." A few months later she was appearing in both media, on radio with Hope and then with Sinatra on the "Hit Parade" show and in her first film, which eventually led to thirty-nine movies with leading men like Sinatra, Jimmy Cagney, Kirk Douglas, Clark Gable, James Garner, Cary Grant, Rex Harrison, Rock Hudson, Gordon MacRae, Ronald Reagan, and Jimmy Stewart, and to her election as Hollywood's Number One Box Office Star.

Movies and acting became the second phase of a career that had begun with music and dancing back in Cincinnati, where she was born Doris Kappelhoff. Her father, choral master of St. Mary's Catholic Church, loved classical music, played the organ, and taught piano. However, his influence on his daughter was minimal. Instead of the piano, she took up dancing, making her first public appearance as a dancer in a kindergarten minstrel show. Her performance was a spotty one: She wet her pants. A few years later, as half the dance team of Doris and Jerry, she did much better, winning a $500 prize and a trip to Hollywood. But before she could leave, a train hit the car in which she was riding, and two broken legs ended her dancing career.

Confined to her home, she began listening to and singing along with records by her musical idol, Ella Fitzgerald. A firm believer in her own abilities, Doris decided to become a singer. She worked hard at it, always remembering the advice of her first teacher to "communicate on a personal basis, make sense out of the lyrics and sing as though you are playing a scene." Never a belter of songs, Doris forever after concentrated on the soft, intimate ballads on which she could use her limited voice to best advantage, later imbuing songs like "When I Fall in Love," "Secret Love," and her biggest hit, "Que Será, Será," with her unique blend of sexiness and tomboyishness.

In her early days, one of the numbers she sang best was "Day by Day." That song inspired Barney Rapp, leader of the first big band with which she worked, to change her name from the unromatic "Kappelhoff" to "Day." Doris never liked the new name. "It sounds like a headliner at the Gaiety Burlesque," she told her biographer, A. E. Hotchner. "It sounds phony." She still prefers some of the kooky nicknames created by her Hollywood cohorts—"Clara Bixby," "Eunice," "Do-Do," and even "Suzie Creamcheese."

Naturalness (she never tried to hide her freckles), honesty, and a deep-seated faith in herself and in some sort of a God (for years she was deeply involved with Christian Science) have always remained with her. "Nobody can make me believe what I don't feel," she told Hotchner, adding, "I always show exactly how I feel. I am what I am," although the "America's wholesome virgin" image that was created for her was, she admits, "more make-believe than any film part I have ever played."

In the 1960s and '70s, her well-received TV series (she had shied away from the medium for longer than almost any other major film star) gave her a chance to play a more mature, glamorous role. But glamour has never obsessed her.

On the other hand, happy homes and marriages have, though three of her marriages failed. Her first, to trombonist Al Jorden, who later committed suicide, brought her a son, Terry, who became a successful record producer. Her second, to saxist George Weidler, brought heartaches, and her third, to her manager, Marty Melcher, brought her bankruptcy (though after his death she won a judgment of more than twenty million dollars from his former business associates).

Despite her problems, her faith has never wavered. During the mid-1970s, looking as stunning as ever, she indicated she would like to sing again, perhaps to fulfill an ambition expressed some years ago—to be able to emote like Etta James, the great rhythm and blues shouter. "It must be wonderful to have that freedom—throwing your head back and closing your eyes and just going!" she exclaimed. And maybe one of these days she'll do it. And then again maybe she won't. Either way, it won't be the end of her world. For, as Doris Day sang more than twenty years ago, "Que Será, Será"—"Whatever Will Be, Will Be."

(1922–   )

John Denver

"Selling the notion of pastoral isolation to a mass audience."

The New York *Times* described him as "Peter Pan in granny glasses." *Time* magazine called him "the Tom Sawyer of rock." And John Denver (born Henry John Deutschendorf, Jr.), who claims he's not an especially good singer because his voice is too thin and too limited, thinks of himself as basically "a communicator" and just keeps on grinning as he continues to spread gallons upon gallons of his musical honey over millions of records and TV tubes.

His longtime producer, Milt Okun, marvels at Denver's attitude toward his work. "He's the only star I've ever worked with who feels he's a worker and not a star. On shows, his guest stars may come late and need to be catered to. Not John. He'll even arrive early just to tune his guitar."

Denver's success on records has been phenomenal. Two albums, *John Denver's Greatest Hits* and *Back Home Again,* have each sold over three million; on one three-day weekend they sold a total of four hundred thousand copies. And *Billboard*'s 1975 year-end charts placed him number one for top singles, easy listening, overall artist, and for the top country album.

Though his parents (his father was an army career colonel) felt entertaining "wasn't something you do for a living," John received a guitar when he was a youngster and played it to gain friends and recognition at the various schools he attended, including Texas Tech, where he studied for two and a half years to become an architect before splitting because, as he told Chet Flippo in *Rolling Stone,* "Singing was the thing that I did that was easy and made me feel good." For a while he sang folk songs in minor clubs in Los Angeles; then he flew to New York to audition as Chad Mitchell's replacement in that mid-1960s popular folk trio. Said Okum, "We auditioned hundreds, but John stood out. He didn't sound especially good—really not as good as Chad then. But he just radiated personality and music, and he improved the group radically."

The group helped Denver, too. "They were really professional," he later remarked. And he was encouraged to write songs. One of his earliest, "Leaving on a Jet Plane," was turned into a huge hit by a Peter, Paul and Mary recording. When the trio dissolved in 1968, Denver settled in Aspen, Colorado. He worked as a single and continued to write songs. More hits followed: "Take Me Home, Country Roads," "I'd Rather Be a Cowboy," and "Rocky Mountain High." Still, Denver finds taking credit for his songs a bit difficult, because, as he told Noel Coppage in *Stereo Review,* "I don't write songs. They come to me and say, 'O.K., you're the one. I want you to put this down.'" Some songs

Rock's Tom Sawyer

have been easier to put down than others. It took him nine months to complete "Rocky Mountain High," but he finished another big hit, "Annie's Song," in ten minutes and "on a ski lift" at that!

Annie is his wife, with whom he often skis in Aspen, Colorado, where they live with their adopted son, Zachary. Frolicking with them is pure joy for Denver. And so is singing his songs about love and nature and tranquility to his predominantly white, semisophisticated, middle-class audiences.

Some critics have faulted his music for being plastic and Pollyannish and, too far removed from what they regard as reality. Robert Christgau in *The Village Voice* called him "a rank hypocrite" for "selling the notion of pastoral isolation to a mass audience." But Milt Okun insists that Denver is for real. "What you see is what's there. He evokes the American countryside the way Elgar wrote about the plains of England and Mussorgsky put Russian peasant song into opera," Okun told Maureen Orth of *Newsweek*.

Denver sees himself as fulfilling almost a messianic need. "Everyone else is talking about how hard life is," he told Grace Lichtenstein in the New York *Times,* "and here I am singing about how good it is to be alive . . . That gives them [people] support in feeling those things." And that, John Denver believes, is precisely the role of a "really far-out" communicator.

(1943–   )

Neil Diamond

A balance between sexy superstar and nice boy from Brooklyn.

He has a broad appeal to an audience that cuts across age levels, sophistication levels, and the traditional musical-preference categories. When his twenty performances at New York's Winter Garden Theater sold out in 1972, it was said that rock had conquered Broadway. But Neil Diamond's music was rock domesticated for everyone; his singing combined rawness and control; his manner and look struck a balance between sexy superstar and nice boy from Brooklyn.

Diamond sings his own songs—middle-of-the-road, autobiographical, suffering, memorable—from the simple sing-along lyric of "Song Sung Blue" to the stream-of-consciousness poetry of "I Am . . . I Said." Musically they might be three simple chords, the complexity in the rhythms calling on influences as varied as Latin, African, rock, country, and gospel.

Each of his record albums, with its picture of Diamond's handsome, brooding face, sold more than one million copies. In live performance, however, with his aching baritone building dynamic energy, he makes his songs even more vibrant and immediate than they seem on his albums.

Some critics, who use the words *schlock* and *pompous* in referring to his concert style, don't like his sense of melodrama. Diamond likes to be backed by a thirty-five-piece string section as well as a seven-piece rock band because strings make him cry. Critics may deride the slick professionalism, but they admit it works.

Diamond began his career with a seven-year, relatively unsuccessful stint writing songs for New York publishers. Then he started singing his songs and was heard by executives at Bang Records. The first three he recorded were hits: "Solitary Man," "Cherry, Cherry," "I Got the Feeling." More hits followed on UNI—"Sweet Caroline," "Holly Holy," "Soolaimon," "Cracklin' Rosie," "Play Me." He had a following now and went on tour for six years. Then, at the peak of his fame after the Winter Garden engagement, Diamond announced a sabbatical from personal appearances (which lasted forty months) to catch up with the self he'd lost touring. He signed a contract with Columbia Records guaranteeing him one million dollars on each of five records over the next five years, and he wrote the score for the movie *Jonathan Livingstone Seagull.*

Some predicted that he would be forgotten if he stayed out of the tour circuit for long. But the day after his 1976 "return" concert was announced the box-office manager of the 2,400-seat Sacramento theater was flooded with more than 30,000 orders. Diamond made a triumphant tour of New Zealand and

Australia, then in the spring and summer swung across the United States and Canada.

"I had secretly hoped when I finished at the Winter Garden that I would never have to come back and perform," he said. "But then I got itchy about wanting to be in front of an audience again. It's the only real test of whether a song works. A concert is like a lollipop after I finish the hard work, which is writing the songs for an album."

In 1976, after his divorce, his psychotherapy sessions to give him confidence, and his second marriage, Diamond announced, "This will probably be my last major tour ever. My goal now is not just to be a complete songwriter or complete performer but a complete person, which includes being a complete husband and father." But even his most trusting fans and friends remained unconvinced that their King of Diamonds would really trump his own career.

(1941–   )   Neil

Rock and roll pioneer

Fats Domino

A combination of dignity and bruised innocence.

With a voice and accent as rich and warm as the life of his city of New Orleans, Antoine "Fats" Domino, a fine all-around entertainer, has often been wrongly relegated to the narrow category of "honored rock and roll pioneer." Actually, Domino was never truly a rock singer; instead, he rates as a gifted and genial pop-jazz vocalist who excels in the phrasing of the lyrics of adult romantic ballads.

His road to success was difficult and painful. While in his teens, and just breaking in on the piano, he was earning rent money by working in a bedspring factory when one awful day a pile of springs fell on him, mangling his hands. Slowly and patiently Domino retrained his hands for his instrument, despite pronouncements of doctors who said he would never play again. "I guess I fooled them," he announced a few years later, when in 1949 and barely out of his teens he recorded his first single, "The Fat Man." The record featured his rollicking boogie-woogie piano and Dave Bartholomew's hot little band, with whom Fats had been playing in New Orleans roadhouses, bars, and dance joints. And only five years later, he was introduced at a jazz festival by fellow Orleanian Louis Armstrong as "a man deserving of membership in the Hall of Fame." A year later, he became a national personality with his recording of "Ain't That a Shame."

Although Fats's 1949–57 recordings (which netted him most of his many gold records) are now considered examples of "early rock" or "early soul," they are actually samples of a local blend of tough, small band jazz and rhythm and blues, meant primarily for dancing. Whether singing blues, *patois* rhythm songs, or evergreen ballads, Domino's vocals have always exuded a friendly confidence. His most famous recording, his 1956 version of "Blueberry Hill," reveals a combination of dignity and bruised innocence, typical of Fats's ability to add new dimensions to average pop songs.

In the years following the 1950s "golden age" of rock, Domino's record-selling power declined. But the easygoing, though sometimes impulsive Domino continued to find lucrative club work, especially in Las Vegas, where once, miserable over his heavy losses at the gambling tables, he cheered himself up by going out and buying a new Cadillac.

Known to hold conversations made up of titles of his songs with his friends, Fats might choose one, "Be My Guest," as his motto, for his audiences during his more-than-thirty-years career have been made to feel extremely comfortable and at ease by his warmth, his rum-smooth vocals, and his infectious mixture of rough-and-ready jazz and gentle blues.

(1929–   )

Jimmy Dorsey

He was stuck with the band.

"You just can't be any nicer than he was and still be a success as an orchestra leader," Ray McKinley, his longtime drummer, recently commented about his former boss Jimmy Dorsey. Jimmy indeed was the nice, easygoing Dorsey who sat in the sax section while his younger, more dynamic brother, Tommy, led the smartly swinging Dorsey Brothers Orchestra of the mid-1930s. But one night in 1935, while the band was playing at the Glen Island Casino in New Rochelle, New York, Jimmy caustically questioned a tempo his brother was setting, whereupon Tommy blew his top, stalked off the bandstand and left the band.

"Jimmy never wanted to be a leader," points out Bob Eberly, the band's singer and Dorsey's friend. "He was much too shy." But he was stuck with the band. The brothers' split soon stretched over three thousand miles. While Tommy was organizing a rival band in New York, Jimmy transferred his inherited group to Hollywood to play for an old friend, Bing Crosby, on his "Kraft Music Hall" radio series. Except as accompaniment, the band was heard little and made few personal appearances away from the West Coast. Eventually it emerged from its subordinate role, and by the early 1940s, with pert, pretty, dimply Helen O'Connell and handsome Bob Eberly singing songs like "Amapola," "Tangerine," and "Green Eyes" on records and appearing in movies like *The Fleet's In,* the band attained top-class status.

Of course Jimmy was featured too—on both sax and clarinet—neither, by the way, his original instrument. When Jimmy was six, his father, a music instructor in their hometown of Shenandoah, Pennsylvania, had taught him the trumpet. By the time he was twelve, Jimmy, then playing professionally (he said he enjoyed bringing home the money even more than playing), switched to the sax because the town had too many trumpeters.

Four years later he and Tommy had their own jazz band, first known as Dorsey's Novelty Six, then as Dorsey's Wild Canaries. Soon his talents on sax and clarinet brought him an offer to join the Scranton Sirens, the area's top band. He accepted and immediately suggested hiring "the younger brother." Years later their mother recalled, "That's the way it always was. Whenever Jimmy joined a band, he'd always tell the leader right away about his kid brother, the trombone player."

The pattern prevailed. Jimmy led the way into more important bands: the California Ramblers, Jean Goldkette, Paul Whiteman, Red Nichols and His

Five Pennies, Andre Kostelanetz, and other top radio and recording orchestras
in New York's studios. There the brothers remained throughout the early 1930s,
sometimes using other studio musicians, such as Glenn Miller and Bunny Berigan, to record as the Dorsey Brothers Orchestra, which also accompanied singers
like Bing Crosby, Mildred Bailey, and the Boswell Sisters. In 1934 they quit
the studio grind and formed what was to have been a permanent band (Miller
wrote their arrangements and played trombone). That lasted only a year—until
that evening when Tommy exploded on the Glen Island Casino bandstand.

In later years Tommy and Jimmy got together again, first in a 1947 movie,
The Fabulous Dorseys, loosely based on their lives, and later in 1953, when
the big-band business was in the doldrums and they decided to combine their
overheads. But that reunion ended abruptly in 1956 with Tommy's tragic death.
Jimmy, already quite ill, seemed to lose his will to live, and six months later
he succumbed to cancer.

(1904–1957)

The older Dorsey and his fans

Tommy Dorsey

Probably the greatest all-around dance band of all time.

Frank Sinatra once said of the bandleader who helped make him famous: "I learned about dynamics and phrasing and style from the way he played his horn. Tommy Dorsey was a real education to me in every possible way."

Teacher and pupil worked together for almost three years, and though Sinatra may never have recognized it, much of Tommy's personality also seems to have rubbed off on him. For Dorsey definitely was a man of action and energy, a man with a temper that rose and subsided abruptly, a compulsive man (a lover of toy electric trains, he stacked his garage with more train paraphernalia than he could unpack). He was strong-willed and seldom harnessed his emotions. He could be very gentle and kind, as well as brusque and ugly, telling people off, using vicious language, even throwing punches at them. But though often intolerant, he could also show much compassion. He had a sharp sense of humor, even about himself. He was a gracious and generous companion who loved to be surrounded by friends. He had numerous interests and a great thrist for knowledge (his biggest regret in life was his lack of a college education). He had a driving ambition to excel, which he did.

That drive had been instilled in him by his music-teaching father in their hometown of Shenandoah, Pennsylvania. It developed into an intensely competitive streak that, interestingly, did not infect his older, more passive and almost as successful brother, Jimmy, who seldom retaliated when young Tommy did things like sliding down a banister, feet first, right into Jimmy and knocking him to the floor. Two hours later all would be forgiven, and they would be blowing their horns, side by side, in the local band.

Together they developed into outstanding musicians, Tommy into one of the great trombonists of all time, with a gorgeous tone and superb breath control that let him blow long, effortless phrases. From the mid-1920s to the mid-1930s he played in the bands of Jean Goldkette and Paul Whiteman and in New York's recording and radio studios. In 1934 he and Jimmy formed the Dorsey Brothers Orchestra, but after a year of many brutal arguments Tommy stalked off the famous Glen Island Casino bandstand, leaving the band to Jimmy.

His competitive drive still alive, Tommy soon developed probably the greatest all-around dance band of all time. It combined Tommy's penchant for perfection with his flair for remantic ballads (which almost always featured his gorgeous trombone solos) and the sort of big-band jazz that appealed to audiences of all ages. Always appreciative, never jealous of talent, Dorsey proudly featured

The Sentimental Gentleman of Swing

new singers like Jack Leonard, Sinatra, Jo Stafford, and the Pied Pipers, great jazz soloists like Bunny Berigan, Ziggy Elman, Bud Freeman, and Buddy Rich and outstanding arrangements by Sy Oliver, Axel Stordahl, and Paul Weston.

But still Tommy was not satisfied. Although he was leading the greatest band around, he wanted to compete in other ways. He didn't like the way his booking office handled his band, so he started booking it himself. Certain journalists bugged him, so he began publishing his own music magazine. He saw no reason for promoting songs for music publishers, so he formed his own publishing company. And finally, after the big bands began to lose popularity in the latter 1940s, Dorsey felt record companies were not doing right by him, and he began producing his own.

But no matter how strong-willed, competitive, and active he remained, he could not stem the decline of the big bands' appeal. During the mid-1950s, after he and Jimmy had rejoined forces, their band was given a short transfusion by one of their many admirers, Jackie Gleason, who featured them on "Stage Show," his summer-replacement TV series, which presented on national television, for the very first time, two comparatively unknown singers—Connie Francis and Elvis Presley.

The strain of fighting losing battles had begun to show on Tommy. His third marriage had deteriorated into the most unhappy of all, and his wife was suing him for divorce. The thought of losing custody of his two young children, whom he adored, must have been unbearable. On November 26, 1956, Tommy Dorsey went to bed after eating a large meal and taking some sleeping pills. It's just possible, when be began choking in his sleep, that he had neither the ability nor the desire to wake up. In any case, he never did.

(1905–1956)

He never pretended he was a great musician.

"Many people didn't listen to him as much as they looked at him," one of the members of Eddy Duchin's orchestra once remarked. "He was the only musician I've ever known who could play a thirty-two-bar solo with thirty-two mistakes and get an ovation afterward."

No doubt about it, Eddy Duchin, leader of one of the most successful sweet bands during the 1930s, and a remarkably handsome and charming man, ingratiated himself with his followers, especially with the rich women who danced in the smart supper clubs that vied for his orchestra's services. Seated at his piano, dressed stylishly in tails, he would weave to and fro over his instrument, seeming to coax every nuance from its keys, his winning smile captivating those impressionable society dolls who probably fancied that a major chord would some day be promoted to lieutenant colonel.

Duchin was thoroughly aware of his role. He never pretended he was a great musician and did, in fact, turn over many musical responsibilities to his subordinates. He claimed that for him music was "inspirational rather than mechanical. I close my eyes, hum to myself, and then play what I happen to feel inside of me."

He measured his achievement not so much by musical as by commercial standards. "Dance music is primarily for dancing," he one stated. "If the crowd finds your music easy to dance to, you're a success."

Such success came early to Duchin. At the age of nineteen, while enrolled at the Massachusetts College of Pharmacy near his native Cambridge, he auditioned for Leo Reisman's orchestra, then enjoying tremendous popularity in New York's posh Central Park Casino. His seemingly facile technique and beaming personality won him the job from among a large corps of aspirants, and his flashy style and personality so captivated the customers that three years later, much to Reisman's chagrin, Duchin himself had taken over the prestigious engagement.

Duchin personalized the playing of his instrument as no other dance-band pianist before him had done. Visually his approach, with its sexy, undulating swaying, was unique. But so was his musical approach, which emphasized his crossed-hands technique of playing the melody in the bass register with his right hand while his left hand ploddingly pressed down the chords where his right hand was supposed to be. The resultant emphasis on melody in the lower register exuded musical masculinity.

Eddy

Throughout the 1930s Duchin's orchestra played primarily in hotels like the Waldorf-Astoria in New York and other so-called "swank spots." It also appeared on several radio series and in two films. The polite, personable Duchin was soon accepted socially by the country's bluer bloods, married well and was blessed with a son named Peter, who was to follow very successfully in his father's musical footsteps.

Early in the 1940s Eddy took his orchestra on a memorable South American tour but soon thereafter left his musicians to accept a commission in the Navy. Deeply patriotic, he paid little attention to music during his time in the service. By the end of the war his popularity had waned. So, unfortunately, had his health, and in 1951 he died of leukemia. Five years later *The Eddy Duchin Story,* starring Tyrone Power, paid a cinematic tribute to one of the dance-band era's most colorful maestros.

(1910–1951)

Jimmy Durante

"The song gotta come from da heart."

The sandpaper voice with its range of about four notes and its uncompromising Old New "Yawk" accent never qualified Jimmy Durante as a real singer. But whenever he sat down at the piano, pushed his battered hat to the back of his head and shouldered his way into one of his upbeat, generally nonsensical songs, audiences loved him. Gusto and the kind of professional polish that make an artist look as if he's in the business just for the fun of it made up for his lack of vocal equipment. And Jimmy Durante had another secret for success: As he wrote and as he sang a hundred thousand times, "The Song Gotta Come from da Heart."

The son of Bartholomew Durante, a barber who left Salerno, Italy, and settled in New York's Bowery district, Jimmy had his sights set on becoming a concert pianist. But his ambitions for a classical career ended when, still a teenager, he got a job playing ragtime in a Chinese nightclub, earning twenty-five dollars weekly, money he turned over to his mother.

After a few years of playing at Coney Island during the summer and in Harlem nightclubs during the winter, Durante teamed up with a glossy dandy of a song-and-dance man named Eddie Jackson and a first-rate vaudevillian and part owner of a nightclub, Lou Clayton. The three opened their own Club Durante in New York under Clayton's able direction and, as performers and clubowners, made a nice bundle. Jimmy, characteristically, shared his prosperity with his family, treated his wife like a duchess, and subsidized old friends.

But the Depression hit show business hard, and after Clayton, Jackson, and Durante starred in two Broadway musicals, the Gershwins' *Show Girl* (1929) and Cole Porter's *The New Yorkers* (1930), they realized that together they couldn't make it to the top of their narrowing field. Jimmy could do it, but he'd have to go it alone.

It could have ended right there, like a lot of show-business stories, but Jimmy couldn't bear to leave his pals behind. So with Clayton as his manager and Jackson contributing material, Jimmy's career blossomed. Starting in 1931, he appeared in numerous movies and two years later returned to Broadway.

But no matter the medium—movies, the theater, nightclubs—Durante's act didn't vary much. His half-sung songs, including his own "Inka Dinka Doo," and his straight-ahead, saloon-style piano weren't sophisticated, but they made people feel good. "Lemme hear dat band!" he'd cry, strutting across the stage (he was never much of a dancer). He was never known to tell an off-color

"Good night, Mrs. Calabash, wherever you are."

story or to indulge in racial or religious jokes. Instead, he made fun of himself. Not a bad-looking fellow, he called attention to his nose, exaggerated it, glorified it, used it to pick out tunes on the piano, and made it his trademark. His act climaxed when he'd attack his piano, eventually reducing it to splintered rubble. "I don't know how many pianos I've murdered over the years," he once said.

In 1947 the diminutive Jimmy teamed with the most unlikely partner of his career—the majestic Wagnerian soprano Helen Traubel. The lovable buffoon and the good-natured diva toured internationally to sell-out throngs, closing each performance with a spirited duet rendition of, naturally, "The Song Gotta Come from da Heart."

Jimmy hosted his own television variety show for years, and, still looking after his old pals, he usually brought out his old partner Eddie Jackson for a few high-stepping moments.

For audiences who had missed Jimmy's golden vaudeville days, his gentle essence was best revealed in the close of each television show. After the laughter and the mayhem with the piano Jimmy's kind face appeared in close-up as he croaked his mysterious tag line, "Good night, Mrs. Calabash, wherever you are!"

Turning from the camera, the rumpled little man moved slowly, as if his feet hurt, across the stage into a pool of light, stopping for a lingering wave at the audience that had loved him for so long.

(1893–   )

He half-sang, half-whined his free verse lyrics in a nasal voice like the sound of a dog with a leg tangled in barbed wire.

At twenty, Robert Zimmerman was a skinny, ordinary-looking (except for his startlingly blue eyes), blazingly ambitious middle-class Jewish kid from Hibbing, Minnesota, in search of a mystique.

From Bo Diddley, Chuck Berry, Leadbelly, and some other singers of blues, country-western, and folk music, he acquired his musical tastes and style. From Welsh poet Dylan Thomas, he borrowed a pretentious new last name. Woody Guthrie provided the finishing touch: Dylan's first trip to New York, in 1960, was a pilgrimage to the bedside of that man, whom he called his god. He patterned his dress, his drawl, his mannerisms, and his music after those of his idol. He hung around the lower East Side, sleeping in subways and crash pads, singing in Village coffeehouses for nickels and dimes. If it bothered him that nobody took him seriously, he never let on. He knew he was serious.

The cat went through a lot of lives in the next decade. He was "discovered" by Columbia's John Hammond, who heard him accidentally during another folk singer's rehearsal. Hammond signed him and set up his first recording sessions. His earliest hits—"Blowin' in the Wind," "Don't Think Twice, It's All Right," "Mr. Tambourine Man," "Like a Rolling Stone"—were practically instant standards. For the next several years he was constantly on the road, fulfilling demands to appear on network television, at folk festivals, in concerts all over the United States and in Europe, as well. The boy who, in his teens, had been a chronic runaway was traveling first class and making a musical and social impression on millions of young Americans, who seemingly hung on to and were willingly swayed by his philosophical songs, dedicated to the life-style that made him to some a Messiah.

While the mystique mushroomed, the only clues to what Bob Dylan was really like were to be found in the torrent of lyrics that poured from him in record numbers of syllables to the bar. By 1965 he had written over two hundred songs—some filled with adolescent self-pity, many in righteous protest against social issues: the hypocrisy of organized religion ("With God on Our Side"); the military mentality ("A Hard Rain's A-Gonna Fall"); the civil rights movement ("Only a Pawn in the Game"); the brutality of professional boxing ("Who Killed Davey Moore?"); the generation gap ("The Times They Are A-Changin' "); right-wingers ("Talking John Birch Blues"); the drug culture ("Mr. Tambourine Man"). He half-sang, half-whined his free verse lyrics in a

Dylan

nasal voice likened by one reviewer to the sound of a dog with a leg tangled in barbed wire. Songwriter Don McLean called it "a voice that came from you and me."

In 1965, to the dismay of purist folk music fans, he traded his acoustic guitar for an electric one and a backup band. Zap—he was a rock and roll star! In *Don't Look Back,* a documentary that followed him onstage and off during a 1966 tour in England, he was clearly under enormous pressures, internal and ex. "The pressures of fame," he said, "did weird things to my head. I was on the road for almost five years. It wore me down. I was on drugs." He was well along the road taken by Joplin and Hendrix when he got lucky and nearly killed himself on his motorcycle in upstate New York.

The accident forced him to lie back and get himself together. Two years later he emerged in an unexpected new incarnation: country-western-styled singer *(John Wesley Harding, Nashville Skyline)*. In 1971 he returned to the Judaism on which he had turned his back and changed his name back to Zimmerman (though professionally he remained Dylan). On his thirtieth birthday, he was a tourist at the wailing wall in Jerusalem.

In the 1970s, helped in part by his wife, former fashion model Sarah Lowndes, and their five children, he seemed to have mellowed. His songs, as always, dealt more with questions than with answers, and the "real" Bob Dylan (or Dylans, the clues point to multiple personalities) remained shrouded in myth. He seemed determined not to repeat himself and continued to surprise his public. When accusations of his having abandoned all political commitment were at their height, he surfaced unexpectedly at George Harrison's star-studded benefit concert for Bangladesh and caused a near-riot in Madison Square Garden. His latest protest songs concerned George Jackson, Rubin "Hurricane" Carter, and Joey Gallo, but his rage seemed more muted than in the early years.

Some critics (including Allen Ginsberg, who authored the liner notes) consider his 1975 album, *Desire*, the most revelatory of his career; in "Sara" he wrote of "Staying up for days in the Chelsea Hotel, writing 'Sad Eyed Lady of the Low-land' for you." He also returned to the road in 1975, with a caravan of seventy musicians, filmmakers, and technicians. Their *Rolling Thunder Revue* toured New England with a three-hour show that seemed motivated more by love than by profit. Performing with old friends and new—Joan Baez, Ramblin' Jack Elliott, Ronee Blakley, Joni Mitchell, and others—Dylan seemed freer, looser, happier than ever before.

And the impact of the more mature Dylan broadened even more during the 1970s. Accepted even by members of an older generation he once had seemed so intent upon criticizing, his lyrics, slightly altered from one of his songs, "It's Alright Ma, I'm Only Bleeding," became one of the climactic points of Jimmy Carter's 1976 nomination speech. "We have an America," stated the candidate, "that in Bob Dylan's phrase is busy being born, not busy dying."

(1941–   )

The Eagles

Alternately wistful love laments and stabbing allegories full of double meaning.

California's tanned, sun-soaked teenagers lived during the early 1960s in a state of innocence—surfing, dancing, listening to their transistor radios, and racing their souped-up Thunderbirds—all according to the gospel as dispensed by the Beach Boys. But a decade later that blond innocence had faded into a darker street-hipness that passed for maturity. Decadence and escape became the by-words of their living in the 1970s, and no musical group expressed those themes more fluently than did the Eagles with such songs as "Life in the Fast Lane" and "Hotel California."

In 1971, two members of Linda Ronstadt's backup band, lean and rangy Detroit rhythm guitarist Glenn Frey and sharply groomed Texas drummer Don Henley, joined forces to form a band forged from country and rock elements, with equal emphasis on each style. To accomplish this goal, they enlisted a shy Nebraskan bassist, Randy Meisner, and a Minnesota native with an overrid-

The Eagles

ing fondness for bluegrass, Bernie Leadon, who could play nearly every stringed instrument in the rock pantheon.

Success came almost immediately. Their debut album, *Eagles* (they took their name from Hopi Indian mythology, though Frey claimed it sounded more like a Detroit street gang), launched their first three hits in 1972. It also introduced the Eagles' two main songwriting streams: lush, melodic ballads rich in four-part harmony and heartbreak stories, and fast, hard rock and roll, paced by forceful guitar lines and kicked along by heavy bass and drum beats. Both styles had their devotees and both proved equally lucrative. By combining them, the Eagles could double their potential fans. Thus, their first six albums, *Eagles, Desperado, On the Border, One of These Nights, Greatest Hits,* and *Hotel California* sold over twenty-seven million copies and garnered three Grammys.

Besides bringing them financial prosperity and fan adulation, the Eagles' music, alternately wistful love laments and stabbing allegories full of double meaning (which Penny Rose in the New York *Times* called "stylish and intelligent music"), established them as leaders of a small Southern California song-writing clique that included Linda Ronstadt, Neil Young, Jackson Browne, and Warren Zevon. While utilizing the crystalline production and mellow country fullness of what music critics termed the "L.A. sound," the Eagles invariably progressed beyond the worst of that sound: its repetition of ideas and chords blending into a boring sameness. For the Eagles were the innovators of that sound and style, not its followers.

While their music explored the limits of their Los Angeles territorial stake, the Eagles' lineup, during their first seven years, underwent several changes. In 1974, Don Felder, a family man from Florida, became the fifth Eagle. Leadon and Meisner, victims of too many hotel rooms and early planes, departed in 1975 and 1977 respectively, replaced by Joe Walsh and Timothy B. Schmit.

But, despite having to break in new members, the group's output remained prodigious. In an interview in Britain's *Melody Maker,* Frey told Chris Charlesworth, "We work so much because it's therapeutic. Sometimes it's easier to be the underdog. Being an Eagle can be a handicap. Your life is not your own anymore. But what keeps me going is to make my singing and my music a little better each time. At this point, it's either grow or stagnate, and we won't do that."

Bob Eberly and Helen O'Connell

Virile and romantic (and) strictly cutsie-pie.

They were the most popular singing couple of the big band era, and four records on which Bob Eberly and Helen O'Connell shared the spotlight with the Jimmy Dorsey band—"Green Eyes," "Tangerine," "Yours," and "Amapola"—still stand out as four of the era's longest-lasting hits.

They sang on the same recordings, yet they seldom actually dueted. The formula was simple: First Bob sang the song as a slow ballad; then Helen burst forth with her rhythmic version of the same tune. The contrast was dramatic. Handsome, dark-haired Bob had a voice that was virile and romantic; his rich baritone emoted legato phrases warmly, even passionately. Blond, dimpled, pug-nosed Helen had just the opposite approach, strictly cutsie-pie, as she coyly, and sometimes affectedly, blurted forth her clipped, rhythmic, more forceful renditions of a song that Bob had just finished caressing so tenderly.

Helen and Bob

Romantic Eberly and O'Connell

Bob, whose mother played piano at the silent movies and whose father often led the sing-a-longs, was discovered by the Dorsey band while singing at a policemen's benefit in Troy, New York, near his hometown of Hoosick Falls. His easygoing, self-deprecating manner and witty personality endeared him to his fellow workers, while his emotional treatment of ballads like "I Understand," "I'm Glad There Is You," "Maria Elena," and "I Get Along Without You Very Well" resulted in his becoming the most popular of all pre-Sinatra boy band singers. He was encouraged to break away from Dorsey for a career as a single, and for years he was admired for not deserting the band that had given him his start. "But," Eberly admitted later on, "it wasn't a matter of loyalty on my part. I just didn't have the ambition and that's because, I realize now, I never had enough self-confidence." However, his rival with the other Dorsey band, Frank Sinatra, *did* have enough self-confidence; in fact, he admitted that the main reason for his cutting out when he did was "to get there before Bob Eberly could."

Helen, on the other hand, colder, more calculating and more confident than Bob, came on much stronger and eventually achieved greater commercial success. When, early in 1939, she joined Dorsey's band it was a wish come true for she had dreamed of working with it since her early days as a band singer back in Lima, Ohio. Helen stayed with the band until about the time in 1943 that Bob, with whom she was always very close, personally as well as musically, was drafted into the Army. Her first big record was a ballad, "All of Me," but later she became better known for rhythmic novelties like "Six Lessons from Madam LaZonga" and "Arthur Murray Taught Me Dancing in a Hurry," and of course for the sides she made with Eberly. She continued to record on her own after she left the band, then went into radio and television where her good looks and confident manner helped her land the role of hostess of NBC's "Today" show and of several beauty pageants.

Bob's three years in the Army hurt his career as other, nondrafted singers like Sinatra, Como, and Haymes replaced him in the hearts of America's teenagers and the innards of the country's jukeboxes. But his impact on other singers remained, though he must have cringed in the late 1940s when a young lass complimented him after a performance for sounding "so much like Dick Haymes," who long before had cited Eberly as his early inspiration.

During the 1960s and '70s, the team of Eberly and O'Connell continued to make personal appearances, featuring Bob's witticisms, Helen's still stunning looks, and some of the most enjoyable singing around from two sparkling performers, loved and admired as much by their loyal fans as by their combined nine grandchildren.

(Bob Eberly: 1916–   )
(Helen O'Connell: 1920–   )

Billy Eckstine

The first black singer to become a national sex symbol.

At its zenith in the mid-1950s, his fame equaled that of any popular singer of his time. First dubbed "The Sepia Sinatra," then "The Great Mr. B.," Billy Eckstine had a host of imitators, set trends in male fashions, and was pursued by bobby soxers. Responsible for a new and influential style of romantic singing, he was also the first black singer to become a national sex symbol and to make the front cover of *Life* magazine.

The handsome, charming man with the warm and sometimes alarmingly wobbly baritone was no overnight success. He had attended Howard University in Washington, D.C., then drifted into show business during the Depression, working nightclubs as a combination M.C. and dancer-singer. When he joined Earl Hines's band in 1939, it took more than a year until the blues recording of "Jelly, Jelly" established him as the band's chief asset. There were follow-

Mr. B.

ups in the same vein, but Eckstine, who, ironically, disliked to sing blues, showed that he had other strings on his bow with ballads like "Somehow," "You Don't Know What Love Is," and "Skylark."

A while after he had left Hines to go out on his own, Billy decided to form a big band. He knew and admired Dizzy Gillespie and Charlie Parker and was able to talk them, the co-founders of the jazz style known as bebop, into joining him. Other budding stars followed suit. During the three years of its existence, the band sported such talents as trumpeters Fats Navarro and Miles Davis, saxophonists Gene Ammons, Dexter Gordon, and Sonny Stitt, drummer Art Blakey, and a shy, young ex-Hines vocalist named Sarah Vaughan.

Eckstine laid his popularity on the line to enable his young and often wild crew to play uncompromising jazz and, having picked up trumpet and valve trombone, sometimes joined in himself. But even the growing Eckstine charisma couldn't make the band commercially viable, and the immature behavior of some of the musicians was trying his considerable patience. "I decided to do a single and go hear Dizzy for kicks," he said after disbanding.

Bebop's loss was Eckstine's gain. Unfettered by the band, he soon produced a string of hits, mostly stylized, smooth romantic ballads like "Prisoner of Love," "Everything I Have Is Yours," "Fools Rush In," and "I Apologize." Along with what Duke Ellington dubbed Eckstine's "sensuous semantics" went a style of dress that had hip young men wearing shirts with Mr. B roll collars and jackets draped off the body. When Billy and Duke worked on the same bill, the bandleader recalled, "neither of us wore the same suit twice . . . by the third week, people were buying tickets just to see the sartorial changes."

In the late 1970s, still the essence of casual hip elegance, Eckstine was dividing his time between engagements in places like Las Vegas and Miami, an occasional jazz reunion, working on his golf, and playing the guitar, which he had recently taken up. The years had been kind to his voice, and the old magic with the ladies still worked. Fads don't last, but talent does.

(1914–   )

Nelson Eddy and Jeanette MacDonald

All America responded to the wholesome and enchanting new pair.

He was tall, blond, and handsome. She was slender, properly pretty, with red-gold hair and green eyes. They made beautiful music together, such beautiful music that their eight mid-1930s to early-1940s film musicals were still popular in revivals around the world in the 1970s.

Nelson Eddy and Jeanette MacDonald both made films with other costars, had separate concert and opera careers, recorded copiously on their own. Eddy was also a top radio attraction. But when he blended his rich, virile baritone with her creamy, easy-flowing soprano in the tuneful, sentimental songs of Victor Herbert and Sigmund Romberg, amid apple blossoms, towering Canadian Rock-

MacDonald and Eddy in *Maytime*

ies, and boots and saddles, their togetherness reigned supreme. They were "America's Sweethearts" and, though laughed at by the rock generation for the costumed stuffiness and stilted drama of their operetta roles, for the majority of their public they forever after deserved their sentimental billing.

Eddy had the all-American good looks and vibrant voice that drew female fans in droves. Miss MacDonald's somewhat sugary appeal was less physical. As *Newsweek* reported, it was "not based on bathing suit allure. Mainly she made it on her voice. Her president-of-the-PTA prettiness never got the ladies' backs up."

Jeanette was born in Philadelphia. Nelson moved there from Providence, Rhode Island, at age fourteen. But their paths did not cross. The former church-choir boy soprano worked variously as police reporter, ad salesman, copywriter, studied voice when he had funds, learned operatic arias from phonograph records when he didn't. Jeanette passed up high school parties in order to concentrate on a theatrical career. By the time she had moved to New York and made it from a Broadway chorus and small parts to a featured role in *Fantastic Fricasee* in Greenwich Village and subsequent Broadway musicals, Eddy had made his operatic debut in *Pagliacci* at New York's Metropolitan Opera House and was on his way up in the serious music world. An MGM contract in 1933 shifted his direction. After appearing in two forgettable movies, he was cast as the lead in Herbert's *Naughty Marietta*. According to a New York *Times* report, he was warned by producer Hunt Stromberg that because one of its songs, "Ah! Sweet Mystery of Life," was the theme of Hollywood's Forest Lawn Cemetery, "he would have to sing it well enough to re-establish its identity." Not only did Nelson Eddy re-establish its identity, he sang it so fervently to—and with—the girl from Philadelphia that all America responded to the wholesome and enchanting new pair.

Naughty Marietta won an Academy Award in 1935 and sent "America's Sweethearts" singing their romantic way through seven more fairy-tale films— *Rose Marie, Maytime, The Girl of the Golden West, Sweethearts, New Moon, Bitter Sweet, I Married an Angel.* The last ended their screen romance in 1942.

Miss MacDonald pursued an opera and concert career before retiring. Eddy found a new singing partner, Gale Sherwood, and, though preferring to do new songs, continued his successful career with her in nightclubs singing the old favorites. "These are what they yell for," he told an interviewer, "and they want them straight. We tried kidding 'Indian Love Call' and they wouldn't stand for it." No fan of the MacDonald-Eddy films himself, the baritone star never saw one ("I was too ashamed of them") until caught unawares by a TV rerun. "I think it was *Maytime*," he told newsman Paul Meskil. "But no matter what it was, I was dressed up in one of those silly suits with frills at the cuffs. I whistled and said, 'Get him! Ain't he pretty!' "

(Nelson Eddy: 1901–1967)
(Jeanette MacDonald: 1901–1965)

Cliff "Ukulele Ike" Edwards

A combination of minstrel and Dutch uncle.

One of the star entertainers of the 1920s, a headliner on the vaudeville circuit and a major recording artist, he was also a trailblazing vocalist, quite possibly the first "pop-jazz" singer. Anticipating Bing Crosby by several years, he combined a smooth, fluid sense of beat and rhythm with a casual, folksy delivery and a liking for jazz evinced by his frequent additions of jazz "scat" choruses and vocal imitations of "hot" instruments.

Cliff "Ukulele Ike" Edwards was born in Hannibal, Missouri, and by his early teens was singing in St. Louis saloons for nickels. He next toured with

Ukulele Ike

carnivals and then managed to get on the vaudeville trail, strumming his ukulele and singing in his easy, comfortable style. During this period he and pianist Bobby Carleton popularized "Ja-Da," one of the 1920s great hits.

While working in a Chicago cafe he received his famous moniker from a waiter called Spot, who couldn't remember the entertainer's given name. "Ukulele Ike" seemed to fit Edwards' musical personality: He was a combination of minstrel and Dutch uncle.

By the mid-1920s he was an established vaudeville star, and he also made many successful forays as a featured performer in Broadway musicals and revues, among them *Lady Be Good, Sunny,* and the *Ziegfeld Follies of 1927.* But what made Edwards a national figure was his phenomenal popularity on records. He introduced "Toot, Toot, Tootsie!" before Al Jolson appropriated the tune, and he scored with "Sleepy Time Gal," "I Cried for You," and "June Night," among other huge sellers. He was adventurous and tasteful in his choice of accompanying musicians for his records; he often used Red Nichols, Miff Mole, Eddie Lang, Arthur "the Baron" Schutt (a pianist much admired by "Fats" Waller), and other notable jazzmen.

In 1928, while playing the Orpheum Theater in Los Angeles, Edwards was approached by Irving Thalberg, the boy wonder producer of MGM film studios, and was signed to appear in *The Hollywood Revue of 1929,* where he introduced "Singin' in the Rain."

But the Great Depression, which began that same year, left Edwards without his two prime vehicles. Recording companies collapsed in bankruptcy and vaudeville was dead by 1935. Though he was in demand for cameo appearances and supporting roles in early sound pictures (between 1929 and 1931 he performed in twenty-three films), his cheery vocalizing seemed inappropriate during the grim Depression. In addition to his declining professional career, he also had to deal with a morphine addiction, dating from the 1920s, for which he later substituted a growing dependence on alcohol.

A personal friendship with Walt Disney resulted in his making a limited comeback as the voice for the character of Jiminy Cricket in the 1940 Disney cartoon feature *Pinocchio,* in which he sang—superbly—"When You Wish Upon a Star." He obtained occasional picture work and was regularly featured on the Rudy Vallee radio program through the late 1940s, but after that his employment was sporadic.

His last years were troubled by illness. The Disney organization paid him a monthly stipend, and there were also contributions from musicians who had worked with him in his great days. He was confined in a nursing home when the star he had wished upon finally went out.

(1895–1971)

Roy Eldridge

Still taking risks, still challenging himself, still full of fire.

Jazz critics customarily have described him as "the link between Louis Armstrong and Dizzy Gillespie," but that's only half the story of the fiery, dynamic trumpeter, singer, and bandleader aptly nicknamed "Little Jazz," whose career has spanned six decades and who influenced a generation of trumpeters.

Roy Eldridge played his first professional job on drums at the age of six, took up trumpet at ten, and ran away from home with a touring carnival at fifteen. When the show was stranded in Arkansas, far from his native Pittsburgh, Roy worked his way home. Within months, he was leader of his own band of youngsters and soon was playing with the best bands in the Midwest. He came to New York in 1930 and caught Louis Armstrong live for the first time—and indelible experience.

Up to then he had, by his own admission, been concentrating on speed and technique. ("He's as fast as greased lightning, but he isn't saying anything,"

Roy

judged the great drummer Chick Webb.) Hearing Louis, Roy became aware
of the importance of also "telling a story" in his playing. He even went beyond
Louis in exploring the upper ranges and increasing the mobility and flexibility
of the trumpet, injecting a crackling, sparkling "edge" to his tone that made
his sound easily identifiable. By 1935 he had created a new style which captivated,
among others, young Dizzy Gillespie, who made it his business to catch every
Teddy Hill band broadcast featuring Roy. It was not just his speed and range
and tone and power that so impressed his peers but also his sophisticated harmonic imagination, inspired by his idols, the great saxophonists Benny Carter
and Coleman Hawkins. Roy had played in Fletcher Henderson's band in the
late 1920s and went back to it in 1936, leaving a year later to form his own
eight-piece group in Chicago. Records and radio further spread the message
among musicians and aficionados, but it was in 1941, when he joined the big
band of his friend Gene Krupa, that Roy rose to national prominence, not,
incidentally, as one of the first black musicians to work in a white band and
not just as a featured attraction but instead as a regular bandsman.

It was tough to live within the often capricious unwritten rules of racial
prejudice, when, among other things, black musicians were forced to live in
separate hotels and not permitted to mingle with the crowds. "One night,"
Roy recalled, "the tension got so bad I flipped . . . I started trembling, ran
off the stand and threw up. They carried me to the doctor. I had 105 fever;
my nerves were shot." Meanwhile, customers were asking for refunds because
Roy wasn't in the band, and they wanted to hear hits like "Let Me Off Uptown,"
his famous duet with singer Anita O'Day, and "Rockin' Chair" and "After
You've Gone," which featured his brilliant trumpeting. When he returned to
the band, as he wryly puts it, "they let me sit at the bar."

Roy worked with Krupa and Artie Shaw, leading his own bands intermittently
through 1949, and was also featured with Jazz at the Philharmonic. Following
a 1950 European tour with Benny Goodman, he settled in Paris for a year,
coming to terms with the fact that the advent of bebop had removed him from
the front ranks of jazz modernists. He returned to America a year later, as
fiercely competitive as ever, ready to match skills with all comers. From then
on, right through to the late 1970s, he was still reaching for the high notes
whether they came easily or not, still taking risks, still challenging himself,
stillfull of fire and the desire to assert himself, which even serious eye trouble
could not dim.

(1911–   )

Duke Ellington

It would take a convention of Ellington friends and relatives, pooling their knowledge, to put Ellington together.

"If you're going to play good jazz," Duke Ellington once explained, "you've got to have a plan of what's going to happen. There has to be intent. It's like an act of murder: You play with intent to commit something."

Early Duke

Duke Ellington committed more "somethings" in jazz than any other person who ever practiced and tried to perfect this particular art. This regal man with the fertile mind, the facile tongue, and the flamboyant showmanship was a composer, arranger, pianist, and orchestra leader. And as each of these he showed such imagination, such originality, such musical know-how and spirit that almost every jazz player will agree with critic Ralph Gleason that Duke's was "the greatest single talent to be produced in the history of jazz."

Duke, born Edward Kennedy Ellington in Washington, D.C., just before the turn of the century, was raised in a comfortable home. His father was a naval blueprint expert, but Edward's designs were on music. He was an innovator even then. His continual creation of the kind of harmonically advanced chords that later typified his music amazed and distressed his teacher, who soon gave up trying to make him play legitimate exercises. Securing a job as one of five pianists in a sixty-piece orchestra, he was fired for continually improvising. So he formed his own five-piece orchestra in which he was the only pianist.

During his very early career he had also earned money as a soda jerk, and the great pride with which he wore his nattily starched uniform reportedly earned him his "Duke" nickname. He dedicated his first musical composition, which he called "The Soda Fountain Rag," to his counter mopper-upper. From then on his pen never stopped dripping notes. Alone, and occasionally with members of his orchestra, he composed such never-to-be-forgotten pieces as "Mood Indigo," "Creole Love Call," "Black and Tan Fantasy," and "The Mooche," songs like "It Don't Mean a Thing (If It Ain't Got That Swing)," "In My Solitude," "Sophisticated Lady," "I Let a Song Go Out of My Heart," "I Got It Bad and That Ain't Good," "Don't Get Around Much Anymore," "I'm Beginning to See the Light," and "Satin Doll." He wrote scores for movies *(Anatomy of a Murder* and *Paris Blues)* and for musical revues *(Jump for Joy)*. And he wrote and arranged ambitious, extended works like *Black, Brown and Beige, A Drum Is a Woman, The Far East Suite,* and finally some intricate religious works, often using large choral groups and orchestras, that were performed in concert halls and cathedrals throughout the world.

But Ellington did more than compose and arrange great music; he also played it with his magnificent orchestra, hailed by critics as the greatest of all time. One reason it sounded so good was because its personnel remained constant. Besides being rewarded by their close association with a man they revered and considered a genius, the musicians, unlike those in almost every other band, were assured a week's salary whether they worked or not. Fortunately for Duke, the steady income from his songs enabled him to meet such payrolls, and he admitted that in some ways he considered his band a luxury. "Without the musicians," he explained, "I would have nobody to play the things I write so that I can hear what they sound like."

That Ellington sound, with its full voicings, its startling chords, its unique blending of various instruments, its exciting rhythms, from the most primitive

Latter Duke

to the most complex, permeated all his music, beginning with such seemingly simple early pieces as "The Mooche," through his dozens of pop hits, to his various suites and finally to his extended and highly emotional religious works.

He was intensely proud of his musicians, and he often composed pieces that would set off the individualistic styles of saxophonists Johnny Hodges, Harry Carney, and Ben Webster, trumpeters Bubber Miley, Cootie Williams, Rex Stewart, and Cat Anderson, and trombonists "Tricky Sam" Nanton, Lawrence Brown, and Juan Tizol. Some of these men had been with him since the late 1920s when the band had scored its first major hit in Harlem's Cotton Club and radio broadcasts from there brought the band national attention. However, until the 1940s prevalent racial attitudes kept the band out of most top spots. Years later, queried how he felt about such exclusions, Ellington replied philosophically: "I merely took the energy it takes to pout and wrote some blues." A creative genius, often a dreamer, he was also a realist who insisted that "nothing is worth worrying about. I never worry, but I do become concerned." The difference? "You worry about things you can't do anything about, but you become concerned about things you can do something about. And then you do them!"

However, Duke and his men were noted for lack of one concern: punctuality. Rehersals, even recording sessions, might start hours late, with Ellington invariably the last to show. Sometimes his excuse would be that he had to finish a complex score. Apparently he wrote well under pressure. He dashed off "Mood Indigo" in a quarter of an hour, a last-minute creation for an impending record date.

His life-style was as unorthodox as his music. He seldom went to bed before 6 A.M. and seldom rose before midafternoon. He loved to eat, loved women, invariably kissed close friends four times, twice on each cheek. He socialized frequently, enthralling companions with his wit. But his innermost feelings were almost always hidden behind a supercharming facade. Many people thought they knew the complete Ellington; few—perhaps not even his son Mercer, who later was to take over his father's band and drastically alter its style, his sister Ruth, his musical alter ego Billy Strayhorn, or his wife Evie—really did. As his close friend Irving Townsend pointed out in the *Atlantic Monthly,* "It would take a convention of Ellington friends and relatives, pooling their knowledge of him, to put Ellington together." For Duke refused ever to be pinned down. "The secret of Duke's security," Townsend decided, "was constant movement."

Until he succumbed to lung cancer in 1974 Ellington never stood still. And yet, as his admiring friend Count Basie insisted, "He doesn't have to move an inch. Duke is definitely a statue in American music."

(1899–1974)

Ruth Etting

She specialized in sad songs whose urgent lyrics reflected the unhappiness that lay beneath her smile.

With a voice like velvet, the sunny-faced girl from Nebraska wheat field country led the parade of torch singers of the late 1920s and early '30s, filling theaters, nightclubs, air waves, and disc grooves with mournful laments of lost loves, broken hearts, and "Dancing with Tears in My Eyes." Ruth Etting sang in so compelling a way that at the peak of her radio and stage career she was making the highest salary ever paid an "ether artist," as radio singers were often called.

She specialized in sad songs, like "Ten Cents a Dance," "Mean to Me,"

"Love me or leave me."

and "Love Me or Leave Me," whose urgent lyrics reflected the unhappiness that lay beneath her smile, her sweet manner, her all-work-little-play life. For the major part of her career—1922–37—the blue-eyed girl from David City, Nebraska, was married to, managed and jealously guarded by a denizen of Chicago's tough subculture, the self-styled "Colonel" Martin (Moe) Snyder (nicknamed "the Gimp"), feared by not only his wife but also agents and producers with whom he "negotiated" his adored "Mommy's" rise to show business success.

Show business, however, had not been Ruth Etting's original goal. After finishing high school, she left David City to study art in Chicago. In an art-related job she was assigned to design a costume for the chorus girls at a nightclub. Soon her stunning figure, pretty face, and curly blond hair won her an offer of a chorus line job. Despite the fact that she knew nothing about dancing, she accepted the job—and learned later. Next she was asked to fill in for a featured vocalist who fell ill. Knowing nothing about singing, she said yes just in time to slip out of her costume and into the star's polo outfit, step on stage and warble, "Hats Off to the Polo Girl." It was a neat feat, especially since the singer she replaced was a man. She was soon a featured singer, moving on to more important nightclubs that gave her radio exposure. Her first appearance on Chicago's WLS drew so much fan mail that the station gave her a twice-a-week singing spot for over a year. A record company official heard her and signed her for recordings. Chicago movie theater magnates Balaban and Katz starred her in their newest innovation—live stage presentations with flicks—at their McVickers Theater.

Flo Ziegfeld heard one of her records and, sight unseen, cast her in his 1927 Follies. She sang again in the 1931 Follies after appearing in the 1930 show *Simple Simon,* where her hit song, "Ten Cents a Dance," moved columnist George Ross to write: "It was the most memorable one the Etting girl ever did." Films followed, two with Eddie Cantor. Radio guest appearances led to shows for Chesterfield, Oldsmobile, and Kellogg.

But weary of the Gimp's jealousy, in 1937 Ruth Etting won a divorce from Snyder and freedom to seek happiness with pianist Myrl Alderman. A year later, the Gimp shot Alderman. He recovered, and during Snyder's subsequent trial and conviction for attempted murder, Alderman and Miss Etting were married.

Though she had renounced her career, reportedly burning all her music, to concentrate on her new marriage, Ruth Etting tried the comeback trail via radio and clubs in the late 1940s. By the mid-1950s she had reached the "tribute" stage, with the release of the film based on her life called *Love Me or Leave Me.* With James Cagney as Snyder, another velvet-voiced singer, a girl born the same year Ruth Etting married the Gimp, played her role and sang her songs. Her name: Doris Day.

(1898–1978)

Bill Evans

"I have no use for the bathroom noises of the artist."

The creator of the most influential jazz piano style of the 1960s, Bill Evans achieved considerable popular recognition without attempting to adapt his essentially introspective and highly sophisticated music to the demands of the market place.

One reason for this success is the rare harmonic and melodic beauty of his playing, which makes that playing accessible to the listener who may have no real comprehension of its musical subtleties. In performance, Evans has appeared to be a study in total absorption, with no line of patter and no introductions of tunes or players. A fleeting smile acknowledging applause and a deep bow at the end of a set may be the total extent of extramusical communication

Bill

with his audience. Seldom is anything else needed; his piano has done all the talking.

Evans' style makes the instrument sing. A master of dynamic shadings and rhythmic contrasts, he infuses his music with a lyricism that never becomes blatant, yet provides the emotional content to balance the intellectual component of his art. Above all, Evans is a master of harmony, and this aspect of his music has had a pronounced influence on other pianists, among them such younger luminaries as McCoy Tyner, Chick Corea, and Herbie Hancock.

Though decidedly a modernist, Evans prefers discipline and structure to so-called freedom. His extensive repertoire consits of traditional show tunes and jazz standards, interspersed with his own compositions in the idiom, among which the charming "Waltz for Debby" has become a classic. "I have no use for the bathroom noises of the artist," he bluntly said when asked his opinion of the avant-garde jazz of the later 1960s. Nevertheless, not a conservative, he has experimented with twelve-tone rows and made startling use of overdubbing techniques, notably on the album *Conversations with Myself.*

Born in Plainfield, New Jersey, Evans studied flute, violin, and piano as a child, graduated from Southeastern Louisiana College, and after his 1954 discharge from the Army began to work in New York, rapidly gaining the respect and admiration of his peers. His records with George Russell brought him critical acclaim, but the real breakthrough came when he joined Miles Davis' prestigious sextet for ten months in 1958. "I sure learned a lot from Bill. He plays the piano the way it should be played," said Davis, usually stingy with praise.

Since then, Evans has worked almost exclusively with his own trio, which took off in earnest when the brilliant bassist Scott LaFaro came aboard in 1959: The interplay between these two changed the role of the bass in jazz. In 1961 LaFaro was killed in a car crash at age twenty-five, but Evans eventually found a worthy successor in Eddie Gomez, who joined in 1966.

For years, Evans struggled with the demon of drug addiction. It is a tribute to his artistic dedication and discipline that he nevertheless maintained a consistently high level of creativity. By the early 1970s, free at last, he embarked on a new marriage and, at age forty-six, became the proud father of a son.

In 1976, Evans teamed with pop singer Tony Bennet for the first of several highly acclaimed duet albums. Finally secure in both his music and himself, he had emerged as one of jazz's most successful performers, respected by his peers and idolized by his ever-growing public.

(1929–   )

The Everly Brothers

Too old to be newcomers and still too young to settle for their reputation as pioneers.

From 1957 to 1962, in a string of nearly two dozen hit records (among them: "Bye Bye Love," "Cathy's Clown," "Til I Kissed You," "All I Have to Do Is Dream," "Bird Dog," "Wake Up Little Susie"), Phil and Don Everly of Brownie, Kentucky, made special contributions to the story of rock. Their high, tight, clean vocal harmonies were studied by young John Lennon and Paul McCartney; the brothers' success showed the artistic advantages of mixing ele-

Phil and Don Everly

ments of pop, country, and rock into a new, homogeneous whole; their original songs ("When Will I Be Loved" was revived by Linda Ronstant in 1975) provided material for future singers to interpret.

The Everly Brothers became entertainers at a very early age, traveling the Midwest and South with their father Ike and mother Margaret, both country performers. Phil and Don's first radio broadcast was over station KMA in Shenandoah, Iowa, when they were six and eight. They became a regular part of their parents' programs as well as having shows of their own where Don told jokes and Phil read the commercial announcements (the sponsor manufactured rat poison).

This gypsy life lasted for a decade of summers, until the Everlys graduated from high school and their parents decided to retire. Sticking with music, Phil and Don moved to Nashville in hopes of getting a recording contract. One of their demonstration tapes reached Archie Bleyer's small, adventurous Cadence label in New York. Bleyer flew to Nashville and recorded the brothers singing "Bye Bye Love." Then, as was his custom, Bleyer took the record home to his teenaged daughter Jackie, to gauge its potential by her reaction. She was enthusiastic (so much so that she later married Phil; they have since divorced). Despite initial disc jockey resistance to what was considered a "country" record, "Bye Bye Love" took off and the Everlys were suddenly stars.

Their red-hot period ended around 1962, mostly because the Everlys were not careful about the kind of material they recorded and because their early novelty and freshness became commonplace as more and more singers and songwriters integrated pop, rock, and country styles. The brothers continued to tour but recorded success eluded them, though they found consistent welcome and respect in England. Then personal pressures and work frustrations resulted in an early 1960s drug-related suicide attempt by Don in London.

By that time the brothers, still young men, were exhausted with nearly thirty years of show business behind them. Rushed through childhood they found adulthood baffling and anticlimactic. Too old to be newcomers and still too young to settle for their reputation as pioneers, their aimless careers made them tense and volatile.

In 1974 the Everlys formally announced the end of their professional relationship, though both continued to record solo albums.

(Don Everly: 1937–   )
(Phil Everly: 1939–   )

Percy Faith

He dazzled audiences with his big, symphonic sound.

Listening to any of the forty Percy Faith albums still available on Columbia Records may provide insight into Faith's romantic nature and gregarious personality, but they shed not one clue into the tragedies that marred the beginning and end of his long, illustrious career.

The sound associated with Percy Faith was consistently virtuosic in terms of orchestral textures. He dazzled audiences with his big, symphonic sound; he played Cupid with his lush mood music; he even won over some diehard rock fans with his infectious contemporary pulse. He was one of Hollywood's most gifted hyphenations: composer-conductor-arranger. The orchestra was his instrument and, quite literally, he "played" it.

At the outset his musical career was headed in a different playing direction. Born in Toronto, Canada, he began studying violin at age seven, but soon

Percy Faith

switched to piano. While a student at the Toronto Conservatory, he made his debut as a concert pianist at Massey Hall. At eighteen, his future as a keyboard artist seemed assured until a tragic accident intervened. The clothing of his three-year-old sister caught fire, and Percy, responding instinctively, beat out the flames with his hands. They were burned so severely he could no longer tolerate the long hours of practice required of a concert pianist.

Percy was heartbroken. But he was also resilient. He shifted his major at the conservatory and began an intensive study of composition and arranging. Shortly after graduation he organized his own string ensemble, which became a fixture on the CBC, the Canadian Broadcasting Corporation. At the same time, he began arranging for some of the leading bands and combos in the Toronto area.

It wasn't long before Percy was engaged by the CBC as a staff arranger and conductor, nor was it long before he had his own program, *Music by Faith.* For seven years (1933–40) it reigned as the most popular musical show on the network and by 1938 one of the most popular in its neighbor to the south.

When Joseph Pasternak, conductor of the top-rated radio show "The Carnation Contented Hour," died suddenly Percy filled in for three weeks, making such an impression that the network brass tendered him an offer he couldn't refuse.

He moved to New York in 1940, became an American citizen that year, and continued to perfect the opulent string sound that became his trademark. In 1947 he became musical director of "The Coca-Cola Show," and shortly thereafter he inherited "The Woolworth Hour."

In 1960 the lure of film scoring drew Percy west, and from that point on he was blessed with the Midas touch. Three of his Columbia albums, *Viva, Bouquet,* and *Themes for Young Lovers,* exceeded sales of a million dollars each. His arrangements of "Because of You," "Cold, Cold Heart," and "Rags to Riches" for Tony Bennett also turned to gold. His 1955 score for the film *Love Me or Leave Me* earned an Academy Award nomination, and his arrangement of "Theme from a Summer Place" won a Grammy and stayed on the charts for the entire year of 1960.

His reputation as an orchestrator grew in a community brimming with first-rate arrangers. The studio musicians enjoyed working for him because he knew what he wanted, knew how to achieve it, and, as drummer Earl Palmer recalls, "he was a warm individual, no pretentiousness, no ego tantrums. He loved to mix with the 'cats,' joke with them, and especially enjoyed reminiscing about the old days. He was beautiful."

But beneath the joking and the camaraderie, Percy was slowly and painfully dying of cancer, and he knew it. As his condition worsened, he maintained his rigorous touring and recording schedule. Then just six weeks after he had completed his *Summer Place '76* album, the pain subsided forever. Percy had lost his battle with cancer.

(1908–1976)

Arthur Fiedler

The strongest of all bridges between popular and classical music.

He visited dives in London to get the true feeling for the sound of rock music before conducting a full symphony that played the music of the Beatles. He flew to New Orleans to conduct Al Hirt's six-piece Dixieland combo in a nightclub. He rides police patrol cars, chases fire engines, and in 235 cities has been named honorary fire chief.

Hardly sounds like one of the greatest conductors of symphony orchestras. But he is. Specifically, he is Arthur Fiedler, a zestful, talented, innovative musician, who through his Boston Pops Orchestra concerts and recordings has created the strongest of all bridges between popular and classical music.

The classics came first in his life. He was born in Boston, moved, when he was sixteen, to his family's native Vienna and then went to Berlin, where he

"Mr. Quackenbush"

continued his musical studies at the Royal Academy of Music. But he yearned for more than just the traditionally stuffy approach to music. Life's other pleasures—girls and other adventures—fascinated him too, and so he left his comfortable home to play pop tunes in pit orchestras. When World War I erupted, his dual citizenship (Austrian and American) made him eligible for the German draft. Not considering fighting a war one of his pleasures, he returned to America and at the age of twenty followed his father's footsteps to a violin chair in the Boston Symphony.

Eventually, just sitting there, one of twenty violinists in a section, bored him. In 1924 he formed a small orchestral group, the Boston Sinfonietta; in 1929 he inaugurated the semiclassic open-air Esplanade Concerts. His engaging manner led to an appointment in 1930 as conductor of the Boston Pops, which from that time spent ten weeks every spring combining snippets of classical music with snatches of Victor Herbert, John Philip Sousa, George Gershwin, Cole Porter, Duke Ellington, Glenn Miller, Dixieland jazz, rock, and many other forms of pop music.

In 1935 Fiedler's Boston Pops Orchestra began recording for RCA with a two-sided disc of "The Carioca" and "The Continental." His version of "Jalousie," an unknown tune he bought for fifteen cents at a clearance sale in a Boston music store, became the first orchestral recording ever to sell a million copies. His albums have included a continuing best seller, *Gaîté Parisienne,* the intriguing *Classical Music for People Who Hate Classical Music,* two volumes of *Greatest Hits of the '70s,* and many dozen more.

Ever on the lookout for something new and daring, he presented the first black concert pianist, the first Afro-American Music Night, the first children's morning concerts, and the first conducting appearance of a twenty-two-year-old Harvard student named Leonard Bernstein.

A natural showman who delights audiences with little asides as he conducts and who once assumed the role of a stuffy "Mr. Quackenbush" to promote his concerts on radio, he has been rewarded, because of his musical skills, with eight honorary Doctorate of Music degrees, plus invitations to conduct leading symphonies throughout the world. Robin Moore in his excellent biography, *Fiedler,* quotes an associate: "Arthur can step up there and make an ordinary orchestra sound good, a good orchestra—well, the regular conductor might be hesitant about inviting him back." Another admirer recently described Fiedler as "a God-like figure who turned into a human being," and one Pops musician looked upon him as "a colleague rather than a taskmaster."

After more than eighty years of spirited living that included several heart attacks and hospitalizations that forced him to cancel some appearances, his drive to conduct and entertain the world over had not diminished by one decibel. Nor had his zest for life's other blessings, which include a wife and three musically talented children, one of them the leader of a rock band. And how has Fiedler felt about that? "I agree with Rossini, who once said, 'All music is wonderful except the boring kind! ' " Obviously, Fiedler's tastes and interests have spanned the rock of all ages.

(1894–   )

Gracie Fields

The House of Commons called a recess so MPs could hear one of her radio broadcasts.

Part of what has made Gracie Fields "our Gracie" to millions of Britons and a perennial favorite entertainer in the United States as well has been her steadfast refusal ever to become, as she put it, "brown shoe." "When you're very poor you have just one pair of shoes," she once told an interviewer, "and that has to be black, of course. But when you get very grand you buy a second pair, and they're brown."

Gracie

Gracie Fields has long been wealthy enough to afford that second pair of shoes, but she has never allowed it to make her "very grand." The melodious soprano voice and flair for homespun comedy that made her one of Britian's highest-paid stars of musical stage and screen during the 1930s have always spoken first and most directly to the common folk with whom she grew up.

One of four children born to a mother with unfulfilled theatrical ambitions, young Grace Stansfield was singing for pennies at six on the streets of her native Rochdale, a mill town in Lancashire, northern England. At twelve she ran away from school to join a children's touring vaudeville company, only to be marched home by the truant officer. The rest of her training seems to have been in doing songs and comedy routines for fellow workers at a local mill.

She worked her way up through the music halls, finally scoring her first London success in 1922 in a review called *Mr. Tower of London.* By the time her first film, *Sally in Our Alley,* came along nearly a decade later, Gracie Fields was on her way to stardom. Her voice was equally at home with ballads, sacred songs, and novelties such as "The Biggest Aspidistra in the World." Sales of her records ran into millions.

One film followed another: *Living on the Bright Side, Sing as We Go, Smiling Along, Shipyard Sally.* All were hits, making Gracie "one of the family" for millions. It's even said that the House of Commons called a recess one day so MPs could hear one of her radio broadcasts.

During World War II, first in England, then in Canada and the United States, she campaigned vigorously in support of the war effort, touring, recording, and broadcasting. Veterans recalled the very sound of "our Gracie" singing "There'll always be an England, and England will be free" as a dramatic boost for troop morale.

She was a favorite on American radio in the early 1940s, and thereafter spent much of her time shuttling back and forth between the two countries.

After the war her popularity continued. Her recording of "Now Is the Hour," sung in straightforwardly sentimental style, was a worldwide hit. In recent years she has lived in retirement on the Isle of Capri, with occasional nostalgic visits to England.

What keeps a Gracie Fields popular with so many people so long? One long-time colleague has cited her "stubborn refusal to become sophisticated." But leave it to Gracie herself to supply the last word:

"I'm not clever, you know," she said during a recent London visit—she had come to sing "The Lord's Prayer" at a friend's funeral. "I just sing. I'm a housewife. I enjoy being with *people.* There's nothing I love better than sitting in a bus or a tram car . . . I want to look at other people. They interest me."

They always have. No brown shoes for our Gracie.

(1898–   )

The 5th Dimension

"You can't sing a color."

When curvaceous Marilyn McCoo was crowned Miss Bronze California of 1962, one of the photographers on hand to immortalize the event was Lamonte McLemore, an erstwhile drummer with show business aspirations which, it turned out, were shared by the beauteous contest winner. The two explored possible avenues toward their goal and, when the next year's contest rolled around, its winner, Florence LaRue, was recruited as the third member of a group that would become the 5th Dimension.

The next two members to join, Ron Towson and Billy Davis, Jr., had been hometown cronies of McLemore in the St. Louis ghetto. Towson had been singing in church choirs and gospel groups since the age of six. In his teens, he sang with Nat Cole and in the famed Wings Over Jordan Gospel Singers

The 5th Dimension: Ron Towson, Florence LaRue, Billy Davis, Jr., Lamonte McLemore, and Marilyn McCoo

and placed third in the Metropolitan Opera auditions. After college, he organized his own gospel group.

Davis, also from a gospel background, was a cousin of McLemore's. With his arrival in Los Angeles, the group began rehearsing and, very soon, recording—as the Versatiles. Under the dedicated management of Marc Gordon, they soon had a major hit, "Go Where You Wanta Go," and a new name, the 5th Dimension.

Their determined efforts, pleasing harmonies, and pizazz-filled delivery earned them a huge following, gold records, several Grammys for "Up, Up and Away" and "Aquarius/Let the Sun Shine In" and the label of "the black group that sings white." When black students picketing a 1968 concert asked, "Why are you playing that honky music?" Towson defended the group with, "You can't sing a color. People sing styles."

In 1973 their Establishment orientation became official when they accepted President Nixon's invitation to perform at the White House before fifty state governors. (The inclusion of "Up, Up and Away" in the program was approved only after it was explained that the lyrics referred not to drugs but to a balloon.)

In November 1975, after a decade of refining its sound, choreography, costumes, and patter, the group lost two members when McCoo and Davis, who were married in 1973, left to do their own thing as a double. They were replaced by Danny Beard and Marjorie Barnes, whose musical talent and sense of showmanship kept the group's dimensions just about the same.

Although all the members continued to participate in business decisions, manager Gordon remained its guiding force. (He and Florence LaRue were married in 1969 in the gondola of a balloon, ninety feet off the ground.) Gordon has kept the group alive and kicking via engagements in clubs and fairs and on television. If in the future their new directions should fail to keep them soaring up, up and away, they at least seem destined to be here, here to stay.

"Singing with him is surely an exciting rhythmic adventure!"

The titles of some of Eddie Fisher's most popular records reflect rather accurately the turbulent life of the young singer who, during the early 1950s, replaced Frank Sinatra in the hearts of the country's female teenagers as their new Prince of Passionate Puberty.

"Forgive Me" could have been sung to Debbie Reynolds after he had left her to marry Liz Taylor. "Bring Back the Thrill" could have been his imploring incantation to Liz when she left him. "Wish You Were Here" could have been his melodic yen for Connie Stevens, after she, his third wife, had departed.

"Oh! My Pa-pa!"

And "Turn Back the Hands of Time" might have been his lament after his fourth wife, more than a generation his junior, trod down the same, well-traveled path away from Eddie's bed and board.

"Oh! My Pa-Pa!" and "Heart" could have been dedicated to comedian Eddie Cantor, who had become Fisher's father figure after hearing Eddie's heartfelt emoting at Grossinger's. Cantor immediately designated Eddie as one of his "discoveries" and launched him on his career. And the title of Fisher's biggest hit record, "Any Time," reflects rather accurately his unpredictably wandering rhythmic beat that for years musicians tried valiantly to follow as he gaily and unconcernedly created his own time by decimating or elongating musical measures. As one famous singer remarked after trying to complete a duet with Eddie, "Singing with him is surely an exciting rhythmic adventure!"

Fisher was a gentle, soft-spoken, likable sort of guy with an appeal that featured a "gee-whiz-is-this-really-happening-to-me?" boyish charm, which obviously impressed the millions of young American misses who yearned to mother him as their older sisters had mothered Sinatra. His musical approach, however, was much more virile. Unlike Sinatra, who crooned intimately and softly, Fisher was more of a belter who used his naturally rich, bell-like voice to project his songs with infectious enthusiasm. His overall approach reminded one of the singing styles of Cantor and his vaudevillian confreres, who, unaided by microphones, had been forced to sing vigorously, with undiminished volume, to reach audiences in the rear rows of large theaters. Thus, Eddie's singing, with its unsubtle shading, not to mention occasional difficulties with time and even intonation, impressed music critics and musicians a good deal less than it did his adoring teenage fans.

His talents had first been recognized publicly when, at the age of thirteen, he won first place on "The Children's Hour" radio show in his native Philadelphia. He sang in local clubs with no national recognition for the next eight years. Then in 1949 Cantor dropped in at Grossinger's, heard Fisher sing, loved him, and young Eddie's future was assured. The next year Fisher had a record in the top ten, and his 1951 induction into the Army barely slowed his impetus, as Eddie continued to record, turning out hit after hit. He succeeded in selling a cool seven million records while still in uniform! In 1953 he began his four-year starring spot on the coast-to-coast television series "Coke Time," and three years later appeared with his then wife, Debbie Reynolds, in his first major film role in *Bundle of Joy*.

With the advent of rock, Eddie's popularity began to decline, though his discs sold well enough to keep him recording. However, his series of matrimonial adventures and financial crises succeeded in keeping his name and his face, if not his voice, in front of the American public.

(1928–   )

Ella Fitzgerald

"I used to think that people would think I was big-headed if I went into a record store and asked for my own records."

As she came off the stage of the Newport Jazz Festival, the cheers of the standing crowd resounding everywhere, Ella Fitzgerald turned to an old friend and asked, semipleadingly, "Did I do all right?"

That's Ella for you—starred in concert halls, with symphony orchestras, on recordings and on television specials, at music festivals all over the world, recipient of hundreds of standing ovations, and acclaimed just about everywhere as the greatest female pop singer who ever lived. And yet, despite all that adulation, she is still not entirely sure of just how great she is—not as sure as Ira Gershwin, who gushed, "I never knew how good our songs were until I heard Ella sing them"; or Richard Rodgers: "Whatever it is Ella does to my songs, they sound

Ella with the band of Chick Webb (lower left)

better"; or Bing Crosby: "Man, woman, and child, Ella is the greatest!" or Frank Sinatra, who has declared that "Ella Fitzgerald is as good a musician and vocalist as anyone is going to hear for the next one hundred years!"

Ella's inability, or perhaps unwillingness, to grasp how great she is stems from both innate modesty and her enthusiastic recognition of the qualities of *other* singers, such as Billie Holiday, whom she once asked for an autograph. She admires Sarah Vaughan's natural voice, Sinatra's phrasing, Nat Cole's warmth but never consciously tries to imitate another singer (except for her impressions of Louis Armstrong), although she does admit that she was influenced at the start by Connee Boswell.

Born in Newport News, Virginia, and raised in Yonkers, New York, Ella never thought seriously about becoming a singer until one night in 1934 during an amateur contest at the Harlem Opera House. About to compete as a dancer, she panicked and her legs grew wobbly. So instead of dancing she reportedly sang one of Connee's tunes, "The Object of My Affection," and won first prize. A man named Bardu Ali, who fronted Chick Webb's band while the leader sat at the drums, heard Ella that night and kept raving about her to Webb, who finally agreed to try her out on a 1935 Yale dance with the stipulation that "if the college kids like her, she stays."

Stay she did and three years later gave Chick his first big hit record, "A-Tisket, A-Tasket," which she wrote herself with Van Alexander, the band's arranger. When Chick died in 1939 Ella fronted the band but finally grew tired of the grind, and in 1942 she began her career as a solo performer.

For the next ten years she made her reputation primarily as a jazz singer. Said Met Torme: "I always thought that if there were such a thing as a potion for jazz, Ella Fitzgerald swallowed it at birth." She recorded for Decca, played jazz clubs, and toured with Jazz at the Philharmonic, Norman Granz's troupe. But it was not until 1955, when the musically sensitive, commercially astute Granz started managing her and recording her on his Verve label, that she became an international headliner. While appreciating her jazz talents, he recognized the need for broadening her repertoire and appeal. He turned her from the more mundane Tin Pan Alley tunes to more sophisticated musical-comedy songs. Ella considers *The Cole Porter Song Book,* their first recording collaboration, "the turning point in my life." Other multirecord sets featuring the songs of the Gershwins, Rodgers and Hart, Irving Berlin, Duke Ellington, and Harold Arlen followed. "Doing all those musical comedy tunes and all those songbooks," she recently confided, "helped me get into spots I'd never been able to play before. What's good about it, too, is that now I can also sing jazz for people who never listened before."

Listening to Ella can be a changing emotional experience. She will make you cry with ballads like "Misty" or "Angel Eyes," make you laugh with hilarious imitations of Louis Armstrong singing "Hello, Dolly!" or "Mack the Knife" or make you stomp your feet and shout with glee through "The Lady Is a

Tramp" or "How High the Moon." She constantly changes not just her moods but also her repertoire, mixing musical comedy and jazz tunes with the most current rock songs, ever-willing to keep her ears open to the world around her, still as anxious as ever to satisfy her varied audiences' tastes. In England her most requested song is "Everytime We Say Goodbye," in Germany it's "Mack the Knife," in Italy it's "How High the Moon," in France it's "Mr. Paganini," in South America it's "Hello, Dolly!" and for her older fans everywhere it's always "A-Tisket, A-Tasket."

As for her own tastes: "Mostly I like pretty things. I like the type of songs that are relaxed and tell a story. I love to listen to other singers and to get the feeling of how the other singer is feeling inside. When I come home and I'm tired, I put on a bunch of my favorite records, and I just sit there and relax and listen."

She seldom listens to her own records—because she doesn't own many of them. "I used to think that people would think I was big-headed if I went into a record store and asked for my own records. So I never went."

"A-Tisket, A-Tasket!"

Attentive audiences please her greatly, especially those that keep so very quiet as she caresses a ballad. She appreciates tremendously the loyalties of her old fans and is equally thrilled by the attentions of her newest ones. "I cannot describe the feeling I get," she confessed to Wayna Warga of the Los Angeles *Times,* "when I look up and out to an audience and see some young people watching, listening and deep in concentration."

During recent years, serious eye problems had made it more difficult for Ella to look back at her audiences. Finally she gave in to wearing glasses on stage. The move improved both her sight and her performances. "Now I can look out again and see the people I'm singing to, and that's very important to me."

Approaching her sixtieth year, Ella set a new goal—to perform as closely as possible to people, preferably in her own little club near her home in Beverly Hills, California. "I'd call it 'Ella's.' I'll be the hostess. I've got a cousin who cooks out of this world, so we'll serve food early only. Later a trio will begin playing. And I'll go out on the stage, sit on a stool and sing. Sing all the special songs and lyrics I've grown to love." To quote from her *Gershwin Song Books:* "Who could ask for anything more, who could ask for anything more?"

(1918–   )

Roberta Flack

"Nobody is going to use me up."

"I can play 1940s music, blues, gospel, sing a cappella, ballads, boogie, lull you to sleep, give you opera, sing dirty or sexy. What's me is whatever I'm doing," Roberta Flack recently told writer Frederick Douglas Murphy in *Black Stars* magazine.

And just what has this multitalented lady been doing? In addition to creating top-selling, award-winning singles and albums that display her warm, rich, gutsy voice and musician-like phrasing, she has performed as a concert pianist, conducted an opera, played with symphony orchestras, sung and played in both wee clubs and huge concert halls, devoted years to studying and teaching, and has even scored for motion pictures and television.

In connection with her recording career, she has gradually taken over all its creative aspects herself—selecting material, conducting, arranging and supervising and editing her own sessions. Why? Because she has become increasingly disenchanted with some of the industry's criteria and motives. Emphasizing

Roberta

that her aim is to make a *musical* contribution, "not money," she insists that she "is not about to be bossed, bullied, coerced, or coddled into being what and who I am not. Nobody is going to use me up. I am going to be who and what I am, not what agents, promoters, record companies, producers, or the public would have me be."

Abrasive words they may be, especially from someone who at first meeting comes across as a tender, shy romanticist. But underneath lies great strength and stubbornness plus a dedication to her responsibilities as a caring human being, a dedication that led her to spend seven years teaching both music and grammar to culturally deprived children in the Washington area and spurred her to work for her Ph.D. while preparing a textbook that would help other teachers understand the language of the ghetto.

Roberta displayed her talent and determination at an early age in the small North Carolina town of Black Mountain. At four she began picking out tunes on an old, battered piano. At nine she was given formal music lessons. At thirteen she won second place in a statewide piano contest and at fifteen a scholarship to Howard University, from which she was graduated in three years. The seven years of teaching followed, during which time she was discovered by jazz pianist Les McCann, in the late 1960s, while earning extra money working as a singing pianist in a local nightclub. He immediately arranged for an audition with Atlantic Records, where her recordings soon attracted not merely the general public, mesmerized by her emotional output, but even more importantly her fellow performers because of their artistic input.

Two of her recordings, "The First Time Ever I Saw Your Face" and "Killing Me Softly with His Song," won successive Grammy Album of the Year awards for outstanding artistic creativity. And the former has literally been "out of this world": When the astronauts flew to the moon for the first time, they took along a copy of the mellow-sounding, aptly titled song reportedly to "soothe their nerves."

And yet, despite such overwhelming acceptance, Roberta stubbornly refuses to rest on her laurels or to compromise her goal of perfection. Recently, it took her one full year to complete an album, much to the frustrations of both fans and record company executives. But she remained adamant. "When my songs come out," she explained to writer Murphy, "I have to be able to listen to them on the radio without having to duck up under the car seat."

Fortunately, so far, Roberta has never had to duck.

(1940–   )

Lester Flatt and Earl Scruggs

Country gentlemen in the quiet, dignified way common among southern highlanders.

When Lester Flatt and Earl Scruggs broke up their celebrated twenty-one-year partnership in 1969, it marked the end of an era in country music, and the end of one of the most successful teams in the music's history.

The two had first met in 1945 when Bill Monroe, long known as "the father of bluegrass," hired the nineteen-year-old Scruggs to play banjo for his Blue Grass Boys, and the shy kid from North Carolina brought his revolutionary banjo-playing style to the group that included a fine songwriter and smooth singer named Lester Flatt, whom Monroe had hired in the previous year.

This was a band ablaze with energy. Every member contributed enormously, no one more than Scruggs, who revolutionized the technique of playing the five-string banjo with a driving, syncopated roll, achieved by using his thumb.

Both Flatt and Scruggs left Monroe within weeks of each other in 1948

Earl Scruggs and Lester Flatt

and within a few months had formed their own band, the Foggy Mountain Boys, which was to become the most popular and well-known bluegrass band in the world. Their recording career began almost immediately, and by 1955, as members of the Grand Ole Opry, they were spreading their homey music and humor all over radioland.

Both men, reserved in manner and action, country gentlemen in the quiet, dignified way common among southern highlanders, expressed themselves primarily through their music. Flatt, the ever-relaxed spokesman on stage, was reserved and reticent off, though behind Scruggs's painfully shy slow-talking façade lay an extremely active and restless mind.

Despite several hit records in the 1960s ("Ballad of Jed Clampett," "Foggy Mountain Breakdown," and the theme from the film *Bonnie and Clyde*), they had begun to lose their confident, energetic manner. They grew listless and their performances perfunctory. In disagreement about their musical directions, and lacking enthusiasm for their music, they dissolved their partnership in 1969, each forming his own band, pursuing his own style. Flatt put together a basically old-time bluegrass ensemble with all acoustic instruments, featuring his laid-back vocals, while Scruggs spread out more. He contributed themes and sound-tracks for "The Beverly Hillbillies" and *Bonnie and Clyde*, and teamed with his folk/rock-oriented sons to push at the barriers of country music and bluegrass with heavy electric instrumentation, drums, and modern material. Explained Scruggs, "I wanted to do something a little more exciting. I wasn't going to let myself go down with stale music, because I still wanted to play music; it's part of my life and always has been."

Ill health plagued both of them during the 1970s, though their later performances with their own bands occasionally showed flashes of the greatness that once had been theirs, when they were spreading the gospel of bluegrass far and wide, when there was nobody like them. Nobody.

(Lester Flatt: 1914–1979)
(Earl Scruggs: 1924–   )

Fleetwood Mac

Smooth but not sappy, energetic but not nerve-wracking.

The five members of the pop-rock phenomenon, Fleetwood Mac, were certain they'd achieved supergroup status when, in describing their commercial impact, the U.S. music press dropped the accepted metallic (gold, platinum) record sales lexicon and began comparing their extraordinary reception at the cash register to . . . hamburgers.

In November 1976, as the band was nearing sales of four million for its breakthrough *Fleetwood Mac* album, *Crawdaddy* magazine ran a cover story on the group with the title "Big Mac." And when Fleetwood Mac swept *Rolling Stone*'s 1977 Reader Poll, the headline, "Over a Million Sold," reaffirmed the fast-food-like appeal of the band's output. By the beginning of 1978, its follow-up album, *Rumours,* which was to spawn four hit singles, had topped the charts for over six straight months and went on to capture a Grammy as Album of the Year.

How had a rank-and-file, blues-oriented British rock band grown to be one of the biggest successes in pop music history? The best guess is that a fresh, effervescent, California pop sound had casually merged with the crisp, dead-sure attack of blues-filtered British rock (two strong elements on 1960s AM radio) to create a synthesis that was smooth but not sappy, energetic but not nerve-wracking, and accessible, yet not syrupy. The up-tempo songs felt good streaming out of car radios, and the ballads had a calming influence in the suburban living room. Businessmen in their forties, many weaned on Elvis, and who hadn't bought a record since, were strolling into electric bazaars to purchase *Rumours.* Rock and roll had at last become a part of the mainstream entertainment consciousness, on a par with Hollywood, Las Vegas, television, and baseball.

Fleetwood Mac had been formed in 1967 from remnants of John Mayall's Bluesbreakers: drummer Mick Fleetwood, melancholy bassist John McVie, and guitarist Peter Green. (The group's appellation is a hybrid of Mick's and John's last names.) Jeremy Spencer soon joined as guitarist/vocalist, later supplemented by Danny Kirwan. When McVie married pianist/vocalist Christine Perfect in 1970, it seemed only logical that she come aboard as well.

From there the band underwent no less than four additional configurations before reaching its present status. The eccentric Green left to do a solo album. Kirwan was fired. Lead guitarist/vocalist/writer Bob Welch, hired in 1971, lasted three years, retired and became a solo star managed by Fleetwood. His departure precipitated the most significant personnel change of all: the addition of San Franciscans Lindsey Buckingham and Stevie Nicks. The combination of their distinctive reedy vocals, Lindsey's fluid guitar work, and the well-honed strengths of the Fleetwood-McVie core proved a magical alloy of California pop-rock and the cutting edge of British roll. Their inaugural collaboration on the *Fleetwood Mac* album produced three huge hit singles, "Over My Head," "Say You Love Me," and Nick's famous "Rhiannon."

But while the band's commercial woes were being resolved, internal tensions rose to soap opera proportions. Christine and John dissolved their marriage. Steve and Lindsey terminated their longtime love relationship, and Mick and his wife were temporarily separated. "We were all in pretty bad shape," admitted Stevie, who was being hailed as the most charismatic woman in rock since the emergence of Grace Slick a decade earlier.

Amazingly, the group endured intact, in part because both Christine and Stevie were able to adapt to the unique pressures on a woman in a male-dominated rock world. "Before Stevie," Christine has pointed out, "I was the only girl, and I was also with John twenty-four hours a day—for years—and that's exactly why everything went wrong. So I had to decide: either I'll be lonely or I'll damn well adapt enough to be like a big sister, to be with the guys and still retain their respect."

Insists the normally bubbly Ms. Nicks: "The last thing I need to hear is one more person saying 'Isn't Stevie cute.' I'm not responsible for the way I look, but I am responsible for what I do creatively."

"Winning on our own personal charm is most important," adds the intense but genial Mick. "The money is great, but in a lot of ways it has nothing to do with money. The thing is, we are all tremendously pleased with ourselves."

In trying to explain how everything finally worked out all right, Lindsey recently confided that "nobody knew what was gonna happen, but that's the way Fleetwood Mac has always been—played everything by instinct; by feel rather than calculation. I guess we've gotten there; realized the dream, whatever the dream was."

Fleetwood Mac: Christine Perfect McVie, John McVie, Stevie Nicks, Mick Fleetwood, Lindsey Buckingham

Tennessee Ernie Ford

"A satiric sophistication to hill-country wit."

"Bless your little pea-pickin' hearts, this is ole pea-picker here" became familiar to millions of radio listeners and television viewers over two decades as the greeting of Ernest Jennings "Tennessee" Ford, a warm and ingratiating vocalist and a relaxed, genial personality.

Ford's early 1950s recordings of "Shotgun Boogie," "River of No Return," "The Cry of the Wild Goose," and especially "Sixteen Tons," featuring country-style singing over a quasi-rock beat, helped to make listeners in northern urban

The Ole Pea-picker

centers more conscious of country music and eventually led to a greater acceptance of the music by them, of country ideas, forms, and styles. Doubling as a
humorist, who, according to one reviewer, brought "a satiric sophistication to
hill-country wit," Ford became the first hillbilly entertainer to play the London
Palladium, his performances and personality winning him a devoted fan in
the august person of Her Majesty, Queen Elizabeth II.

His pliant but forceful baritone has often been applied to sacred music as
well as pop songs: "Of all the singing I do, the hymns, spirituals, and gospel
songs not only give me great pleasure but seem to be something that truly
needs to be done. People may get all steamed up about big new love songs
that come along, but let's not forget that hymns and spirituals are the finest
love songs of them all."

In 1937, when he was eighteen, Ford badgered the staff at radio station
WOPI in his hometown of Bristol, Tennessee, until he was hired as an announcer
at a salary of ten dollars a week. He was also taking private lessons in singing,
and that same year he studied vocal technique at the Cincinnati Conservatory
of Music.

When the United States entered World War II in 1941, Ford, who was then
announcing for a Knoxville, Tennessee, station, joined the Army Air Corps
and flew combat missions as a bombardier. In 1945 he married; the postwar
recession forced him to travel to California in a beat-up car with his bride,
looking for radio work. He became a "hillbilly" disc jockey for a Pasadena
station. During his first day on the job, "just for the heck of it, I ran into the
studio while Cliffie Stone's show was on the air, exchanged a few jokes, sang
a hymn with the quartet, and left. It was just for fun—didn't pay a thing."

Two years later Ford was a regular supporting player on the Stone program
and had also signed a recording contract after a talent scout heard him singing
along with records on his show. He scored with "Shotgun Boogie," and in
1955 "Sixteen Tons" became the fastest and biggest-selling "overnight smash"
of the time. "I didn't particularly like the record," he recalled, "but then the
only other record I didn't particularly like was 'Shotgun Boogie.' "

Through the late 1950s and mid-1960s Ford starred in various radio and
television musical variety programs. Toward the end of the latter decade he
curtailed his entertainment activities to devote more time to his family, to fishing
and to his 540-acre cattle ranch near Clear Lake, California. But he continued
to remain active as a recording artist, maintaining a loyal following among
both pop and country fans, who admired the "pea-picker" for his way with
almost any kind of song.

(1919–   )

Helen Forrest

"I _had_ to sing with a band."

In Gordon Jenkins' special piece of material recalling her years as one of the greatest of all big band vocalists, Helen Forrest sings, "The only thing I dreamed about was how to sell a song. But did I use my head and get happily wed? No, I _had_ to sing with a band."

And sing she did, with three of the best of them—with Artie Shaw, Benny Goodman, and Harry James. (She also got wed, though not happily.) Generally recognized as one of the best, if not _the_ best of big band vocalists, she was especially good with a ballad, phrasing each with warmth, a feeling for the melodic nuance and the understanding of a lyric, via a voice that projected a sensuous aura of emotional urgency.

Helen surrounded by Dick Haymes and Harry James

If, as she sang in the Jenkins arrangement, she *had* to sing with a band, it wasn't apparent that day back in Atlantic City when ten-year-old Helen Fogel had to be zealously coaxed to sing a tune with brother Ed's band at a dance marathon. But that gave her a start that led to singing in high school musicals. Eventually hooked on singing, but seeing no future in Atlantic City, she went to New York where, as Bonnie Blue, she sang with Bunny's (Berigan's) Blue Boys on CBS. Artie Shaw heard her, offered her a job, and in the summer of 1938 she joined his band as co-vocalist with Billie Holiday, who soon left to start her solo career.

After Shaw broke up his band late in 1939, Helen joined Benny Goodman's. Often asked to compare the two rival clarinet-playing maestros, she recalls, "Artie played a pretty, romantic, inspirational clarinet, and Benny would drive a band." And, although she had minor hits with Shaw, like "All the Things You Are," and with Goodman, like "The Man I Love," neither leader saw the potential of extending her bandstand bit beyond the in-tempo chorus—no more, no less than expected of the unemancipated girl band singer of the day.

With James it was another ball game. Helen's warm singing, which reflected her personality so well, blended beautifully with Harry's schmaltzy approach to ballads. From the opening audition, when members of the band applauded after the first number, it was obvious that they were superb musical mates. Harry built arrangements around Helen, featuring her as a star instead of just another band soloist. Years later, she was still "thanking Harry for letting me really develop even further as a singer." In addition, a strong, warm, personal relationship also developed between the two of them.

Together they recorded a series of World War II hits: "But Not for Me," "He's My Guy," "I Don't Want to Walk Without You," "I Had the Craziest Dream," and "I've Heard That Song Before." Then, after the war, when big bands began to fade away, Helen started a second career as a solo performer on radio and in nightclubs, where one critic, after hearing a particularly passionate performance, labeled her "The First of the New Red Hot Mamas."

Year in and year out, she continued to maintain her high musical standards, a devotion to perfection instilled in her by her three band-leading bosses. In the closing bars of the Jenkins arrangement that she continues to feature in her nightclub act, Helen sings: "When all's said and done, it's been lots of fun, and I'm sure that you'll all understand. But I remember it, I'm not sorry a bit, 'cause I *had* to sing with a band."

For such a sense of urgency, Messrs. Shaw, Goodman, and James, and their millions of fans, will remain forever grateful.

(1917–   )

Peter Frampton

"Performing is the only drug I need."

"I think I've finally become a rock star for the right reason," Peter Frampton told the New York *Post* in June 1977. "I served a long musical apprenticeship playing with lots of bands to get where I am today. Before, I didn't feel good because people liked me for my looks; now I am confident that it is my music."

And what a rock star the small, elfin, 115-pounder with the tousled hair and the "gee-whiz-is-it-really-me?" expression certainly had become! During 1976 he generated over fifty million dollars in revenues. He played before a million-and-a-half people, and his *Frampton Comes Alive* album sold three million copies and placed number one on the pop album charts for a record-breaking fifteen weeks. Naturally the results thrilled him. But they also left him a little anxious, not just because he wasn't sure if he could ever equal, let alone top success, but because, he announced almost naïvely, "I hope setting this record doesn't mean I'm going to get kidnapped."

Frampton

His early life had been comfortable and secure in his Bromley, England, home where his parents (his mother was a frustrated actress, his father an art teacher) encouraged him to sing, to write songs, and even to set up a small recording studio, using their bathroom for an echo chamber. When his father brought home an album by Django Reinhardt, the great gypsy jazz guitarist, young Frampton became so hooked on the instrument that soon more than half his record collection consisted of albums by such jazz guitar greats as Reinhardt, George Benson, Kenny Burrell, Wes Montgomery, and Joe Pass. Delving deeper into music, he studied classical guitar for four years and later became one of London recording studios' most sought-after sidemen.

Early in his career he had surfaced as a sixteen-year-old teeny-bopper's idol, called "the Face," with a group called the Herd, which specialized in cuteness and gooey pop tunes. From there he had graduated to a hard rock group, Humble Pie, and then in 1971, after strong disagreements with its leader about the group's musical approach, left and formed his own unit. Success came slowly—in fact, after having recorded four LPs, he found himself eighty thousand dollars in debt to his good friend and personal manager, Dee Anthony, bouncing some checks, and ready to sell off his possessions. And then came *Frampton Comes Alive!*

Never has one album done so much for one artist. Culled from live performances, it projected an excitement and immediacy that the previous four albums, all cut in more arid recording studio atmospheres, had been unable to. Its reception ignited an entire Frampton craze. But, unlike many other rock stars, Frampton (he has never used drugs because he is frightened to death of them. "Performing is the only drug I need.") took his newly found fame in stride, "more enraptured than trapped by it," according to *People's* Jim Jerome. "Suddenly I'm the most sought-after music person there is—it seems quite ridiculous."

In the late 1970s it became even worse than "ridiculous" for Frampton. "There were so many demands on my time, talent, and presence," he told writer Diane Judge, "I almost went mad. I wasn't creating. I was frightened and lonely." He mentioned his depression and the terrible feeling "that my life was out of control."

He couldn't "control" the terrible reviews of *Sgt. Pepper's Lonely Hearts Club Band,* a motion picture in which he appeared, and which he probably wished he'd never made. Nor could he control the car that crashed into a tree, almost ending his life. But during his recuperation he was able to put things into perspective. "I realized everything had been output. What I needed was input." The terrible tension seemed to have slackened; the driving pressure to constantly please others had diminished. And what had become his greatest desire? "I can't wait to go to my house upstate and sit on the lawn and listen to the bugs go zsit! zsit!"

(1950–   )

Aretha Franklin

In between her hits there were many misses.

Her life has had its ups and downs and she has made her share of mistakes, but Aretha Franklin has never even come close to losing the title her public bestowed on her, "Lady Soul," so strong is her emotional hold on the millions of followers mesmerized by her powerful blending of blues and gospel music.

She was born in Memphis but moved to Detroit with her family when she was two. At the age of seven she started singing in the choir of that city's Bethel Baptist Church, of which her father, the Reverend C. L. Franklin, was pastor. As a teenager Aretha was featured as singer in the group that accompanied her father on his tremendously successful evangelistic tours, shouting out gospel messages to the receptive congregations, a style of singing she later carried into more pop-styled music as she blended the gospel beat and rhythm with blues melodies.

Aretha

Aretha

At eighteen she signed with Columbia Records after having been brought to the attention of John Hammond, one of music's great talent discoverers. For seven years she recorded, with very little success, "white" pop songs, jazz, and novelties. In 1967 she switched to Atlantic Records, where the company's astute vice-president, Jerry Wexler, became her producer. "I had been cutting rhythm-and-blues records for fifteen years," Wexler said recently, "and I recorded her in a manner that I thought was consistent with her essence, which was rhythm and blues—soul gospel rhythm and blues." The approach worked. Beginning with "Never Loved a Man the Way I Love You" and "Respect," one big hit followed another. She proceeded to win numerous Grammys, nine for rhythm and blues, one for gospel, but none for strictly pop recordings.

Yet, in between her hits there were many misses. Her inconsistency was attributed to personal problems, including a falling-out with her father and the breakup of a stormy marriage. Her weight soared with her problems. She ignited a small riot at a Denver concert when she walked out in the middle because the producer had paid her only half of her twenty-thousand-dollar fee. In 1970 she was arrested at a Rome airport on a promoter's charge that she was running out on her concert engagement after she had fainted at the end of her first of two scheduled performances.

Certainly her health was not good. She suffered from emotional upsets, aggravated by alcohol, and she remained secluded in hospitals several times. But with the help of Ken Cunningham, who had taken over guiding her career, she got herself back on her feet.

She became more and more involved with the secular world around her. Her success on records resulted in bookings into some of the country's largest and most posh nightclubs. A move to a mini-estate in Encino, California, from a twenty-three-room house on Manhattan's fashionable East Side coincided with a decision to concentrate on nightclubs and hotel engagements and give fewer concerts. She dyed her hair red and began wearing glamorous, skintight gowns that showed off her exciting, new, svelte figure. She made regular appearances on TV shows and became "commercial" enough to be featured on a TV jingle. But a lot of her fans objected. They didn't want what one critic called "a pretty girl, singing pretty songs" and another described as "a sexy Las Vegas entertainer."

And yet Aretha never really lost what she had to begin with: that ability to bare her soul through her music. What she had gained, however, was a greater awareness of herself and, thanks to her newfound peace of mind at home and some professional counseling, a great deal more self-confidence. By the mid-1970s she was putting everything together. As she grew more extroverted, earlier criticisms like "great voice, dull show" disappeared. Instead, as one writer put it, "She wasn't merely singing; she was more like bearing witness to a reality."

Certainly, many of the titles of the songs she has sung seem to bear witness to the trials of her life and of her career: "Chain of Fools," "Bridge Over Troubled Water," "Amazing Grace," "Ain't Nothing Like the Real Thing," and her hit album, *Young, Gifted and Black*. But, as critic Albert Goldman once noted, "Natural Woman" (which Wexler commissioned from Carole King for Aretha) should be her theme song. For, he said, "None of the famous Negro singers has epitomized normal female soul or free expression of the full range of feminine feelings" the way Aretha Franklin has. And possibly none ever will.

(1942–   )

Judy Garland

"It never occurred to anybody that I might have feelings."

Barely five feet one inch in stature, she was one of the tallest talents this country has ever produced. On stage, she owned every inch of the theater—from the footlights, where she sat like a waif crooning her ritualistic closer, "Over the Rainbow," to the last row in the balcony, where every syllable reached pure and sure. "When she was good," famed author and screen writer Budd Schulberg eulogized, "she was so very, very special that we laughed with her and cried with her and begged for love in a marriage of requited love never before experienced in the theater."

She was born Frances Gumm in Grand Rapids, Minnesota—not in a trunk, but into a family of vaudevillians. Her mother played the piano while her two sisters, billed as "The Gumm Sisters," sang and danced. Judy joined the act at three, by walking on stage to sing impromptu choruses of "Jingle Bells" until her father carried her off.

When the act was inadvertently billed on a Chicago marquee as "The Glumm Sisters," little Frances became Judy Garland. Her father, whom she adored, died when she was twelve. Her mother, later described by Judy as "the real-life Wicked Witch of the West," was the first in a succession of people determined to cash in on the talent of the chubby little girl with the big voice and the eyes that begged, "Love me, please."

She was thirteen when L. B. Mayer put her under contract and into her first MGM picture, a short entitled *Every Sunday.* Her rendition of "Dear Mr. Gable" ("You Made Me Love You") in *Broadway Melody of 1938* drew attention, but it was as the wistful Dorothy in the classic *The Wizard of Oz* that she became a star. That role won her a special Oscar in 1940.

To the studio, Judy was not a child but a property. "It never occurred to anybody," she said in retrospect, "that I might have feelings." During the next eleven years, MGM starred her in twenty movies, including the Andy Hardy series with Mickey Rooney. To dispose of her baby fat, which, said studio executives, made her look "like a monster," they fed her amphetamines and, when rest was essential, barbiturates. At twenty-one, a sizable chunk of her $150,000-a-picture salary was going to the psychiatrist with whom she had daily sessions.

In 1945, after a short-lived marriage to composer David Rose, she married Vincente Minnelli. He directed her in *The Pirate, Meet Me in St. Louis,* and *The Clock,* the latter her first nonsinging dramatic role. In 1946 they had a

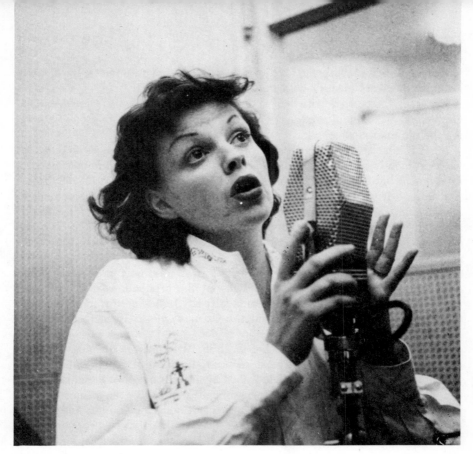

Judy

daughter, Liza. By 1948 such films as *For Me and My Gal, Girl Crazy, The Harvey Girls,* and *Easter Parade* had made her the leading star of musical films. That year she failed to show up for work on three films and wound up in a sanatorium after a nervous breakdown. She recovered and made two more pictures, *In the Good Old Summertime* and *Summer Stock,* for MGM. In 1950, when the studio fired her for "temperamental" behavior during the filming of *Annie Get Your Gun,* she attempted suicide.

In 1951 she made the first of many comebacks ("a Lady Lazarus," Budd Schulberg called her) at the London Palladium, under the aegis of Sid Luft, who became her third husband. Nobody could have anticipated the electrifying impact, the amazing chemistry that resulted when Judy Garland worked before a live audience. Through twenty-six numbers she clowned, danced, talked, and sang, using the mike like a trumpet, while her frenzied fans went wild. "She communicates for the audience," was Jerry Lewis' explanation of her extraordinary appeal. "All the things people can't say for themselves. All the stout women identify with her, the losers in love identify with her, the insomniacs, the alcoholics and pill takers identify with her." Certainly her delivery of the two songs most closely associated with her—"Over the Rainbow" and "The Man That Got Away"—communicated overwhelming feelings of vulnerability and a longing for the unattainable.

In 1951 she also set a vaudeville record of 184 performances in nineteen weeks at New York's famed Palace. Her voice was already beginning to deteriorate, but her growing mastery of performance, the dramatic, exquisitely timed transitions—from soft, tender ballads with intimate piano accompaniment to all-stops-out, belt-'em-to-the-balcony "up" songs backed by the full blasting orchestra—compensated for the vibrato that sometimes got away. "A Garland audience doesn't just listen," Spencer Tracy once said. "They have their arms around her when she works."

In 1954 Luft produced her "comeback" movie, a remake of *A Star Is Born* costarring James Mason. Fans adored it, but the production so far exceeded its budget that it was not a commercial success. Judy's performance won her an Academy Award nomination, but the Oscar went to Grace Kelly for *The Country Girl.*

Illness and overweight plagued her until, in 1959, doctors diagnosed her ailment as hepatitis—attributed, at least in part, to the years of uppers and downers. But in 1961 the comeback trail led once again to London's Palladium, then to a Carnegie Hall concert that one reviewer called "probably the greatest evening in show business history." During a subsequent sixteen-city tour, Judy told a reporter, "A really great reception makes me feel like I have a great big warm heating pad all over me. I truly have a great love for an audience, and I used to want to prove it to them by giving them blood. Now I want to give them two hours of just POW!"

In 1963, after twelve stormy years with Luft, she divorced him. She signed with CBS for a weekly television show, but the schedule was too tight for her temperament, the screen too tiny for her talent. When the network dropped the show after one season, her career and her health began an irreversible decline.

Audiences still chanted, "We love you, Judy!" but now some came out of a morbid curiosity. Would she show? If she did, would she make it through the performance? The suspense added to the emotionalism of the evening; nobody knew that better than Judy. Emotion, she once said, was her business.

In all, there were five marriages, three children (two by Luft), thirty-six films, three nervous breakdowns, countless suicide attempts, and legions of people who will never forget the magic of witnessing a Garland performance. When she died, at forty-seven, twenty-one thousand mourners filed past the bier where her body lay in state. "You only have one life to live," she once remarked on her television show. To the contrary, she lived many lives. Until, as Ray Bolger— who, as the Scarecrow, danced with Dorothy down the yellow brick road to Oz—put it, "she just plain wore out."

(1922–1969)

"There's these eighty-eight keys. The guy who made it must have had *something* in mind.

Erroll Garner can thank the Pittsburgh local of the American Federation of Musicians for making him what he became, one of the great and most original-sounding pianists in jazz history. Not that the Pittsburgh AFM ever did anything positive for him. Because he could not read music it just refused to allow him to join, barring him from playing with local bands.

"I'll play here some day," Garner vowed, "and I'll play like a whole band and I won't play with *none* of you."

That is the genesis of a style that combined elements of a Hollywood sound score, a symphony orchestra, a jazz band, and most of the great jazz piano soloists—a synthesis, a history done with assistance from no one. Adamantly illiterate musically, Garner based his life on improvisation in all areas; he refused

Errol

to make social plans in advance, he cooked by taste, and he was convinced he could learn more about playing golf on his own than with the help of a pro. Thus, whenever he walked out on the stage at his concerts, with the spring-toed jauntiness of a boxer (a profession he once considered), sat down at the piano and thumped out a series of introductory chords, there was always an even chance that he would not know what his first selection would be.

But then his face would light up, his eyebrows waggle, his great curved jib of a nose rise exultantly as though it had just caught the downdraft of all the perfumes of Araby, a vast happy grin slicing his face as appreciative grunts rumbled out of him, as, in the words of a Belgian critic, "he dominates the keyboard, masters it and imposes his own laws on it."

Garner had taught himself enough on the family piano by the time he was seven to make nickels and dimes playing for neighbors. When he was eleven he was sneaking out of the house to play on a riverboat with a band led by the legendary Fate Marable. His family tried to make him take lessons, but his teachers gave up when they found he was memorizing his exercise books and then faking his lessons.

Moving to New York in the 1940s, he settled on Fifty-second Street and at one time held three jobs simultaneously in three different clubs: as accompanist to Billy Daniels, accompanist to Billie Holiday, and pianist in Slam Stewart's trio. He remained an itinerant jazz-club musician until 1956, when his LP, "Concert by the Sea," recorded at Carmel, California, became a best seller at a time when jazz was fashionably on the rise. By then he had acquired as manager a pocket-sized virago named Martha Glaser, who mothered him as sternly as she rode herd on those who hired him. Miss Glaser turned Garner into a major concert attraction, even booking him with major symphony orchestras. And he turned himself into a major composer when he wrote "Misty," one of many original pieces.

His ideas came from everything—"a big color, the sound of water and wind or a flash of something cool." He was fond of highly theatrical bravura effects that would show off the full resources of the piano.

"There's these eighty-eight keys," he once said in explaining his urge to make his instrument sound like an entire orchestra. "The guy who made it must have had *something* in mind."

Ben Webster, a saxophonist who explored his instrument as deeply as Garner explored his, once ran into Garner eating oysters in a New York musicians' hangout. "Take care of yourself, Erroll," the ebullient Webster cried, hoisting the pianist in a bearlike hug. "You're the last of us. You're the whole story." But "the last of us, the whole story," suffered a fatel cardiac arrest in an ambulance on the way to a Los Angeles hospital right after New Year's Day 1977, and the world of jazz lost one of its purist, most pixieish, most productive pianists.

(1921–1977)

Stan Getz

He remained a jazzman to the core.

"I want to communicate with people," said Stan Getz, "but I won't put on funny hats to do it." He never had to; the beguiling tone of his tenor saxophone (early in his career, he was nicknamed "The Sound") and his very special way of caressing a melody sufficed to bring him great popular success even in an era dominated by rock groups and singers rather than instrumentalists.

Getz moved into star orbit via his 1962 recording of "Desafinado," which set off the bossa nova fad and made him a wealthy man. Two years later he had an even bigger hit in "The Girl from Ipanema," also a bossa nova, but this time in collaboration with the Brazilian singer Astrud Gilberto, the only performance by a jazz artist ever to win the prestigious Record of the Year

Early Stan

Grammy award. With his lovely Swedish wife, Monica, and his children from this and an earlier union, Getz moved into a stately mansion in Irvington, New York, once occupied by George Gershwin, but he remained a jazzman to the core and did not permit material success to dilute his music.

Born in Philadelphia and raised in the Bronx, the son of a Russian immigrant tailor (the family name was originally Gayetzky), young Stanley was recommended for a scholarship to Juilliard by his high school bandmaster. But the boy, who had made his professional debut at fifteen with a swing band, left school a year later to go on the road with Jack Teagarden, who had to become Stan's legal guardian to permit the minor to travel. Already possessing a virtuoso technique, he further polished his musicianship through stints with many fine bands, among them Stan Kenton's and Benny Goodman's, and made his breakthrough with Woody Herman's newly formed Second Herd in 1947. Here, the brash, bright disciple of the great tenor saxist Lester Young helped create the celebrated "Four Brothers" sax section sound and, with the help of such men as Al Cohn, Zoot Sims, and Serge Chaloff, made the jazz public sit up and take notice with a beautifully conceived and executed solo on "Early Autumn," which established him as one of the leading stylists of cool jazz.

Getz formed his own group in 1949 and continued to grow in musical stature. But all was not well on the personal front. Drug addiction, the scourge of so many jazzmen of his generation, had taken hold, and things came to a head in 1954 in Seattle. Getz attempted to hold up a drug store, and was arrested. Overcome by remorse, he returned to apologize and had to spend several months in prison.

"None of us knew what we were getting into, what a messy scene it was," he explained. "We were young and working hard, staying up all night and looking for false stimulation." His career regained momentum after a period of convalescence and cure in Sweden, and though he later settled in Denmark for almost three years (1958–61), records sustained his reputation at home. Not long after his return, his masterful playing on *Focus,* an extended work created for him by Eddie Sauter, further secured his position at the apex of his profession. And then came "Desafinado," a melody tailor-made for Getz's bittersweet lyricism.

As he entered his fifties, Getz had retained his boyish good looks and continued to surround himself with fresh, stimulating young talent while broadening his musical horizons by adopting, in carefully considered moderation, some of the electronic devices being utilized in so-called "fusion jazz." Meanwhile, his personality also underwent change: his volatile and sometimes abrasive temper had simmered down, and while no further popular successes of the magnitude of the bossa nova hits seemed likely to materialize, Stan Getz remained among the few committed jazz players fortunate enough to have found room at the top, and to have been able to stay there.

(1927–   )

Dizzy Gillespie

". . . And not only that, I'm a good dancer, and I'm funny!"

"I'm sort of like what Willie Mays is to baseball. I can do a lot of things and do them well, but I'm not necessarily the best at any of them. I have range and facility on my horn. I can read well. I can lead a trumpet section and a band, too. I can follow vocalists. I'm at home with all sorts of rhythms. And not only that, I'm a good dancer, and I'm funny!"

That's what Dizzy Gillespie thinks of himself. One of the three most influential trumpeters in the history of jazz (Louis Armstrong and Roy Eldridge are the others), he has been one of that instrument's most musically inventive and entertaining joys, and, in the opinion of jazz-pianist-turned-symphony-conductor André Previn, he is "the perfect jazz musician. He is a great trumpet player. He's inventive. He swings, and he has a sense of humor that jazz should have. And he has developed the proper perspective that comes from maturity and confidence."

Back in his young days in Cheraw, South Carolina, John Birks Gillespie had developed enough confidence by the time he was fourteen to borrow a neighbor's trumpet and begin to teach himself how to blow it. Blessed with an unusually keen ear, he also began to discover harmony. "I was always messing

Diz

around the piano. And today I still think like a piano player. When I'm playing my horn, I actually visualize the notes of each chord on the piano."

Before emigrating North at the age of eighteen he did study some harmony and theory at Laurinburg Institute. On one of his first jobs with Teddy Hill's band, he filled the trumpet chair that had just been vacated by his first idol, Roy Eldridge. (It was, the musicians of Hill's band who dubbed him "Dizzy" because on a stormy Atlantic crossing he ate continuously while they were sick.) Other gigs followed, some of them short-lived because of Dizzy's nonprofessional antics, such as throwing spitballs at leader Cab Calloway. He also played with Benny Carter, Charlie Barnet, Earl Hines, Ella Fitzgerald, and even Duke Ellington for a short while. "And I hung around Minton's [a Harlem gathering spot for musicians]. I learned a lot from the guys there; mostly they'd tell me what I was doing wrong." He has always been a good listener. "I'd use the elements and then play them the way I *felt* them. That's the way jazz is: You listen, but you don't copy. You just adapt things to suit your own personality."

Dizzy's development zoomed after he met the late Charlie Parker in Kansas City. "We attracted each other like a magnet. I remember in 1940 we blew all night in a hotel room out there." Together these two amazingly inventive, resourceful, talented musicians initiated a whole new style of jazz called bop, revolutionary both harmonically and rhythmically. "I influenced Bird harmonically. He taught me a new way of phrasing percussively, I guess you'd call it, and hooking phrases together." The resultant bop style, which permeated his small groups and his two big bands, extended musical phrases à la Parker and musical harmonies à la Gillespie. At the same time it also developed into a fad, with musicians latching onto Dizzy's supposed idiosyncrasies, such as his beret, goatee, and heavy-rimmed glasses. "But I wore them for good reasons," he recently explained. "I was always losing hats and a beret fit into my pocket. I didn't shave under my lower lip so that I wouldn't get ingrown hairs. And I had my glasses made with heavier frames because I was always sitting on the others and breaking them."

He plays his famed uptilted trumpet for another sensible reason. "I like the way it sounds better. Once at a birthday party for Lorraine [his wife] somebody bent it, and I had it straightened the next day. But then I started thinking about how good it sounded bent, so I had a horn made up especially that way."

He has blown his horn to telling effect throughout the entire world, interspersing his brilliant musical displays with his "down-home," imaginative wit. Once he started his own "Dizzy for President" movement and threatened to slug anyone who called him "a dark horse." In a more serious vein he reflects on the lasting impression he would like to leave: "I don't care if people say what I play isn't the greatest they ever heard. But I do want them to say it's not in bad taste." Dizzy should definitely have his wish.

(1917–   )

Jean Goldkette

One of the most important of all pioneering dance bands.

He gave his name to probably the greatest white dance band of the 1920s, an aggregation of some of the most creative jazz musicians and arrangers ever assembled. Stars like Bix Beiderbecke, Frank Trumbauer, Jimmy and Tommy Dorsey studded its ranks.

Though its nominal leader, Jean Goldkette did not lead the band, neither out front with a baton nor from the piano, his chosen instrument. He confined his "leading" to the business end of the band, appearing with it only to conduct its occasional concerts.

A native of Valenciennes, France, Goldkette emigrated to America as a young boy in 1911. A concert pianist with a penchant for business, he took over Detroit's Greystone Ballroom in the 1920s and became an entrepreneur of jazz-oriented dance bands. One was a top black outfit, McKinney's Cotton Pickers, another the Orange Blossoms, which evolved into the Casa Loma Band, chief white pace-setter for the swing era.

But Goldkette wanted something more: a band, according to its pianist Itzy Riskin, that would be "the Paul Whiteman of the West." How this serious, quiet man, with his courtliness and gentle manner, ever wound up with the exact antithesis of the formal, well-disciplined Whiteman orchestra may be ex-

The Goldkette band: Bill Challis, Spiegel Wilcox, Irving Riskin, Bix Beiderbecke, Don Murray, Howdy Quicksell, Doc Ryker, Chauncey Morehouse, Fred Farrar, Ray Ludwig, Bill Rank, Frank Trumbauer, Steve Brown

plained in part by the fact that he left the hiring and rehearsing to jazz-oriented members Fred "Fuzzy" Farrar and Russ Morgan, who brought in several fellow Pennsylvania jazz musicians, including the Dorseys. Farrar once told *Metronome* magazine: "We used to go up to Jean's office every week for our pay, but outside of that we hardly ever saw him."

Farrar conducted at rehearsals, where solos, section choruses, and tempos were worked out cooperatively. This kind of input gave the band its special dynamism and originality. Later Bix and Trumbauer contributed their inspired improvising and fresh ideas, and arranger Bill Challis harmonized their solos, particularly those of Bix, for the brass and sax sections.

The band abounded in innovations that in time became standard equipment for swing bands. For example, every man, not just the rhythm section, had to play rhythmically; that is, melody and harmony had to have a beat. It introduced the "flare," a dramatic opening up of sound by the horns at a phrase end. It used a full "sock" chorus, a tune's climax driven home by the full band. Most of the band's recordings, however, were a terrible disappointment. The recording director's idea of putting Goldkette music into Whiteman and Nat Shilkret molds bombed. Yet, a few sides gave some idea of the band's terrific drive and fire: "Clementine," "My Pretty Girl," "Sunny Disposish," "Dinah."

During its three years of glory, 1925–27, the Goldkette band forsook the Greystone periodically to tour the East and Midwest, play colleges and engage top bands, including Duke Ellington's, in battles of music. It lost more "battles" than it won, not musically but commercially, because it could not "entertain" with funny hats and hokum. Eventually, the imbalance between receipts and disbursements forced Goldkette to disband. The men scattered, some to Whiteman. Goldkette continued as an entrepreneur and performer in both popular and classical fields, with special emphasis on the development of a symphony to perform American music. His last hurrah: a 1939 concert at which he conducted a ninety-piece orchestra in New York City's famed Carnegie Hall. After that—some performances but mostly memories for him and for those who had been thrilled by one of the most important of all pioneering dance bands.

(1899–1962)

Benny Goodman

"I'm completely absorbed in what I'm doing. And I expect other people to be, too."

More than anyone else, Benny Goodman launched the big swing band craze. His brilliant, intensely rhythmic jazz clarinet sparked his fourteen-piece band that burst onto the pop music scene in the summer of 1935 with high-swinging arrangements that spotlighted pulsating ensemble passages and brilliant solos by trumpeter Bunny Berigan, pianist Jess Stacy, drummer Gene Krupa, and others. Later, Goodman featured performers like pianist Teddy Wilson, vibra-

Benny

phonist Lionel Hampton (two of the first black musicians in a white band), trumpeters Harry James and Ziggy Elman, and vocalist Peggy Lee, all of whom went on to become stars in their own right. During the swing era, his band won most of the major polls, and in January 1938 became the first jazz band to play in Carnegie Hall, an event he celebrated forty years later in the same hall as he once again regaled a packed house with his spirited playing and flowing technique.

His bands, more or less permanent at first but organized for shorter periods after the big-band era, have always rated a rung or two above most others because of Goodman's penchant for, and insistence on, musical perfection and because, as more than one of his musicians has explained, "He plays so great that he's constantly inspiring you to try to play as great as he does."

The music world first became aware of Goodman's fiery clarinet when, in August 1925, he was hired to play in Ben Pollack's top-rated band. Recordings, especially those with Red Nichols and His Five Pennies during the late 1920s and early '30s, brought even greater recognition. Soon he settled into New York's financially rewarding but musically stultifying radio and recording studio rut, eventually emerging in 1933 to form the band that two years later would ignite the swing band craze and would carry him first to national and then to international fame.

Born and raised in Chicago's Jewish ghetto, son of a Russian immigrant tailor, the self-made Goodman has often appeared to be much cooler and less emotional than his playing—often to the point of seeming not to care about those around him. And yet those closest to him have invariably found him to be warm, caring, loyal and, when not immersed in his music, witty and charming. He has been especially good to his family: brother Harry played bass in his band, brother Irving the trumpet, brother Freddy was road manager, brother Gene handled the music, and sister Ethel ran his office.

Others have found him less caring, especially some of his own musicians who have been unable to penetrate his shield of fogginess and who have taken as personal insults his lack of reaction that borders on rudeness. And Benny doesn't blame them. "It's true," he recently admitted. "You know that when I play music that's all I think about. I'm completely absorbed in what I'm doing. And I expect other people to be, too." Once Frank Sinatra pointed out to Goodman, "Every time I see you, you're practicing. Why?" To which Benny replied with typical candor, "So that if I'm not great, I'm at least good."

Benny's dedication to his music has rewarded him handsomely—with roles in half a dozen movies, star spots on many radio and TV series and specials, dozens of top-selling recordings and posh homes in New York, Stamford, Connecticut, and on St. Maarten island in the Caribbean. He has been the subject of a full-length biography, *The Kingdom of Swing,* co-authored by Goodman and Irving Kolodin; of a movie, *The Benny Goodman Story,* in which he was portrayed by Steve Allen; and of many tales about his apparent fogginess. Peggy

The Goodman band, circa 1936: bassist Harry Goodman, drummer Gene Krupa, trumpeters Harry Geller, Ralph Muzzillo, Nate Kazebier, pianist Jess Stacy, trombonists Joe Harris, Red Ballard, guitarist Allan Reuss, vocalist Helen Ward, Goodman, saxists Dick Clark, Bill Depew, Hymie Shertzer, Arthur Rollini

Goodman, circa 1975

Lee has told of the time she and Goodman got into a taxi. "We were going to a restaurant, but Benny never told the driver where to go. We just sat there. Finally the driver turned around, and just then Benny looked up and said, 'Oh yes, how much do I owe you?' " And Goodman himself recalls a wintery day in Manhattan when he saw a convertible roadster with no top filled with snow after an all-night storm. "I was thinking, 'Poor guy!' and then suddenly I realized—it was *my* car!"

Goodman's preoccupation has mostly centered around his music. But he can become occupied with things other than swing—with chamber music, for example, which he now plays well and often. Or with golf, in which he shoots in the eighties, despite a sciatica condition. Or with bridge, which he used to play with his late wife, the former Alice Hammond, with exasperating detachment. Or with his two talented daughters, pianist Rachel and cellist Benjie. Or with watching sporting events on television in one of his homes, where he practices daily but which he still leaves many times a year to perform in concerts all over the world—in Russia, Japan, England, South America, and in so many more places where he and his clarinet, partners now for more than fifty years, continue to swing as high and as mighty as ever.

(1909–   )

Glen Gray

The first swing band to capture the fancies of the era's influential college kids.

He was probably the handsomest man ever to lead a band, yet for years six-foot-four, dimpled, mustachioed Glen Gray sat in the Casa Loma Orchestra's sax section while a debonair fiddle-player stood up front and played the role of the maestro. But then along came Benny Goodman, proving that horn-blowers could make effective front-men. And so, in 1937, Glen Gray (Knoblaugh) followed his example, picked up his sax, and took his rightful place in front of one of the most popular big bands of the 1930s.

Actually, Glen Gray and the Casa Loma Orchestra paved the way for the successes of Goodman and others, for this was the first swing band to capture the fancies of the era's influential college kids. Its flashy, often stiffly played, up-tempoed performances of Gene Gifford's and Larry Clinton's original instrumentals like "Casa Loma Stomp" and "Maniac's Ball" and its mid-tempoed

The Glen Gray Orchestra; trumpeters Sonny Dunham, Grady Watts, Bobby Jones, drummer Tony Briglia, pianist Joe Hall, trombonists Pee Wee Hunt, Billy Rauch, guitarist Gene Gifford, bassist Stan Dennis, saxists Pat Davis, Clarence Hutchenrider, Glen Gray, Kenny Sargent, conductor Mel Jensen

rhythm novelties featuring vocalist-trombonist Peewee Hunt contrasted effectively with its moody, ultra-slow-tempoed ballads, such as "Under a Blanket of Blue" and "It's the Talk of the Town," which spotlighted Kenny Sargent, the most romantic-looking and -sounding band singer of the early 1930s.

Though hours of intensive rehearsing resulted in precise playing, the band's musicality was limited by several poor readers and, with the exception of clarinetist Clarence Hutchenrider and, occasionally, trumpeters Sonny Dunham and Grady Watts, by a paucity of first-rate soloists. It did, however, project a fine *esprit de corps*. Always immaculately garbed, often in tails, its members charmed the college kids, most of whom probably never even suspected that off the bandstand their idols swung a good deal more than their music.

Originally, as one of Jean Goldkette's Detroit-based groups, the band bore the name of a cocktail, calling themselves the Orange Blossoms. They later changed their name to the Casa Loma Orchestra in honor of an elegant Canadian nightclub into which they had been booked but which never opened. Reorganized as a corporation in 1929, with Gray as president, they were then booked into New York's Roseland Ballroom. There they were heard by Bob Stevens of Okeh Records, who immediately recorded the first of several hundred sides they were to make for Okeh, Brunswick, Victor, and Decca Records.

A 1932 appearance at Yale made such an impression on the manager of the Glen Island Casino that he engaged them for the summers of 1933 and 1934. The band, through its appearance at this romantic spot and its many radio broadcasts from there, captivated its young collegiate followers so completely that Camel cigarettes, anxious to capture the suddenly spurting college market, hired the band for its "Camel Caravan" coast-to-coast radio series. And then in 1935, when New York's Paramount Theater decided to launch its stage band policy, it picked the Casa Loma Orchestra as its first attraction.

Gray managed to keep the band in shape for several years. But some members tired of the grind and left, and when singer Sargent left to become a disc jockey, the band's primary romantic appeal went with him. Gray tried injecting some spark by hiring top jazz soloists like Red Nichols and Bobby Hackett, but the band was never again the same, and when it appeared in 1944 at the Paramount it played just three numbers as an "added attraction" to featured singer Andy Russell.

The band broke up in 1950, but six years later Gray assembled some top studio musicians to record excellent re-creations of the biggest hits of the Casa Loma and other top orchestras of the swing era.

(1906–1963)

Woody Guthrie

"A wispy, raspy-voiced musical spokesman for the downtrodden."

"I hate a song that makes you think you're not any good," said Woody Guthrie, whose renditions of his own songs influenced so many socially conscious singers of the 1960s and '70s. "I hate a song that makes you think that you are born to lose. Bound to lose. No good for nothing. Because you are either too old or too young or too fat or too slim or too ugly or too this or too that. Songs that run you down or songs that poke fun at you on account of your bad luck or your hard traveling. I am out to fight those kinds of songs to my very last breath of air and my last drop of blood."

Nothing ever made Woody feel that he was a loser—not the succession of tragedies that hit him in childhood when his father's land-trading business went

"This land is your land . . ."

bankrupt, three of the family's houses were destroyed (two by fire, one by cyclone), his sister was killed in an oil-stove explosion and his mother was institutionalized with Huntington's chorea; not the dust storms that swept across Oklahoma, nor the Depression; not even his contraction of the same disease that killed his mother.

He found beauty and hope even in migrant camps and Hoovervilles. He sang, cheerfully, "So Long, It's Been Good to Know You." He celebrated the "union maid" who "never was afraid/ Of goons and ginks and company finks/ And the sheriffs that made the raids." And he summed it all up in "This Land Is Your Land":

> This land is your land, this land is my land,
> From California to New York island
> From the redwood forest to the Gulfstream waters,
> This land was made for you and me. ©

How could anyone with that vision feel like a loser?

The man who saw it this way was small, bushy-haired, simple, and unpretentious. He was born in Okemah, Oklahoma, which he remembered as "one of the singingest, square-dancingest, drinkingest, yellingest, preachingest, walkingest, talkingest, laughingest, cryingest, shootingest, fist-fightingest, bleedingest, gamblingest, gun-, club- and razor-carryingest of our ranch and farm towns because it blossomed out into one of our first Oil Boom Towns."

He heard lonesome old ballads from his mother, honky-tonky blues and wild hollers from his father and other men in the town. He learned his guitar style from records by the Carter Family, learned their songs and used some for his own purposes (he took the melody for his "Reuben James" from the Carters' "Wildwood Flower"). He listened to Jimmie Rodgers, too, and when he first took to the road after the family was broken up by the succession of tragedies that engulfed them in Okemah he "played in barbershops, at shine stands, in front of shows, around the pool halls, and rattled the bones, done jig dances, sang and played with Negroes, Indians, whites, farmers, town folks, truck drivers, and with every kind of singer you can think of."

First he went to California, where he got a radio program on KFVD in Los Angeles and became deeply involved with unions. Late in the 1930s he moved to New York, where he lived with Leadbelly, the great black blues singer and twelve-string guitarist. With Pete Seeger, Lee Hays, Millard Lampell, and others he formed the Almanac Singers. He wrote and sang blues, ballads, and children's songs, songs advocating public power, songs deploring the treatment of migrant workers.

He wrote more than a thousand songs. Usually he turned out two songs a day and his ideas came from everywhere.

"Anything worth discussing was worth a song to him," his friend Pete Seeger said, "news off the front page, sights and sounds of the countrysides he traveled through, and thoughts brought to mind by reading anything from Rabelais to Will Rogers."

He was described as "a rusty-voiced Homer" and "a wispy, raspy-voiced musical spokesman for the downtrodden." "Rusty" and "raspy" were all right with Woody.

"I had rather sound like the ashcans of the early morning," he said, "like the cab drivers cursing at one another, like the longshoremen yelling, like the cowhands whooping and like the lone wolf barking."

In his vision of America he was a true descendant of Walt Whitman, and before the early stages of the fatal illness that hospitalized him in 1952 and killed him fifteen years later he had planted the seeds that inspired a legion of young followers, most notably Bob Dylan, and left his own heritor in his son, Arlo.

"I am out to sing songs that will prove to you that this is your world," said Woody, "and that if it has hit you pretty hard and knocked you for a dozen loops, no matter how hard it's run you down and rolled over you, no matter what color, what size you are, how you are built, I am out to sing the songs that make you take pride in yourself and your work. And the songs I sing are made up for the most part by all sorts of folks just about like you."

(1912–1967)

"The master of distillation and understatement."

He was as gentle as the lovely sounds that flowed from the bell of his trumpet. Bobby Hackett, master of the melodic horn and, according to composer Alec Wilder, one of his many admirers, also "the master of distillation and understatement," projected his personality through his playing. As Wilder pointed out to writer Whitney Balliett in *The New Yorker,* Bobby "is never aggressive or noisy; rather he is tender and witty."

Held by his fellow jazz musicians as one of the best, Hackett, who was once described as looking like the groom on a wedding cake, was heard publicly most often in a nonjazz setting—as featured player of a 1950s series of huge-selling lush mood albums produced and conducted by Jackie Gleason. The rotund comedian made a fortune from the six albums, but Bobby himself realized so little that he resignedly repeated drummer-friend Cozy Cole's observation: "The big ones keep eating the little ones." Hackett was also featured on several records with the Glenn Miller band, most notably for his famous cornet solo on "A String of Pearls." Some of his staunchest jazz fans criticized him for having "sold out" by joining such a "commercial" outfit. "Hell, I didn't sell *out,*" insisted Hackett, who had been having financial problems when Miller invited him to join up and enjoy a regular income. "I sold *in!*"

Some tooth extractions made it impossible for Hackett to blow his horn during his first months with the band, so Miller let him play his other instrument, the guitar, until his gums had healed. Bobby had been playing guitar, ukulele, banjo, violin, and trumpet since the age of twelve but, after hearing some Louis Armstrong records, decided to concentrate on trumpet. Many jazz writers have insisted that Bobby was influenced by Bix Beiderbecke, because of their similarly relaxed, pure-sounding, melodic styles, but Hackett insisted, "My inspiration was always Louis!"

Hackett first attracted attention while playing a gig at Boston's Theatrical Club, where visiting jazz players would drop by for jam sessions. His mentor, clarinetist Pee Wee Russell, encouraged him to come to New York, where he played guitar in Joe Marsala's small band at the Hickory House before beginning a two-year hitch (1938 and 1939) as trumpet-playing leader at Nick's, the famous Dixieland jazz spot. Success encouraged him to join the burgeoning big band brigade. The move was a disaster. The easygoing Hackett had trouble disciplining his musicians and himself (for his last thirty years he was a recovering alcoholic), and the band collapsed. To revive his finances, he joined Horace Heidt and His Musical Knights but soon left "that musical circus" and returned home

Bobby with idol Satchmo

totally discouraged. And then came Miller's call and "two of my happiest years."

When Glenn went into the Army, Bobby went into New York's radio and recording studios, where, except for an early spell with the Casa Loma band, he remained for twenty years. A diabetic, he decided in the mid-1960s to forego his hectic schedule and settled down in Chatham, Massachusetts, with his wife, children, and grandchildren, playing in a small club with his own group, and emerging occasionally for trips with Benny Goodman, Tony Bennett, and to appear on TV and in jazz concerts. Though his health continued to deteriorate, he remained as warm and as gentle as the sound of his horn, stilled forever in the spring of 1976 by the persistency of his illness.

(1915–1976)

Merle Haggard

It was not one of the finest country music voices ever, but it was among the most moving.

Kris Kristofferson once said about him: "That man has already written some of the best folk songs that have ever been done. I think now, when we speak of Merle Haggard, we aren't talking about how he's going to come out in the CMA (Country Music Association) awards this year; we're talking about posterity."

Merle Haggard has often inspired such superlative descriptions, but despite the fact that stardom and acclaim have been granted him, Merle Ronald Haggard has persisted in being the truth-seeking-bordering-on-defiant writer and artist who preferred fishing alone to playing golf with music industry cronies.

It seems as though with every song he has focused his piercing blue eyes on not only his audience but also his own stardom and material successes, as if saying, "I've made it, you've put me there, but I haven't lost sight of who I am or where I came from."

Born in Bakersfield, son of one of the thousands of Okie immigrant families who moved to California, the problems of his poor, hard childhood were intensified by the death of his father when Merle was nine. He eventually resorted to petty crime and ended up in San Quentin. While serving his sentence he was inspired by Johnny Cash's celebrated performance at the prison and turned to music. He drew heavily on the style of the tremendously influential country-western singer Lefty Frizzell and, like Frizzell, kept his voice deep, slurring, with a rich vibrato, with each phrase filled with genuine and carefully expressed emotion. It was not one of the finest country music voices ever, but it was among the most moving.

After his release from prison in 1960, Merle was guided by Fuzzy Owen, who later became his personal manager. Fuzzy liked Merle's style and helped him to record on the Tally label, and later, in 1965, secured him a Capitol recording contract. In the next five years Merle had nine number one singles on the country charts, including "The Fugitive," "Branded Man," and "The Legend of Bonnie and Clyde." He was on his way.

During his almost fifteen-year career, Merle has remained remarkably consistent in both his writing and performance, changed only by the growing maturity and ease in his already rich voice. His material, however, changes constantly. His work ranges from love songs such as "Always Wanting You" to descriptions of his early involvement in low living like "Swinging Doors" to a patriotic ditty, one of his most famous numbers, "Okie from Muskogee." Haggard has also recorded two tribute albums, to Jimmie Rodgers and Bob Wills, which became landmarks in country music.

When asked how he wanted to be remembered, Merle answered, "As a writer, I guess. Somebody who did some living and wrote songs about what he knew, just like Jimmie and Hank did. That's all."

(1937–   )

Merle (right) and Chet Atkins

Bill Haley

He became a hero to the rebel young, first in America and then all over the world.

He was the first great star of rock and roll and more than likely the inventor of the form. In 1951 he fused white country-western and black rhythm and blues deliberately, three years before Elvis Presley did it accidentally.

Bill Haley was a slightly chubby, genial twenty-four-year-old in 1951, leader of a mildly popular regional country band, the Saddlemen, working, as he put it, "in a little place called the Twin Bar in Gloucester City, New Jersey. We used to like rhythm and blues, too, and I think these were some of the moments when rock and roll really started. In those days, if you were country-western you didn't *dare* sing anything else. [But] more as a joke than anything else, one night—laughing about it and kidding—we did a rhythm and blues tune that had been around a long time . . . 'Rock the Joint.' We put the two styles together, and it was our first hit in the rock and roll field."

Haley was an astute bandleader, and he continued his experiment. "Around the early 1950s the musical world was striving for something new. The days of the soloist and the big bands had gone. About the only thing that was making any noise was progressive jazz, but this just went above the heads of the average listener. I felt that if I could take a beat that the listeners could clap to as well as dance [to], this would be what they were after."

Renaming his band Bill Haley and the Comets, he purposefully developed a new style, utilizing various instruments to get the effect of the big bands' brass and reeds. The electric guitar, as played by Fran Beecher, formerly of the Benny Goodman Sextet, imitated the brass, and for his "reed section" Haley featured the facile pop-jazz saxophonist Rudy Pompelli.

Haley's first national hit was "Crazy, Man, Crazy" in 1953, followed by "Shake, Rattle and Roll," a copy of Joe Turner's earthy original, and, in 1955, the song that was to become Haley's and the music's anthem, "Rock Around the Clock."

His success was enormous and took Haley by surprise. He became a hero to the rebel young, first in America and then all over the world. His initial tour of England in 1957 triggered a hysteria that caused Queen Elizabeth II to order a Buckingham Palace private screening of Haley's film short, *Rock Around the Clock,* to see who was causing such disturbances.

Yet by 1958 Haley, who never really looked like a rock and roll singer, and his band were in popular decline, considered old-fashioned. The ideas he formulated were presented with greater fire and greater depth by Elvis Presley, Little Richard, Fats Domino, and Chuck Berry.

Haley retreated to Europe for many years but was coaxed back to the United States in 1969 for a nostalgic concert, at which he received an eight-minute standing ovation. He was puffier about the waist and face, but he and the band performed with experience and drive. He was the good wise king returned, and his subjects hailed him as teacher and father.

A remarkable combination of practical bandleader, popular music catalyst, and gentleman, Haley told an audience soon after his restoration began: "When I'm seventy-five, and if you can still clap your hands and I can still hold a guitar, we'll still have rock and roll."

(1927–   )

"Rock around the clock . . ."

Lionel Hampton

"I want to be remembered most for spreading happiness and good will."

The enthusiasm and the rhythmic excitement he has projected on vibes, drums, or piano have brought Lionel Hampton standing ovations from audiences all over the world and have invariably inspired his musicians to rise to ever greater swinging heights.

Such enthusiasm for music manifested itself early. "Back in Chicago, my parents bought me drums every Christmas—usually two, because I'd break one on the first day. When I wasn't drumming, I'd use the rungs of chairs." He learned about drumming at Holy Rosary Academy and about harmony and marimbas from Major N. Clark Smith, one of Teddy Roosevelt's Rough Riders, a black man who directed the Chicago *Defender's* Newspaper Boys Band.

After his family moved to Los Angeles, Lionel's training helped him get a job with Les Hite's fine band, which in 1930 backed Louis Armstrong on some of his greatest sides, sides that contain the first jazz vibraphone on records.

"There was a set over in the corner of the studio and Louis asked me, 'You play that thing?' and I said, 'Sure!' If you listen closely you can even hear me playing jazz behind Louis' vocal on 'Just a Gigolo.'"

Lionel's late wife, Gladys, who played such an important, supportive role throughout his career, encouraged Hampton to buy a set of vibes and to form his own group. While it was playing at a small nightclub in the summer of 1936, Benny Goodman, Gene Krupa, and Teddy Wilson dropped in, and soon all four were participating in a monumental jam session. The next day Goodman offered Hampton a job, playing vibes, sometimes singing with the quartet and occasionally filling in on drums with the full band. "That's what I really wanted to do!" Hampton said. And he also recorded with his own all-star pickup groups that produced some of the best sides in swing history. (In the mid-1970s he formed his own record company that presented him playing with many more jazz stars.)

In 1940, when an ailing Goodman disbanded, Hampton organized a brilliant big band that at times included discoveries like Illinois Jacquet, Quincy Jones, Charles Mingus, Dinah Washington, and Joe Williams. Hamp specialized in working his musicians and his audiences into rhythmic frenzies. Once in Harlem's Apollo Theater, during the finale of his big hit, "Flying Home," his fans reacted with such rhythmic passion that their stomping and jumping cracked the theater's balcony and everybody had to go home.

To most of the world, Hampton may have seemed the epitome of the uninhib-

Hamp

ited, carefree, sometimes almost childlike jazz musician. But he has also cared deeply about other matters—about religion, about the cause of Israel (for which he worked hard and visited so often that he became a celebrity there), about human rights and even about politics. A Republican, he proudly has taken some credit for suggesting in 1958 to the New York State committee that it consider Nelson Rockefeller as the party's gubernatorial candidate. When Rockefeller accepted the nomination, Hampton's band "played him on" to the podium. A strong friendship resulted. "Forever after I played the music and he made the speeches."

Hampton's new ties helped secure important loans for Harlem housing developments. The Lionel Hampton House was completed in the 1960s; the Gladys Hampton House is scheduled to be Harlem's tallest building. Are these the monuments for which Lionel wants most to be remembered? Not quite. "I want to be remembered most for spreading happiness and good will."

(1913–   )

Coleman Hawkins

He knew very well that he had created a landmark of jazz improvisation.

Justly called "The Father of the Tenor Sax," Coleman Hawkins did more than establish his instrument's claim to serious musical attention. He was one of the great masters of jazz. His huge sound, command of harmony, driving beat, and fertile imagination carried him to the top by the late 1920s, and there he remained, often challenged but never dislodged, until the end of a rich career that spanned six decades.

Hawkins, who liked to tease interviewers, once claimed to have entered the world aboard an ocean liner carrying his parents home from a visit to Europe. The truth was less romantic. Born in St. Joseph, Missouri, he started piano lessons at five, soon added cello, and zeroed in on the saxophone at nine. He left college to join singer Mamie Smith's touring Jazz Hounds. When he joined Fletcher Henderson's band in 1923, he had the technique of a virtuoso but a conception rooted in ragtime and vaudeville rather than genuine jazz. Louis Armstrong, who joined the band in 1924, ignited Hawkins' creative spark.

Within a few years he became the pace setter on tenor, balancing a churning drive on fast tempos with the rhapsodic, romantic ballad style heralded by his 1929 recording of "One Hour." Proud and fiercely competitive, Hawkins delighted in cutting down all comers in the legendary jam sessions of the day, but early in 1934, tiring of the hectic life of a traveling bandsman, he sent a characteristically terse wire to Jack Hylton, Britain's Paul Whiteman. It read: "Am interested in coming to London." Soon he was on his way, spending the next five years as the foremost jazz missionary to the Europeans. For the first time, he was treated with the respect due a great artist and acquired the manner and tastes of a cosmopolitan *bon vivant.*

And that manner and those tastes remained with Hawkins, coloring his life for the next three decades. In the late 1950s his apartment commanded a magnificent view of Central Park, his closets bulged with two-hundred-dollar suits and handmade shoes; his stereo equipment was the best money could buy, worthy of his collection of complete operas; he bought a new Chrysler Imperial every year, considering Cadillacs too vulgar and Rolls-Royces too conspicuous, and drank only the best scotch, cognac, and wines. But he also loved to prepare and devour great quantities of basic soul food and took a schoolboy's pleasure in instigating arguments among his colleagues, roaring with laughter as they went at each other.

When he prudently came home months before the outbreak of the Second

"Father of the Tenor Sax"

World War younger rivals had laid claim to his crown. But he settled all disputes with his most famous record, "Body and Soul." "It was nothing special," he insisted, "just something I used as an encore to get off the stand." But he knew very well that he had created a landmark of jazz improvisation.

When bebop reared its impertinent head, most jazz elders turned their backs on the rule-breaking upstarts. But Hawkins, long in the habit of listening to and learning from everything, hired and encouraged the boppers. "To me, bop was just music," he said. The association kept him on his creative toes.

"The older he gets, the better he gets," said one of his few peers, Johnny Hodges. "If ever you think he's through, you find he's just gone right on ahead again." Loved and admired by musicians of all persuasions and ages, Hawkins might well have settled gracefully into the role of Old Master. But he resented every symptom of advancing age. He drank more and ate less. He let his hair and beard grow freely, and in his last years looked like a grizzled Old Testament prophet. But the sound was still there and so, astonishingly, was the facility— almost to the end. And, of course, his influence lives on forever.

(1901 *–1969)

* While most sources give 1904, the birth certificate shows 1901.

Isaac Hayes

"I can still relate to the dudes on the block."

"Success has placed me on a high level of society," he says, "but I can still relate to the dudes on the block. The money, the fame is just the fringe. Isaac Hayes is *roots.*"

Those roots first took hold in a tin shack about forty miles outside Memphis, where he was born. After his mother died (when he was a year and a half old) and his father abandoned him, nobody would have given odds that this "raggedy little cat" would grow up to win an Oscar, a Grammy, and the presidency of a production company called Hot Buttered Soul, Ltd.

His sharecropper grandparents took him in, but Isaac was mostly on his own. He attended school erratically, picked cotton and scrounged for menial jobs, anything to survive. He learned to live in abandoned cars in junkyards.

His career as a juvenile delinquent seemed promising when he discovered music. It gave him, he says, the self-respect he got nowhere else. It made him feel like *somebody.* He taught himself to play the piano and sang to his own accompaniment (trying to sound like his idol, Nat Cole). When his piano playing got him hired as a backup man for Stax Records in Memphis, Hayes, barely out of his teens, was already married, with an infant to support.

He summoned to Memphis an old high school buddy, Dave Porter, who wrote lyrics, and he began writing music. The Hayes-and-Porter team produced over two hundred hits for Stax artist—hits like "Hold On, I'm Coming," an instant soul standard; "B-A-B-Y"; and a gold record, "Soul Man." Their style of soul was cooler, more staccato, than the traditional wailers and keeners. It came to be called "The Memphis Sound."

Hayes was frustrated at not being able to sing his own compositions. He finally got his chance through Enterprise Records, a subsidiary of Stax. His first album, *Presenting Isaac Hayes,* was released in 1968 and went unnoticed. His second, *Hot Buttered Soul,* made him a star.

His narrative introductions to each number—"rap sessions," he called them—became his trademark. *Hot Buttered Soul* sold over three and a half million copies; his next two albums—*The Isaac Hayes Movement* and *Isaac Hayes . . . To Be Continued*—earned platinum records, with sales surpassing two million dollars. In 1972 he won his Oscar and Grammy—for "The Theme from Shaft."

His childhood deprivations amply justify, he believes, his love of flamboyant clothes and luxury cars. "I like luxury, man. I never had any." He designs his own clothes and wears the jewel-studded velvet caftans, furs, and capes offstage as well as on. Otherwise, his life-style is simple. He neither drinks nor smokes and abhors drugs of any kind. He eats only health food and often works—some say compulsively—twenty hours a day. He lives with his third wife, Mignon, in Memphis; his five children are from previous marriages.

His concert tours, in which he "raps" with organ accompaniment, draw capacity crowds. He co-produced, starred in, and scored one movie, *Two Tough Guys,* and plans to do another. He is continually widening his horizons because, he says, "Once you make it, it's not over. The real test is whether you can *sustain.* Every day I have to know that I can stay on this perch until I decide to step down."

(1942–   )

Hayes

Dick Haymes

"If you're going to be a male singer, don't be half a man!"

"I appreciate what you're telling me about how you want me to sing. But I don't want to sound like Frank. I want to be me and nobody else."

That's what Dick Haymes told Tommy Dorsey in September 1942, when he succeeded Frank Sinatra as the band's featured vocalist. It was strong stuff from a young singer to a seasoned veteran. But even in those days, the baby-faced Haymes with the virile, grown-up-man-sounding baritone voice, insisted upon doing things his way. Such an intransigent attitude may not have been a good one insofar as his later personal life was concerned, but in relation to his singing career, it proved to be the best way.

Dick took his singing seriously. "Singing and show business," he once insisted, "are just like any other career, like law and medicine." Well educated in private schools, he had been impressed with the fundamentals of his craft by his mother, Marguerite Haymes, one of the era's best teachers of vocal technique, and those who saw him during his first important assignment in 1940 as boy singer in the Harry James band recall how conscious he was about correct breathing, voice projection, and other vocal techniques.

A young man of various talents—acting, singing, and songwriting—he had approached James hoping that the leader would play some of the songs he had composed. As Harry later recalled, "I didn't think much of the songs, but I sure liked the way Dick sang them." And with Sinatra just having left the band, James offered the job to Haymes.

His singing, deeper and more resonant than Sinatra's and admittedly influenced by Bob Eberly, still stands out as some of the big band era's most impressive, especially on ballads like "A Sinner Kissed an Angel," "I'll Get By," and "You've Changed." (Years later other singers would feel complimented if told, "You have a sound like Dick Haymes.") He stayed with James for almost two years, then joined Benny Goodman for four months, followed by six with Dorsey, all six during a recording ban, so that he could then only be heard on live radio broadcasts. But he had already made a deep impression on movie moguls, and in 1945 he starred in two pictures, *State Fair* and *Diamond Horseshoe*. Suddenly he had changed from just a band singer into a singing star, one of Sinatra's most potent challengers.

He made a dozen films and a lot of hit records, like "Little White Lies," "You'll Never Know," and "The More I See You," and was starred on several national radio series. During his career he also married a lot of wives, six in

Dick

all, including some of Hollywood's most glamorous stars, like Joanne Dru, Nora Eddington, and Rita Hayworth. "When I sang, 'Our Love Is Here to Stay,' no one would take me seriously, and who could blame them," he once quipped.

Unfortunately, success was not "here to stay" either. Caught up in the Hollywood dream world in which he often averaged $25,000 weekly from movies, radio, and recording royalties, the intelligent, articulate, charming, sensitive Haymes later confessed to Clive Hirschhorn of the London *Sunday Express,* "I was blessed with too much too quickly. I believed nothing could go wrong and when in the mid-fifties I was on the skids, I wouldn't face the fact." He began to drink too much. He incurred debts of close to half a million dollars. He was having trouble with the immigration department, which used his Buenos Aires birthplace (his father was a traveling cattle breeder) to try to deport him. Finally he declared bankruptcy. "I figured I'd worn out my welcome in the business," he later told writer Gene Lees, "and so I went away [first to Spain, then to England] to try to find myself."

What he also found was an attractive sixth wife, Wendy Jones, who eventually bore him the fifth and sixth of his children. With her support, he cut out excesses, went on a health kick, started doing vocal as well as physical exercises, and in a few years he was singing as well as ever. He returned to America in 1972, a more mature performer and a human being as charming and enthusiastic as ever, and made some tremendously impressive recordings and TV and club appearances, following the advice he had expostulated back in 1947: "If you're going to be a male singer, don't be half a man!"

(1916–   )

Ted Heath

"British bands have to play in all styles in order to survive."

"Listen to my music," was Ted Heath's slogan and the title of his autobiography. It was not quite a plea and not really a command but a firm, polite suggestion that typified the manner of Heath himself. Everything about Heath and his music was neat and precise, never obsequious but never overly aggressive. He could shrug off his big band, the most universally popular band ever developed in England, as "just a swing band." But at the same time he would insist that "British musicianship is the best in the world."

When Heath, a trombonist, formed his unit in 1944 he was, at forty-four, one of the oldest musicians to start a big band and certainly the oldest to organize a highly successful one, a band that regularly packed the London Palladium with three thousand enthusiastic fans for a series of monthly concerts that ran on for more than a decade.

Born of poor parents in the Wandsworth section of London, he learned to play a horn at six and a year later was playing in brass band contests. He switched to the trombone at twelve. After World War I, when unemployment was rife in England, he played with itinerant street musicians and was once arrested for obstructing the sidewalk.

But in 1920 he landed an indoor job with Jack Hylton's orchestra at the Queen's Hall Roof Garden, and for almost a quarter of a century he was one of the top sidemen in England. He played with the bands of Bert Firman, Sidney Lipton, Bert Ambrose, and Geraldo, among other leading groups.

Early in the 1940s, Heath began writing songs with his wife, Moira (with whom he had five children). The royalties from those songs helped him float a band of his own, which had become an all-star group when, in 1944, the BBC asked him to do a monthly radio program from the Palladium.

A stocky, clean-featured, quiet-spoken man, with a trim mustache and a pronounced stoop, Heath put together a band that was a mixture of the swinging elements of Benny Goodman or Woody Herman, the lush tonal colors of Glenn Miller (whose Army Air Force Band served as Heath's basic model), and the crisp, slambang showmanship of Waring's Pennsylvanians in its heyday, a combination that was the result of both necessity and Heath's well-trained instinct.

"British bands have to be jacks of all trades," he once said. "There is just a limited area in Britain in which to play and so you find yourself coming back to some major cities about once a month. Under these circumstances, British bands have to play in all styles in order to survive. It may be swing for dancing one night, society music the next, and a stage show or concert the next. We can't play only what we'd like to play all the time the way Kenton or Basie or Les Brown do."

Yet, whatever Heath did, he did exceptionally well, as though trying to prove his oft-expressed opinion that "British musicianship is the best in the world."

(1900–1969)

Heath with Horne (Lena, that is)

Fletcher Henderson

A study in frustration.

At its peak, roughly from 1924 to 1934, his band contained some of the greatest soloists in jazz—Louis Armstrong, Coleman Hawkins, Benny Carter, Rex Stewart, Jimmy Harrison, and others too numerous to mention—and Fletcher Henderson himself was one of the chief architects of big band jazz.

The son of college teachers in Georgia, Henderson came to New York in 1920 to do postgraduate work in chemistry, playing a little piano on the side. Within two years he had become a full-time musician, active in the budding black recording field. In 1923 he and his colleagues were leaving a recording session when they got word of an opening for a band at a nearby club, auditioned for it as a lark and, to their astonishment, landed the job. Soon thereafter the personable, handsome, well-spoken Henderson and his band were hired by the prestigious Roseland Ballroom on Broadway, which remained their main stamping, and stomping ground for the next decade or so.

A well-schooled musician but indifferent pianist, Henderson at first left arranging chores to his lead saxophonist, Don Redman, who formulated the basic style perfected by Henderson soon after Redman left the band in 1927. Like many great ideas, the Henderson formula was simple: contrasting brass and reed passages, plenty of solo space for featured players, a knack for inventing catchy rhythmic phrases (called "riffs"), an ability to score section passages that retained the flavor of improvised solos, and a sense of structure and development.

But Henderson was a lax disciplinarian and poor administrator, and the band became notorious for its exploits. For an important record date, the last man arrived two and a half hours after the scheduled starting time, but the band managed to record three sides in the remaining half hour. The men were heavy drinkers. When the band went on road trips, it traveled in the biggest, fastest cars available, Henderson himself setting the pace. In 1928 his Packard roadster landed in a ditch, and the bandleader suffered severe concussions. After the accident, his disinterest in business matters became even more pronounced, and his wife, Leora, took over most administrative matters. (Henderson's nickname, "Smack," derived from the sound of kissing, had reference to his fondness for pretty ladies.)

In late 1934, hurt by the Depression and incompetent booking agents as well as his own indifference, Henderson's band broke up, but within a year he headed one of the best outfits of his career, with Roy Eldridge, Chu Berry,

The 1936 Fletcher Henderson band: Chu Berry at far left, Sid Catlett fourth from left, Roy Eldridge leaning on piano at right, Henderson pointing the baton

Ben Webster, and Sid Catlett in its ranks. His reputation as an arranger was then at its height, boosted by the well-publicized work he was doing for the new Benny Goodman band. He was responsible for many of Goodman's best things, including "King Porter Stomp" and "Sometimes I'm Happy." In 1939, his fortunes at their lowest ebb, he became Goodman's pianist and staff arranger, but two years later he once again headed his own band, financed by Goodman. In 1948, however, he was touring as Ethel Waters' accompanist, a role he had filled at the very dawn of his career. A stroke in 1950 resulted in partial paralysis. He never played again, and Goodman starred in a benefit for him.

Henderson launched and furthered the careers of many great players, but his own has been well summarized by his friend and admirer John Hammond as "a study in frustration." His best work was popularized by Goodman rather than by his own band; he lost key jobs to other black bands, such as Jimmie Lunceford's and Cab Calloway's, due to his lack of showmanship, and he failed to exploit his biggest hit, "Christopher Columbus." According to many of his alumni, the band's records failed to capture the excitement of its live performances, due in part to his inability to impose discipline on his men. Nevertheless, Henderson's achievements in shaping the language of big band jazz (abetted by his gifted younger brother Horace) made an indelible contribution to jazz history.

(1897–1952)

Jimi Hendrix

One of the most exciting and most eulogized of all rock musicians.

"May you never hear surf music again," Jimi Hendrix proclaimed on *Are You Experienced?*, his first album. After hearing Hendrix's style of electric-guitar playing, no rock player would ever again approach the instrument in quite the same way. Coupling various modes of distortion—wah-wah, super volume, feedback, and every other gimmick in the book—with a basic style rooted in pure blues, Hendrix became such a giant that even his few acknowledged peers, such as Eric Clapton, Jeff Beck, and Peter Townshend, have owned up to being intimidated by him.

He was a large man with a master guitarist's enormous hands. One of the first stars to wear an Afro, he dressed in a style as flamboyant and unruly as his playing: Velvets and satins took their places next to do-rags and pointy-toed shoes. Yet, flashy as he was, from his beginnings, as a sideman for such rhythm and blues giants as Little Richard and the Isley Brothers, until the end of his career, he was, by all accounts, a shy person.

Apparently troubled psychologically from the time he left his native Seattle to join the Army in 1965 until his death six years later, he relied heavily on drugs, though generally steering clear of the more pernicious kind. Nevertheless, a combination of Bob Dylan records and LSD seems to have inspired him to move beyond the straightforward twelve- and thirty-two-bar forms in which he had been schooled.

Discharged from the Army after breaking an ankle during his twenty-sixth parachute jump, Hendrix migrated to New York's Greenwich Village, appearing in small clubs. In 1966 he traveled from there to London, where he achieved his first major recognition, then returned the next year to America. There at the Monterey Jazz Festival his natural exuberance resulted in an incident that would haunt him the rest of his life. After performing all his normal tricks—playing between his legs, behind his back, and with his teeth—he poured lighter fluid on his guitar and lit it. No one ever let him forget what he had done. When he wasn't being assaulted for letting his fans down by not burning his instrument, he was being impugned for having engaged in such a shoddy gimmick in the first place.

The pressures began to mount on Hendrix. Blacks started chastising him for playing with white musicians to primarily white audiences. And so he formed Band of Gypsies, composed entirely of black players. But the group didn't last long, disbanding in the summer of 1970. Confused in many ways, he still talked optimistically about his future. "Something new has to come," he told an interviewer for England's music weekly, *Melody Maker,* "and Jimi Hendrix will be there."

But Jimi Hendrix never made it "there." After a night of drinking, Hendrix, only twenty-eight years of age, made the mistake of taking too many sleeping pills. The reaction caused him to vomit in his sleep. Unable to rouse himself, he choked to death, and the life and career of one of the most exciting and most eulogized of all rock musicians, whose talents and influence are still revealed in the dozen or so albums and three movies he made, came to a tragic end.

(1942–1970)

Jimi

Woody Herman

"You can do any damn thing you want if you have the courage and the ability."

"If I thought there weren't any more challenges in life, I would have thrown in the towel. But as long as there is a challenge, living is fun!"

More than any other leader, Woody Herman, while fronting his band for over forty years, met the challenge of changing musical tastes head-on and invariably came out a winner. He managed to change his musical directions without ever sacrificing his musical integrity. By his own admission he was "a good organizer and a good editor," which meant that he selected and nurtured musicians and steered them down the narrow path bordered by their and the public's often divergent musical tastes.

His first band, "The Band That Played the Blues," organized in 1936, featured semi-Dixieland jazz, such as its famous "Woodchoppers' Ball." The next one patterned its style on Duke Ellington's music. His most successful band, the mid-1940s First Herd, which won numerous polls, produced hard-driving, progressive swing numbers like "Caldonia," "Apple Honey," "Bijou," and "Northwest Passage," as well as "Ebony Concerto," written especially for the band by Igor Stravinsky. Next came Woody's flirtation with the more subdued, introverted bop. And in later years, as jazz and rock music began to blend, Woody was there waiting for them with bands composed of immensely talented musicians, many of them two generations his juniors, all well in tune with the musical times and, according to Herman, capable of creating music more exciting than any of the predecessors ever could. He never ceased to express his admiration for the skills of his "kids," skills that he attributed to the advances in music education ("They can learn in two or three semesters what it took us years to figure out") and to music's new freedoms ("So many barriers have been broken down. You can do any damn thing you want if you have the courage and the ability").

Woodrow Charles Herman first evinced his own courage and ability when at the age of six he started dancing on vaudeville stages in his native Milwaukee. Three years later he was blowing the sax professionally and a bit later the clarinet. He also developed a warm, personal singing style, which he brought into bands like Tom Gerun's, where he shared vocal honors with Ginny Sims and Tony Martin, and the Isham Jones band, in which he was so popular and respected among its sidemen that, when Jones quit, they elected Woody as leader of their cooperative venture.

Herman's popularity among musicians has never waned. Warm, generous, compassionate, always taking his music, but seldom himself, seriously, he has

Woody

won the respect and love of just about every musician who has ever worked for him, including such future stars as Ralph Burns, Stan Getz, Neal Hefti, and Zoot Sims. Explained his longtime arranger and pianist, Nat Pierce, "We never feel we're actually working *for* the man. It's more like working *with* him."

For a while in 1977 it looked as if none of his men would ever work with Woody again. While driving through Kansas one March night, he fell asleep at the wheel and crashed head-on into another car. Hospitalized for weeks with multiple injuries, he doggedly regained his health, eventually leading his band while still moving about on crutches.

And still he kept looking ahead. "I want to keep my out-take greater than my in-take," he said. And with his young band he was recording music of the younger generation, including contemporary pieces written especially for him by Chick Corea and Steely Dan. Obviously refusing to rest on his laurels, he regularly replied, with his ever-youthful optimism, whenever asked which of his many bands was his favorite, "The band I'm going to have next year."

(1913–   )

The Earl

Earl Hines

Any pianists with the audacity to run up against this cat will still get bruised.

"He can go on for ninety years and never be out of date," Count Basie once said about Earl Hines, the great jazz pianist, whose powerful, rhythmic style of playing during a career of over half a century has enthralled fans, inspired many imitators, and mesmerized musicians throughout the world. "You get bruised running up against a cat like that."

Some of the bruises produced by such unflagging longevity have been Hines's. When his career took a sudden upward sweep in the mid-1960s after he had been out of the public eye for almost fifteen years, young listeners, who were hearing this handsome, energetic, extroverted entertainer for the first time, wanted to know if he was the son of the Earl Hines whose band their parents had heard at the Grand Terrace in Chicago in the 1930s. Hines found, as his career took on fresh momentum as he was entering his sixties, that he had become an anomaly.

"The young don't believe I'm me," he said, "and the old are too tired to come and see."

There have been so many significant way stations in Hines's long career that it is not surprising anyone might think there have been several Earl Hineses. As a child in Pittsburgh he wanted to be a trumpeter. But he never learned to blow the horn correctly, and he complained that it hurt behind his ears. So he shifted to piano, although he still wanted his piano to penetrate the ensemble the way a trumpet would. The result was an attack full of brilliance and ringing tones that became identified as "trumpet style" piano, a style to which Hines applied the finishing touches when he moved to Chicago in the mid-1920s and began playing with Louis Armstrong.

Until he formed his own big band in 1929 Hines, for all his brilliance, played somewhat in the shadows of Armstrong and Jimmie Noone, the clarinetist, who was one of Benny Goodman's influences. But all through the 1930s when Hines's band played at the Grand Terrace and was heard regularly on radio throughout the Midwest (introduced with cries of "Fatha Hines! Fatha Hines!"), he was one of the top bandleaders in the country, particularly in the years before the swing era began. And in the 1940s as swing was dying out, Hines's band became an incubator for the emerging bebop movement. In 1942 his band included Charlie Parker, Dizzy Gillespie, Billy Eckstine, and Sarah Vaughan, who was both singer and second pianist.

After these stars went out on their own, Hines unsuccessfully tried leading a large, concert-type band that included a string section of eight women. Then in 1949 Hines rejoined his old pal Louis Armstrong. But within two years he had tired of the sextet's endless one-nighters, and so he settled down on the West Coast and for the next fourteen years was buried in a Dixieland band.

Seemingly forgotten, he was on the verge of leaving the music business in 1964 when he was asked to fly East to play in one of a series of innovative jazz concerts. It was his first real concert recital. The reviews were ecstatic, and his career was revitalized almost instantaneously. "From then on," he said, "I had a new spirit, a new life."

He was rushed from recording studio to concert hall to nightclub to jazz festival. He made a triumphant tour of the Soviet Union in 1966 for the State Department. As he approached his seventy-fifth birthday his energy seemed boundless and his playing was as brilliant and inventive as ever. Any pianists with the audacity to run up against this cat will still get bruised.

(1905–   )

Billie Holiday

"I've been told that nobody sings the word 'hunger' like I do."

"The only time she's at ease and at rest with herself is when she sings," said Carmen McRae—quite a singer herself—about Billie Holiday.

As Billie put it, "I don't think I'm singing. I feel like I'm playing a horn. I try to improvise like Lester Young, like Louis Armstrong, or someone else I admire. What comes out is what I feel. I have to change a tune to my own way of doing it. That's all I know."

Considered by many the greatest of female jazz singers, Billie was born in Baltimore, the child of a jazz guitarist and a maid. "Mom and Pop were just a couple of kids when they got married. He was eighteen, she was sixteen, and I was three." These opening lines of *Lady Sings the Blues* set the tone for Billie's frank and often lurid autobiography. Raped at ten, she was sent to a home for girls where, as punishment, she was locked in a room with a child

Later Billie

who had died in an accident. She satisfied her craving for music by running errands for a madam in whose parlor she could listen to records by Bessie Smith and Louis Armstrong, her idols.

A bit later, in New York, she served four months in jail for prostitution. She was fourteen. In the winter of 1932, she and her mother were starving in Harlem. One cold night, Billie walked down Seventh Avenue, "going into every joint" to find work dancing or singing. At Jerry Preston's Log Cabin she tried to dance but was told she stunk. She asked the piano player to strike up a tune she knew and sang. "The customers stopped drinking. They turned around and watched. All of them started crying. Preston came over and said, 'Kid, you win.'"

It was here that John Hammond, the well-known discoverer of jazz talents, heard Billie and arranged her record debut. It was a flop, but less than two years later Hammond had her back in a studio, this time with splendid backing from handpicked jazzmen. "What a Little Moonlight Can Do" and other classics-to-be set the pattern for dozens of unforgettable records, many of which rank with the best jazz has to offer.

In 1937 Billie joined Count Basie's band for a year, then sang for eight months with Artie Shaw as the first black vocalist featured with a white band. Shaw and the men in the band loved her, but the road was paved with prejudice. "Eating was a mess, sleeping was a problem, but the biggest drag of all was a simple little thing like finding a place to go to the bathroom," she wrote. A trumpet player who stuck up for her was kicked in the mouth. But the last straw was an engagement at New York's Lincoln Hotel, where she was told to use the back entrance. After that, Billie was on her own, no longer "somebody's damn vocalist."

By 1940 she was on the way to stardom. From the start, she had the gift of infusing the often tawdry lyrics of popular songs with such honest, open emotion that they were transformed into art. She had a small voice and no musical training, but she projected like a great jazz instrumentalist. "She had the greatest conception of a beat I've ever heard," said accompanist Bobby Tucker.

At New York's Café Society, a club with a liberal clientele, she found that she could do offbeat material like "Strange Fruit," a bone-chilling song about lynching. After a tiff with her mother, the only person in the world she felt secure with, she and lyricist Arthur Herzog came up with "God Bless the Child," a moving "message" song that later became a hit with young people in the late 1960s.

By then Billie had been dead for nearly ten years, a victim of heroin, the unreasonable attitude of society toward addiction (especially if the addict was black and famous), and of her own inner demons. Hounded by the police, she had been "busted" and served a year in prison in 1947–48. When she came out, she was refused a cabaret card, the license without which one could not work in a place serving liquor in New York. But her 1948 comeback Carnegie

Earlier Billie

Hall concert was a triumph. Shortly thereafter, however, she was tried and acquitted on another narcotics charge. Somehow she always got involved with the wrong men, and while she had a generous nature, she was hot-tempered and insecure. After her mother's death, friends said, she felt completely alone and isolated.

Her voice was beginning to show the strain of years of abuse, though strangely this cracked instrument remained capable of producing incredibly moving sounds. And there was still more than a trace of the striking beauty that had once been hers. In 1957 she was reunited with Lester Young, who had dubbed her "Lady Day," on a remarkable television show, "The Sound of Jazz."

In March 1959 Billie attended Lester's funeral. She wanted to sing, but his family thought her too notorious. Outside, friends tried to console her. "They wouldn't let me sing. Those m_____s wouldn't let me sing," she said over and over between tears. Ten weeks later she was hospitalized and seemed to be making progress when a "friend" smuggled her some dope. Billie was arrested on what became her deathbed. "They even took my damn comic books," she told a musician who was permitted to visit. Years later her life story was vulgarized in a film. She had become a legend.

"I've been told that nobody sings the word 'hunger' like I do. Or the word 'love,' " she once said. That was right. She knew what those words meant, and she made the listener understand.

(1915–1959)

Buddy Holly

True style and a winning way.

He looked very unlike a hero—a skinny, gawky kid in thick-framed glasses. His popular career lasted barely two years. He died in the crash of a chartered light plane with rockers Ritchie Valens ("Donna") and The Big Bopper ("Chantilly Lace") while on a tour; the three of them wanted to arrive at the next town early to have their shirts laundered.

But Charles Hardin "Buddy" Holly left such a lasting musical impression that in 1967 the London *Sunday Times* magazine named him one of twenty

Buddy

"Lost Heroes" (among the others were Lawrence of Arabia and John F. Kennedy) whose early deaths permanently bereft their generations.

Best remembered for "Peggy Sue" (which John Lennon recorded in tribute in 1975) and "That'll Be the Day," Holly took his country/western musical background, added his liking for blues, and topped them off with a southwestern variety of rock beat. A "good ol' boy" at heart, Holly never quite lost his Texas accent and used it to good effect with stretchings, bendings and syncopated extensions of vowels and syllables to create rhythm tensions and relaxations. His technique was matched by an instinct for knowing how to phrase a lyric line.

Born in Lubbock, Texas, Holly was playing the guitar at the age of nine. As a teenager he appeared on local radio as a country singer but after an appearance in town by Elvis Presley (then known as "The Hillbilly Cat") Holly changed his style to rock. In 1956 he was recorded in Nashville as a Presley-style singer but the material was mediocre. Holly returned to Lubbock and began writing his own songs. He took two of them, "Peggy Sue" and "I'm Looking for Someone to Love," to the Clovis, New Mexico, recording studios owned by Norman Petty. The soft-spoken and astute Petty—"Buddy had something great going for him but even he wasn't sure what it was"—became Holly's producer and business manager. It was under his direction that nearly all of Holly's best recordings were made: "Oh, Boy!" "Maybe Baby," "Not Fade Away," "Everyday," "Heartbeat." They also established the southwestern rock style known as "Tex-Mex."

After the drummer in his combo, the Crickets, married the real life Peggy Sue, Holly moved to New York. He seems to have been lonely and unsure of himself in Manhattan and uncomfortable with the new smooth-pop recordings he was making where he was backed by string sections. In his apartment and in visits to his parents in Lubbock, he sang "Tex-Mex" versions of rock and country tunes into a home tape recorder, as if to comfort himself. Despite a still-remembered successful tour of England in 1958, he didn't have a hit and was somewhat fatalistic when he signed on with a 1959 American tour.

Then he was dead at twenty-three. His single in release, which became a hit at the time of his death, was titled, "It Doesn't Matter Anymore." But Buddy Holly's story did matter: in 1978 it was told in a highly acclaimed, full-length motion picture. And his songs and vocal style continued to be copied and admired—not from sentiment only, but because the boy from Lubbock, Texas, had true style and a winning way.

(1936–1959)

Libby Holman

"A mixture of sugar, graphite, and raw whiskey."

An admiring critic once lauded Libby Holman's deep, sultry voice as "a mixture of sugar, graphite, and raw whiskey"—an apt leitmotiv both for the great torch songs she popularized in the 1920s and '30s and for a career as stormy as anything in their lyrics.

Things didn't start that way. The Cincinnati-born brunette, who was once determined to become a lawyer, turned up on Broadway in 1925, attracting little notice in a spate of short-lived revues. Discouraged, she was thinking of heading home when songwriter Howard Dietz helped her land a role in *The Little Show,* opposite Clifton Webb and Fred Allen.

Almost overnight, Libby Holman was the hottest thing on Broadway. Her voice and sense of drama turned the show's two big songs, "Can't We Be Friends" and "Moanin' Low," into an emotional feast for the likes of critic Brooks Atkinson, who rhapsodized in print over "the dark purple menace of

"Moanin' Low!"

Libby Holman in the blues." A new revue, *Three's a Crowd,* yielded more Holman magic in "Body and Soul" and "Something to Remember You By."

Then, abruptly, tragedy struck. Her husband, heir to the Reynolds tobacco empire, was shot to death with Libby apparently present. She was eventually cleared of all charges, remarried, and returned to Broadway. But her name and career had been tainted.

Now nothing seemed to go right for her. The magic was gone. She sought new direction—and found it after hearing the black singers, Leadbelly and Josh White. "What d'you want to learn our songs for?" an incredulous White demanded when Libby asked him to teach her. "Anyway, a white woman can't sing our songs." Then he heard her sing, and a four-year working partnership was born.

Adversity, though, was never far off. In 1945 Libby and her second husband separated, and shortly thereafter he died of an overdose of sleeping pills. Then another blow, with her son's death in a mountain-climbing accident. Libby carried on, opening her own one-woman show, *Blues, Ballads and Sin Songs,* heavily featuring her newly acquired folk repertoire.

But the torch singer image stuck with her, and with it the stigma of scandal. Libby Holman's public appearances, mostly for charities and benefits, became less and less frequent throughout the 1960s. She receded from public view, an elusive, troubled woman.

A small circle of intimates knew her as a gracious, compassionate friend, who quietly adopted two children, befriended many, and gave freely of her wealth. She formed a close friendship with actor Montgomery Clift and was reportedly distraught over his death in 1966. Her life became ever more secluded.

Then, one June morning in 1971 she was found dead in the front seat of her car in the garage of her 112-acre Connecticut farm, an apparent suicide.

Libby Holman's death, like her tempestuous life, had been foreshadowed in the torch song lyrics of those early, blighted years:

. . . what lies before me
The future is stormy
A winter that's gray and old;
unless there's magic
the end will be tragic
and echo a tale that's been told so often . . .©

(1906–1971)

"She has given glamour manners."

"She is probably the most physically attractive singer in the business," wrote John J. O'Connor of Lena Horne in the New York *Times,* September 1973. "Her style leans less toward energetic belting than simmering insinuation, sometimes a touch mean, sometimes sassy, always sexy, always dazzling."

No doubt about it, the way Lena moves when she sings—even such minuscule mannerisms as dilating her nostrils one or two millimeters, or switching a hip one and a half degrees starboard—can underscore a musical phrase more emphatically and more dramatically than any boisterous blast from an entire brass section. As New York *Times* critic John S. Wilson noted in a concert review, "She actually made a John Denver song sound sexy!" But he also praised her musical ability: "She swings openly or with subtlety—really swings much more so than many singers who are considered primarily jazz singers."

Lena

Sometimes shy and not always too sure of herself, Lena admitted on the CBS TV show "Who's Who" in June 1977 that "I wish I could sing as free as Aretha Franklin." And she added, "I could never sing the blues. I was a Catholic."

Her performances by some have been considered a bit too studied. On the same program she admitted that "for many years I was just locked in." Recently she appeared to have lost some of her vocal inhibitions; her records made in 1977 displayed a freedom less evident in her previous works.

Though she has developed into a first-rate, all-around singer, Lena remains, above all, the consummate entertainer. "I'm a visual performer," she once told writer Dick Kleiner, trying to explain why her records seldom landed on the pop charts, "and records aren't visual."

Indeed, Lena's first venture into show business was basically visual. At age sixteen she migrated from her Brooklyn, New York, home to Harlem's Cotton Club to work as a chorine. Bandleader Noble Sissle heard her and offered her a job, and she made a few records with him, using her full name of "Helena Horne." That was changed in 1937 to Helena Jones, when she married Louis Jones, a printer, with whom she had a daughter and a son. Three years later she joined the all-white band of Charlie Barnet and recorded with him also.

Her band singing career ended when talent-developer John Hammond suggested to Barney Josephson, head of Greenwich Village's Café Society club, that he engage Lena as a solo act. She was a big hit. Encouraged, she decided to try Hollywood and all on her own landed a job at the Little Troc. For weeks she packed the room, then moved on to the larger, more prestigious Mocambo. Movie scouts moved in. First came an unbilled appearance in *Panama Hattie;* then MGM signed her to the first long-term contract ever offered a black performer and starred her in *Cabin in the Sky* and *Stormy Weather.*

After nearly a decade, and twelve films with Metro, she returned to New York and broke all attendance records at the swank Savoy-Plaza. Meanwhile, her marriage to Jones having ended, she married her musical director, Lennie Hayton, a white man, whose coaching and encouragement had helped her develop new-found confidence in her singing. Their marriage proved to be one of Hollywood's best, though bigoted neighbors necessitated their keeping a shotgun in their home. "I wanted to kill anyone who invaded my yard," she admitted years later.

To her other professional triumphs she added a Broadway success; in 1957 she was starred in *Jamaica.* In the 1960s and '70s she concertized in top spots like the London Palladium and New York's Carnegie Hall, was starred on numerous TV specials, continued to record, to fight for civil rights (her grandmother had enlisted her in the NAACP when she was only two), and to live up to the late Elsa Maxwell's apt description of her: "She has put poise into seduction, dignity into daring; she has given glamour manners."

(1917–   )

The Ink Spots

The whole proved to be much more successful than the individual parts.

Musicians used to make fun of them and the way they exaggerated their singing with a high tenor characterized by a seemingly uncontrollable tremolo emoting the melody, followed by an overconfidential baritone talking words of love. But the general public loved them and accepted the Ink Spots as possibly the most popular, though not the best, of all male vocal groups of the late 1930s and early '40s.

In his book, *The Ink Spots,* original quartet member Ivory "Deek" Watson describes how the group got its name.

Originally called The King, Jack and the Jesters, it performed for two years at WLW in Cincinnati, a state away from the members' hometown of Indianapolis. Summoning their courage, the group, which included Jerry Daniels, Charlie Faqua, Orville "Hoppy" Jones, and Watson, went to New York and were sitting in their manager's office when they noticed some ink spots that had spilled from a pen. "What an idea for a name for the group!" Watson reports someone exclaimed. "Why not call us the Black Dots or the Old Black Joes?" a couple of members remonstrated. But the Ink Spots they became.

In the mid-1930s they recorded a couple of dozen jivey sides for Decca, all typical of the sort of lightweight swing sounds that many black groups of the

The Ink Spots (Bill Kenny is at the left of mike)

period were singing. Then Jerry Daniels took sick, and long, lanky Bill Kenny came in. With his high falsetto voice carressing each ballad with all the apparent passion and sincerity of a medicine man, followed by "Hoppy" Jones reciting the same romantic lyrics in a deep baritone voice with the relaxed assurance of an auditioning mortician, they produced a highly stylized, easily identifiable musical image. Following their first big record hit, "If I Didn't Care," they were inundated with offers for personal appearances. In the fall of 1939 they appeared as the "extra added attraction" to Glenn Miller at New York's Paramount Theater then stayed on for many more weeks as the star attraction. So successful did they suddenly become that, according to Watson, they played engagements simultaneously at the Paramount, the Apollo Theater in Harlem, and the Famous Door nightclub in mid-Manhattan, and, according to Watson, used an ambulance to rush them from engagement to engagement.

During the early 1940s they recorded more hits: "Whispering Grass," "Maybe," "We Three," "Java Five," and "Do I Worry." They were reportedly making $15,000 each per week and carried an entourage of four personal valets, a uniform valet, and a private barber and masseur. They engaged in wild crap games (Watson claims to have lost $100,000 in one night), bought posh homes, and appeared in two movies.

But the high living and the string of record hits ended after their 1946 version of "For Sentimental Reasons." Jones had died in 1944 as the result of an epileptic seizure, and for a while they worked as a trio. They began squabbling among themselves, spurred on by managers who hoped to get larger percentages from three pies, and apparently convinced they could be making more money as individuals than as a group. But the whole proved to be much more successful than the individual parts, and though the members struck out on their own, each using the name "The Ink Spots" (as even other, nonrelated singers started to do), the original members gradually faded into the same sort of obscurity, and in 1978, when Bill Kenny died at age fifty-five, not a living trace of the original Ink Spots remained.

Burl Ives

"A fat man who likes to sit around and sing."

In 1938 a booking agent, who had never been west of the Hudson River, brushed him off with, "We're not interested in hillbilly acts." To the man he rejected, folk singing was a neglected art, one that Burl Ives wanted to bring to the American people—those who *didn't* live in the regions where the music originated.

Burl Icle Ivanhoe Ives, whom poet Carl Sandburg has called "the mightiest ballad singer of any century," was raised in the "Bible Belt" of Illinois, the son of hard-working but dirt-poor tenant farmers. He and his five siblings were known as "The Singing Ives"; Burl debuted at the age of four, singing "Barbara Allen" at a reunion at an old soldiers' home. He soon learned to play the banjo and guitar and in later years would do much of his own arranging.

The young Burl Ives carried 240 pounds on a six-foot frame and dreamed

Burl

of playing or coaching pro football. Instead, he dropped out of Eastern Illinois College in his junior year because "my feet were itchin' to see this country and the people, and studyin' wasn't doin' it." His vagabond trek took him to forty-six states and Mexico and Canada. He sang for his meals and lodgings while collecting a repertoire of five hundred folk tunes: cowboy songs, sea chanteys, songs of the steel mills and of lumberjacks.

During a brief return to college, he was urged by a singing teacher to go to New York, where he landed some nonsinging parts—first off, later on, the great White Way. Soon he was playing featured roles and starring in his own radio show, "The Wayfarin' Stranger," on CBS. The show was named for one of several ballads with which he was closely identified. Some others: "Big Rock Candy Mountain," "Foggy, Foggy Dew," and his famous "Blue-Tail Fly." *Wayfarin' Stranger* was also the title of his autobiography, published in 1948.

Drafted during World War II, he starred in Irving Berlin's *This Is the Army*. After a medical discharge, he continued to entertain the troups with his mellow, easygoing renditions of folk ballads.

In the postwar 1940s he was much in demand in clubs, concerts, on Broadway and, inevitably, in fourteen motion pictures. His greatest portrayal, both on the stage and in the movie, was that of Big Daddy in *Cat on a Hot Tin Roof.* His role in *The Big Country* won him an Academy Award in 1958. But throughout the 1940s, '50s, and '60s, he never stopped recording ballads and folk songs, many of which became hits.

Self-effacing (he describes himself as "a fat man who likes to sit around and sing"), Ives now lives with his second wife, Dorothy, in Santa Barbara. During a 1974 concert tour, the audience shouted for all the old favorites, and he sang them all. In his own words, "Ballad singing has been going on ever since people sang at all. It comes up like an underground stream and then goes back again. But it always exists."

(1909–   )

Mahalia Jackson

"Anybody singing the blues is in a deep pit yelling for help . . ."

The gospel music purists thought she had become too commercial, but the rest of her record-buyers seemed to prefer her more pop-oriented albums. And so Mahalia Jackson, Queen of the Gospel Singers, was faced with a dilemma: Which group should she try to please?

Her solution was simple: Please them both. And so she proceeded to record some albums that included pop songs and well-known hymns and anthems, backed by large, lush orchestras, as well as other albums of only gospel songs with just a down-home piano-player and a couple of rhythm instruments that projected the pure gospel music on which she had been raised and which she, more than any other singer in history, spread around the world.

"The vocal, physical, spiritual, symbol of gospel music," Tony Heilbut called her in his book *The Gospel Sound*. "Her huge [260 pounds], noble proportions, her face contorted into something like the Mad Duchess, her soft speaking voice and huge, rich contralto, all made her gospel's superstar." And "a belter and a shouter," is how Henry Pleasants described her in *The Great American Popular Singers*. "She was never happier than when pouring it on and out, the breath heavy on the vocal cords, extracting every decibel of chest and head resonance."

Queen of the
Gospel Singers

She began singing at the age of five in the local New Orleans church in which her stevedore father preached on Sundays. Two cousins, with whom she lived after her mother died, introduced her to the blues recordings of Bessie and Mamie Smith and Ma Rainey. Though musicologists have insisted that their style infiltrated her singing, a proud and sometimes haughty Mahalia would never acknowledge such secular influences.

When she was eighteen, she moved to Chicago, where she sang with the Greater Baptist Choir and the Johnson Gospel Singers. In 1945 she began recording for Apollo and soon her fame spread. She toured Denmark, England, and France, singing mostly for white audiences, and in 1950 made her debut in Carnegie Hall. She also sang for the Empress of Japan, the Prime Minister of India, President Eisenhower, and at President Kennedy's inauguration, on the steps of the Lincoln Memorial just before the Reverend Martin Luther King, Jr., delivered his famous "I Have a Dream" speech, and at King's funeral.

Her Apollo records sold well, though they brought her shockingly low financial rewards. And so when Columbia Records began wooing her, she signed with them, made many top-selling albums, and was rewarded with her own radio and TV series. She was encouraged to sing some blues and possibly become "the next Bessie Smith," But she refused because, for her, spirituals expressed hope while "the blues are sad and stay that way. Anybody singing the blues is in a deep pit yelling for help and I'm simply not in that position."

But she did veer from her pure gospel format. She recorded with large orchestras, like Duke Ellington's, which shocked some of her purist followers, and Percy Faith's huge ensemble, which accompanied her on *The Power and the Glory* album that contained no gospel songs, only hymns and anthems. "But," avers her producer, Irving Townsend, "she always told me that was her favorite of *all* her albums."

Such commercial ventures made Mahalia a lot of money, though she spent little of it on material things, except on some rather inhuman human leeches who made her personal life miserable. But she did invest wisely in financially successful ventures like "Mahalia's Beauty Salon," "Mahalia's Flower Shop," "Mahalia's Chicken Dinners," and income-yielding real estate holdings. Still, she never forgot her oldest and purist audiences and more than once, after having earned something like ten thousand dollars in one night from a concert promoter, she would show up the next night in some small-town church and sing for free.

"I don't work for money. I sing because I love to sing," she told *The Melody Maker*'s Max Jones in 1969. When she died a few years later, she left two legacies, an estate reportedly worth over a million dollars, and recordings and memories of some of the most heartfelt, emotional, and rewarding singing the world has ever known.

Mahalia Jackson certainly did have it both ways.

(1911–1972)

Harry James

"I have a degree in mass psychology."

"I want to have a band that really swings and that's easy to dance to all the time," said Harry James late in 1938 when he left Benny Goodman's orchestra to form his own. And that's exactly what he created: one of the most swinging, one of the most danceable, and what became in the mid 1940s the most popular orchestra in America.

His own trumpet, brilliant and biting on swing tunes, soothing and syrupy on ballads, brought a highly personalized sound to his band. But of equal importance, for dancers especially, was Harry's innate knack of playing the right tunes at precisely the right tempos for the right people. "I have," he once boasted facetiously, "a degree in mass psychology." When composer Jule Styne demonstrated "I Don't Want to Walk Without You," Harry agreed to record it but insisted on playing it at a slower tempo than Styne had played it. It became a hit. When Styne returned a few months later with "I've Heard That Song Before," Harry opted for a faster tempo. The recording proved to be the first million-seller in Columbia Records' history.

Harry's feeling for tempos stemmed from his earliest musical years. At age six he was playing drums in a traveling Texas circus that included his mother

Harry, mid-1970s and still blowing strong

World War II idol James

and his bandmaster father. As soon as Harry was old enough, his father taught him his own instrument, the trumpet. Not willing to settle for a circus career, young James left and began playing with local Texas dance bands. Years later he reported that he "almost joined Lawrence Welk who was traveling in the territory. But I couldn't play enough instruments for him. He had a seven-piece band and everybody was playing four or five instruments."

In 1935 bandleader Ben Pollack, who had previously discovered Benny Goodman, Glenn Miller, and Jack Teagarden, heard James and hired him. A writer for *Metronome* magazine heard James on a radio show, had no idea who he was, but raved about him. Others began talking about him, and Benny Goodman got the word and sent for him. He joined the Goodman band right after New Year's Day of 1937, and from then until late in 1938, when he left to start his own band, he was featured on a slew of swing selections. When he did leave, he did so with Goodman's blessings and even a loan from the frugal leader, who had grown fond of the lean, hard-working, enthusiastic, outgoing twenty-two-year-old.

The new band struggled for a year and a half. For seven of those months it featured a young singer whom Harry had discovered as a singing M.C. in a New Jersey roadhouse. Frank Sinatra became the first of several excellent James singers that included Dick Haymes, Helen Forrest, and Kitty Kallen. But it took a singer who never worked with the band to inspire its first hit record. Smitten by Judy Garland's singing of "You Made Me Love You," Harry recorded his own version of the ballad, featuring his schmaltzy trumpet in place of Judy's voice. It became his first big hit, and spurred by its success he began to concentrate more on sentimental songs beamed at couples separated by the draft and eventually by the war itself.

Out they poured—"I Don't Want to Walk Without You," "He's My Guy," "That Soldier of Mine," "I Cried for You," "It's Been a Long, Long Time," and many more. To embellish the romantic mood, Harry added dozens of string players. By the mid-1940s he had captured the number one spot in just about every popularity poll, had been featured in several movies, and had taken a glamorous movie star, Betty Grable, as his second wife (his first was vocalist Louise Tobin).

Harry's intense interest in music and baseball (he was once a big league prospect and for years worked out with his favorite team, the St. Louis Cardinals) was diluted by love of horse racing, golf, and the higher-flying Hollywood life, and some felt that his music suffered. Yet at times, especially during the 1960s when Buddy Rich helped spark his band, he would blow as brilliantly as ever, and his band was working regularly well into the late 1970s, when he joyously announced, "We've got offers for more jobs today than we've had in over twenty years. The kids are coming out to listen and dance, and the older folks are saying, 'Hey, it's time we had some fun too!' " And Harry James seemed delighted to indulge both groups.

(1916–   )

Jefferson (Airplane) Starship

"I can't write about Gerald Ford bumping his head."

The first of the San Francisco rock bands to achieve national fame and acclaim was Jefferson Airplane. Retaining its popularity even after the San Francisco music scene had begun to fade, the group came back so strong in 1975, under its new name of Jefferson Starship, that it achieved something the Airplane had never been able to. It produced the country's number one selling album.

The group was organized in 1965 in the days of Haight-Ashbury and flower power. Guitarist-vocalist Marty Balin came up with the idea of playing folk music on electric instruments—the way the Byrds had down in Los Angeles—and adding the San Francisco message of love. He met guitarist Paul Kantner, and together they molded a style that included not just folk music but also bits of country and classical music and rhythm and blues, all propelled by a hard-driving acid rock beat. After they added four more members, including singer Signe Anderson and lead guitarist Jorma Kaukonen, the Jefferson Airplane was almost ready to take off.

Balin's sweet, rich voice added a dimension of gentleness foreign to most other rock groups. When beautiful, serene Grace Slick joined the group, replacing the pregnant Anderson, she provided contrast to Balin's sweetness with her distinctive sound and style—a loud, ear-catching voice and (often) a longshoreman's vocabulary. And she brought with her something of immediate tangible value: two big songs, "Somebody to Love" and "White Rabbit." The latter song, a musical psychedelic trip, described by New York *Times* writer Barbara Howes as "a distillation of Lewis Carroll and Maurice Ravel etched in acid imagery," became the group's first hit. By 1968 they were all on the cover of *Life* magazine. They appeared as stars of the Monterey Pop Festival and at Woodstock, and they were at Altamont with the Rolling Stones.

Members came and went, while Slick and Kantner remained as the group's nucleus. And the money came and went too—coming in because the group remained such a big draw and going out to pay for the expensive light show that augmented the group's psychedelic imagery; to lawyers for various drug arrests; for expensive cars and clothes, chartered planes and champagne; and to maintain the mansion that Grace and Paul bought in San Francisco, in which they, their daughter, China, and other musicians sometimes lived.

In 1970 Paul created a concept album, *Blows Against the Empire,* in which the revamped group fantasized about hijacking a starship to create a life in outer space. On its back cover he thanked the musicians who helped him record

"Jefferson (Airplane) Starship"

the album, calling them "Jefferson Starship." That casual mention resulted in the group's changing its name.

The new group, with new personnel, came up with two big hit albums, *Dragon Gold*, which sold over a million copies, and *Red Octopus*, which sold twice that number and topped the album charts.

Though the group has often been identified with hard rock, most of the songs in its latter and most successful albums centered around love. To their fans they have at various times expressed their devotion and gratitude by giving free concerts, a rarity in an age of money-grabbing rock groups.

Of course, their way of expressing love has sometimes surprised some sedate listeners. That may be because, as Kantner told Rowes, "We are trying to create songs which reflect the different experiences of living in this society." One aspect of American life that they tend to de-emphasize is politics. As Slick noted in 1976: "Politics don't provoke many epic rock and roll songs today. I can't write about Gerald Ford bumping his head."

Elton John

"I just leaped on the piano in celebration and that was it. I was free at last."

On stage, sporting flamboyant finery accessorized with one of his two hundred pairs of fancy glasses, he sings and plays the piano in assertive style, ending by flinging away the piano bench and doing a handstand on the keys or by lying down on his back and playing the piano with his feet.

Elton John, top pop music superstar of the early 1970s, living the fantasy life of a onetime fat, nearsighted wallflower, was earning seven million dollars a year in 1975, according to *Time* magazine, and spending money as flamboyantly as he dressed, driving up to Cartier's in his Rolls-Royce to purchase seven thousand dollars' worth of gifts.

He says his audience—a cross section that includes young, old, freaky, straight, the masses, the celebrated—knows that he is having fun with rock, and there is a mood of laughter at his concerts. But Elton John is not a joke. He is part clown, part artist, and there is a real respect in the applause he receives for the songs he writes with lyricist Bernie Taupin. Several number one hits, including "Rocket Man," "Honky Cat," and "Goodbye Yellow Brick Road," attest to the fact that Elton John must be taken seriously. The wild clothes? While he admits they enhance his showmanship, he insists that they are a reaction to a restricted youth, that he wears them because he didn't have any fun, didn't indulge in any childhood games or adolescent nonsense until he was twenty-one.

He was born Reginald Kenneth Dwight in Pinner, Middlesex, England. His father, a squadron leader in the Royal Air Force, was, according to Elton, "very snobbish and sort of stiff." He even disapproved of "in" school clothes, boyish horsing around, and pop music. It was John's mother, however, who provided Elton with his early interest in rock when she brought home records by Bill Haley and Elvis Presley.

Young Reggie Dwight played the piano by ear from the time he was four and entered the Royal Academy of Music in London at age eleven. Five years later he left the Academy to play in blues and rock bands. One such band provided the raw material for his stage name: He combined the first names of singer John Baldry and saxophonist Elton Dean to create the first stage of his metamorphosis.

In 1967, soon after adopting his new moniker, he met Taupin, and they started writing songs together. Music publisher Dick James signed them as a writing team and soon recognized that the best performer of the Taupin-John songs was Elton John himself.

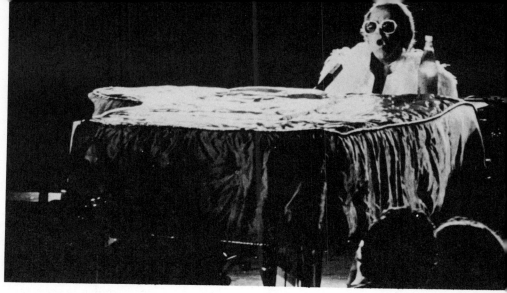

The many moods of Elton

Just before Elton made his American debut, on August 25, 1970, he lost a lot of weight and put himself into the kind of mod garb his former plumpness had denied him. He said later: "I went to the Troubador Club in Los Angeles dressed in the most outrageous gear I could find. No one believed that I would actually go on stage and play like that. But I did, for the first time, and was so overjoyed I just leaped on the piano in celebration and that was it. I was free at last."

He was free, and his star soared. His records became smash hits; his ninth album, *Goodbye Yellow Brick Road,* produced in 1973, sold two million copies in the United States within six months; he won a film role, Pinball Wizard, in *Tommy;* and his concerts sold out.

According to Taupin, their music's strongest motif, focused on human relationships unhappily missed or lost, reflects Elton's thinking. That John has not always been the happy-go-lucky person some believed him to be became apparent in a mid-1978 television interview with David Frost, to whom he admitted that he prefers soccer to pop music, that he'd gladly trade the stage for playing soccer at Wembley, that he quit his career for a while "because I had to have four bodyguards," that at age twenty-one he had attempted "a Woody Allen type of suicide, I left the windows wide open without knowing it," that "inanimate objects give me more pleasure than people." He also recognized that he was not responsible enough to himself for his own happiness because "I'm always trying to make others happy. I won't let anybody get close to me. I live alone in a thirty-six-room house and I can't go into the kitchen because the alarms are on." And who might be responsible for this twentieth-century Pagliaccio's apparent misery? "I'm my own worst enemy," he told Frost.

(1947–   )

Al Jolson

He would sing almost anytime, anywhere for anyone who'd let him know how great he was.

He referred to himself as "The World's Greatest Entertainer," and he thoroughly believed it. For many years, especially during the mid and latter 1920s, the response of fans and even fellow performers seemed to prove him right. For Al Jolson could captivate almost any audience, with his ringing voice, his passionate, pleading style of singing, arms outstretched, often "begging" on one knee— the complete master of almost every all-stops-out gimmick known to show business.

He could make you adore his "Mammy," slobber over his "Sonny Boy," wish you were really down in Dixie floating on his fictitious "Swanee" river and convince you that the greatest weather of all was his "April Showers." Judged by social and musical standards fifty years after his time, Jolson may seem corny and his black-face performances more than just slightly offensive, but during his premicrophonic period, when singing and emotions were projected strictly on a one-to-one basis from performer to audience and before today's social attitudes had developed, Jolson was indeed a masterful singer and the consummate showman.

Born Asa Yoelson in Russia, the son of a rabbi, he was raised in Washington, D.C., then migrated to New York, where his forcefully projected musical enthusiasm captivated audiences in theaters and nightclubs and won a wide following for his recordings and radio performances. In 1927 Hollywood starred him in the first "talkie," *The Jazz Singer* (though he actually never sang jazz), and a generation later honored him with *The Jolson Story,* for which he supplied the singing voice for Larry Parks's Jolson portrayal.

The real Jolson, according to those who knew him best, was one of the most egocentric entertainers of all time. He would sing almost anytime, anywhere for anyone who'd let him know how great he was. In fact, his entire life revolved around making love to audiences while fully expecting and even demanding their love in return. Such a passion for constant popular approval, however, destroyed three marriages (including his celebrated one to Ruby Keller), precluded all but a few strong friendships, aroused resentment among many colleagues and indirectly led to his death when, at age sixty-four, he insisted, against the advice of physicians and friends, on continuing a long barnstorming tour of Korea, where he could enjoy the sort of adulation from home-starved GIs that he was beginning to find increasingly difficult to arouse in audiences back in the States.

"M-a-m-m-y!"

Fellow performer and friend George Burns, in Michael Freedland's book *Jolson,* summed up the singer's penchant for approval with: "It was easy enough to make Jolson happy at home. You had to cheer him at breakfast, applaud wildly at lunch, and give him a standing ovation for dinner." And, despite his waning popularity in later years, Jolson remained convinced that his way of singing was the right way. "I haven't changed my style or my delivery in fifty years!" he boasted.

And just what was that "style"? Friend George Jessel summed it up during his eulogy at Jolson's funeral: "A man vibrant and pulsating with youth, authority, and courage, who marched on the stage, head held high and with the look of a Roman emperor. He had a gaiety that was militant, uninhibited, and unafraid."

(1886–1950)

Quincy Jones

"When they scraped my brain, they scraped all the b.s. out of me."

"I'll run for anything except Governor of Mississippi," announced bright-eyed, quick-witted, and multitalented Quincy Jones when asked in the early 1960s if he'd accept a nomination for a governorship in the Recording Academy. That response, flip as it was, typified the realistic, sensitive but "never-take-yourself-too-seriously" attitude of this highly successful conductor, composer, arranger, trumpeter, pianist, singer, and record producer and executive, who has blended so wonderfully well the melodic and rhythmic aspects of jazz, rock, and rhythm and blues. Both creative and pragmatic, he has been described by friend and writer Gene Lees as "a shrewd, determined, ambitious man who keeps his own counsel and never takes a step, as he once said of himself, 'before I'm ready.' "

Quincy Delight Jones, better known simply as "Q" to his close friends, started getting ready as the ten-year-old member of a church vocal quartet in Seattle. Inspired by the blues bands of Louis Jordan and Eddie "Cleanhead" Vinson, he took up the trumpet and at fourteen was playing his horn and singing in a soft, misty, Nat Cole manner in the small band he had formed with his sixteen-year-old pal Ray Charles. "It was a great learning experience," he later recalled. "We played everything: schottisches, blues, even Sousa marches." And when Ray began to show Quincy how to arrange, "that's when I became really and permanently hooked on music!"

His talent was matched by his faith in his abilities. Some months later, when Count Basie was passing through Seattle with his seven-piece group, young Quincy offered him some of his arrangements to play. The Count liked them, and later, when he re-formed his big band, Quincy became one of its chief arrangers.

Meanwhile, determined to learn all he could about music, he studied for a year and a half on a scholarship at Boston's Berklee School of Music, sometimes attending as many as ten classes a day, then playing nights in local strip joints.

Next came two years trumpeting and arranging for Lionel Hampton's band, followed by two years in New York devoted entirely to arranging. In 1956 he joined Dizzy Gillespie's band, toured with it in Europe, then remained in Paris to work as musical director of Barclay Records, a jazz label, and to study serious composition with Nadia Boulanger, who had also taught Aaron Copland, Leonard Bernstein, and Roger Sessions. He returned to the States and in 1959 organized an all-star band for Harold Arlen's blues opera, *Free and Easy*. But the high payroll, plus an unsuccessful European tour, left him $100,000 in

"Q"

debt. So he accepted a job as producer at Mercury Records, stayed there for seven years and became the first black vice-president of a major record company.

Still his arranging pen continued to flow. He wrote impressive scores for Frank Sinatra, Peggy Lee, Sarah Vaughan, Dinah Washington, and Basie and Gillespie. His zooming reputation attracted Hollywood producers, and soon he was composing and arranging for such films as *The Pawnbroker, In the Heat of the Night, In Cold Blood, The Anderson Tapes,* and *The New Centurions.* He received several Oscar nominations, but in 1972, annoyed and frustrated by the movies' restrictions and musical typecasting, he quit films and decided to regroup, concentrating on his recording career. Winner of four Grammys, he made a slew of hit albums, like *Walking in Space, Smackwater Jack, Gulama-tari,* and *Body Heat,* that spanned jazz, rock, rhythm and blues and middle-of-the-road pop music. And he also functioned as producer and executive for A&M Records.

In 1972 he suffered the first of two cranial aneurisms. His close brushes with death changed some of his values. "When they scraped my brain, they scraped all the b.s. out of me," he later said. Grateful for his past, delighted with his present ("My five kids keep my head in the present!"), he was busy in the mid-1970s combining the past and the present with his future. Hired to write the score for the TV movie version of Alex Haley's *Roots,* he spent days and nights delving into black history and sociology along with the evolution of jazz and the blues. He found it to be a fascinating and broadening assignment. And when it was completed, he just kept on recording and producing, and, most of all, "enjoying every minute" of the precious, productive life that a few years earlier had almost been taken away from him.

(1933–   )

The soothing sounds of talent night in a lunatic asylum.

He created a blend of ricky-ticky Dixie and the soothing sounds of talent night in a lunatic asylum, and it added up to just the kind of spunky irreverence the nation needed in 1942.

Spike Jones, a highly successful radio and recording-studio drummer in Los Angeles, took a tune written originally for a Donald Duck cartoon and, with the help of a rubber "razzer" that emitted heartfelt Bronx cheers, turned out one of the great pieces of musical propaganda of all time. "Der Fuehrer's Face" was an instant hit with everybody from the GIs to the folks back home to President Franklin D. Roosevelt. The record sold one and a half million copies and enabled Spike Jones and his bunch of fellow disaffected studio musicians to become one of the most famous and successful musical novelty acts.

Spike and His City Slickers

Lindley Armstrong Jones was born in Long Beach, California, and was at once nicknamed Spike, probably because his father was a station agent for the Southern Pacific Railroad. When Spike was eleven his mother gave him his first set of drums. After high school he played in nightclubs and dance bands, and by twenty-five he was playing regularly with John Scott Trotter's Orchestra on the Bing Crosby radio show. A streak of oddball creativity led him to build a personal arsenal of strange percussion "instruments," beginning with a set of tuned cowbells and eventually including washboards, auto horns, and pistols.

With other musicians who, like Jones, were bored with the commerical arrangements of the day, he held informal weekly sessions in which they spoofed the music they played for a living. Victor Records was sufficiently amused by their versions of "Pretty Red Wing" and "Sloppy Lagoon" to sign them to a contract, but, as Jones later explained, "We were too corny for sophisticated people and too sophisticated for corny people."

Nothing happened until the summer of 1942, when the zany defiance of "Der Fuehrer's Face" caught on, enabling the maverick bandsmen to quit their studio jobs. As Spike Jones and His City Slickers, they followed up with assaults on other songs. "Cocktails for Two" was embellished with a chorus consisting entirely of hiccups, right on key, of course. "You Always Hurt the One You Love" subjected the loved one to an assortment of indignities that included shooting, poisoning, and hanging. And "Pass the Biscuits, Mirandy" became the locker-room war cry of the 1946 St. Louis Cardinals, leading them to a National League pennant and a World Series championship.

In 1947 Jones assembled a successful two-hour "Musical Depreciation Revue" complete with an octave of Flit guns in E-flat, a "crashophone," which produced the sound of breaking glass, and a live goat, trained to bleat in the key of C. In the 1950s Spike Jones and His City Slickers had their own television show. With their bizarre instruments, manic energy, and polished comic showmanship, the City Slickers were always visually exciting, often hilarious.

In the 1960s Jones left comedy behind and began making records in a straight Dixieland style—competent but not very original. His true genius had been revealed in his ability to make his countrymen smile when there wasn't much to smile at.

During World War II the men of a U.S. aircraft carrier adopted the City Slickers' version of "The Sheik of Araby" as their theme song and played the record over the P.A. system whenever the crews scrambled for their planes. For many of those fliers, the infectious razz-ma-tazz of Spike Jones was the last music they ever heard.

(1911–1964)

Tom Jones

He collects middle-aged ladies.

In the mid-1960s, when long hair, reed-thin bodies, and unisex clothing began to make sexuality ambiguous, and any male with a mature voice was suspected of being over thirty and untrustworthy, Tom Jones burst on the scene with a frankly carnal, rich baritone voice, and an emphasis on sexuality that set him apart from the mainstream of rock, and made him one of the most imitated singers among the also-rans who populate the lounges of the Catskills and Las Vegas.

Thomas Jones Woodward was born on June 7, 1940, in the South Wales mining town of Pontypridd that also sired Richard Burton. When he was only three his mother took him to the local store to sing for shillings and later sent him out to sing "Ghost Riders in the Sky" and "Mule Train" at ladies' clubs and local weddings.

Tom

A Teddy boy in his teens, he married a local girl at sixteen and fathered a son at seventeen. Determined not to work in the mines, he labored at construction jobs by day and sang the workingmen's clubs by night. In 1963 he was discovered by Gordon Mills, a local boy who had moved to London to be a songwriter. Home for a visit, Mills convinced "Tiger Tom," as he billed himself, to come to London under Mills's management. After the inevitable scuffle, and a name change to capitalize on the film *Tom Jones,* Mills wrote him a song (with Les Reed), "It's Not Unusual," that hit the top of the British charts a week after its release in 1965. It sold three million copies and was number one in thirteen countries.

After the usual tours and TV shows, Jones found himself back in the working-men's clubs again. Rock audiences and Tom Jones were not connecting. But then in November 1966, Mills noticed that the more mature women who caught his act responded powerfully to the Jones sexuality, and in a flash he decided to aim Jones at this new and hungry market. The connection was made and soon Jones's hits were coming hot and heavy—"What's New Pussycat," "Green Green Grass of Home," "Love Me Tonight."

Tom settled into a seventeen-room house in London, had his nose fixed, teeth capped, and his hair curled. In 1969, his hour-long television show, "This Is Tom Jones," premiered on ABC, and thanks to the exposure it afforded him, Jones sold out everywhere on his American tour in 1969. Mobs of women screamed and danced on tabletops. Harassed husbands desperately scrambled for autographs. He had to be rushed from stages to freight elevators and secret staircases under cover of total darkness.

Despite the self-conscious sex-machine posturing and the provocative tightly wrapped trousers, Jones's style has been based solidly on the less manufactured, more traditional black gospel and rhythm and blues music. As a boy he collected records by such artists as Muddy Waters and Big Bill Broonzy. Today he collects middle-aged ladies who are totally captivated by such an unabashed masculine image. As for Jones himself, he has remained very much the Pontypridd boy, married to the same Pontypridd girl, avoiding the inevitable carnal distractions at every hand, most comfortable with pubs and hotel TV sets when he's on the road, and very much a homebody when he's not, a tender "Tiger Tom" in his sumptuous Bel Air, California, home.

(1940–   )

Janis Joplin

"People like their blues singers dead."

She introduced classic-style blues singing to the rock of the 1960s. Like her idol Bessie Smith, whose 1920s recordings inspired her, Janis Joplin's vocal phrasing imitated the sounds of "hot jazz" instruments: the broad glissando of the trombone, the liquid flutter of the clarinet, the bite and command of the trumpet. It was ironic that she dwelt in a musical world of guitars and drums.

Her contribution to contemporary popular music was never fully realized because of the fury of her personality. Though she had passion and power, she had little discipline in her life or in music. Janis Joplin was a victim, not only of her fame and the whore/earth mother image invented by "underground culture" propagandists, but by her own wayward indulgence. She was often

Janis

careless about and abusive to her talent and confused and bitter about her relationship with her audience.

As a child in Port Arthur, Texas, she showed signs of the self-centered and insatiable desire for attention that was eventually to destroy her. In later years she claimed the townspeople persecuted her for being "different," but there is reason to believe she provoked some of the hostility as a means of being noticed.

At seventeen she heard records by Bessie Smith and immediately became a blues fan, learning several of Smith's songs and performing locally. The following year she went to California and entered the early "underground culture." When she returned to Port Arthur in 1965 she was an exhausted narcotics user. The retreat to her hometown was one of her occasional attempts to put her life in order; she dressed primly and enrolled at college as a sociology major.

That same year a friend was organizing rock concerts at the Fillmore Auditorium in San Francisco. A band named Big Brother and the Holding Company was looking for an additional singer. The friend recommended Janis, who was again working small clubs in Texas. She was auditioned and selected. When the group played the Monterey Pop Festival in 1967, she was immediately hailed as a star. She was raw, emotional, flamboyant, and quite overpowering on stage singing "Piece of My Heart."

In 1968 she left Big Brother—never very much of a band—and organized a new backing group that wasn't much better. She sang harder and harder to no great effect except to cause some of her fans and friendly critics to have second thoughts about her use of her talent. Her excess of zeal was abetted and complicated by her continuing use of drugs, plus alcohol and casual sexual encounters.

She made a last effort to put her artistic and personal life in order in 1970. She finally found a good backing group, toned down her volume, showed taste and humor in her selection of material, worked on an album, *Pearl,* that was to be her finest, and planned to marry. Then she accidently shot an overdose of heroin into her arm and died. She was twenty-seven.

Her career was brief and, except for a few isolated recordings such as "Me and Bobby McGee," not satisfying to herself or her admirers. She typified rock performers who hurry to cannibalize themselves before the hungry audience does. "People like their blues singers dead," she once commented, and on another occasion mused, "I'm going to write a song about making love to twenty-five thousand people at a concert and then going back to my room alone."

(1943–1970)

Louis Jordan

He never threw away one single word of a lyric or wasted a musical note.

Long before the term gained currency, Louis Jordan "crossed over" from the rhythm-and-blues field to the front ranks of show business. In his heyday—roughly from 1941 to 1951—he sold some fifteen million records, was featured in Hollywood musicals, and charmed black and white audiences with his masterful rhythmic comedy.

A short, compact bundle of energy, Jordan never stopped working, from the moment he bounded on stage until he took his final bow. "I get tired," he confessed, "but I love it. Just give me the chance to get tired." He never threw away one single word of a lyric or wasted a musical note. His art, like Fats Waller's, was a blend of visual showmanship, an original, rhythmically

"Mr. Personality"

supercharged vocal style, solid musicianship, and infectious humor. He was justly nicknamed "Mr. Personality."

Jordan's father had been a bandleader and music teacher in Brinkley, Arkansas, and gave his son a thorough grounding in traditional music. While attending Arkansas Baptist College, young Louis spent his summer vacations touring with the Rabbitfoot Minstrels, doubling as clarinetist and utility entertainer. He then pursued a career as big-band sideman, which culminated in a stay with Chick Webb, whom he left in 1938 to form his own group, the Tympany Five.

While working at the Capitol Lounge in Chicago in 1941, Jordan introduced "I'm Gonna Move to the Outskirts of Town." It became his first million-selling record, and the four-week engagement was stretched to thirty-two weeks. A string of hits ensued, including "Caldonia," "Saturday Night Fish Fry," "Let the Good Times Roll," "Choo Choo Ch' Boogie," which sold two million records, and that marvelous mock sermon on the pitfalls of courtship, "Beware."

Jordan acted out the story of each song, and he had a knack for finding fresh material, encouraging unknown writers to approach him (and penning some excellent songs himself). In one year, he said, he listened to over two hundred songs, selecting twenty-five of them for use. The hit "Run, Joe" was a case in point. While getting a checkup, he discovered that his doctor wrote calypso songs, left the office with a stack of them and picked out the right one.

In addition to his special talent for bringing blues and novelty material to life, Jordan was a convincing ballad-singer—"Don't Let the Sun Catch You Crying" was as big a hit for him as it would become years later for Ray Charles, on whom he had considerable influence. And he always sandwiched hot samples of his jazz alto saxophone playing between vocals. His bands (he expanded to seven pieces in 1942, and briefly to big-band size ten years later) consistently supplied good music as well as zestful entertainment.

With all the energy Jordan expended on his work, he still found time for his favorite cause, fighting juvenile delinquency. He put on free concerts for teenagers, combining them with "Youth Forums," in which he urged the youngsters to come to terms with their problems.

Though he deserved better, Jordan's popularity declined as new musical styles came into vogue. Health problems defeated several valiant comeback attempts, forcing him into periodic retirement. Yet he never became bitter, kept working when he could, and patiently waited for the lucky break that never materialized. In the early 1970s, his career flared briefly, following a rousing appearance at the Newport Jazz Festival.

Although he was almost forgotten by a new generation of black performers whose success he had helped make possible, Louis Jordan had brought happiness to millions with his genuinely musical brand of joyful entertainment. To paraphrase one of his hits, whenever he lit up a stage or a jukebox, the good times rolled.

(1908–1975)

Sammy Kaye

Sweeten romantic songs with simpering saxes and slurping trombones.

"From my observation, the dancing public, ninety-nine per cent of it, comes to a place of dancing for dancing and romance," Sammy Kaye once announced, justifying his band's extreme emphasis on sweet rather than swing music. Disgruntled music critics put it a little differently: "His appeal is definitely not to lovers of music nearly so much as it is to just plain lovers."

Music purists agreed with the critics. So did many of his own musicians, who at one time became so fed up with the band's mechanical approach to music and Kaye's fetish for perfection, that they left en masse. But Sammy had his formula down so pat that he immediately organized another successful group, while the malcontents struggled to find new jobs elsewhere.

Sammy

Kaye's formula was simple. Sweeten romantic songs with simpering saxes and slurping trombones, set off by dainty, muted trumpets, and climax each arrangement with full ensemble sounds. Spice it all with a few catchy tricks, like singing, instead of announcing song titles, and personalize each tune with a vocal refrain by one or more of the half dozen or so singers in the band. Sammy called it all "Swing and Sway with Sammy Kaye," and it worked so well that his became one of the most popular of all big bands.

His analytical mind had been honed at Ohio University where he had studied for a degree in civil engineering. There he also organized his first band. During its first major postgraduate engagement at Cleveland's Hotel Statler, the manager noted that the band was commnicating with the people better than was Sammy, who had never lost his parents' Czechoslovakian accent. "He took me aside," Kaye recalled years later, "and said he didn't want to hurt my feelings, but he wondered, if he agreed to pay for them, whether I'd take elocution lessons. I did, and they helped me a lot. But now I wonder, when I look at Lawrence Welk's success on TV, whether I made a mistake taking those lessons!"

Kaye made very few mistakes during his career. A realist, he was not averse to using other leaders' tricks, like Kay Kyser's singing song titles or the exaggerated vibratos of Guy Lombardo's saxes. Each move was carefully planned to win fans and make money. His hit records, like "Daddy" and "Harbor Lights" and "It Isn't Fair," were carefully conceived and executed.

His "Sunday Serenade" radio series, successful for twelve successive years, was designed to bring relaxed, soothing sounds to the millions of conservative Americans, his biggest fans, who may have resented the more *au courant* swing music as an intrusion into their Sabbath. And his "So You Want to Lead a Band" routine, which he featured in theaters, dance halls, on radio and on TV, was calculated to bridge the gap between his band and his fans by bringing some of those fans right into the band itself. The gimmick proved to be a huge success as contestants vied to impress their fellow audience members by waving a baton at the Kaye musicians, with the winner receiving a sumptuous prize, a Sammy Kaye baton.

Sammy wasn't a tightwad, just a good businessman. His musicians always traveled first class, and Sammy himself traveled among entertainment's elite. During the 1960s and 1970s, while still occasionally leading a band and recording, he spent much time playing golf and overseeing his music publishing and other very successful business investments that had turned this once poor son of immigrant parents into one of the half dozen richest of all big-time bandleaders.

(1910–   )

Stan Kenton

"Some people with lots of nervous energy could feel what we were doing, but nobody else could."

"Every performance was an exercise in sustained hysteria," wrote Carol Easton in *Straight Ahead,* her incisive biography of bandleader Stan Kenton. "His intensity, his total commitment to his music was awesome to behold. The vulnerability on his face was like a public confession."

Few performers have ever been more dedicated to their art or have suffered more for it than Stanley Newcomb Kenton. For nearly two generations his progressive style of big band jazz attracted thousands upon thousands of performing and nonperforming converts. And yet by the mid-1970s, when others his age had retired, he was still holding forth in high school and college clinics and making personal appearances with bands composed of musicians who could have been his grandsons, selling the brand of overwhelming, thunderous, musi-

Stan in action

Stan at ease

cally advanced jazz that he remained convinced was the *right* approach to his art.

And six-foot-six Stan was quite a convincer. On the bandstand his wild gesticulations emphasized every nuance of his music. Off the bandstand he talked intensely for hours to anyone willing to listen long enough, explaining, extolling and, if necessary, trying to justify his progressive approach to music.

His own childhood in Los Angeles focused more on sports than on music until some talented cousins visited him when he was fourteen, played some jazz, and he was hooked. Even then a person of action, he soon formed his own high school band. Recordings of Earl Hines helped Stan develop the driving piano style that he displayed in solo gigs in small clubs and later in the bands of Everett Hoagland, Hal Grayson, Gus Arnheim, and Vido Musso. In 1941 he formed a band to play his own arrangements. On one of the band's first one-nighters, the reaction of the kids so impressed the manager of the Rendezvous in Balboa Beach that he hired the band for the 1941 summer season.

During the next four decades Stan worked so intensely selling his music that more than once the constant emotional and physical strain led to breakdowns. His talent and dedication evoked great respect from his musicians, such as future jazz stars Maynard Ferguson, Stan Getz, Bud Shank, Bill Holman, Pete Rugolo, and Shelly Manne, who recently noted that "Stan was so personal, always one of the fellows, and yet nobody ever lost any respect for him. And he was so wonderful with the public, too. He never fluffed anybody off."

But others raved in a different vein. Eddie Condon suggested that Stan's ponderous music "ought only to be played close to elephants and listened to by clowns." And fellow bandleader Charlie Barnet claimed that Kenton's heavy-handed, nonswinging approach "killed the dance band business," a charge that Stan himself never denied. "It was much too stiff," he later admitted. "Some people with lots of nervous energy could feel what we were doing, but nobody else could."

For once Stan was underselling his music. During his band's thirty-five-year history, millions shared and even became addicted to his progressive sounds. He had his share of hit records—"Artistry in Rhythm," "Eager Beaver," "And Her Tears Flowed Like Wine"—and probably the most loyal, devoted fans of any band ever. It was they who continued to support him when, in the late 1960s, Capitol Records dropped him but permitted him to issue through his own company, Creative World, Inc., forty albums of music he had recorded for them. To these he added many more by his band of the 1970s.

But by the latter 1970s the killing pace almost ended his life. A bad fall in a parking lot during a 1977 tour resulted in serious head injuries. Hospitalized for months, Kenton was brought back to the bandstand much too soon by his driving desire and dedication. Gaunt, tired-looking, unable to concentrate, and suffering from occasional loss of memory, he distressed his many friends and admirers with his refusal to relax and even retire, apparently unwilling to forsake his musical cause and to die anywhere except on the bandstand.

(1912–   )

B. B. King

A magnificently casual stage presence—loose, easy, beautifully timed.

"Blues is what I do best," said the veteran B. B. King, whose guitar playing and blues singing have inspired many much younger performers. "If Frank Sinatra can be tops in his field, Nat Cole in his, Bach and Beethoven in theirs, why can't I be great and known for it in blues?"

That was in 1968 when he had just arrived as a major headline performer after twenty years of working "the chitlin' circuit." During those twenty years he had played dances in back-country shacks and neonlit city bars, developing a magnificently casual stage presence—loose, easy, beautifully timed and always in complete control of his performance and his audience.

B.B. is not his name. He was born Riley B. King on a cotton plantation in Itta Bena, a small town on the Mississippi delta, where he walked five miles a day to a school. But his family needed money, and so he started picking cotton—as much as four hundred pounds a day—and then began singing the blues for money, "so I could eat regular." He was influenced by the records of Blind Lemon Jefferson, and, after serving in the Army in World War II, he became a singing disc jockey on WDIA in Memphis where he was billed as "The Blues Boy from Beale Street," which was shortened to "Blues Boy" and then to "B.B."

He began recording in 1949 and, a year later, had a hit, "Three O'Clock Blues." Spurred by this success, he gave up his disc jockey job and went on the road. For almost twenty years he played more than 300 one-night stands each year. One year he did 342 "and that's enough to kill you," he said.

He sang the blues in a voice that had a touch of huskiness and with diction that was precise without being ostentatiously careful. As a guitarist, he was an extraordinary virtuoso, playing on an instrument he called Lucille.

He grew up admiring Count Basie's band and the way Jimmy Rushing sang with it. His guitar playing has been strongly affected by the famous French gypsy Django Reinhardt and by the first of the great amplified guitarists, Charlie Christian.

"You can still hear a little of Django in my playing," he once admitted. "But you also hear T-Bone Walker and Lonnie Johnson. The influence of a lot of great musicians that have been around me over the years has rubbed off on me. I don't copy them. But I can take things I've heard them play and put B. B. King in them and it comes out bluesy."

And, in the same way, some who have heard B. B. King have had him rub off on them. In the mid-1960s, when King's career was in a slump, a young

"Blues Is King . . . King Is Soul"

and popular guitarist, Mike Bloomfield, helped bring King to the attention of youthful white audiences by playing in King's style and extolling him during his concert appearances. And over in England the Rolling Stones admitted to using King as a basis for their early playing.

Gradually, more and more rock guitarists became influenced, both directly and indirectly by King, so that from the late 1960s on, the basic technique of rock guitar playing reflected his style. At a Newport Jazz Festival, one of them, Johnny Winter, made a big mistake: he went up against King in a "cutting" contest. Almost every other rock guitarist would have suffered a similar fate.

In May 1977 he became the first popular singer to receive an honorary degree from Yale. The citation read: "You are prominent among those who have made great performances in music from their own lives. In your rendition of the blues you have always taken us beyond entertainment to the deeper message of suffering and endurance that gave rise to your form. In recognition of your particular and personal contribution to our American culture, Yale is honored to confer upon you the degree of Doctor of Music."

B.B.'s business card puts it more simply. "Blues is King," reads a line in the upper left-hand corner. "King is Soul."

(1925–   )

Carole King

A woman of many talents, not the least of which is surviving.

Her second album, released in 1971, made musical history, selling over ten million copies in just two years—more than any Beatles album. On its cover, her youthful appearance and peaceful pose belied years of struggle in the pop-music jungle. Ever since she was sixteen, prodigiously cranking out hits in a "musical chicken coop" in New York's Brill Building, her music had been making other people rich. By 1963 more than two hundred of her songs had been recorded by artists as diverse as Steve Lawrence ("Go Away, Little Girl"), Bobby Vee ("Take Good Care of My Baby"), and Little Eva ("Locomotion"). She is a woman of many talents, not the least of which is surviving.

At Queens College, Carol Klein was a middle-class Jewish girl from Brooklyn whose after-school hours were spent recording demos of her songs by the dozen. Some became hits—for other people. At the end of her freshman year a chemistry major named Gerry Goffin became her lyricist and husband. The newlyweds quit school and joined a stable of would-be songwriters working for Aldon Music, a publishing firm owned by Al Nevins and Don Kirshner (known in the trade as "The Man with the Golden Ear," referring to his genius for anticipating commercial trends). There, in what she later described as "a little cubbyhole with just enough room for a piano, a bench, and maybe a chair for the lyricist— if you were lucky," she and Gerry wrote a succession of hits. The first was "Will You Love Me Tomorrow?" recorded in 1960 by the Shirelles. For two years scarcely a week went by without a Goffin-King song appearing on the charts. (Ringo Starr paid fellow Beatles John and Paul the compliment of being "fantastic composers, right up there in the Gerry Goffin–Carole King class.")

In 1966 they contributed songs to the Monkees, another Kirshner brainchild. Their biggest hit of 1967 was Aretha Franklin's recording of their "Natural Woman." But in 1968 Carole and Gerry separated. Carole moved to the West Coast with her two daughters in search of "a new identity," which she found with dizzying speed. Her first album as a performer—*Writer: Carole King*— was recorded on Lou Adler's Ode label in 1970. On it she sang and played piano, backed by a group called the City. It included bassist Charles Larkey, whom she later married and with whom she has a daughter. The album was a modest success but fell far short of preparing the industry or the public for the encore. *Tapestry* was a *tour de force,* with music, vocals, piano, keyboards, and more than half of the lyrics by Carole King. The National Academy of Recording Arts and Sciences awarded her Grammys for the best album, best song ("You've Got a Friend"), best record ("It's Too Late"), and best pop

Carole

female vocal performance of 1971. "It was Carole King's year," said *Newsday*'s Robert Christgau, "and only a sorehead could gainsay these choices."

Since 1971 Carole King albums have appeared regularly. Frequently the lyrics, as well as the music, are her own. Like her life-style, her lyrics are simple and direct; love and friendship are favorite themes. She rarely appears in concert and even more rarely grants interviews, pleading that her lyrics (such as "My friend, there's no end to the music") speak for her. With eloquence and insight they do.

(1941–   )

Wayne King

Music for easy dancing, easy listening, and easy remembering.

The old folks liked him more than the young folks, and little wonder, for Wayne King specialized in playing music for easy dancing, easy listening, and easy remembering. His was one of the most popular orchestras of the 1930s, especially in the Midwest, where people liked their music on the conservative side.

King was a hard worker. While attending Valparaiso University he commuted nightly to his saxophone-playing job with a local Chicago band. He also doubled in an insurance firm and as a garage and railroad mechanic.

He was playing with Del Lampe's band in Chicago's Trianon Ballroom when its sister dance emporium, the Aragon, was opened in 1927, and Lampe formed a second band fronted by King. And so in the Aragon began the career of a band that belied the title of its first recording, "To Be Forgotten." A year later, in 1930, King recorded "The Waltz You Saved for Me," his syrupy theme song, which he had composed, and in the following year an emerging ballad called "Star Dust."

King's fortunes began to flourish in 1931 when he was approached by a brother and sister, who were manufacturing cosmetics on a modest scale in the back of their house. They hired Wayne and his orchestra for a weekly commercial radio show named after their products. With King's soft, melodious alto sax featured along with snippets of sentimental poetry readings, "The Lady Esther Serenade" drew so many listeners that it graduated from a local radio show to one of the country's most-listened-to programs. Not only did the manufacturing family amass a fortune, but King, who had taken the job at five hundred dollars per program, wound up getting fifteen thousand a week!

By then he had become firmly established as "The Waltz King," appearing in chic hotel rooms as well as in ballrooms throughout America. Occasionally his band would play peppier tunes, and one of them, "Josephine," written by King and two others, became his biggest hit record. But otherwise King, a hard-nosed businessman who sincerely believed his music was good music, wisely refused to change his format. He did spice up his radio show for a while with one of popular music's great singers, Buddy Clark, and, while he was a captain in the U. S. Army, he had Bob Eberly singing in his unit. But otherwise it was "schmaltz as usual."

During the early 1970s, Trigger Alpert, Glenn Miller's former bassist and then highly successful portrait photographer, took some pictures of King. "He looked absolutely fantastic," Trigger reported. "He had a band bus that looked

The Waltz King

as big as an apartment, and you could see he still loved the adoration of his fans. He told me that women still wanted to kiss his saxophone, and that he planned to will it to the Smithsonian Institution."

Which is precisely where musicians, somewhat more modern than King, believed it had belonged, even when he was playing it.

(1901–   )

The Kingston Trio

Uniform button-down collars, striped shirts, and thick doses of college humor.

The folk music craze of the late 1950s and early '60s was largely due to the success of the Kingston Trio. Though roundly damned at the time by purists for being false and "show-bizzy," they presented and popularized (though often compromising the texts of) native American songs of fable, brag, adventure, and romance. They inspired thousands of young people to take up the guitar; they created an audience that Bob Dylan and, later, the Beatles inherited.

The original members of the Trio were Dave Guard, Nick Reynolds, and Bob Shane. Guard, who was to be the "acknowledged leader" of the group, was a friend of Shane's; both had grown up in Hawaii. As college students in California, Guard was enrolled at Stanford University while Shane and his acquaintance, Nick Reynolds, were attending Menlo Business College.

Guard was the catalyst of the group, which appealed primarily to college kids, and he selected its name "as a combination of something that sounded Ivy League and also had something to do with calypso—that's what we were singing then—so we chose Kingston, from the town in Jamaica where they have rum. The stuff we were singing then really gassed us, even though the harmonies were strictly Whiffenpoof."

The Trio first sang at campus hangouts for free beer. It dropped its calypso programs when the style became saturated with amateur and professional groups and at Guard's insistence switched to American folk tunes. They polished their act and, after an appearance at the Purple Onion club in San Francisco, were signed to a recording contract. Their first single, "Tom Dooley," was a national sensation and sparked the folk mania.

Many hits followed: "M.T.A.," "Worried Man Blues," "Where Have All the Flowers Gone," and "Scotch and Soda," a witty, sophisticated jazz ballad original by Guard.

Despite their whopping success with the public, the Trio came in for increasing amounts of criticism from knowledgeable folk fans, and there was increased pressure from competing performers in the field. The trappings of the Trio's success—uniform button-down collars, striped shirts, and thick doses of college humor—increasingly disturbed Guard, who in 1960 announced his intention of leaving the group due to a "conflict of interest" regarding the presentation of the act. He wanted more authenticity while Shane and Reynolds were leery of jeopardizing a group career that was worth millions of dollars a year. Guard departed with a $300,000 quit-sum, formed a quintet called the Whiskeyhill

Kingston Trio's Bob Shane, Nick Guard, Dave Reynolds

Singers, which flopped, and later wandered to Australia as a vocal coach and musical arranger.

Nick Reynolds commented wryly on the departure: "Yes, it's all over. We had to give up the secret handshake, and he had to turn in his striped shirts." Guard was replaced by John Stuart.

The Trio continued to have hits, like "Greenback Dollar," until 1965, but they were displaced, first by Peter, Paul and Mary—another slick folk group—then by Bob Dylan and finally by the Beatles. Acknowledging changing tastes and times, and frankly admitting they were "no longer creative," the Trio officially disbanded in 1967.

Gladys Knight and The Pips

"I used to think if I could have a whole hot dog to myself, that would be style."

During a performance at the Waldorf-Astoria Hotel in the early 1970s, one of the Pips fanned himself with his hand and called out to the others: "Say, can I get a handkerchief? I'm really workin' up a sweat." Gladys Knight corrected him: "Honey, when you are in Georgia you 'sweat.' When you are at the Waldorf, you 'perspire.'"

Gladys Knight and the Pips (her brother Merald and cousins William Guest and Edward Patten) have known lowdown sweat and hightone perspiration through a career that began when they were children in Atlanta, Georgia, and took them through twenty, mostly rough, years. Then, in 1972, Gladys' smoky voice, adaptability to different kinds of material, emotional range, and subtle phrasing of lyric lines, resembling in all these characteristics the great Lena Horne, finally brought the group to national fame.

Showered with recording industry and show business awards, selling millions of records—"Imagination," "The Way We Were," "If I Were Your Woman," "Midnight Train to Georgia"—the group, in a few rewarding years, made up for all the lean and hungry ones. They also maintained strong loyalties to their large families, refusing to appear on certain holidays, like the Fourth of July, because such days are reserved for family picnics. "I like the people I love to be around me," Gladys says. "I can't get enough of them. I like to touch."

At a family gathering when she was eight, "everybody was supposed to get up and entertain. So my sister and Merald and my cousins and me, we began to sing and kind of fool around. And another cousin—everybody called him Pip—said, 'I can get you people some work.' He got us bookings in clubs and lodges, that sort of thing."

The group went to New York in the early 1960s—with nearly a decade of professional experience behind them—and found the town hard to handle. They came close to starvation. "That was what we called the two-hot-dog time. This place sold two hot dogs for a quarter, and there were days when two hot dogs were all the food the four of us had. I used to think if I could have a whole hot dog to myself, that would be style."

Their early recordings, like "Every Beat of My Heart," were popular but brought them few rewards. They recorded for various small labels, seldom receiving royalties. One label didn't tell them they were releasing the record; another folded when the Internal Revenue Service foreclosed; and even when they signed with the powerful Motown Records of Detroit they found themselves given low priority on the artist roster. Ironically, their major hits began to come all at once as their association with Motown drew to a close. Singing with Buddah, a New York label, the Pips continued their streak of million-selling records and bookings in the best clubs as well as making numerous television appearances, bidding farewell to the two-hot-dog days and welcoming the steak-and-potatoes years.

Although stars, the Pips have continued to conduct themselves by lady-and-gentleman standards. They still form a prayer circle before each performance, as they did when they were kids. Gladys once told an interviewer, who was astonished that she had shown up on time for the appointment, "I'm not big enough to be late," and she expressed in four words the determination that have enabled the group to survive their long and ugly apprenticeship and to enjoy their bravely won fame: "We will be *heard.*"

Gladys and her Pips

Andre Kostelanetz

"My heavens, we are being heard in Alaska and San Francisco—what shall we do?"

Even among those select figures able to span the gulf between popular and classical music Andre Kostelanetz is special: he pioneered the use of radio and records to bring quality music of both sorts to a wide and varied public.

The diminutive, Russian-born maestro summed it up himself thus: "We are living at a time when to spead the gospel is very appropriate—radio, television, and records can reach in one evening as many people as someone in another century reached in two lives."

A simple formula—but one which has guided a great career. Trained at St. Petersburg, the young Kostelanetz plunged into the infant medium of radio shortly after his arrival in the United States in the early 1920s. He soon had a regular show of his own.

"It was very experimental," the conductor recalled. "I remember thinking, 'My heavens, we are being heard in Alaska and San Francisco—what shall we do?' We could not possibly have known at that time whether what we were doing was right or wrong."

Judged on popularity alone it was eminently right. The idea of programs mixing popular and concert music, played and sung by stars of both worlds, drew an ever-expanding audience. Throughout the 1930s and '40s Kostelanetz stocked his orchestras with great jazz musicians like the Dorsey Brothers, Benny Goodman, and Artie Shaw, blending their talents with those of pop singers like Kay Thompson and Tony Martin, and of classical artists like Jascha Heifetz, Arthur Rubinstein, and his future wife, soprano Lily Pons.

In those years Kostelanetz made his first records, some of them intricate jazz-flavored scores. From the start he took an active hand in achieving good recordings, devising special seating plans and microphone placements for the effects he wanted. He himself wrote many of the musical arrangements; respected writers like Gordon Jenkins, Eddie Sauter, Raymond Scott, and Claude Thornhill contributed additional scores.

"It didn't take me long to realize that music is not what we play in the studio, but what comes out on the air or on records," the maestro said.

During World War II he and Miss Pons traveled widely, conducting orchestras of U.S. servicemen from Germany to Burma and China. "I learned a great lesson from that," he said. "I realized that audiences loved to hear great melodies from Broadway shows but also responded enthusiastically to a movement from a symphony. They were *interested* in both."

This revelation carried over into civilain life, with Kostelanetz's famed New York Philharmonic Promenade Concerts at Lincoln Center and to outdoor concerts in Central Park, which have drawn audiences estimated at 150,000 or more. The recordings continued, and with the coming of television the Kostelanetz touch found yet another outlet.

Could there be anything left undone in so illustrious a career? A shake of the head. "Just more of the same, I think. We are still battling the great battle to increase concert audiences. In the long run, after all, the best way to hear music is face to face.

"I'd like to be remembered as a musician and conductor who has done a great deal to interest as many people as possible in music. That would make me happy."

(1901–   )

Kosty

Kris Kristofferson

"I was always chained to that damned Rhodes Scholarship. I had to break away."

A balladeer of the dispossessed, the troubadour of losing and losers, he brought a gentle intensity to his portraits of frustration, defeat, and lost romance, which challenged the orthodoxy of country music and compelled it to look at the sorrows of living without sentimentalizing them.

Hailed as a poet, leader of the "Nashville Underground," and one of the foremost singer-songwriters of the 1960s and '70s, Kristofferson remarked soon after his discovery in 1969, "I got a brilliant future behind me," a comment on his life's crowded but anticlimactic first thirty-three turmoil-filled years of his life.

Born in Brownsville, Texas, he moved with his family to California in the early 1950s. "Country music wasn't as popular out there as it is now. I was buying Hank Williams records, and I was really considered a square."

After graduation from college, where he was active in sports and the ROTC (his father was a major general in the Air Force), he won a short story contest in the *Atlantic Monthly* magazine and a Rhodes Scholarship to Oxford University. He had already started to write songs and play the guitar. While in England he was signed by a personal manager who sought to turn him into "Kris Carson." Kristofferson's attempt to portray a Presley-style rocker was a huge failure.

He earned a degree in literature from Oxford, joined the American Army, trained as a paratrooper and helicopter pilot and spent three tours of duty in Germany. While performing in a military club he was advised by a fellow pilot with contacts in Nashville to submit his early songs to a publisher. Transferring back to the United States (where he turned down an offer to become an English literature instructor at West Point), Kristofferson spent a giddy, galvanizing two weeks in "Music City U.S.A.," meeting songwriters, singing and playing and getting to know the city.

"I bailed out in Nashville. When I started writing songs again, I felt like I'd come back to life." He abandoned his army career to devote all his time to music.

He built up a catalog of songs that were to make him famous: "Me and Bobby McGee," "Sunday Mornin' Comin' Down," and "Help Me Make It Through the Night" among them. But he was also soon broke, forced to take menial jobs as a drudge in a recording studio, where he met Johnny Cash ("They had to tell me who he was"), and as a sweeper in a saloon. "Well, you really made it to the top there, son. Janitor in a bar. But the beauty of

Kris

droppin' to the bottom is that it wipes the slate clean; I was always chained to that damned Rhodes Scholarship. I had to break away."

He was financially desperate when a phone call came from country star Roger Miller, telling him to come to California. Miller recorded "Me and Bobby McGee," as did dozens of other performers. Johnny Cash became one of his boosters and sponsors. Almost overnight Kristofferson was a major Nashville figure, and he became a nationally known personality through his own recordings and film roles, including *Blume in Love, Alice Doesn't Live Here Anymore,* and *A Star Is Born.* "Some of the characters I play come dangerously close to reality," he recently admitted. His subsequent marriage to singer Rita Coolidge, with whom he often performed, helped to sober him up and settle him down.

His career as an actor, in which he showed natural inclination and quickly acquired technique, sometimes tended to overshadow his later musical activities. Artistically and commercially successful, he was no longer the loser, loner, or outsider. He settled comfortably, if sometimes with less inspiration, into the life of a star, of a "talent conglomerate: songwriter, poet, singer, movie star, sex symbol." But he has remained an intelligent, perceptive man with a wry wit, who, recently commenting on the times when "I was doing too much of everything in excess," including drinking, quipped, "I'm better now, I think. I can't remember, so I can't be sure." Often called a poet, he would agree with a remark by the rakehell bard Lord Byron: "I woke up one morning and found myself famous."

(1936–   )

Gene Krupa

He made the drummer "a high-priced guy."

"I succeeded in doing two things in my life," Gene Krupa admitted. "First of all, I made the drummer a high-priced guy, and secondly, I was able to project enough so that people were drawn to jazz."

Krupa, the most popular jazz drummer of all time, achieved both these goals in the years 1935 to 1938 as the gum-chewing, hair-waving drummer in Benny Goodman's band. The youngest of four children and the only one not given musical training, he had begun preparing for the priesthood when he was sidetracked by the call of the drums. "I was working at a soda fountain one summer in a small joint and sometimes, when the drummer wanted to dance with his wife, he'd ask me to sit in." When the drummer took sick, Gene took his job.

Better jobs with bigger bands followed, culminating in the gig with Goodman, who recently called Krupa "an inspiration to the band." However, back in 1938, Goodman had been calling him less favorable names. The two had a falling-out (some attributed it to Goodman's jealousy; others to Krupa's ambition), and Gene left to form his own band. For five years it was starred in top spots all over the country, in movies, and on many hit recordings, some featuring Gene's drums and others his rhythmic singer, Anita O'Day, and his powerhouse trumpeter, Roy Eldridge. But in 1943 Krupa's career collapsed when Gene was arrested and jailed in San Francisco for possession of marijuana and allegedly impairing the morals of a minor. The minor (his valet) recanted, however, and the charge was dropped. Gene was freed, but the episode fortified the distorted claims of those who couldn't imagine how anyone could drum with such gusto without being "a dope fiend." The incident itself was grossly distorted in the movie *The Gene Krupa Story,* starring Sal Mineo as a totally inaccurate, cocky Krupa. Actually Gene was always extremely modest and polite, well disciplined, deeply dedicated to music, and greatly respected by his fellow musicians. Upon his release from jail, he was hired by Tommy Dorsey and soon thereafter by his old boss, Goodman. A few months later he made his debut with his new band, which combined a large string section's sonorities with the emerging bop sounds.

When the big bands began disbanding in the early 1950s, Krupa formed a quartet, which he led for almost twenty years. He occasionally took time off to tour throughout Europe and Asia, as well as in the United States, with Jazz at the Philharmonic, Norman Granz's troupe of jazz all-stars, whose concerts often climaxed with stirring drum duels between Krupa and Buddy Rich.

Following the death of his first wife, the former Ethel Mae Fawcett, whom he had married, divorced, and remarried, he and his new wife, Patty, adopted a girl and a retarded boy. Spending at least half his time in his Yonkers, New York, home, he became deeply involved in work for retarded children, captaining a softball team (he had always been an avid baseball fan) that played for his newfound cause. But a combination of debilitating illnesses slowed his softball and drumming careers. Shortly before he died, he appeared in Carnegie Hall with the original Goodman Quartet. Though obviously in pain and very weak, he still managed one more time to inspire the group to great emotional and musical heights. In July 1973 he was honored by a host of fellow drummers during a special ceremony in the midst of the Newport Jazz Festival. Their tribute to him as a warm, decent man, an outstanding dedicated and creative artist, and, in fact, as the drummer who had made many of them "high-priced guys," came just in time. A few months later he was gone.

(1909–1973)

Gene

Kay Kyser

He focused on more than just the music itself.

"Evenin' folks, how y'all?" oozed the southern drawl over the airwaves as Kay Kyser began another of his broadcasts that successfully blended his personal charm and his band's mixture of novelty tunes and ballads. How successfully? When Glenn Miller, at the height of his popularity, was asked if he envied any other leader, he replied, "Yes, one, Kay Kyser." The reason? Because Kyser's band at a million dollars a year was the only one outgrossing Miller's.

Bespectacled, craggy-faced, sweet-talking James Kay Kyser had set out to become a lawyer. But something occurred during his undergraduate days at the University of North Carolina to change his mind: He formed a band, a band that became so successful in the Southeast that he forgot about the legal bar and concentrated solely on the musical ones.

Actually, Kyser focused on more than just the music itself. Bright and witty he compensated for his lack of talent as an instrumentalist by coming up with novel ideas that attracted people to his band. On its first major engagement at the Miramar Hotel in Santa Monica, California, he invited dancers to "Swing and Sway with Music Played Kay Kyser's Way." That "way" featured the singing of (instead of the usual announcing of) song titles to introduce each selection, plus a few bars of the band's theme song, "Thinking of You," vamped before each vocal chorus while the singer's name was being announced, a gimmick later successfully copied by other bandleaders.

What it lacked in musicality, the band more than made up for with its showmanship, built around Kyser's personality and fertile brain. During a 1938 engagement at Chicago's famed Blackhawk Restaurant, Kay and a young Music Corporation of America executive named Lew Wasserman, who later was to become chairman of the MCA board, concocted a local radio game show in which members of the audience were asked to identify songs that the band was playing. (A young pageboy named David Susskind helped line up the contestants.) Thanks to Kyser's wit and warmth and ingratiating personality, his Kollege of Musical Knowledge became successful enough to attract a national sponsor and for several years thereafter reigned as one of radio's highest rated programs.

With so much important airtime, music publishers turned to Kyser to plug their songs, which he also recorded. Thus, he came up with such big hits as "Three Little Fishies," "Who Wouldn't Love You," "Strip Polka," "Praise the Lord and Pass the Ammunition," and "On a Slow Boat to China." Kay

Dean of the Kollege of Music Knowledge

featured his singers, and he had some good ones, romantic crooners like Harry Babbitt and Michael Douglas (who later became daytime TV talk show host Mike Douglas), comedians like Ish Kabibble and Sully Mason, and various girls like Julie Conway, Trudy Erwin, Lucy Ann Polk, Jane Russell (who recorded one song with the band), Ginny Sims, the band's most important singer, and the beautiful and intelligent Georgia Southern, whom Kay married and who mothered their three children.

The band always had a family feel. Kay would never hire a musician unless the band members approved. But he remained very much in charge, driving his men hard but with patience, urging them on with such homey exhortations as, "Hoppy, jumpy, skippy!" On the bandstand he may have acted like a buffoon, but according to his longtime arranger, George Duning, "Off the bandstand Kay was a practical but shrewd businessman, an unassuming person of clean habits and simple tastes." He was also very religious, and after the big band era devoted his life to his family and to another successful career with the Christian Science Church, first as a reader and eventually as national head of its Film and Broadcast Division.

(1906–   )

Frankie Laine

"The first he-man singer . . . who the blue-collar guys could identify with."

"I sang pretty and I sang often. But all I got out of it was a plate of spaghetti."

That's how Frankie Laine described his lack of success, during almost twenty years of trying hard to show the world how well he could sing. When success did finally come to him, it couldn't have happened, as his many friends pointed out, to a nicer, friendlier, more unassuming guy. Mitch Miller, who produced such Laine hits as "That's My Desire," "Lucky Ol' Sun," "Jezebel," "Mule Train," and "I Believe," described the virile-sounding, extroverted Laine as "a great guy—the first real he-man singer, the first singer, other than those doing country songs, who the blue-collar guys could identify with."

Frankie L.

Born Frank Paul Lo Vecchio, the big, barrel-chested Laine had always loved music, especially jazz, and so during the 1930s he hung around New York jazz clubs, hoping he'd be asked to sing. His emotional phrasing impressed Bobby Hackett and Joe Marsala, who occasionally invited him to "sit in." But the city's club owners weren't convinced, and so Frankie, who once had won a 145-hour dance marathon, moved on to Chicago where he taught dancing at the Aragon Ballroom "so I could get in free to hear Perry Como singing with the Ted Weems band." When Weems didn't accept Como's suggestion that Laine be hired as his replacement, Perry recommended Frankie to his old boss, Freddie Carlone. He got the job but left after a few days, unable to adjust his jazz-tinged singing to the Lombardo-like simperings of the band.

Next, a return to New York where Frankie settled for another gig, singing on radio station WINS at five dollars a week and at small, well-hidden clubs in nearby New Jersey. Some months later he had graduated to the College Inn in Cleveland where he introduced an unknown girl singer, June Hart, so exuberantly that she was hired to replace him. No sore loser, he hung around the club because he loved to listen to her, especially when she sang a song called "That's My Desire."

Three years later, two and a half of which he had spent working in a defense plant ("When I got that first paycheck for sixty-eight bucks, I gave up singing altogether!"), he was invited to "sit in" at Billy Berg's, the Hollywood hangout for musicians. "I was singing 'Rockin' Chair' "Laine recalled, "when some guy jumped up and acted real excited. I could see him talking with Billy [Berg] and I could feel he liked what I was doing. It turned out the guy was Hoagy Carmichael, who only wrote the song. He liked the way I did it so much that he got Billy to give me a regular job.

"One night at Berg's I decided to try out 'That's My Desire.' It broke up the joint. It was the greatest hand I'd ever gotten." Mercury Records headman Berle Adams heard him, signed him, recorded the tune, it became a smash hit, and Frankie was on his way. When Mercury producer Mitch Miller went over to Columbia Records, Frankie went too, and a series of big, "he-man" hits followed.

A quarter of a century later, neither his powerhouse singing nor his warm, personal style had changed much. "When you succeed that late in life," Miller pointed out, "you know how to take it." Laine continued to play top spots throughout the world, interspersing oft-requested big hits with the kind of quality tunes that jazz musicians, with whom he continued to associate, liked to play. "It's the pulse and the beat in what I sing that counts," he once explained. "I just use my voice instead of a horn."

(1913–   )

Lambert, Hendricks and Ross

A swinging antidote to the raucous and/or pretentious vocalisms.

Scat, the art of instrumentalized jazz singing, was not new when the vocal trio of Dave Lambert, Jon Hendricks, and Annie Ross made its debut in 1958. Louis Armstrong invented it, Cab Calloway popularized it, Leo Watson surrealized it, and Dizzy Gillespie transformed it into bebop.

But nothing like the swinging threesome had been heard before. Taking their cue from Eddie Jefferson and King Pleasure, who had hit upon the idea of setting words to famous jazz solos, they recast Count Basie's classic big band records in vocal terms, emulating both section and solo passages with such élan that they were soon acclaimed as "the hottest new group in jazz."

Lambert, the senior member, was a pioneer bebop singer who had worked with the bands of Gene Krupa and Charlie Barnet. A gifted vocal arranger, he devised choral backgrounds for Charlie Parker and achieved considerable success in the commercial jingle business. A bearded pixie of a man, he was the soul of kindness, always willing to lend struggling singers a helping hand.

Hendricks, one of seventeen siblings, had sung in his father's church in Toledo, Ohio, taught himself drums, and eked out a living as a performer while attending law school before moving to New York. A facile and clever rhymer, he had a knack for devising lyrics to improvised jazz solos and had joined with Lambert in some unsuccessful recording ventures.

Annie Ross, born Annabelle Short into a Scottish theatrical family, was raised in the United States by her aunt, singer-actress Ella Logan, made her debut at five in the "Our Gang" films, and played Judy Garland's kid sister in *Presenting Lily Mars.* She sang jazz in Paris boîtes, worked briefly with Lionel Hampton's band, appeared in the successful revue *Cranks* in London and on Broadway, and made her jazz reputation singing her own zany lyrics to the bebop instrumental "Twisted."

Annie was among the thirteen singers assembled by Lambert and Hendricks to record their Basie transcriptions. It didn't work. "We sounded like an operatic choir," said Hendricks. But Annie so impressed the partners that they redid the project as a trio, beefed up by multi-taping. The resultant album, *Sing a Song of Basie,* was an instant hit. The tape gimmick was dispensed with, and for four swinging years, LH&R basked in success, on records and in person.

A typical LH&R piece featured effective teamwork sparked by Annie's great range and uncanny ability to imitate high-note trumpet "shakes"; tricky lyrics

Dave Lambert, Annie Ross,
Jon Hendricks

by Hendricks (dubbed "the James Joyce of jazz" by *Time* magazine) delivered in his machine-gun style; and Lambert's deft arranging touches and humorous singing. They soon went beyond Basie for material, and such Hendricks originals as "Gimme That Wine" further enhanced the repertoire.

Annie left for reasons of health in early 1962. A worthy successor was found in the charming person of the Ceylonese actress Yolande Bavan, and the group's name was changed accordingly. Lambert left two years later, and in 1964 Hendricks resumed his career as a single performer, while writing more clever lyrics and sometimes working as a journalist.

Resuming her interrupted stage career, Annie Ross was a big hit in the London production of *Threepenny Opera.* Dave Lambert, always the good samaritan, was killed while changing a tire for a stranger on the Connecticut Turnpike.

The LH&R formula was bound to exhaust its potential, but in its heyday, the group's pleasing blend of hip verbal wit and clever musicality provided a swinging antidote to the raucous and/or pretentious vocalisms of rock.

(Dave Lambert: 1917–1966)
(Jon Hendricks: 1921–   )
(Annie Ross: 1930–   )

Eddie Lang

The soul of an Italian artist and the drive of an American jazzman.

Born Salvatore Massaro in South Philadelphia, quiet, soft-spoken Eddie Lang played his guitar with the soul of an Italian artist and the drive of an American jazzman. Originally a violinist, he phrased as if he were playing a melody instrument, while producing a strong, full sound from his acoustic guitar, sometimes sounding as if he were actually plucking up each string to form each note. His "breaks" (short, ad-lib solos between written ensembles or longer solos)—whether a four-note single-string phrase or a sensitively wrought chord progression—were like minicompositions, in perfect rapport with what preceded and followed them. His longer solos, using the melody simply stated, showed his innate taste and musical feeling. His taste, sensitivity, and technique, unmatched

Guitarist Lang

by any guitarist before him, made him the favorite of his late 1920s and early 1930s jazz peers, and he was constantly being asked to perform and record with them. Never a very good reader, he had an amazingly retentive ear and needed to hear a song—even a full arrangement—only once before it became part of his musical memory.

Earlier in the 1920s he had blended his solid rhythm chords and big-toned single-string solos with the horns of the Dorsey Brothers in the Scranton Sirens, a vigorous Pennsylvania coal-area dance band. During one of its out-of-state engagements at the Beaux Arts Cafe in Atlantic City, who should come by to sit in but an old boyhood chum, Joe Venuti, with whom Lang had previously played violin duets. This time they tried a different combination, Venuti still on fiddle, accompanied by Lang's guitar. Thus began one of the most famous and distinguished duos in the history of jazz.

Together they made many records, on their own and also with the bands of Jean Goldkette and Paul Whiteman. Eddie also recorded as a sideman with Bix Beiderbecke, Red Nichols, the Dorsey Brothers, the Boswell Sisters, and others. And as "Blind Willie Dunn" he waxed a dozen "down-home" duets with Lonnie Johnson, the legendary New Orleans guitarist, who, according to jazz historian Leonard Feather, averred that "Lang could play guitar better than anyone I knew: The sides I made with him were my greatest experience."

By 1931 Eddie was playing regularly with Whiteman, and when band singer Bing Crosby left to go out on his own, he asked Lang to become his accompanist. It was a happy and successful relationship that ended all too soon and abruptly when Lang developed a fatal embolism following a tonsillectomy that he had been postponing for several years because of a fear of doctors. Crosby, who had been urging the operation, later said simply, "I sure wish I hadn't."

(1902–1933)

Mario Lanza

He squandered what once promised to be *the* glorious contemporary voice of opera for too many helpings of spaghetti.

Everything about him was big: his voice, his physique, his furniture-smashing bouts, his income, his appetite. His Caruso-like tenor was so emotionally stirring and powerful it made bobby-soxers, presumably unfamiliar with Caruso and "Celeste Aida" and "Vesti la giubba," scream for more; inspired fans to drive hundreds of miles for his autograph; propelled him into top slots on both classical and popular music charts; made his concert tours the most lucrative of any since Nelson Eddy's, and turned Mario Lanza into a top moneymaking film star. His 1951 smash film, *The Great Caruso,* grossed a reported five million dollars for MGM. In 1951, referring to his new radio program, "The Mario Lanza Show," Variety called him "one of the hottest properties in the film and disc field." His recording of "Be My Love" sold a million and a half copies. His "The Loveliest Night of the Year" also passed the million sales mark.

Predictions were rife that Lanza, inheritor of the Caruso mantle, would be the greatest tenor of his time, even of the century. Had he loved to sing more than he loved to eat, he might have proved them right. Known first in his South Philadelphia neighborhood as Alfred Arnold Cocozza—Freddie for short—Lanza was the son of an opera-loving disabled World War I veteran and a mother who reportedly yearned for an opera career. Besides absorbing arias and the Caruso sound from records, Mario took part in the usual inner city capers, went in for weight lifting and boxing, and played baseball and semipro football.

Having sung along with Caruso records from childhood, he burst into song on his own, at either age twelve or twenty (accounts vary), studied briefly, was heard by Boston Symphony conductor Serge Koussevitzky and invited to sing at the Berkshire Music Festival in the summer of 1942. Poised then for a concert and opera career, he was drafted into the Air Force and sang in two service shows, *On the Beam* and *Winged Victory.* After his discharge and fifteen months' study with an opera teacher, he hit the concert trail. MGM's Louis B. Mayer heard him at the Hollywood Bowl and gave him a seven-year contract, assuring him he'd be "a singing Clark Gable" some day. As his popularity zoomed with his first three films—*That Midnight Kiss* (1949), *Toast of New Orleans* (1951), *The Great Caruso* (1951)—so did his weight. Dieting problems postponed his fourth, *Because You Are Mine.* In 1952 he recorded the songs

Lanza

for *The Student Prince* but did not report for its filming. The recordings "sang" instead for nonsinging Edmund Purdom cast in the Lanza role. His recordings came to his own rescue when he mouthed the lyrics with them for his 1954 TV debut on "Shower of Stars." Weight loss, it was said, had impaired his voice. He did sing "live" on a subsequent "Shower of Stars," but missed engagements, cancellations, and alienations became as much his routine as overeating, frantic dieting, and destructive temper explosions.

In 1953 Mario left with his wife and four children for Rome, where he made three more films, gave his fans new songs to cherish, like "Arrivederci Roma," and died there of an embolism in the heart at age thirty-eight. Hung with the

Caruso identity and ill-trained to cope with the demands of a Caruso-like career, Mario Lanza had squandered what once promised to be *the* glorious contemporary voice of opera for too many helpings of spaghetti.

(1922 *–1959)

---

* Lanza told columnist Art Buchwald in Rome: "MGM had me born in 1921, the year Caruso died. They were trying to say on the day he died another star was born . . . I wasn't born in the year Caruso died and now that I am no longer under contract I don't mind saying it."

Steve Lawrence and Eydie Gorme

There was no competition. Rock won out easily.

"The real talent of this world . . . should stop apologizing for being great," Eydie Gorme told Paul Rosenfeld of the Los Angeles *Times* in the fall of 1976, while putting in a plug for higher musical standards. "I'm waiting for the white charger to come along and take all the nontalents to jail."

If there is an aura of resentment to this indictment of some of the musically limited performers of the 1960s and '70s, perhaps it is justified. Perennially outspoken Eydie Gorme, one of the truly great popular singers of the age, has been singled out by many of her peers, including Ella Fitzgerald, Frank Sinatra, and Jo Stafford, as one whose talents they most admire. Projecting tremendous warmth and emotion through a gloriously clear voice that spans several octaves and features a pulsating vibrato, she has been described as "the singer Barbra Streisand would like to sound like, but can't!"

She and husband Steve Lawrence, another singer of exquisite taste, warm phrasing, and fine technique, found themselves coming into their own during the early 1960s just when rock music was finding itself in the same situation. There was no competition. Rock won out easily. But neither Steve nor Eydie would give in. Both continued to sing in their mature musical manner the kind of "class" songs in which they believed, and in the mid-1970s, their "Our

Eydie and Steve

Love Is Here to Stay" TV special, containing a full hour of songs by George
and Ira Gershwin, won an Emmy. Two similar top-notch specials, one featuring
the music of Irving Berlin, the other of Cole Porter, followed.

But in between not enough was heard of them. They did establish a following
in Las Vegas, and they toured the theater-in-the-round circuit successfully, and
they appeared as guests on numerous TV shows. But unlike other singers of
their age and musical beliefs who did compromise, Steve and Eydie steadfastly
refused to knuckled under to the rock sounds. Consequently their record sales
diminished drastically, and, by the mid-1970s, apparently frustrated, Eydie
shifted her recording activities from the pop to the Latin scene, where she
found enthusiastic if limited acceptance.

Their lives had become closely entwined ever since they began performing
together in the early 1950s as members of Steve Allen's "Tonight Show." They
soon fell in love, married, and then raised a family. Before then, Steve, the
son of a Brooklyn house painter who was also a cantor, had made a few recordings
on a minor label. Eydie, the daughter of Turks who had moved to the Bronx,
had sung with the bands of Tommy Tucker and Tex Beneke, and had given a
hint of things-to-come with an impressive, last-minute substitute appearance
for an ailing Billy Daniels in New York's Copacabana. Both had auditioned
for Arthur Godfrey's "Talent Scouts" TV show. Steve had made it on the
third try; Eydie had failed four times.

The summer after their December 1957 marriage, they took over as hosts
of Allen's summer replacement show, and audiences began to realize that Steve
especially could do more than just sing. A natural actor, he was soon cast in
the lead of the Broadway production of *What Makes Sammy Run,* received
an "I think Lawrence could be the biggest musical star on Broadway" rave
from critic William Goldman, and was nominated for a Tony.

Eydie won an award, a Grammy, in 1966 for an emotion-charged rendition
of "If He Walked Into My Life," that packed all the wallop of Judy Garland
at her best. But thereafter, they seldom made even the bottom of the top hundred
record charts. Still, they didn't starve—far from it, in fact! Steve, an astute
businessman, had invested their money wisely and Eydie even caught the fever
and, according to one associate, "became quite knowledgeable about such things
as stock options." Playing Las Vegas regularly, touring, and guesting occasionally
on TV, they seemed content to live comfortably in their Beverly Hills home
with their two sons. Feeling no financial pressure to forsake their artistic convictions by latching on to the music of the "no-talents," they could afford to sit
and wait for the musical pendulum to swing their way again. As Eydie told
Paul Rosenfeld, "I don't want to appeal to everybody. [After all] everybody
doesn't appeal to me."

(Steve Lawrence: 1935–   )
(Eydie Gorme: 1931–   )

Leadbelly

His musical genius was almost equaled by his talent for self-destruction.

From the day he was delivered by voodoo-conjuring midwives in a Louisiana swamp, Huddie Ledbetter's life was pure melodrama. As the self-proclaimed "King o' the Twelve-String Guitar," he had no challengers, but his musical genius was almost equaled by his talent for self-destruction. He was cruelly victimized by racists in the South and, later, in the North, but Leadbelly was his own worst enemy.

His mother was half Cherokee, his father a hard-working, hard-drinking farmer, his paternal grandparents killed by the Klan. At six he got his first

Huddie Ledbetter

instrument, an accordion, and witnessed his first murder (of a black man by a drunken redneck). At sixteen he mastered the six- and twelve-string guitars, bass, harmonica, and piano, as well as the accordion, and was playing and singing in a deep, guttural, passion-filled voice in the streets, saloons, and whore-houses of Shreveport.

He became a ramblin' man, drifting from job to job: oil field roustabout, cotton picker, railroad brakeman. Everywhere he went, he added new folk songs to his repertoire, field hollers, work songs, ballads, and spirituals. From Blind Lemon Jefferson, he learned the blues.

He was a dedicated hellraiser who saw himself as being pursued by trouble. In fact, it was his pursuit of women and whiskey that usually got him into trouble. His physique was as powerful as his voice. When drunk and/or provoked, he was liable to lose all control. In 1917 he killed a man in a fight and wound up in the notorious Sugar Land Prison near Houston. On special occasions, he was allowed to perform for the inmates. Asked to do so when the governor toured the facility, he improvised a song that contained lyrics as:

I'se your servant compose this song.
Please Gov'nor Neff lemme go back home.

Please Honorable Gov'nor be good an' kind,
If you don' get a pardon, will you cut my time?

Leadbelly had already served six years of a thirty-year sentence. The pardon was granted.

He stayed out of serious trouble for a few years, but in 1930 he stabbed a man, again during a fight. Halfway through a ten-year prison term, he sang his way out a second time, adapting his "pardon song" for the governor of Louisiana ("Boss, help me get out o' this ol' place. I just naturally don't like it!").

Folklorists John and Alan Lomax became his mentors and took him to New York to record commercially. There, the *Herald-Tribune* announced his arrival with a story headed SWEET SINGER OF THE SWAMPLANDS HERE TO DO A FEW TUNES BETWEEN HOMICIDES. The liberals lapped it up and adopted him, like some exotic pet, and other folk singers, for whom he had been an invisible legend, listened even more intently to the man whose unrelenting musical passion had already influenced so many of them.

A country boy, he was never at home in the city, or at the universities where he concertized. His depressions and drinking and brawling became more fre-quent. During World War II he shined shoes and washed dishes in the Village. At his last concert, in Paris, the year he died, his audience was thirty people— in a four-thousand-seat house. Thirty years later, his records have become clas-sics, his life story a legend, immortalized in the mid-1970s by a sanitized (PG) film. Leadbelly's true story would be rated X.

(1888–1949)

Led Zeppelin

"That incredible energy and power that flows when we come together on a stage—like ESP."

Many critics believed Led Zeppelin would quickly become the *Hindenburg* of heavy metal rock music, once aloft with their first LP, "Led Zeppelin Volume I" (1968). But singer lyricist Robert Plant, guitarist Jimmy Page, drummer John Bonham, and bassist/keyboardist John Paul Jones knew they were setting new standards for sheer pulverizing power and precision—and, ultimately, profits (twenty-four million albums sold, fifteen million dollars in concert grosses)—with their music and delirious in-person performances.

"For once," says Plant, a closet intellectual, "we were all on board the same ship, going the same way, expressing the same feelings." Plant's strident, lyrically imaginative vocals have dominated the band's LPs. But Plant has benefited from a driving, ominously powerful rhythm section in Bonham and Jones, and from the stinging, stalking blues-rock inventions of guitarist Page. "We always try to lull our fans into a sense of beauty and tranquility," explains Plant, "then capture them with the ferociousness of our music."

As with the Rolling Stones (Jagger/Richard), The Who (Daltry/Townshend) and, most notably, Lennon and McCartney of the Beatles, the source of Led

Led Zeppelin's Plant and Page

Zeppelin's dynamism has been a creative tension flowing between the jigsaw meshing of its leaders, Plant and Page. The son of a civil engineer, Plant is the flamboyant, impishly extroverted showman who, since his Birmingham, England, school days, has "always enjoyed the way words could be put together." He left home as a teenager, he remembers, "with one foot in academia and the other in bohemia." He soon found himself firmly planted in the latter, shouting blues and playing harmonica with the local Band of Joy, with Bonham, a muscular, rugged local boy, on drums. "It was then," adds Plant, "that I first discovered and lived the blues as I had known them from the music of Muddy Waters and Howlin' Wolf."

Page grew up in a working class part of London, a frail, withdrawn youth who, as a teenager, became, in his own words, "a blend of rebel and loner at art school." He spent long hours at night adapting r&b guitar riffs onto his own fretboard at home, most often those of Otis Spann and B. B. King. By the mid-1960s, after leaving art school, he had become a celebrated sessions player who backed, among others, the Rolling Stones, The Who, and Burt Bacharach. In 1966 he joined the Yardbirds, the germinally influential rock group, and when it broke up in 1968, he formed his own group. He soon asked Jones, a well-groomed, methodical, and precise player and producer to join, and, at the urging of a friend familiar with the Band of Joy, took on Plant and Bonham.

Though he has admitted "there is a lot of aggression in my music," the gentle and diffident Page has added, "It does provide great release for me."

A near-fatal, mid-1975 automobile crash involving Plant forced a long delay in the groups colosally lucrative touring schedule, though it did manage to record its seventh platinum LP, "Presence," during Plant's convalescence. Then one day, while still hobbling on a cane, Plant met the other three musicians in a tiny club on the island of Jersey. There they plugged into some small amps—unrecognized—and found, recalls Plant, "We were the old Zeppelin again. That incredible energy and power that flows when we come together on a stage—like ESP—was still there in enormous quantities. That was our true reaffirmation, in the wake of near-disaster, our mighty fist raised against the storm—and on and on we rocked." Their subsequent rocking included another top-selling LP, "The Song Remains the Same," also the title of their film, consisting of old concert footage cum fantasy sequences, full of violent nightmares and harcissism, that attracted huge, young audiences. This was followed by an SRO tour, as Led Zeppelin continued to pillage and plunder the land, as ever the most puissant rock group on earth.

Peggy Lee

She seems to be most concerned with love.

Her vague, often sexy-looking stare can be deceiving. For, although Peggy Lee is a very emotional, sensuous, and sensitive singer and a very warm, witty, and caring person, she is also a polished, studied, cool performer who knows precisely who she is, what she is doing and why.

One of the world's top pop singers for thirty years, she has been described by critic Gene Lees as "the most mature, the most authoritative, the most sensitive, and the most consistently intelligent female singer of popular music in America." And writer Henry Pleasants adds, "What you get from Peggy Lee is not just a song superlatively well sung. It is a production."

Certainly few, if any, pop singers ever become as totally immersed in the preparation and production of their acts as she does. With Peggy, whom writer Philip Oakes described in the London *Times* as "a big, buttery blonde with platinum hair and an oddly impassive face," nothing is left to chance. The selection of material, its presentation, including musical arrangements, stage lighting, audio, and even the choice of musicians, all come under her sharp review. What's more, she methodically logs details of every one of her performances for future reference.

The feelings Peggy projects in her numbers run the gamut from good, strong, healthy sex to cute, pixieish humor, to sweet, little-girl sentimentality. But she seems to be most concerned with love (love of all kinds: light, heavy, happy, dismal), with presenting those various feelings through her songs and with receiving love in return from those close to her, including her audiences. She loves people easily, making her quite vulnerable.

During her early days, when she was just plain Norma Jean Egstrom in her native Jamestown, North Dakota, she found so little love that soon after graduating from high school and selling her graduation watch, she left home to begin her career in earnest. First she sang with Jack Wardlaw's band, then with Will Osborne's, and eventually in 1941 with Benny Goodman. "I learned more about music from the men I worked with in bands than I've learned anywhere else," she once said. "They taught me discipline and the value of rehearsing and how to train."

With Goodman she made her first recordings, including her first big hit, "Why Don't You Do Right," a song she had heard an old blues singer, Lil Green, perform on a record and which she induced Goodman to record.

Her career with Goodman ended after she married guitarist Dave Barbour,

Peggy

and they settled in Hollywood to raise their baby girl, Nicki, and to write songs like "It's a Good Day," "I Don't Know Enough About You," and one of her biggest record hits, "Mañana." She has also written songs with Duke Ellington, Quincy Jones, Michel Legrand, Johnny Mandel, Victor Young, and other fine composers. But, of course, it has been her singing that has brought her everlasting fame—exemplified on such recordings as "Lover," "Fever," and "Is That All There Is," which in 1969 won two Grammys.

She has toured extensively throughout America and Europe, almost always playing to packed houses. She has appeared on numerous TV shows and has continued to record, though less successfully in recent years. Despite her great popularity, acceptance by her public remains very important to her, and she works hard to get it, often to the point of utter exhaustion. (For years, plagued by a respiratory ailment, she required a portable oxygen tent at all her engagements.) Relating well to audiences invariably buoys her spirits. "Appreciation," she once said, "is the best vitamin I've found."

In turn, she appreciates good musicianship and insists on it from her co-workers, who she feels should share one of her strongest beliefs: "I've been given a talent, and I feel a responsibility to try to improve the presentation of it."

Unlike most of the middle-of-the-road singers who first flourished in the 1940s and '50s, Peggy attempts to remain musically *au courant*. She sings many songs by young, contemporary composers, sometimes to the dismay of those who prefer the Peggy Lee they once knew. But she has no intentions of growing as old as the attitudes of some of those early fans. "I'm not looking back in longing or in anger," she insists. "But you know, when you compare what was then with what is now, believe me, *these* are the good old days!"

(1920–   )

Michel Legrand

"I just sit there, glued to the piano bench, and I don't move from it, even if I feel like an old lemon."

He has written a slew of hit songs, scores for dozens of movies, and has arranged and conducted for some of the world's most famous singers. But what Michel Legrand likes to do most of all, he insists, is to "sit down at the piano and play some jazz!"

Boyish-looking, despite a few gray hairs, and trim, primarily because he plays so much tennis, the very personable, outgoing Legrand has emerged as one of the most prolific, talented, and successful quadruple threats (composer, arranger, conductor, and performer) in popular music. A child prodigy, son of a French pop musician, he entered the Paris Conservatory when he was only eleven years old and studied there for nine years. His first major musical assignment involved him directly with jazz: scoring and conducting an album featuring Dizzy Gillespie and a huge orchestra. That and another very lush, elegantly orchestrated album, *I Love Paris,* which he wrote "because some Americans wanted something 'French-sounding,' " gained him international recognition. Soon he was conducting and creating warm, romantic arrangements for such top pop singers as Julie Andrews, Harry Belafonte, Maurice Chevalier (who brought him to America for the first time), Petula Clark, Lena Horne, Barbra Streisand, Sarah Vaughan, and Andy Williams.

His total musical output is prodigious. He has conducted, arranged, and/or performed on close to a hundred record albums, composed close to fifty movie scores, plus several hundred popular songs. Happily married and father of three children, he easily uses his family or what he considers the need to play tennis as excuses for not working.

Though he finds writing songs a real chore that almost invariably leads to procrastination, he has managed to discipline himself when working on a movie score. Involved with many others, he becomes all business, working every day from ten to one and two to eight and often hating it. "But it's the only way. I just sit there, glued to the piano bench, and I don't move from it, even if I feel dry like an old lemon. Finally I find that ideas have sunk in and I start to create." A composer, he points out, must condition himself like an athlete if he expects to function efficiently and realize his full potential.

Legrand's "realized potential" is mighty impressive. His hit songs include "What Are You Doing the Rest of Your Life," "I Will Wait for You," "Watch What Happens," and "The Windmills of Your Mind," some of which come

Michel

from some of his successful movie and TV scores, such as *The Umbrellas of Cherbourg, The Thomas Crown Affair, The Summer of '42, Portnoy's Complaint,* and *Brian's Song.* Though obviously proficient at creating made-to-order scores, Legrand has an even more important personal goal: he wants to satisfy himself.

He has already satisfied enough of his fellow artists to have won three Grammys and two Oscars and enough of the record-buying public to emerge a wealthy man. But such success is not all that he wants out of life. He wants to express himself more spontaneously, more for his own gratification. "That's why I love to play jazz. It's so free and adventurous, and the limits are so very wide. When we improvise, we surprise even ourselves, and what I really love to do *is* to surprise myself. That's *really* great!"

(1932–   )

He seemed the very essence of all that was wrong with this new rock and roll music.

Rockabilly, a word that came out of Memphis in the mid-1950s, described a new wave of music sweeping the country, a mixture of the rhythm and out-front emotion of black blues with the vocal intensity of white "hillbilly" music. And it also described Jerry Lee Lewis.

Between 1957 and 1958 the brash native of Ferriday, Louisiana, had four million-sellers in a row in the dawning days of rock: "Whole Lotta Shakin' Goin' On," "Great Balls of Fire," "Breathless," and "High School Confidential." But the basis for his appeal was in his personal appearances: singing in a frenzied, sexual, yet somehow intimate tenor, clowning with the piano, pounding it, abusing it with demonic energy, his long, curly blond hair weaving as his head flailed from side to side. To the parents of the teenagers who adored him he seemed the very essence of all that was wrong with this new rock and roll music.

Their parents' fears seemed to have been realized when in 1958 it became

Jerry Lee

known that his recent (third) marriage was to his thirteen-year-old second cousin, a fact which fans, promoters, and record company executives generally found appalling. At twenty-three he became rock and roll's first has-been.

He was down but not out. An alcoholic, an insomniac, a compulsive performer, he never quit what he calls "the greatest live show on earth." His word to promoters—and he almost always kept his word—was: "Just point me to the piano and give me my money, and in fifteen minutes I'll have them shaking, shouting, shivering, and shacking."

After playing years of small clubs and having little success on records, he decided to return to his roots and try his hand at country music. The result was his 1968 recording, "Another Place, Another Time," a classic country honky-tonk song about drinkin' and cheatin', and it vaulted him back onto the top of the charts and into the public eye once more. The rock and roll has-been became a country music star.

A man of boundless, flaming energy on stage and off, it's a wonder he didn't burn himself out. A contemporary writer described him in a nutshell: "His private moments are rare, his introspective ones almost nil. He simply lives to live."

Restless, churning with emotion and seemingly unbounded talent, possessor of a famous ego of unparalleled proportions—which is part of his charm and his drive—he once described his future: "I've been the Greatest Live Show on Earth for the past fifteen years and I'll keep on being the Greatest Live Show on Earth until they put me six feet under. And even then I might find a way to keep hanging in!" More recently, apparently haunted by the specter of religious damnation, he told Peter Guralnick in the New York *Times,* "Had I known then what I know now, I would never have played my first note on the piano."

(1935–   )

A surefire mix of sentimentality, ham, and show biz know-how.

In the 1920s and 1930s pollsters were not out counting the number of yes-sayers to the most famous question in show business, "Is everybody happy?" as posed in his gruff, semisinging, semitalking voice by vaudevillian-bandleader Ted Lewis. But the yes-sayers must have been in the millions, for "The High-Hatted Tragedian of Song" made a fortune asking that question during five of the six decades he played his squealing clarinet and projected his hammy histrionics in theaters, nightclubs, and hotel spas here and abroad.

According to UP writer Frederick Othman, Lewis first asked the question of patrons at Rector's, a post New York restaurant of the teens and 1920s, because the out-and-out request for applause, part of his act in Coney Island, seemed inappropriate in such a respectable spot.

Lured by the romance of show business, Lewis, born Theodore Leopold Friedman, ran away from his respectable business-oriented Circleville, Ohio, family while still in his teens, to play his clarinet for hootchy-kootchy dancers in carnivals and work his way up through novelty-ragtime bands, burlesque, and vaudeville. Before "arriving," he acquired a new name on a theater marquee too small for "Lewis and Friedman": He and his partner Eddie Lewis became "Lewis and Lewis." When the duo split, young Friedman became singing bandleader Ted Lewis. He surrounded himself with attractive singing and dancing talents and, billed as "The High-Hatted Tragedian of Song," he plied his trade, a surefire mix of sentimentality, ham, and show biz know-how, in front of a colorful show band, which at various times housed topflight jazzmen. The longest-staying were cornetist Muggsy Spanier and trombonist George Brunis. Shorter-term members included clarinetists Don Murray and Frank Teschmacher and alto sax star Jimmy Dorsey. After his 1929 New Year's Eve imitation of the boss's corny clarinet style, however, Jimmy was out of the band. Another imitator of many years earlier, Benny Goodman, had, at age twelve in 1921, played a Lewis solo note for note on a Chicago theater "Jazz Night" program. Ten years later he was tapped by Lewis, along with saxist Bud Freeman, Spanier, and Fats Waller (a rare example of a "mixed" group in 1931), for some recordings that yielded at least one notable disc: "Dallas Blues" and "Royal Garden Blues."

Actually, as a jazz musician, Lewis was never in the same league with his sidemen. But he was a canny showman capitalizing on jazz ballyhoo, who starred not only in his own act, but also in Broadway revues; who recorded copiously, and who made several films, including *Show of Shows* and *Is Everybody*

"Is everybody happy?"

Happy? In his battered top hat, won in a crap game, he entranced audiences with his half-whispered, lump-in-throat talking delivery of songs like his theme, "When My Baby Smiles at Me," his great showstopper, "Me and My Shadow," and a potpourri of optimistic songs, like "I'm the Medicine Man for the Blues," "Keep a Little Sunshine in Your Heart," and "Dip Your Brush in Sunshine," softening up every audience for an effervescing affirmative when Lewis asked them, just one more time, "Is everybody happy?"

(1892–1971)

"Men's fashion has finally caught up with me."

He said he cried all the way to the bank. Wladziu (pronounced Vla-ja) Valentino (for the great screen lover) Liberace (pronounced Lib-er-AH-chee), known to his friends as Lee, was one of the show-business phenomena of the 1950s, one of the biggest stars on the mid-1950s television screen, selling out concert performances so regularly that, for tax purposes, he purposely limited his income to $750,000 a year.

He played the piano well enough to be offered the leadership of Eddy Duchin's band in 1942 when Duchin went into the Navy (Liberace turned the offer down) but not well enough to satisfy music critics, who complained of "slackness of rhythms, wrong tempos, distorted phrasing, and excess of prettification." His trademarks included candelabra on the piano, excessive dimpling, mischievous wink, and a wild wardrobe that was not matched (or even approached) until the rock groups of the 1970s got into outlandish costuming. The New York *Times* television critic described him as "a childish mound of sequins bent on seducing every mother who felt she had been disappointed by her son."

"Look me over," he would say, preening in front of his audience with a great show of teeth and dimples as he made his entrance in an ostentatious costume that he admitted weighed thirty pounds. "I didn't get dressed like this to go unnoticed."

His primary appeal was to women of middle age, who pursued him as avidly and ingeniously as any of the teenaged groupies who later followed the rock groups. They screamed and sighed at his renditions of romantic bits and pieces of Gershwin, Chopin, Liszt, and such stickily sentimental items as "O, Promise Me" and "Let Me Call You Sweetheart."

"My whole trick," he said, "is to keep the tune well out in front. If I play Tchaikovsky, I play his melodies and skip his spiritual struggle."

When critics complained that he cut the classics (Vladimir Horowitz took eight minutes to play a movement of Beethoven's "Moonlight Sonata;" Librace got through it in three), he admitted that he condensed.

"I have to know just how many notes my audience will stand for," he explained. "If there's any time left over, I fill in with a lot of runs up and down the keys."

The son of an Italian-French horn player, Liberace was born in West Milwaukee, Wisconsin, where he led a five-piece combo in high school. At sixteen, calling himself Walter Busterkeys, he did a concert tour of Wisconsin high

Wladziu Valentino Liberace

schools, where he found that most audiences were less interested in classics or jazz than in comfortable, sentimental middle-area music. On that premise he built himself into a major nightclub and hotel performer. But by 1946, even an income of forty thousand dollars a year did not seem enough to compensate for playing to drunks. He quit the clubs and tried to get into records, into films, on television, with no success until KLAC in Los Angeles took a chance on his TV show in 1951 and struck gold.

"I knew that once I got the chance to look into that camera real hard," he said, "the country would know me for a friend."

After his peak of popularity had passed, Liberace was able to maintain his Hollywood home with its piano-shaped swimming pool, piano-shaped beds, and 188 miniature pianos by supplementing his performances with a line of men's clothing based on his wardrobe, because, he declared, "men's fashion has finally caught up with me."

(1920–   )

Scaring the devil out of everyone with his eccentric behavior and by singing flamingly obscene lyrics.

Standing atop the piano, his arms spread wide, the beams of the spotlights broken into thousands of spitting flashes by the tiny mirrors on his costume, his polished coiffure fresh from the beauty parlor, Richard Penniman screeched to the hysterical audience with fine gospel fervor: "I want you all to know that I am king of rock and roll!" He then proceeded to stake his claim with amazing funk.

Little Richard has been, all at once, rock's first and most notable zany, a ferociously talented singer, a jackhammer piano player, and a man obviously in love with the idea of stardom.

Raised in Macon, Georgia, he sang and danced on street corners for pennies, peddled home brew medicine in tent shows, joined a touring gospel group in the South, won a rhythm and blues talent contest, made eight go-nowhere sides for RCA, and returned to Macon in temporary defeat. He washed dishes at the local Greyhound bus station and dreamed his dreams.

In 1955 he auditioned for Specialty, a small Los Angeles-based label; a recording session was scheduled. Penniman nearly ruined it by scaring the devil out of everyone with his eccentric behavior and by singing flamingly obscene lyrics to what eventually became his first hit, "Tutti Frutti," with its famous opening line of syncopated gibberish: "A-wop-bop-a-lu-bop, a-wop-bam-boom!"

From 1955 to 1959 Little Richard made rock history with "Long Tall Sally," "Rip It Up," "Ready Teddy," "Keep A' Knockin'," "Good Golly, Miss Molly," "Lucille," and others. Then, while en route to Australia by air for a tour, the plane's engines began to conk out. Richard vowed to God that, if spared, he would devote the rest of his life to church work. The plane landed. Penniman took his band to the shore, where he tossed his diamond rings into the sea. After the tour was completed, he sold his Cadillacs and apartment houses, enrolled in a theological school in Alabama, and became a preacher. He made half a dozen gospel albums, changing his raspy, grinding vocal style into a deliberate imitation of smoothie pop singer Johnny Mathis (!).

But the lure of show business was too strong to resist, and by the early 1960s he was touring again. While appearing in England he met and was so impressed by a scruffy quartet that he placed an overseas call to Art Ruppe, head of Specialty Records, and advised him to sign the Beatles. Ruppe wanted Richard back but wasn't interested in British groups.

Little Richard Penniman

Returning to America, Richard put together a band that included a boy-wizard guitarist, Jimi Hendrix, who displeased his leader one day by showing up for rehearsal wearing a dazzling shirt. "Take that thing off!" Richard shrieked, *"I'm* the only one who's allowed to be pretty!"

Richard's comeback was slow but steady. His influence on British rockers was strong, especially on the Beatles (whom he taught to use his famous falsetto whoop), and their respectful testimonials brought him attention. A 1970 album, *The Rill Thing,* sold well, and at his increasing concert dates he gleefully bowled over audiences with his steady intensity and yahoo antics. By the early 1970s he was again a star.

And then it happened again. In 1975 the violent deaths of friends and a brother seemed to him that God was trying to tell him something and so he forsook rock and roll and became an evangelist, telling his new followers that "Jesus wanted me to say no to the lowest so I can look to the highest." He disdained makeup, sequins, and his foot-high pompadour, donned a three-piece suit and went to work as a salesman for the Memorial Bible Company of Nashville.

Little Richard had become Brother Richard.

(1935–   )

Guy Lombardo

"The place was so empty we had to get four waiters and a guy out of the kitchen to clap."

"The Sweetest Music This Side of Heaven," which came out of London, Ontario, and became indelibly associated for decades with New Year's Eve, has turned out to be one of the most consistent, long-lived, and most imitated sounds of the twentieth century. Guy Lombardo, a violinist who spent most of his career dancing with his baton, and his younger brothers, Carmen, a saxophonist, and Lebert, a trumpeter, had organized the Royal Canadians when they were teenagers back in Canada. By the mid-1920s, they had migrated to Cleveland, Ohio, where their distinctively soft, purry, bouncy sounds gained them a local reputation via their broadcasts over station WTAM.

Their style revolved around Carmen's tremulous saxophone sound, which he had adapted from that of his original instrument, the flute, Lebert's clipped, muted trumpeting, and the schottische rhythm that Guy said the band invented. Their unusual and distinctive sound, that also included Carmen's famed wavering vocals, dominated the years preceding the Swing Era.

By 1927 the Royal Canadians' reputation had spread and they were lured away from Cleveland to Chicago by the Granada Cafe with an offer of more money. On arriving in the Windy City, Guy found that most of the time for dance band broadcasts (a prime means of exposure) had already been taken. So he went to a new radio station, WBBM, which agreed to put the band on the air for fifteen minutes a night starting at 9 P.M.

And so at nine o'clock on Wednesday, November 16, 1927, a notable date in dance band history, Lombardo, acting as bandleader, announcer, and engineer, threw a switch, and the band was on the air.

"The place was so empty," Guy recalled," "we had to get four waiters and a guy out of the kitchen to clap." When he flipped the switch back again at nine-fifteen to take the band off the air, a call came through from WBBM headquarters: "Keep on playing." So Lombardo threw the switch once more and played. Soon came another call, this one from the president of WBBM: "Keep on playing until sign-off at 1 A.M.!" The band kept on playing, and by midnight the Granada was filled with people who had heard the band on the air.

On the next day, Wrigley's Chewing Gum and Florsheim Shoes each signed the band for their own half-hour sponsored broadcasts. And during the following week, station KSTP in St. Paul put a wire into the Granada, creating the first radio network for a dance band.

The Lombardos: Guy with the baton, Carmen the saxist nearest Guy, Liebert the trumpeter behind Carmen, Victor the saxist at extreme right

Two years later the Royal Canadians, by then an established favorite at midwestern colleges ("We had all the college kids until Benny Goodman came along," Guy once claimed), moved to the Roosevelt Grill in New York where they remained for more than thirty years, except for an early 1930s, three-year stint at the Cocoanut Grove in Los Angeles. The move East had been instigated by William Paley, head of the Columbia Broadcasting System, who had lined up a radio series, sponsored by Robert Burns Panatella Cigars, for the band. In honor of Burns, the band introduced "Auld Lang Syne" as its new theme, "a song we used to play," Lombardo recalls, "when we were performing for people of Scottish descent back in Canada."

Paley also asked the band to broadcast on CBS from eleven-thirty to midnight on New Year's Eve, closing out 1929. The National Broadcasting Company countered by inviting Lombardo to play from midnight to twelve-thirty welcoming in 1930. This back-to-back parlay continued until 1954, when Lombardo moved his New Year's Eve program to television, where for more than another generation his band blew in each new year.

In addition to its radio shows and personal appearances (it broke the all-time record at Harlem's Savoy Ballroom), the band made numerous recordings, introducing a slew of hit tunes like "Boo Hoo," "Sweethearts on Parade," "Coquette," and "Seems Like Old Times," all written by Carmen, and "You're Driving Me Crazy," "Gimme a Little Kiss," "Little White Lies," "Heartaches," "Annie Doesn't Live Here Anymore," and many others. Guy was always extremely selective about songs he would or would not play. "There's nothing like a bad song to ruin a singer or a band," he insisted.

In the mid-1930s, when the swing bands had lured away many of Lombardo's younger fans (but not Louis Armstrong, who continued to call the Royal Canadians "my inspirators"), Guy and his family, which now included another brother, Victor, and a sister, Rosemarie, continued to play the "class" spots, their music still slow and dreamy and sentimental. "We play for lovers, not acrobats," Lombardo muttered disdainfully.

Though his band was still going strong in 1954, Guy, who had become an avid speedboat racer in the 1940s, winning the coveted Gold Cup in 1946, entered still another field. He succeeded Mike Todd as producer of musical shows at Jones Beach on Long Island. But still he and his Royal Canadians never stopped playing, and never stopped touring either. In 1977, approaching his seventy fifth birthday, the perpetually polite, ever-enthusiastic Lombardo was still following a rigorous routine of one-nighters, often traveling from town to town by bus—just like in the old days. "The only thing I dread is a night I don't have to work," he told Frank Meyer of *Variety*. "I'll keep on working forever." Shortly thereafter he became sick and a few weeks later in a Houston hospital he failed to rally from a heart attack. But his music didn't stop. Brother Lebert took command and first inserted brother Victor and then his own son, Bill, as frontman, who began to modernize the music just a little bit.

Shorty after Guy's death Hubert Saal in *Newsweek* concluded a piece titled "Father New Year" with: "Warm and unpretentious, Lombardo's music evoked the good old days. He used to joke, 'When I go, I'll take New Year's Eve with me.' Not quite. But the cup of kindness may not seem so full without him."

(1902–1977)

Jimmie Lunceford

Thrilling to hear and a joy to watch.

If there was ever a big band that personified the musical excitement and fun of the swing era, Jimmie Lunceford's was the one. Thrilling to hear with its irresistibility pulsating ensemble sounds, it was also a joy to watch as its musicians projected their obvious delight by urging each other on, tossing trumpets into the air in unison (and catching them), slipping their trombone slides skyward, and generally having themselves one big and very contagious ball upon their bandstand.

Individually, the band may have boasted of fewer outstanding musicians than some of its rivals. But as Sy Oliver, the great arranger responsible for much of its music, noted, "The whole was three times as great as the individual

Jimmie and his men

components. The band played way over its head simply because of its tremendous spirit."

Its impact on audiences was almost impossible to match. In a famous Battle of the Bands late in 1940 in New York, during which twenty-eight groups, including Benny Goodman's, Count Basie's, Glenn Miller's and Les Brown's, were allotted fifteen minutes each, only Lunceford's created such a hysterical crowd reaction that the show couldn't go on until the band returned for an encore.

Its unique esprit de corps began in the late 1920s when the big, handsome Lunceford, a graduate of Fisk University, formed his band, enlisting some musicians whom he had previously taught both music and athletics in a Memphis High School. Less flamboyant than most bandleaders, Jimmie sometimes gave the impression of a schoolteacher. But, according to Oliver, "He was consistent in everything he did, and that gave the fellows a feeling of security."

And that sort of feeling is precisely what they needed, considering their back-breaking schedule that called for about two hundred one-nighters a year, during which they covered forty thousand miles, seldom settling in any one spot for more than a week at a time. Segregation kept them out of most of the best spots with their important radio outlets. So the band concentrated on recordings, turning out a series of swinging masterpieces, including "My Blue Heaven," "Four or Five Times," "Margie," "Tain't What You Do," "What's Your Story, Morning Glory," and Oliver's jumping theme, "For Dancers Only."

Sy's loose, easy-swinging arrangements and singing provided the band with much of its character, though other instrumentalists who doubled as singers, notably Willie Smith, Joe Thomas, and Trummy Young, also stood out. And so did Jimmy Crawford, a tremendous drummer, who sparked a forever-swinging rhythm section.

More than any other band, Lunceford's invariably sounded loose and relaxed, yet always swung. For this, Oliver's arrangements, as well as some by Eddie Wilcox, Billy Moore, and Gerald Wilson, were partially responsible. But perhaps even more of the credit goes to the band's seemingly never-ebbing spirit that, despite relatively low pay and the often intolerable living conditions foisted on the black bands of the 1930s, managed to last until the late 1930s. But then, as times began to change and as the musicians began to mature and raise families and think about their individual futures, that great spirit did begin to ebb. One by one, the stars started to flow away, until by mid-1947, when Jimmie was felled by a heart attack, the almost totally revised group bore little resemblance to the great Lunceford band that had thrilled musicians and fans for a full decade.

(1902–1947)

Loretta Lynn

"I've seen things, and that's *almost* the same as doing them.

"Everyone says all my songs are about myself. That's not completely true, because if I did all the things I write about, I wouldn't be here, I'd be all worn out in some old people's home. But I've seen things, and that's *almost* the same as doing them."

Loretta Lynn has indeed seen things in her well-publicized rise from—in the words of her most famous song—a "Coal Miner's Daughter" to international superstar.

Born to the family of an impoverished coal miner in Butcher Holler—near Paintsville—Kentucky, Loretta Webb became a bride at thirteen, a mother at fourteen, and a grandmother at twenty-eight, and worked her way up from singing in seedy bars to the Grand Ole Opry, and onto network television appearances, as well as a cover story in *Newsweek* in 1974.

Loretta

Chronically underweight—she has barely tipped the scales at ninety pounds—
her health was a continual problem as she reached her heights in the late 1960s
and early 1970s, and this, combined with her enormous financial success, caused
her to cut back on personal appearances sharply as the 1970s progressed.

Her voice was a marvel. Originally heavily derived from the tight, restrained
style of Kitty Wells, it eventually took on an extremely distinctive feel of its
own: breathily sensuous one moment, sassy the next, loving and tender the
next.

Perhaps the greatest contradiction in a contradictory career was the material
she chose to sing. It often seemed a shame to waste that marvelous voice on
such gimmicky fluff as "Don't Come Home A-Drinkin' with Lovin' on Your
Mind," "You Ain't Woman Enough to Take My Man," "Your Squaw Is on
the Warpath," and "The Pill." Yet it is no coincidence that these songs were
chosen and were big hits—they reflect the sentiments of a lot of women who,
as Loretta says, have been kept "barefoot and pregnant over the years," but
who are not yet ready for women's liberation.

Loretta was able to touch this vast untapped market, claiming it for her
own: "I tried aiming my show at the women. They could see I was Loretta

Loretta

Lynn, a mother and a wife and a daughter, who had feelings just like other women. Sure I wanted men to like me, but the women were something special. Most of my songs were from the women's point of view. In the old days, country music was directed at the man: truck-driving songs, easy women, cheating songs. I remember how excited I got back in 1952, the first time I heard Kitty Wells sing 'It Wasn't God Who Made Honky-Tonk Angels.' See, Kitty was presenting the woman's point of view, which is different from the man's. And I always remembered that when I started writing songs."

If the songs themselves were inconsequential, their implication was not, and Loretta Lynn became something of a woman's champion in a field not known for championship of women's rights.

Still, as a singer, her warm, rich, throbbing voice seemed far better, though too infrequently, showcased by more typical lovelorn country ballads like "Blue Kentucky Girl" and "Here I Am Again," where both sexes were touched by her moving, sincere, and plaintive voice.

It is a bit ironic that as domestic as she is, Loretta Lynn has been considered an important factor in opening up the field of country music for women, including her younger sister, who, as Crystal Gayle, became quite a star in her own right. Yet there is little question that Loretta's career has gone beyond her poor-mountaineer-made-good success story, and beyond the only occasionally superior material she wrote and recorded. She flung wide the door which Kitty Wells had opened, and country music became infinitely richer for it.

(1936 (?)–   )

The Mamas and the Papas

A subtlety to rock that eliminated the pile-drive pulse of most other rock groups.

"Pop music is just long hours, hard work, and a lot of drugs." That assessment—which purports to sum up yesterday's work ethic and today's counterculture—was made by Mama Cass Elliot in *Rolling Stone* in 1971, three years after the Mamas and the Papas broke up, and three years before her own untimely demise.

The statement is symptomatic of much of the rock side of the pop scene—particularly its ephemeral nature. The Mamas and the Papas burst on the scene in 1965, blazed across the musical firmament, then seemingly burned themselves out in 1968.

But during their brief, intense fling, the Mamas and the Papas made a tremendous impact on the pop scene with their slick folk-rock blend. Their first hit, *Monday, Monday,* sold nearly 170,000 copies the first day it went on sale. During 1967 and '68, their singles and albums were consistently on the charts, and three of their albums turned gold by going over the million-dollar sales mark.

The group appeared on every major TV music and variety show, enjoyed SRO concerts in most American cities, and headlined all the big rock festivals. They were bright, witty, outrageous, financially independent. The world was their collective oyster, yet as the 1960s came to a close, so did the Mamas and the Papas.

At the time, leader John Phillips offered this post-mortem: "Groups are just about through. The individual composer and the singer is it." However, that was merely an evasive response to a reporter from the Los Angeles *Times.* The truth of the matter was twofold: the desire by Cass Elliot to pursue an individual career, and the personal problems stemming from the marriage of two of the members, John Phillips and Michelle Gilliam. But that's like writing the final chapter before introducing the cast of characters.

Group founder, John Phillips, was born in 1935 at Parris Island, South Carolina, where his father was a career officer with the Marines. John grew up in Virginia, entered a Catholic private school and by his midteens had won state honors in track and basketball. He was awarded an appointment to the U.S. Naval Academy, but a sports injury and his growing attachment to folk music caused him to quit school and head for Greenwich Village, New York, in 1957.

John was a member of an up and coming folk trio, the Journeymen, when Michelle Gilliam came into his life in 1962. Michelle was born in Long Beach,

The Mamas and the Papas: Dennis Doherty, Cass Elliot, John and Michelle Phillips

California, in 1944, and after high school decided to pursue a modeling career in New York. Following a whirlwind courtship, John and Michelle were married and she began singing with him and the Journeymen.

Dennis Doherty came to New York by way of Halifax, Nova Scotia, where he was born in 1941. He had appeared in Canada with a group called the Halifax Three, singing and playing trombone, guitar, and bass. Like musicians in all fields, Dennis knew he had to make it in New York. Shortly after arriving there he joined a band called the Mugwumps, which contained another recent émigré to the Big Apple, Cass Elliot.

Cassandra had started out as Ellen Cohen in Baltimore in 1943. Her parents were quite well-to-do and they had elaborate plans to send their daughter to "one of the more important eastern colleges," but Ellen changed their minds, changed her name, and headed for Greenwich Village.

Phillips—who had been entertaining ideas about a new group after the Journeymen disbanded in 1963—knew whom he could rely on for his vision of a two-male, two-female quartet that would combine the best of folk and rock. He lined up Cass and Dennis to work with him and his wife and they headed for an island in the Caribbean to polish their act.

When they were ready, they made Los Angeles their headquarters and unveiled their sophisticated, four-part harmonies on a pop scene virtually dominated by all-male, hard-rock combos. The Mamas and the Papas astounded the mid-1960s market with a vocal attack that had the bite of a brass section. They showed respect for lyrics with their crisp articulation; their imaginative arrangements showed a penchant for clever passing tones; and above all, with backgrounds steeped in the genteel folk tradition, they brought a subtlety to rock that eliminated the pile driver pulse of most other rock groups.

After they broke up in 1968, Mama Cass became a first-rate star on her own. As she gained renown, she also gained avoirdupois, reaching a peak of 250 pounds. *Time* described her as "a gargantuan, silvery-voiced pop-rock singer"; *Newsweek* referred to "her crystal voice and punch bowl figure." Cass herself once remarked, "I feel hipbones are overrated," and while she would readily admit her age, she never disclosed her weight.

In 1971 the Mamas and the Papas were reunited by Dunhill Records for another album, but nothing was the same. They were all having contractual hassles with Dunhill president Jay Lasker. John and Michelle were divorced (she married their mutual friend, actor-producer Dennis Hopper). Cass and John were in the throes of a personal feud. And most prophetically, they were all actual mamas and papas—even though Michelle was the only married one at the time.

They were never able to re-create that pristine flush of excitement that had made such an indelible impression in the mid-1960s. And as a tragic postscript, Mama Cass died in London, in July 1974, when she choked on a ham sandwich.

The futility of trying to recapture past glories brings to mind a line from one of their biggest hits: "California dreamin'/ on such a winter's day."

Henry Mancini

Three Oscars, five Gold Records, and a record-setting twenty Grammy Awards.

When he enrolled in New York's Juilliard School of Music in 1942, little did Henry Mancini realize that the move would probably save his life. Several months later he was drafted from there and sent to Atlantic City for basic training. Had he remained home in Aliquippa, Pennsylvania, he notes, "I would have wound up with friends and neighbors in the Black Panther infantry division. Its band was almost totally annihilated overseas."

The move also *changed* his life, for in Atlantic City, the tall thin, shy eighteen-year-old met members of the Glenn Miller AAF Band, also taking basic training there. "I never did join the band because Glenn already had enough arrangers and pianists," recalls the man who was to become the country's most popular conductor/composer/arranger. "But I became friendly with one of Glenn's arrangers, Norm Leyden, and after the war he got me a job with the postwar

Mancini and strings

Miller band. There I met Jerry Gray [the band's chief arranger], and when I went to California in 1952, he got me a job composing and arranging for Universal Pictures." (While with the Miller band, Mancini had also met its pretty girl singer, Ginny O'Connor. They are still married.)

Six years later came a typical movie scenario break. "One day I was walking out of the barber shop at Universal and I bumped into Blake Edwards, who was walking into the commissary right next door. We had met a few times before and he was about to start the 'Peter Gunn' series and he was looking for someone to write the score. And there I was!"

The "Peter Gunn" score, replete with big band jazz sounds, established that form of music as the mood-setter for many ensuing TV series. It also established a career for Mancini that eventually garnered him three Oscars, five Gold Records, and a record-setting twenty Grammy awards, plus a never-ending flow of offers to compose original scores for movies and television. He followed his debut with more of the same, notably the rhythmic "Baby Elephant Walk" and "Pink Panther Theme." But once secure and accepted, he was able to diversify, and soon he began composing lovely ballads like "The Days of Wine and Roses" and "Moon River," both with lyrics by Johnny Mercer, plus the title songs for two important movies, *Dear Heart* and *Love Story*.

He recorded all these, and many more—fifty albums in all—for RCA Victor and became a rich man. And he won a record number, twenty, Grammy awards. He also continued composing, and by the mid-1970s had completed over five hundred pusblished works. But despite such complete security, and no need to stray from his happy home, Mancini continued conducting "in-person" concerts, "a welcome change" from composing and arranging, which he eventually found to be "physically tiring." Nevertheless he consistently refused to farm out assignments, as other famous composers and arrangers have done. "I'm very possessive about my work. Every note that has ever been performed by me has been arranged by me," he states with pride. "I've been writing so much that I've developed calcium deposits in my elbow—just like a big league pitcher." Conducting, on the other hand, strains his arm very little, because he spends much of the time standing passively in front of his orchestra, "just listening to the soloists and identifying with the spectators."

Mancini is an expert listener. He likes especially to listen to his daughter, Monica, one of Hollywood's top group vocalists, and also to son Chris's rock group. He's not at all disappointed in the latter's musical taste. "That's his language. I couldn't conceive of his sort of harmonic concepts. But it sounds good to me, and that's the test"—the same test for which Henry has been getting straight "A" rating from millions of avid listeners for the past twenty years.

(1924–   )

Barry Manilow

"When I listen to the hit records I've had, they are romantic," Barry Manilow once admitted to Robert Palmer of the New York *Times,* "but I don't know if that's what's selling them. I hear them on the radio and the productions are interesting to listen to, the songs themselves are well written—I didn't write most of my hits, you know—and the guy singing them sounds like he meant it. I think that feeling, that personal touch, is what's important."

Actually, Manilow, who tends to deprecate his own vocal qualities almost as much as some critics have, claims he never really wanted to be a singer. Arranging was his real interest. "I grew up wanting to be Nelson Riddle," he

Barry

told Robert Windeler of *People.* "I'm only a fair singer, I write nice songs, but I'm a great arranger."

It was his arranging that got him into music's big time in the first place. Music had fascinated him since his early days in a poor Brooklyn neighborhood. At age seven he was playing an accordion. But six years later his new stepfather, Willie Murphy, a truck driver with good musical tastes, rescued him from the corny songs he was pushing forth by buying him a piano and introducing him to the music of Gerry Mulligan, Count Basie, Ted Heath, and other swing artists. Following one year of college, he enrolled in the New York School of Music, switched to Juilliard, got a job in the mail room at CBS, where he gradually drifted into the musical production end, gaining invaluable experience arranging and even conducting for singers of all musical stripes.

His singing career began under duress. He had formed an act with a girl named Jeannie Lucas. She sang and he arranged and played the piano. But on one of their first jobs, the boss insisted that he had bought "a singing duo." What to do? Both sang. Barry wasn't especially happy with the setup and before too long the act broke up. Back in New York he took the job as house pianist at the Continental Baths, where he was asked to accompany a very self-assertive singer named Bette Midler. Three rehearsals almost led to a permanent breach, as each battled to make musical points. But when Bette finally went into her act before a live audience and floored every one of the customers, Barry's skepticism turned to outright admiration.

Soon he became her arranger and musical director. He even produced some of her recordings, including her big hit of "Boogie Woogie Bugle Boy," a song he had learned years earlier while boogie-ing at home to the Andrews Sisters' record of the tune. And as Bette became more famous and her concerts grew longer, Barry helped pad the time by opening her second act with his own solo singing and playing.

Soon he had enough courage to try his own recording date. With close friend Ron Dante he went into the studio. "It was really a toss-up as to who was going to sing, Ron or me," he recently told Merv Griffin. The toss came up Barry. The five-thousand-dollar cost of the session was split by the two, both of whom were beginning to taste success in the jingle business. (Manilow has sung for McDonald's, Kentucky Fried Chicken, and Dr. Pepper, and has written, among others, the State Farm and Stridex jingles.)

Bell Records heard him and signed him, and Clive Davis, who soon bought the label and changed its name to Arista, took a shine to him. It was he who insisted that Barry record an old song called "Mandy" (originally called "Brandy") and who guided him through a slew of hits like "It's a Miracle," "Could It Be Magic," "I Write the Songs," "Trying to Get the Feeling Again," and many more, songs and performances that some have derisively labeled "romantic pop." Insists Manilow with a slight bristle, "I'm trying to bring back intelligent music . . . a little more complicated musically, and lyrically a little deeper."

On a recent Griffin show, he sang a medley of his hits. "I've never done this before," he said after he finished—then kiddingly, "I must be really hot." Some friends claim he doesn't realize how hot he really is. Said one, "To himself, Barry's still zero. He can't believe how enormous a star he is, and he's afraid it's all going to fall apart." He still talks quickly and nervously. His Griffin interview was filled with "you knows" and "I don't knows." He says he phones his adoring mother every day. He appears to long for some of the security of his prepopularity days. He says he likes to go back home—to New York, and "I would love to take the subway again, you know." And so what is he going to do about what he fondly calls his "schlep up the ladder of success?" "I've worked my ass off to get here, and I'm gonna work my ass off to stay here."

(1946–   )

A Brooklyn-born Afro-Cuban-jazz-soul-rock-Middle Eastern flutist.

"You can't be mentally constipated while trying to create music," Herbie Mann, the most popular of all flutists, once told Audrey Arbe of *Soul Sounds* magazine. "You have to be open and loose and be able to take other people's ideas, give and take, and then try to create something and not say I'm only going to go my way and no other way."

Herbie Mann has gone many ways with his music, in almost any direction that he feels his fans, old and hopefully also new, will follow him. "A Brooklyn-born Afro-Cuban-jazz-soul-rock-Middle Eastern flutist" is how Arbe has described him.

The very personable, articulate, and discerning Mann was born Herbert Jay Solomon, son of a Brooklyn furrier. He started playing clarinet, but when swing music's decline diminished the instrument's popularity, he switched to tenor sax, which he didn't like, and finally to the flute, on which, starting in 1957, he won many jazz honors. An astute, talented, and intelligent musician with wide-open ears, he formed an Afro-Cuban jazz group in 1959 but soon latched on to the bossa nova craze of the early 1960s, created a following "mostly among blacks, Puerto Ricans, and Jewish secretaries," he said at the time, and really hit pay dirt with a bluesy rendition of "Comin' Home, Baby." For years he had been listening avidly to records by rhythm and blues artists Ray Charles and Otis Redding; then, after hearing more experimental groups, like the Byrds, and Emerson, Lake and Palmer, expand songs past melodies by improvisation, he announced unabashedly, "I think I can do it better with a good rhythm and blues band."

And so, combining some of the Memphis r&b musicians with his own, he proceeded in 1969 to create his top-selling *Memphis Underground* album that established him as a premier recording artist among jazz/rock fusionists. Then, aware of Duane Allman's popularity, he joined forces in the next year with the rock guitarist for Mann's memorable *Push Push* album. A few years later, for his *London Underground* album, he delved even further into the rock bag by adding to his own group Mick Taylor of the Rolling Stones, Alan Gorey and Ian Mackintosh of the Average White Band, and Aynsley Dunbar of the Mothers of Invention. He took great pride in such amalgamations. "When you can get six or seven people together to at least listen to one another, that's an achievement . . . and to give themselves to somebody else, that's a bigger achievement."

Herbie

Mann not only took from, he also gave musicians to other groups. Two of his most illustrious alumni, Chick Corea and Billy Cobham, moved on to Miles Davis before forming their own groups. Some musicians, Mann has intimated, left him because "they used to think 'Comin' Home, Baby' was the devil, because it was so successful."

To some musicians and jazz fans, Mann, who has sold over ten million singles and albums, has seemed to be too obsessed with success. From 1960 to 1976 he had recorded forty-four albums, most of them highly commercial, one of his more recent even featuring a vocal group so brazenly that Mann admitted that "I had to pick my spots when I was going to come in behind the singers." As musician, writer Sy Johnson has noted, "Herbie Mann is a businessman who very carefully determined where his best chances of success lay and now brings out his 'spring' line as carefully as a Seventh Avenue garment manufacturer. He is different only in degree from Guy Lombardo and Lester Lanin who produce music to order for their clients."

As for Mann, who admittedly has gone directly after the money that has made him very wealthy, he offers not so much an excuse as a pragmatic explanation: "Because I'm not a Charlie Parker, maybe I got bored with my attempt to be profound."

Of such self-recognized creative limitations are musical millionaires made.

(1930–   )

Mantovani

"I wondered what I could do to make an impression in America."

Almost as a counterpoint to the rise of rock and roll in the 1950s was the spreading prevalence of lush string orchestrations of pop tunes. The keystone of the string movement was Annunzio Paolo Mantovani, known professionally as Mantovani. Born in Venice, Mantovani went to England when he was four, grew up and had his basic professional career in that country.

Unlike most idols in pop music, Mantovani was in his mid-forties before lightning struck. Trained as a classical violinist, he had been conducting for broadcasting, recordings theaters, and hotels since 1927. He had started playing violin professionally in a restaurant in Birmingham, England, when he was fifteen, and two years later he had his own band. In 1930 he began concertizing, and, after a concert at Queen's Hall in 1932, he received a note: "Bravo! Well Played!" signed "Tommy Beecham" (later known as Sir Thomas). Meanwhile, his orchestra was growing in popularity, and its records, which emphasized

Annunzio Paolo Mantovani

waltzes, tangos, and other relatively exotic steps (in a period when the box-step foxtrot predominated), began to attract more and more attention.

In 1951 the American branch of his English recording label asked the home office to have Mantovani record an album of waltzes.

"Nothing was said about doing the waltzes with strings," Mantovani has recalled. "But I had always had an ambition to have an orchestra with plenty of strings. I wondered what I could do to make an impression in America when they have the finest orchestras over there. So I said, 'You must give me a big string section.'

"Strings were not being used as they are now," he went on. "I wanted to get a classic string sound with plenty of violas and cellos. I wanted to use close harmonies. I wanted an effect of an overlapping of sound, as though we were playing in a cathedral."

Mantovani got his strings—twenty-eight in an orchestra of forty musicians. One of the waltzes he recorded was "Charmaine," the theme music for the 1926 silent film *What Price Glory.* It caught the ear of the mother of Bill Randle, a Cleveland disc jockey, who relentlessly plugged it into a hit, opening the floodgates for string-based recording groups and launching Mantovani on a twenty-year career as a top-level recording and concert attraction.

In the face of a multiplicity of recording groups diligently trying to ride on his coattails, Mantovani managed to stay far ahead of the pack. To explain the reason for his success, he conceded, "might make me seem conceited. But the reason is this: I've got more heart. And I'm a string man. I know what I want from my string players. I know the capabilities of the violin. I know what it can do. I don't want a soaring phrase that will sound squeaky on top. And," he added, "I've got first-class lads playing for me."

(1905–   )

Mary Martin

"I have a guilt feeling about not singing."

Among the enduring images of show business there is none so vivid as that of sailor-suited Ensign Nellie Forbush washing that man right out of her hair in *South Pacific* or Peter Pan, all mischief and gamin charm, sailing about the stage to the delight of audiences young and old.

For most Americans those roles belong to Mary Martin. From the start, belting out "My Heart Belongs to Daddy" in the 1938 New York production of *Leave It to Me!* she seemed born for the musical comedy stage.

The Texas-born beauty attributed her countless Broadway successes, movies, radio, and TV triumphs to an eternal love affair with her audiences.

"It's a marvelous feeling, to receive this mass outpouring of love," she said. "It's like being hypnotized. I'd go on feeling tired or ill and this love coming

Miss Martin

from the audience would be like adrenalin. You can't help but give out. You can't manufacture this."

Mary Martin's story is a natural, a show business classic. Doing a guest shot at a Los Angeles nightclub she was heard by producer Lawrence Schwab, who brought her to New York for *Leave It to Me!* From there, the Martin chemistry took over.

More than talent, more than just a strong soprano voice, personality, or natural stage presence, she had the ability to touch middle America at its most vulnerable point—its affection for the simple and sentimental. She was wholesome, spirited, feminine, and pretty, but not explicitly sexy; she projected family entertainment incarnate.

Even her attitude toward performing seemed to reflect solid American virtues: "I've never been jealous of a soul in my life. I've never been insecure. I love meeting people. I'm never nervous. I love to talk. I love to sing."

Mary Martin's successes are legion. *One Touch of Venus* at New York's Imperial Theater led to two years touring in *Annie Get Your Gun.* Then came *South Pacific,* costarring with Ezio Pinza, *Peter Pan, The Sound of Music, The Skin of Our Teeth,* and others. She starred in movies, among them *Birth of the Blues,* in which her "Waiter and the Porter and The Upstairs Maid" number with Bing Crosby and Jack Teagarden was an instant hit.

In the late 1960s she toured Vietnam playing *Hello, Dolly!* for U.S. forces there. She returned fatigued and sick, and soon withdrew from performing altogether to be with her husband, Richard Halliday, on their ranch in Brazil.

With Halliday's death in 1973 she returned to California and, inevitably, began talking of a comeback. In 1978 she played a straight dramatic role opposite Anthony Quayle on Broadway. Did that mean she had given up singing? "No darling, I haven't stopped singing," she told an interviewer. "I still have this thing I've had since I was twelve about nourishing your talent or it will be taken away. I have a guilt feeling about not singing. I want to sing again, and I guess I'm just waiting to be turned on."

(1913–   )

Johnny Mathis

"I don't know if you remember me or not, but we met at so-and-so's house."

"He just closed his eyes, tipped back his head, and poured out his heart," is how George Avakian described the singing of Johnny Mathis, whose soft, sensitive, high-pitched, and, to some, effeminate crooning served, during the late 1950s and early '60s, as a musical antidote for those unable to digest the era's barrage of boisterous rock and roll blasters.

Avakian, head album producer for Columbia Records, discovered the tall, thin, athletic Mathis in San Francisco at Ann's 400 Club, a small, gay spot that featured female impersonators. "It was his first singing job," Avakian recalls of that 1955 evening. "Until then he had merely been sitting in at jam sessions. But before he had sung eight bars, I knew I was going to sign him because I felt he could be simply great."

Johnny's father, a former vaudevillian turned chauffeur and handyman, had felt the same about this fourth of his seven children. After teaching him all he could about singing, he turned him over to a local music teacher, Connie Cox, who was so impressed by young Johnny's talents that for six years she taught him for free.

Still, Johnny thought when he grew up he might become an English teacher or an athletic director. A six-letter man in high school sports, he had shared, with future basketball great Bill Russell, a 6' 5½" West Coast high jump record, and had been considered an Olympic Games prospect. But when Avakian said, "Come to New York and make an album," he was on his way.

The album consisted of a dozen standard tunes scored by five top jazz arrangers. It wasn't a big hit, but Avakian and Johnny's hard-working, dedicated manager, Helen Noga, kept pushing for the talent in which they believed so thoroughly. "Besides," Avakian has since pointed out, "he was such a great kid—quiet, unassuming, and extremely well-mannnered, the kind who would never walk through a door ahead of you. And he has never changed."

However, Mathis' approach to singing did change when Mitch Miller, in charge of singles (Avakian headed the albums department), began working with Johnny. He eliminated the emphasis on jazz, and, by adding lush backgrounds to simple songs, concentrated on what he called "Johnny's choirboy quality." The result, according to writer Gilbert Millstein, was "an oddly engaging combination of seductiveness and innocence," as well as a succession of huge hits: "Wonderful! Wonderful!" followed by "It's Not for Me to Say," "Chances Are,"

"My name is Johnny Mathis."

and then one of Johnny's favorites which he also sang in the movie, "Lizzie," "The Twelfth of Never," and finally an album, *Johnny Mathis' Greatest Hits,* that stayed on *Billboard's* top one-hundred charts for an unprecendented seven years.

Johnny had made it big. He played top TV shows and concertized all over the world. For seven more years the record hits continued to pour out; then the flow began to ebb. But in 1978 he re-emerged with a huge hit, a duet with Deniece Williams of "Too Much, Too Little, Too Late." But, Johnny no longer needed the money. Shrewdly investing his earnings, he eventually owned, by his own count, "several apartment buildings, twelve music publishing firms, and an office block with a bank in it." And yet, even at the height of his fame and obvious fortune, he remained, according to Avakian, the same shy, sensitive, well-mannered lad who might go up to someone at a party and say, "I don't know if you remember me or not, but we met at so-and-so's house. My name is Johnny Mathis."

(1935–   )

Marian McPartland

"Marian McPartland has three strikes against her: she's English, white, and a woman."

What's it like being a woman in the supposedly man's world of jazz? It's great, if you'll believe Marian McPartland, one of the most sensitive and still most swinging of all jazz pianists, who once told Whitney Balliett in *The New Yorker,* "I don't feel I've ever been discriminated against jobwise. I have always been paid for what I was worth as a musician. So I feel I've been practicing women's lib for years."

Born Margaret Marian Turner into a conservative British family, she has also practiced as well as performed on the piano since the age of three, when she began picking out traditional tunes by ear. Some years later a boy friend brought some Duke Ellington records to the house and she became "hooked on jazz." Her parents, unapproving of her newfound passion, enrolled her in the sedate, conservative Guildhall School of Music, where she studied piano, composition, harmony, singing, and even violin, while hoping some day to become a jazz player.

When offered a job as part of a piano quartet playing pop tunes in vaudeville houses, she left school. Came World War II, and she volunteered to play for the troops, and was soon assigned to the USO. One night Jimmy McPartland, the famed Chicago jazz trumpeter-turned-soldier, joined her group. As Marian recalls the event, he muttered something like, "Oh my God, a woman piano player! I know she's going to be lousy!" "It happens," she later confessed, "that he was right. I had enthusiasm, and that was about all."

But she also did have something else: an excellent sense of harmony that attracted Jimmy. They played together for several weeks for troops on the front line. Her attractions multiplied and in February 1946 she became Mrs. Jimmy McPartland. Their marriage didn't last, but their mutual respect did. Long after their divorce Jimmy was saying, "There's no one I'd rather be with as a person, as an all-around human being," a sentiment shared by many who have also known her well.

They first lived and played together in Chicago, then in 1949 came to New York, where Marian led her own trio at the Embers and then for several years at the Hickory House. She also played for a while with Benny Goodman, who either didn't appreciate or comprehend her advanced harmonic progressions. "I was very competitive then. I liked to be told I played like a man." She fought hard and succeeded in gaining recognition for her trio as well as for

Marian

all women in jazz, and in the 1970s she wrote an excellent article on the subject included in *Esquire's World of Jazz.*

She also devoted her efforts to the recognition of jazz in general, forming her own Halcyon Records label that featured various worthy pianists, then spreading her talents through classrooms as she embarked on an intensive teaching schedule, visiting grammar and high schools, classrooms and clinics in colleges, and even prisons and detention homes. The enthusiastic responses to her efforts thrilled her, and she takes pride that her encouragements of self-expression may have kept some youngsters out of trouble and helped some older and troubled unfortunates to discover healthy, alternative outlets for their emotions.

Her development as a teacher improved her pianistic skills. "I had to listen to all kinds of music, and to know all about them, too. All that broadened me, and the more confident I became the more I lost my inhibitions."

By the later 1970s Marian McPartland was being acclaimed more and more by her fellow musicians for her tender touch, her harmonic ingenuity, and her swinging jazz beat. A quarter of a century earlier, she may have felt dismayed when critic Leonard Feather wrote that "Marian McPartland has three strikes against her: she's English, white, and a woman." But, once having proved herself, this strikingly handsome lady has been able to state unequivocally, "I don't feel I have any strikes against me whatsoever. In fact, life for me is really a ball!"

(1920–   )

Carmen McRae

"Lyrics are more important than melody to me."

If she had listened to her parents, she might be a concert pianist today, instead of "the only stylist," according to jazz critic Harvey Siders, "who sings in italics . . . the lyric writer's best friend."

Carmen McRae's middle-class Manhattan parents started her on classical piano lessons when she was eight. They applauded when she won several music scholarships but when, in her teens, she announced her intention to emulate Billie Holiday, "my idol, alter ego, and mentor," the parental cheering stopped.

She loved to sing and play popular songs for her fellow students at Julia Richmond High School. They loved it too. "I never studied voice at all," she said years later. "I was just one of those show-off brats who liked to entertain all the time."

An admiring mentor, Irene Kitchings (then married to Teddy Wilson), introduced the starry-eyed seventeen-year-old Carmen to Lady Day. "The bud of my ambition to be a singer," Carmen says, "opened up under Billie's approach . . . her penchant for taking the ordinary and illuminating it, bringing magic to the mundane and passion to prosaic material."

Through a friend, she got her first musical job as a singing pianist in a Chicago nightclub. "I knew only eight songs and I could only play them in the key of F. That made it sort of difficult for me, because I couldn't sing them all in that key, but I guess it worked out because I stayed there for seventeen weeks. That gave me the confidence I needed, and I also got to learn how to play in another key, the key of C!"

She began to study some more and to compose. During World War II she was featured with the Count Basie and Benny Carter bands. In 1946 and '47 she sang with the Mercer Ellington band and made her first records with it as Carmen Clarke. (She was then married to drummer Kenny Clarke, later known for his Jazz Messenger.) Later she worked in clubs around the country as an intermission pianist. To support herself between gigs, she worked as a typist and as a chorus girl. In 1953 she made her first records under her own name, some sensitive ballads with Dutch accordionist Mat Mathews on the little-known Stardust label.

By the mid-1950s, better club bookings, concert dates, rave reviews, and a major recording contract with Decca had come her way. She was maturing into what Johnny Magnus called "A Method Singer . . . like an eloquent viola . . . her tone mellow and true and a quality you want to live with." But even

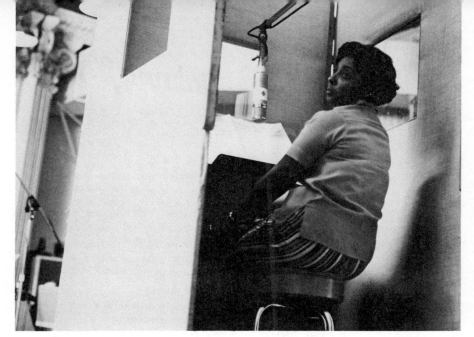

Carmen

as she was becoming perhaps the most versatile of all jazz singers, she was insisting that "being typed is a form of death," that "jazz is much more of a horn thing than a voice." In fact, Carmen does with her voice what every good horn player aspires to: She makes a statement, develops it, recapitulates it and takes it out.

"Lyrics," she believes, "are more important than melody to me. Some guy took a long time, maybe months or years to write it, and I figure that's the way he'd like to hear it."

Her following in the 1960s was solid but limited; why she has never achieved success on the scale of, say, Ella Fitzgerald's, not even Ella can say. "Rating by talent," says Ella of Carmen, "a thousand beautiful things should have happened to her."

In 1967 she moved from New York to Beverly Hills, hoping for some film parts. "If they don't develop," she said, "I've lived through a few mirages. I've a new husband and a new home and I really want to roost."

The film roles failed to materialize, the husband *de*materialized, and Carmen lives now with her poodle, Alfie. Still, Carmen's life today is pretty much on Carmen's terms. She cuts a couple of albums a year, works where and when she pleases and, when laying back, most enjoys "doin' *nothing!*"

On stage, her once-glamorous image is earthier now—but even in caftans and close-cropped hair, the Rushmore-like profile, the eloquent hands, the thousand-year-old eyes and the elegant presence make her the quintessential (but hip!) African Queen.

(1922–   )

Johnny Mercer

He took his responsibilities seriously, but his performing talents lightly.

He was warm, witty, tremendously talented and deeply admired and appreciated by all who came in contact with him on both a professional and personal level. Though Johnny Mercer achieved greatest fame as probably the finest all-around lyricist of the twentieth century, he was also a distinctive and delightful singer of often clever and always joyous rhythm tunes, and one of the smartest and most successful music businessmen, one of the founders in 1942 of Capitol Records, where he seemed to care even more about his artists' opportunities to create than his stockholders' chances for higher dividends.

The round-faced, puckish Mercer with the wide-awake southern drawl cared most of all about music and people. Friends tell the story of how years after his father's small bank had failed during the Depression of the 1930s, Johnny, having sold his interest in Capitol Records ("After a while, it stopped being fun," he explained later), quietly, unbeknown even to his wife, Ginger, searched out the investors and repaid each of them, or their heirs, in full.

He took his responsibilities seriously, but his performing talents lightly, projecting a lighthearted, devil-may-care aura into the songs, mostly his own, that he recorded or sang on his radio shows. His dozens of records included some memorable duets with Bing Crosby, one of his greatest admirers, with Jack Teagarden (their "Fare Thee Well to Harlem" became a jazz classic), with Ginger Rogers, Nat Cole, Bobby Darin, and others. And he also sang on records with the bands of Paul Whiteman, the Dorsey Brothers, and Benny Goodman.

His words graced the melodies of many of pop music's greatest composers, most of whom sought him out as a collaborator—Harold Arlen, Hoagy Carmichael, Duke Ellington, Jerome Kern, Henry Mancini, Jimmy McHugh, Arthur Schwartz, Jimmy Van Heusen, Harry Warren, Richard Whiting, and more. His total output of over fifteen hundred songs included "Accentuate the Positive," his own philosophy; "And the Angels Sing," a Jewish frählich that he wrote to order for Benny Goodman, who, Mercer once stated, "believed in me long before the others did"; "Blues in the Night"; "Come Rain or Come Shine," from one of six scores he wrote for Broadway musicals; "Dream," one of the few songs for which he wrote both words and music; "G.I. Jive," which he wrote in ten minutes; "I'm an Old Cowhand"; "Jeepers Creepers," which he sang on many personal appearances; "Laura," according to him, "the most recorded of all my songs"; "One for My Baby"; "Satin Doll"; "Skylark";

"You Must Have Been a Beautiful Baby"; and the three songs that won him Oscars, "On the Atchison, Topeka and the Santa Fe," "Days of Wine and Roses," and "Moon River."

Many of Mercer's hits were written for the movies. He had migrated to Hollywood in 1935, leaving the Whiteman band to try his hand at writing for films and also singing and acting in them. How successful was he in his thespian role? "I made two pictures and I was never in another; that's a pretty good answer," he once replied with typical candor.

An acting career had been an early ambition, which is why he had left his comfortable home in the late 1920s for a try at Broadway. When he failed to gain even a minor role in a revue called *Garrick Gaieties,* he decided to try contributing a song instead. It was accepted, and his career as a songwriter was officially launched.

Mercer's simple, direct, unpretentious qualities pervaded his singing, his writing, and his life-style. He was deeply loved by his wife of almost fifty years and his two children, and so respected by his peers that they elected him the first president of their Songwriters Hall of Fame. He died in June 1976, following the removal of a brain tumor, leaving a musical legacy that projected, to quote close friend and writer Bob Bach, "a native humor, a keen insight into the nation's speech habits, and an originality of thought as refreshing as the scent of magnolias."

(1909–1976)

"You've got to accentuate the positive!"

Mabel Mercer

"I can't bear to listen to myself."

When she sings, sitting in a straight-backed chair, a long, colorful shawl around her shoulders, Mabel Mercer exudes a regal aura. In her mid-seventies, she is still a handsome woman, her posture erect, her diction precise, yet easy and natural.

A queen-mother figure not just in appearance but in reality, Miss Mercer has been the learning source for a remarkable span of popular singers. Frank Sinatra has said that Mabel Mercer "taught me everything I know." Her other "students" have included Nat "King" Cole, Billie Holiday (who almost lost a job because she kept sneaking out to hear Miss Mercer), Leontyne Price, Eileen Farrell, Peggy Lee, Mel Torme, Lena Horne, and Bobby Short.

She has also gathered around her a flock of songwriters who would prefer to have her rather than anyone else sing their songs. Alec Wilder, whose "While We're Young" was first sung by Miss Mercer, has called her "the guardian of the tenuous dreams created by writers of songs." She introduced Bart Howard's "Fly Me to the Moon," Edward Redding's "The End of a Love Affair," and many songs by Cy Coleman. She found and kept alive an impressive number of songs that might otherwise have been forgotten—"Little Girl Blue," which she nursed for years after it made its debut in Rodgers and Hart's *Jumbo* in 1935; "By Myself" from the 1937 show *Between the Devil;* and "Remind Me," which was buried in a 1940 Abbott and Costello film, *One Night in the Tropics.*

Despite all this, Miss Mercer tends to be self-deprecating. "I've always been shy of singing," she says. "It's a great surprise to me when people say nice things. I can't bear to listen to myself. I won't listen to my records."

For many years her soft soprano voice sensitively caressed the sophisticated songs whose lyrics were heightened by her intelligent interpretations. In later years, though, her voice deepened and became less certain.

"As my voice got lower and lower," she explained, "I had to compensate for the notes I couldn't make anymore. It gave me a chance to talk the story of a song. People say, 'Why, she can't sing for toffee!' I say, 'I know that—I'm telling a story.' "

Miss Mercer was born into a vaudeville family in Staffordshire, England. Her father was a black American who died before she was born, her mother a white Welsh singer and actress. Mabel joined the family act as a dancer when she was fourteen. She began singing in Paris when a male quartet that had lost a tenor asked her to fill in. When the quartet broke up, Miss Mercer

Mabel Mercer, circa 1933

continued on her own as a singer and was a fixture at Bricktop's, a favorite Paris club for the international set, from 1931 until she came to New York in 1938 to perform at Le Ruban Bleu. In the early 1940s she established herself at Tony's, a small club on West Fifty-second Street, where her followers flocked to hear her until the building was torn down in 1949. Since then she has had several "homes," including Downstairs at the Upstairs, and the St. Regis Hotel.

Over half a century she has collected more than a thousand songs that she likes. But she admits that there are a lot of good songs that are not for her. "I can't get anything out of them," declares this singer who has shown so many other singers how to get the most out of so many songs.

(1900–   )

Sometimes brash and loud, she was always very direct and completely unphony.

"I just stand up and holler and hope that my voice holds out," explained Ethel Merman in her autobiography, *Who Could Ask for Anything More*. And that's exactly what's been happening. For more than sixty years, the most enduring and dynamic star of the musical theater has been standing up and hollering and delighting audiences, composers, and fellow performers. And her voice has held out.

Young Ethel Zimmerman began unleashing her vocal cords when she was only five years old, singing in her family's Lutheran church in the Astoria section of New York City. Self-assured even then, she began entertaining the troops at Long Island's Camp Mills when she was only eight, while also singing in local amateur shows. But she was also a realist who knew that she'd better learn something more than singing. So she took up shorthand and typing, and soon became secretary to the president of the B. K. Vacuum Booster Brake Company.

But still she kept hollering, evenings and on weekends, to supplement her income. While singing in a Manhattan bistro, she was discovered by a talent scout who found her enough work so that she could break away from the brake company and who convinced her to drop the "Zim" from Zimmerman.

During her first important engagement in the stage show at the Brooklyn Paramount Theater, she was heard by Broadway producer Vinton Freedley, then casting with his partner, Alex A. Aarons, for their forthcoming musical comedy *Girl Crazy*. Impressed, he arranged for an audition with the show's composer, George Gershwin, who, after hearing young Ethel belt out a few numbers in her unique, unorthodox way, said, "Don't ever go near a teacher. He'll only ruin you." Forever after she heeded his advice.

She got the job and on opening night, October 15, 1930, she stopped the show cold with the very first line of her very first song, "Sam and Delilah," as she belted "Delila . . . was a fff-loozy!" And she was able to top all this with her first-act finale of "I Got Rhythm," the song with which forever after she was closely identified.

Merman's energy was incredible. While appearing evenings in *Girl Crazy*, she spent her days at Paramount's Astoria studios making not only short film subjects, but also her feature film debut in *Follow the Leader*. But that wasn't all. After each performance of *Girl Crazy* she would hie herself over to perform

"I Got Rhythu-u-um-m-m!"

at the then ultra-chic Central Park Casino, where she was backed by Leo Reisman's Orchestra, with young Eddy Duchin at the piano.

From then on her career became a nonstop series of successes. She starred in a dozen more Broadway shows, including *Anything Goes, Panama Hattie, Annie Get Your Gun, Call Me Madam,* and *Gypsy,* and also appeared in fifteen movies. Record-wise, though, she was less successful, for her dynamism and charm needed to be seen as well as heard.

Her talents remained in constant demand, especially by composers, who loved the straightforward, energetic way in which she treated their material. Cole Porter stated, "I'd rather write for Ethel Merman than for anyone else in the world." He wrote five shows for her: *Anything Goes, Red Hot and Blue!, Du Barry was a Lady, Panama Hattie,* and *Something for the Boys.* Irving Berlin wrote *Annie Get Your Gun* and *Call Me Madam.* And she helped turn their best songs into all-time hits: "You're the Top," "I Get a Kick Out of You," "Anything Goes," and "It's D'lovely" for Porter; "They Say It's Wonderful" and "There's No Business Like Show Business" for Berlin.

Her personality matched her performing style. Sometimes brash and loud, she was always very direct and completely unphony, admired and respected by her fellow performers both as an artist and as a person. And one thing she wasn't was shy. In discussing her concern "for making people understand the lyric I sing" she unabashedly stated, "I honestly don't think there's anyone in the business who can top me at that." Or as friend and admirer Cole Porter had already written for her, "You're the top !"

(1909–   )

Bette Midler

Through all her performances shone her outrageous, often totally uninhibited personality.

The "Divine Miss M" is one of those self-created personalities who took an improbable appearance and an average talent and, by the sheer force of her dreams and desires, burst out of the pack, demanding our love and attention.

Combining the torch singing of Helen Morgan, the gospel quality of Aretha Franklin, and the uninhibited vigor of Janis Joplin, Bette Midler created a driving, "I-will-not-be-denied" singing personality that was embellished in personal appearances with the brassiness and "put-on" sexuality of a Mae West or a Sophie Tucker.

Born in Honolulu, Bette was raised in Aier, which she has described as "a slum right near Pearl Harbor." Miserable as a child, the only Jewish girl in her grade school, she was withdrawn. She read a lot, often living in daydreams where she eventually created the "Divine Miss M" who would permit her to act out all her fantasies on stage.

The Divine Miss M

"By the time I was a senior in high school," she reports, "I was completely stagestruck and had made up my mind that eventually I would come to New York." When she made the move in 1965 she felt "like I was finally free."

First she acted in off-off Broadway shows, then landed a job in the chorus of *Fiddler on the Roof,* eventually graduating to a featured role. Meanwhile she was also playing in clubs, looking for new "old" material, like Helen Morgan's torch songs, to add to her act. Steve Ostrow, owner of the Continental Baths, liked her and gave her weekends at his club, a gathering spot for gays. Responding to them, she grew more outrageous; the Helen Morgan part began shrinking as the Mae West personality took over. May Okun wrote in the New York *News* Sunday magazine: "The 'gays' saw in her a rebellious, kindred spirit. Her big belting voice, imitating, parodying, wallowing in the past but making it all sound new, her campy clothes, letting it all hang out, made them forget their longtime devotion to . . . Garland, Davis, and Tallulah."

She took on a coach, Bill Hennesy, who helped organize her wild, frenzied performing and developed it into an act. But perhaps even more important, certainly from a musical standpoint, was her relationship with the young accompanist who joined her at the Baths. It was Barry Manilow who arranged her first big hit, "Boogie Woogie Bugle Boy," and it was Barry Manilow, equally talented and in his own quieter way just as forceful as Bette, who helped develop her musically. As Bette described them, they were "two Jewish kids with incredible egos" and often they would yell and scream at each other, letting out their deepest emotions, yet at the same time bringing out the best in one another.

Bette's fame began spreading. She moved from the Baths to Upstairs at the Downstairs. Suddenly, it seemed, all of New York night life was turning out for her. She appeared regularly on "The Tonight Show," went with host Johnny Carson to Las Vegas, returned to New York an even bigger star.

Through all her performances shone her outrageous, often totally uninhibited personality. In 1973, Atlantic Records attempted to capture her performance inside a studio, replacing Manilow with an "in-house" producer. The sessions weren't making it. Then someone brought in a tape of a concert with Manilow conducting his own arrangements and Midler performing superbly. He was brought in, the special Midler quality was recaptured, and the album, *The Divine Miss M,* turned out to be a smash, and Bette was awarded a Grammy as the Best New Performer of 1973.

Meanwhile, Manilow was making it on his own as performer/composer/conductor. The beautiful chemistry between Bette and Barry was thereby disturbed, and in 1974 she retreated to her Greenwich Village apartment. Then in 1975 she emerged again, bright and saucy as ever, a big hit in her Broadway show, *Clams on the Half Shell,* and in numerous concerts. In 1976 she recorded another album, *Songs for the New Depression,* her career was again blossoming, and once again the Divine Miss M had recaptured the love and attention for which she had always so fervently yearned.

(c.1945–   )

A stern, dogmatic, hard-nosed taskmaster, he worked equally hard at controlling his musicians and his emotions.

He had always possessed two major assets: (1) He knew exactly what he wanted, and (2) He knew exactly how to get it. And then in 1939, when Glenn Miller discovered exactly what his public wanted, he completed the formula that allowed him to create the most popular big band of all time.

Success as a bandleader had eluded him before then. When he organized his first band in 1937, he tried to compete on the same swinging level with

The Glenn Miller band at the Cafe Rouge: (front row) Ray Eberle, Hal Dickenson, Chuck Goldstein, Ralph Brewster, Marion Hutton; (second row) Paul Tanner, Jim Priddy, Frank D'Anolfo, Miller, Wilbur Schwartz, Al Klink, Skip Martin, Ernie Caceres, Tex Beneke; (back row) Ray Anthony, Johnny Best, Dale McMickle, Billy May, Bill Conway, Doc Goldberg, Maurice Purtill, Chummy MacGregor

friends and former fellow studio musicians Benny Goodman, Artie Shaw, and Tommy and Jimmy Dorsey, each already well established with his band, and each an outstanding soloist in his own right. But Glenn, never an outstanding trombone soloist, failed miserably. A realist, he recognized that the sound of his own horn wasn't enough. So he created a new band with a new sound that focused on five reeds—one clarinet and four saxes—and on ballads instead of swing numbers. Its impact on the public far exceeded even his fondest hopes, and almost forty years later, long after Major Glenn Miller had disappeared in a plane over the English Channel, that "Glenn Miller Sound" still stood out as the most evocative and most memorable reminder of the big band era.

Some music purists claimed that Miller's music sounded too mechanical, that Glenn adhered too strictly to a formula. What they failed to realize was that as good as Miller was as an arranger, he was an even better businessman. A brilliant organizer, who had formed bands for the Dorsey Brothers and Ray Noble before starting his own, he was also a topflight administrator with a cool, calculating approach that subjugated emotional wishes to pragmatic needs. In fact, during the three quarters of a year that he spent at the University of Colorado, he flunked music, but gained high grades in mathematics!

His family had moved to Colorado when Glenn, who had been born in Clarinda, Iowa, was in his late teens. Financially deprived (they had all lived in a sod hut for a while), Glenn had been instilled with the work ethic, with success and financial security as ultimate goals. He milked cows, worked in a beet factory, and jerked sodas before settling on music as a career. He played in territory bands, eventually moved to Los Angeles where his roommate, Ted Mack, then a saxophonist in Ben Pollack's band and later majordomo of TV's "Amateur Hour," got him a job with Pollack, one of the top bands of the late 1920s. Later came studio and theater pit jobs in New York, recording sessions with Red Nichols, and eventually organizing and arranging for the Dorseys and Noble.

Finally he decided to do unto himself what he had done unto others: He organized his own band. Success arrived in the spring of 1939 during an engagement at the Glen Island Casino, and soon kids throughout the land were naming Miller's their number one band.

Hit record followed hit record: "Moonlight Serenade" (the theme he had written as an arranging exercise), "In the Mood," "A String of Pearls," "Tuxedo Junction," "At Last," "Chattanooga Choo Choo," "Serenade in Blue," "Don't Sit under the Apple Tree," and on and on. His repertoire mixed ballads that featured his reed sound and Ray Eberle's singing with simple, easily understood swing numbers that often spotted Glenn's favorite singing tenor saxist, Tex Beneke, Marion Hutton and the Modernaires, and lots of visual showmanship by the entire band.

In theaters, in ballrooms, in hotel supper rooms, and on his commercial radio series that ran uninterruptedly for almost three years, ending only in

Glenn with Frank D'Anolfo, Maurice Purtill, Wilbur Schwartz, Al Klink

Glenn

September 1942, after Glenn had enlisted in the Army, Miller's music remained a model of musical consistency. A stern, dogmatic, hard-nosed taskmaster, he worked equally hard at controlling his musicians and his emotions, showing and sharing with few people the warmth and love that he kept so tightly muted. He remained especially close and devoted to his wife, Helen; his quasi-biographical movie, *The Glenn Miller Story,* recaptured that relationship admirably, even though, while June Allyson portrayed the real Helen Miller effectively, Jimmy Stewart's wishy-washy "Glenn" was only pure Jimmy Stewart.

Within the band, he was strictly the father figure, regularly dispensing discipline, sage musical advice, and expertise. His "children's" reactions varied. Singer Marion Hutton said, "With the band I felt I was just a thing, that's all." Tex Beneke, while admitting that Miller was "strict" and "tough on musicians," emphasized that "I loved the man. He taught me so much." Drummer Maurice Purtill, one of the few sidemen close to Glenn, summed up with, "Never in the music business was there a smarter cat. He had it all covered. And everybody knows how generous he was. He tried to be rough, but that was just a pose."

When it came to things outside himself, however, Glenn hid very little. He made his likes and dislikes very obvious. He never hesitated to say what was on his mind. And though he always respected and encouraged outstanding musicianship, he never denied that his primary goal as a bandleader was public acceptance.

He was also very patriotic, which is why, after having been turned down for a commission in the Navy shortly after World War II began, he fought until he gained a captaincy in the Army—all this despite being classified "non-draftable." In the service, he organized one of the greatest bands of all time, and never let up pressure on Washington until his band was booked into what he felt was the most important engagement of his lifetime: playing live for the soldiers in England and France. His dedication to his men and his goals induced him to attempt a flight across the English Channel, despite treacherous weather conditions and an innate fear of flying, to make sure his musicians would be well taken care of when they arrived a few days later. As he entered the tiny plane he reportedly asked, "Where the hell are the parachutes?" To which a fellow officer retorted, "What's the matter, Miller, do you want to live forever?" That "forever" lasted less than an hour: the plane and Glenn Miller were never heard from again.

Not so his music, however. Thirty-five years after that fatal 1944 flight, the sound of Glenn Miller was still being heard all over the world, played live by the official Glenn Miller Orchestra, and via records that continued to sell in the hundreds of thousands, year in and year out, bringing back fond memories to all those millions who agree with *All in the Family's* Archie and Edith Bunker's opening lines: "Boy, the way Glenn Miller played! . . . Those were the days!"

(1904–1944)

Mitch Miller

His apparent double standard shocked some music purists.

"If you don't reach your audience, you're nothing!" Mitch Miller recently proclaimed. By his own proclamation, he was really "something" because he emphatically reached not just one, but two kinds of audiences: those enthralled by his mastery of the oboe and the English horn, which he played in symphonies, chamber music groups, and leading pop studio orchestras, and those who bought the millions of the ultra-commercial records, complete with various gimmicks, that he produced for Columbia throughout the fifties.

His apparent double standard shocked some music purists. But the pragmatic Miller felt no qualms. As a classical musician, he remained eternally pure. But as a pop performer and producer, he insisted that "it's perfectly all right to do anything so long as it makes the result more palatable."

Most palatable and successful of all his endeavors were his million-seller "Sing-a-Long with Mitch" albums. These simple and direct chorus renditions of very well-known songs made active participants of formerly passive listeners as they joyously joined Mitch's enthusiastic chorus emoting songs like "Tzena-Tzena," "The Yellow Rose of Texas," "The Bridge on the River Kwai," "The Children's Marching Song," and "Do-Re-Mi."

Mitch

Miller remains proud of those recordings—the way his singers phrased like members of an orchestra, the clarity of their articulation and the brilliance of their sound. A forerunner in modernizing recording techniques, he once insisted that "anybody who doesn't take advantage of advances in electronics is an idiot."

Mitch has always believed in forging ahead as quickly as possible. After he took up the oboe as a twelve-year-old member of his high school orchestra (all the other instruments had been assigned), he applied himself so diligently that he was soon offered scholarship lessons at the famed Eastman School of Music in his hometown of Rochester, New York. At fifteen he had become a member of the Eastman Symphony and five years later he was concertizing in New York City. In 1936 he began an eleven-year tenure as a staff musician at CBS, playing under Andre Kostelanetz and Percy Faith, and eventually winding up as the most respected and sought-after oboe and English horn player in town.

An artist but also a practical businessman, Mitch relates that "I was always raising hell on record dates because so much time was being wasted." Such an unusual musician's attitude attracted John Hammond, who was then supervising sessions for Mercury Records, and who needed someone to produce some dates in a hurry. So he called on Mitch, who was soon also producing classical recordings for Keynote, children's records for Golden, and more pop sides for Mercury. He became so successful that in 1950 Columbia Records asked him to take over its pop record department. There he nurtured and supervised the careers of Tony Bennett, Rosemary Clooney, Frankie Laine, Johnny Mathis, Guy Mitchell, and Johnny Ray, among others, spicing their recordings with what were in those days such unusual sounds as a tinny, tinkling harpsichord, French horns whooping in unison, galloping horses' hooves and even the sound of a bull whip swirling through the air.

During the mid 1970s, long after his recording career had ended and he was conducting orchestras in various parts of the world, he was asked to briefly analyze his success. "It's simple," he said. "It's like being a good cook. Everyone can go to a grocery store and buy the same ingredients. It's how you put them together and how you season them that makes your dish a success or a disaster."

(1911–   )

Roger Miller

A spectacular job fitting more words-per-line-per-song than many folks ever had dreamed possible.

"Erick is so small that the city limits signs are back to back. Its population is fifteen hundred rakes and tractors." Whether it be in the well-turned verse of a song or in the whimsical description of his hometown, the natural poetry of Roger Miller is omnipresent. From a tangled and wordy English he makes lyrical and sometimes circular sense, leaving his listeners shaking their heads yet understanding perfectly what he has just said or sung.

Roger Dean Miller was born in Fort Worth, Texas, but before he was one, his family had moved to Erick, Oklahoma. His facility with the English language was demonstrated at the age of five when he wrote his first song for his classmates,

The King of the Road

all occupants of a one-room schoolhouse. He sums up his early education with the typical Miller alacrity:

"This school I went to had thirty-seven students, me and thirty-six Indians. One time we had a school dance and it rained for thirty-six days straight. During recess we used to play cowboys and Indians and things got pretty wild from my standpoint."

Roger had left school by the end of the eighth grade and began working odd jobs, among them ranch-handing and dehorning cattle. During this time he managed to polish up his musical act, so that by the time he enlisted in the Army his jeep-driving status was quickly commuted to a stint in the Special Services, entertaining troops in a country band. And entertained the troops must have been, for Roger played not only guitar, but drums and fiddle, and sang much of his own material.

Once discharged from the Army (which Roger refers to as his college education—"Korea, Clash of '52') he made his move to Nashville. Using up his pocketful of cash to stay one night in a posh hotel, Miller then took a job at the same hotel as a bellhop, working for tips and entertaining elevator riders with snatches of newly written songs. Encouraged by the receptions to some of his efforts, he set himself to the serious task of writing songs and presenting them to artists and publishers. Finally, in the late 1950s, Ray Price recorded a Roger Miller song, "Invitation to the Blues," and soon after, Miller became a writer for the Nashville-based Faron Young Organization.

Roger's own recording career began in the early 1960s with "When Two Worlds Collide." But he had already moved to Hollywood and was pursuing acting when things really started moving with his original songs. People were beginning to listen to the man who could do a spectacular job fitting more words-per-line-per-song than many folks ever had dreamed possible. By 1966, Miller had recorded numerous hits: "Dang Me," "Chug-A-Lug," "King of the Road," "Kansas City Star," "England Swings," and "Husbands and Wives." In two years, 1965 and 1966, he walked off with an unprecedented total of eleven Grammy awards.

Then came what Miller has described as a "dry period" of songwriting for himself. "It had all come so easy to me, writing songs. Then it got so hard I just couldn't do it. So I stopped writing for four or five years." But Miller made a brilliant comeback in 1973 with an album entitled *Dear Folks, Sorry I Haven't Written Lately* and in that same year was named to the Nashville Songwriters Association Hall of Fame, as he once again began giving both his pop and country audiences a little wisdom, a lot of wit, and a raft of unforgettable songs.

(1936–   )

The Mills Brothers

"One of the most spontaneous-sounding groups of all time."

"They are the kind of guys," Sy Oliver was saying about the Mills Brothers, for whom he had arranged many recording sessions, "who tip their hats when they meet a lady."

That may not sound like much, but it describes elegantly the brothers who for more than fifty years projected one of the politest and still one of the most propulsive of all group singing styles. Their sound was always rich, well modulated, beautifully blended, and forever swinging. Over a period of half a century they almost miraculously never lost the joyous conviviality that permeated all their hit recordings, "Up the Lazy River," "Paper Doll," "I'll Be Around," "Till Then," "You Always Hurt the One You Love," "Glow-Worm," and "You're Nobody Till Somebody Loves You." An admiring Artie Shaw described them as "one of the most spontaneous-sounding groups of all time. Every time they sing a song they sound as if they're doing it for the first time."

The Mills Brothers (second from bottom is actually the Mills father)

The first time they ever started singing together was as kids back in 1922 in their hometown of Piqua, Ohio. Their house had been filled with music. Mother and Father Mills had dabbled in opera, and all four of the brothers, John, Herbert, Harry, and Donald, sang in the church choir along with their three sisters. When John came in possession of a guitar, the four boys began fooling around with popular music, imitating musical instruments as well as singing the words. During a 1925 audition with a band at Cincinnati radio station WLW, the band didn't get the job, but the brothers did, and soon they were singing at the station under various names on various shows. Talent developer and agent Tom Rockwell heard them and arranged for an audition with the CBS network. They were signed by William Paley on the spot and given their own show as well as a three-year contract, the first such break for any black artists.

They also began making records, first on Brunswick and then Decca, mostly with just a guitar, but sometimes coupled with artists like Louis Armstrong, the Boswell Sisters, Cab Calloway, Duke Ellington, and later on with Count Basie. During the period of 1925 to 1975 they estimate that they recorded a total of 2,490 songs!

Tragedy struck in 1936 when John, who sang the oompah bass parts and played the guitar, died of pneumonia. They worked as a trio for a while, auditioning replacements in the meantime. Then one day, according to *Ebony* writer Louis Robinson, their father, John, Sr., walked in and announced, "Everybody out. I'm taking over." And he stayed on for the next twenty years, singing John, Jr's "oompah" parts. When he retired in 1956 the brothers returned to their trio format.

Their sound changed little; the warm, musical vocal blend, interspersed with occasional imitations of horns, remained one of the joys of popular music. Off stage they have blended a bit less, for each leads his own personal life. As their longtime record producer Tom Mack has noted, "They're all beautiful but very different. Herb is the quiet one; he keeps to himself and takes care of his golf and family. Harry remains the spokesman; he's the most talkative, ebullient, and the charmer. Donald is somewhere between the two; he is a great family man and in that respect the most prolific."

By the mid-1970s, all three had settled comfortably in their West Coast homes, financially secure and emerging from time to time to work in top clubs and television. On a recent *Tonight* show, an admiring Johnny Carson asked them how much longer they planned to stay around, to which brother Harry politely quipped, "As long as people want us. At our age we have nothing better to do."

(Herbert: 1913–   )
(Harry: 1913–   )
(Donald: 1915–   )

Charles Mingus

President Carter gave him a warm hug.

A big, shaggy bear of a man given to volcanic outbursts of temper; complex, proud, unpredictable, and fiercely individualistic: that was Charles Mingus, bassist, composer, bandleader, and creator of one of the most personal bodies of music in the annals of the highly personal music called jazz.

Born in Arizona and raised in Watts, the black sector of Los Angeles, Mingus first played trombone, then cello, but his early musical development was handicapped by incompetent teachers. His parents were religious, and the music of the black holiness church was almost all he heard as a child. In his early teens, a friend, trombonist Britt Woodman, introduced him to the music of Duke Ellington. "I never heard music like that in church," he remembered. "I nearly jumped out of the bleachers. Britt had to hold me."

Ellington became—and remained—one of Mingus' musical heroes. He took up bass, this time under first-rate teachers, and soon became a professional musician. After working with Louis Armstrong and Kid Ory, among others,

Mingus

he came to the fore as a member of Lionel Hampton's big band, notably with his composition, arrangement, and solo feature, "Mingus Fingers." He further established his reputation through a stint with Red Norvo's trio, and also worked with two of his idols, Art Tatum and Charlie Parker. By the mid-1950s, he had settled in New York and begun to lead his own groups.

Mingus soon evolved his concept of the "jazz workshop," performing regular repertoire as well as works in progress in a unique setting characterized by his exhortations (and occasionaly bawling out) of his sidemen, stop-and-go performance procedures, and other unorthodox methods. His groups became incubators for new jazz talent, and he also demonstrated an uncanny ability, akin to Ellington's, of coaxing extraordinary performances from players of modest or even insignificant ability.

"Mingus' musical personality is so exaltingly forceful that he can uplift almost any musician and transcend almost any material," writer Nat Hentoff has noted. Demanding the utmost from himself as well as from his players, Mingus was a hard taskmaster. His compositions, which ran the gamut of emotions and incorporated stylistic devices from traditional to avant garde, remained in a constant state of flux in performance. At any given moment, Mingus would call for sudden changes in tempo, key, or solo order, keeping players and listeners in suspense, and he has been known to stop the music in midair if something annoys him. A consummate virtuoso (he has been dubbed "the Segovia of the bass"), he extended the expressive potentials of the instrument remarkably. His compositions reflected his character—from tender vignettes to straightforward soul music through ideological statements to complex, full-scale suites.

"I play and write me," he once explained, "the way I feel. And I'm changing all the time. I've got to go inside, as far inside myself as I can. I'm going to get through and find out the kind of man I am—or die."

In the late 1960s, after a melodramatic eviction from his loft apartment, Mingus went into a psychological slump. Exceedingly angry, he denounced the word "jazz" as racist, and refused to be called a jazz musician. But he re-emerged a few years later, was awarded a Guggenheim fellowship, wrote scores for films and TV and won worldwide acclaim. In the late 1970s a serious illness confined him to a wheelchair, in which he sat on the White House lawn during a June 1978 jazz concert. During the proceedings, promoter George Wein acknowledged Mingus' presence, whereupon President Carter walked over to the surprised and obviously touched Mingus and gave him a warm hug as the hundreds of jazz fans cheered.

For once, the man who acted so often as though he felt the whole world, especially the Establishment, was against him, must have realized for certain how much he was loved and respected. He had found what kind of man he was. Six months later he died, and the New York *Times* spread his picture over two columns of its front page.

(1922–1979)

Liza Minnelli

A waif in a Halston gown.

From the first, Liza Minnelli has known how to stand her ground and, sooner or later, to triumph. Her family's pet boxer puppy nipped her when she was a child and, a family friend recalls, "She looked over at the dog so hurt, and then she crawled over and bit the dog on the leg!"

With this combination of vulnerability, imagination, and spunk, Liza survived challenges that might have broken frailer spirits and, not satisfied with mere survival, bloomed, gloriously, as a singer, dancer, and actress with her own personal magic.

Being the daughter of eminent film director Vincente Minnelli and the brilliant, tormented Judy Garland was a mixed blessing. There were wondrous advantages like dressing up in movie costumes, riding the camera boom with her father

Liza

as he lined up shots, peeking at Fred Astaire, Gene Kelly, and Cyd Charisse at rehearsal and then practicing their numbers in front of a mirror at home. At three, Liza made her professional debut in a toddle-on role in *In the Good Old Summertime,* directed by Vincente Minnelli and starring Judy Garland.

But when she was just a young child Liza's parents divorced, her mother soon remarried, and Liza was caught up in an uncertain, nomadic life. They had either lots of money or, more frequently, none at all.

"I don't really remember having any childhood," Liza recalls. "I always had responsibilities and never felt free." By the time she was sixteen she had attended more than twenty schools, and by the time she was seventeen she had dropped out in favor of a chorus-line "gypsy" apprenticeship and landed a job as the third lead in an off-Broadway revival of *Best Foot Forward.* After that she toured with her mother in one of the famous Garland "comebacks."

Anyone who thought that Liza was coasting on the strength of her parents' reputations was set straight when, at nineteen, she won a Tony Award for the best actress in an otherwise forgettable musical, *Flora, the Red Menace.* She was the youngest performer ever to receive the honor. Soon afterward she made her solo nightclub debut at the Shoreham in Washington, D.C., earned her first adult screen credit in 1968 in a featured role in *Charlie Bubbles* and, a year later, playing a lovable, even admirable kook in *The Sterile Cuckoo,* won her first Academy Award nomination.

When she was twenty-five, Liza burst forth as a first-magnitude star with her singing, dancing, and acting performance in the film *Cabaret.* To no one's surprise she walked off with the Oscar for her breathtaking characterization of Sally Bowles.

Liza is a total performer. Her broad-shouldered, long-legged body, her eloquent, doe-eyed face, and her dynamic but superbly controlled gestures are as essential to her performance as her voice. It's a good voice, well trained and supple and, when she chooses, hauntingly reminiscent of her mother's; but, as a voice, it is not especially distinctive. Liza's genius is in what she does with her voice, in her surefooted instinct for the drama of a phrase, and in the way her confident professionalism plays against her half-expressed appeal for love.

"I love attention and I want everything," says Liza. "But, listen, I know show biz ain't all singin' and dancin'." Though she's one of the world's highest-paid and most sought-after artists, Liza works single-mindedly and disciplines herself like a hungry beginner. She still puts in six weeks of tough rehearsal to polish a new act for Las Vegas.

Not content with being merely an echo of her mother, Liza drove herself toward excellence on her own terms. Now a star in her own right, a waif in a Halston gown, Liza stands her ground, in triumph.

(1946–   )

Joni Mitchell

"I felt that maybe I hadn't done enough scuffling."

"We are stardust, we are golden," she wrote in the euphoric afterglow of Woodstock, in the song that became the anthem of the "Woodstock generation," "and we've got to get ourselves back to the garden."

The garden turned out to be permanently off limits. While some of her most talented contemporaries chose to self-destruct rather than grow up, Joni Mitchell put aside childish things and created, in the words of one devotee, "metaphoric excursions-through-life trips that are common to us all."

She was born Roberta Joan Anderson in Fort Macleod, in the foothills of the Canadian Rockies. As a child, she had "star eyes," dreaming first of becoming a glamorous ballerina, then a great painter. But during her first year at the

Joni

Alberta College of Art, she began picking up pocket money singing in a nearby Saskatoon coffeehouse, accompanying herself on a ukulele. En route to an appearance at the Mariposa Folk Festival in Ontario, she wrote her first song, which, performed at the festival, created a minor sensation. She never returned to art school.

Influenced by early exposure to jazz artists like Lambert, Hendrix and Ross, Miles Davis and, later, to Bob Dylan, she kept working at her songs and her instruments: guitar, piano and, most elusive of all, her extraordinary voice— raw, untrained, leaping from octave to octave like a reckless mountain climber. Ironically, her first successful songs were often credited to the artists who recorded them: Many people still assume that "Clouds" and "Both Sides Now" were composed by Judy Collins. In fact, Mitchell's work has such broad appeal that she may be the only composer whose songs have been recorded by both Dylan and Sinatra.

In 1965 she married Chuck Mitchell and moved with him to Detroit. "The magic of crossing the border," as she calls it, and developing relationships with fellow artists such as James Taylor and Graham Nash, threw her creative energies and her confidence as a performer into high gear. In 1968 she recorded her first album, *Songs to a Seagull.* Since then she has recorded many more albums, including the widely acclaimed *Court and Spark, For the Roses, Blue, Ladies of the Canyon,* and *Miles of Aisles,* recorded live during an infrequent tour with the jazz-oriented L. A. Express.

Her successful personal appearances created a dilemma. "To suddenly often be the center of attention," she said, "threatened the writer in me." She began to feel "separated from my audience and my times, separated by affluence and convenience . . . I felt that maybe I hadn't done enough scuffling." Her songs became more and more personal. Once divorced and, as documented in her lyrics, many times burned, she continued to explore the themes of loneliness, love, values, guilt, freedom, and what she called her main interest in life: "human relationships, human interaction, and the exchange of feelings."

Already hailed by the New York *Times* as "one of the most genuinely gifted composers North America has yet developed," she believes that her best work is still ahead. "I'm almost a pianist now, and the same thing with the guitar." She continues to draw; the art on some of her album covers is her own. And she remains, proudly, a Canadian, planning to settle "in my old years" on her land north of Vancouver. Happily for her fans, that time is far in the future.

(1943–   )

Modern Jazz Quartet

"Four morticians who have just been told that their rates are too high."

When the Modern Jazz Quartet took its final bow after a concert in Sydney, Australia, on July 16, 1974, it officially concluded a twenty-two-year career, longer than any other small jazz group's. The only change in the quartet during those twenty-two years occurred in 1955 when Connie Kay replaced drummer Kenny Clarke, who had moved to Europe. For the last nineteen years, the personnel remained the same—Kay, John Lewis, pianist and musical director, Milt Jackson, vibes, and Percy Heath, bass.

MJQ members Jackson, Kay, Lewis, and Heath

They had all come together after World War II in Dizzy Gillespie's big band where, at times, the rhythm section (i.e., the quartet) had opportunities to perform by itself because the band's trumpet parts were so difficult that the rhythm section had to fill in while the full band rested. They began recording as the Modern Jazz Quartet in 1952. But outside of the recording studio they had trouble coping with the usual jazz jobs because of the soft, delicate interplay of their instruments.

"We tried to play a dance," Lewis recalled, "but the audio equipment was so poor that the dancers couldn't hear us over the shuffle of feet. So that was the end of dances for us. Then we went into the Embers, a restaurant, but the rattle of dishes was so loud that we quit after a few nights."

By this process of elimination, the quartet became primarily a concert attraction and this, in turn, had an effect on how and what the group played. Most of its book was written by Lewis, who mixed a strong classical orientation with a consuming interest in jazz, and who worked closely in the 1960s with Gunther Schuller in the creation of their so-called "Third Stream Music."

The subtlety of much of his writing has, as Whitney Balliett said, "misled the unknowing into regarding it as a cocktail group and the knowing into scoffing at it as staid and stuffy." This apparent staidness was reinforced by their habit of performing in morning coats and striped pants, which led one observer to remark that they looked like "four morticians who have just been told that their rates are too high."

Both their style and appearance were reflections of the personality of John Lewis, whose stiffly erect carriage and soft, precise manner of speech might suggest a diplomat, a banker, or a lawyer. Percy Heath shone, the most outgoing of the four, a gleam of pleasure constantly lurking in his eyes. Connie Kay, a big, seemingly stolid man sat behind his drums with rarely a change of expression. Milt Jackson became the activist. When he was in the Army in 1943 during race riots in his hometown, Detroit, he wanted to organize a troop to go there and fight instead of fighting other people overseas.

From the earliest days of the Quartet, it was thought that there must be dissension within the group because it was believed that Lewis' classical inclinations were stifling Jackson's free-swinging instincts. But if there were such differences, they never became apparent. In fact, Jackson declared in 1971 that "the only way we'd break up would be somebody getting sick." Yet it was Jackson who, three years later, broke up the group. Annoyed that the Quartet was not making as much money as some rock groups, he insisted on going out on his own to try to collect some of that big bread. He never collected it, but record buyers who collected and retained the MJQ's numerous Atlantic records can still listen with pleasure to some of the most delicate, relaxed, and musically interesting performances in the history of jazz.

Thelonious Monk

"I don't believe in the word 'try.' I believe in the word 'do.' "

Even within a music so individualistic as jazz, Thelonious Monk's iconoclasm stands out. True to his own dictum, "Play yourself!" the pianist-composer spent many years in semiobscurity, but reached the top without having made the slightest concession to convention, secure in the knowledge that some day the world would beat a path to his door.

Monk's music sounds like no other. First considered weird and arcane (he was dubbed "The High Priest of Bebop" and "The Mad Monk"), it was eventually acclaimed for its directness and mastery of form. "When you learn one of his pieces," said pianist Dick Katz, "you can't learn just the melody and chords; you have to remember the inner voicings and rhythms exactly. Everything is so carefully interrelated—his works are *compositions.*"

Born in a North Carolina hamlet, Monk was brought to New York at the age of two, started to play piano by ear at six, and had some formal lessons at eleven. While still in his teens, he joined the band of a touring evangelist

Monk

("She healed, we played," was his typically terse recollection). This was one of his few steady jobs until he was able to have his own groups, since he lived by the whims of his biological clock, staying up for three days and sleeping through the next two when it suited him. "Monk sleeps, eats, and speaks only when he feels like it," a friend once said. He lived for more than forty years in the same small New York apartment, first with his mother and siblings, then with his wife and two children, grudgingly agreeing to move only when the building was about to be demolished.

In 1940, Teddy Hill, the ex-bandleader and manager of Minton's Playhouse, a Harlem nightspot catering to musicians, hired Monk for the house band, letting him come and go as he pleased. Here, Monk developed his original ideas in the congenial company of Charlie Christian, Dizzy Gillespie, and other young experimenters. Already, his absorption in music was total: "He just doesn't seem to be present unless he's actually talking to you, and then, in the middle of a conversation, his mind is somewhere else," Hill noted.

Coleman Hawkins, a confirmed Monk fan, gave the pianist his first and only job on Fifty-second Street, which in 1944 led to his commercial recording debut. But most of the work Monk was able to find was out of the limelight, even after bebop had been accepted. This was due not only to his intransigence (he walked out on one job because the sound of a note on the piano upset him; on another, he ripped off and tossed aside an annoyingly squeaky pedal assembly) but also because he insisted on going his own musical way. "Most bebop turns out to be like Dixieland," he told George Simon in a rare 1948 interview, explaining that most modernists didn't play thoughtfully. And he told a musician who found a Monk arrangement hard to play: "You have an instrument, don't you? Either play it or throw it away!"

Though many musicians played Monk's tunes, in particular the famous " 'Round Midnight," most had little regard for his unorthodox approach to the piano. But after he began to record regularly, from 1947 on, his reputation grew. Ten years later, he had a long, successful stand at New York's Five Spot, where the management tolerated his habitual tardiness. In 1964 he was a *Time* magazine cover story. Under the firm but gentle guidance of his devoted wife, he began to tour worldwide, learning to show up on time for work, and joining the select inner circle of jazz giants. In 1974 he took a sabbatical, and made only single concert appearances in each of the following years. In 1975 he was awarded a Guggenheim fellowship.

"I don't believe in the word 'try,' " he once said. "I believe in the word 'do.' " Thelonious Monk's life and music are all of a piece, created by a true original.

(1917–   )

> "If that fiddle's cutting good and they're playing pretty harmonies, it will make cold chills run over me."

Bluegrass music. Somehow it suggests a wilder yet simpler time, with the fire and drive of the five-string banjo, the bluesy wail of the fiddle, and the eerie, moving singing often called the "high, lonesome sound" of bluegrass. It is the archaic, stubborn, proud music of a people and a region. And it is the music of a man, Bill Monroe, who said of his creation with typical terseness: "To me bluegrass is really the country music. It was meant for country people."

Like many country music performers, Monroe knew country life: "If you was raised on a farm you would know of hard times. On Saturday I would

Bill Monroe (front center) backed by "Bijou," Lester Flatt, "Stringbean," Jim Shumate, Sally Ann Forrester

get a nickel to buy some candy and that's all I got all week. And one pair of shoes a year and two pairs of overalls. If you plowed for your father it felt good to your feet to follow that plow and stay in that furrow with the fresh ground turning over there. You didn't mind."

Those times behind the plow gave Bill Monroe a good bit of time to think and to create. A painfully shy child, he learned to express his inner drives through the mandolin, a little-used instrument he was relegated to by seven older musical children, and he was to revolutionize the use of this instrument in country music with his fiery style. Raised in the bluegrass region of Kentucky (hence the name of his band and, ultimately, the entire musical genre he was to create), Monroe learned from his elder brothers, from a fiddling uncle he celebrated in song ("Uncle Pen"), and from a black guitarist and fiddler named Arnold Schultz, who gave to bluegrass the powerful touch of blues which is one of its most distinct elements.

Bill and his elder brother Charlie, a strong guitarist and singer, formally teamed up in 1935 as the Monroe Brothers, and in the three short years they existed as a band they electrified audiences across the entire Southeast, adding a drive and an excitement not known before to duet singing.

Each brother formed his own band in 1938, and in 1939 Bill and his Blue Grass Boys won a job on the "Grand Ole Opry" and Monroe's debut performance on the "Opry" presaged what was to come: numerous ovations for an old blues number, "Muleskinner Blues," which contained in it all the elements—save one—which typify bluegrass: it was high-pitched, with a crackling yodel; the fiddle was mournful, bluesy, yet somehow driven; the guitar pulsated with a syncopated rhythm.

The missing element was the banjo. Always willing to allow talented musicians to propel the group's music in new directions, Monroe added a quiet kid from North Carolina named Earl Scruggs in 1945. This solidified the sound and style of bluegrass music, and the music of this 1945–48 version of the Blue Grass Boys (in addition to Monroe and Scruggs, Lester Flatt on guitar and Chubby Wise on fiddle) has ever since been the standard against which all others have been compared.

As popular as they were—and they were tremendously popular—all fads shift and change, and by the late 1950's few but Monroe's most loyal fans stuck by him. Fewer and fewer good musicians came his way, and those who did didn't stay long: too much time between jobs. Yet right at this dark time another whole wave of interest was building. As one so inspired by Monroe, mandolinist Ralph Rinzler (who eventually became Monroe's biographer) was a leader among city-bred folk musicians who saw the greatness in Monroe's music: "For me it was like going into another world. I was fascinated by the totally different life-style—dinner on the grounds, different speech patterns—a whole different way of life. The whole idea of it really astounded me—that this existed."

His discovery was followed by that of many others, and bluegrass was revived to the point that what looked like an exquisite but dying art form grew to enormous popularity within the decade. The ringing banjo filled TV and film soundtracks, the fiddle made a huge comeback in all popular music, and the term "bluegrass" grew beyond musical boundaries to express a certain mystical sense of rural paradise, of a certain solid, unchanging "old-timeyness" in a swiftly changing and increasingly urban society.

Yet although he accepted the role of "Father of Bluegrass" with a certain regal pride, Bill Monroe never lost sight of the ultimate objectives of his music: "If a man listening will let it, bluegrass will transmit right into your heart. If you love music and you listen close, it will come right into you. If that fiddle's cutting good and they're playing pretty harmonies, it will make cold chills run over me and I've heard it many times. If you really love bluegrass music it will dig in a long ways. If you take time to listen close to the words and the melody, it will do something for you."

(1911–   )

Vaughn

Vaughn, more than so-so

Vaughn Monroe

Virility and vitality with touches of tenderness tossed in.

His style of singing has often been imitated and perhaps too often caricatured, but performers might have served mankind better had they instead tried to emulate the style of Vaughn Monroe, the man. For few bandleaders have ever been accorded such personal respect as this handsome six-footer who led a successful band in the 1940s and became a top singing star on records.

"No one ever wanted to leave the band," reported one of his musicians, "because he always treated us so well." Unlike other leaders, Vaughn did not make his men pay for their uniforms. Instead of riding in uncomfortable buses, they traveled first class by Pullman or by plane. If a musician needed money, Monroe would lend it to him without interest. And, according to another side-man, "If any guy had any problem, Vaughn would always ask, 'What can I do to help?' "

Barbara Hodgkins, in an interview in *Metronome,* found him to be "one of the most polite, pleasant, and peaceful citizens in the music business—a very normal person in a crazy world." And this from a critic, who like many others, really didn't appreciate his rather stiff, semioperatic (he had studied voice formally at Carnegie Tech and the New England Conservatory), nasal way of singing that caused one writer to wonder whether by opening his mouth more, less sound might be forced out through his nose.

But the general public, especially the feminine majority, pooh-poohed such nit-picking. For them, his voice projected virility and vitality with touches of tenderness tossed in. He was, in a way, the Robert Goulet of his day.

He first attracted national attention when he brought his band down from Boston and into Frank Dailey's Meadowbrook, a famous big band spot not far from New York City. He was an instant hit in person (he had a great smile and a shy, gentlemanly charm), as well as on the air (he broadcast many times each week from Meadowbrook), and on records with songs like "Racing with the Moon" (his theme), "When the Lights Go on Again All over the World," and "There, I've Said It Again." Though rough at first, his band improved dramatically, thanks in part to Vaughn's dedication (he played occasional trumpet and admired and respected good musicianship), and because he had the good sense to engage good players, including a then young, unknown trombonist and arranger named Ray Conniff.

But after a while he became disenchanted leading a band. "The band business isn't an artistic thing," he complained. "It's strictly a business." And so in the late 1940s, he broke up his band to concentrate on a career as a solo singer, a timely move since big bands were on the way out, anyway. He continued to record more hits—"Riders in the Sky" and "Ballerina" were his biggest—and he appeared regularly on radio for Camel Cigarettes. Then, when television took over, RCA invited him to become its spokesman, a role he fufilled with taste and conviction, imbuing his corporate image with the same sort of virile gentlemanliness that had characterized his entire career.

(1911–1973)

Wes Montgomery

He had endeared himself to legions of nonjazz listeners without sacrificing his jazz stature.

He discovered guitarist Charlie Christian on a Benny Goodman record in 1943. The record was "Solo Flight." It changed the course of his life. Not quite twenty, he was married and had a day job in his home city of Indianapolis. Becoming a professional musician, let alone a headliner, never entered his mind. But Christian's guitar magic had entered it and would not go away. So he bought a $350 guitar, amplifier, some picks, listened to more of Christian's recorded solos, and started practicing. When neighbors complained, he substituted his thumb for the pick to soften the sound on the strings.

But there was nothing soft about John Leslie (Wes) Montgomery's determination to learn the guitar, or about his playing. It was strong and full-toned, with the thumb—a method eschewed by most guitarists. And it was ear-catching from his first emergence as a musician working in small groups in local nightspots, through a two-year hitch with Lionel Hampton's band, to his further emergence into the spotlight in 1959 when he worked with his brothers, pianist

Wes

Charles and bassist Monk, in a group called the Mastersounds, and to his almost total dominance of the field in the 1960s.

An astute record producer, Creed Taylor, had seen the great commercial sense of combining Wes's blues- and jazz-oriented guitar with pop and rock beats in big orchestral settings that would woo listeners normally frightened off by the word jazz. It worked. Album after album rolled out (e.g., *Movin' Wes, Goin' Out of My Head, Down Here on the Ground, California Dreaming*), copping top spots on the music trade charts. In 1965 Montgomery was nominated for two Grammy awards. His *Goin' Out of My Head* was voted the best instrumental of 1966. He was the top-selling jazz recording artist of 1967, and voted best jazz guitarist of 1968 in a *Down Beat* poll. For five years running, musicians voted him top jazz guitarist in the *Playboy* "All Stars' All Stars" poll.

A modest man, more family- than fame-minded, Wes played primarily for the sheer love of playing. He enjoyed working in small groups such as his own trio (*Round Midnight* album) and the Wynton Kelly Trio with whom he recorded *(Smokin' at the Half Note)* and appeared in concerts and at jazz clubs. Jazz buffs have their own memories of Wes among his peers, leaning back slightly in his chair, his face happy, his guitar lying across his lap as he stroked out throbbing blues or chorus after chorus of exciting improvisations, using "impossible" successions of octaves, thumb flying.

In an interview in *The Christian Science Monitor* in the spring of 1968, he pointed out that his concessions to public taste stopped with "rock flavor," and that he always used jazzmen in his rhythm section in the big-orchestra recordings (usually pianist Herbie Hancock, bassist Ron Carter, drummer Grady Tate). He stressed that "to make it in this world" an artist had to find a way to the buyers' market.

In another three weeks, home again in Indianapolis with his wife and family of five daughters and two sons, after a tour, Wes Montgomery died suddenly of a heart attack. Only forty-five, he had, with a late start and just a few playing years, made jazz history in a rock-dominated music scene. And with the genuine sweetness of his tone, respect for melody and simple figurations, he had endeared himself to legions of nonjazz listeners without sacrificing his jazz stature and Charlie Christian discipleship.

(1925–1968)

Helen Morgan

Her notoriety offered a startling contrast to her sweet, clear voice and her soft, delicate beauty.

The claim that Helen Morgan had on the consciousness of America in the 1920s and '30s was based almost as much on her troubles with the law and her drinking as it was on the stunning achievement of her performance in 1928 as Julie in the original company of *Show Boat.* One of the most popular singing stars of her era, her notoriety offered a startling contrast to her sweet, clear voice and her soft, delicate beauty.

She was discovered singing from the cowcatcher of a locomotive in the railroad yards of Danville, Illinois, by a flamboyant writer, Amy Leslie, who was writing a feature on railroad wives for the Chicago *Daily News.* Miss Leslie persuaded Helen's mother that she had the theatrical connections necessary to take the twelve-year-old Helen in hand and launch her career.

Soon Amy had arranged a tryout engagement at the French Trocadero in Montreal where Helen sang the French Canadian folk songs she already knew. By week's end she was packing the place. One night, an enthusiastic customer set the little girl on top of the upright piano so she could be seen and heard

"He's just my Bill . . ."

by the eager customers in the back of the room, and from then on she was to continue misusing pianos in that fashion.

Helen's career as a child performer was aborted abruptly by a visit to the Troc by members of the Gerry Society, a group that fought against child exploitation in show business. So she and her mother returned to Chicago and in 1913 Helen began and ended her high school education.

Following a succession of menial jobs that included inserting prizes into Cracker Jack boxes, she landed a singing engagement at a small club, the Green Mill, and later entered several beauty contests, winning the titles of Miss Illinois and then Miss Mount Royal in Canada, for which she was rewarded with a trip to New York City where she was greeted by the mayor and driven down Broadway in a limousine. But true stardom was still to come her way. She managed to land a job in the chorus of a Ziegfeld musical, *Sally,* and after 570 performances, she went to work for Billy Rose in his first nightclub, the Backstage Club. There she made her first acquaintance with the underworld characters who infested the nightclub business during Prohibition, and who later were to get her into trouble.

In 1924 she appeared in *George White's Scandals* and two years later joined the cast of another Broadway revue, *Americana,* for which Philip Charig wrote a song, "Nobody Wants Me," especially for her. Famed composer Jerome Kern came to see the show and was so enchanted by Helen's performance of the song from the top of an upright piano in the orchestra pit that he decided she'd be perfect for the role of Julie in his 1928 production of *Show Boat.* The rest became history. Helen sang "Bill" and "Can't Help Lovin' Dat Man" in the tremendously successful Broadway production and continued to sing them and play Julie until the end of her life.

She became such a big star that the nightclub in which she sang and which she partially owned carried her name. Accordingly, she, rather than any of her unsavory, lesser-known partners, was the one who was served with summonses for violations of the existing Prohibition laws. She was arrested twice and acquitted both times, but the strain and notoriety upset the timid girl and intensified her growing dependence upon brandy for relief.

In 1929 she successfully portrayed an aging stripper in the movie *Applause,* and appeared in her second Jerome Kern and Oscar Hammerstein show, *Sweet Adeline,* which included her dramatic rendition of the torch song, "Why Was I Born?" But from then on her career and life went downhill. Helen Morgan, for whom the expression "torch singer" could have been coined, carried the torch for several men and a peace of mind she could never possess. A gentle, generous, sweet, kind, timid little girl at heart, she seemed unable to cope with the growing sordidness and reality of her real life. Even her brandy could no longer bring her relief, and at age forty-one her torch and her life had burned out.

(1900–1941)

Jelly Roll Morton

Resplendent in diamonds, big cars, and flashing thousand-dollar bills.

Music filled New Orleans at the turn of the century, music of brass bands, string bands, dance orchestras, marching bands, ragtime, and the blues.

Jelly Roll Morton, descendant of French settlers and African-Creoles, heard it all, and by combining the informality and relaxed improvisations of the blues with the formal structure and patterns of ragtime, created a new style of music called New Orleans jazz. He is considered to be the first jazz composer to have put his works into musical notation and ultimately orchestrations for ten- and eleven-piece bands.

Like Duke Ellington, pianist/composer Morton (born Ferdinand La Menthe in New Orleans) could have maintained a band just to play his own compositions. Among the nearly hundred that swung from his powerful fingers—but always with delicate touch—several found a permanent place in the jazz and swing

Jelly Roll

repertoire, such as "Jelly Roll Blues," "Wolverine Blues" (titled originally by Jelly as "Wolverines"), "Milenburg Joys," "Kansas City Stomp," "The Pearls," "King Porter Stomp." Jelly seldom appreciated what happened to them in the transition from his pen into the horns of other musicians. His constant assertions that no one knew how to play them right struck other musicians as arrogant, self-righteous boasting. But Jelly was both dogmatic and a perfectionist who had set out to be a king when, at fourteen, he joined the company of "professors" in Storyville, New Orleans' Tenderloin District, where these solo pianists played long, but not too loud, in the high-class "mansions" catering to white trade.

As a young boy Ferd had tried various instruments around the house (his father, Ed La Menthe, was a music lover and trombonist of sorts) and had become expert on the guitar. But, inspired by a pianist at the French Opera House and a ragtime player at a party, he took up the study of piano. After his father left home, and his mother later died, Ferd started proving his pianistic skills in the District. Banished thereupon from home by his grandmother as unfit company for his two younger sisters, he went all-out to prove he could be king of everything by means of what the District had taught him. And so, using the last name of his stepfather, Willie Morton, he began playing honky-tonks in Mississippi Gulf Coast towns and developing skills as a pool player, gambler, and hustler. He traveled farther and farther, sometimes via vaudeville and minstrel shows. In one show he got his nickname Jelly Roll. As related in Alan Lomax's *Mr. Jelly Roll,* Morton topped the comedian's brag, "I'm Sweet Papa Cream Puff," by starting his boast with "I'm Sweet Papa Jelly Roll."

In Los Angeles in the years 1917–22, Morton applied his talents to bandleading, a step which brought him to seven years of plenty in Chicago marked by extensive recording: piano solos for Gennett and the now-historic Red Hot Peppers Band sides for Victor. As that company's "No. 1 Hot Band," it played top midwestern college and hotel dates. Resplendent in diamonds (even a diamond-filled tooth), big cars, and flashing thousand-dollar bills, Jelly cut a kingly figure. But in the dawning swing era, this proud Creole leader and his elegantly turned-out ragtime-blues were thought old-fashioned, and tossed aside. He spent lean years of the 1930s as part-owner and piano player in a second-floor Washington nightclub. Then in 1938, three years before he died in California, a signal honor assured his immortality. Alan Lomax supervised Jelly's recording of his music and his life story for the Library of Congress, an unprecedented documentary of and by a jazz pioneer, whose pure New Orleans jazz delineates elegantly and expertly the exotic, good-time atmosphere of the city of its birth.

(c. 1885–1941)

Gerry Mulligan

He has never underblown his blasts at things of which he disapproves.

One of the greatest jazz creators, one of the founders of its cool school, has never been willing to be cut off from pop music. Gerry Mulligan, arranger, composer, multi-award-winning baritone saxist and small group and big band leader, has refused to create and play his music in an artistic vacuum, unresponsive to the emotions of his listeners. Unlike other modern jazz musicians, who approach the public with a "take-it-or-leave-it" attitude, the tall, slim, personable Mulligan has insisted that "you've got to reach people on a personal level if you expect to reach them musically. And if the sound you're making is attractive and colorful, instead of harsh and ugly, you've got a much better chance of reaching them and holding them." However, he has consistently refused to sacrifice his musical integrity just to win over an audience.

Though one of the creators of the cool sound, Mulligan has never affected a cool personality. His enthusiasm almost stunted his musical career when at the age of seven he tried writing new music instead of playing the warhorses

Gerry

his piano teacher had assigned him. "She claimed I was always changing the music, so she quit." Four years later, Gerry's musical adventures received another rejection. He had arranged Rodgers and Hart's "Lover" for the school band. "But the nun in charge wouldn't let us play it, not because of the music, but because of the song's title!"

In addition to arranging and playing piano, Gerry had begun learning the trumpet, but when he heard Artie Shaw play clarinet, he immediately switched instruments. Later, when he grew big enough to hold it, he took up the baritone sax and became so immersed in music that he quit high school before graduation "so that I'd get a chance to play before being drafted." But the war's sudden end kept him a civilian anyway.

His reputation as an arranger grew around Philadelphia, and Tommy Tucker gave him a job. After three months the maestro of the basically sweet band told Gerry, "You've outgrown us already." So young Mulligan graduated to more adventuresome bands, to those of Elliot Lawrence, Gene Krupa, and eventually to Claude Thornhill, a topflight arranger, "who taught me the greatest lesson in dynamics, the art of *under* blowing, or controlled violence, while still getting a full, rich sound." Forever after, that characteristic was to permeate all of Mulligan's music.

Meanwhile, he had also been playing with and arranging for small jazz groups. In 1949 he wrote many of, and performed on all, the selections in the Miles Davis' Nontet's famous *Birth of the Cool* album. Then he hitchhiked to the West Coast to write for Stan Kenton. But his underblowing style didn't fit Kenton's bombastic blasting. "There was no way I could please him." So Gerry tried pleasing himself instead by organizing a small group. "Our first gig was at a club with a bad piano that had only sixty-six keys. So I decided to go with just bass and drums."

The piano-less rhythm section, which was to become a fixture with Gerry, blended ideally with the underplayed horns of Mulligan, trumpeter Chet Baker (later replaced by trombonist Bob Brookmeyer), and in the early 1960s with Gerry's wonderfully relaxed big band. Five years, on and off, with Dave Brubeck followed. "We were hired to do a jazz concert together for one night. I turned out to be the man who came to dinner." More and more guest appearances ensued. "But it became deadly because I couldn't play my own compositions. My main concern has been to get more recognition as a composer." In the late 1970s he had formed a new band to play his own works. It drew rave notices.

What recognition Mulligan has not received through his music has come via his tongue. Very articulate, he has never underblown his blasts at things of which he disapproves—like the limitations of electronic instruments, or jazz musicians sloughing off their audiences, or their "too-much-with-it" disdain of jazz's traditions. He likes to paraphrase Lillian Hellman's famous dictum about her conscience: "I can't cut my *tastes* to fit this year's fashions."

(1927–   )

Anthony Newley

Nothing looked so inviting as stopping the world and getting off.

In the early 1960s "Stop the World, I Want to Get Off" became the national protest, and the singer-actor-songwriter-mime who first promulgated it in his smash hit musical became a hero of those antihero times. That musical and its successor, *The Roar of the Greasepaint, The Smell of the Crowd,* gave the United States a new British star to applaud: Anthony Newley. His impersonation of "Littlechap" fighting the world had special appeal in that time of national calamities and cataclysmic social upheavals. Nothing looked so inviting as stopping the world and getting off.

Though hardly known outside of Britain before *Stop* opened on Broadway, Newley was already one of England's top rock-and-roll singers and recording stars. He hadn't aimed for that niche. In fact, since he quit school at fourteen, he had played in children's films, including the role of the Artful Dodger in *Oliver Twist,* and made, in all, some forty minor movies before fame touched him. An only child of a broken home, Newley first felt the lure of the stage during evacuation from buzz-bombed London and a stay in Brighton with a

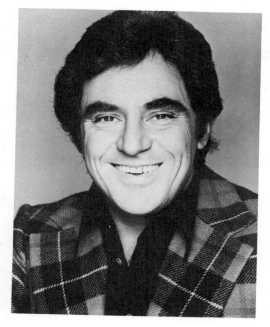

England's Tony

retired music hall performer, who encouraged him to develop his show business talents.

He became a rock-and-roll singer by portraying a rock-and-roll singer in the film, *Idle on Parade*. One song he sang, "I've Waited so Long," made him an overnight idol of British teenagers.

"I'm not a trained musician or singer," he once told an interviewer, "but I can turn out a song." He turned out "What Kind of Fool Am I?" so successfully that twenty-seven different recordings of it had fairly blanketed the United States before *Stop the World*, in which it was featured, got to New York. It was subsequently recorded by an estimated seventy-five vocalists, such as Tony Bennett and Ella Fitzgerald, and has reportedly provided Newley and his song- and play-writing collaborater Leslie Bricusse an annual income of over eight thousand dollars for life. His use of "damn" in the lyric in his own recording of it bothered some radio stations, so London Records, the company that first issued it, put out a damn-less version for disc jockeys.

And the Newley Cockney accent filled the American air waves as his albums and singles continued to pour out, including another big hit, "Who Can I Turn To?" and other songs from *Roar of the Greasepaint*. In 1973 he recorded an album of his original songs titled *Ain't It Funny*. He has played such prestigious spots as Caesar's Palace in Las Vegas and the Empire Room of New York's Waldorf-Astoria.

In spite of his popularity as a singer, mime, and star of his innovative musicals, critics have not always warmed to him. They have cited unsettling mannerisms, for example, his habit of "hunching" his head, as one critic wrote, as if to make it disappear into his body like a snapping turtle. Others have mentioned his overdone Cockneyisms ("die" for "day"), his high-note quavers, his "bleat." Even so, Newley has had his own TV show on WNBC in New York, has appeared in American films (e.g., *Dr. Doolittle*), and has moved into another career interest: directing films. In experimenting with erotic themes, he is exploiting an interest as popular in the mid and late 1970s, perhaps, as stopping the world was in the 1960s.

(1931–   )

Red Nichols

His martinet ways had earned him the disapproval of every freewheeling jazzman who crossed his path.

A ubiquitous presence on the New York dance music scene of the Roaring Twenties, cornetist Red Nichols was the most active recording bandleader in early white jazz, presiding over a vast variety of star-studded studio groups. The most famous among these was known by the punning title of Red Nichols and His Five Pennies, though it often consisted of many more than five pieces.

As a player, Nichols stood in the shadow of his idol, Bix Beiderbecke, whom he copied assiduosly, if a bit too meticulously. His reputation, once very great, underwent drastic critical revision when black jazz came into its own, but Nichols was responsible for introducing an impressive number of important musicians to the listening public. Moreover, he gave them a chance to play their jazz without commercial restrictions.

Red Nichols

Ernest Loring Nichols was the son of a bandmaster and music teacher from Ogden, Utah. The father, a strict disciplinarian, started the boy on cornet at four, insisting on an hour of practice each day before breakfast. If little Red didn't do his duty, he got nothing to eat until lunchtime. Red joined his father's band at twelve, becoming its featured soloist before leaving home at eighteen.

His arrival in New York was perfectly timed. Dance music was a most viable commodity, and Nichols found himself in demand for recording, radio, and pit band work. The habits inculcated by his unbringing proved useful: he was never late for a job, kept the other musicians in line, and could read and execute anything put on music paper.

And he was an expert talent spotter. Early associates included Eddie Lang, Miff Mole, Joe Venuti, and the Dorsey Brothers, and when the jazz invasion from the hinterlands hit New York, he picked the best. Benny Goodman, Gene Krupa, Jack Teagarden, Eddie Condon, Glenn Miller (his favored arranger), Joe Sullivan, Pee Wee Russell, and Dave Tough all worked for him, not only on records, but also in the pit bands of such important Broadway shows as *Girl Crazy* and *Rain or Shine*. "I was the businessman of the group," he said later. "I always tried to get the best men I could."

His fortunes declined during the next decade, most of which found him leading a second-string road band. In 1942, unable to earn enough as a musician to pay for the treatment needed by a daughter stricken with polio, he threw in the towel and went to work as a welder in a San Francisco shipyard. The revival of interest in traditional jazz soon led him back to music, however, and then a most unlikely turn of events returned him to the limelight.

In 1959, *The Five Pennies,* a film purportedly based on his life, was released. It starred Danny Kaye, and the madcap, nonconformist character he portrayed had nothing whatever to do with the real Nichols, whose martinet ways had earned him the disapproval of every freewheeling jazzman who crossed his path. The film, for which the real Nichols soundtracked Kaye's simulated playing, made him famous once again, and he acquired a loyal following for the revived Five Pennies, purveyors of rather bland Dixieland that had little in common with the fresh, experimental music of his heyday.

That music, critical neglect notwithstanding, was a genuine contribution to jazz, and earned Red Nichols—temperamentally anomalous to jazz—a respectable place in its annals.

(1905–1965)

The ultimate in tasteful, high-class dance band music.

His music matched the quality of Ray Noble the man: smart, elegant, graceful, suave, and sophisticated. Like him, it was also lean, trim, and devoid of unnecessary fat. And for dance band fans and musicians of the early and mid-1930s, it represented the ultimate in tasteful, high-class dance band music.

The son of a prominent London surgeon, the well-educated young man was appointed in 1929 to the post of musical director of E.M.I., the worldwide recording outfit. There he inherited the original New Mayfair house band from an American expatriate named Carroll Gibbons. "It consisted very largely of his own lads who, in those affluent days, used to arrive at the studio in riding breeches, fresh from a session on horseback in Hyde Park," he told jazz historian Neil McCaffrey. Replacing most of the horsemen with a group of all-star musicians from other London bands, Noble proceeded to whip the outfit into superb shape. Playing almost entirely his own arrangements, and featuring the intimate singing of Al Bowlly, Ray Noble, and the New Mayfair Orchestra, which existed in the recording studio only (the men retained their regular nighttime jobs), he produced a series of beautifully scored and superbly recorded sides. Among them were several songs that Ray wrote: "By the Fireside," "Love Is the Sweetest Thing," "The Very Thought of You," and the band's closing theme, "Goodnight, Sweetheart." These and others caught the fancy of American dance band enthusiasts and entrepreneurs who wanted to import the entire band. But the musicians' union said, "Nothing doing," so Noble hired Glenn Miller, already a highly respected arranger, to organize and rehearse an American all-star band for him. It included such great sidemen as Miller, Charlie Spivak, Claude Thornhill, Bud Freeman, and Will Bradley.

The band debuted early in 1935 in the swank Rainbow Room atop New York's Radio City, where it was starred for two years, and also recorded many fine sides for RCA Victor. With both Noble and Miller arranging, the band projected two distinct and different styles. Ray continued to create beautiful ballad moods that featured Al Bowlly, who had been permitted to immigrate with him, while Glenn contributed more rousing, semi-Dixieland versions of jazz favorites on which the instrumentalists soloed.

Eventually, though, personal, rather than musical friction, tore the band apart. Ray and Glenn were equally strong-willed, and when some of the musicians, led by Glenn, insisted that Noble had failed to live up to certain promises,

Ray surrounded by his trombone section of Glenn Miller
and Will Brady

Ray Noble's band in the Rainbow Room: (front row) Al Bowlly, Fritz Prospero,
Nick Pisani, Danny D'Andrea, George Van Eps, Noble, Claude Thornhill; (back
row) Glenn Miller, Will Bradley, Charlie Spivak, Pee Wee Erwin, Bill Harty,
Jim Cannon, Delmar Kaplan, Johnny Mince, Milt Yaner, Bud Freeman

the rift became irreparable. By the late 1936 most of the stars had left, with Miller, Bradley, Spivak, and Thornhill eventually forming their own bands. Noble accepted an offer as musical director on the "Burns and Allen" radio show in Hollywood, where he also assumed a rather charming, bumbling comedic role that he continued several years later on "The Edgar Bergen and Charlie McCarthy Show." With his new, less impressive West Coast band, he recorded several sides, including a memorable version of "Linda" with singer Buddy Clark.

Well-heeled financially (all those royalties from his songs didn't hurt one bit), he retired in the 1950s to the Isle of Jersey, off the English coast, then returned in the early 1970s to America, living out the remainder of his life in Santa Barbara, California, in quiet serenity.

(1903–1977)

Pure joy, not only to hear, but also to watch.

They used to call it "The Soft, Subtle Swing of Red Norvo and His Orchestra," and they were so right. For never was there a band that swung so delicately and so tastefully, never attacking the listener, as so many high-voltage bands would do, but rather insinuating itself, via its light, airy lilt, into his consciousness.

His musical style typifies Red Norvo himself: a gentle, undemanding, understanding man who has never blustered his way into trying to get people to listen to his music. "Just show your listeners you're interested in them by giving them a little something, like just a few bars of a tune they know, and you'd be amazed how much they want to be with you," he once philosophized.

His gentle, forever swinging way of playing on the xylophone and, more recently, the vibraphone has always been pure joy, not only to hear, but also to watch. He makes both visual and musical contact, as he hunches over his instrument, head bent down, looking out at his audience, it seems, through his eyebrows, a quizzical smile on his face, his hands gliding effortlessly, with almost no vertical motion, over his instrument, as he coaxes one series of melodic, swing notes after another from his instrument. "It's a funny thing," he once pointed out, "but it seems about half the people who go to hear jazz get the message through their eyes."

He has been entertaining the general public for over half a century, and enthralling and often amazing his fellow musicians, who marvel not only at his dexterity and swinging ways, but also at his ability to keep up with progressive changes in musical styles.

He was given piano lessons at an early age in his hometown of Beardsville, Illinois, but they ended when he insisted upon playing by ear only. Then one day he traded a pony for a xylophone he had seen in the local music store and taught himself how to play the instrument. By 1926 he was knocking off nonjazz novelties with Paul Ash's band, while sitting entranced between shows in his dressing room listening to jazz records. In 1929 he formed his own band, then decided to go back to college for a fourth time, quit, and landed a job with NBC in Chicago where he was heard and hired by Paul Whiteman, with whom he traveled to New York.

While with the band he fell in love with its star vocalist, Mildred Bailey, and they were married and settled in the Big Apple. A group of 1934 recordings by his all-star group, that included Artie Shaw, Bunny Berigan, and Charlie

Red—the soft, subtle swinger

Barnet, established Red as a major jazz artist. The next year he organized a magnificent non-all-star septet with brilliant arrangements by Eddie Sauter, which soon developed into an eleven-piece orchestra that became one of the Swing Era's greatest delights. When travels persistently took him away from his bride, she joined the band, and as "Mr. and Mrs. Swing" they played major spots throughout the country and recorded brilliant sides for Brunswick Records.

Eventually the draft decimated the band, and so Red organized a light, swinging septet, heard by few because of the recording ban. In 1944 he switched to the more popular vibraphone, joined Benny Goodman, with whom he recorded several quintet sides, and then Woody Herman's great First Herd. Tired of traveling, he settled on the West Coast and from then on fronted small jazz groups, including a memorable trio of Tal Farlow, Charles Mingus, and Norvo, while also appearing from time to time with Goodman and his smaller groups.

But his life was not all joy. One of his sons committed suicide. His second wife (Red and Mildred were divorced in the late 1940s), to whom he was tremendously devoted, died of a lingering illness, and in the early 1970s, after having played a tune in one key while his group played in another, he realized he was losing his hearing. And yet his warmth and gentleness and caring ways never left him. And of course neither did his immense talent, which, with the help of a hearing aid, continued to establish Red Norvo as one of the great jazz creators of all time.

(1908–   )

Anita O'Day

Taking more risks than perhaps any other singer.

Girl singers with big bands had traditionally been sweet-looking things in pretty evening gowns and stylish hairdos when Anita O'Day joined Gene Krupa's band in 1941. She was different. She favored mannish tailored suits, reflecting her desire to be accepted as a member of the band rather than a bandstand ornament. And she sang with a difference, too. Her husky voice and offhand, offbeat, always swinging delivery were elements of a truly original approach, and after a few years with Krupa and a stint with Stan Kenton's band, she was able to establish herself as one of the leading and most durable of jazz song stylists.

Born Anita Colton in Chicago (she took the O'Day name because "it was pig Latin for dough, and I wanted to make some"), she was weaned musically on Mildred Bailey and Billie Holiday records, though she claims her primary influence was Martha Raye, "her rhythm, her freedom, and her sound." At thirteen she dropped out of high school. Tall enough to lie about her age, she entered walkathons, those grotesque and grueling Depression "entertainments"; her longest walk took 3,248 hours. She finished second in four out of six contests, completing one of 2,228 hours with Frankie Lo Presto, later known as Frankie Laine, and bringing home the prize money to her separated mother.

She started to sing in bars for the same economic reasons, but soon began to enjoy and learn from the work of the jazzmen she encountered. At nineteen, she was singing at one of Chicago's hottest jazz spots, The Three Deuces, often garbed in a belted raincoat. During the Krupa years, she specialized in blues and novelty numbers, such as her famous duet with Roy Eldridge (the band's trumpet star), "Let Me Off Uptown." But she could also make a tender ballad like "Skylark" her own.

Anita didn't just sing like a jazz musician, she lived like one. "The narcotics thing was just there; it was happening," she told Leonard Feather. "Kept me in and out of trouble for twenty years; cost me a couple of very nice houses, the Jaguar, the self-respect, everything . . . It's like quicksand. You never get out."

Eventually she did get out. By then she had spawned a school of singers whose most illustrious graduates were June Christy (whom she recommended as her Kenton successor) and Chris Connor, another Kenton alumnae. And her career had seen ups and downs, the most notable up resulting from her appearance in the 1958 Newport Jazz Festival film *Jazz on a Summer's Day*,

Anita

in which she presented a new, ultra-feminine image, replete with big straw hat trimmed with real ostrich feathers, sleeveless blue linen dress, and elegant long white gloves. Singing better than ever, she stole the show, and a series of excellent albums for Norman Granz ensued. Yet she didn't overcome her chief problem until 1967, after she had nearly died from an overdose of narcotics. "That was my cue," she said. She moved to Hawaii for a while, removing herself from the pitfalls of the music environment. After she returned, jobs were often scarce.

Anita O'Day never indulged in self-pity. She kept up her appearance well and always presented a tough, insouciant, wisecracking exterior to the world. "It gets to be so heavy, you just pack it all down and walk on top," she told Feather in 1973. "You keep the spirit up and go right on."

In the mid-1970s and in her mid-fifties, working again with some regularity, Anita O'Day was still singing with the urgency, conviction, and adventurousness that had been hallmarks of her style. Taking more risks than perhaps any other singer, she kept her accompanists and listeners on their toes with sudden shifts in tempo, meter, or key, singing as fast as any musician could play, or in contrast, managing to imbue even the slowest tempo with rhythmic tension.

At the dawn of her career, Anita O'Day wanted to sing like a jazz musician. Through a topsy-turvy career, she never swerved from that desire.

(1919–   )

Joe "King" Oliver

The first of the black New Orleans bandleaders to make it big.

He was "Papa Joe" to Louis Armstrong. He was "King" to fellow musicians and to the crowds who loved his cornet-playing, in the early years of the century, when they heard it in the parades forever filling the streets of New Orleans, in clubs of Storyville, the city's famous red-light district, or at dances in the Tulane University gym.

A creative, dynamic player with bands like the Melrose, Olympia, and Onward, a star of trombonist Kid Ory's group where he was first billed as "King," then as leader of his own band in the District, Joe Oliver became the first of the black New Orleans bandleaders to make it big in Chicago in the 1920s: He played top nightspots, he made recordings, those vital communications means just opening up for black bands. It was a tremendous triumph for the boy born on a plantation near Donaldsonville, Louisiana, where his mother was a cook. Blinded in one eye in childhood, Joe Oliver grew up in New Orleans, working as a yard boy and in later years as a butler for the affluent. But with a chance to study music, he found the way to express his individuality and eventually to escape the more suffocating confines of segregation.

In most of his band pictures Oliver presents a portly and dignified figure, standing, cornet in hand, among his musicians, a sober but kindly expression on his face. It belies his reputation of being "a riot," fond of jokes, eating, and playing pool. He loved to ape various human and animal sounds on his horn with an array of mutes, cups, bottles, glasses, buckets. They were his "inventions," which, like many of his musical ideas, others frequently appropriated or adapted and purveyed as their own. New Orleans trumpeter Mutt Carey called him the greatest "freak" trumpet player he ever heard. And in his heyday in the Windy City fans packed the South Side cabarets—Royal Gardens, Dreamland, Pekin, Lincoln Gardens—to hear King Oliver and his Creole Jazz Band. Wherever they appeared, they just about blew the roof off with their sizzling New Orleans-style ensemble playing and those hot-as-pistols two-cornet "breaks" Oliver and his young protégé Louis Armstrong ripped out with breathtaking fire and precision. "Breaks" gave musicians a brief interval for solo glory.

Back home in New Orleans, Oliver had helped the fatherless Armstrong improve his cornet technique, played duets with him. Armstrong gratefully ran errands for the King's wife, Stella, and when his idol sent for him to join his band in 1922, Armstrong had come running. Pupil inevitably outdistanced teacher, and after Armstrong summoned enough courage to leave his mentor

Joe "the King"

in 1924, Oliver could acknowledge that Louis played better than he did.

His crown wobbly, the King regrouped for more recordings as the Savannah Syncopators, and still drew fans during his stay at the Plantation Cafe. But New Orleans-style jazz was on the wane and New York had superseded Chicago as the jazz caldron. With pickup groups in New York, Oliver made more of his-style records, but he couldn't get a toehold in the new "Swing." The Depression 1930s saw him scuffling for jobs in the South. In time, tooth and gum problems forced him to give up playing, and the King wound up with a menial 9 A.M.-to-midnight job in Savannah. It was in the kind of place he'd once enthusiastically patronized: a pool hall. Though his letters to his sister expressed optimism and faith in the Lord, Oliver died a forgotten jazz pioneer. But his creative contributions are attested to by his nearly forty recordings, by his compositions like "Dippermouth," "West End Blues," "Doctor Jazz," which have enriched jazz literature and performance, and, most of all perhaps, by having been Papa Joe to number one: Louis Armstrong.

(1885–1938)

He had never studied arranging and so just wrote more or less as he felt like writing.

For many years he helped top singers and bandleaders achieve greatness by creating for them some of the finest arrangements in the history of popular music. And then in the early 1970s he finally decided to help himself. So big, handsome, barrel-chested Sy Oliver began writing arrangements for his own lightly swinging mini-big band, reminiscent of the great big bands, like Tommy Dorsey's and Jimmie Lunceford's, to which he had supplied so many memorable charts.

The list of stars who sought his arranging talents is impressive. In addition to Dorsey and Lunceford, it includes Louis Armstrong, Bing Crosby, Sammy Davis, Jr., Ella Fitzgerald, Peggy Lee, the Mills Brothers, and Jackie Gleason, for whom he scored some lush mood albums, and Frank Sinatra, for whom he arranged a batch of swinging sides, and many more.

Swinging was always Sy's forte. He set the loose, relaxed style of the Lunceford band when he joined it in 1933 as arranger, trumpeter, and vocalist, after having worked for Al Sears, Zack White, and other bands near his hometown of Zanesville, Ohio. Both his parents had taught him music, but, as a kid, Sy preferred playing baseball and boxing. However, when his father died while Sy was still in his teens, he needed to make a steady living. And so he began to concentrate on music.

His relaxed, loping arrangements for Lunceford had a style all their own, perhaps because he had never studied arranging and so just wrote more or less as he felt like writing. Oliver tends to deprecate his famed Lunceford arrangements of tunes like "Four or Five Times," which featured his soft sexy singing, "Swanee River," "My Blue Heaven," and his own tunes, "For Dancers Only" and "'Tain't What You Do," often cited as among the best in jazz history. "Hell," he says, "those guys played so well that anybody could have written for that band."

But others saw it differently. When word got out in 1939 that Oliver was leaving Lunceford, ostensibly to complete his college education, the line of leaders wanting to hire him formed at the right. The winner, Tommy Dorsey, sealed his bid with "Whatever you've been making for Lunceford, I'll pay you five thousand dollars a year more." Little did Dorsey or anyone else know at the

Sy

time that when a young, eager Oliver joined Lunceford, he had been paid $2.50 per arrangement!

With Dorsey, Sy continued to write not only swinging arrangements of standards like "For You" and "On the Sunny Side of the Street," but also of his own tunes, like "Opus One" and "Well, Git It," and some on which he also sang, like "Dream of You" and "Yes, Indeed!"

Came the war, and Sy was drafted into the Army where he wrote for radio shows put on by the Special Services Division. After his discharge, he led, but soon chucked, a not very successful band and decided to settle in the recording studios, where he began arranging for all those top artists. But the commercial grind bugged him, and so in 1968 he migrated to Paris where for two years he served as musical director of the Olympia Theater. Upon his return to New York, he tried once more to complete his education, but a course in New Life Styles at the New School convinced him that at sixty maybe he couldn't become a lawyer after all. "So I decided to stick to music and see if I could make a nine-piece band sound like a fourteen-piece band." He succeeded, played some of New York's best clubs, including several successive years in the prestigious Rainbow Room, and, when others were worrying about social security checks, began a new life as one of the most gracious and talented gentlemen ever to lead a band.

(1910–   )

"The audience out there wants to know if you are fish or fowl."

"California is awful good. It's the economics. The working people get more per capita income and more livin' margin. So I would say they rank with the best of them."

Such an evaluation comes from one of the shrewdest, most dedicated businessmen in Central California, who also happens to be a superstar of country music. For one of the field's all-time hit-makers and heartbreakers, Alvis Edgar Owens, Jr. (most often called "Buck") stands as head mogul over an ever-growing music business empire. And the amazing thing is, he's doing it not where you'd think—not in Nashville, Tennessee—but right in Bakersfield, California.

Buck Owens has come a long way. Born the son of a Sherman, Texas, sharecropper, another child of the Great Depression, he readily recalls his rough beginnings: "We lived in North Texas just on the outskirts of the Dust Bowl. In 1938, when I was eight years old, my whole family—aunts and uncles, folks, brothers and sisters—we all piled into a 1933 Ford and headed West. We broke down in Phoenix and settled right there."

Buck attended high school only through the ninth grade, leaving because "I was big enough and strong enough to do a man's work and get a man's pay." He began teaching himself guitar and various other instruments and within a year became good enough to take on a nightly radio show. For a while he also hauled produce between California and Arizona, and gradually became acquainted with Bakersfield, then just beginning to be a thriving center of country music.

Buck recalls one of his first gigs in a Bakersfield club: "The singer didn't make it one night and the owner said if I wanted my job to start singing fast. I started singing fast."

Meanwhile, he had been augmenting his income by traveling daytimes down to Los Angeles to play on sessions at Capitol Records. There he was signed in March 1957 to record as a featured singer. Influenced by rock and rollers Elvis Presley and Fats Domino, he concentrated on a more rhythmic approach than other country singers had been using. Acceptance came slowly, but beginning with "Under Your Spell" in the late 1950s, such Buck Owens' hard-driving country records as "Excuse Me," "Above and Beyond," "Act Naturally," "Together Again," and "I've Got a Tiger by the Tail" began to top the country music charts.

Well established on the West Coast, Owens declined to make the expected move to country music's capital, Nashville. Instead, he decided to build his own smaller empire in Bakersfield, which eventually began to be referred to as *"Buck*ersfield."

Despite increasing emphasis on his numerous business enterprises like recording studios, publishing companies, a booking agency, and artist management, Owens continued to perform regularly on records, in concerts, and eventually on television. A commercial success? Assuredly so! And yet he kept working hard to maintain his original image, that of a genuine, down-home country performer. As he once explained to writer Jeff Young, "Image is a very strange and tough thing. The audience out there wants to know if you are fish or fowl. If you have a record that breaks over into the pop category, that's okay. But if the country people think you've gone over into the pop area totally, then they'll think you deserted them. And then you do have a problem."

(1929–   )

Buck

Patti Page

"Now I find that when a lot of people are laughing and talking when I'm singing, they aren't necessarily laughing at me."

When the anonymous singing star of the Tulsa, Oklahoma, radio show, "Meet Patti Page," sponsored by the Page Company, the local dairy, suddenly became too ill to perform, plump Katy Fowler, an apprentice in the art department, filled in and sounded so good that from then on *she* became "Patti Page."

Clara Ann (Katy) Fowler, the tenth of eleven children of a struggling Oklahoma family, never dreamed in the early 1940s, when she was out there picking cotton to supplement her parents' income, that ten years later she would become the most popular girl singer of the 1950s. But that's just what happened, thanks to an astute manager, some imagination and, of course, her warm voice and simple phrasing, featuring, wrote columnist Harriet Van Horne, "a melancholy vibrato that evokes the old-time ballad singers from the hill country."

The manager, Jack Rael, heard her in Tulsa, got her a job with Jimmy Joy's band, which he was then managing, followed by a steady engagement on Don McNeill's famed "Breakfast Club" radio series. He also secured her a recording date with Mercury Records for which she first cut some jazz-tinged sides (among her favorites in those days were Count Basie, Nat Cole, and Ella Fitzgerald) before she and Jack came up with the novel idea of including more than one Patti Page voice on a record.

And how did they do that in the days before tape recording? Simply by replaying the acetate recording of the first voice onto a second acetate while Patti supplied the additional voice. The result was "Confess," her first record hit. Encouraged, they doubled their efforts and came out with an even bigger hit, "With My Eyes Wide Open I'm Dreaming," that featured four Patti Pages!

Innovative record producer Mitch Miller, who worked with Patti throughout most of her career, credits her and Rael, with whom she maintained a superb working relationship for many years, for their imaginative breakthrough. "Patti was a real worker, a real pro," he recalls. Others have noted that only once during her entire career did she miss an engagement, often singing with the sorest of throats. For years distressingly shy in front of audiences, she worked hard to lose weight and her stage fright, admitting to writer Bob Salmaggi, "I may look good, I suppose, and act as if I'm terribly relaxed, but if you knew what was going through my mind!"

During the early 1950s, her record hits tumbled out, one on top of another: "Tennessee Waltz," which had been released as a throw-in on back of "Boogie

The former Katy Fowler

Woogie Santa Claus," which was supposed to have been the hit, "How Much Is That Doggie in the Window," "I Went to Your Wedding," "Mockin' Bird Hill," and the tune that became her theme, "This Is My Song." Her own favorite, remembered by practically no one except Patti: "Roses Remind Me of You."

She began her television career as a summer replacement for Perry Como, then went on to "The Big Record" and eventually "The Patti Page Show." Like Como, she always came across as an effortless singer: she reportedly never took a lesson, never practiced, and never found it necessary to warm up her voice before a performance. By 1961, when she scored a major triumph at New York's Copacabana, where ten years previously she had bombed because of her stage fright, she realized that success had helped her attain an even greater feeling of relaxation and objectivity. "Now," she explained, "I find that when a lot of people are laughing and talking when I'm singing, they aren't necessarily laughing at me. They're just having fun." Which is precisely what the former Katy Fowler has always wanted them to have.

(1927–   )

Charlie Parker

The hero of a generation of hipsters.

One of the most inspired and influential improvisers in the history of jazz, Charlie Parker was also one of its most enduring legends and, with trumpeter Dizzy Gillespie, the chief creator of the musical style called bop, or bebop.

Parker's short, explosive yet productive life began in Kansas City, Missouri, where nightlife flourished under the corrupt rule of Boss Pendergast. When Charles was given an alto sax at age eleven, he began to sneak out at night to drink in the sights and sounds, catching up on his sleep in school, which he left at fifteen ("I spent three years in high school and wound up a freshman"). The mature-looking Parker became a full-fledged professional when he lied about his age and joined the musicians' union.

But the youngest pro in a town bursting with jazz talent showed no signs of budding genius and was often ridiculed by his peers. Determination and the inspiration of Count Basie's saxophonist, Lester Young, whose records Parker studied like the Bible, eventually changed such ridicule to respect. In 1939 he went to New York, the jazz mecca, and was sufficiently original to impress musicians but too unorthodox to find steady work. Returning home, he joined and made his first records with the best band in town, Jay McShann's. In 1943 he played in Earl Hines's band with Dizzy Gillespie, and the two became inseparable. They worked out a new way of playing marked by lightning-fast execution, improvisation based on the harmonic rather than melodic line of tunes, and unexpected rhythmic accents. After a stay with Billy Eckstine's fabled band, he and Gillespie joined forces as a team on New York's Fifty-second Street, setting the jazz world on its ear, in person and on records, with their revolutionary and often puzzling sounds.

By 1946 Parker's addiction to heroin (he'd been initiated by "friends" at fifteen) removed him from the jazz scene and placed him in a psychiatric hospital. Released in early 1947, he embarked on the most productive and successful four years of his career. He visited Europe twice and realized a dream: recording and touring with a string section. His final years were brightened by a happy marriage (his fourth) but plagued by ill health. Parker died, apparently of a stroke, at the age of thirty-four. But so ravaged had his body become through his drug addiction and other self-destructive ways that the medical examiner estimated his age at fifty-five!

His huge appetite for life—for music, women, food, drink, and drugs—had

Bird with Miles Davis

literally consumed Parker but not before his brilliant and highly original approach to jazz had been absorbed into the mainstream of American music. As a man Parker was as complex and unpredictable as his music: warm and generous or as devious as the most fiendish con man, victim and victimizer in turn. Nevertheless, he remains the hero of a generation of hipsters and the idol and inspiration of countless jazz musicians throughout the world, including such latter-day jazz stars as Stan Getz, Miles Davis, John Coltrane, "Cannonball" Adderley, and many more.

(1920–1955)

Dolly Parton

"Where it really counts I am not artificial."

"I'm aware I'm not in style, but it don't bother me," country singer Dolly Parton told Robert Windeler of *People*. "I like looking as if I came out of a fairy tale."

"I enjoy the way I look, but it's like a joke," she admitted to *Soho News*. "It's a plaything. It's like playing show business."

"Part of the magic of me, I think, is that I look totally one way—an overall artificial look—but I *am* totally another," she explained to Neil Hickey of *TV Guide*. "Where it really counts, I am not artificial."

"My inner sadness and joy are as real as my hair and my nails are fake," she insisted to Pete Axthelm of *Newsweek*. To Barbara Walters on TV she referred to "my ridiculous image." But, she added, "I'm sure of myself and my talent, so I can make fun of myself."

There seems to have been at least as much written about the way singer Dolly looks as there has been about the way she sounds. That's not too surprising, though, when one considers her fantastic figure, tightly wrapped in gawdy costumes and topped by some of the most outrageous wigs east of Mae West. After all, sight often more than sound seemed to attract many music writers during the mid-1970s. And Miss Parton is *some* visual attraction!

Time magazine did take the time to describe her vocal qualities: "a high, accurate chirp that is sometimes tremulous with passion or nasal with determination or sweetly childlike with tenderness." And the New York *Times*'s John Rockwell, in one of several Parton pieces, called her "not only a singer but an unmatched songwriter and an abundant personality as well." The admiring Rockwell also noted that "Dolly Parton is at the brink of a radical shift in direction, one that should, if there is any justice in pop heaven, make her one of the great stars of American entertainment."

The shift to which he was alluding was away from the tightly constricted world of pure country music, in which she had been raised, toward a more rock-oriented approach, exemplified, rhythmically, by a shift from a relaxed emphasis on the second and fourth beat of a measure to the more ponderous pounding of the first and third beats, so indigenous to commercial contemporary top chart sellers. "I can make more money in the pop field," she freely admitted to Barbara Walters. "Millions rather than thousands."

Most of the songs she has sung have been her own. "I started writing songs

Dolly

before I ever went to school," she told writer Jerry Bailey. "My momma would write them down for me." At six she was playing a homemade guitar in her hometown of Locust Ridge, Tennessee; at eight, a real one. And at ten she came down out of the mountains to sing in a Knoxville radio station. She was an instant hit, then went down to Louisiana to make her first record, "Puppy Love," written by her and her uncle. It was an instant flop. But undismayed ("I had ambition and it burned inside of me," she told Chet Flippo of *Rolling Stone*), she packed her cardboard suitcase full of her songs and set out for Nashville. Her uncle helped her get a contract with Monument Records with whom she fought zealously to be permitted to sing country songs, despite their thinking that nobody would be convinced by her little-girl sound. But she won out and also won a spot on a local TV station.

Veteran country singer Porter Wagoner saw her and when Norma Jean, his partner, left the act to get married, he invited Dolly to replace her. Together they made many RCA hit records. But soon she began yearning to go in other musical directions. And so she did. The move meant some sharp breaks, including one away from her back-up group, composed mostly of relatives, to a more modern-sounding, more musically sophisticated band. And she also took on a high-powered personal manager and public relations outfit. "I have a lot of big dreams," she told Flippo, "and before I had a lot of people who couldn't dream as big as me." And referring to her more sophisticated approach to music: "This is a new freedom to me. Just total self-expression and daring to be brave, just to really see music the way I totally feel it."

According to author Douglas Green of *Country Roots,* she still "retains much of the traditional country style in her currently popular sound—one of the gifted and sensitive few who are able to combine the old and the new." And those who have known her best point out that, as a person, Dolly Parton remains the same simple, straightforward, unassuming, often very naïve girl, who still stops off in diners to eat with the guys in the band, and who keeps insisting, "I don't want to leave the country but to take the country with me wherever I go. I am Dolly Parton from the mountains. That's what I'll remain."

(1946–   )

Les Paul and Mary Ford

"If you feel like Lester Young and then go to a Fred Waring session, you have to go through a decompression chamber first!"

His innate enthusiasm permeated everything he ever did, and so it is no wonder that Les Paul became the most influential, the richest, and probably the happiest guitar player the world has ever known.

Of course talent helped too. Les had plenty of that, and he applied it to all sorts of music, especially to the jazz, of which he became one of that music's outstanding players, and which always remained his true love. Back in 1930 he had recorded down-home blues with Georgia White, and then a few years later, as "Rhubarb Red," he was playing hillbilly harmonica and guitar over several Midwest radio stations.

By then he had plunged deep into musical schizophrenia. Starting at six each morning, the Rhubarb Red of him took over. Then in the afternoon, as Les Paul, he would plink-plank-plunk pop tunes over other stations. And finally each evening he'd go out and jam at sessions with some of the world's greatest

Mary and Les

jazz musicians centered in Chicago, all of whom welcomed the driving, soulful, and often humorous and technically amazing pickings of the rambunctious red-head who reminded them of his musical idol, Django Reinhardt, the great French gypsy guitarist. "It was a funny scene," he recalled later, "telling somebody like Art Tatum at four in the morning that I had to cut out to go to work. But of course I wouldn't tell them where I was going!"

Les (his real name is Lester Pollfuss) continued his split existence after he joined Fred Waring's Pennsylvanians in 1938. Nights he'd jam up in Harlem with all the jazz greats. "If you feel like Lester Young and then go to a Fred Waring session, you have to go through a decompression chamber first!"

In 1941 he went to Los Angeles and appeared regularly on Bing Crosby's radio program, worked with Judy Garland, and also guested on numerous top shows. Following a hitch with Meredith Willson's Armed Forces Radio Band, he returned to the Los Angeles studio scene, starring with close friend Nat King Cole on the first and most famous "Jazz at the Philharmonic" record date and playing other jazz sessions, while also appearing regularly on NBC as "Rhubarb Red and His Ozark Apple Knockers." Merle Travers recommended a girl, Coleen Summers, for that show. Les liked her, changed her name to Mary Lou, and for five years "she traveled everywhere with me."

He had made some successful records, "Lover" and "Brazil," when a bad auto accident suddenly cut two years out of his career. On his first comeback appearance at his family's Wisconsin tavern, his brother booked an incompetent guitarist, so Les hit upon the idea of Mary Lou, who played a little guitar, coming out of the audience and joining the group. She was a big hit, whereupon Les, who had been experimenting with multiple-recording techniques in a studio in his Hollywood garage ("Bing, Mel Torme, and everybody used to drop by."), hit upon the idea of overdubbing Mary Lou's voice and his guitar. Soon they were married; she changed her name to Mary Ford ("We needed something that sounded rich") and together they recorded "How High the Moon," the first of a gang of Les Paul and Mary Ford hits, that included "Tiger Rag," "The World Is Waiting for the Sunrise," "I'm Sitting on Top of the World," and "Vaya Con Dios." Meanwhile, Les, dissatisfied with the sameness of guitar sounds, had designed the first solid-body, amplified guitar, the daddy of all the millions of amplified instruments that were soon to mushroom all over the music world. "It was merely a piece of four-by-four wood with strings!" He kept refining the instrument and it caught on so big that there were soon eight different Les Paul models!

In 1962, Les and Mary split up. "The pace was just too rough for her. I was working all the time." Mary remarried and lived on the West Coast until her death, brought on by several diseases, in September 1977. From 1964 to 1974, Les stopped playing altogether and just invented. He developed sound-on-sound and eight-track recording processes. "In three years I had made over a million dollars." But the rock-infested music scene, which ironically his inventions had helped create and sustain, had diminished his enthusiasm for performing publicly.

Then one evening in 1974 he received an SOS from friend and guitarist Bucky Pizzarelli who had had a run-in with partner George Barnes. Les subbed and when he saw the reaction on the listeners he realized that jazz had at last come out from behind all those rocks. Thrilled by the reactions, "especially those of the college kids," to his playing, he flew out of retirement. He played in jazz joints, in major concert halls, and in Nashville's Grand Ole Opry. Two years later he was touring with two of rock's biggest stars, Jeff Beck and John McLaughlin, both tremendous Les Paul fans. And with his old pal, Chet Atkins, he recorded a Grammy-winning album, "Chester and Lester." Its opening selection was a song he had recorded as a duet with Bing Crosby more than thirty years earlier. Its title couldn't have been more meaningful: "It's Been a Long, Long Time"!

(Les Paul: 1923–   )
(Mary Ford: 1928–1977)

Peter, Paul and Mary

Disparate in temperament, attitudes, backgrounds, and ever musical timbres.

It's the Tale of Three Singers—Peter, Paul and Mary—disparate in temperament, attitudes, backgrounds, and even musical timbres, and yet the most popular and successful of all the many American singing groups of the 1960s.

Peter Yarrow, energetic, ambitious, driven, Brooklyn-born, graduate of Cornell where he studied, taught and promoted folk music, anxious for a solo career, auditioned early in the 1960s for famed folk-singers' manager Albert Grossman, who politely urged young Yarrow "to organize a group instead." In a Greenwich Village picture gallery of folk singers, Peter saw a photo of an unusually attractive girl with long, blond hair. How would she do? "Mary Travers would be fine," Grossman told him, "that is, if you could get her to work."

Mary Ellin Travers, daughter of two Greenwich Village writers with left-wing leanings and friends, including Paul Robeson, who once sang her to sleep when she was a tot, sang at the age of fourteen on Pete Seeger records, sometimes performed at parties, but had neither eyes nor ears for a career. But when Peter Yarrow persuaded her to try singing a few songs together and maybe form a trio, he piqued her interest enough for her to suggest that they "go across the street to the Gaslight Club and listen to Paul Stookey."

Conservative, ex-Mormon Noel "Paul" Stookey out of Birmingham, Michigan, had led his own rock group, the Birds of Paradise, at Michigan State before migrating to New York, where he was working daytimes for a photochemical company and nights as a stand-up comedian, also sang and played guitar and occasionally strummed accompaniments for the tall girl with the long, blond hair when she would drop in from her house across the street.

When Peter, Paul and Mary got together for the first time, they found out each was singing a different version of any number of folk songs. Inexperienced and frustrated, they finally settled on the supersimple "Mary Had a Little Lamb" as their audition tune for Grossman. He immediately recommended the experienced and talented musical director, Milt Okun, who had already trained other groups very successfully, to try to make order out of their chaos. According to Mary, "Milt had pity on us. I couldn't read a note and we were all slow learners. But he was a great disciplinarian and he had wonderful taste and patience beyond belief." His patience could well have been taxed by the bickering that Mary reported went on as she and Peter matched strong wills to see who could control the group. "Only Paul was mature enough not to push for it,"

Peter, Paul and Mary

she realized. Perhaps their strongest adhesive became their total commitment to the emerging civil rights movement into which they channeled much of their boundless energy via innumerable appearances on behalf of the cause.

Both visually and aurally the trio projected a contagious excitement. The blend of Peter's piercing high tenor, Mary's booming low alto, and Paul's more subdued baritone, though not always perfectly balanced because of the great disparity of their timbres, produced an arresting sound that had a distinctive, often biting edge. Obviously carried away by their own spirited performances, the trio readily touched the millions of college kids who came to hear their concerts, and who identified easily with them and the subject matter of their songs. Record hit followed record hit: "If I Had a Hammer," "Blowin' in the

Wind," "Puff, the Magic Dragon," "Leavin' on a Jet Plane," and many more, "all songs," Mary pointed out, "that each of us really believed in."

Their success was sustained until the late 1960s, when their philosophical beliefs had grown so divergent that they seldom agreed on anything anymore. Paul, deeply immersed in religion, began spouting his Christian doctrines even during their concerts. Mary fought bitterly with him, but she couldn't control him any more than she had been able to control Peter. The battle ended when Paul withdrew, forsaking folk music for religious songs. Peter and Mary embarked on only moderately successful solo careers. In 1978 all three got together again for a brief, heart-warming concert fling. But that's all it was—a short fling, for the ideas and the sounds of the 1960s had already gone on their own way. And so had the trio of Peter, Paul and Mary.

(Peter: 1938–   )
(Paul: 1937–   )
(Mary: 1937–   )

Oscar Peterson

The rock-conditioned audience got the message.

The unique power and joy of Oscar Peterson's talent was perhaps never more strikingly apparent than on a 1972 Newport Jazz Festival program when this monumental pianist's appearance was sandwiched between the raw horn and percussion power of the Cannonball Adderley Quintet and the electronic voltage of a larger group called Mahavishnu. Mahavishnu's refrigerator-size black generating "boxes" were already on the Carnegie Hall stage when Oscar sat down at the concert grand and began to play. With only the power of his ideas, his arms, and his two hands, he unraveled themes and counterthemes, sped up and down the keys much as Art Tatum did, perhaps with even greater force; tumbled out chords and convoluted patterns with design and precision, threw down enormous glissandos and from storms of notes struck sudden whisper-soft passages; and then finally repeated chordal figures to build a furiously swinging beat. The rock-conditioned audience got the message.

Oscar

Jazz for Peterson has never been a casual kind of fun music. Instead, it has been real fun, the kind of fun in which only a player in full command of the music and his instrument (he started studying seriously at the age of seven) can indulge.

Before he began traveling coast to coast, continent to continent, playing concerts, clubs, festivals, Peterson had stayed put for twenty-four years in his native Montreal, Canada, studying and practicing the piano. He didn't even have to leave the house for his first playing dates, for the musical Petersons—father, mother, three daughters, and two sons—had a family orchestra. Young Oscar balanced his playing and study of the classics with listening to jazz, later studying it also. During his high school years he won an amateur contest and was subsequently featured on a weekly radio program over Montreal's CKAC, then later joined Johnny Holmes's band. The recordings he made with Holmes began to catch the public's ear and later Oscar organized his own trio.

In the beginning he used the piano-guitar-bass instrumentation, just like the trio of Nat "King" Cole, the major influence on his piano playing. He also sang occasionally. Later Peterson dropped the guitar in favor of drums, and in this context won perhaps his greatest fame with his longtime associates, bassist Ray Brown and drummer Ed Thigpen.

Oscar made his U.S. debut as a pianist in 1949 with a Norman Granz "Jazz at the Philharmonic" concert at Carnegie Hall. This led to tours with JATP, recordings, and a continuing association with Granz as his personal manager. Under Granz, Peterson's recording output reached almost unclassifiable proportions, a veritable cavalcade of performances with his peers, from the great Louis Armstrong to Jon Faddis, the young trumpet star of the latter 1970s. A consistent poll winner in the 1950s for his piano virtuosity, Peterson began winning recognition for composing when in 1965 the Recording Academy nominated his "Canadian Suite" for a Grammy. New recognition of his international status as a jazz artist awaited him in 1974 when he was booked to tour the Soviet Union, but a courageous and independent thinker and actor, he canceled the tour when he felt he was receiving what he considered cavalier treatment from Soviet officialdom. Four years later, his popularity still undiminished, he won the first of two successive Grammys.

Peterson has remained a firm believer in truth and the importance of roots, both personal and musical. He has spoken out boldly against some sorts of questionable "avant-garde" explorations that ignore the basics of jazz. And as for the emergence of power through electronics in music, Peterson continues to have faith in the power of his own two hands, as opposed to that generated by electronic pianos. As he told British writer Les Tomkins, "When the tubes go, and the transistors fail, there's only one place to go." No electric power failure will ever still Oscar Peterson.

(1925–   )

Edith Piaf

"You have to send the elevator back down so others may get to the top."

"She has genius, she is inimitable," Jean Cocteau said of his close friend Edith Piaf. "It was she who beheld lovers folded in each other's arms who still knew how to suffer and to die. How was this tiny person able to bring from her heart the great sad songs of the night? And when she sang, it was more than a voice. It was like an April nightingale."

This "tiny person" was, in fact, barely four feet ten inches tall and weighed, at best, ninety-nine pounds. To Cocteau, she may have been an "April nightingale" but to her worldwide legion of followers she was "The Sparrow," a name suggested by her frail, bedraggled appearance ("piaf" is French slang for "sparrow"). Wearing a simple, short black dress that was her performing uniform, Miss Piaf sang in a strong, keening voice (it has been called "the voice of

The Sparrow

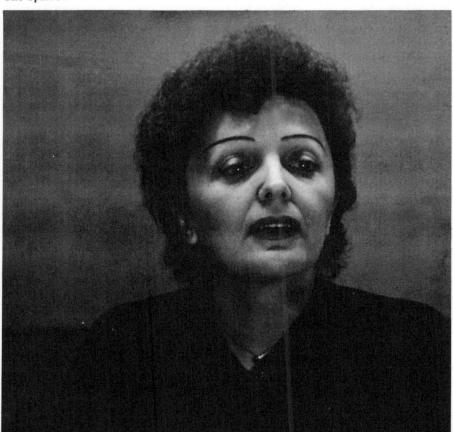

every woman's innermost anguish") of the tragedies of love and the tragedies of life, both subjects with which she was very familiar. And yet the best known of all the songs she sang, one for which she wrote the words—"La Vie en Rose"—was a song of happiness in love.

She had an almost unbearably miserable childhood. Born on a narrow sidewalk in Paris at 5 A.M. with two policemen serving as midwives, she was named Edith Giovanna Gassion and turned over to her grandmother, who ran a brothel. She contracted meningitis, which left her temporarily blind. For a while, she traveled with her father, an acrobat, sleeping in hallways and in trunks. Her only solace and only companion was a doll to which she clung desperately.

At the age of sixteen, she had a child by a soldier who was transferred before the baby was born. The child died in infancy and Miss Piaf began singing outside of sidewalk cafes. In 1937, when she was twenty-two, she was heard by Louis Leplee, a small-time impresario. It was Leplee who named her "Piaf" and suggested the simple black dress. At her first cabaret performance for Leplee, Maurice Chevalier, who was in the audience, cried out, "Cette mome—elle en a dans le ventre!" ("That kid—she's got it inside!"). "Ventre" was a word that stayed with Piaf. People said that she sang from her gut ("ventre") or hit them in theirs.

Within two years she was being acclaimed as one of France's great music hall singers. But although her professional life became one triumph after another, she continued to live the life of personal tragedy to which she had been born. In 1947 she fell in love with Marcel Cerdan, the boxer. Two years later he was killed in a plane crash. She married Jacques Pills, a singer, in 1952, but the memory of Cerdan still haunted her and they were divorced in 1957. During the 1950s, she was wracked by illness, was injured in three automobile accidents. Yet she continued to perform on what the French press called "suicide tours." She was scheduled to open in New York in a show called *Piaf!* on October 3, 1963, but she became so ill that she could not make the trip. Eight days after the scheduled opening, she was dead.

Despite her own troubles, she was always lending support and help to other musicians and singers, among them Yves Montand and Charles Azhavour. "When you are on top," she once said, "you have to send the elevator back down so others may get to the top."

Edith Piaf? There are many who may never have heard of her. And yet, according to the August 27, 1977, issue of *Billboard*, New York's prestigious Liberty Music Shop reported that along with Sinatra's, the most requested records from nostalgia fans were those of Edith Piaf.

(1915–1963)

The Platters

Deliberately and, for some, overly sentimental.

Led by the distinctive tenor of Tony Williams, the Platters was the last and possibly the greatest of the major romantic vocal groups, singing in a style first developed in the 1930s by the Mills Brothers and later revised by the Ink Spots. The quintet's style was deliberately and, for some, overly sentimental but the performances were delivered with the precision and attack of concert musicians. Though their career as successful recording artists lasted only from 1955 to 1959, the Platters' original recordings were still popular twenty years later.

Tony Williams, son of an Elizabeth, New Jersey, minister, sang in church choirs. As a youth he studied formal vocal techniques with a private tutor and learned to expand his voice while also learning ways to sustain and protect it. "Tony could hit high C while everybody else was looking for it," his wife

The Platters

Helen recalled, "and he could sing night after night without getting hoarse; he had so much technique he could even sing over a bad cold."

Williams formed the Platters in 1952 while he was a teenager. Early members came and went but the final personnel consisted of Williams, David Lynch, Paul Robi, Herbert Reed, and Zola Taylor. They had recorded an album and a few singles for the King label combine in Cincinnati but were not notably successful. In 1954 the group followed Williams' sister, Linda Hayes, who had a hit record, "Yes, I Know," to Los Angeles, where they met her manager, Buck Ram, who rehearsed them, wrote special material tailored to them, and secured a recording contract. In 1955 they hit with "Only You," and followed it up with "The Great Pretender," "The Magic Touch," "I'm Sorry," "Twilight Time," "Smoke Gets in Your Eyes," "My Prayer," and others, all marked by Williams' four-octave vocal range and craftsmanship of performance.

The group toured extensively in the United States and overseas. In Rome, Williams had an audience with the Pope. In North Africa the group entertained at a French Foreign Legion outpost in Tunisia, and in the Far East they performed for the King and Queen of Thailand. Then in 1959 Williams left the group to pursue a solo career. He returned briefly in 1962 but left again as, one by one, the original members also departed, being replaced by Ram-groomed substitutes. Of the original personnel, Taylor, Robi, and Reed made occasional appearances with their own groups, billing themselves as Platter alumni, while Lynch abandoned show business altogether.

In 1967 Tony Williams and his wife Helen formed their own Platters group for personal appearances and world tours. On one occasion they received a special clearance from the Department of Defense so that they could perform inside the nuclear submarine U.S.S. *John Adams* while it was submerged four hundred feet off the island of Guam.

The estrangement between Williams and Ram, which had been building since the early 1960s, continued to grow with the years; each claimed the major share of credit for the success of the original group (the success would have been impossible without their combined talents), and they entered into frequent legal wrangles over the rights to the use of the quintet's name. Both parties continued to operate Platters groups into the mid-1970s, though none ever projected the original spirit that had permeated one of the most popular of pre-Beatles vocal groups.

Ben Pollack

Controversy often surrounded the short, squat, tense, ambitious, and at times pugnacious little drummer.

"If you want to hear a *really* good drummer with a great beat," Glenn Miller once enthused, "go hear Ben Pollack!"

"Ben Pollack, he really wasn't that great a drummer," Benny Goodman recently insisted.

Both Miller and Goodman knew Pollack and his drumming well, for both were members of the band that they and many others agree was one of the greatest and most important of all the big bands. Yet, their disagreement about his talents is not unexpected, for controversy often surrounded the short, squat, tense, ambitious, and at times pugnacious little drummer from Chicago who led the orchestra that in the late 1920s discovered Miller and Goodman, as well as future star musicians Bud Freeman, Jimmy McPartland, and Jack Teagarden, and then in the 1930s introduced Harry James to the big time.

The band featured pulsating ensemble sounds, created by arrangers, Fud Livingston and Miller, that were unmatched by any other white band of its time, save possibly that of Jean Goldkette. It also highlighted solos by the young

The Ben Pollack band on the MGM lot: Pollack at far left; young Benny Goodman fifth from left; young Glenn Miller far right. Costumed actors are Henry Wallthall, Lionel Barrymore, and Owen Moore

instrumentalists (Goodman was only sixteen when he joined the band) whom Pollack discovered and, unlike other leaders of the era, was willing and proud to feature.

Pollack's intense, driving personality was reflected in his forceful drumming. He started his bandleading career late in 1924 when he assured the owner of the Venice Ballroom in Los Angeles that he could do a better job than the incumbent leader. And he was right. Within a year, the Pollack band had become the musical talk of the town, and it aroused the same sort of reaction when in 1926 it moved to Chicago, Pollack's hometown, and then in 1928 to New York, where it appeared in several top clubs, in the Broadway musical, *Hello, Daddy!* and recorded for RCA Victor.

And yet, despite such success, Pollack never seemed to find contentment. At the Little Club, he fought with Lillian Roth, the star of the show. His penchant for fault-finding irritated his own musicians, including Goodman, who quit the band twice, once after Pollack had criticized him in front of the other musicians for having dust on his shoes! Others drifted away: Miller, Teagarden, Freeman, McPartland. Then in 1934 the entire band quit, fed up with Ben's devoting most of his time and energies to the career of the band's singer, Doris Robbins, who became his wife, instead of to the band itself.

But their walkout didn't mean the end of their music. Held together by Gil Rodin, Pollack's right-hand man, eight of the alumni formed a cooperation, elected Rodin president, installed Bob Crosby as their frontman, and for years thereafter the Pollack brand of music flourished in what was called "The Best Dixieland Band in the Land."

As for Ben, in 1936 he organized another band that featured more future stars like pianist Freddy Slack, clarinetist Irving Fazola, and Harry James. Then in 1942 he organized a band for comedian Chico Marx and uncovered a young drummer who also sang. His name: Mel Torme. Later Pollack tried other businesses—heading a talent agency, a record company, and a nightclub. But he was never very successful and he became increasingly embittered, even going so far as to petulantly institute unsuccessful lawsuits against successful big bands for having "stolen" his musical style.

Greatly respected as an organizer, but as Goodman later asserted, "not the easiest guy in the world to get along with," Pollack gradually drifted into a relative obscurity that was shockingly terminated when one night, all alone in his Palm Springs home, he hanged himself.

(1903–1971)

Elvis Presley

A highly public and furtively private person.

Without him, much of American musical and social history of the last twenty-five years is inexplicable. Though Elvis Presley did not create rock or its corollary, "the youth culture," he personified them during his early career, and the colossal impact of his fame and success continued to influence both.

All that glory could bring to a man had come to Presley before he died under somewhat mysterious circumstances in his Tennessee mansion during the summer of 1977: worldwide recognition, a rajah's income, the love of adoring women everywhere and, perhaps the most sought-after of all, the respect of his professional peers. His vocal style and stage personality had impressed themselves on nearly every rock singer and musician who came after him. As John

Elvis

Lennon recalled, "Nothing really happened to me until Elvis." But the worship could be taken to loony lengths: A Nashville musician once found a pair of Presley's socks left behind at a recording session and had them bronzed.

Throughout his fabulous career, Presley became simultaneously a highly public and furtively private person. When not appearing in concert, he lived in well-guarded seclusion at Graceland, his mansion, on Elvis Presley Boulevard in his adopted home of Memphis. Most of his friends and associates—former and current—rated him as generous, intelligent, sentimental, polite, and basically shy. His public vs. his private life was the music industry's dichotomy of Superman vs. Clark Kent. Though for a time he seemed to be able to commute easily between the two roles, his reclusive behavior and bulbous physical appearance during his later years lent credence to the reports that he had become a troubled man who sought relief through prescribed drugs and perhaps alcohol.

Elvis was born in Tupelo, Mississippi, where his father took whatever work was to be had during the Great Depression. His mother doted on her only child (a twin was stillborn) and the boy adored her in return.

The family moved to Memphis ("We were broke, man, broke . . . We left Tupelo overnight. Things had to be better") and for a time was on relief. Elvis had already been affected by music, from seeing preachers wiggle at singing services of the First Assembly of God Church in Tupelo, then from listening to country music over the radio, and finally from a $12.50 guitar his father gave him. In Memphis, the Presleys lived near the black part of town and the impressionable boy was quick to appreciate blues and jump records that he heard.

In 1953, while working as a truck driver for the Crown Electric Company, Presley went to Sun Records and paid four dollars to make an acetate disc of "My Happiness" and "That's When Your Heartaches Begin" as a present for his mother. A year later he was called in for a commercial test—he ran from Crown's offices to the studios—and despite an unsuccessful beginning to the session it ended in an impromptu version of a jump blues, "That's All Right, Mama." Sun released it as a single and Presley, holding a copy, burst into tears: "This is what I've always wanted; my very own record with my very own name on it." Sam Phillips, head of Sun Records, recently remarked that Elvis combined innocence with impudence. "He looked so clumsy and totally uncoordinated back then. And that was the beauty of it: he was being himself."

He began to tour the county fair and barn-dance circuit as "The Hillbilly Cat" and was spotted by Steve Sholes of RCA Victor Records and by a ballyhoo promoter named Colonel Tom Parker, once described as "the toughest manager since Cardinal Richelieu," who began a campaign to advance his client that was a shrewd mixture of fertilizer and hard bargaining.

Sholes recorded Presley in Nashville on January 10, 1956, and his first release, "Heartbreak Hotel," quickly became the first of a long line of gold records. Its sales were helped by Elvis' first TV appearance on January 28 on the Dorsey Brothers' "Stage Show" series and by subsequent guest spots on "The Ed Sullivan

Elvis on his first national television show flanked by Tommy and Jimmy Dorsey

Show." Within a few months Presley had conquered the nation through records, radio, television, and personal appearances. On stage, with his then-scandalous hip-shaking and bumps, he was a hot, quick animal. (TV censors permitted cameramen to shoot him only above the waist!) Wherever he went, he was greeted with hysterical screams and squeals. His responses to all these emotional and professional pressures were made with admirable tact, discipline, and patience. Throughout his entire career, he remained a gentleman, low-born, hard-working, and high-flying.

Record hit followed record hit: "Hound Dog," "Don't Be Cruel," "Love Me Tender," "All Shook Up," "Jailhouse Rock," and on and on. Naturally Hollywood wanted him. His films became enormous moneymakers and his performance in *King Creole* (1958) brought a grudging admission from movie critics—that he could indeed act. Of the thirty-one movies he made, Presley's personal favorites were those in which he sang less and acted more.

Drafted into the Army in 1958, he returned in 1960 to resume a career which, though lucrative, floundered artistically as he made a series of Grade C movie musicals and recorded banal songs. The stifling of his talents as an actor and, soon after, the death of his mother were perhaps the two major sorrows in his life.

In 1968, disgusted with Hollywood, he made plans to return to personal appearances; a television special and a triumphant performance in Las Vegas, plus a 1969 recording session in Memphis that was exciting and fruitful (at long last he was again singing good material), brought a tidal wave of good feeling from his old fans and new converts.

Upon his return to public performing ("I really missed the audience contact— the people"), Presley experienced the supreme pleasure of reliving his youth while still a comparatively young, though by then an experienced, man. His voice had mellowed to an anisette baritone and his phrasing had become more assured than ever. And when the ladies began screaming for him, he heard the sounds of three generations: his original fans, their daughters, and their daughters' daughters.

But it all ended—too soon and too abruptly—when he was found dead— eight automobiles, six motorcycles, two airplanes, sixteen TV sets, and many millions of dollars richer—inside his huge mansion, behind his estate's imposing, protective walls, walls that could protect him so well from everything outside but from so little inside of him—from the terrible tortures that seemed to have seized him, bent on leadening his effervescent spirit and deadening forever the voice that had made him his generation's most revered performer.

(1935–1977)

Charley Pride

"I'm no different from any other country artist, other than the pigmentation of my skin."

"I said to myself, 'Why can't I sing the kind of music I love?' I believe you should be your own individual self and not be molded into what somebody thinks you should be. Country music is the music I chose to sing, and I feel that I'm a *true* country artist. I'm no different from any other country artist, other than the pigmentation of my skin."

This kind of individualism and determination is hardly atypical of the country singer, many—perhaps most—of whom used music as an escape from the grinding poverty of their youth. But it is remarkable indeed in Charley Pride, the son of a Sledge, Mississippi, sharecropper who, in addition to being a topnotch country singer, is also black, a more than serious roadblock in a competitive

Charlie

field already strewn with roadblocks, in a society not known for its enlightenment.

Actually Charley Pride didn't even consider country music as his means of escape, at least not until he had exhausted the possibilities of that other—and for blacks, infinitely more attainable—common route: professional athletics, in his case baseball.

Pride struggled for years in the minors and the semipros, and in fact it was while in the role of struggling ballplayer that Charley Pride the country singer was discovered in 1963, in a Helena, Montana, tavern where he sang at night, while working for Anaconda Mining during the day and playing semipro ball on the weekends.

Encouraged by his discoverer, country singer Red Sovine, Pride eventually moved to Nashville—not until a final unsuccessful tryout with the New York Mets in 1964—and teamed up with a superpromoter named Jack Johnson, who has carefully overseen Pride's career ever since. Johnson made the rounds of record company executives, all of whom had predictable reactions: enthusiasm after hearing his tapes, shock and rejection after seeing his picture.

For Charley Pride's voice was pure country, very much a baritone Hank Williams, and it was Chet Atkins at RCA who eventually decided to take the chance. Johnson called the still-naïve Pride and "told me I was going to be on RCA Records. I said, 'Is that good?' They kid me a lot about that now."

The gamble, of course, paid off, and by the mid-1970s Pride had become a country music institution, with two-score albums, awards including Entertainer of the Year, and dozens of hits such as "The Snakes Crawl at Night," "All I Have to Offer You Is Me," and "Kiss an Angel Good Morning." In fact, Charley Pride had become a pretty hip commodity, and even spawned a batch of imitators—black men and women attempting to sing country music—none of whom could match his authentic sound.

Pride, with Johnson's aid, was extremely careful to maintain a pleasant, non-threatening, nonpolitical image, yet he was well aware of his groundbreaking role: "I'm sure Jackie Robinson would have loved to have been just another baseball player. But society put him in the position of being the first known Negro in the major leagues. I came along years later and I'm in the same position. And it's slowly breaking down."

Charley Pride's race was at first a hindrance and then a help to his career. He eventually reached a point where his talents as a singer and an entertainer were all that mattered.

His acceptance opened the door for a host of black singers, as well as country singers of other ethnic minorities like chicanos Johnny Rodriguez and Freddy Fender (Baldemar Huerta) and "Texas Jewboy" Kinky Friedman. Yet he also feels, rightly, that the point has long been made: "After twenty RCA albums I don't think I have to prove anything to anybody anymore."

(1938–   )

Ma Rainey

"Really an ugly woman . . . but when she opened her mouth, that was it."

The origins of the blues are obscure, and we know practically nothing of the men and women whose transformation of life experience into words and music gradually took the particular shape and form we call blues. But we do know that Ma Rainey's right to the title "Mother of the Blues," under which she was billed on stage and records, was not challenged, though hers was a time when others who might have laid claim to it were still around.

Gertrude Malissa Pridgett was born in Columbus, Georgia. Her parents had been in show business. She made her first stage appearance in 1898, when she was twelve. Six years later, she married William "Pa" Rainey, a dancer, comedian, and singer featured with the famous Rabbit Foot Minstrels. The newlyweds became an act, and since he was "Pa," Gertrude, at the ripe old age of eighteen, became "Ma" Rainey. She was a plain girl, so the premature sobriquet did not seem incongruous.

At this time, the blues were not yet part of professional black shows, but a rural folk music. Many years later, Ma told of first hearing the blues in a

Ma Rainey and her Georgia Jazz Band

small Missouri town. A young girl came to the show's tent one morning "and began to sing about the man who'd left her." The strange and poignant song moved Ma; she learned it and used it as an encore. The response was so great that the song soon became her special feature. She heard other, similar blues on her travels and adapted these as well, making this folk music part of her more sophisticated professional art.

It came easy, for Ma was of the folk herself. The poet and scholar Sterling Brown described her as "very simple and direct . . . Ma really *knew* her people. She would moan, and the audience would moan with her. She had them in the palm of her hand." Champion Jack Dupree, the blues singer and pianist, saw her as "really an ugly woman . . . but when she opened her mouth, that was it. You forgot everything. What a personality she had!"

Photographs show a kind, even a sweet face; if not ugly, then certainly far from pretty. Her body was short and squat, her hair unruly, and her teeth lined with gold. But she used what she had with a sure sense of drama. Her gowns were extravagant. She wore necklaces made of gold pieces and genuine diamonds. An inevitable headband, feather boas and plumes, long earrings, tiaras, and the like rounded out an extraordinary getup. For a time, her act opened with her emerging from a giant Victrola. Musicians found her a kind and generous employer. Her entourage always included a handsome young man with very specific duties. "She didn't care for nothin' but young men, and there was always a bottle of moonshine under the bed," said Chippie Hill, the blues singer.

Ma made the first of her ninety-odd recorded sides in late 1923, when she was thirty-seven, and the last exactly five years later, all of them for Paramount, one of the leading labels catering to black audiences. Unlike Bessie Smith (contrary to persistent legend, Ma did not discover Bessie, but certainly influenced her), she never achieved much popularity beyond the South, and by the time she stopped recording, her down-home style had gone out of fashion. She continued to tour until 1933, when her mother and sister died in quick succession and she retired to keep house for her brother. A good businesswoman, she operated two theaters in Rome, Georgia, until her death.

Ma Rainey's art may have temporarily gone out of fashion, but it will never go out of style. She was indeed the mother of classic blues—a seminal figure in American music.

(1886–1939)

Johnnie Ray

"The kid who never quite made it in time to be picked for the team or on anyone's side for a snowfight."

"He was one of the first performers to let it all hang out," reports record producer Mitch Miller, who helped Johnnie Ray parlay a torrent of musical tears into one of the 1950s' most successful singing careers. The willowy, wispy Ray, whose recordings of "Cry" and "The Little White Cloud That Cried" catapulted him to instant fame, seemed to release all his pent-up emotions through his supercharged singing.

"I was an unhappy, frustrated kid growing up in Oregon," he has noted. Son of a father who fiddled at barn dances and a mother who played piano and sang in the choir, he had always loved music, even picking out "Rock of Ages" on the piano when he was only two years old. But when he was twelve, a freak accident—some supposedly friendly Boy Scouts tossed him high in a

"Cry! . . . Cry!! . . . Cry!!! . . ."

blanket and dropped him—left him deaf. A hearing aid partially restored his hearing, but his impediment destroyed his self-confidence and dropped the bright, sensitive teenager to the bottom of his class, "where I was ostracized even more." He became, in his own words, "the kid who never quite made it in time to be picked for the team or on anyone's side for a snowfight."

Disconsolate and insecure he wandered through Oregon, singing occasionally in school shows and even appearing on a radio program with an emerging Jane Powell. Eventually, at the age of seventeen, he set out for Hollywood, drifting in and out of nonmusical jobs like welder, laborer, bellhop, gas pumper, busboy, soda jerk, and movie extra. In 1945 he got a job playing piano in what he described as "an upholstered sewer," the sort of rundown nightclubs in which for the next six years he was to play and sing in a combination jazz and hillbilly style (he has listed Billie Holiday, Kay Starr, and Little Miss Cornshucks as his major influences).

While performing in 1951 for seventy-five dollars a week at the Flame, a Detroit club that catered mostly to blacks, he was heard by Danny Kessler of Okeh Records, who sized him up as a rhythm and blues singer and offered to record him. When he heard the news, Johnnie, true to his emerging image, broke down and cried. His first recording, "Whiskey and Gin," released later that year, caught the ear of Mitch Miller, producer for the parent Columbia label. Convinced that Ray's raw passion could be refined into a highly commercial package appealing to a much larger segment of the record-buying public, Miller recorded Johnnie with slick, polished backgrounds supporting his unabashed emotional outpourings of songs like "Cry," "The Little White Cloud That Cried," which Ray wrote, and "(Here Am I) Broken Hearted."

The impact of the lachrymose lyrics delivered so passionately by the tall, thin lad with the hearing aid created powerful reactions, ranging from passionate squealing and screaming to one caustic critic's "At least *he* can turn that hearing aid off!" Tabbed "The Prince of Wails," he was booked into New York's famed Copacabana, where he overwhelmed the generally hard-hearted customers. "And Johnnie himself was overwhelmed by his sudden success," reports Miller. "But he rolled with it. He was really just a great kid!"

For five years he maintained his popularity. Then a series of bad breaks, including trumped-up charges that questioned his sexual preferences, and a bout with tuberculosis, reduced his appeal and his record sales. But the mid-1970s nostalgia boom raised his stock again. He scored a huge triumph in Great Britain that helped to spark renewed interest in him at home. Throughout it all, he remained the same shy, modest man. Asked to analyze his appeal, he said simply, "I guess I just show people the emotion they're afraid to show."

(1927–   )

Otis Redding

"He would have to put his dental plate on the little radiator to warm it up before he could sing."

He was a $1.25-an-hour oil well driller in his hometown of Macon, Georgia, dreaming occasionally of being another Little Richard. A few years later, in the mid-1960s, he was the brightest hope of black "soul" music. Then, in the Christmas month of 1967, he was dead.

Otis Reddings's musical career began with his winning fifteen Saturday night amateur contests in a row at a Macon club; on the sixteenth Saturday the management asked him not to compete, so as to give others a chance. In the early 1960s, still very much under the Little Richard influence, he recorded "Shout Bama Lama" for a small midwestern label but the single was not successful. Determined to participate in the music business in some form, he became road manager and valet to Johnny Jenkins and His Pinetoppers, a regional southern band signed to the fledgling Stax label in Memphis.

When a 1964 Jenkins recording session finished ahead of schedule, Redding asked to be allowed to record a number of his own. At first he tried "Shout Bama Lama" but the recording director told him, "We don't need another Little Richard." Redding then tried his own ballad, "These Arms of Mine." The single was released and became his first hit.

Otis

A frequent visitor to Stax, publicist Richard Gersh, recalls that Redding was "a good kid—straight—very eager to learn. He wanted to better himself. He was very interested in the production end—he wanted to know how everything worked. You could see him consciously studying engineers and producers to learn their techniques."

Once Redding had combined his acquired knowledge of production techniques with his newly personal singing style, he let his talent roar. Other hits followed: "Fa Fa Fa Fa (Sad Song)," "Mr. Pitiful," and the bravura "I've Been Loving You Too Long," as well as a passionate reworking of the standard ballad "Try a Little Tenderness." He often came to recording sessions with tunes only half-finished, whistling "head" arrangements of lines for the brass and sax sections to play, making up lyrics as he went along and punctuating his vocals with gasps, grunts, and spoken asides. His feverish pronunciation of "got to" as "*gat*-tuh, *gat*-tuh, *gat*-tuh" was quickly imitated by other singers.

Redding personified the "Memphis Sound" of the middle and late 1960s—rural, genial, blues-based, erotic, funny, tender, and flexible. The down-home qualities of his recordings were aided by the informality that prevailed at Stax. Deanie Parker, a publicity officer with the label almost from its inception, recalled that "the tiny studio we had in those days would *boil* in the summer, so the musicians would record with their shirts off, sometimes even in their underwear. And in the winter, when Otis came in from outside, he would have to put his dental plate on the little radiator to warm it up before he could sing."

Redding was always an unaffected man. He happened to be in New York when Booker T and The MG's, Stax artists who often backed him on records, received a last-minute booking on a Sunday afternoon for a small audience at Hunter College. One of the MG's phoned him at his hotel and asked him to drop by, since they thought the program could use a couple of vocals. Otis thought that was a good idea too. He showed up, sang two songs that left the audience limp with cheering, and departed as casually as he had come.

Though Redding's recordings consistently "crossed over" from rhythm and blues markets to the general, predominantly white pop market, he was not for many years a familiar figure to white audiences. Then in 1967 he appeared at the Monterey Pop Festival, where his performance was overwhelming; in a matter of weeks his reputation had increased and his career seemed headed for major expansion.

At the end of 1967, on the verge of becoming a national star, he began a new tour from which he never returned. His last performance was on a midwestern television program where, ironically, he sang "Knock on Wood." The next evening his small plane, in which he was flying to make the next tour date on schedule, was blinded by fog and swallowed by a freezing Wisconsin lake. Black music—and American music in general—had lost one of its best talents. As a final irony, his greatest hit record, the Grammy-winning "Sittin' On the Dock of the Bay," was a posthumous honor.

(1941–1967)

Helen Reddy

"Everybody in the United States had two cars and a refrigerator, and I was determined to be there."

She is small (5'3"), slight (107 pounds), and nondescript enough in appearance to be easily overlooked in a crowd. But when that intense, country voice belts out, "I am strong/I am invincible/I am *woman,*" you know that Helen Reddy is very much a star. She has many Gold Records, sell-out concert appearances and television appearances to prove it. Still, some critics are unconvinced. Writing in *Newsday,* April 23, 1973, Robert Christgau thought "Woman" "not a very good record, overorchestrated and overwritten and dishonest."

When she won her Grammy for that record (over competition that included Roberta Flack and Barbara Streisand), her acceptance speech acknowledged the help of her husband-manager, "because he makes my success possible, and God, because *She* makes *everything* possible." Some people loved the remark;

Helen

others hated it. Personally as well as professionally, Helen has seldom not inspired neutrality.

Born to show business parents (both acted and her father was also a theatrical producer) in Melbourne, Australia, Helen yearned for the limelight from childhood. "I could sing in tune, and I had this tremendous ego." At twenty-one, she had her own weekly television show in Sydney. Her ambition, far from satisfied, continued to grow. "I wanted to be a star," she says, "rich and famous. I *knew* I'd be one. I'd seen all those movies; everybody in the United States had two cars and a refrigerator, and I was determined to be there."

She thought she was on her way in 1966 when she won a national talent contest. The prize was a trip to New York, four hundred dollars and an audition with Mercury Records. She cut some sides that were released but caused little reaction. Mercury let her go. Down to her last twelve dollars, "I thought, 'This is it. It's over.' But it was also my birthday, and some friends gave me a party. That night changed my life, and my luck, because Jeff Wald crashed the party."

Wald, then a talent agent for William Morris, is Pygmalion to Reddy's almost-completed Galatea. His ambition matched hers; soon they were married, and the bookings got better—but the Big Time eluded them until a spot on "The Tonight Show" brought her to the attention of Capitol Records, which signed her to a contract. "I Believe in Music" and its flip side, "I Don't Know How to Love Him," were her first real hits. Then came "I Am Woman."

Helen wrote the lyrics to "Woman" because "I've always rejected songs like 'Take me back, baby/I'm on my knees/Begging you, please' . . . it's not my concept of womanhood . . . I've experienced a lot of life and couldn't have survived unless I had been pretty strong."

Although "Woman" became, for some, the anthem of the Women's Movement, Helen thinks of herself as "a singer, who has had my consciousness raised . . . not a card-carrying women's libber." Her other hits include "Delta Dawn," "Leave Me Alone," and "Angie Baby"—Gold Records all. In the cut-throat competition of show business, the team of Reddy and Wald may be, after all, "invincible."

(1941–   )

One of country music's most talented and most natural-sounding performers.

When his light plane crashed that stormy night in July 1964, it added fuel to the fire that makes for country music legend: a young performer whose career is snuffed out just as he seems on the verge of breaking through to new and exciting musical plateaus.

For Jim Reeves, former minor league pitcher and radio announcer out of Panola County, Texas, was at this very time bucking all trends, as he had done throughout his career, and was threatening to become an international star of major proportions. He had already arrived as a country singer, and was finding acceptance in the larger pop field, and even as an actor. His film, *Kimberly Jim,* had been a huge success (especially, of all places, in South Africa),

Jim

and more movies were planned for the tall, handsome, rich-voiced singer with the athletic build and the million-dollar smile.

Reeves began bucking trends at the start of his career, singing in an ultrasweet, smooth, masculine voice which has been called the "velvet touch." It was exactly the kind of voice one would not have expected to succeed in the two eras of country music in which he thrived, and which were so inimical to his style: first the post-Hank Williams era that glorified the high, tight, lonesome honky-tonk wail Hank made famous; and later the rockabilly era of Elvis and Carl Perkins and Jerry Lee Lewis. Both sytles were poles apart from Reeves's easygoing, full-voiced, clean and precise style.

His voice was extremely affective: intimate and romantic, and although his early record successes were with up-tempoed numbers like "Mexican Joe" and "Bimbo," he is best remembered for slow, soft, extremely personal ballads like "Four Walls" and "He'll Have to Go."

Yet just as the smoother "Nashville Sound" was coming to prominence in the late 1950s, beating back the nemesis of rockabilly, Reeves took another bold step, especially considering he was a member of that bastion of conservatism, the Grand Ole Opry: he began using trumpets and violins, not exactly going pop—he would have made a superb soft-pop singer, much as Eddy Arnold had become—but bringing country music a lot closer to the borders of mainstream American music.

His widow Mary—now an influential Nashville executive—recalls: "We felt it wouldn't hurt to try it. Jim had reservations about it too. He really did. But he wanted to try it because he liked to try new things, and we felt that it would, if it was accepted, help the whole country music scene to be bigger and bigger. He had a lot of letters on it, a lot of fans who didn't like it because they felt he was getting away from the country sound. But as a whole it worked out much better for him and for country music. It worked."

In fact, his whole life and career were working magnificently until that fateful night in 1964. And yet, for more than a decade after his death, his records continued to be hits, poignant reminders of one of country music's most talented and most natural-sounding performers.

(1924–1964)

Django Reinhardt

The first European jazz musician to have an influence on American jazz musicians.

If a genius is a natural phenomenon (no one can study to be a genius), Django Reinhardt, a self-taught guitarist, was the ultimate genius—a child of nature. He was a gypsy, born in Belgium, raised in a traveling gypsy caravan. He could neither read nor write and he was so illiterate musically that he knew nothing about scales, notes, or keys. When Duke Ellington once asked him in what key he wanted to play "Tiger Rag," Reinhardt replied impatiently, "There's no key! You just go ahead and I'll follow."

Jean Cocteau called him "an offspring of the air." Yet, despite such an ephem-

Django Reinhardt (front center) with Stéphane Grappelly and other members of the Hot Club of France Quartet

eral background, Reinhardt was the first European jazz musician to have an influence on American jazz musicians.

He accomplished this despite what might have been an insuperable handicap. When he was eighteen, the *roulotte,* or gyspy wagon, in which he lived with his mother and father and his pregnant wife, which was filled with artificial flowers to be sold the next day at a cemetery, caught fire. In seconds, the wagon was engulfed in flames. Reinhardt's right leg was burned so badly that the doctors wanted to amputate, but Reinhardt refused. Worse yet for a guitarist, the fourth and fifth fingers of his left hand were seared together. They healed as a paralyzed, useless claw.

But Django's life was his guitar. He devised a new chording technique to compensate for the fingers he could not use. Soon he was playing again and traveling with his brother, Joseph, also a guitarist. In Toulon he heard jazz for the first time, when an artist, Émile Savitry, played records for him by Louis Armstrong, Duke Ellington, and Joe Venuti. When Django heard Armstrong's "Dallas Blues," he put his head in his hands and wept.

In 1934 the Hot Club of France asked him to form an all-string quintet— three guitars, violin, and string bass—with Stéphane Grappelly, a violinist with whom Django frequently played. Reinhardt was the focal point of this unprecedented jazz group.

In the 1940s he became interested in bebop and when he made his first trip to the United States in 1946, his first words on getting off the plane were, "Ou est Dizzy?" (a reference to Dizzy Gillespie). He also tried to shift from his usual acoustic guitar to the new electric guitar but the magic he produced acoustically never came out of the electric instrument. This, combined with his efforts to inject bebop into his playing, made his visit to America a disappointment. But he continued to play successfully in France until his death, at forty-three, from a cerebral hemorrhage.

Reinhardt's playing was strongly emotional, an inexhaustible well of fluently expressed ideas that might be fiery and explosive or warm and intimate. Some of this came from his gypsy background, from the flamenco music that was part of his heritage, a heritage that also affected his personal life. He never lost the gypsy's wandering instincts. When he was playing with an orchestra, he might leave the stand in the middle of a number and not be seen again for weeks. Although he had a small apartment, he often slept on park benches or roamed around all night.

"He was just a simple person," one of his musical associates, Roger Kay, once said, "who liked his music better than anything else and played only the way he wanted to play."

(1910–1953)

Buddy Rich

"Did you come to see my teeth or hear me play?"

"People come up to me," Buddy Rich was telling writer Whitney Balliett, "and say, 'How come you don't smile when you're up there playing?' I say, 'Did you come to see my teeth or hear me play?' If you like my playing, never mind *me*."

The trouble is, it's just about impossible not to mind Buddy Rich one way or another, both on or off the bandstand. He's an overpowering drummer, whose prodigious technique, applied to an ever-driving beat, makes the difficult seem ordinary and the impossible seem possible. Yet, he has never taken a lesson and never practices. Asked by Balliett where his speed came from, he replied, "I don't know. Maybe it's greased elbows, and maybe it's because the Man upstairs talked to my hands and said, 'Be fast.'"

Some years ago at the Newport Jazz Festival, he climaxed an afternoon of successive appearances of leading drummers with such an extraordinary display of virtuosity that before he had finished, all of the other participants reappeared from backstage to gaze and listen in amazement and disbelief at what they were hearing.

Away from the bandstand, however, many people would rather not listen to Buddy. Described years ago by writer Bob Bach as "cocky, brashly outspoken, and brutally sarcastic," he has managed to maintain his image for three decades with consistently snotty remarks to his audiences and interviewers, including good friend and admirer Johnny Carson, on whose TV show he has frequently appeared and where he has projected his aggressiveness physically by busting boards with his hands. (He is a First Degree Black Belt in karate.)

However, off the bandstand he kids with wife Marie, daughter Cathy, and friends about being "too nice" and "ruining my image," and reacts with kindness and often gentleness to those who demand nothing from him except his friendship. As one writer noted, "Unpressed, he can be a delight; pressed too hard he can become a disaster." He is especially considerate of children and the rights of blacks. "I only have trouble with grown-ups," he once said. In another interview he remarked, "I never have trouble with blacks, only with whites." When Gene Krupa was fast losing his health and life, Rich organized a party of Gene's closest friends that created the kind of emotional warmth that Buddy outwardly repudiates.

Krupa has often been cited as Rich's first inspiration. Not true. Buddy started playing drums professionally when he was two years old, long before he had

Buddy, circa 1978

ever heard of Gene. Known as "Baby Traps," he appeared as part of his parents' vaudeville team. Wearing a Buster Brown collar and a sailor suit, he played "The Stars and Stripes Forever" on a snare drum. He soon became the main part of the act, dancing, drumming, and singing, forsaking a formal education to tour the country, reportedly making as much as a thousand dollars a week.

But jazz drumming, not vaudeville, was what he wanted. While in his late teens he sat in one afternoon with Joe Marsala's Dixieland-type band in New York's Hickory House. That night Marsala offered him a permanent job. From there he joined Bunny Berigan, "a fun-loving band with music second," and then hit the really big time with Artie Shaw, who years later admitted that Rich's "enormous youth, enormous energy, and enormous vitality made the band into practically a new band overnight." When Shaw took off alone for Mexico, leaving his men stranded, Rich joined Tommy Dorsey, also sparking that band to greater heights. He stayed for six years, with two years off to serve as a Marine judo instructor. Rich told writer Balliett that he and the equally cocky Dorsey "never really got along. He resented my talking back but respected what I played." But apparently Buddy did get along with a third cocky member of the band, because when Rich left late in 1945 to start his own band, Dorsey's former boy vocalist, Frank Sinatra, backed him to the tune of fifty thousand dollars.

But Sinatra's investment didn't pay off. Buddy didn't like to play for dancing, the *dancers* didn't like his music or his attitude, and Buddy gave up and joined Norman Granz's Jazz at the Philharmonic touring troupe. He stayed with it for several years, followed by three separate, lengthy engagements with an appreciative Harry James, who noted: "For the first time I felt I had a drummer who was driving *me*. Till then, I'd always felt *I* had to carry the band."

But Buddy still wanted his own band. In 1966 he got it, and from then on, with a few time-outs, he kept leading exciting outfits composed mostly of young musicians playing modern, swinging arrangements. But though the style of the music had changed, Buddy hadn't. He still insisted on doing things his way, and only his way. Would he ever play for dancing? "Hell, no!" he snarled. "My band is too good to be danced to and ignored!" Ignore Buddy Rich? Impossible.

(1917–   )

Charlie Rich

Perhaps the bluesiest of the white rockabillies.

Blues singer. At least up until 1975 that's the way pop/country singer Charlie Rich described himself, and truly it's not at all inaccurate.

Born in rural Arkansas, Rich grew up on the music of the great black bluesman Jimmy Reed, and from his earliest days as a musician was a blues, or pop, or even occasionally a jazz musician. He played tenor sax in high school, where he says he found his "bluesiness," and jazz piano in the Army. Only with the tremendous success of two pop hits—produced in Nashville—did he begin to be categorized as a country singer, a position that both he and the average country music fan found uncomfortable.

When in the late 1950s Rich signed on with Sun Records—the small Memphis label that within four years produced Elvis Presley, Carl Perkins, Jerry Lee Lewis, and Johnny Cash—he was widely touted as Elvis' heir apparent, the next and perhaps the bluesiest of the white rockabillies. But for some reason or combination of reasons—perhaps changing times or tastes, perhaps choice of material, perhaps his unwillingness to leave his family for extended, grueling road tours—the big Charlie Rich breakthrough on Sun never happened, and he spent the next fifteen years playing small clubs, drifting from label to label, impressing producers and musicians alike with his prodigious talent, but scoring his biggest (though not especially big) success with blues, rather than country material.

"Paying dues" is a popular expression for time spent working toward the big time, and Charlie really paid his: twenty years of sometimes slick, sometimes seamy clubs and a whirling carousel of record labels, and never-ending frustration. Maybe the world—outside of the music community, where everyone was sure he had what it took—just finally caught up with Charlie Rich.

A move to Epic Records brought him together with Billy Sherrill, the super country producer who brought in two back-to-back million sellers for Charlie in 1973 and 1974: "Behind Closed Doors" and "The Most Beautiful Girl," and the so-often-predicted success at last became a reality.

Sherrill's production and its location tended to label the records as country, although his songs—the two big hits in particular—sold hugely in every field, for they contained a touch of flavoring from every style.

Yet, ultimately, Rich's self-assessment as a blues singer is the most accurate (and revealing). And his blandish hit records have never really done him justice. His magnetism as a performer is far better communicated in live performance, especially when he sings blues-tinged songs, than in the production-heavy, syrupy, country-type ballads that made him famous at last.

(1932–   )

The Silver Fox

Few have cared so much about the history of a musical form.

Strange, in a way, that the career of one of America's most respected—and knowledgeable—entertainers should have been influenced not by other entertainers, but by folklorists J. Frank Dobie, John A. Lomax, and Oscar J. Fox: "During my university days they influenced the direction of my career, not knowing it at the time, of course. During those years I didn't think anybody *paid* anybody to sing!"

Yet this is exactly the case of Woodward Maurice Ritter, who picked up the familiar nickname of Tex only after leaving the academic world (including a year in law school at Northwestern) for the Broadway stage, where he costarred in *Green Grow the Lilacs,* which later was made into the musical, *Oklahoma,* and appeared in a half dozen other productions.

Personable, handsome, articulate, very popular on radio ("The Lone Star Ranger" on station WOR, "Cowboy Tom's Roundup" on station WINS, and the "WHN Barn Dance," all New York City radio stations) as well as on stage, and an authentic Texan with a big drawl and skill in the saddle, Ritter was a natural to follow Gene Autry onto the silver screen in singing cowboy roles, and he went to Hollywood to appear in some eighty-five films between 1935 and 1945. In addition, his big, deep, extremely distinctive voice helped him become a big record seller in the 1940s, with songs like "Jealous Heart," "You Two Timed Me One Time too Often," and "There's a New Moon Over My Shoulder."

Although a man of learning and of great fame, Ritter was also a man of simple tastes, and he remained level-headed and gracious, and genuinely concerned with others (his fatal heart attack came while on an errand of mercy typical of him: trying to bail a musician out of the Nashville jail) throughout his long career. A tireless worker, he was on the road constantly in the late 1940s and early 1950s, and at one time was the most-traveled entertainer in America.

In 1952 Dmitri Tiomkin chose Ritter over a host of others because of the authentic, earthy quality of his voice, and his rendition of "Do Not Forsake Me" from the film *High Noon* won an Academy Award the following year; while at the other end of the spectrum, Tex recorded a series of children's records of cowboy songs, with which thousands of youngsters grew up.

Ritter had always actively been involved in the preservation of country music and cowboy lore, and he was one of the few performers to work tirelessly for the creation of the Country Music Hall of Fame (of which he became a member in 1964) and the library housed in the basement of that building.

Warm, slow-talking with a drawl that thickened as the years went by, with a deep, resonant, frequently imitated singing voice and a distinctive snort for a laugh, Tex Ritter not only achieved success in four different entertainment media, but also, perhaps more importantly, constantly strove to compel the music industry around him to preserve its own ever-receding past.

Few have cared so much about the history of a musical form (especially entertainers, who rarely look back, choosing to create rather than to preserve), and fewer still have done so much to help in its preservation. Yet this was a main focus of Tex Ritter's life, both public and private.

More than anything else, this was the essential Tex Ritter.

(1905–1974)

Tex

Was there ever anyone who sang "Ol' Man River" with such overwhelming power?

Was there ever anyone who sang the beautiful Negro spirituals with more grandeur and depth of feeling than this multigifted American, the first concert artist to present—in 1925—a program of music arranged and composed exclusively by blacks? Or was there ever anyone who sang "Ol' Man River" with such overwhelming power? From the time in 1928 when this commanding six-foot-three former All-American football star and Phi Beta Kappa alumnus of Rutgers University and Columbia University Law School debuted the Jerome Kern classic in *Show Boat* at London's Drury Lane Theatre, it became his identifying song the world over. In 1957, under a U.S. travel ban, he even sang it by telephone, notes biographer Edwin Hoyt, to audiences in England, changing "tired of livin' and skeered of dyin' " to "I must keep fightin' until I'm dyin'."

Paul Robeson fought racism all his life, as an artist and increasingly in the post-World War II years as an activist. From the mid-1920s through the '40s his magnificent bass-baritone thrilled millions in this country and overseas. His starring in Shakespeare's *Othello* shook up Broadway audiences in the mid-1940s. He was the first black actor to play the role on Broadway—for 296 record-setting performances. That and his other stage triumphs, beginning with Eugene O'Neill's *All God's Chillun Got Wings* and *The Emperor Jones,* his eleven British and Hollywood films (e.g., *Show Boat, The Emperor Jones, Song of Freedom, Proud Valley*), his countless recordings and concerts, made him in his day the most famous and lionized black man in the world.

After a twelve-year residence in England, where he had concertized and performed widely, and in Europe and Russia as well, he returned to the States in 1939 a hero. In November of that year he electrified radio audiences with his singing of the rousing "Ballad for Americans." He included it on his concert programs (some two hundred in the 1945, 1946, and 1947 seasons) with the spirituals, and folk songs of other lands: he had mastered over twenty European, Asian, and African languages. He sang and performed to aid the war effort. But his activities on behalf of left-wing organizations, and his militant advocacy of American Negro rights and the liberation of African colonies, combined with his outspoken defense of the Soviet Union in pre-détente United States, alarmed an America gripped by fear of Communism.

Progressively, concert halls and theaters closed their doors to him. His records disappeared from music stores. In 1950 the State Department canceled his pass-

"I loved his integrity, decency, and courage."

port. By 1952 his income had dropped from over $100,000 in 1947 to well under $10,000. Black churches provided almost his only stage. Finally, in 1958, a Supreme Court ruling opened the way for the return of his passport. He gave his first Carnegie Hall concert in eleven years, made an album of uncontroversial songs for Vanguard, and again concertized triumphantly in Britain, Europe, the Soviet Union, Australia, and New Zealand. Suffering mounting ill health, however, he returned home in 1963, unheralded.

By 1965 signs of Robeson's "rehabilitation" were showing. Friends staged a "Salute to Paul Robeson" at Carnegie Hall. But after his wife's death the same year, he went to live, ill and in seclusion, with his sister in Philadelphia and there, almost nine years later, after a lingering illness, he died.

Reporting on the January 1976 funeral of this enormously talented, uncompromising artist and man, son of a former slave who had graduated from Lincoln University and become a minister, and a schoolteacher mother, Carlyle Douglas wrote in *Ebony* magazine: "There were . . . people who loved him because he sang of them and to them with a voice unmatched in its combination of technical mastery and natural beauty." And he quoted a white mourner: " 'I loved his voice. I loved his integrity, decency, and courage.' "

(1898–1976)

His impish charisma and innate talent, coupled with an intense drive to carry on, sustained his popularity.

Did anyone suspect when the frail, tubercular young fellow materialized in Bristol, Tennessee, on August 4, 1927, to "make a record" that he would eventually sing and yodel his way to being remembered as "The Father of Country Music"? Did he leave any impression on that warm summer day that everything about his musical presence, right down to his exact lyrics and lilting falsetto at line's end would eventually be emulated and re-presented to avid fans by the likes of such luminaries as Hank Snow, Lefty Frizzel, and Gene Autry?

Perhaps Ralph S. Peer, the Victor talent scout who had announced in local newspapers his impending visit to Bristol to find recording artists, felt the magic when the slight Jimmie Rodgers stepped forward and sang "The Soldier's Sweetheart" into the portable microphone. Victor released the song two months later, with a flip side of "Sleep, Baby, Sleep," also sung by Rodgers, and sales figures soared. James Charles Rodgers, railroad man from Mississippi, was well on his way to being one of the first stars of country music.

Jimmie was born on December 8, 1897, in Meridian, Mississippi. His father was a section foreman on the Mobile and Ohio Railroad, and before he was fourteen Jimmie had left school and joined his father in the yards, working as a water boy. There he became exposed to the black music that determined so much of his later style. The workers taught the pale, but enthusiastic young boy the basics of banjo and guitar, and it wasn't long before Jimmie Rodgers was crooning to an admiring crowd of railroad men, many of whom would cover for him in his duties so that he might be free to perform.

Jimmie stayed working on the railroads, doing everything from water boy to brakeman, but always with instrument in hand and a song on his lips. By 1919 he had perfected his "blue yodel" which would later become his trademark. But his health was rapidly failing, and Jimmie Rodgers found himself doing less and less railroad work and more and more singing.

By the time he married his wife, Carrie, in 1920 Rodgers' facility on guitar and performing ability had become well developed. He finally left the railroad in 1925 and began devoting himself seriously to music. In 1926 he formed the Jimmie Rodgers Entertainers who played on radio station WWNC in Asheville, North Carolina, but they soon disbanded. Then in 1927 Carrie spotted the Ralph Peer ad in a local paper, and Jimmie answered it.

Following Victor's release of Jimmie Rodgers' "The Soldier's Sweetheart,"

Jimmie

Peer shrewdly steered Rodgers' career. Hit records followed hit records, some with jazz-style backup ("Waiting for a Train"), some showing off his novelty whistle-yodel ("Hobo Bill's Last Ride"), some with Hawaiian musicians ("The One Rose That's Left in My Heart"). Within two years, Jimmie had become a star, no longer traveling from town to town, but ensconced instead in a fifty-thousand-dollar mansion in Kerrville, Texas. He called it "Blue Yodeler's Paradise," and while the rest of the nation was crashing into financial depression, Jimmie and his wife and young daughter Anita were able to enjoy a resplendent life.

But then came Jimmie's own depression: a bout with tuberculosis. His impish charisma and innate talent, coupled with an intense drive to carry on, sustained his popularity as he continued during the early 1930s to perform and record. But by the late spring of 1933, he was in such poor shape that a bed had to be set up in the studio for him to use between songs for much-needed rest. By May 24 he had recorded twelve songs, bringing his total to one hundred and eleven in the short span of six years. Two days later, Jimmie Rodgers, the small man who yodeled and sang out of the side of his mouth and never knew how much his distinctive guitar runs and bluesy asides would influence all of country music, died in his room at the Taft Hotel in the heart of New York City. He was only thirty-five.

(1897–1933)

Mick, with Keith Richard (left)

The Rolling Stones

The only successful survivors of the Nostalgic "British rock invasion" of the mid-1960s.

In 1964 an English pop music newspaper headline over a photo of the group read: WE'RE UGLY, MATEY, BUT WE'RE DOWN TO EARTH. The photo showed thick-lipped singer Mick Jagger, hollow-eyed bassist Bill Wyman, and poker-faced drummer Charlie Watts, while guitarists Keith Richard and Brian Jones looked like debauched elves. The Rolling Stones, then and now, meant to look sinister, and it is a mixture of their black-influenced music, Jagger's sensational stage presence, and their image as *machismo* outlaws that made them, following the demise of the Beatles, the most popular and analyzed rock group in the world.

How much of their image is real and what part of it is shrewd play-acting is open to interpretation. All evidence of Jagger's personal life suggests it is unlikely that he will ever be accused of doing a spontaneous good deed. He is bright, narcissistic, manipulative, and secretive. "I don't *care* how the public

The Stones: Mick Jagger, Keith Richard, Charlie Watts, Bill Wyman, and Brian Jones

sees me," he told John Rockwell of the New York *Times* "I don't want to be known as anything. I never give money to charities—but I wouldn't tell you if I did." Richard, a talented and conscientious musician, is tough and cynical and presents an ominous, death-oriented demeanor. Brian Jones, long before his death in 1969, was masochistic and spent much of his career with the Stones in a love-hate power struggle with Jagger. Drummer Charlie Watts and bassist Bill Wyman have been kept in the background, though without their rhythm synthesis—the tightest and most effective in any rock band of the last twenty years—the Rolling Stones' sound could not exist.

The group was formed in 1963. Jagger was leader of an amateur band and Richard a promising guitarist. Both were avid collectors of American blues records. After hearing Brian Jones (then playing with a group called Blues Incorporated), they determined to establish a no-nonsense band whose inspiration and direction would be that of black American bluesmen like Muddy Waters, Elmore James, and Slim Harpo—names barely known in England and familiar only to white cognoscenti in the United States. "Did the Stones rip off the black originators?" John Rockwell once asked. Answered Jagger, "We haven't ripped off black music at all . . . We simply played what we liked to play because we loved it. I don't think our versions are 'as good' in certain ways; they're just different. They're not the originals, but then you usually find that the black versions you know aren't the originals either. They used to rip each other off something rotten." Charlie Watts was recruited against his better judgment; he didn't see himself as a full-time musician and, besides, considered himself a jazz drummer; he claimed the relentless hammering required in rock hurt his wrists. Bassist Bill Wayman also had misgivings but joined because he was tired of playing with tiddlywink dance groups.

The Rolling Stones might have been no more than an interesting cult band but Jagger's stage personality and the refreshing and exciting unfamiliarity of their sound quickly brought them many fans in London, among them the Beatles. John Lennon and Paul McCartney, rolling along in a taxi one day, hailed Andrew Loog Oldham, the Stones' nineteen-year-old manager, and bundled him into the taxi after Oldham complained that the Stones, scheduled for a recording date, had no material ready. Arriving at the club where the Stones were rehearsing, Lennon and McCartney dashed off "I Wanna Be Your Man," the Stones' second record and their first hit.

In 1965, "(I Can't Get No) Satisfaction" became a worldwide smash and established them as a major group. At the same time they turned away from their original rhythm and blues inspiration and adopted a more pop sound, due to Jagger and Richard—being jealous of the Beatles' success—writing the group's material. By the end of the 1960s their songs became increasingly hostile, sneering, violent, and morbid, and the group was looked on as a threat to society in Britain and the United States.

Between 1967 and 1969 the band experienced a series of personal and artistic disasters: *Their Satanic Majesties Request* was a blowsy and feeble attempt to match the Beatles' *Sgt. Pepper* album; Jagger, Richard, and Jones were sent to jail for possession of narcotics (all were subsequently freed); Brian Jones's death by drowning revealed him to be a debilitated addict whose consumption of drugs and alcohol had affected his brain tissues; and, at an open-air concert in Altamont, California, a motorcycle gang member retained by the Stones as a security guard murdered a man in the audience.

The Stones retreated first to England and then to France (to avoid the homicidal British tax rates) and did not appear in public for two years, maintaining their popularity by recordings. Regarded as messiahs by spokesman and partisans of the "revolutionary youth culture," their return to public performing was eagerly awaited. When the band nervously resumed touring in 1971 they found immediate and overwhelming acceptance.

Since then the Stones have settled into a lucrative and comfortable pattern of semiannual touring interspered with new albums. The musical power of the band has been diminished by repetition of old themes in their subsequent material. Jagger, a superb performer, has satellitized the band, which is now more or less his backup group. Charlie Watts commented some time ago: "We were . . . when Brian was alive, a family in a way. But sometimes now I'm not sure I even know the others." Bill Wyman, who once complained of Jagger and Richards running "a closed shop" when it came to writing songs for the band, has released two solo albums; the second showed him to have a sense of humor, talent for arrangements, and a desire to move away from the certified "Stones sound."

Although the Stones have come far from where they started, there remains some doubt whether they have gone where they meant to go. They did intend to become world figures, and that is what they are. But by the mid-1970s what had once been a truly exciting and creative rock band had become to some of its admiring purists more of a company of marionette entertainers, often working on separate stages, and neither their audiences nor the Stones—so dependent on each other for so long—seemed to know exactly who was pulling the strings.

Some of their enthusiasm and wonderful cohesion did seem to be returning in 1977 with the arrival of guitarist Ron Wood, and a three-column New York *Times* headline quoted them saying, "It's Time for More Energy in Music." By then, they had become a semisacred group, worshipped as virtually the only successful survivors of the nostalgic "British rock invasion" of the mid-1960s, with an audience composed of one generation that grew up with them and another growing up with the Stones' reputation.

Though sometimes criticized for laziness in their recording, they continued to be surprisingly adaptable. Their 1978 album, *Some Girls,* which sold five million copies, contained the hit single "Miss You," which combined the Stones' early rhythm and blues influences with a touch of disco, while not compromising either style. But in the final analysis, what has really kept them successful for so long has been their bitter, sometimes amoral, sometimes brutal antihero image.

Linda Ronstadt

"I've always been a bit of a closet housewife."

It used to be that Linda Ronstadt's emotional vocal outburst—alternately wistful and scorching on ballads, gutsy and rip-roaring on rock and roll—were merely public outlets for her many private hurts. Songs like "Love Has No Pride," "Heart Like a Wheel," and "Faithless Love" were evidences of her well-chronicled, unhappy romances with her managers, producers, and musicians. In fact, *Rolling Stone* labeled the shapely, five-foot-two singer with the free-flowing dark hair "rock and roll's most eligible woman."

But the open window to her private life was closed after she found a psychiatrist "who really put me on the right track. If it wasn't for him I probably would have quit," she told Cameron Crowe in a *Rolling Stone* interview. "Anyone can hurt my feelings; it's not very hard to do. But they don't get a second chance. I try to walk that fine line between being strong and trying to avoid becoming callous. As soon as you're callous you not only shut out the pain but all the good stuff too."

That "good stuff," namely her newly found strength, was soon reflected in the quality of her records, which became more confident with each outing, as well as in the one place that the business part of the music business insists it counts the most: in the sales column. By the late 1970s, more than seventeen million people had bought her Elektra/Asylum recordings. Five albums, *Don't Cry Now, Heart Like a Wheel, Hasten Down the Wind, Prisoner in Disguise,* and *Simple Dreams,* each sold more than a million copies. And in 1975 she won a Grammy for "I Can't Help It If I'm Still in Love With You" and in 1976 for "Hasten Down the Wind."

The road to such success began early. A singer "since I was two," Linda left her parents and three siblings in Tucson at age eighteen, after a single semester at Arizona State College, for Hollywood's recording studios. The story goes that she took with her no more than thirty dollars and her parents' blessings. After three years of scrambling, Linda and her band, the Stone Poneys, had themselves a big hit album, *Different Drums.* But the Poneys soon hoofed off in different directions, while Linda remained in the LA corral. There she recorded flawed, though promising, albums and assembled some powerhouse backup groups, one of which, containing Glenn Frey, Don Henley, Bernie Leadon, and Randy Meisner, later gained fame on its own as the Eagles.

Despite her obvious talent, it wasn't until the flailing singer merged forces with the smooth, cool professionalism of former English pop-singer-turned-

Linda

record-producer, Peter Asher, that her efforts began to attract major attention. "Peter," Linda revealed to Crowe, "was the first person willing to work with me as an equal. I didn't have to fight for my ideas. All of a sudden, making records became so much more fun." And the rest became a matter of simple arithmetic: better discs equals more sales equals number one.

With her success came a far less frantic approach to life. Like any successful recording star, she naturally spent many, many hours in the studios. In demand for personal appearances almost everywhere, she also toured in her custom-outfitted luxury bus, complete with tapestried ceilings and five separate stereo systems. But perhaps most satisfying and surely most relaxing of all had become living in her new home, a split-level, $200,000 house on the beach at Malibu, where she regularly jogs three miles a day. Far less dependent than ever before on others,—though she did spend a good deal of time with California Governor Jerry Brown—she told Crowe, "I'm learning how to live by myself and I love it." And to Lisa Robinson of *Hit Parader* she confided, "I really like the whole idea of domesticity. I've always been a bit of a closet housewife anyway." The "Simple Dreams" of Linda Ronstadt had in fact become a reality.

(1946–)

Diana Ross and the Supremes

It wasn't spontaneous, but it sure was exciting.

They may not always have been supreme, but they certainly were durable. This trio of girls, up from the slums of Detroit, was the first group to bring the world the slick, pseudo-rhythm and blues Motown Sound. They were ahead of Little Stevie Wonder, ahead of the Temptations, their "brother" group who went to Motown as the Primes, bringing the Supremes along as the "Primettes."

"Finish high school first," Motown president Berry Gordy had told the girls. Then he had hired them to type for his fledgling record company and to sing backup vocals. They made nine records of their own which flopped before they cut "Where Did Our Love Go?" in 1954, with Diana Ross singing lead. It went straight to number one best seller in the country and the pattern was set.

Their next four records, all emphatic, rhythmic, with a danceable tune, strong bass lines, and a somewhat watered-down blues for a pop market became number one best sellers. And any of the three girls could sing lead. "I always did the ballads," Mary recalls. "Florence [Ballard] did the real up-tempo things and Diana did the screaming."

The Supremes took classes at Motown in dancing, grooming, and manners. They opened at the Copacabana in New York in 1965, dressed in sophisticated, identical evening gowns, moving as one to choreography they'd learned in Detroit. It wasn't spontaneous, but it sure was exciting.

"We always symbolized beautiful black young women," Mary says. "We're still representing beautiful black women in America." Their conduct had to be impeccable too. For eight years, a chaperone toured with them; for much of the time it was Diana's mother.

Fan clubs sprang up and stayed steadfast. In 1965 astronauts Cooper and Conrad asked Gemini control to pipe "Where Did Our Love Go?" to them in outer space. On Broadway, *Hair* had three black girls dance a time step standing in different parts of one expansive glittery dress, and nobody had to be told who was being kidded.

The Supremes didn't stay the same three girls and they didn't stay that famous. Motown replaced Flo with Cindy Birdsong and Flo later sued unsuccessfully. Before she died in 1976, she was feeding her three daughters on Aid to Dependent Children. Mary stayed on because "I love the good times and the bad times. I figure you're going to have some of those anyway."

Diana (center) and the other Supremes

But the best times of all came to Diana Ross, the determined refugee from Detroit's ghetto, who had originally badgered Gordy into hiring the group. During the years after her departure in 1970 from the group, she established herself as a $25,000-a-week-and-up performer. She appeared in the country's top clubs, starred in several TV specials and in two movies. Her Oscar-nominated portrayal of Billie Holiday in *Lady Sings the Blues* was acclaimed for its range and sensitivity. In 1976, *Billboard* magazine acclaimed her Top Female Performer of the Century. Two years later, she received some rave notices for her performance in the movie version of *The Wiz*. Diana was surely reigning supreme!

And what happened to the other Supremes without Diana and her exceptional talents and infectious enthusiam? Their popularity predictably began to wane. Numerous replacements, though talented, never projected Diana's dynamism. Ironically, the Supremes' final big hit in 1970 had been titled "Someday We'll Be Together." Years later it became more and more evident that such a prediction would never come true.

(Diana Ross: 1944–   )

Jimmy Rushing

"I'd never been out on a floor. But I got out there and broke it up. I was a singer from then on."

Visually, Jimmy Rushing lived up to his nickname, "Mr. Five by Five" (theoretically, five feet tall and very close to five feet wide, topped by a round, cherubic face, heavy-lidded eyes, and a broad, half-moon smile). But it was not this striking image that made him one of the most memorable performers to come out of the rich jazz milieu of the Southwest during the 1920s and '30s. He sang with a bright, penetrating sound and a warm, emotional involvement that led some jazz experts to view him as the greatest of all male jazz singers.

Novelist, Ralph Ellison, who grew up in Oklahoma City when Rushing was singing there with Walter Page's Blue Devils, remembers that voice: "When you stood on the rise of the school grounds two blocks to the east," he recalled, "you could hear it jetting from the dance hall like a blue flame in the dark; now soaring high above the trumpets and the trombones, now skimming the froth of reeds and rhythm as it called some woman's anguished name—or demanded in a high, thin passionately lyrical line, 'Baaaaaay-bay, Bay-aaaaaay-bay! Tell me what's the matter now!'—above the shouting of the swinging band."

At first, growing up in Oklahoma city, where he was born, Rushing was not sure what musical direction he wanted to take. His father played trumpet. His mother sang. Young Jimmy taught himself to play the violin. "But, man!" he exclaimed, "I had to do more than that to get across what I wanted to say." He got the clue from his uncle, Wesley Manning, a blues pianist and singer who worked in a sporting house.

Jimmy was footloose and twenty-one in California when he got his first professional music job as a pianist, playing intermissions in an after-hours club.

"One night a headliner girl by the name of Carlyn Williams asked me to sing a song," he recalled. "I'd never been out on a floor. But I got out there and broke it up. I was a singer from then on."

Three years later he returned to Oklahoma City and began singing with Walter Page's Blue Devils. A year later Count Basie joined the band and, in 1931, when Page broke up the Blue Devils, Rushing, Basie, and Page all moved into Bennie Moten's Kansas City band, one of the most popular in the Southwest.

When Moten died in 1935, the three musicians stayed together in a nine-piece band led by Basie at the Reno Club in Kansas City where they played seven nights a week for fifteen dollars. It was a discouraging period and Basie

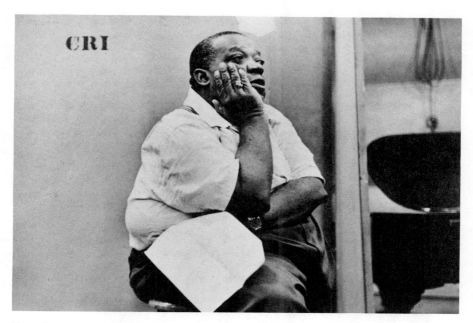

"Sent for you yesterday!"

admitted that he would have given up if Rushing had not urged him to "stick with it."

They stuck long enough to attract New York agents and in 1936 the Basie band, expanded to thirteen pieces, left Kansas City for Chicago, New York and, eventually, fame. Rushing, who had been a ballad singer when he first started singing, was singing both ballads and blues in Kansas City. But once the Basie band went on the road, he was urged to concentrate on the blues. This led to such classic performances as "Good Morning Blues," "Sent for You Yesterday," "Goin' to Chicago," and "Harvard Blues." According to Ellison, his beginnings as a ballad singer gave Rushing's blues their special poignance.

"One of the significant aspects of his art," Ellison pointed out, "is the imposition of a romantic lyricism upon the blues tradition, a lyricism which is not of the Deep South but of the Southwest, a romanticism native to the frontier."

Rushing had a simpler self-analysis. A simple man with simple tastes, except perhaps when it came to eating, he once explained, "I don't know what kind of blues singer you'd call me. I just sing 'em."

(1903–1972)

Pee Wee

Pee Wee Russell

"A passionate, jilted bullfrog—with a beat."

This lovable, quixotic clarinet-player not only survived all the Dixieland-style groups he was locked into most of the 1920s, '30s, and '40s, but in the 1960s, Charles Ellsworth Pee Wee Russell actually escaped them to play successfully compositions by such moderns as John Coltrane and Ornette Coleman in a thoroughly un-Dixie group—a feat equaled by few, if any, other Dixieland musicians. As a matter of fact, there was nothing ever predictable about Pee Wee. Though he conversed mostly in monosyllabic grunts and a few stammering phrases, he knew whereof he spoke.

And his playing was not much different. It consisted primarily of long wails, ruminative or brisk rumblings in the lower register, or treble pipings that sent notes glancing off the melody at startling angles. One critic once described his style as sounding like "a passionate, jilted bullfrog—with a beat"! Certainly he emoted both emotion and rhythm, and yet though he may have sounded weird and uncertain at times, Pee Wee knew what he was doing and where he was going.

He traveled as a respected and important confrere of musicians like Jack Teagarden, Bobby Hackett, Bud Freeman, Muggsy Spanier, and Eddie Condon with whom he recorded and appeared in clubs on New York's Fifty-second Street and at Nick's in Greenwich Village. Classic examples of his playing on the Commodore sides of the late 1930s (reissued in recent years on Mainstream's *Pee Wee Russell: A Legend*) reveal a doggedly, unchanging Russell compared with his blowing three decades later on the Russell-Brown *New Groove* and *Ask Me Now* albums.

His highly individualistic, lonesome-sounding clarinet style seems to reflect his early emotions. An only child, born in St. Louis to a forty-year-old former newspaperwoman mother and hotel-steward father, Ellsworth grew up, he once confessed, with a feeling of being an afterthought. Fortunately he was given a chance to study various instruments, and he settled on the clarinet. School held less charm for him than playing music, and after a year at a military academy, a move designed to curb his wandering interests, he was back in St. Louis and in 1922 joined the dance band of a local leader, Herbert Berger, who tagged him "Pee Wee," a nickname that fit his tall, perennially undernourished-looking frame and long-nosed, long face with its apologetic, shy-beagle expression.

He continued working with various bands in the area. In 1925 he joined Bix Beiderbecke for a job near Chicago, then remained in the Windy City until early 1927, when he joined Red Nichols in New York, which became his home for the next forty-two years. Often undernourished and overliquified, he almost died in 1951, but then made an almost miraculous recovery that seemed to fill him with renewed confidence. Though by the 1960s the clarinet had gone the way of the dodo as a relevant working jazz instrument, Russell refused to retire it. Instead, he added his unique voice to those of the avant-garde. Unexpectedly it seemed to fit handsomely. His sounds and quirky original-ity, always as challenging as the avant-garde's, had finally brought him full circle, from Dixie to modern, and made his the truly inimitable clarinet voice in all jazz.

(1906–1969)

Santana

"I wasn't inspiring enough to keep myself and my friends progressing."

"At Roseland they played until the crowd could no longer stand up; at the Palladium they played until the crowd refused to sit. Both audiences went home happy," reported Stan Meises in a 1977 New York *Daily News* review of concerts on successive nights by Santana, whose music has been as exciting to dance to as to listen to.

Personal appearances have played an important part in the success of this San Francisco group that in the late 1960s became the first to fuse Latin and Cuban rhythms with those of rhythm and blues. Their exciting blend, offset at times by softer, more intimate singing, had attracted the more "in" listeners to the small clubs to which the group was relegated. But then late in the decade,

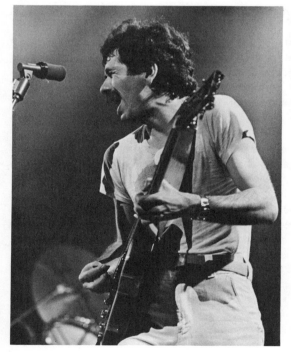

Carlos

two important appearances suddenly zoomed the group into the national spot-light. "Few people had ever heard of them," reports Irwin Stambler in his *Encyclopedia of Pop, Rock and Soul* about Santana's 1968 stint at the Fillmore West, "but after a few minutes' exposure to the group's pile-driving Afro-Latin beat, the audience stopped its conversations and other distractions to listen intently. When the set was over the group was given a standing ovation." A year later at the famous Woodstock Festival, according to Stambler, Santana's appearance left the crowd "screaming for more, and that set was one of the most gripping parts of the documentary of the festival."

Such audience response attracted Columbia Records and soon Santana was recording several albums that became top sellers and suddenly the group had become an international hit.

Musical success had not been one of Mexican-born Carlos Santana's early dreams. "My father had been a musician so I was exposed to music early, but I never thought of playing in a band until I was angry enough," Santana told John Swenson in *Crawdaddy.* He was working as a dishwasher "and I was very angry because I was doing my job so well that they fired the other guy who was working with me and I had to do the work of two. Then one night I saw the Grateful Dead pull up to the Fillmore in limousines and I said to myself, 'If they can do it, I can do it.' "

And "do it" Carlos Santana did. Following the successes at Fillmore West and Woodstock, his band began recording for Columbia, immediately producing two hit albums, *Santana* and *Abraxas,* and eventually following up with several more.

But Santana wasn't satisfied. At times he would leave his group to perform with others. Jazz trumpeter Miles Davis attracted him both as a musician and as a person. He began to withdraw more; he became, according to a Columbia executive, "even *more* difficult to interview than Miles!" To Swenson, Santana later admitted, "I used to get angry a lot. It was because of me that the original band broke up. I wasn't inspiring enough to keep myself and my friends progress-ing."

Then one day he found spiritual inspiration in the person of a guru, Sri Chimnoy, and his attitude began to change drastically. He became more content and less edgy. A new manager, Bill Graham, the successful West Coast impresa-rio, helped to put his career into perspective. His new group produced more hit singles and albums, but success alone did not satisfy Santana. "I want prog-ress, not success," he explained. "The band is going to fall if we don't have a goal to aspire to, like Tarzan reaching for another vine to carry him forward. I find myself looking to transcend myself—if not, if music becomes self-aggran-dizement, I'll leave because I'll eventually suffer from it." Then what would he do? He could return to his roots. "I could be a *good* dishwasher," he said.

Sauter-Finegan

"If things are getting that bad, we'd better start our own band."

Time magazine called it "the most original band heard in the U.S. in years." Pop music writers and more sophisticated fans hailed it as the most musically innovative orchestra of the 1950s. But Eddie Sauter and Bill Finegan, co-leaders of an organization that featured their own imaginative compositions and brilliant arrangements, full of harmonically rich, unusual voicings that sometimes extended even beyond the range of a piano keyboard, and instruments like tubas, tympanis, glockenspiels, piccolos, recorders, and even kazoos, have since claimed, "We had no high-blown purpose to prove anything. Our purpose was survival."

Both Sauter and Finegan had survived very well during the dance band era—Eddie as arranger for Red Norvo, Ray McKinley, Artie Shaw, and Benny Goodman, whose style he changed in the early 1940s, and later for Ray McKinley; and Bill as one of the chief writers for the highly regimented Glenn Miller, who admired Finegan's work so much that he permitted him to write anything he felt like writing. (Later Bill also arranged for Tommy Dorsey and others.)

But as the bands faded, so did the demand for their services. Shy and unassertive, they too faded from the scene—Eddie to his home in New York's Rockland County, and for a year into a tuberculosis sanatorium, and Bill to France to

Eddie and Bill

study at the Paris Conservatory and to arrange for European groups that appreciated his talents.

Across the sea they maintained a mutal admiration society. "Bill's inner workings are like a Swiss watch," Sauter exclaimed, while Finegan agreed with his old boss Glenn Miller that his innovative partner was "always just about ten years ahead of his time!" They kept corresponding, often bewailing the fate of the sort of popular music each respected. "The capper came," Finegan said years later, "when Eddie, just as a gag, sent me a letter on the back of a rejection slip he had received from Ralph Flanagan," a leader/arranger who, many cognoscenti agreed, couldn't shine Sauter's shoes. "I was outraged. If things are getting that bad, I thought, we'd better start our own band."

Sauter agreed it wasn't such a bad idea, so Bill returned to America, and the two began writing. With only themselves to please, they released all their musical inhibitions. The result: an electrifying barrage of instrumental outpourings, first captured late in 1952 on a series of RCA Victor recordings, like "Doodle Town Fifers," "April in Paris," "Moonlight on the Ganges," "Nina Never Knew." Soon record buyers wanted to see in person what they were hearing on records. So in June 1953 the band took to the road.

But it turned out to be the wrong road. "Instead of playing concerts, as Tommy Dorsey had advised us to, so that people could concentrate on our music," Finegan pointed out years later, "our bookers insisted that we play for dancing." But, though ideal for listening, the band's often intricate arrangements made dancing more difficult. "By December 1955 we were flat broke and owed money all over the place," Sauter later revealed. The band made a few more records, then broke up. This time it was Sauter who took off for Europe, where he conducted and composed for three years for German radio. Upon his return to America, he orchestrated scores for Broadway musicals, composed for movies, and wrote and conducted an album, *Focus,* for Stan Getz that so impressed the saxist that when he won a Grammy, he turned the award over to Sauter.

Finegan turned to teaching and free-lance arranging, contributing occasionally to the orchestra that carried the name of his old leader, Glenn Miller. By the 1970s, both Sauter and Finegan, semiretired, though not of their own volition, could at least look back with satisfaction at their short-lived venture that had served a purpose they claim they hadn't intended: creating and performing original scintillating sounds that were far ahead of their time. And yet, ironically, they had failed to fulfill their self-proclaimed purpose: merely to survive.

(Finegan: 1917–   )
(Sauter: 1914–   )

Neil Sedaka

"Gentle, and civilized, decent—everything that pop is not."

When he was thirteen he started writing songs. At eighteen he had become a top recording star. At twenty-three, and losing his popularity, he retired. And then at thirty-eight, with encouragement from some of his biggest admirers, like Paul McCartney, Alice Cooper, and especially Elton John, who promised to record and promote him on his Rocket label, Neil Sedaka, described by Nik Cohn in *New York* magazine as "gentle, and civilized, decent—everything that pop is not," was back on top again.

From 1959 to 1963, the Brooklyn-born singer with the light, high, relaxed, almost girl-like voice, sold more than twenty-five million teenage-type records, including "Breaking Up Is Hard to Do," "Calendar Girl," "Happy Birthday, Sweet Sixteen," "Oh! Carol," dedicated to Carole King, with whom he was in

Sedaka

love, and "Stairway to Heaven," five of the eight hundred or so songs he has written. But in 1963, in came the Beatles and the harder rock performers, and out went Sedaka's popularity. "It was frustrating writing songs for others and being in the background," he told Beverly Sills on her TV show. "I felt the desire to be out on the stage in front of people again. My ego really needed that."

He had been performing since age eight when he started studying to become a concert pianist. At nine he was already in Juilliard Prep School and at sixteen he won the city-wide Artur Rubinstein competition, and then went on to Juilliard College. But he was also interested in popular music, and so, in addition to practicing piano seven hours a day, he kept writing songs. When he asked his mother if she would grant him a leave of absence from his piano-practicing to concentrate on a pop music career, she said, "I'll give you six months."

Recording artists liked his songs. "But nobody wanted to record my voice. Then Steve Sholes, who discovered Presley, heard me sing a song called 'The Diary.'" Sholes invited Sedaka to record it. "It was a hit. I was going on nineteen, and that was the end of my classical music." To this day he still harbors some guilt feeling about having deserted classical music.

For the next four years, hit followed hit record. Then came the harder rock era and Neil's enforced sabbatical as a performer. "But in 1970 music became more melodic and people were looking for the original performance: how a song was conceived. They wanted to hear how the composer himself wanted it to be interpreted. And there were such great people like James Taylor and Carole King and Paul Simon. That's when I decided to make a comeback as a performer."

Not too sure of being accepted again by American audiences, Sekada decided to try making a new name for himself with a new generation in a different place. So he went to England. "It would be sort of the back door to America. I had to start in very dumpy places and had to sing my old songs from my first career. I felt kind of squeamish about it because I wanted to come back to contemporary music and audiences and I didn't want to have to rely on my name being a name from the past." He was a big hit in England, especially singing his new material. And so he returned to the States.

His comeback, which included big-selling albums like *Sedaka's Back* and *The Hungry Years,* brought him greater self-assurance. He admits he has never been much of an exhibitionist or very outgoing and was "frightened for years to talk with an audience." But now he devotes the first part of a concert to talking about songwriting and about his children, Mark and Dara, the latter a teenager who has been writing songs since she was nine and recently started her own recording career. He finds family life "wonderful, therapeutic, relaxing— the only thing that has kept me sane." And he even includes his songs in his family. "Each song," he told Ms. Sills in his poetic way, "is almost like one of my children that lives and breathes every time I sing it."

(1939–   )

Pete Seeger

An uncanny mixture of saint, propagandist, cornball, and hero.

The tall, skinny man walks on stage and slings a five-string banjo over his shoulder. The neck of the instrument is as thin as his own. He taps his foot and his fingers begin to fly over the strings, as accurate as a sewing machine, as delicate as the flutter of wings. He is barely able to sing the first lines of his opening song before the audience smothers the words with tidal waves of applause—for he is the minstrel, the prodigal, the loved one, an uncanny mixture of saint, propagandist, cornball, and hero. He is Pete Seeger.

The world's most respected folk singer, Seeger also has had an enormous effect on contemporary pop and rock music. He was a direct inspiration to Bob Dylan, Joan Baez, the Kingston Trio, and other stars of the folk music boom of the late 1950s and early '60s. His influence carried over into the formation of "folk-rock"—the Byrds' 1966 recording of Seeger's "Turn! Turn! Turn!" being an example. He insisted that music belonged to "the people" and that it was cathartic. As he told J. C. Barden in *High Fidelity* magazine in 1963, "I feel I'm building a healthy musical life for people who seem to have lost it

"Goodnight, Irene!"

somewhere in the machine age." His attitude may be seen as a contributing factor to the sentiments of the many pop and rock stars who proclaim their identification with their audiences.

Seeger's fascination with folk music began with his attendance at a North Carolina folk festival in 1935. The following year he enrolled at Harvard University, where he sometimes played banjo with a campus jazz band. But he left in 1938 to wander about the country as a folk singer; during his travels he met and performed with two giants of the genre, Woody Guthrie and Huddie "Leadbelly" Ledbetter.

When America entered World War II, Seeger served as a corporal in the Army's Special Services (entertainment) branch. "I was singing at hospitals full of wounded men," he told *Women's Wear Daily* interviewer Mort Sheinman in 1972, "and I remember one guy in a plaster cast from his nose to his toes, but I could see those toes beating rhythm to my music."

Besides excelling on the five-string banjo, Seeger was accomplished with the recorder, a pipe instrument dating from the Elizabethan age, and he was also a commanding twelve-string guitarist. His voluminious recordings over a twenty-year period have demonstrated his gigantic repetoire—classic Scots/Irish/English ballads, pioneer ditties, Appalachian murder narratives, children's rhymes, sea chanties, black spirituals, railroad tales, lullabyes, cowboy yodels, field hollers, and historic and contemporary propaganda broadsides, as well as his own compositions like "Where Have All the Flowers Gone?" and the delightful instrumentals "Living in the Country" and "The Goofing-off Suite."

In 1948, Seeger formed and led what was perhaps the finest of all American folk groups, the Weavers, whose recordings of "Kisses Sweeter Than Wine," "Tzena, Tzena, Tzena," "On Top of Old Smokey," "Wimoweh," and "Good Night, Irene" were national hits and reminded the country of the richness and variety of folk music.

From the late 1950s on, Seeger has devoted most of his musical time to solo concert appearances, making world tours well into the 1970s, but always finding time to encourage and promote younger folk singers and writers. An openhearted, sometimes naïve man, Seeger cares little for financial success. His personal and musical passion has been the quality of life, coupled with a fondness for and a faith in the average citizen. Seeger's emotional generosity and companionship with his audiences around the world has invariably been returned affectionately by the hundreds of thousands of people he has entertained and inspired.

(1919–   )

Ben Selvin

The most prolific recording artist of all time.

Would he be another Mischa Elman? Or another J. P. Morgan? That career choice lay before the young New Yorker with an ear for music and an eye for money. He wound up with an earful and an eyeful of each, for Ben Selvin became not only a "name" violinist and bandleader, he also became a very wealthy man and the most prolific recording artist of all time.

During a career that spanned seventeen years (1917 to 1934), he recorded, by his own count, a total of nine thousand discs, many times more than those of Bing Crosby, his nearest American competitor. The intense, still energetic Selvin has estimated it would take fifty days and eight uninterrupted hours of listening each day to hear all nine thousand of them.

He began his career as a violinist in combos playing colorful off-off-Broadway clubs. His business acumen surfaced in the band of Charles Strickland, a strict

Ben

New Englander who frowned on musicians accepting tips from customers. Persuading Strickland to lift his ban, young Selvin began to double as the band's "financial adjuster." Soon the musicians' incomes soared. Some months later, Selvin parlayed his "financial adjusting" into a sort of one-man conglomerate by garnering coatroom, parking lot, cigarette, and men's room concessions on a summer job in New Jersey.

His first job as a leader, in 1917, set a seven-year record at the Moulin Rouge on Broadway. "And I never again was a sideman," he proudly noted many years later. In 1919 he set another record with his orchestra's Victor version of "Dardanella," the first instrumental million-record seller. He also recorded for many other labels under a variety of "adjusted names," telling an interviewer, "People kept writing in and telling me some other orchestra was stealing my style." Little wonder for such confusion, because, according to Brian Rust's *The American Dance Band Discography,* Ben Selvin recorded under one hundred and four very different names, like Selvin's Novelty Orchestra, Selvin's Syncopatic Melodists, the Knickerbockers, the Harmonians, the Broadway Bandits, Perry's Hot Dogs, Barney Trimble and His Oklahomans, and the Bar Harbor and Newport Society orchestras. Using the city's top musicians, like the Dorsey Brothers, Benny Goodman, Bunny Berigan, Mannie Klein, Joe Venuti, and Eddie Lang, as his sidemen, it seems he just never stopped recording.

Finally in 1934, after seven years with Columbia Records as combination conductor and executive, he joined a new company as vice-president in charge of recording and programming. Muzak was its name, and during his dozen years with the company, Selvin set a soft, unobtrusive musical style that became a "storehold" (as opposed to "household") commodity throughout the land.

In 1947 he rejoined Columbia as director of artists and repertoire in Hollywood, where he produced many hit records with Doris Day, Dinah Shore, Frank Sinatra, and others. In 1952 he moved on to RCA Victor for an eleven-year stay, leaving in 1963 to join 3M Company, the audio tape firm, as a consultant.

During the mid-1970s, smartly tailored, quip-of-tongue and twinkling-of-eye as ever, as well as independently wealthy, he had become immersed in another long run: a so-called "retirement," full of new music ventures like New York's Senior Citizens Orchestra, unofficially the one hundred and fifth orchestra to be led by ever-young Ben Selvin.

(1898–   )

Artie Shaw

"I just didn't want to be just a half-assed human being in order to become a whole-assed musician."

"If variety is the spice of life, I guess I've had a pretty spicy life," big-time bandleader Artie Shaw has admitted. And, of course, he is right, for the handsome, garrulous, often intellectualizing and contentious clarinetist led a dozen different bands during a dozen and a half years, has essayed a half a dozen different careers, and has been married eight times to, among others, such glamorous ladies as Lana Turner, Ava Gardner, Kathleen Winsor, Doris Dowling, and Evelyn Keyes. "I've been blessed or cursed with a large curiosity bump," he once explained.

His curiosity got him started in the music business in the first place. That was back in New Haven, Connecticut, where he was raised, and where as a

Artie then

youngster he would follow musicians around, trying to figure out how they played and hoping they'd ask him to play with them. When they finally did, they were impressed enough to invite him on to their bandwagons, though one of his first leaders, Irving Aaronson, remarked, after young Artie had tried to show he could also sing, "That kid's got the personality of a dead lox!"

Shaw's musical curiosity also gave him his start as a leader. In 1935, after he had established himself alongside Benny Goodman and the Dorseys and Glenn Miller as one of New York's most successful studio musicians, he wondered how a different kind of orchestra would sound—just he himself on clarinet plus a string quartet and a rhythm section. So he organized the group, and it debuted at a jazz concert in New York's Imperial Theater, where it caused such a sensation that band bookers prevailed upon him to challenge Goodman's supremacy. At first it was no contest; the public wouldn't buy a swing band with strings. And so Artie organized an orthodox band of the usual brass, saxes, and rhythm, recorded "Begin the Beguine," and suddenly found himself locked in combat with Goodman, the reigning "King of Swing."

But the free-spirited, ever-self-analyzing Shaw could not withstand the pressure of such competitive popularity. "I don't want to be King of anything!" he exclaimed, when publicists dubbed him "King of the Clarinet." And he railed out against his adoring fans, calling them "morons." He suffered a couple of nervous collapses. Late in 1939 he remarked, "I'm unhappy in the music business. Maybe I don't even belong in it. I like the music—love it and live it, in fact—but for me the business part just plain stinks!"

Shortly thereafter, right in the middle of an immensely successful engagement in the famed Cafe Rouge of New York's Pennsylvania Hotel, "I just got up and walked away in the middle of the night, leaving all the debris behind."

He flew to Mexico, stranding a band that soon broke up. He insisted he'd be gone for a long time, but a few months later he flew to Hollywood, formed an even larger band, including a full string section, and made more successful records, among them his famed rendition of "Star Dust." A few months later, he disbanded again, soon formed yet another group, disbanded once more, and enlisted in the Navy, where he organized a great service band that included Claude Thornhill, Dave Tough, Sam Donahue, and Max Kaminsky. It toured the Pacific and survived seventeen bombing attacks. But Shaw could survive neither the physical nor the emotional pressures, including the resentments of some of his own men, many of whom considered him an intellectual snob, and he was discharged for health reasons.

Back on land, he organized still more bands. The 1944 edition included such embryonic stars as Mel Torme and Ray Conniff. His 1947 edition again had strings. His 1949 edition featured bop sounds but didn't last long, and Artie retired to a farm until 1953, when he formed his last group. And why did he unretire? "I went back only to feed some cows," he later told the AP's Bob

Artie now

Thomas. "They were eating their way through my money. I earned enough to keep the farm going, and then I quit again."

Thereafter, Shaw refused ever to play his clarinet again. Instead, he concentrated on his nonmusical careers, as farmer, author (his autobiographical *The Trouble with Cinderella* was a best seller), gunsmith, and movie distributor and producer, limiting his public appearances to TV talk shows on which he could expound on his many careers and theories about living. It would have been impossible, he noted, to combine music with any of his new careers, for "music is such a horrendously all-consuming discipline, and I just didn't want to be just a half-assed human being in order to become a whole-assed musician. That's why I gave it up."

(1910–   )

George Shearing

The musicianship has remained uncompromisingly fine.

He once wrote an article called "I Turned Down the Gift of Sight," explaining how he had refused offers from people who wanted to bequeath him their eyes, because "I am a completely happy man. My life today fits me."

To his enormous credit, George Shearing has adjusted himself to lifelong blindness with grace and ingenuity. Born into a large working-class English family, he began studying classical music at the age of five at a London school for the blind. In his teens, he discovered the sound of jazz through the records of Art Tatum, Teddy Wilson, and Fats Waller. His extraordinary talent brought the offer of a university scholarship, which he regretfully declined in order to earn one pound sterling a week, and tips, playing jazz piano in a Lambeth pub.

At eighteen, he joined the Claude Bampton All-Blind Band. When the group was jamming one night in a London club, jazz critic Leonard Feather happened in and was so impressed with Shearing's playing that he arranged a recording session. The records caught on quickly; by the time Shearing was nineteen, he was an established "name" in England, in demand as a performer (with Ted Heath's Orchestra for a time) and an arranger.

During World War II he played at military bases and even in air-raid shelters; at one such underground concert he met Beatrice "Trixie" Bayes, whom he married in 1941. After the war, they settled in New York City and Shearing formed a trio, then a quartet and, finally, the quintet with the distinctive sound (piano, drums, bass, guitar, and vibraphone) that soon became popular throughout the United States *Billboard*'s 1950 jazz poll awarded the group second place in the "favorite small instrumental group" category, and Shearing's sensitive, intimate style won the approval of jazz fans whose ears couldn't accommodate hardcore bop.

The quintet's personnel changed many times during its history, most radically when Shearing relocated to Los Angeles in 1961. But the musicianship remained uncompromisingly fine, reflecting the leader's own perfectionism. Between club engagements, concert dates, recording sessions, international tours, and radio and television appearances, Shearing continued to arrange and compose (his best-known song is "Lullaby of Birdland") and to explore new avenues of musical expression. A series of popular "mood music" albums with strings, brass choir, and such titles as "White Satin" and "Velvet Carpet" broadened his audience while incurring the wrath of some purist fans.

George

Shearing is a member of the board of directors of the Hadley School for the Blind in Illinois, and of Guide Dogs for the Blind in San Rafael, California. The latter facility was the setting for a moving 1975 documentary, in which Shearing starred, about his selection of a second golden retriever guide dog after the death of the dog that for twelve years he had called "the other half of my life."

Shearing's eminently listenable style has prompted charges of "Commercial!" from some jazz critics, but none fail to acknowledge his craftsmanship, especially his soft, gentle touch coupled with a seemingly effortless, yet astounding technique that have been displayed more and more recently in solo settings, many in the New York area. When he appeared in Los Angeles recently, Leonard Feather, Shearing's onetime mentor, wrote, "God bless George Shearing and all the true exponents of the very grand piano, who defend us from the inroads of the Fender-Rhodes brigade."

Amen.

(1919–   )

Dinah

Dinah Shore

"If you're going to keep up with the musical times, it's important to retain your awe as a fan."

"The music part of my show is pure joy—the rest is just plain fun." Dinah Shore, describing how she felt about her successful syndicated television series, "Dinah!" once again expressed her unbridled enthusiasm for the entertainment form she has always loved most: music.

It was that way back in Nashville, Tennessee, when as a teenager she stuck close to the radio, struck by the wonderful sounds of jazz, blues, and gospel music, and especially inspired by Billie Holiday ("I cried the first time I heard her!"), Maxine Sullivan, and Frances Langford and by numerous jazz musicians ("The great ones still knock me out!"). For a while she even dreamed of trying to become a jazz singer, but, as she later explained, "I wanted to work and I wanted to sing, and I knew that the more I could sing the more I would improve." So, with more jobs available along the pop route, she went that way.

Frances Rose Shore, she of the soft, soothing, velvety voice, began singing publicly on Nashville's WSM radio station, standing six feet away from the mike, so as not to overload it with her soon-to-be-forsaken blues-belting style. A name change accompanied the style change: Fanny Rose Shore became Dinah Shore, in deference to the title of her theme song.

After her graduation with a degree in sociology from Vanderbilt University, where she was a cheerleader, she hied herself to New York. There at station WNEW, she received fine coaching from Jimmy Rich, who at the same time was also helping another young singer, named Frank Sinatra, who would pop up on the station now and then. Dinah, though, became a regular, singing five days a week for free, "just to get the experience and exposure." It paid off.

Though auditions for jobs with the bands of Benny Goodman, Tommy Dorsey, Bob Crosby, and Jimmy Dorsey netted nothing, her singing did impress band-leader Leo Reisman enough to let her sing one chorus of "Hurry Home" with his band at New York's Strand Theater, and Xavier Cugat to sing on several of his recordings. But the big break came when NBC, after having heard her on WNEW, offered her a job and eventually starred her on the highly successful "Chamber Music Society of Lower Basin Street" radio series. Back came Tommy Dorsey with an offer to join his band, but the very bright and pragmatic Dinah refused the honor. "I think I'm on my way in radio and that's where I'd like to be," she rationalized.

And how right she was! Soon Ben Bernie featured her on his show and Eddie Cantor built her up on his. By 1941 she was recording regularly on Bluebird records, hitting big with "Yes, My Darling Daughter" and following up with "Blues in the Night" and intimate ballads like "You'd Be So Nice to Come Home To" and her own favorite, "He's My Guy."

During the war years she became the musical darling of millions of guys in the service, not just because of her records and radio shows, but also because of her many, many personal appearances at camps in the United States and later right out front near the firing lines in the European theater.

After the war she settled on the West Coast with husband George Montgomery, continued to star on her radio series, and then, when TV came in, switched over to that medium. Her warm, gracious, informal, "me-to-you" personality was ideally suited to the intimate home screen, and by the late 1950s her series for Chevrolet cars, always ending with her blowing her famous "M—wah!" kiss, had registered at the top of ratings. Unfortunately, though, changing tastes of the early 1960s in both music (rock was starting to take over) and television (situation comedies and violent dramas became the rage) siphoned off the audiences of high quality but expensive musical variety shows, and Dinah's and others' gradually faded from the screen.

In 1971, Dinah made a strong television comeback with her "Dinah's Place," a straight talk show on which the rest of the country discovered what those close to her had always known: that she is an especially intelligent, articulate, well-read and well-bred lady. But missing was an ingredient that meant much to her: music. And so in 1974 she started an even more ambitious series called simply "Dinah!" on which she intermingled conversation about current topics with performances of current music.

The opportunity to return to her first love thrilled her. "Music is so exciting today," she exclaimed late in 1976. "There are so many good writers. I love the strange, wonderful rhythmic and melodic patterns of today's music, and I want to try to lead the way for it on TV."

In her sumptuous Beverly Hills home she keeps a Wurlitzer jukebox stocked with all the latest records, including many by comparatively unknown, young singers. For just like the young girl back in Nashville, inspired by what she was hearing on the radio, Dinah Shore has never stopped listening. "If you're going to keep up with the musical times," she points out, "it's important to retain your awe as a fan." Which may just be why she has been able to maintain that wonderfully youthful outlook and appearance that have made her such a joyous performer and human being for so many years.

(1922–   )

Carly Simon

"I was feeling that the only way I could get anyone's attention or love was by being the black sheep."

From the start of her recording career, Carly Simon has proved herself to be that rare artist who can express feelings that most of us have but don't know how to define. Sexily provocative, with a rich and expressive voice that conveys positive energy charges, she has also related to her audiences via her self-revealing lyrics and melodies that catch the ear easily. Popular and peer recognition came quickly when her first single, "That's the Way I've Always Heard It Should Be," written with Jacob Brackman, helped her win a 1971 Grammy as Best New Artist.

There are those who are quick to say that she always had it easy growing up as one of four children of well-to-do publisher Richard Simon in affluent Riverdale and Stamford, Connecticut. In fact, Albert Grossman, who once managed Bob Dylan and Peter, Paul and Mary, turned her down as a client because

Carly

he told her that on a scale of ten her talent rated only nine since she hadn't suffered enough. But, as she has pointed out in conversation and in her songs, "Rich kids can suffer in different ways."

While at Sarah Lawrence, she and her sister Lucy (now a recording artist in her own right) sang around Greenwich Village clubs as the Simon Sisters and made several records. But Carly's fear of flying prevented them from touring far from home and soon Lucy got married. So Carly, who had dropped out of college, floundered around in a series of dull jobs. "For a long time," she recalls, "I was feeling that the only way I could get anyone's attention or love was by being the black sheep who wasn't making any money, didn't have a job, didn't fit in."

Brackman, an old friend, came to the rescue by urging her to start taking songwriting seriously. She made a demonstration record that impressed Jac Holzman, then president of Elektra. But again jitters hit Carly when the record company urged her to start performing in person as soon as that first single made the charts. "There's just too much anxiety involved in performing for me," she says. "I like to relate to people on a one-to-one basis best of all, and in an audience there are just too many people that I have to relate to."

To make matters more nerve-wracking, at her debut as Cat Stevens' opening act at the Los Angeles Troubador, Carly was told that her idol, James Taylor, was in the audience. The two had vaguely known each other as children vacationing with their parents on Martha's Vineyard. Carly triumphed on stage and afterward James dropped by to chat. The ensuing courtship led to their marriage on November 3, 1972.

Now the mother of two, Carly insists: "Just because James and I are married it's not a natural condition that we should perform together. We didn't start our careers as a team and we don't want to be the Ozzie and Harriet of rock."

Of Carly's half dozen gold records (four albums, two singles), "You're So Vain" spurred the most talk in the pop world as people tried to guess just who it was that "walked into the party like you were walking onto a yacht." Carly always smiles mysteriously when people suggest that it might be Mick Jagger or Warren Beatty. "It's about a lot of people" is all that she'll say.

Listeners do identify with her songs because she writes from a very honest point of view. She explains: "All the songs kind of come out of an experience. I don't consciously set out to put a message across or sit down to write a hit single." "I work for love," she told Nancy Naglin of *Crawdaddy*. "I see myself as a bottomless pit, that I'll just never get enough love. Anything I have ever done has been for love."

(1944–   )

Simon and Garfunkel

From the start, they seemed a most unlikely pairing.

The year was 1970. "Bridge over Troubled Water" was Columbia Records' hottest product and well on its way to becoming one of the top-selling albums in the company's long history. Across the nation, stores could scarcely keep ahead of the clamorous demand for the record, while critics, journalists, politicians, and even clergymen praised its title song for its inspirational value. From ten thousand car radios there blared a bold anthem to charity and brotherhood:

> When you're weary, feeling small
> When tears are in your eyes
> I will dry them all . . .
> I'm on your side, when times get rough . . .
> And friends just can't be found,
> Like a bridge over troubled water . . .
> I will ease your mind©

With "Bridge over Troubled Water," a folk-rock singing duo with the almost comically cumbersome name of Simon and Garfunkel had achieved the impossible: They had become a household word. Ironically, at the vẽry moment that Paul Simon and Art Garfunkel's career together was peaking, they were making plans to dissolve a professional partnership that had existed, on and off, since 1957. They were throwing away—according to some of the best minds in the record business—thirteen years of fruitful struggle simply because of a "slight" personality conflict and some crazy notions about pursuing solo careers. What no one understood, however, was that right up until their dramatic parting, Simon and Garfunkel had remained fierce individualists. Indeed, that dogged quality was and continues to be one of the secrets behind their many successes.

From the start, they seemed a most unlikely pairing. Simon, a soft, sinuous baritone and the writer for the two, was a dark-haired, pale, and conspicuously shy man, admittedly extremely self-conscious about his short stature. (He is approximately five feet, four inches tall.) Simon's gloomy reticence was in sharp contrast to the boyish casualness of the blond, bushy-haired Garfunkel, whose choirboy tenor added a much-needed airiness to his partner's often saturnine songs.

They co-wrote their first song, "The Girl for Me," in 1955. Two years later they scored a modest regional hit with "Hey! Schoolgirl," recorded for Big Records under the pseudonym of Tom and Jerry. From 1964 to 1970 they produced a slew of hits, including "The Sounds of Silence," "Homeward Bound,"

"Tom and Jerry"—pre-Simon and Garfunkel

"I Am a Rock," "The Boxer," "Bridge over Troubled Water," and "Mrs. Robinson," the unofficial theme song from the smash 1970 film *The Graduate*.

Happily, after their breakup, each released a number of solo albums that were well received by critics and consumers alike. The artistic differences that sparked so much creative combustion during their alliance become more clearly delineated in their individual efforts and the public was fascinated.

Simon's LPs, among them his early *The Paul Simon Song Book* (released in England in 1966) and the post-breakup *Paul Simon, There's Goes Rhymin' Simon* and *Still Crazy After All These Years*, featured finely crafted, meticulously arranged but essentially grim songs that bespoke an unsentimental and frequently fatalistic view of the world. Even when writing a (serious) love song, he was most comfortable confessing that even an ideal relationship troubled him—he couldn't "get used to something so right."

On the other hand, the material Garfunkel selected for his first two solo albums virtually epitomized dulcet romanticism, even in the face of tragedy. Most of the songs on his *Angel Clare* and *Breakaway* albums were love ballads sung to lush accompaniment.

Since their days growing up together in Forest Hills, Queens, New York, there has been a definite tension between them. The problem apparently grew grave in 1969 when Garfunkel accepted a role in the film version of *Catch-22*, deciding his musical career would temporarily take a back seat to his acting aspirations. Occasionally thereafter, they appeared together on records and at concerts. But their often disparate ambitions and attitudes broadened the gap, and with each finding success in different ways, and later even on different record labels, there seemed little desire or need to include the "and" in "Simon and Garfunkel."

Simon's own attitude, reflected in his songwriting, underwent a striking metamorphosis after he had reached the age of thirty. "The Beatles wrote about their age," he pointed out. "That's what I'm doing. I can't stay writing the same lyrics I wrote when I was twenty-three. So much of what I hear on the radio is *boring*. I think that part of the reason is it's not real. It may be real—maybe—if you're eighteen, but not if you're thirty. People thirty years old wonder why they're not getting off on popular music the way they once did, and it's because nobody is singing for *them*."

Though now wealthy and surely a celebrity, Simon insists that the biggest thrill in his life occurred when he was sixteen years old—"when I stole home in the bottom of the eleventh inning of a high school baseball game. I believe that I *peaked* at that moment. I truly believe that was it and don't think I have done anything greater since then."

(Simon: 1941–   )
(Garfunkel: 1941–   )

Paul and Art

Nina Simone

A very tough shield created to protest a soft and frightened girl.

When Nina Simone plays the piano or sings, pendant earrings framing the strikingly full, firm features of a classic Nubian beauty, the result is less a performance than a battle of wills—hers and her listeners'. Her art is based on building a mood and drawing her audience into that mood. Sometimes this is more difficult than it is at other times. But, at best, it is always a challenge. And the emotional involvement of challenge is what Nina Simone has brought to every moment of her life.

"Music gets me worked up," she once said. "I can't sing a song without meaning it. I used to hate music because every night I'd give, give, give. And then I'd go to bed and hear a tune go on and on and on in my head. I was blowing my mind."

"Nina Simone" is actually a figment of the imagination, a very tough shield created to protect a soft and frightened girl named Eunice Waymon. Eunice grew up in the wealthy town of Tryon, North Carolina, the sixth of eight children, born to a fervently religious mother and living in extreme poverty, complicated by the fact that she was, as she puts it, "the most outstandingly talented little girl in town—and I was colored."

By the time she was four, she was playing the piano. Soon she was giving recitals in the white library, across the tracks. "I was tense and scared of those white people," she said. "I was split in half. I love Bach but the music was never a joy, never a pleasure."

But with the help of local white supporters, she went to a girls' boarding school in Asheville and had two years at Juilliard. Then, when the money ran out, she went home to her family, who had moved to Philadelphia. There she gave piano lessons and worked in a vocal studio until she was offered a summer job in an Atlantic City nightclub. To spare her mother the embarrassment of having it known that her daughter was working in such a place, Eunice called herself Nina Simone.

This was her first contact with pop music and, although she had been hired as a pianist, when she found she was expected to sing, she tried that too. Everything was worth trying then.

"I'd play any piece of pop music to death," she said. "I'd improvise, turn it around, sing an obligato. In my first two years in show business, I was letting so much out—all the things I'd always held in. I'd feel better after playing. It was like having a good cry."

Eunice Waymon/Nina Simone

Out of this came the mood-building Nina Simone style. At first she sang pop songs—"Porgy," the record that brought her national attention in 1959, "Little Girl Blue." Then she began to express more personal feelings—the "feeling of being imprisoned."

"I've known about the silence that makes that prison," she said. "Any black person does." She broke the silence with "Mississippi Goddam," a protest against the violence in the South in the mid-1960s. And "Four Women"—biting vignettes in which the circumstances and outlooks of four women are related to gradations of skin color. Both were banned on radio.

By the 1970s, Nina Simone was finding the challenge of living in the United States more than she could take. She lived outside the country much of the time. Her marriage to Andrew Stroud, a onetime New York City detective who became her manager and by whom she had a daughter, Lisa, broke up. While they were married, she felt that the pressures that had buried Eunice Waymon and created Nina Simone were diminishing. But with the end of the marriage, Nina once more became dominant.

"Nina takes care of Eunice," the mind behind both Nina and Eunice has pointed out.

(1933–   )

Frank and Tommy Dorsey: the band's new boy singer

"I Get a Kick Out of You!"

Frank Sinatra

Girls wanted to smother him; older women wanted to mother him; jealous male partners wanted to shoot him.

His friends—and he has had many of the, some real, too many merely hangers-on—have called him "the most mercurial man" they have ever known. One moment he may be warm gracious, compassionate, caring, deeply concerned, the tenderest of humans. And then suddenly he can turn and become churlish, cruel, crude, distressingly inconsiderate, and brutally cold.

This is Frank Sinatra, a man of a million moods, to many eyes and ears the most important musical performer of the past half century, a singer whose sensitive and highly personal phrasing has convinced millions of listeners that each one of them is the only person in the world to whom he is directing his musical message of romance.

And when he does sing a ballad, such could be precisely his intent. Personal communication is certainly his forte. "I'm more conscious of the words in a song than I am of the melody," he once explained. There has never been a more touching, more tender singer of love songs. On a strictly one-to-one basis, Sinatra, not only as a singer, but often as a human being, has been just beautiful. But on a less personal basis he can be and too often has been something else.

The dichotomy between his personal and public life has been reflected in his singing. What has been referred to as his "Las Vegas personality," brash, cocky, "Man-am-I-with-it!" has too often pervaded his superhip and sometimes quite disrespectful interpretations of the most highly respected songs. It is the Sinatra dealing impersonally with a large public, strangely concerned with making a "mucho-macho" impression, the direct antithesis of the man who has done so many good things for so many people, quietly, compassionately, with deep, honest feeling and conviction and who once insisted, "More than anything I expect and hope from people is kindness. If I don't get it, it upsets me."

No group of people has upset him more than journalists, who know little of the many good deeds he keeps private, and who therefore have exploited his more public and less charitable affairs. Ironically, his first job as a teenager in hometown Hoboken, New Jersey, was that of a copyboy on the local newspaper. For a while he thought of becoming a sports writer or a boxer. "My dad even wanted me to be a civil engineer," he recently told television interviewer Bill Boggs. But when, as a member of the Hoboken Four, he won a "Major Bowes and His Original Amateur Hour," he began to concentrate on music.

"I sang at night with little combinations, sometimes through a megaphone." Daytimes he often emigrated across the river, singing for free whenever he could be heard, and occasionally filling in when a regular singer failed to show at New York's WNEW radio station, one of whose executives described him as "a polite pusher interested in himself." But when bandleader Harry James, after having heard him on a broadcast, also became interested in the skinny, cocky kid with the intense eyes and soft, crooning voice, Sinatra entered the big time.

He made his first records, "From the Bottom of My Heart" and "Melancholy Mood," on July 13, 1939, as the James band's boy vocalist. He stayed with the band for seven months, respected and well liked by its leader and sidemen. Then in February 1940 he left, with James's blessing, to join Tommy Dorsey's then more successful band for the higher salary ($125 as opposed to $75 a week) required to support himself and pregnant wife Nancy. "I wanted to sing with Dorsey more than anything else." With Dorsey, both his singing style and his career blossomed. He later described his two and a half years with Dorsey as "a real education in music, in business, in every way." He was one of the few band members not awed by the domineering Dorsey. "When Frank joined," arranger Sy Oliver reported, "he just moved right in and took charge. He had an awful lot of assurance for a youngster."

Certainly his confidence must have been buoyed by the shrieking, hysterical reactions his soft, often tentative-sounding crooning created among bobby-soxers. Hit records, some with the Pied Pipers, others alone with the Dorsey band, poured forth: "I'll Never Smile Again," "This Love of Mine," "Everything Happens to Me," "Polka Dots and Moonbeams," "Oh, Look at Me Now," and "Let's Get Away from It All," the last rather prophetic when late in the summer of 1942 Sinatra left Dorsey, with some bitterness on both sides, to begin his illustrious solo career.

A two-year musicians' strike at first limited his recording output but failed to slow the impetus of his popularity. In February 1943 he was signed as the star of Lucky Strike's "Your Hit Parade" program, and the whole country heard him regularly. When he made his first major solo stage appearance at New York's Paramount Theater, the colossal reception turned the costar on the bill, Benny Goodman, the King of Swing, into something more resembling a pawn. His first club appearance at New York's Riobamba resulted in a near riot. The popularity of the shy-looking, soft-singing, bow-tied boy was overwhelming. Girls wanted to smother him; older women wanted to mother him; jealous male partners wanted to shoot him.

Because of a damaged ear, he was rejected for military service. Loyal and concerned, he toured for the USO and campaigned diligently, traveling to various trouble spots at home, to combat juvenile delinquency and to preach racial tolerance.

When the recording ban was lifted in November 1944, Sinatra began making a series of superb recordings for Columbia—soft and gentle like "Try a Little Tenderness" and "Nancy," dedicated to his first child, and more ambitious, like the eloquent "Soliloquy" from *Carousel.* He also made a series of musical movies like *Higher and Higher, Step Lively,* and *Anchors Aweigh,* none of them great artistic masterpieces, and began more and more to live it up, gradually forsaking his boyish image for that of a young Hollywood-type swinger.

The combination of too much singing and possibly too much swinging began to impair his voice. Gradually his poorer performances plus the public's emerging preference for novelty rather than quality songs began to diminish his popularity. By the late 1940s he had lost many fans and for a while he even lost his voice. A tempestuous romance with Ava Gardner, whom he eventually married and divorced, seemed to drain him physically and emotionally. And yet during those troubled times his innate musicianship never deserted him and, despite his obviously weary and strained voice, he recorded, early in 1951, three of the most emotion-charged sides of his entire career—each conceivably addressed directly to Ava—"You're the One," "Love Me," and "I'm a Fool to Want You," the last so self-affecting that, after just one "take," he walked right out of the studio and never returned.

Still, by 1952, Columbia Records, with Mitch Miller producing so many novelty hits, had given up on him. But Columbia Pictures, at Frank's own urging and willingness to work for practically nothing, auditioned him for the role of Maggio in *From Here to Eternity.* The audition and his performance were huge successes. Sinatra won an Oscar and suddenly his records on the Capitol label, with which he had just signed, became big sellers. He was back with the hits again: "I Get a Kick Out of You," "They Can't Take That Away from Me," "In the Wee Small Hours of the Morning," "Young at Heart," "Witchcraft," and on and on—all quality tunes. Sinatra was exultant. "See, you can still show good taste and be appreciated," he gleefully proclaimed.

He grew bigger and bigger, starring in hit movies like *High Society, Guys and Dolls, Pal Joey* and *The Man with the Golden Arm.* "If I ever deserved a prize," he said to Bill Boggs, "it should have been for *The Man with the Golden Arm.* We wanted to show the misery of drugs."

In December 1960 he formed his own Reprise Records and recorded exactly what he felt like recording: ballads with Gordon Jenkins, nostalgia with Sy Oliver, and swing tunes with Nelson Riddle, Billy May, Neal Hefti, and the entire Count Basie band, with whom he also appeared in concerts. The personal, sensitive, me-to-you crooning approach surfaced only occasionally. Instead, he performed more often like a jazz soloist, swinging along with his favorite musicians to mass audiences. The older he grew, the more intent he seemed to become to project his swinger's image. To some, his high-flying conduct appeared almost self-destructive. And maybe he knew it. "When the vibrato starts to widen and the breath starts to give out," he announced one day, "when that happens, I'll say good-bye." Not long thereafter, it did happen, and, following a much-publicized 1971 farewell concert, Sinatra did say good-bye and retired.

His many record fans were crushed. Some refused to believe he could stay away from singing too long. His close friend, Dean Martin, clearly predicted the early return that two years later brought Sinatra, by then a beefier, bulgier belter of songs back into circulation. More hit records, more SRO concerts, more television and nightclub appearances, more adulation and hysteria, and much more money followed. Though his large and powerfully protective entourage made him almost personally unreachable, his musical communicativeness never stopped.

Martin explained the reason for his return, simply and logically: "He loves singing too much to tire of it. He always sings, he always has, and he always will."

How true—and how fortunate!

(1915–   )

Sly and the Family Stone

By turns personally willful, arrogant, and furtive, his music became more introspective.

He combined the rhythms of black "soul" music with harmonic and compositional aspects of jazz and white pop. His alchemical mixture of the forms was aided by his brilliant talents as an arranger and by his comprehensive background as a record producer, recording studio engineer, and innovative radio station disc jockey. His understanding and experience of the technical, commercial, and cathartic components of popular music resulted in a blazingly creative and successful series of recordings between 1968 and 1970: "Dance to the Music," "Everyday People," "Sing a Simple Song," "Stand!" "Thank You (faletinmibimicelfagin)," the throbbing "I Want to Take You Higher," and the delicate and elegant "Everybody Is a Star."

Sylvester "Sly" Stewart had the technical training in music, a wowser sense

Sly and the Family Stone

of stage presentation (the Family Stone was an immensely exciting group visually), and an elfin personal charm that made him hard to resist.

He recalled that at the age of four he found rhythm: "That's all I had to play with. No toys." His mother was the dominant personal and musical influence on his life; she placed him in a family gospel group. From there he went to a pop vocal quintet that had a minor hit. Then he enrolled at Vallejo Junior College in California where he studied theory and composition under David Frolich, who had played for a while with Dave Brubeck's Quartet. As Stewart told Andrew Furnival in *Music Scene* magazine in 1973: "That helped me more than anything, more than the rhythm . . . Between him and my parents, that's about it. It was Frohlich's interpretation of Walter Piston's *Harmony* [textbook] and his psychological way of getting along with people, regardless of the type of person, that turned me on."

After graduation he went to San Francisco, where he won local fame at two black stations as an unusual disc jockey who varied orthodox all-black programming with insertions of Beatle records and other recordings by white groups he admired. He tried forming his own group, the Stoners, but was not successful. Shortly after the attempt, he became a producer and house songwriter for a small label and hit several times with records by a white group, the Beau Brummels. Stewart formed another group, the Family Stone, which included his brother and sister and a white saxophonist and drummer. Hyperenergic, he wrote and arranged furiously for the Family Stone—as well as choreographing them—and they hit in 1968 with "Dance to the Music."

For the next two years he was at his musical peak. Then, suddenly, in 1970, the zip and dash of his music faded. He released a manic and morbid album, "There's a Riot Goin' On," and began to demonstrate personality quirks that were at odds with his formerly cheerful, affectionate nature. He and the group began showing up hours late—or not at all—for concerts; his popularity suffered and his professional reputation was heavily damaged. By turns personally willful, arrogant, and furtive, his music became more introspective without revealing what troubled or concerned him. His personality change has never been explained, but it could have been a result of a mixture of physical exhaustion brought on by high living, and emotional stress, intensified by the speed and intensity of his sudden rise to stardom.

In the early 1970s he recovered his equilibrium somewhat, and started to rebuild his career; his occasional use of his powerful charm had maintained his mystique. But his musical efforts to recapture his former audacious brilliance seemed mechanical and calculated; only traces of his original magic could be heard. Though he was still popular, his talent was in limbo, and he seemed to be paying off a mortgage on his future by taking a lien on the accomplishments of his past.

(1944–   )

Bessie Smith

"You didn't turn your head when she was on."

Rightly known as "The Empress of the Blues," Bessie Smith was the greatest blues singer in the classic tradition, and beyond that, one of the foremost artists in the annals of jazz.

"Bessie Smith was a fabulous deal to watch," recalled New Orleans guitarist Danny Barker. "She was a large, pretty woman, and she dominated the stage. You didn't turn your head when she was on. You just watched Bessie. She could bring about mass hypnotism."

Born in Chattanooga, Tennessee, Bessie began singing at an early age; by her midteens, she was touring with minstrel shows and in vaudeville, and soon established herself as a solo act. In 1923, when she made her first records, black singers had been recording blues for some three years, but most of these had been of the polite vaudeville type. Bessie's powerful voice and intense, deeply felt delivery were revelatory.

The Empress of the Blues

Through the next decade, accompanied by some outstanding musicians, like Louis Armstrong, she recorded one hundred and sixty songs, mostly blues but also some pop tunes like "Nobody Knows You When You're Down and Out" and "After You've Gone." Her blues, like most of the genre, dealt with various aspects of love, treated with a directness, sexual frankness, and humor far removed from the romantic treacle of pop song lyrics, but she also sang about other things. Her own "Backwater Blues," inspired by firsthand observation of the effects of a Mississippi flood, became one of her masterpieces. In fact, whatever material Bessie dealt with she brought to life.

In the wake of her successful records, Bessie achieved stardom in the world of black entertainment. During her lifetime, with the exception of jazz musicians and a few knowledgeable devotees, her audience was almost exclusively black. She toured with her own shows in her own Pullman car, headlined at such major theaters as Harlem's Apollo, and starred in a 1929 film short, *St. Louis Blues.*

As the blues declined in popularity, Bessie moved with the times, changing her repertoire to popular songs, and though her career had its ups and downs, the stories about her voice deteriorating and jobs growing scarce are no more true than the much publicized fiction blaming her death from injuries suffered in an automobile accident in Mississippi on racial prejudice. Her death, ironically, came just at a time when the blues were being rediscovered. Some of her best records were about to be reissued, and she had been set to record again for the first time in four years.

Bessie Smith's personal life was tempestuous. A commanding presence off stage as well as on, she could be generous to a fault, especially to members of her family, but she was also intensely jealous, short-tempered, and proud. She made and spent a great deal of money, though, like most black performers of her time, she was exploited by unscrupulous business interests.

"Bessie Smith," wrote her biographer, Chris Albertson, "cared remarkably little for the good opinion of others; she sought acceptance as a human being, but she would not alter her ways to gain it." These "ways" included both heavy drinking and sexual promiscuity.

For all that, she was a consistently disciplined performer, as her recorded legacy bears out. She was in firm control of her rich, full voice, had remarkable pitch control, superb natural diction (every word she sang could be clearly understood; something by no means common to all blues singers), and a matchlessly dramatic, intense manner of projecting her material.

In 1970, Columbia Records—the only company for which she ever recorded—initiated an ambitious reissue project, presenting her entire output on five double albums. Within two years, more than two hundred thousand copies of these had been sold, and a new generation of listeners had become aware of the incomparable artistry of Bessie Smith.

One result of all this attention was that—much belatedly—a headstone was placed on Bessie's unmarked grave. The inscription reads: "The Greatest Blues Singer in the World Will Never Stop Singing."

(1894–1937)

Kate Smith

Stokowski whistled the aria for her.

In 1939, when he was presenting her to King George VI and Queen Elizabeth of England at a White House reception, President Franklin D. Roosevelt—a consummate showman himself—said: "Your Majesties, this is Kate Smith—this is America."

From 1931 onward, the portly singer did indeed seem to personify the country: idealistic, generous, homespun, sentimental, emotional, and proud. Her renderings of Irving Berlin's "God Bless America" in 1938 sparked a grass-roots movement resulting in proposed congressional legislation to have the song named

"When the moon comes over the mountain."

as the national anthem. Typically, she asked that the proposal be dropped; she had too much respect for "The Star-Spangled Banner."

As a young girl hoping to be a professional singer, she had appeared in a local theater in Washington, D.C., her program consisting of "songs folks like to hear" and topped off with a hot Charleston dance. She was already obese at fifteen and her parents, fearful that she would never marry (a fear that proved to be unwarranted), urged her to a career in nursing. After a bitter argument with her family she temporarily surrendered her dreams, but she soon left nursing to go to New York, where she appeared in small roles in two Broadway musicals, *Honeymoon Lane* (1926) and *Flyin' High* (1930).

She was approached by Ted Collins of the Columbia Phonograph Company to record in 1930. A year later he became her manager (on a permanent hand-shake contract) and placed her on CBS radio opposite NBC's phenomenally popular "Amos 'n' Andy" comedy series. She was so immediately successful that NBC switched its comedy program to another evening.

Throughout the 1930s her broadcasts grew in popularity and number. She had a regular weekly hour program and five daily commentary shows. Her theme song, "When the Moon Comes Over the Mountain," exemplified the sturdy, safe, and sure material she most often sang, and her belief in the *bel canto* theory: "The best way to sing a song is as near to the composer's intentions as possible . . . it's his ideas I am embellishing . . . Intelligent analysis of [his] intention automatically ensure[s] sincerity."

During a rehersal for a performance in which she was to sing an aria from *La Bohème,* she asked Leopold Stokowski, conductor of the symphony orchestra, to whistle a passage for her since she wasn't quite sure of the melody. Stokowski looked perplexed. She explained that she couldn't read music but relied on her ear and sense of perfect pitch. Stokowski whistled the aria for her.

In 1950 she was one of the first major entertainers to have her own television program, and her recording career continued well into the 1960s. In her autobiography (1960) she devoted a chapter to "the career woman" and expressed ideas and sentiments that forecast some aspects of the "women's liberation" movement, and she surprised her fans with some kind words for rock and roll: "If [it] is well done, by a voice that is neither manufactured nor has no music in it at all, and if the beat is executed correctly, there's nothing so terribly wrong with that kind of music."

She continued to make guest appearances on television in the early and middle 1970s, sometimes singing pop-rock, still affectionate and generous to the audience, still Kate Smith and still—in many good and comforting ways—America.

(1909–   )

Willie (the Lion) Smith

"When the Lion roared, you never knew what was in store."

Of all the great pianist-entertainers bred by Harlem in the early days of the century, none was as flamboyantly individual as William Henry Joseph Bonaparte Bertholoff Smith, known to all and sundry as "the Lion." Wit, bon vivant, raconteur, and virtuoso musician, he ranks with Fats Waller, James P. Johnson, and the other giants of Harlem's "stride" school of jazz piano.

Like its originator, the Lion's style was a heterodox mixture: baroque-like counterpoint, filigree, flights of harmonic fancy redolent of Debussy—all mounted astride a rhythmic foundation of irresistible power and momentum.

Born into a large, rather rootless family in Goshen, New York, just before the turn of the century, young Smith did combat service in World War I. On his return, he quickly became a familiar and colorful Harlem figure, playing and leading the small backing band on Mamie Smith's 1920 recording of "Crazy Blues," generally considered the first blues record by a black artist.

No Harlem rent party was complete without the Lion at the keyboard, derby cocked and cigar jutting, taking on all comers. As another piano great, Joe

Willie, "the Lion"

.embered it, "He was the most unpredictable pianist ever. I mean,
layed, or Fats or James P., we'd usually have a pretty good idea
coming. But when the Lion roared, you never knew what was in

emingly disparate creeds, astrology and Judaism, dominated his per-
. Decades before it became fashionable to do so, he was speaking of
d bad "vibrations" and their effect on his music making. Indeed, there
nes when he turned down work at one club or another because he
he "vibes" inimical.

u might as well try making love to each member of a girl quartet at
ame time as to try playing your music when the vibrations are wrong,"
his way of putting it. "If people learned to watch out for themselves by
dying the planets, there would be fewer wars rushing folks into the ground."
Equally strong was the Lion's love of Judaism. In his autobiography, *Music
on My Mine,* he said he had actually been Bar Mitzvahed at thirteen and later
served as cantor at a Harlem synagogue.

Willie seemed to have a fresh tale, too, for everyone curious about how he
came to be called the Lion. Sometimes it was for valor in the great war, sometimes
a contraction of "the Lion of Judah," betokening his devotion to Judaism. He
told at least one interviewer that James P. Johnson had dubbed him thus for
"my spunk and enterprise."

If his name was open to dispute, the Lion's musicianship was not. His compositions, among them "Echoes of Spring," "Passionette," "Morning Air," and "Portrait of the Duke," for his lifelong friend and admirer Duke Ellington, reflect
imagination and flair for the exotic. Smith remained popular and active until
late in life, recording, making club appearances, and touring.

Ellington, whose piece "Portrait of the Lion" repaid Willie's compliment in
kind, hailed the Lion's style as a key influence on his own playing and that
of most of the great pianists.

"He is wonderful," the Duke wrote in his *Music Is My Mistress,* "and I
love him. I can't think of anything good enough to say about the Lion, Willie
the Lion, Willie the Lion Smith."

(1897–1973)

Hank Snow

"Why has everybody gotten away from the rhinestones and the flash?"

"Occasionally I'll wear a straight western-cut suit, but I'll always go back to rhinestones. I talk to the public, and if I've heard it once I've heard it a thousand times: 'Why has everybody gotten away from the rhinestones and the flash?' The audience expects it and they miss it. They really do."

Through country music's rockabilly era and the pop-country era and the "progressive" era, Hank Snow has stuck to his gaudy rhinestone-encrusted suits, each one seemingly more garish than the last. Yet it is easy to pick up on this idiosyncrasy while ignoring what it reveals about the man: his self-assurance, his commitment to tradition, his pride—in an era of increasing blandness—in his extremely distinct image, and most of all his deep and genuine devotion to his public.

Hank

Hank Snow was born in rural Nova Scotia, and like many country singers used music as an escape from an improverished childhood. The records of Vernon Dalhart and especially the "Mississippi Blue Yodeler" Jimmie Rodgers were of tremendous inspiration to him, and while still in his teens he became the Yodeling Ranger on Canadian radio, struggling in that role for more than a decade before moving to the States in 1950 and joining the Grand Ole Opry.

Hank's glory years were the early 1950s (although a number-one record in 1974 prompted RCA to extend his contract to cover a full fifty years, 1935–85), when he racked up a string of hits such as "I'm Moving On," "Rhumba Boogie," "Bluebird Island," "Now and Then There's a Fool Such as I," and "I Don't Hurt Any More."

His style of that period was to remain unchanged throughout the years that followed: simple but eloquent steel guitar and fiddle (and occasionally his own acoustic guitar picking) merely complementing his voice, one of the most distinctive and imitated in country music. His resonant baritone with its heavy vibrato and back-of-the-palate tone combined with his faultless enunciation and unusual Canadian accent provided him with instant recognizability over the air and on record.

It was consistent with his combined distinctiveness and independence that he became an outspoken spokesman for traditional country music in the 1970s, often railing against the semi-factory approach to recording which had become prevalent in Nashville: "They use the same group of musicians on every record, with the exception of a few people who are carrying their own bands. And, with the exception of the artists who *are* different and do have a style, you're hearing the same music over and over on every record you buy."

This is the quintessential Hank Snow: proud of being distinct while at the same time proud of being a part of traditional country music as a whole, and committed to the preservation of both.

(1914–   )

Jo Stafford

"My sound was perfect—but boring, too."

"If you'd been trained to march, it would take you a long time to learn how to Lindy Hop," Jo Stafford was saying in the sumptuous Beverly Hills home she shares with Paul Weston, her husband of over a quarter of a century. One of the most technically correct of all pop singers with superb pitch and magnificent control, as well as exquisite musical taste, she was explaining why it took several years for her to express much warmth as a singer.

"Sure, you're right," she said, "When I was with Tommy Dorsey's band, my sound was perfect—but boring, too. The notes meant more to me than the words. But that's the way I had been trained."

The training had begun on a tract of land called "Lease 35" in Coalinga, California, where Jo Elizabeth Stafford lived with her family. Her mother played a five-string banjo and helped Jo and her sisters develop their pure delivery

Jo

as an act aptly named the Stafford Sisters. After marriage broke up the act, Jo joined the Pied Pipers, then a vocal octet. Tommy Dorsey hired them, then fired them because he couldn't afford that many singers. In 1941, after they'd cut their group in half, he rehired them, with Frank Sinatra added, and they made a batch of hit sides: "There Are Such Things," "Street of Dreams," "Oh, Look at Me Now," and the famous "I'll Never Smile Again."

Jo was also featured as a soloist with the band—on ballads like "Embraceable You" and "Who Can I Turn to," and on more rhythmic numbers like "For You" and "Yes, Indeed." But she considered herself "first and foremost a lead singer in a group. That takes a certain amount of subjugation; you're fitting what you're doing to what others are doing—to lead them but not to stick out."

But starting in 1943, Jo did begin to stick out on her own. Working with Dorsey, she had absorbed some of his as well as Sinatra's warm phrasing. She left the Pied Pipers and at Johnny Mercer's request began recording for his new Capitol label, singing ballads like "Tumbling Tumbleweeds" and doubling as comedienne Cinderella Q. Stump on Red Ingles' hit recording of "Timtay-shun." Later, in the mid-1950s, she turned in even more hilarious performances as the horrendously off-key, beat-skipping "Darlene Edwards," wife of the equally exasperating pianist "Jonathan Edwards" (Paul Weston).

Throughout the 1940s, she starred on radio, notably on "The Chesterfield Supper Club" series which she shared with Perry Como. She switched to Columbia Records and turned out a slew of hits: "Shrimp Boats," "You Belong to Me," "Make Love to Me," and "Jambalaya" among others. After marrying Weston in 1952, she turned to television, slimming down what had been a large body, and starring on "The Jo Stafford Show."

Then followed a period of semiretirement, as she devoted most of her time to her two children, Timothy and Amy, both musically talented and embarking on their own careers during the mid-1970s. "I even passed up a ten-year contract at Las Vegas to be with them," she relates rather proudly.

A warm, caring person, totally unlike the "cold" singer of her Dorsey years, she volunteered her talent for public service broadcasts like the Youth Program of "The Voice of America" and Radio Free Luxembourg, whose director, Frank Lee, declared, "In her own quiet way, Jo Stafford is selling America to Europe." And, it might be noted, Jo Stafford, for more than thirty years, has been selling good taste, encased in a superb technique, to popular music everywhere.

(1920–   )

The Staple Singers

"The white man hasn't had the black experience and now we're trying to give it to him."

"Pop had a guitar that some man had loaned to him. He had loaned the man some money and the man had left his guitar as security. He never claimed it, so Pop played it when the whole family gathered to sing."

Thus his daughter Cleotha describes the circumstance that eventually led Roebuck "Pop" Staples to become one of gospel music's boldest composers and who, with his son and daughters, was to win world fame as the Staple Singers.

Roebuck Staples came from a farm family in the Mississippi Delta, a region

Roebuck Staples and family

THE STAPLE SINGERS

long noted for blues singers and guitarists like the tortured Robert Johnson and the folk gospeler Blind Willie Johnson. "I taught myself guitar by listening closely to others," Roebuck remembered. "Then I'd try to figure out what I heard them do. It was strictly ear-playing."

By 1946 Roebuck had moved his wife and family to Chicago, where he worked in the stockyards and steel mills by day and sang gospel at home in the evenings for comfort and relaxation. His children joined in—son Purvis and daughters Cleotha and the gifted Mavis (youngest daughter Yvonne would eventually replace Purvis in the professional group).

The family became so popular singing on the "church circuit" that Roebuck resigned his day jobs; father and children made regional and national tours, traveling by car so that they could be close together.

Distinquished by their subtle harmonies, novel arrangements, and Roebuck's guitar playing, the Staples also featured Mavis' masterful vocals, rich in imagination and inventive in technique.

By the mid-1960s the Staples were recording for major labels, and Roebuck had begun to write songs like "Why (Am I Treated so Bad)?" and "Long Walk to D.C.," which altered the concepts and intent of gospel music. He made it a vehicle for expressing the social hopes of the black man for first-class citizenship. Where traditional gospel looked upon Christianity as an earthy aid for life's troubles, pointing to a perfect hereafter, Roebuck insisted that gospel be used to provide for the here-and-now. If American democracy and Christian ethics were, as they had been proclaimed, inseparable, then it was impossible to have either or both without full equality for American blacks. Roebuck's daring and forceful conception of a new role for gospel came to be known musically as "soul-folk."

Roebuck's definition of gospel—"the truth and nothing else but!"—was amplified by Purvis: "We're trying to carry a freedom message. The white man hasn't had the black experience and now we're trying to give it to him."

Roebuck's forging of "soul-folk," with its accommodations of pop and rock forms (a practice that would be followed by most gospel groups), lost the Staples some of their support in the more conservative elements of the black church, but the group has continued to receive broad—black and white—acclaim. Roebuck's material has reflected changing social conditions and attitudes, notably in his arresting song, "I Like the Things About Me (That I Once Despised)."

"It pleased God to put a guitar in my hands and a song on the lips of my children," Roebuck said, "and we aim to please God through our music." A man of talent and will, "Pop" Staples has done his utmost to see that God's work is done on earth—and done right.

Kay Starr

"The ad agency in New York wanted a bigger name."

The country music craze of the 1970s amuses Katheryn (sic) La Verne Starks. When she began singing, that kind of music was a novelty north of the Mason-Dixon Line, and Kay wanted to be more than just a novelty. And so she decountrified her style, changed her name to Kay Starr, and became one of the biggest recording stars of the 1940s and '50s.

She had started belting out songs in her oversized voice as a nine-year-old, winning amateur contests in hometown Dallas. "They liked me on station WRR," she says, "and they gave me a fifteen-minute program—but no pay. All I had to show for those solo programs was a bundle of fan mail."

By the time she was fifteen, her family had moved to Memphis, where the famed jazz violinist Joe Venuti, then leading a dance orchestra, heard her and hired her for a summer tour. When Venuti's old pal Glenn Miller needed a one-week replacement for a hospitalized Marion Hutton, the young and very scared singer got the job. She cut two records with the orchestra, "Baby Me"

Kay

and "Love with a Capital 'You,'" which some critics insist contain the best singing on any Miller record.

When Marion returned the next week, "Mom and I packed our bags and got back home to Memphis with just three cents to our name," Kay still recalls. She returned to Tech High, graduated, then sang for almost two years with Charlie Barnet's band, with whom she recorded two memorable V-Discs for the armed forces, "Sharecroppin' Blues" and "Nobody Knows the Trouble I've Seen," as well as several commercial sides.

She worked next for Bob Crosby. As his vocalist, she was approached by Camel cigarettes to star in a weekly radio show, but at the last minute the deal fell through. "The ad agency in New York wanted a bigger name," she says, "and there I was again." Her "inside" (business) reputation was solid by then, however, and she recorded some good sellers for Capitol.

A throat infection stilled her voice for a year, but the plucky singer studied new arrangements and trends so thoroughly that when she began recording again (in a throatier, huskier voice), the public "discovered" her at long last. Each of her Capitol releases seemed to be a bigger hit than the last one. They included "I'm the Lonesomest Gal in Town," "Angry," "Side by Side," "Bonaparte's Retreat," "Changing Partners," "Someday Sweetheart" and her golden "Wheel of Fortune."

Her phenomenal energy still undimmed, Kay appeared during the 1970s in Vegas, Tahoe, and on talk shoes, and recorded two country/western albums on Crescendo—*Kay Starr Country* and *Back to the Roots.* Her ability to enjoy life to the hilt may reflect her American Indian and Irish heritage; or it may simply be, as she puts it, "I love to sing—especially songs that have to do with real life. A good singer tells a story to music." Kay's still telling her stories.

(1922–   )

Barbra Streisand

"I was afraid that if I learned to type I'd become a secretary."

As a youngster in the Williamsburg section of Brooklyn, Barbra Streisand announced that she would become a famous actress. By age twenty she had starred in a major Broadway hit. Within another decade, true to prediction, she was at the top, an actress-singer-comedienne of spectacular talent and a superstar of awesome wealth and power.

She had also alienated hosts of admirers along the way with a mercurial temperament and the same vaulting ego that had enabled her to scale such heights.

Barbra

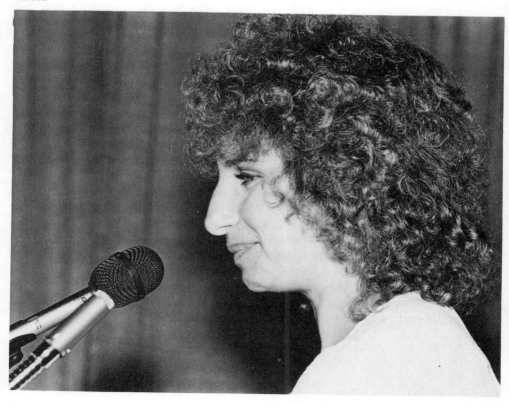

From the start, first singing around Greenwich Village clubs, then playing Miss Marmelstein, wallflower secretary of her first Broadway hit, *I Can Get It for You Wholesale,* Streisand seemed to break all the established show business success rules.

She was not beautiful. In fact, as columnist Norton Mockridge put it, "She's ungainly, she has scrawny legs, angular arms, a flat façade, and a face that sometimes looks as though it came right out of *Mad* magazine." But he hailed her "great, soaring, spectacular voice . . ."

There was to her a flavor, a tone, which *Newsweek*'s Joseph Morgenstern admiringly termed "pure oddball." It allowed her to sing an old chestnut like "Happy Days Are Here Again" as a lover's dirge, leaving nary a dry eye in sight. And oddball or not, it sold millions of albums.

Barbara Joan Streisand—the second "a" was dropped later—grew up in circumstances hardly suggesting such singularity. One of three children, she was raised by her mother. "We weren't *poor* poor," she has said, "but we didn't have anything." She refused her mother's entreaties to study typing and stenography: "At sixteen I knew I would be famous. I knew I had talent and I was afraid that if I learned to type I'd become a secretary."

The young singer worked at several New York clubs, winding up at the Blue Angel, famed incubator for promising talent. There Broadway producer David Merrick saw her and signed her to play Miss Marmelstein, a role that could almost have been drawn from her high school days as a self-confessed ugly duckling.

Film critic Molly Haskell saw that role as a key to the Streisand mystique, hailing her "way—perhaps a genius—for exploiting the public's knowledge of her real-life background to help rationalize her screen persona . . . able to symbolize ugliness without making audiences want to avert their eyes."

Her film debut came in *Funny Girl,* in which she had also starred on Broadway. Whatever its merits, and those of the others which followed—*Funny Lady, Hello, Dolly!* in which she sang an engaging duet with Louis Armstrong, *The Way We Were,* or the hugely publicized but critically disastrous *A Star Is Born*— Streisand's personality and voice have remained distinctive, if controversial.

The voice, when kept under control and given material appropriate to its textures, can be warm and caressing. Despite lapses into stridency and overdramatization, Streisand at her best seems able to inhibit and personalize a song in a highly distinctive and poignant way. And her apparent self-confidence appears limitless. In 1976 she invaded the classical music world when she recorded an album of Lieder and classical art songs. The critics sneered. One outraged writer decried the record as "scandalous." It sold in the millions.

For all the criticism, all the charges of artificiality in the singing, all the gossip and her reported contempt for press and fans alike, Barbra Streisand continued to dominant box offices, record sales, and just about all the rest of show business.

Whither Barbra from there? Perhaps in the end only her audiences will decide, as an earlier Streisand said they would. "The audience is the best judge of anything," she told *Newsweek*'s Morgenstern in 1970. "They cannot be lied to . . . the slightest tinge of falseness, they go back from you, they retreat . . . individually they may be a bunch of asses but together as a whole they are . . . the wisest thing."

(1942–   )

Art Tatum

> **"The more I hear him, the more I want to give up the piano altogether and drive a milk truck."**

His ability to play the piano so outdistanced that of his contemporaries in the jazz field—and astonished concert pianists Leopold Godowsky and Vladimir Horowitz as well—that it defied categorization. And description. According to jazz historian Leonard Feather, Mary Lou Williams once tried to explain with: "Art Tatum does everything the other pianists try to do—and can't." Another fine pianist, Eddie Heywood, said, "The more I hear him, the more I want to give up the piano altogether and drive a milk truck." Even Slam Stewart, a close associate and the original bassist in the Art Tatum Trio, still found it hard, some thirty years later, to convey in words the true measure of this brilliant, visually handicapped pianist. "Playing with Art Tatum was one of the most beautiful experiences in music I ever had. He was a wonderful man. One of a kind," Stewart has said. "We played mainly on Fifty-second Street in New York at the Three Deuces. All our numbers were 'head' things, we never used written music. Art had no sight at all in one eye, and just a little vision in the other. Art was an excellent pinochle player. He would hold the cards up close to his good eye and that way he could make them out." Pinochle, along with other elements of his life-style, such as his fondness for

Art

beer and food, and a tendency to be heavy, presented an image that contrasted sharply with his gossamer touch and grace of style as a pianist.

A native of Toledo, Ohio, Tatum began music study on the violin at age thirteen, then switched to piano as his career instrument. Would he play jazz or classical music? Tugged in both directions, he solved the dilemma by combining both. Within the limits of the jazz vehicles then available, such as thirty-two-bar pop tunes, and ten-inch 78-rpm discs, he succeeded remarkably. He debuted on a Toledo radio station and in local clubs. Jazz clubs were to be throughout his life the main public forum for his talent. He was playing music that should have been performed on concert stages, but the time was the 1930s and '40s, and Art Tatum was black and played jazz, however classically tinged and exquisite.

After coming to New York in 1932 as accompanist for singer Adelaide Hall and recording with her, Tatum began creating, at the Onyx Club, his lifelong reputation for incredible pianistic feats. They are well documented on his many recordings, with his trio, other groups, and as a solo pianist. Preeminently a soloist, he used the keyboard as an orchestra, as witness, for example, his spectacular orchestral development of "Tiger Rag." He also obviously enjoyed investing such nineteenth-century romantic salon pieces as Massenet's "Elegie" and Dvorak's "Humoresque" with rich overlays of rhythmic and harmonic embroidery; and, with classical devices, transforming pop tunes into salon pieces. A joyous performer, he deluged his improvisations with runs and embellishments, and engaged in often breathtaking thrust and parry of melodic, harmonic, and rhythmic ideas. But he always swung, lightheartedly and irresistibly.

His playing opened a whole new world and breed of jazz pianists, who idolized and imitated their common idol, enthralled not only with his inventiveness and technique, but also with his amazingly light touch. But few, perhaps none, ever expect to match the special genius and the sweetness of soul that poured through his fleet and precocious fingers that were stilled only after a losing battle with uremia. As Slam said, "He was one of a kind. We miss him."

(1910–1956)

James Taylor

"This all started with me singing lullabies to soothe myself."

At the age of twenty-two he was *Time* magazine's cover story. Chosen as the foremost exponent of a softer, more introspective and intimate music after the psychedelic excesses of the late 1960s, James Taylor hit big with his second album *Sweet Baby James,* which sold over three million copies. Albums like *Mud Slide Slim, Walking Man,* and *Gorilla* have insured Taylor's place as one of America's foremost singer/songwriters.

Although the tall, handsome, retiring Taylor himself has always shied away from interviews, he reveals himself in songs that temper emotional intensity with sharp wit. He explained recently: "There's no sense in holding anything back. I can only write about myself anyway. It's the personal gratification of songwriting that makes it all worthwhile: navigation through life by self-expression. I mean this all started with me singing lullabies to soothe myself."

The second oldest of five children, James grew up in North Carolina, where his doctor father was dean of medicine at the University of North Carolina. Summers were spent on Martha's Vineyard, where at age fifteen James and guitarist Danny ("Kootch") Kortchmar won a local hootenanny contest.

After finishing high school, the eighteen-year-old headed for New York with "Kootch" to form a band called the Flying Machine. One year and countless career frustrations later, Taylor flew to London where a self-made demo tape wound up in the hands of Peter Asher, the former half of Peter and Gordon and then head of A&R for the Beatles' Apple Records. Impressed by the demo, Asher asked Paul McCartney to listen and McCartney approved Apple's signing the young American.

That first album, *James Taylor,* hardly broke any sales records, but a year later back in the States and signed to Warner Brothers, James recorded *Sweet Baby James.* "Fire and Rain" from that álbum hit the top of the charts and helped make James a household name. Writing at that time, critic Danny Goldberg perceived: "He brings to his audiences the finest gift that any artist can give—the reassurance that they're not alone in their fantasies, their sadness, and their soul. By being very honest—faithful to himself—he expressed universal feelings through a crystal voice of ages."

The early media-created image of Taylor emphasized his darker, conflicted side. His adolescence had been troubled and he, like a number of other of his contemporaries, had a drug problem. But even in those early albums, his sense

James

of humor and earthiness came through. On the same album as "Fire and Rain," which poignantly presents his feelings on the death of a friend, there is a song called "Steamroller." This hard-driving blues shows how Taylor's debt to rhythm and blues is as strong as to folk, and its lyrics are as funny and raunchy as any blues sung by Bessie Smith.

On November 3, 1972, Taylor announced to his delighted audience at the Radio City Music Hall concert that a few hours earlier he and Carly Simon had wed. Though they have no intention of combining careers, they have been appearing now and then as backup singers on each other's recordings. One of James's most recent efforts, "Handy Man," won him a Grammy in 1978.

Now the parents of two children, the Taylors divide their time between the house they built (James did much of the carpentry himself) on Martha's Vineyard and wherever their careers take them.

A devoted husband and father, James's face lights up when he says things like, "I love being with my family. I want to spend quite a bit of time with them and the rest working on perfecting my recording technique."

(1948–   )

Jack Teagarden

"Sort of the Yogi Berra of jazz."

"He has everything a good jazz musician needs to have: a beautiful sound, a wonderful melodic sense, a deep feeling, a swinging beat, and the ability to make everything, even the most difficult things, sound relaxed and easy."

Saxophonist Gerry Mulligan, who himself comes close to having all those attributes, was talking about one of the most admired and respected of all jazz musicians, Jack Teagarden, the trombonist whom, Mulligan said at the time, he "hoped to have the honor of recording with someday." Unfortunately that "someday" never arrived, for soon thereafter Teagarden was found dead in a hotel room in New Orleans, the city in which, during the early 1920s, a young Teagarden had first attracted attention as an early and stellar example of that city's "bluesy" style of jazz.

He hadn't always played trombone, because when he was five years old and already interested in music, his arms weren't long enough to negotiate the length of the instrument's slide. So he took up the baritone horn. But a few years and many inches later he was blowing his "trambone," as he liked to call it, and at fifteen he was appearing professionally with Terry Shand's band, and right after that with the legendary Peck Kelley in Houston, not too far from his hometown of Vernon, Texas. Later he played with the famed New Orleans Rhythm Kings before migrating in 1927 to New York where his lazy, super-relaxed, bluesy playing captivated musicians.

At an early morning jam session, Gil Rodin, the playing-manager of Ben Pollack's great band, was so knocked out by Teagarden that he woke Pollack out of a sleep to come hear him. "We just had to have him," Rodin remarked years later. It meant dismissing the regular trombonist, but Glenn Miller never questioned the wisdom of hiring his replacement, for like almost every trombone player who has ever lived he was completely captivated by Teagarden's style and technique. (On a Metronome 1941 All-Star recording date, Tommy Dorsey refused to play a jazz solo, "not when you've got Jack in the same studio!" he declared.)

During his five years (1928–33) with Pollack, Teagarden recorded with numerous groups, including Red Nichols and His Five Pennies and a Benny Goodman-led outfit called the Charleston Chasers with which Jack sang and played trombone on the most memorable of all his sides, "Basin Street Blues." From 1933 to 1938 he was featured in Paul Whiteman's band and then in 1939, with the big band boom well underway, he formed his own large orchestra. Featuring Jack's singing and playing, it was very impressive; commercially, though, it

Jack

never amounted to much, in part because the shy, not very communicative Teagarden never related very well with his audiences. But his relaxed charm and personal integrity, so typical of his music, endeared him to all who were privileged to have known him. And his closest friends all agreed with Red Nichols' description of Jack: "Warm and comfortable like an old shoe."

But old shoes have never been very salable and so after a couple of years Jack reduced his outfit to a small jazz band with which he seemed to feel more at ease. From 1947 to 1951 he played with Louis Armstrong, two giants who admired and respected one another and who produced some of the greatest jazz of all time together. But Jack tired of Armstrong's constant touring, and for the remaining years of his life he seemed resigned to fronting various small groups, none of them outstanding or worthy of one of the greatest talents that jazz has ever produced.

During the late 1970s, Benny Goodman was reminiscing fondly about his old friend: "Jack was so great! He was a real peasant-type player—sort of the Yogi Berra of jazz—down-to-earth and warm and wonderful—not especially intellectual or thinking, but just full of such natural talent!"

(1905–1964)

"We're adaptable, we dress sharply, and we work hard."

There are plenty of groups in the music business that wish they could earn just what the Temptations have been spending on their wardrobe each year. With their suits averaging five hundred dollars apiece (and that does *not* include a second pair of pants), the annual cost of their sartorial splendor exceeds twenty-five thousand!

And there must be plenty of groups on the scene whose total recorded output will never equal the number of Gold Records the Temptations can boast: over two dozen. Yet, founder Otis Williams is disarmingly level-headed, down-to-earth and, yes, even modest.

"You know, we've been together so many years, and I've seem so many comings and goings, it has made me more dedicated to my profession. As a matter of fact, I find myself speaking to new or up-and-coming groups, and it's frustrating to see them make mistakes we made years ago and not be able to help them. I guess they have to learn for themselves—especially how to take direction."

The fact that the Temptations have endured and prospered since 1960 is eloquent testimony to *their* ability to take direction. Not that they haven't had internal hassles. They've gone through so many changes that to name their original personnel would make an interesting pop music trivia question.

In the beginning there were Otis Williams, Paul Williams, Eddie Kendricks, Melvin Franklin, and David Ruffin. Another interesting bit of trivia is the fact that their original group name was the Primes. (And to carry that historical fact one step further, their sister group on the Motown label, the Primettes, evolved into the Supremes.)

There was so much traffic in and out of the group that today Mel Franklin is the only other Temptation—along with Otis Williams—who can claim original membership. Included among the replacements was star lead David Ruffin—a tremendous box-office draw—who decided to make it as a single.

Now that might have proved demoralizing for a lesser group. Not just the inconsistencies of personnel, but the constant rehearsals to break in new members, and the adjustments in arrangements to make sure that the old keys fit the new blends.

But the Temptations were made of sturdy stuff. Changes notwithstanding, any traditions they initiated were perpetuated intact. They have always been a highly disciplined organization whose vocal precision was eventually matched

The Temptations

by the same fastidiousness in choreography. And in addition, they were fortunate in having Berry Gordy—prime mover behind Motown Records—as their mentor. Gordy not only managed them for their first decade, but also produced and released a slew of their hit records on his Gordy label.

Their durability, of course, cannot be attributed to direction alone. Versatility in style and variety of material allowed them to cross over from their original rhythm and blues classification to more lucrative markets. As Williams put it, "There is no accurate pigeonhole for us—just call our sound *music.*"

Billboard, the bible of the record industry, has listed dozens of their recordings, including their Grammy-winning "Cloud Nine" and "Papa Was a Rolling Stone," among the top ten on pop, as well as rhythm and blues charts. But one can also hear their recordings on middle-of-the-road or easy-listening radio stations in addition to those outlets specializing in rhythm and blues, soul, gospel, and rock.

"That's the secret of our success, I guess. We're adaptable, we dress sharply, and we work hard at putting on a complete show." Originally they modeled themselves after a number of rhythm and blues vocal combos: the Flamingos, the Five Keys, the Cadillacs, the Moonglows. But in 1967 they added the extra dimension of dancing. "Now we carry a full-time choreographer plus a five-piece band, and we have charts for up to fourteen pieces. We're prepared for anything."

That's for sure. As one reviewer noted, "If two-a-day vaudeville comes back, the Temptations are a good bet to top the bill at the Palace."

Sister Rosetta Tharpe

An unforgivable sin: She took her gospel songs into nightclubs.

"I've been robbed, cheated, married three times," said Sister Rosetta Tharpe, "but God is so good! Oh, yes!"

Yet despite this declaration for God, despite the fact that both her parents were active preachers in the Pentecostal Church and her mother, Katie Bell Nubin, lived for singing and Jesus, Sister Rosetta committed an unforgivable sin: She took her gospel songs into nightclubs and sang them with jazz bands.

Because of this, she was one of the first gospel singers to reach a wide audience outside the black churches. But she was also widely criticized by churchgoers and other gospel singers who refused to mix religious singing with such worldly surroundings.

Sister Tharpe's problem was that she achieved success—and, in churchly eyes, notoriety—as a show business personality. By the time she was six, she had been playing guitar and singing with her mother at Holiness conventions in and around her native Arkansas. As she grew older, she developed a high, sweet voice along with guitar and singing styles that were colored by the blues, swinging like a jazz band, all projected with lively, boisterous showmanship.

In 1938 she made her first records, which included "Rock Me" and one of her greatest successes, "This Train." With just her guitar as accompaniment, these records became the biggest gospel hits of the 1930s. Soon she was singing with big bands, with Cab Calloway and Lucky Millinder. She became a headliner at such famous nightclubs as the Cotton Club in Harlem and Cafe Society in Greenwich Village.

"She was a true Holy Roller," recalled Barney Josephson, the owner of Cafe Society. "Her fervor was so true, so real. It was no put-on. And she played a hell of a guitar. The way she stroked her guitar, she put an awful lot of sex in it."

Her popularity continued through World War II when she and the Golden Gate Quartet were the only black religious singers on V-Discs. She made a series of records with Sammy Price, the boogie-woogie pianist, one of which, "Strange Things Happening Every Day," hit the top ten. When she married Russell Morrison, former manager of the Ink Spots, in 1951, twenty-five thousand guests paid to attend the outdoor gospel wedding.

For several years after the war, Sister Tharpe was teamed with Marie Knight, a contralto whose rich voice provided a counterpoint to Sister Tharpe's more piercing, energetic sound. But when Madame Marie decided to concentrate on the blues, the team broke up. Sister Tharpe did not want to sing the blues. Instead, she toured through rural churches and Catskill resorts, shedding much of her earlier show business aura and turning to evangelism and nostalgia.

While she was touring Europe in 1970, she suffered a stroke which, on her return home to Philadelphia, resulted in the amputation of one leg. Within two years she was performing again, walking on crutches. But she became haunted by a fear of dying. Her mother, who had died in 1969, was constantly on her mind.

She had not recorded since her mother's death, but a recording session was arranged for her in October 1973. She planned to re-record some of the songs she had done at her earliest sessions thirty-five years before. But she never made the records. The day of the session, she suffered another stroke and died the next morning.

"Pray for me, children," she had been singing at her last concerts. "I don't want to die."

(c. 1916–1973)

Sister Rosetta

Claude Thornhill

"I wonder if the world will ever know how much it had in this beautiful man."
—Duke Ellington.

There wasn't a dreamier, more musical band in the world to dance to than Claude Thornhill's. Its rich, mellow, dramatic sonorities that featured as many as seven unison clarinets set against French horns, interspersed with bits of Claude's delicate piano tinklings, and then climaxed by brilliant, goose-bump-raising singing brasses, made it very easy for a guy to fall in love with any girl who might happen to be in his arms that night, and vice versa.

Yet Thornhill's was more than a romanticist's dream band. It was also a jazz musician's dream band that played equally unusual and imaginative arrangements, interspersed with fine jazz soloists, that were written by young Gil Evans and Gerry Mulligan and by Claude himself.

So much emphasis on unique, not always familiar musical sounds made it more difficult for Thornhill to match the successes of his good friends and admirers like the Dorseys, Glenn Miller, Benny Goodman, and Artie Shaw with whom Claude had worked regularly as pianist and arranger during the early 1930s in New York's radio and recording studios. Though just as serious about his music as they were, the cherubic, relaxed, and thoroughly lovable Thornhill was less of a conformer and more of a flake than any of them. Which one of them, for example, would have dared to register his displeasure the way Claude did in 1935 when he was a member of Ray Noble's in New York's

Claude

swank Rainbow Room and the musicians, about ready to go home, were summoned back from their dressing room to play more music for a "preferred" customer? Waiting until the rest of the band was well into its first number, Claude meandered nonchalantly back onto his piano stool, impeccably garbed like the rest of the band, with one exception: he was wearing no trousers.

Claude's nonconforming ways may have been a continuing revolt against a dominating mother who, back home in Terre Haute, Indiana, had kept insisting that her four-year-old son master the piano. By twelve he had become good enough to lead his own dance band, and at fifteen he was receiving rave notices for his innovative accompaniments of silent movies at the local theater. For the next few years he played in dance bands before settling down in New York's studios. His first national recognition came in 1937 when he arranged, conducted, and played piano for Maxine Sullivan, a young singer he had discovered, on her big hit recording of a swinging version of "Loch Lomond."

After a two-year stint as musical director of "The Bob Hope Show" on radio, Claude formed his own band. At first its career seemed haunted. The night before its major debut at a swank club, the place burned down. Some months later the men arrived for the third night of a lengthy engagement to find the club padlocked; the owner had absconded with all the money. But with financial and moral support from his good friend Glenn Miller, Claude persevered, and his early 1941 debut at Glen Island Casino drew raves. So did recordings like "Where or When," "Autumn Nocturne," and Claude's original, haunting theme song, "Snowfall."

His blossoming career nipped by a three-year hitch in the Navy, during which he was cited several times for bravery while leading a fine service band in the Pacific theater, resumed when he reorganized in 1946 with twelve of his sixteen former musicians and arrangers welcoming the chance to rejoin, so esteemed was he both as a leader and as a person. The band was magnificent, mixing those gorgeous ballads (its recording of "A Sunday Kind of Love" was a big hit) with big band versions of progressive jazz. Thelonious Monk acclaimed it as "the only really good band I've heard in years."

But by the early 1950s, big bands began to fade and Claude, beset also by personal problems, slid into semi-obscurity, appearing mostly in the hinterlands with smaller units that sometimes sounded good but more often were like watered-down distortions. Then in the mid-1960s, Claude returned to the New York area. No longer drinking, living a healthy country life with his third wife, he was making plans for a comeback, beginning with an engagement at Atlantic City's famed Steel Pier, when he was felled by two massive heart attacks. His loss as a musical creator and lovable human being was eloquently expressed by a mourning Duke Ellington with "I wonder if the world will ever know how much it had in this beautiful man." Like the great Duke himself, only time will tell.

(1909–1965)

"Music began to be sung and played not for posterity, but for prosperity."

The cute little four-year-old boy in the sailor suit sang "You're Driving Me Crazy" with the Coon-Sanders band in Chicago's Blackhawk Restaurant and everybody cheered. "Then," recalls Mel Torme, "Carlton Coon put me on his knee while he played drums, and every Monday night I was featured with the band."

A year later at the age of five he had moved on up to the College Inn of the Hotel Sherman singing with the bands of Louis Panico, Frankie Masters, and Buddy Rogers, and at the age of eight he was playing drums in his school's drum and bugle corps.

Mel Torme was a precocious kid all right, but eventually he turned out to be much more than that. In addition to becoming one of the most musical and most admired of all pop singers, and a first-rate drummer, he learned to play the piano, to arrange, to lead a vocal group called the Meltones, to compose such hit songs as "Born to Be Blue," "A Stranger in Town," and "The Christmas Song," to act (he was nominated for an Emmy), to produce TV shows, and even to author several books plus articles for leading publications.

Among all those talents he became best known for his singing. He wasn't blessed with a great voice box but he compensated by phrasing magnificently and always singing in exquisite taste. Himself a "wise guy" during his early days, he was offended by nicknames created by other "wise guys," like "The Velvet Fog," "Mr. Butterscotch," and "The Kid with the Gauze in His Jaws."

But he was still just plain Mel Torme when he started what he called "my first serious singing job with the Chico Marx band. I had a vocal group there called 'The Revellis,' named after the character Chico portrayed in the Marx Brothers' movies." While the band was playing at the Roxy Theater in New York, he impressed an RKO talent scout. "He took me up to the roof of the theater and gave me a screen test right there." By August 1943, Mel was in Hollywood, playing the juvenile lead in *Higher and Higher*. He was more interested, though, in singing, so in 1945 he formed the Meltones, which provided backgrounds for some Bing Crosby records, made a few records of their own, notably "Born to Be Blue" and "It Happened in Monterey," and finally gained national recognition for their spirited singing on Artie Shaw's recording of "What Is This Thing Called Love?"

However, it took two other name bandleaders to recognize Torme's talents as a soloist. "Les Brown and Woody Herman kept telling Carlos Gastel (one

Mel Torme and the Meltones, circa 1948

of Hollywood's top personal managers) that they felt I could make it as a soloist. Carlos listened and got me a recording contract." One of Torme's first sides, "You're Driving Me Crazy," became one of his big hits. But the biggest turned out to be "Blue Moon," which he sang in *Words and Music,* the biographical movie about composers Richard Rodgers and Lorenz Hart.

Good quality songs have always attracted Torme, who always wanted to be "a jazz-oriented singer." But by the time he arrived on the recording scene, jazz was on the way out, and, as he puts it, "the music business had become purely the business. Music began to be sung and played not for posterity, but for prosperity." Mel's efforts were lauded by musicians, but ignored by the general public. "Finally I realized that fighting the anti-intellectuals in the business was, to quote Bob Dylan, like 'blowin' in the wind.' "

Still Mel hung in there, refusing to compromise. He worked regularly in top clubs, performed in concerts all over the world and on occasional TV shows, always to critical acclaim. As his voice kept maturing, he kept singing better and better. In 1976 he and Ella Fitzgerald caused such a sensation with their ad-lib scat singing on the Grammy awards TV special that he received five offers from recording companies. Even his "anti-intellectuals" began to recognize that music as good and tasteful and creative as Torme's might be truly commercial after all.

(1925–   )

Sophie Tucker

She looked up at the Royal Box and yelled, "Hi, ya, King."

She came on stage like hellzapoppin', a 192-pound diamond-spangled bombshell, drenched in satins, jewels, beads, feathers, and furs, waved her chiffon handkerchief and roared into "Some of these days . . ." And audiences ranging from tired businessmen to monarchs roared back their approval. It went on like that for close to sixty years in theater after cabaret after nightclub, coast to coast, continent to continent. Faces of teenagers in her audience at Chicago's Circle Theater in the 1920s were red when she sang Irving Berlin's "All Alone"—they thought it was suggestive. Faces in later years just smiled and yelled for more when she sang her double entendre songs like "There's No Business Like That Certain Business," or "I May Be Getting Older Every Day (But Getting Younger Every Night)."

Everything about Sophie Tucker was big: her voice, her figure, her heart, her income. In the millionaire entertainer class, she gave away much of her fortune to charity. Her bigheartedness—and informality—keyed her performing. At her first Command Performance in London in the 1930s, she looked up at the Royal Box and yelled, "Hi, ya, King." At another in later years, she looked up at the Royal Box and, overwhelmed with emotion, burst out crying. Sophie never held back one atom of herself, on stage or off. She answered every fan letter and telegram personally and kept in touch with a list of seven thousand friends. She kept track of her own fame more avidly than any press agent and in 1955 delivered eight hundred scrapbooks of her clippings, notices, and memorabilia to the New York Public Library. She sold her records and her book, *Some of These Days,* after her performances and gave the proceeds to charity.

She began her career as Sophie Abuza (in fleeing Russia her father, Charles Kalish, had obtained the passport of an Italian) serving twenty-five-cent gefilte fish dinners to customers at the Abuza family hotel in Hartford, Connecticut, and doubling as singer. After an impecunious and short-lived teenage marriage to Louis Tuck, she added "er" to the name and took off for New York. She sang "coon songs" in blackface on small vaudeville circuits, stopped the Ziegfeld Follies of 1909 show, and was on her way, successively and successfully from "World-renowned Coon Shouter," "The Mary Garden of Ragtime," "Queen of Jazz" to "The Last of the Red Hot Mommas." She gave her last performance in 1965 at New York's Latin Quarter.

The Last of the Red
Hot Mamas

Sophie preferred nightclubs to revues, live audiences to radio and TV. Her type of material kept her pretty much off radio, though she appeared on some TV specials and on "the Ed Sullivan Show."

Her two marriages, after the luckless teen venture, ended in divorce, but the last sixteen years of her life she lived in a Chippendale-furnished Park Avenue apartment, surrounded by the only small things in her life: a collection of three thousand minatures. Always seeking new material, new gowns, new settings for her act, she had planned, during the mid-1960s, to blast into space as "The Gold Momma," a new image of the old Red Hot Momma, and no doubt still singing "Some of these days . . ." But, unfortunately, increasing ill health pursued her, and early in 1966, *some* of these days of Sophie Tucker's life and career had become *none* of these days.

(1887–1966)

Ike and Tina Turner

"I used to ask him to let me sing. He'd say okay but never call me to the stage."

He was the leader of a rhythm and blues combo playing small, tough clubs on the black "southern circuit." She was Annie Mae Bullock, living in St. Louis and hoping to become a professional singer. They met and married. Their professional and personal relationship seemed to be something like that between the fictional Svengali, the ominous Hungarian vocal coach and hypnotist, and his prize pupil, Trilby, whom he transformed into an international singing sensation.

Lean and cold-eyed Ike Turner was a hardworking keyboardist, songwriter, arranger, singer, and producer. Born in Clarksdale, Mississippi, he was attracted to the piano in "a church lady's house" where he was allowed to play in exchange for chopping her firewood. "At that time I didn't really know what a piano was. All I knew was that when I pushed down on the keys it made a sound I liked." When he came home one day with a high-marks report card from school his parents presented him with his own piano.

In the mid-1950s Ike and his combo, the Kings of Rhythm, had a hit with a Turner original, "Rocket 88," for which, he later said, he never received more than forty dollars. He took the combo on the road, sharing dates with blues champions like B. B. King and Howlin' Wolf.

Annie Mae Bullock was a patron in a St. Louis club where Ike's band was playing. "I used to ask him to let me sing. He'd say okay but never call me to the stage. One night . . . I took the microphone and started to sing. Ike was shocked! I did several numbers with them that night and later I joined the group."

Married shortly thereafter, the Turners, under Ike's direction, expanded the Kings of Rhythm into the Ike and Tina Turner Revue, complete with a horn and reed section and the Ikettes, a trio of girl dancers and backup singers. Tina was a blazingly attractive woman with a voice somewhere between a whiskey rasp and a baby's cry, and with Ike's coaching, her erotic posings and antics on stage made the Revue a hot act on the black touring circuit.

Through the 1950s and into the early 1960s the Turners made hit records that were largely confined to the rhythm and blues market: "A Fool in Love" and "I Think It's Gonna Work Out Fine." Then, in 1965, Phil Spector, the white whiz kid pop producer, applied his grandiose "wall of sound" theory to a Turner single, "River Deep, Mountain High," which stands as perhaps the

Ike and Tina

finest of Tina's vocal performances. Though not a hit in the United States, it was hailed in England, for, like many black groups, the Turners were more appreciated abroad than at home. When Spector returned to the United States for a new record production contract, he insisted that "River Deep, Mountain High" be reissued. Around the same time the Rolling Stones, also Turner fans, chose them for their opening act on an American tour, and they were exposed, for the first time, to a new, mass, white audience.

In 1971 the Turners were signed to a major American label and had several hits, "Honky Tonk Woman," "Nutbush City Limits," "Come Together," and "Proud Mary," as well as making major concert tours of the United States and Europe.

By 1974, Ike and Tina were issuing solo albums. Hers were flamboyant, brilliant, and thrilling. His were introspective, intriguing, and low-key. Ike opened the Bolic Sound Studios and concentrated on producing while Tina, in 1975, appeared in the film version of *Tommy,* the rock opera by The Who, in which she played the Acid Queen.

Strains in their marriage and the demands of their individual careers culminated in a 1976 announcement that they would go their separate ways. Svengali was probing the sources of his hypnotic power, while Trilby had found that her stardom was not induced, but natural.

(Ike: 1933–   )
(Tina: 1938–   )

Joe Turner

"We were doing that kind of music before they even *called* it rock and roll."

"Blues shouter" is the way this energetic, spontaneous purveyor of the blues is tagged. Not strumming a guitar like blues singers of the rural South, or beating an amplified guitar like urban blues and rock and roll singers, he just stands up at a mike and lines out the often earthy lyrics in an urgent, slightly dry voice, frequently flecked with humor.

The virile, handsome Joe Turner of the early singing years began shouting blues in clubs of his native Kansas City. The story is told by pianist Mary Lou Williams in Nat Shapiro and Nat Hentoff's *Hear Me Talkin' to Ya* that at the Sunset, a small jazz club where he tended bar, Joe Turner, inspired by the club's pianist Pete Johnson, often burst into the blues right in the middle of serving drinks. In the same work, Jo Jones, sometime drummer at the Sunset, remembered the indefatigable Turner singing there, then going to a club across the street to sing, and returning much later to resume singing at the Sunset.

Discovered by John Hammond in the late 1930s, Turner was brought to

Joe

New York along with other Kansas City musicians, including his piano-playing partner, Pete Johnson. They were featured in Hammond's "From Spirituals to Swing" concert at Carnegie Hall in 1938. Besides Johnson, there were two other boogie-woogie pianists on the program, Albert Ammons and Meade Lux Lewis. Shortly after, and for several years, the three boogie-woogie pianists and Turner headlined at Barney Josephson's popular New York night spots, Cafe Society Downtown and Cafe Society Uptown. They also performed their hearty and hypnotic blues in theaters across the United States. Turner also recorded extensively with such jazz greats as Benny Carter, Art Tatum, and Joe Sullivan. He composed most of his own songs (i.e., "Well Oh Well," "Corrine, Corrina," "Since I Was Your Man," and with Pete Johnson, "Piney Brown Blues," "Roll 'Em Pete," "Cherry Red."). In 1945 he won the Esquire Silver Award. But in the post-World War II years bop was in, Joe Turner's blues shouting, and boogie-woogie piano, out.

However, in the early 1950s, music known as rhythm and blues, from which white rock and roll took much of its inspiration, began to catch on, and Joe Turner was again on the rise. With his first big hit on Atlantic Records, "Chains of Love," he became a top-selling rhythm and blues artist. He told writer Frank Kofsky he recorded "Shake, Rattle and Roll," one of his big hits, ten weeks before rock and roll star Bill Haley and His Comets made it. "We were doing that kind of music," he said, "before they even *called* it rock and roll."

After appearing in the film *Shake, Rattle and Roll,* in 1956, Turner toured Europe, in 1958 and 1965. In the late 1960s he recorded a spate of great blues, many his own, for ABC BluesWay and Flying Dutchman BluesTime labels. Backed on these albums by contemporary-style groups made up of guitars, Fender bass, tenor sax and harmonica, piano, and drums, Joe's singing came on just as full of conviction, urgency, and hear-me-talkin' as when it was egged on by the relentless eight-to-the-bar boogie-woogie pianos. One reason for Turner's never-say-die ability to ride the crests of recurring blues waves is indicated in Jo Jones's story. It is also indicated by an incident told by Barry Ulanov in his book *Duke Ellington.* Turner was featured in Ellington's revue, *Jump for Joy.* After his fifteen minutes on stage shouting the blues—and dressed, of all things, like a cop—Turner would go to a neighboring bar and sing duets with his own records on the jukebox.

(1911–   )

For the first time, soft, sexy singing was wafted out and beyond the first row.

The very first of the crooners, Hubert Prior (Rudy) Vallee, was always controversial. Women adored his soft, nasal, intimate style of singing; jealous men often ridiculed it. Those whom he treated kindly and compassionately loved him. Others—and they were generally in the majority—resented his impatience, intolerance, and often snobbish ways. Though an inveterate romanticist constantly chasing women (his third wife insisted "his whole life has been one of a pursuit of romance for romance itself"), he admittedly "never had the good fortune to look impressive or commanding." "But I have compensated!" he explained in *My Time Is Your Time,* the autobiography he wrote with Gil McKean. "In some sort of reverse reasoning I have accomplished a feeling of satisfaction— to have become a popular figure when my appearance, to many people at least, in no way indicated that I might be the personality that had won their approbation through a microphone."

Actually, such approbation first arrived not through a microphone but through a megaphone, when Rudy, trying to reach dancers in the rear of the ballroom on Maine's Old Orchard Pier one evening in 1925 decided to sing through the cut-down cheerleader's megaphone he had stuck into the bell of his baritone sax to project sound. For the first time, soft, sexy singing was wafted out and beyond the first row. The era of the crooners had been born and Rudy Vallee was its sire.

When he was only thirteen Rudy had sung professionally for the first time, receiving ten dollars for a public rendition of "The Sunshine of Your Smile." The son of a Westbrook, Maine, pharmacist, whose ancestors had migrated with General Lafayette to America, he broke away early from behind his dad's drug counter into the world of music. First he played drums in the town band; then he switched to sax and was hooked on the horn after hearing Rudy Wiedoft, the era's top virtuoso, whose first name he immediately adopted. His sax-playing and eventually his singing helped him through his early college days at the University of Maine, and then later on to a degree from Yale.

In 1928 he decided to try for the big time. He went to New York, played some dates for Ben Bernie and a week with Vincent Lopez for a cool fourteen dollars. When Bert Lown, who fronted various bands, needed a unit for a new club, the Heigh-Ho, he contacted Vallee who said he'd take the job only if he could be the leader. Lown agreed and on January 8, 1928, Vallee and some other Yalies began an immensely successful engagement at the club. Smarter,

"My time is your time . . ."

by his own admission, than most musicians, he immediately seized the opportunity to prove that he could do more than the average leader, spicing his performances with funny hats and dramatic presentations of war song medleys while gunpowder exploded at crucial stages. When the management decided to broadcast from the club, Rudy not only sang and led the band but also announced the programs, beginning with the soon-to-be-familiar "Heigh-ho, everybody. This is Rudy Vallee announcing and directing the Yale Collegians from the Heigh-Ho Club at Thirty-five East Fifty-third Street in New York City."

Those broadcasts boomed the club's business and Vallee's career. He made a series of hit records, beginning with "Deep Night," and going on to his theme song, "My Time Is Your Time," "I'm Just a Vagabond Lover," "Life Is Just a Bowl of Cherries," "Betty Co-Ed," and songs associated with his two colleges, "The Maine Stein Song" and Yale's "The Whiffenpoof Song."

The next year, on October 29, just two days after the collapse of the stock market, he began his immensely successful ten-year series of commercial broadcasts for Fleischmann's Yeast on which he featured, some for the first time on radio, stars like Jack Benny, Edgar Bergen, Milton Berle, Fanny Brice, Burns and Allen, Eddie Cantor, Bob Hope, Red Skelton, and Orson Welles. He also appeared in *George White's Scandals* and made his first movie, *The Vagabond Lover,* which he later admitted was "the prize turkey of the year . . . and is now shown only in penitentiaries and comfort stations." However, he did appear to advantage in comedic roles in later films like *The Palm Beach Story* and *Time Out for Rhythm*.

His quest for success and acclaim seemed insatiable. So that he could be heard by more people on his personal appearances, he conceived the idea of combining a microphone borrowed from NBC, a homemade amplifier, and the speakers from a couple of radios to create the first portable p.a. system. His invention pleased him not only because of what it accomplished for his performance, but also because it showed off his "practical mind, a quality I have always had, to the displeasure of those who would set me down as a purely artistic and impractical fellow."

His practical mind made him a mint of money. But his intense intolerance made him few friends. "I have the patience of a saint," he boasted in *My Time Is Your Time*, for which struggling, young, and infinitely less rich McKean received only one third of the royalties, "but cannot tolerate repeated stupidity or inattention." When guests visited his sumptuous lodge (the doorbell played the opening bars of "My Time Is Your Time"), they were presented with a seven-page rule-book outlining what was expected of them regarding cleanliness and neatness, with the sarcastic observation that "of course most people apparently aren't brought up any longer to be thoughtful and neat." He called his radio production associates "bird-brains, lightweights, and knuckleheads," and during his hitch as a bandmaster in the Coast Guard he railed, and perhaps quite justifiably, at the incompetence of many fellow officers.

After the war, with Sinatra and Como and other singers firmly entrenched, Rudy forsook crooning for comedy. But a nightclub routine and tour failed miserably, with an aggravated Vallee going so far as to pick fistfights with his audiences, whom he labeled "mean, vicious, cruel individuals whose natures, inflamed by alcohol, lead them to consider the entertainer out there on the floor, who is trying to earn a living, fair game for their sadistic torture."

Comparatively little was heard from Vallee during the 1950s, but in 1961 he scored a big hit as the prissy board chairman in the Broadway smash comedy *How to Succeed in Business Without Really Trying*, a role which he repeated just as successfully in the 1967 movie version. He achieved national attention in the 1970s when he attempted to run for mayor of Los Angeles and to have the name of his street changed to Rue de Vallee (some neighbors might have found Avenue N.E. Humility more appropriate!), and in 1976 returned to New York, the city of his first major triumph for a thoroughly untriumphant two-hour, one-man review of his career. In 1961, while discussing a possible retirement, Vallee had stated, "I don't feel I have to *prove* myself anymore." But at the age of seventy-five, he was still trying to do so. Unfortunately, almost nobody seemed to care.

(1901–   )

Sarah Vaughan

"I give her a song and she makes ten songs out of it."

To performing artists, the most valued praise comes from their professional peers. Sarah Vaughan has received unstinting kudos from the likes of Tony Bennett, Ella Fitzgerald, and Billy Eckstine. She was paid the ultimate tribute by that paradigm of singers, Frank Sinatra, when he said of her: "Sassy sings so good, I want to cut my wrist with a dull blade and let her sing me to death . . ." Michel Legrand has called her "the best jazz person I have ever met in my life. I gave her a song, and she makes ten songs out of it. She is like a fantastic jazz instrumental soloist."

At times, her fascination with jazz improvisation disappointed those who would prefer hearing her magnificent, full-bodied, sensuous voice "straight," without any tricks or trimmings—a voice "whose richness and range," *The New Yorker* writer Whitney Balliett has pointed out, "are exhilarating in themselves." Labeling her "a singer of phenomenal technique," he added that "she really doesn't need songs . . . She could simply sing, inventing as she goes along."

Sarah Vaughan certainly treasures those accolades, but she equally values the audiences who have given her their version of appreciation. She was perhaps most moved by a standing ovation she received after a show in the remote town of Maseru, the capital of the new state of Lesotho in Africa. Her audience had come a thousand miles in every conceivable kind of conveyance just to hear "The Divine Sarah" sing.

"As far as I'm concerned, an appreciative audience is the highest form of

Sassy

honor I can receive," says Miss Vaughan. "Nothing ever quite matches the feeling I get inside when an audience really shows me that they care for me. I sure care for them."

This mutual respect between audience and performer began in Newark, New Jersey, where Sarah Lois Vaughan was born. Both parents were musical. Sarah's mother sang in the choir at Mt. Zion Baptist Church. Her father sang for fun and played his guitar whenever he could, between working as a carpenter for a living. Sarah sang in the church choir with her mother, who hoped that after eight years of studying the piano, her daughter would become a concert artist, never dreaming that it would be her voice and not her fingers that one day would bring her to the stage of Carnegie Hall.

When she was only eighteen she entered an amateur contest on a dare. The prize was ten dollars and a week's engagement at the famed Apollo Theater in Harlem. Sarah sang "Body and Soul" and won hands down. Earl "Fatha" Hines remembers the event well: "She just came out there, cool as a cucumber, never moved a muscle, just sang." Billy Eckstine, Hines's lead singer at the time, convinced his boss to hire her. Later, Sarah credited Billy with being the most important musical influence in her life.

Ella Fitzgerald, the Apollo headliner that week, was also very impressed with the young singer. She took Sarah under her wing and showed her the tricky ropes of the music business. Her advice helped Sarah survive tough years on the road, during which she fought bad bookings and Jim Crow. When racists at a Chicago nightclub pelted her with fruit, she came close to quitting but "for some reason," she says, "I hung on."

From 1944 to 1945, Sarah sang and played piano with Eckstine's band, which included such horn men as Dizzy Gillespie, Charlie Parker, and Gene Ammons. These men may account for that "two-octave slide trombone of a voice" she has—a voice whose pitch and range reminded Leonard Feather of "a soprano, a contralto, and a coloratura; a singer with the spontaneity of Ella, the soul of Aretha, the warmth of Peggy, and the impeccable phrasing of Carmen."

When Eckstine broke up his band, Sarah, or "Sassy," as she was nicknamed, began her illustrious career as a solo performer, recording many memorable sides, including her famous versions of "Tenderly" and "Misty." During the late 1960s she had withdrawn somewhat from musical circulation, but by the mid-1970s she was back again in greater form than ever, captivating her admirers, who filled Carnegie Hall every time she was starred there as part of the Newport Jazz Festival and in 1979 during three SRO concerts there in nine days. She has never denied how much appreciative audiences mean to her. "It's their response that gets me going and keeps me going," she recently stated. And they feel exactly the same way about her.

(1924–   )

And now, miraculously, here was the originator.

There have been times through the years when Joe Venuti's antics as a clown and practical joker have all but obscured his fame as single-handed pioneer of the jazz violin and, to many, its greatest exponent.

But no wonder. Something irreverent in the Venuti makeup seems to delight in confounding attempts to pin him down, just as it loves deflating pomposity or demolishing a phony. Even the date of his birth, on a ship carrying his parents and their seven children to the United States sometime around the turn of the century, has remained a bit of a mystery—largely because Joe tells a different story to each person who asks.

He grew up in Philadelphia, began violin lessons as soon as he was large enough to hold the instrument, and, barely into his teens, met and became friends with a schoolmate who was to profoundly affect his life. Salvatore Massaro, too, had studied the violin, but his first love was the guitar. Later, as Eddie Lang, he was to team with Venuti in one of the most extraordinary instrumental duos jazz has produced.

From the start the two friends seemed able to anticipate each other's ideas

Joe

and moods. They heard harmonies the same way, shared a flair for tone color. Though their early careers took them separate ways, they were happiest when playing together.

Venuti's fame soon spread beyond Philadelphia. While working regularly with Jean Goldkette and then Roger Wolfe Kahn, he also became the busiest of the free-lancers, often in tandem with Lang. They recorded with Red Nichols and Miff Mole, Bix Beiderbecke and Frank Trumbauer, Adrian Rollini and the Dorsey brothers, producing an exquisitely crafted jazz chamber music.

As Venuti's fame grew, so did his reputation for prankery. Whether passing out peashooters to a band backing a scantily clad chorus line, dumping a piano out of an apartment window to "find out its natural key," or auditioning for an important job dressed as a gypsy, bandanna and all, Venuti was unmistakably and outrageously Venuti.

Toward the end of the 1920s the Venuti-Lang team joined Paul Whiteman's orchestra and appeared together in the film *King of Jazz*. He soon became a popular figure in radio and continued to make records, settling on the West Coast. But as music fashions changed there seemed ever less place for the violin in jazz; Venuti receded from view. As a leader of a big band during the early 1940s he was only semisuccessful. The great days seemed behind him.

Then, in the late 1960s, the unexpected happened. Touring here and abroad with a new quartet, Venuti spurred a new generation's interest. There had been other jazz violinists in the meantime—Stuff Smith, Stéphane Grappelly, and Ray Nance among them—and now, miraculously, here was the originator.

His playing recovered much of the old fire, and his appearances highlighted many jazz concerts and festivals. He recorded as a timeless peer with Ruby Braff, Marian McPartland, Zoot Sims, and many other latter-day jazz greats. In his seventies—or was it eighties?—Joe Venuti was finding himself once again a celebrity.

The zany jokes and roughhouse gags had been supplanted by a fatherly twinkle in the eye, but the ferocity, musicianship, and crackling technique had, if anything, intensified with age and time. Whitney Balliett, of *The New Yorker,* summed him up with awe as "a great, squat, square bustling haystack of a man with a trombone of a voice and a huge Roman head . . . his style is plunging but assured. He fashions frequent and enormous intervals, wild bent notes, and roaring double stops. His tone can be sweet and gypsy-like or rough and hurrying, and his sense of dynamics is a marvel . . . they don't make Venutis anymore." And then all of a sudden in September 1978 it happened. The seemingly forever lighthearted Venuti had told few people what he knew too well: He had cancer. He just kept on living his life to the fullest playing at concerts and in clubs all over the world—he even continued to smoke— until this bear of a man could no longer battle the only enemy he probably ever had.

(1898–1978)

"Fats" Waller

He made his whole life an agreeable joke.

The "harmful little armful" with the big innocent eyes and the cocked derby hat; the poet laureate of the tough and tender Harlem "stride" piano style who described himself as "Mrs. Waller's 285 pounds of jam, jive, and *everythin'* "; the gifted wit and angel-touched popular composer—Thomas Wright "Fats" Waller was all of these.

Born in New York in 1904, he early acquired his "Fats" nickname by his voracious appetite. "Naw, *naw,* sir," he told an interviewer years later, "I never ran away from home. There was too much good food on that table."

At the age of ten he was playing the family harmonium (a wheezy, nasal reed organ) and dodging his devoutly religious parents' complaints that he was

"Every honey bee fills with jealousy . . ."

sneaking ragtime and jazz phrasing into his rendering of hymns. Shortly after, his brother bought him an upright piano that became Tom's treasure.

When his mother died in 1920—the great sorrow of Waller's life—he turned to music full-time. The "stride" piano style, featuring a boisterous left hand keeping and teasing the rhythm while the right hand traced rainbows, was at its height. Stride's two most formidable practitioners, James P. Johnson and Willie "the Lion" Smith, became Waller's teachers and patrons. By 1925 he was known and admired by George Gershwin, Irving Berlin, and Paul Whiteman, as well as being a favorite on the Harlem "rent-party" circuit and beginning a recording career.

In that same period Waller became so proficient on the organ that by 1927 he could say, in a rare moment of immodesty, "I am now the finest jazz organist alive." He was in fact the first great jazz organist; it always remained his preferred instrument, calling forth his best efforts and soothing and subduing his restless personality.

Waller's zesty humor—he made his whole life an agreeable joke—produced some wonderful one-liners. To the radio audience during a broadcast from a swanky hotel: "Don't be fooled, folks, there's nobody here but me and the waiters!" To a Park Avenue matron who wanted a definition of rhythm: "Lady, if you got to ask, you just don't got it." To a bulky comedienne: "Look at all that meat and no potatoes!"

Waller's brilliant piano performances, lava-hot and cool as spring rain, were matched by his talent to casually compose some of the finest American popular melodies—"Ain't Misbehavin'," "Black and Blue," "Honeysuckle Rose," "Squeeze Me," "Keepin' Out of Mischief Now," and "I've Got a Feeling I'm Falling" among them, all of which and many more filled the theater during the long Broadway run in the late 1970s of *Ain't Misbehavin',* the musical revue that honored and projected both Waller's songs and personality.

After 1935, with records, personal appearances, radio broadcasts, and film roles, Waller was a star. He lived a bacchanal life of zany hours, partying, gargantuan meals, and awesome drinking. He botched a 1942 Carnegie Hall recital with his boozing but in 1943 wrote a brilliant score for a Broadway musical. The pace of his life was too fast. Recovering from a bout of pneumonia and exhausted with his generous and patriotic entertaining at army and navy bases, he was returning from Hollywood by train to spend Christmas with his family in New York when he caught a chill in his sleeping car and choked to death in a spasm.

Once, while playing in vaudeville, he watched a chorine undulate across the stage and roared: "Yeah, that's that fine Arabian stuff that your dreams is made of!" So too was Thomas Wright Waller. His living and leaving had already been summarized in his own carefree expression: "One never knows, do one?"

(1904–1943)

To join the band a musician had to be able to sing as well as play an instrument.

It took just a few bars of that smooth-flowing, melodious theme, "Sleep," to wake everyone up: Waring's Pennsylvanians were on the air. And for five years, 1940–45, they broke all records as the most popular show on radio. The way people now tune in the seven-o'clock network news, they used to tune in the fifteen-minute Waring instrumental music and glee club offerings, sponsored five nights a week by Chesterfield. A few years later General Electric lighted up the Waring wares on TV. Waring was the first bandleader with his own TV show. Said to be the most expensive telecast per listener then on the tube, it failed to turn Waring into a Lawrence Welk.

Famous for its glee club, the Waring band began life singing. A small group organized by Tom Waring, Fred's brother, and Poley McClintock, the frog-voiced drummer, always a favorite Waring performer, it featured banjos and vocalizing and was called "Banjazztra." Fred, who reputedly knew at least three ukulele chords, joined on banjo. "Banjazztra" was picked up by Johnny O'Connor, a *Variety* staffer turned artist manager, who booked it into vaudeville spots. Loved and respected by everyone in the business, O'Connor managed the band for over a quarter of a century without a written contract or even a handshake, and steered it to success in theaters, radio, records, films, as it

Fred

metamorphosed into Waring's Pennsylvanians, with Fred out front. During the 1920s, '30s, and '40s, the band filled the air with singing and drew gasps from audiences for its spectacular lighting effects in stage shows, for example, the famous "dancing dominoes." On a darkened stage, the musicians "disappeared" and in their places rose giant dominoes, lights forming the familiar white dots on their "faces."

Early on, the Waring band projected an aura of academe (Fred had attended Penn State). It played and sang college songs, and hymns (family hymn sings had graced the Waring homestead at Tyrone, Pennsylvania, as well as pop tunes.) One of its most famous records was "Collegiate." The band also had an unusual family orientation. Besides the Waring brothers, it included other siblings, such as Priscilla and Rosemary Lane and the McFarland Twins. Tom Waring was not only featured singer for many years, but was also the band's pianist and a composer. Foremost among his tunes: "So Beats My Heart for You." Another popular featured member was trumpetman-singer Johnny "Scat" Davis. In fact, to join the band a musician had to be able to sing as well as play an instrument. To survive in it, both musicians and singers had to bear its leader's verbal blows. To some, even the security of a top job could not compensate for this cavalier treatment. Others were able to cope with such sarcasms as suggesting that his men imitate musicians, and informing singers that any number were waiting to take their places.

The Waring Glee Club, which debuted as a separate group in Billy Rose's Aquacade and was featured on the Chesterfield broadcasts, formed a logical bridge for Waring's move into the choral-singing educational field. He bought an eight hundred-acre summer resort at Shawnee-on-the-Delaware, referred to by some in his employ as Buchenwald-on-the-Delaware, and there in 1947 held his first Music Workshop for choral teachers and directors. Attendance grew to an estimated thousand each summer. In nonsummer months Waring toured with the orchestra, playing leading cities and college campuses, built up a publishing business and, along the way, acquired an invention which he marketed as the Waring Blendor. And in the 1970s, over the whir of the blenders, Waring music could still be heard in the land.

(1900–   )

Dionne Warwick

A kind of elegance, a grace that very few other people have.

"I came along in an era when kids were tired of hearing songs that just said, 'Boo-boo-boo,'" Dionne Warwick once told John S. Wilson of the New York *Times*. "Until then, any Negro singer—except Ella Fitzgerald or Nat Cole, who were jazz or hip pop—was categorized as R&B [rhythm & blues] no matter what they did. I had a different kind of sound that was accepted by both the R&B audience and the pop audience."

Dionne was also possessed of a voice of unusual flexibility and tonal coloration. Thoroughly grounded in musical theory and formal training, she had the background and the equipment to make her association with composer Burt Bacharach and lyricist Hal David one of the most artistically productive as well as

Dionne

commercially successful bodies of work during the 1960s and early '70s.

Among her many hits were "Don't Make Me Over," "Anyone Who Had a Heart," "Valley of the Dolls," "Alfie," the Grammy-winning "Do You Know the Way to San Jose?", "I Say a Little Prayer," "Walk on By," and another Grammy winner, "I'll Never Fall in Love Again," nearly all of which were composed and written by Bacharach and David specifically for Warwicke.

Dionne was born in East Orange, New Jersey. She recalled, in a New York *Post* interview: "We were never hungry. My parents always worked and we always owned our own house. All my life I've had white friends, right around the corner, across the street." Her mother was business manager of the Drinkards, a well-known gospel group, and her father had been a Pullman porter and a chef. He was later director of gospel promotion for Chess Records in New York.

In 1954 Dionne, her sister Dee Dee, and a cousin formed the Gospelaires trio with Dionne as leader. She could read music and was a capable pianist and organist. In 1959 she enrolled at Hartt College of Music at the University of Connecticut, on a scholarship, intending to become a music teacher. The Gospelaires had meanwhile picked up occasional work as background singers on pop recording dates. At one session Dionne was heard by Bacharach, whose compositions were growing increasingly complex and beyond the technique and understanding of most singers. "She had . . . a kind of elegance, a grace that very few other people have," recalled Bacharach in *Ebony* magazine, and he was anxious to write material for her because "she was no play-safe girl. What emotion I could get away with!"

The Warwick-David-Bacharach triumvirate was immediately successful with their venture, in 1961, of "Don't Make Me Over." Other hits followed. In 1963 she conquered Europe, and was introduced by Marlene Dietrich for her triumphant appearance at the Olympia Theater in Paris. In 1966, with Bacharach conducting the orchestra, she gave a recital in Avery Fisher Hall at Lincoln Center in New York that brought her a standing ovation.

Her association with Bacharach and David ended in the early 1970s and the quality of material in her subsequent recordings declined, although her performances remained excellent. She had previously said on several occasions that she planned to "retire" and that she still wished to be a music teacher, and in 1974 she resumed studies toward her master's degree in music. She continued to tour in Europe and the United States to enthusiastic receptions, while maintaining the sentiments she expressed in *Newsweek* in 1966: "Someday I want the kind of loyalty among audiences that Ella Fitzgerald has, so that if I want to stop for two years or ten years I could come back and still be Miss Dionne Warwick . . . What I try to do is not conjured up, not just style . . . I'm pleading the case and you're getting it all, baby, ready or not, here comes all of it."

(1940–   )

Dinah Washington

"I can sing anything, anything at all."

There are all sorts of female singers. Somehow, Dinah Washington, strong, assertive, proud, made most others sound like little girls.

Known to her fans as "The Queen" (short for "Queen of the Blues"), she transcended musical categories, ranging through the fields of blues, jazz, and pop in a style as direct and forthright as the woman herself.

Nurtured on gospel (she began her career as Ruth Jones, playing piano for a church choir) and raised on the blues, she ripened in jazz, and even after she had a string of hit records to her credit, she remained true to her musical instincts.

At fifteen she won an amateur contest at Chicago's Regal Theater and began to sing in nightclubs. Three years later, in 1942, she was heard by a talent manager, Joe Glaser, who gave her (according to most sources) her professional name, and got her a job singing with Lionel Hampton's band. Shortly after

Queen of the Blues

joining Hampton, she made her first records, at a session organized by critic and songwriter Leonard Feather; it produced her first hit, "Evil Gal Blues." In 1946 she left Hampton and embarked on a career as a single attraction, quickly establishing herself as a rhythm and blues star with songs like "I Want to Be Loved" and a number of what were then considered risqué blues.

She captured the jazz audience with some excellent recordings in a jam-session setting, and then moved easily into the pop field with her soulful versions of great standards like "What a Diff'rence a Day Made," as well as more ephemeral songs like "Harbor Lights." Unlike some other recording stars, her strong, forthright delivery and commanding stage presence made her equally effective when heard in person.

The rapport she established with an audience had much in common with the give-and-take of a black sanctified church service, yet she respectfully refused to mix gospel and blues, as Ray Charles did so successfully.

"I like to get inside a tune and make it mean something to the people that listen," she explained "something more than just a set of lyrics and a familiar tune. And I can sing anything, anything at all."

Dinah Washington's personal life was tempestuous. Married seven times ("I change husbands before they change me," she quipped) and famous for extracurricular sexual activities as well, she had a fierce temper and a salty tongue. After she had ridiculed her wigmaker's product from the stage, she was threatened with a lawsuit, but it was less amusing when she cursed the pianist on a bill with her in a famous New York nightclub and refused to appear opposite him.

Ironically, her last marriage, to Detroit Lions halfback Dick "Night Train" Lane, promised to be a happy one when it was cut short by her sudden death at thirty-nine, apparently from a fatal combination of diet pills and alcohol. Plump by nature, she was famous for her periodic crash diets; no doubt, these had a harmful effect on her health.

Dinah Washington died four years younger than Bessie Smith and Billie Holiday, yet her legacy is that of an artist who fulfilled the promise of her talent. Her influence survived in the work of many singers, notably Nancy Wilson, and her records were still heard regularly on radio more than a decade after her death.

(1924–1963)

Ethel Waters

She almost toppled the crown from the reigning queen of the blues singers.

Even after she started singing professionally, she had one dream: to be a wealthy lady's maid and travel around the world.

Instead, she sang her way to world fame from the red-light districts and slum alleys of her childhood in Chester and Philadelphia, Pennsylvania, through rickety second-rate theaters, carnivals, and saloons; from "colored time" to the "white time" of the B. F. Keiths of the vaudeville world; into Harlem clubs and still up and on to London, Hollywood, and Broadway in musicals and dramatic roles that etched her name on the theater's roll of honor with such immortals as Ethel Barrymore, Helen Hayes, and Julie Harris, with whom she starred in *The Member of the Wedding*.

As a skinny, seventeen-year-old, Ethel Waters, at a theater in Baltimore, became the first woman, and second performer, to sing W. C. Handy's "St. Louis Blues." Her style so bowled over her black audiences, she almost toppled the crown from the reigning queen of the blues singers, Bessie Smith. Though performing in her early years as Sweet Mama Stringbean, a blues singer, she later expanded her repertoire to include many kinds of songs. Those forever

"Sweet Mama Stringbean"

associated with her, however—"St. Louis Blues," "Am I Blue" (which she introduced in the film *On with the Show*), "Dinah," "Stormy Weather" (which she introduced in a Cotton Club appearance), "Happiness Is Just a Thing Called Joe" (featured in the filmed version of her Broadway musical success, *Cabin in the Sky)*—all have varying shades of blue in them.

Ethel Waters could express every conceivable emotion with her voice. It could be low and throaty, or high and plaintive. It could whisper or sweet-talk or growl. It could be sad, or sly and full of high spirits. Every consonant and vowel always came out as cleanly and clearly as if she had spent her life at speech school.

But Ethel Waters got the bulk of her schooling on the streets of black urban ghettos. Her mother, full of religious fervor, was only twelve when Ethel was forcibly conceived and brought forth as an illegitimate child. She was brought up by her hard-working grandmother, whom she called "Mom." Her paternal grandmother was a white woman who lived elsewhere in remote comfort. Only when Ethel was able to attend a Catholic school did she find the love and encouragement she longed for. Her faith in God, awakened there, remained the motivating force in her life, taking expression in her later years in her work with the Billy Graham evangelistic crusades.

An artist with many best-selling records to her credit, Miss Waters recorded early discs for Black Swan, where she met Fletcher Henderson and toured with his "Black Swan Jazz Masters" band. Besides singing, she did a mean shimmy, blending it with a song hit of the time, "Shim-Me-Sha-Wabble." She was a hit later in several Negro revues—*Africana, Lew Leslie's Blackbirds of 1930, Rhapsody in Black*—and in Harlem clubs. When she moved to the Broadway musical *As Thousands Cheer,* she sang Irving Berlin's dramatic "Supper Time," a song of a woman whose husband has just been lynched. Ethel Waters knew real-life stories like that—lived her own—and put them into every song she sang. She drew on her own life, also, in her crowning dramatic roles on Broadway as Hagar in *Mamba's Daughters* and Berenice Sadie Brown in *The Member of the Wedding.* Somewhere along the way her ambition to be a lady's maid disappeared in the glory of Ethel Waters being the lady herself.

In her later years, she dwelt more and more on religious themes. When asked to sing "Stormy Weather," she refused. Instead she sang "His Eye Is on the Sparrow." Leaving a Chicago audience during the mid-1970s, she called out, "I want to see you all in heaven. I'll be looking for you."

A short time later she was on the way.

(1900–1977)

Muddy Waters

"I try to take the blues as high as they can go."

Father of the modern urban blues, a seminal influence on such bands as the Rolling Stones and individual guitarists like Eric Clapton and Jimi Hendrix, and a singer of rare dignity and passion, McKinley Morganfield summarized his fifty-year musical career in saying: "I try to take the blues as high as they can go."

As "Muddy Waters" (a childhood nickname that came from his playing in the dirt roads of Clarksdale, Mississippi) he was one of the few blues singers to combine a youthful, deep experience of classic country blues and then adapt it to the bravura sounds of the city in the post-World War II era.

Waters' first instrument was the harmonica; he was playing it in 1928 at backwoods dances in the rural South, where the clientele often brawled and the beverages were near-lethal. In those early years, his night's wages were

McKinley Morganfield/Muddy Waters

fifty cents and a crock of moonshine. By 1932 he became proficient in the "bottleneck" or "slide" style of blues guitar; he met and played with the remarkable Son House and the superb and tragic Robert Johnson. In 1941 Allan Lomax, the discoverer of the legendary Leadbelly, recorded Waters for the folk song archives of the Library of Congress.

Waters moved to Chicago in 1943, and soon became a well-known and popular singer on the city's black South Side. Four years later he made his first commercial recordings, using the then-surprising sound of the electric guitar (he made the switch from acoustic so that he could hear himself in saloons and compete against loud conversation). His records were immediately successful with black audiences, and by the late 1950s he and his band had evolved into the definitive urban blues group, with amplified harmonica and electric bass. They delivered a series of unique performances: "I'm Your Hoochie Coochie Man," "Standing Around Crying," "Tiger in Your Tank," the lazily erotic "I Just Want to Make Love to You," and the rousing jump tune, "Got My Mojo Working."

His records were released in England, where they became favorites of youthful collectors, two of whom, Mick Jagger and Brian Jones, named their band after a Waters record, "Rolling Stone." The group's enormous success and influence on pop music, and its frequent crediting of Waters as one of its major inspirations, brought him attention from white American audiences for the first time in his career. After an album recorded in London with admiring British disciples in the early 1970s, Waters began to make national television appearances, increased his concert bookings, and performed at such swank locations as the St. Regis Hotel in New York. As he neared the age of sixty, his career had suddenly boomed.

Personally Waters remained a mild and down-to-earth man, happy to encourage young white blues musicians, and very much enjoying his role as a patriarch. He once told a friend he was glad success had come late in life: "Now I've got enough money to take care of me, and some left over to spend on my grandchildren."

In a 1971 interview with *Cavalier* magazine, he gave his definition of the blues and his life with them: "I think it's about tellin' a beautiful story . . . something about the hard times you've had, or some lady you've had, and she done drop you . . . I think what we did is tell a good story, expressing ourselves to other people, and when it came out all right, I guess you could say that's all I ever wanted."

(1915–   )

"I'll roll up my sleeves for my wife and let her see the goose-pimples I get just watching myself."

"Our band has been the subject of countless reviews during a career of some forty-five years," Lawrence Welk remarked in 1970. "They have been both flattering and derogatory, witty and dull, friendly and hostile. I guess it's just as well I developed a thick skin early in life."

Critics, nevertheless, once seemed very important to the cheerful North Dakota bandleader of the bubbling music and the bumbling speech. "Part of my education in the music business came when I learned about sending a bottle of champagne to the more influential critics," he has noted. "Suddenly we began to receive much better reviews." In fact, the reviews and the consequent public acclaim grew so ecstatic in the late 1950s that Welk eventually became a millionaire many times over, the suave head of his own music and real estate empire climaxed by the 1971 completion of the Lawrence Welk Plaza, a twenty-one-story California office building and the adjacent sixteen-story luxurious Champagne Towers Apartment Building. Quite an accomplishment for the self-proclaimed "poor, naïve farm boy" from North Dakota who once spoke only German and who was "so self-conscious about my English that for the first fifteen years in the music business I refused to open my mouth in front of an audience."

That "poor, naïve farm boy!"

He left the farm at twenty-one, "convinced that pushing an accordion would be less back-breaking than pushing a plow." Three years later his first band, the Hotsy Totsy Boys, was playing nights in ballrooms and days at station WNAX in Yankton, South Dakota, owned and operated by the Gurnsey Seed and Nursery Company. Quips Welk, "Some of our detractors claim that some of the corn still remains in our music."

Welk was a conscientious leader, bent most of all on pleasing his public, a pragmatic approach to music that never deserted him. "If we showed people a good time, we really slept that night." However from 1927 to 1936 the band may have had many sleepless nights, because these were, according to Welk, "lean years." Then in 1936, for an engagement at Pittsburgh's William Penn Hotel, Lawrence, whose band was playing a prickly, bubbling style of music, decided to dress his men in full dress suits. His fans dubbed his offerings "Champagne Music," and the ensuing bubble never burst!

The band went on to even bigger and better dates, centering its activities for more than a decade in the Midwest, and then in 1951 starring on a local Los Angeles TV show that drew such a large audience that ABC soon signed it for the entire network. It remained there for sixteen successive successful seasons.

"The Lawrence Welk Show," ultra-clean-looking and conservative-sounding, with a "gee-whiz-isn't-everything-just-dandy!" approach, featured pristinelooking and sounding performers like the Lennon Sisters, Norma Zimmer, and accordionist Myron Floren. "I like to play music that puts the girl back in the fellow's arms," Welk explained. Critics who pressed for a more progressive approach couldn't pierce that admittedly thick skin. Nor could the ABC networks chiefs who predicted Welk—after sixteen years of success—was through and dropped his show. Refusing to heed them ("My years of one-nighters taught me what the people really want"), he thumbed his baton in the network's direction, organized his own network, and soon lined up over two hundred stations, far more than ABC had provided to carry his series.

The music remained exactly the same: straight-ahead, completely predictable. He, himself, remains one of his band's biggest fans. "Sometimes when we're home alone," he told *Crawdaddy*, "I'll roll up my sleeves for my wife and let her see the goose-pimples I get just watching myself and my band perform on TV."

Fellow bandleader Woody Herman has offered a logical explanation for Welk's continued popularity: "Maybe it's because the music is in keeping with the times. People don't have to think about it. No effort. It's automatic."

(1903–   )

Paul Weston

"Leading a classical orchestra is eighty per cent acting. Leading a dance orchestra is a waste of time."

Coronet magazine once gave him the romantic-sounding title of "Master of Mood Music," but Paul Weston is also a keen businessman, an expert organizer and, at times, one of the kookiest musicians ever to make a record. And he also happens to be one of the most successful of all conductor/arrangers.

The Springfield, Massachusetts, native who graduated from Dartmouth cum laude and made Phi Beta Kappa, has conducted and arranged for more girl singers than probably any other leader. Take this star dozen, for example: Connee Boswell, Diahann Carroll, Rosemary Clooney, Doris Day, Ella Fitzgerald, Judy Garland, Dinah Shore, Kate Smith, Jo Stafford (his wife), Sarah Vaughan, Margaret Whiting, and Lee Wiley.

Wiley was the first, back in 1940, after he decided to branch out on his own after four years of writing some of the Tommy Dorsey band's finest arrangements. Dinah Shore was next, and the sensitive scores he produced for the

Paul

young Nashville songbird on her first solo sides helped tremendously to launch her career.

In 1941, Weston (his original name was Wetstein) arrived on the West Coast with the Bob Crosby band. The band soon headed back East, but Paul stayed on to arrange songs for Bing Crosby in *Holiday Inn* and two years later to accept the post of musical director of the brand-new Capitol Records label that friend Johnny Mercer and two more of his pals had launched. Freer than ever before to write what he wanted to, he created the first successful series of "mood" records, "Music for Dreaming," "Music for Fireside," "Music for a Rainy Night," etc. Unlike other lush recordings of pop songs, Weston's projected an attractive rhythmic feel along with its romantic sounds. "All I did," he pointed out years later, "was to add strings to a dance band. The reason it still swung was because I used good jazz musicians."

It also happened that Weston knew how to get the most out of his musicians. A superbly organized executive, he prepared carefully for all his sessions, whether for recordings (altogether he turned out more than twenty "mood" albums) or for radio series like "The Johnny Mercer Music Shop" or Jo Stafford's "The Chesterfield Supper Club," or for TV programs like NBC's "The Chevy Show," the Bob Newhart or Danny Kaye or Jonathan Winters or Jim Nabors television programs.

Weston was serious whenever he had to be—for example, during early days of the National Academy of Recording Arts and Sciences, which he helped found and for which he served as its first national president—but he often exhibited a finely honed sense of the ridiculous. During a Columbia Records national sales conference in the early 1950s, he heard an especially awful cocktail pianist playing all wrong chords, skipping beats, and generally murdering one pop standard after another. Using him for a model, he created "Jonathan Winters," an even worse-sounding pianist, and with the help of his wife, Jo Stafford, whom he named "Darlene" and who sang woefully out-of-tune on purpose, created some of the most hilarious recordings of all time.

Weston has also composed several hit songs, "Day By Day," "I Should Care," "Shrimp Boats," a musical portrait of New Orleans, a choral work, and two masses, and in 1971 conducted the premier performance of his symphonic composition, "Memories of Ireland." An intensely honest man who abhors much of the phoniness that has permeated his world of music, Weston recently compared, quite bluntly, the roles of music conductors. "Leading a classical orchestra," he insisted, "is eighty per cent acting. Leading a dance orchestra is a waste of time." And then commenting on what he has done most of, he added, "But conducting for a live television show, well—for that a conductor should also receive a stuntman's check!"

(1912–   )

Paul Whiteman

The master of the grandiose.

He really wasn't exactly what they called him, "The King of Jazz," but Paul Whiteman was by far the most important orchestra leader of the 1920s who, according to noted musicologist Deems Taylor, took jazz "out of the kitchen and moved it upstairs into the parlor."

The parlor is exactly where he himself belonged, because Paul Whiteman was indeed a classy guy. He was warm, generous, enthusiastic, and big in every

The Paul Whiteman orchestra with Roy Bargy and Lenny Hayton at the pianos

way. He sometimes weighed as much as three hundred pounds, and he always thought big and talked big, and, most of all, he acted big. Though a huge success, he, unlike other leaders of the 1920s and '30s, magnanimously shifted the spotlight to his sidemen and singers. As his most illustrious alumnus, Bing Crosby, once noted, "Pops appreciated talent. Any instrumentalists or singers he thought were good he'd hire, whether he needed them or not. He'd fit them in some way."

Bing fit in and so did Mildred Bailey and Morton Downey and Johnny Mercer and, for shorter periods, Dinah Shore and Billie Holiday, and many other singers. His alumni also included great musicians: Bix Beiderbecke, Jimmy and Tommy Dorsey, Jack Teagarden, Joe Venuti, Eddie Lang, Frankie Trumbauer, and Henry Busse, and arrangers Ferde Grofe, Roy Bargy, and Lennie Hayton. And he was the first to encourage George Gershwin to extend his talents beyond a simple popular song, when he commissioned and premiered in 1924 the composer's famed *Rhapsody in Blue* at New York's Aeolian Hall.

Though he liked jazz and proudly featured some of its best players, his orchestra seldom played pure jazz. Instead, he dressed it up with frilly, "concert hall" arrangements, a not-surprising departure, for his own early career as a musician had been spent in concert halls.

Even before he was twenty he had become the first violinist of the Denver Symphony, and soon after of the San Francisco People's Symphony. During World War I, he enlisted in the Navy, where he formed a forty-piece sailor jazz band. Upon his discharge, he organized his first civilian dance orchestra, a nine-piece group that, starting from San Francisco's Fairmont Hotel, wended its way down through a series of the West Coast's swankier hotel rooms, eventually winding up with a smash engagement at the Alexandria in Los Angeles, where, Whiteman recalled, "Charlie Chaplin used to take the stick away from me and Fatty Arbuckle would play the drums."

Soon Whiteman's fame spread East and he was booked for the summer in 1920 at the new Ambassador Hotel in Atlantic City. There, after a slow start, the band, chiefly through word-of-mouth publicity, developed a large following. Among the converts were executives of the Victor Talking Machine Company, who invited the band into their recording studio. Whiteman was slow in accepting the invitation, because, as he later explained, "We were so scared; we postponed the date four times before we made the records." And Whiteman had his group pegged: it required three separate sessions for the band to come up with an acceptable recording of "Whispering," its first big hit in a succession of hundreds upon hundreds of recordings it was to make during the next quarter of a century.

Its hit recording and successful Atlantic City engagement soon paved the way for even more important billings. During 1920 it attracted the cream of New York's Society to the Palais Royal. In 1921 it became the first orchestra to play New York's famed Palace Theater. In 1922 it was featured in *George White's Scandals;* in 1923 in *The Ziegfeld Follies* and in London's Hippodrome.

In 1924 came the famous Aeolian Hall concert, and thereafter long engagements at the Paramount Theater, the Hippodrome, the Paul Whiteman Club (opened especially for the maestro) and the Biltmore Hotel in New York, as well as in top hotels, theaters, and clubs throughout the country. The band was starred in Billy Rose's mammoth New York 1935 production of *Jumbo* and during the next year in the impresarios's even bigger extravaganza at the Texas Sesquicentennial Exhibition where the scenery was sixty feet high and the cast numbered six hundred performers including one hundred and twenty-four long-stemmed show girls.

Such flamboyancy suited Whiteman's style and personality perfectly. He was master of the grandiose manner, though never overbearingly so, and he could be a charmer, as those who saw him in such movies as *The King of Jazz, Thanks a Million, Strike Up the Band, Rhapsody in Blue,* and *The Fabulous Dorseys* would attest. Off-camera, he was perhaps even more gracious and certainly more at ease as he often regaled his many companions—none of whom was ever known to have drunk him under the table—with his sometimes delightfully exaggerated tales.

Business executives loved him and respected him. Corporate heads became his bosom buddies. He was at various times musical director of the National and American Broadcasting companies and host and conductor of numerous radio series. For a while he also performed as a disc jockey for the Mutual Broadcasting System and later for ABC.

During the 1940s, with so many younger leaders serenading the kids, the older Whiteman's personal appearances became less frequent, so that by the time television had become popular he no longer had a set orchestra. Instead, he hired some of New York's top studio musicians who, accustomed to playing under conductors with a more definite downbeat than Whiteman's, willingly followed the baton of his arranger, Glenn Osser, crouched inside the maestro's huge podium, completely hidden from the TV cameras.

Even while well into his sixties and seventies, Whiteman continued to remain very much in view. In 1955 he hosted a TV series that featured over fifty big bands. In 1956 he led a group of his illustrious alumni through a fiftieth-anniversary album. Thereafter, he guest-conducted various orchestras throughout the country. His enthusiasm, his gregariousness, and his love of music never abated, and just before he died, one year and nine months after his seventy-fifth birthday, he was still as chipper as ever, reveling in, and projecting onto others, his own special brand of the Spirit of '76.

(1891–1967)

Margaret Whiting

"I sang simply, and I sounded virginal."

She matured late in life, not physically, but emotionally and musically. And it showed. For in the late-1970s, when Margaret Whiting was more than half a century old, she was singing more warmly, with more expression, and with more musicality than ever before in her close to forty-year career.

And she admitted it. "I sing now as I experience life. I used to sound one-dimensional. I sang in tune. I sang musically. I sang simply, and I sounded virginal. But the more I've experienced life, like finding out what it felt like to be hurt, the more I began to mature musically as well as emotionally. It gets to the point when you finally put your music and your life together."

Maggie, as her many friends call her, experienced music from her early Detroit, Michigan, beginnings. Her father, Richard Whiting, had been writing hit songs even before she was born, beginning in 1920 with "The Japanese Sandman," then on to "Ain't We Got Fun," "Sleepy Time Gal," and "She's Funny That Way." When the movie musical era began, he moved his family to Hollywood, where he composed more big hits, like "On the Good Ship Lollipop," "When Did You Leave Heaven," "Too Marvelous for Words," "My Ideal," "Louise," "Honey," and "Hooray for Hollywood."

The Whiting Hollywood home, recalls Maggie, "was always filled with musical celebrities like the Gershwins, Paul Whiteman, Al Jolson, Eddie Cantor, Maurice Chevalier, Harold Arlen, and Johnny Mercer." It was Mercer who got Dick Whiting's fifteen-year-old daughter to appear on her first radio program, and for the next fifteen years or so she popped up all over the dial singing with Bob Hope, Bob Crosby, Cantor, and on "Your Hit Parade."

"Johnny became my guiding light," she recalls of the cheery friend who, shortly after organizing Capitol Records in 1943, recorded Maggie for the first time as the vocalist on the Freddie Slack band's version of the Mercer-Arlen classic, "That Old Black Magic." After two sides with Billy Butterfield's band that really made her, "Moonlight in Vermont" and her dad's "My Ideal," she joined country singer Jimmy Wakely for a duet on "Slippin' Around" that sold over three million copies. "Maggie is such a pro," a friend recently noted, "that she can sound at home with any kind of popular song, from Gershwin, Berlin, and Rodgers to Stephen Sondheim and Michel Legrand to Barry Manilow and Leon Russell."

Soon she had her own hit records: "It Might as Well Be Spring" and "Come Rain or Come Shine," and then a memorable duet with mentor Mercer of

Maggie

"Baby, It's Cold Outside." She also started playing nightclubs and eventually starring in leads of touring companies of Broadway musicals. Ironically, she had never toured with name bands, as almost all her contemporaries had done—that is, not until 1972, when she toured with the "Cavalcade of Bands" show that also starred Freddy Martin, Bob Crosby, and Frankie Carle. "That's when I got my first taste of living in a bus and out of a suitcase!"

But the strenuous road trip never tired her. She is proud of the good care she has taken of herself. "I don't smoke and I don't drink booze. I feel a singer should stay in shape," said the woman who in her mid-fifties still displayed a remarkable, eye-catching shape.

Her life remained full, too—full of charitable work. She has visited more than twenty-five hundred military installations and in the mid-1970s was still entertaining at veterans hospitals. One of the founders of the Recording Academy in 1957, and an active governor in 1977, she was also taking dramatic lessons, getting involved in politics, reading voraciously, and traveling extensively.

In 1978 she was touring the country and breaking it up with Rosemary Clooney, Rose Marie, and Helen O'Connell. The following year she broke it up all alone in a series of solo concert appearances, projecting more emotion and musicianship than ever before. "All that sort of thing colors your life and your performing and helps you develop. Maybe that's why, as you said, I now sing like a woman instead of like a girl!"

(1924–   )

"Rock performers are always supposed to look angry."

Writer-composer-guitarist Pete Townshend, drummer Keith Moon, singer Roger Daltry, and bassist John Entwhistle caused consternation as The Who from the beginning, in the early 1960s. Admired as perhaps *the* all-stops-out rock band, they were also respected for Townshend's brilliant and ambitious *Tommy,* the first rock opera.

Each of the members contributed his share to the consternation: Daltry, a powerful and resourceful vocalist, baby-eyed and boyish, relishing his role as star. Moon, who once ran over a pedestrian while driving his car backward, and who may also have been responsible for the failure of daredevil Evel Knievel to leap, via motorcycle, thirteen parked buses in England's Wembley Stadium (All the crowd was hushed and awed as Knievel prepared to start his run. Then, just at the crucial moment, came Moon's voice in a hee-haw bray: "Faggot!");Entwhistle, maniacally goofy in his songs and recordings ("Made in Japan" details the hero's disappointment in the origin of manufacture of his car, his clothes and, finally, his wife's private parts); the garrulous and self-analytical Townshend, who frequently embarrassed the rock world—performers and audience—by such statements as: "It strikes me that I'm rather too aged to want fifteen-year-old girls to scream for me; perhaps we're all too old for this business" and "Rock performers are always supposed to look angry; I suppose I was angry when I was twenty-three but I didn't have the faintest idea what I was angry about, and I don't believe anyone else does either; it's more or less a face you put on." Townshend's all-time classic statement came at the end of a New York concert where The Who refused to do an encore. The audience booed; Townshend returned to the stage and, grabbing the microphone, declared: "See here, we've been up on this bloody stage for three hours playing our ballocks off and we're bloody tired, so boo f___ing 'boo' to you, too."

In their early days The Who assaulted the audience with deliberate guitar feedback, with Townshend smashing his guitar, with Moon demolishing his drums, and with smoke bombs being set off. Though hailed as anarchic artists, The Who's stage antics were only an attention getter. The drive of the band came through Townshend's writing; his portraits of off-center characters gave the group an underground following, and when Townshend announced his intention of writing a rock opera the project became the most eagerly followed in pop music. *Tommy* was worth the waiting; it is considered by many the most important album in rock history, besides the Beatles' *Sgt. Pepper.* The Who

The Who: John Entwhistle, Roger Daltry, Keith Moon, Peter Townshend

performed it at the Metropolitan Opera House in New York (the only rock group ever to appear there) and played it in road tours for three years.

Since then the individual members became involved in different projects, though still remaining very much a group. All released solo albums; Moon and Daltry (who played the title role in the movie version of *Tommy*) acted in films; Entwhistle formed a band, Ox, for occasional touring.

Townshend once summed up The Who's life: "We're all dashing about being our own men and establishing our identities, don't you know, and then I get frantic phone calls from the others: 'We've got to get back into the studio and on the road as The Who.' So we do, because we're a band. That's all we really are."

Or really *were*—because in September 1978, Keith Moon was found dead in a London hotel room, a victim of the same sort of high and foolish living associated with the group throughout its entire career. And the Who became the Was.

Lee Wiley

"Devastating sex appeal . . . in an exalted way."

Few singers have been able to raise quite such erotic hopes with the unaided voice as Lee Wiley.

"She has a voice and style," wrote the late George Frazier, Boston's waspish authority on the arts, "that have long since made me extremely eager to go to bed with her."

This proposal—or proposition—was made on the liner of a Wiley album. But Frazier hastened to add that he meant this "in a nice, noble way."

"Although she sings with devastating sex appeal," he clarified, "she does so in an exalted way."

Miss Wiley herself found her manner of singing rather ordinary. "I don't sing gut-bucket," she said. "I don't sing jazz. I just sing. The only vocal trick I've ever done is putting in the vibrato and taking it out. I don't believe in vocal gimmickry and I never had the commercial instincts to concentrate on visual mannerisms."

A tall, striking-looking woman with corn-colored hair and olive skin that she attributed to Cherokee blood, Miss Wiley ran away from her birthplace, Port Gibson, Oklahoma, when she was fifteen and, with the help of a friend of her mother's, found singing jobs in Chicago and New York. By the time she was seventeen, she was singing with Leo Reisman's orchestra, a big name in New York in the late 1920s, and playing dramatic roles on radio.

The early 1930s were a busy period for her. She was on radio on the Paul Whiteman show and the Kraft show with Victor Young, with whom she wrote several songs, including "Any Time, Any Day, Anywhere." There were recordings and nightclub performances—so many that her health collapsed and she had to spend a year in Arizona.

When she returned to New York, she sang on Willard Robison's radio show and cut a series of albums of show tunes by Cole Porter, Rodgers and Hart, and George Gershwin, with jazz backing from some of the many jazz stars who loved her relaxed, laid-back, yet still pulsating style, like Bunny Berigan, Bobby Hackett, Fats Waller, Bud Freeman, and Eddie Condon. The series of recordings gave her an identity as a sophisticated show-tune specialist that she retained for the rest of her life.

In 1944 she married Jess Stacy, the jazz pianist, and became the singer in a big band they formed. "I hocked my jewelry to get things going," she recalled.

Lee

"And I did more than that—the physical work, like driving a car. You can't imagine what it's like driving a car for hours and then having to get up and sing all night. It was a waste of time and years."

The marriage and the band both eventually fell apart and Lee went on singing on her own, fending off constant requests for "Sugar," which she had first recorded in 1940 on the back of her own favorite recording, "Down to Steamboat Tennessee."

For the last twenty-five years of her life, Lee's gently husky voice and sinuous phrasing were heard only sporadically. She was married to a businessman, Nat Tischenkel, and she took engagements or recording sessions only if they suited her, maintaining a policy of independence which may well have kept her from building a big popular following when she was in her heyday.

"I always sang the way I wanted to sing," she once said. "If I didn't like something, I just wouldn't do it. Instead, I'd take a plane to California and sit in the sun."

(1915–1975)

Andy Williams

One of the nicest and most considerate gentlemen in all of show business.

During Robert Kennedy's funeral, when much of the world was in shock, a soft, sweet voice provided the most luminescent balm to its grief. The voice was that of Andy Williams, and the soothing song he sang was "Battle Hymn of the Republic."

During those turbulent 1960s, when many were bewildered by the changes around them, the self-assured, melodic sound of Williams' voice, coupled with his relaxed manner, reaffirmed the values of good, sensible music and living, and once every year the reassuring joys of family ties and roots when his TV Christmas specials would always feature his three brothers and their families with Andy and his wife, Claudine Longet, and their children. And even after

Andy

their divorce in 1975, Claudine would return to share the Christmas program with the man whom many have described as one of the nicest and most considerate gentlemen in all of show business.

H. Andrew Williams, born in Wall Lake, Iowa, was the youngest of those four brothers. Their father, a railway mail clerk and amateur musician, trained his family (there was also a sister) to be the choir of their Presbyterian church. The four boys decided one day that they were too good to remain amateurs, so, when Andy was eight, the Williams Brothers made their professional debut on radio station WHO in Des Moines.

Soon the entire family began moving with the sons' careers—to Chicago, Cincinnati, and finally to Los Angeles after the quartet had been signed to an MGM movie contract. When the war temporarily disbanded the group, young Andy finished high school. Then in 1947 they were reunited and were taken on by top vocal coach, arranger, and singer Kay Thompson to form one of the classiest nightclub acts of all time. When, after several years of playing top clubs, his three brothers married and the group disbanded, Andy set out for New York, where in 1954 he was hired for a two-week engagement on Steve Allen's "The Tonight Show." Since nobody told him to stop coming, he stayed for two and a half years, selecting his own material and participating in all the show's madness.

In 1956 he began his recording career with two hits on the Cadence label, "Walk Hand in Hand" and "Canadian Sunset," followed a few years later by one of his biggest hits, "The Hawaiian Wedding Song." A good showing on two summer replacement TV shows in 1957 and 1958 qualified him for his own series of specials and finally in 1962 with a regular weekly series that won five Emmy awards. From then on he averaged two specials a year and during the 1970s he became the regular host of the recording field's annual "Grammy Awards Show." But perhaps his most important association was with the music of his good friend Henry Mancini, whose soaring melodies, like "Moon River," "Days of Wine and Roses," and "Dear Heart," were so well suited to Williams' equally soaring tenor voice.

A veteran record producer once observed that Andy Williams was the best of a school of tenors who grabbed your attention by singing at the extreme top end of their ranges, and that part of the hold they had on their public was created by the suspense of wondering if the voice would ever break. Andy's, just like his aura of relaxed, self-assurance, never did.

(1936–   )

"He'd come slopping and slouching out on stage, limp as a dishrag."

"You have to have smelled a lot of mule manure to sing like a hillbilly" goes one of Hank Williams' more memorable quotations, a sentiment which not only illustrates his greatest gift as a songwriter—vivid simplicity—and his fierce regional pride, but, even more, helps explain the tremendous changes he wrought in country music in his heyday, changes still being strongly felt.

For despite the widely held supposition that he was the first to nudge open the doors between country and pop music, Hank Williams' entrance into the country music scene in 1946 actually had quite the opposite effect: It synthesized and solidified the "hard" country sound, and caused a surprising and unprecedented revival of the southeastern "hillbilly" style.

For country music in the 1940s was becoming increasingly pop-oriented and slick, and while "old-time" artists like Roy Acuff, whom Williams emulated early in his career, and Molly O'Day were at their peak, the bulk of the public's attention—especially in terms of record sales—went to the big band sound of Bob Wills and His Texas Playboys, the smooth, orchestra-backed sound of Gene Autry, the plaintive, pop-tinged vocals of Eddy Arnold, or the honky-tonk sounds of Al Dexter and Ernest Tubb.

Then along came Hank Williams, who went firmly and bullheadedly against the grain, proudly singing his own songs in an old-fashioned, high, tight, hillbilly voice. Slurring with bluesy intonation, breaking with feeling, yodeling with good cheer, Williams' approach encapsulated the joys and sorrows of country life with his technically limited but spectacularly moving voice.

The enormous success of Hank Williams on record unleashed a tremendous southeastern-sound revival, opening the doors for other stars of the next decade, who either began as Williams imitators or who benefited greatly from the "hillbilly" resurgence that he had invoked.

And others also benefited from his songwriting talents, for an inordinately high proportion of his compositions became country music classics for all to sing: "Your Cheatin' Heart," "Cold Cold Heart," "Jambalaya," "I Can't Help It," "Hey Good Lookin' " and "I'm So Lonesome I Could Cry."

And over and above these songs, and over and above the southeastern-sound revival he spawned, there was another facet to Hank Williams that catapulted him to legendary status. That was his openness, his projection of realness with which anyone could readily identify. On stage he let his whole being show,

Hank Williams (right) with Red Foley

sharing his happy and his bad times with his audience with an unaffected sincerity
that reached to each and every listener.

Part of it was showmanship, most of it was quite genuine, and none of it
escaped his audience. "We got boys who can sing three times as good as him,
people used to tell me," recalls Minnie Pearl. "Sure, but they'd never get that
great cataclysmic reaction from the audience Hank got." Another contemporary
echoes the accuracy of her memory: "Hank didn't have much personality except
when he was singing: that's when his real personality came out. He'd come
slopping and slouching out on stage, limp as a dishrag. But when he picked
up the guitar and started to sing, it was like a charge of electricity had gone
through him. He became three feet taller." Fellow singer Jimmy Dickens put

it more simply: "He just seemed to hypnotize those people. Simplicity, I guess. He brought the people with him, put himself on their level."

As for his personality off stage, the skinny, stooped, balding young man was two different people: shy, cheerful, and uncomplicated when sober; mean and surly when drunk, as he was too often during his hard-living, restless, moody, guilt-ridden later years.

Two stories illustrate these extremes. The first: Hank walking cheerfully into his bank after a long road trip, dumping several fistfulls of bills in front of a bewildered teller, who asked how much he was depositing. "How the hell do I know?" he replied with an irresponsible grin. "My job is to make it, yours is to count it."

The second: A frustrated, self-loathing Williams, with marriage, health, and career failing, increasingly in trouble with alcohol, asking a WSM technician to comment on a line from a new song he was working up—"The silence of a falling star lights up the purple sky." "My God, Hank, that's beautiful; it's really poetry!" gushed the genuinely awestruck technician. "Sheeee-it," snarled Hank, turning away in disgust, walking away without another word.

These wild and well-known shifts in personality, his tremendous popularity and prodigious talents, his identifiability, his roller-coaster rise and fall and sudden death at the age of twenty-nine, all helped make a legend of him, the dominant musical figure of his place and time, a singer who formulated country music for more than an entire decade, and who has left to that slice of Americana a legacy that may never be matched.

(1923–1953)

Joe Williams

"Not a blues singer, but a singer who sings the blues."

In the mid-1950s, as vocal soloist with the Count Basie band, he sang and recorded a blues, "Every Day I Get the Blues." It not only made him a star; it also lifted the Basie band itself into new and ever-widening circles of popularity.

Joe Williams' yearly reunions with his former boss at the Newport Jazz Festival-New York have sent crowds into near frenzies of pleasure. The moment he comes on stage with Basie's fatherly "Here's my number one son" and starts singing "Every Day," the audiences scream, whistle, and applaud. And when he follows it up with his other well-known hit, "Well, All Right, Okay, You Win," his fans let him know they want him to stay on all night. And so do the Basie musicians. They love his singing, and like many others who have known this warm, unassuming, undemanding man, they love him as a person, too.

Joe is direct, as a man and as a performer. Tall, handsome, his tailoring

"Well, All Right, Okay, You Win! . . ."

always tastefully colorful and sharp, he sings right to his audiences in a baritone voice as supple and rich as ever man possessed. He summons all its resources, including a several-octave range and a buoyant, driving beat, to endow whatever he sings with fresh variations of melody, shadings, and surprise falsetto highs and deep-down lows. Usually identified as a blues singer, he has described himself as "not a blues singer, but a singer who sings the blues."

Joe left the Basie band in 1961 for a career as a single. His vocal eloquence on ballads as well as blues and his performing grace have made him a favorite in festivals, concerts, and sophisticated supper clubs here and abroad. With big bands or small, he is a consummate artist, as all his performances attest— in person, on TV, and on his many recordings with Basie, the Thad Jones-Mel Lewis band, and small-group leaders like George Shearing.

Despite his blues-singer reputation, Joe did not set out to be a blues singer. Born in Cordele, Georgia, he was brought to Chicago at the age of two. An only child, he sang to keep from being lonely, to entertain himself. Later he sang in school events, in his church choir. His mother and aunt also were church choir singers. By age ten he had already begun a life of work, running errands, delivering ice. Years later his mother said, "Joe, you didn't have a very good childhood. You had to work so hard all the time. You never had an electric train."

"That's true," he said. "And another thing I never had was a bicycle."

But he had a voice. Inevitably the entertainment world became aware of him, and before long he was singing pop tunes in Chicago nightclubs. He first encountered the blues in 1938 when he heard Joe Turner, the great Kansas City blues shouter. "He was the first one I could understand," he said. He learned lyrics from Turner and began singing blues himself. His mother came one night to hear him perform. "Where did you learn all that?" she asked in astonishment. She knew he'd never had any of the experiences those blues so pungently described.

In his pre-Basie years, Joe sang with several top jazz leaders such as Jimmie Noone, Coleman Hawkins, Andy Kirk, Lionel Hampton. Kirk recalls a Chicago date: "It was at a club on Dearborn just off Randolph. Joe was sitting at a table with some guests. He'd call a number, we'd put mutes in the horns to make the background nice and soft, and he'd sing right there at the table. He's a beautiful ballad singer." At the 1976 Newport Jazz Festival-New York Joe proved he was even more than that: He sang the dramatic role of John Henry in the world premiere of *Big Man: The Legend of John Henry,* a folk musical by the late Cannonball Adderley and his brother Nat. Can the musical theater now ignore this most expressive, buoyant, and lovable singer of blues, ballads—and folk opera?

(1918–   )

Mary Lou Williams

"No one can put a style on me. I change all the time."

Two parallel threads run through Mary Lou Williams' life—her love of God and her love of her music, jazz.

"Jazz is the greatest religion of them all," the pianist once said. "It's a healer of the mind and the soul. The music tells a story. The story originates in the mind, comes through the heart, and out of the fingertips of the musicians. If the mind stops, there will be no ideas—just patterns. If the heart doesn't do its job, the music will be cold."

Miss Williams has been telling her stories for more than half a century, since she was a child prodigy in Pittsburgh, without ever becoming tied to one period or style.

"No one can put a style on me," she insists. "I change all the time. I experiment to keep up with what is going on, to hear what everybody else is doing. I even keep a little ahead of them, like a mirror that shows what will happen next."

Mary Lou

She learned spirituals and ragtime from her mother. Her own career began to take shape in Kansas City in the late 1920s and early '30s when she was the pianist and arranger in Andy Kirk's Twelve Clouds of Joy.

She built her early career on the blues and boogie-woogie—playing "Froggy Bottom" with the Kirk band, writing "Roll 'Em" for Benny Goodman, and creating her own swinging style on originals such as "Twinklin'." By the time bop came along in the 1940s, Miss Williams had left the Kirk band and was leading her own group at Cafe Society in New York. Her New York apartment became a haven for musicians who were major contributors to this new music— Thelonious Monk, Charlie Parker, Tadd Dameron, Bud Powell, Dizzy Gillespie.

But in the 1950s the music went sour for her. She found greed, selfishness, and envy impinging on her musical world. One night in 1954, while she was playing in a club in Paris, she got up from the piano, walked out of the club, and left the music world.

For three years she spent most of her time praying. In 1956 she became a Catholic and took many of her musician friends into the Church with her. Dizzy Gillespie induced her to emerge from her total immersion in the Church to play with his band at the Newport Jazz Festival in 1957. After that, she moved back and forth intermittently between music and the Church until 1969 when, at the urging of a young Jesuit priest, Peter J. O'Brien, she resumed her musical career full-time, playing in rooms such as the Cookery in New York and composing religious music, including a mass which was performed in St. Patrick's Cathedral in New York in 1975. Then in 1978 she began a three-year artist-in-residence stay at Duke University, teaching a course in jazz to one hundred and fifty students, conducting an eighteen-piece jazz band, with occasional weeks off to play for her admirers throughout the country.

Recently, Miss Williams has been disturbed by some of the music that claims to be an extension of the jazz heritage she helped to build.

"After the bop era, our creativeness and progress stopped," she says, "and the newcomers have lost the heritage that we suffered to create.

"But jazz has never died. And when a new modern sound does come forth, all musicians of the era will practically be born playing it. It will still have to come through the spirituals, ragtime, Kansas City swing and bop eras—but it will be a sound never heard before."

(1910–   )

He drew from his musicians great music, true country jazz.

Western swing: a combination of mountain fiddle, big band drums and reeds, prairie lullabies, black blues, mariachi brass, and cowboy singing; the sound that swept the world of country music—and in many ways the nation—in the late 1930s and throughout the 1940s. Bob Wills personified western swing.

Although he could not claim to have invented it on his own, Bob Wills dominated the entire history of the music, developed most of the outstanding musicians, wrote or co-wrote most of the classic songs, led the greatest band in the history of the genre, the Texas Playboys, and gave spirit, sparkle, and instant identifiability to the style with his wisecracky falsetto asides on record and on the air, and with his world-famous trademark, his uninhibited "Aaaaaah-haaa!"

Short, sometimes stout, a huge hat covering his balding crown, a big cigar clenched in his teeth or in his fingers, the other hand ever on his fiddle, his

Bob Wills (front row center) and his Texas Playboys

black eyes flashing with electric intensity, he brought the most out of his musicians on all occasions, and whether leading a fiddle band or a dance orchestra through "San Antonio Rose," his biggest hit, or any of the other songs that he presented with few frills, but much sincerity, he drew from his musicians great music, true country jazz. What's more, he pioneered the use of drums, horns, and electric guitars and steel guitars in country music.

Bob Wills learned the fiddle "in the place between the rivers" near Turkey, Texas, from his father, the region's top fiddle player. And he was also influenced by the field songs of black sharecroppers who "sang blues you never heard before." Bob soon became a champion old-time fiddler, but the boy who "rode horseback from the place between the rivers to Childress to see Bessie Smith" also sang the blues.

Later, an additional love of Dixieland jazz and of the emerging big band sound led Wills to build the Southwest's best band, the Texas Playboys, a free-spirited, improvisational, and swinging group, that at one point numbered twenty-two musicians, but which still managed to retain the informal, free-flowing feeling of pure country music.

After World War II and the decline of the big bands, Wills reverted to a big fiddle band format. At times he would include horns, but most of the time the solos were played by various guitars.

The 1950s and '60s saw a severe decline in interest in western swing. Then, as the music revived in the mid-1970s, Wills suffered two paralyzing strokes. Still the intensity of his creative, innovative, experimental, aggressive spirit continued to shine forth from his flashing black eyes. As the most famous of his former sidemen, steel guitarist Leon McAuliffe, said: "Bob never did wear out at this. His body wore out before his desire did."

(1905–1975)

Teddy Wilson

Reserved, polite, thoughtful, as sparing with his emotions as with his musical notes.

"The ultimate chamber music musician" is how jazz writer John McDonough described famed jazz pianist Teddy Wilson in a 1977 issue of *Down Beat*. And Benny Goodman, for whom Wilson worked for many years, points out, "What I got out of playing with Teddy was something, in a jazz way, like what I got from playing Mozart in a string quartet."

Both in his personal and musical style, Teddy Wilson has invariably exuded sophistication and class. His playing has reflected his personality: reserved, polite, thoughtful, as sparing with his emotions as with his musical notes, a style described by Leonard Feather as "a neat, quietly swinging symmetry, mostly in single-note lines, that was revolutionary in piano jazz [in the 1930s] and influenced countless musicians." So simple and so direct and so effective has Wilson's approach remained that more than forty years after he first attracted attention,

Teddy

he admitted that "I've made a deliberate effort not to change my foundation—just to keep it polished and refined but not to tamper with it basically."

Teddy Wilson might never have emerged as one of the greatest of all jazz pianists had he been able to play the violin in tune. But he became so discouraged while sawing away as a teenager down in Tuskegee, Alabama, that he switched to the keyboard instrument where poor intonation could be blamed not on the piano player but only on the piano tuner. He continued his musical studies at nearby Tallageda College, and then in 1929 moved to Detroit, where he played in local dance bands. Two years later he moved to Chicago, where he worked with Jimmie Noone, the legendary clarinetist, and with Mike McKendrick's band, which backed Louis Armstrong on several recording dates.

Jazz enthusiast John Hammond heard Wilson and in 1933 sent him money to come to New York to play on a recording date led by Benny Carter. Then, a year later, he convinced Benny Goodman to use the relatively unknown pianist on his nine-piece all-star band's record session. Soon Teddy was receiving further recognition as pianist in Willie Bryant's fine band that also included swing stars Cozy Cole and Ben Webster. They joined Goodman and Roy Eldridge in July 1935 on the first of many historic Teddy Wilson recording sessions, initiated and produced by Hammond, which played a key role in launching the career of a virtually unknown singer, Billie Holiday, who appeared on most of the Wilson band's sides.

Teddy's own career took a giant step forward just eleven days after his own group's first session when Goodman recorded the first sides by the Benny Goodman Trio, consisting of Goodman, Wilson, and Gene Krupa, a group that not only played exceptional parlor-type jazz, but which also played a prominent role in breaking down racial barriers. Wilson stayed with Goodman until 1939, when he left to form his own band. Despite some superb arrangements written by Wilson (they so impressed Duke Ellington that he invited Teddy to write for his band—a compliment rarely accorded any arranger), the band lasted only a year. From 1940 to 1944, Teddy led a sextet, and then in 1945 he began concentrating more on teaching at the Juilliard and Manhattan schools of music. He also held staff jobs at radio stations WNEW and WCBS and kept appearing with Goodman in concerts, though their friendship gradually diminished as each tried to preserve his reputation as "champion buck-watcher."

From the 1960s on, Wilson concertized extensively as a soloist, appearing often in the Far East, in Europe, and of course in the United States, performing, it seemed, whenever and wherever he was asked to. And why not? "I still enjoy playing," the then sixty-four-year-old Wilson told writer McDonough in 1977. "What I do for money is exactly what I do for pleasure."

(1912–   )

Stevie Wonder

"I learned who loved me and I learned about those who just said, 'Is he gonna be able to work again?' "

He was born prematurely (he speculates that his blindness may have been caused by "too much oxygen in the incubator") and he's been ahead of his time ever since.

At the age of four, he was playing piano; at five, a toy key-chain harmonica; after that, the drums. His playground was Detroit's east-side ghetto. When he was nine, Ronnie White—a member of the Miracles and big brother of a playmate—introduced him to the center of the local musical action: Motown. It was 1960, and the black record label was just taking off.

Stevie Morris, as he was known then (his full name: Steveland Judkins Morris), began hanging out at the recording studio after school, playing original music on every instrument he could get his hands on. It didn't take Motown long to start recording and promoting their precocious rock and roller as Little Stevie Wonder. When his "Fingertips Part 2" became his first gold record, he was just thirteen.

Stevie's parents treated him just like their four sighted children, even sending him to public schools. But when he became a featured performer, recording and traveling by bus, with the Motown Revue, to appearances at black clubs and theaters all over the country, a private tutor was provided. In the late 1960s he attended the Michigan School for the Blind, where he was exposed for the first time to classical music. "Bein' blind ain't no big problem for me," he has claimed. He watches (or listens to) TV, reads Braille, shops for clothes, even flew an airplane once ("scared the hell out of everybody"). He is constantly telling interviewers how very lucky he considers himself to be. "I don't like to speak of the unfortunate things I went through."

Beginning with *Signed, Sealed and Delivered,* in 1970, Wonder produced a series of increasingly ambitious albums, many in collaboration with his (now former) wife, singer-songwriter Syreeta Wright. When at twenty-one he acquired access to a million-dollar trust account, he rented a recording studio and taped himself as a veritable one-man band, playing piano, drums, harmonica, organ, clavichord, ARP-wired clavinet, and synthesizers, and singing lead and background vocals. The resulting album, *Music on My Mind,* released in 1972, proved to be a virtuoso performance.

Acceptance of the album won Wonder a new contract that allowed him to

Stevie

write and produce for himself, to book his own concerts, to free-lance as he wished. As the opening act in the 1972 Rolling Stones tour of North America, he gained a huge new white following and entrée to more prestigious concert dates, such as Carnegie Hall.

All the while, he was breaking new musical ground in albums such as *Talking Book,* which included the Grammy-winning "You Are the Sunshine of My Life," and *Innervisions,* which won two Grammys, and included "Don't You

Worry 'Bout a Thing." Suddenly, in August 1973, there was plenty to worry about. Stevie suffered severe head injuries in an auto accident and lay in a coma for nearly a week. "I learned who loved me," he says, "and I learned about those who just said, 'Is he gonna be able to work again?' " The accident left him with minor facial scars and a "deeper outlook" on life. He felt, he said, "really peaceful inside for the first time." And he also noted, "The important things in life are the things you feel inside and don't have to rehearse. They just come out."

Following his recovery, Stevie produced his *Fulfillingness First Finale* album, which won several Grammys, one of which he asked to be presented to the family of his idol, the recently deceased Duke Ellington. Then the flow of recordings stopped, and Stevie announced that he planned to move to Africa, "to find out what it's all about, and to find out about the history of its music."

But by the second half of the 1970s, he was still living in Los Angeles with Yolanda Simmons, his secretary, bookkeeper, and the mother of his year-old daughter, Aisha Zakia, whose name means strength and intelligence. By late 1976 he had completed another album, the most ambitious of all his works, *Songs in the Key of Life,* a double LP with twenty-one original cuts, which drew critical raves everywhere. Writing in *People,* Jim Jerome described it as "the affirmation of Wonder's overpowering genius as a composer, lyricist, musician, singer, and producer . . . Lyrically, the LP expresses the Wonder of it all, Stevie's still-innocent yearning for the universe of love: 'If it's magic, why can't we make it everlasting . . . there's enough for everyone.' "

Wonder's extraordinary, multifaceted talent once led Sammy Davis, Jr., to compare his influence on music today to "what Orson Welles was to the movies when he made *Citizen Kane.*" Stevie sees himself more modestly. "My music," he says, "is my way of giving back love."

(1950–   )

Tammy Wynette

Classic repressed country soul.

"I think it's a God-sent blessing I know how to do a *little* bit with hair or I never would have made it on the road," says Tammy Wynette, easily the most famous graduate of McGuire School of Beauty in Tupelo, Mississippi.

The former Wynette Pugh, of Itawamba County, Mississippi, cherished two impossible dreams as she diligently learned to tint, curl, and set: to become a country singer and to meet her idol George Jones, whose moving, pain-haunted voice had earned him the reputation as a country singer's singer.

Not only in Hollywood, but also in Nashville these dreams do sometimes come true. With Loretta Lynn, Tammy developed into one of the top female country singers in terms of all indices: popularity, income, and record sales. And she survived several years of a sometimes blissful, often rocky marriage (which ended in divorce) to her onetime idol George Jones.

Tammy cut her first record in 1966, and shortly thereafter came under the guidance of Nashville's producer with the Midas touch, Billy Sherrill. From their association on Epic Records came "Apartment Number Nine," "I Don't Wanna Play House," and her two giants, "D-I-V-O-R-C-E" and "Stand By Your Man." Both were million-sellers in the country field, and both received a great deal of attention in the film *Five Easy Pieces*. "Monsters"—as the Nashville record industry tends to call them—such as these didn't come Tammy's way over the following years, but she remained a consistent big seller (by herself or in duet with Jones) all the same, and her on-again-off-again marriage to Jones kept her name before the rabid fans.

The Tammy Wynette style—visually and aurally—has been classic repressed country soul. On stage she is so stiff she seems unable to move a muscle, her face a frozen mask of nonexpression. In direct contrast is her voice: not beautiful but intensely moving, breaking with emotion, rising to intense crescendos, falling back to heartbroken whispers; registering the gamut of emotion from loss to anguish, then to anger and determination. Rarely has a light song entered her repertoire, her gut-wrenching voice too fine an instrument to waste on the emotionally trivial. "I prefer ballads," she explained. "I have to have a certain amount of up-tempos for the show, but I can just put more *feelin'* into a ballad."

It was a big change for the little Mississippi hairdresser turned one of the reigning queens of country music. The history of the genre is full of tales of those who made the sudden leap to stardom and couldn't cope: Williams, Frizzell, a score of others. Tammy Wynette, however, seemed to have a handle on things;

Tammy

in fact, her role in their well-publicized (perhaps *too* well-publicized) marriage was that of placator of the wilder of George Jones's impulses. Level-headed and calm, she was able to chart the course of her career with sense and care.

But that voice, that heartstring-tugging voice. Depending on how well her material holds up to historical scrutiny—there is the tendency to blandness of song and to overproduction—history may well view Tammy Wynette not only as a long-popular star, but also as one of the finest and most expressive country singers of all time.

(1942–   )

Lester Young

"By the time I'd packed up my drums, all the pretty girls had left."

It was Billie Holiday who dubbed Lester Young "Pres," short for "President." Bestowed at the height of F. D. R.'s popularity, the nickname was fitting indeed, for with his refreshingly cool approach to jazz, he presided over the second generation of tenor saxophonists as the hotter-sounding Coleman Hawkins had dominated the first. He was, in fact, the earliest influence on the development of what became known as "cool jazz."

Lester's father, a well-schooled musician who played all the instruments and led a touring family band during the 1920s in the still-surviving minstrel tradition, taught his son trumpet, violin, saxophone, and even drums, which he made young Lester play from the time he was ten. Five years later, for extramusical reasons ("By the time I'd packed up my drums, all the pretty girls had left"), Lester switched to sax. By then, the family had moved from New Orleans to Minneapolis, and three years later, when his father insisted on touring Texas, the shy and sensitive boy, who detested the racial mores of the south, went off on his own.

For six years he barnstormed around the Midwest and Southwest. He finally latched on to Count Basie's first band, playing alto sax, then switched to tenor when Fletcher Henderson called on him to replace Hawkins. But he quit after three months because the other musicians tried to get him to play like his illustrious predecessor.

Young's style was in fact the antithesis of Hawkins'. He played without vibrato, employed a lighter, purer tone, and phrased in a manner based on even rather than dotted notes. Basie's band, to which he soon returned, provided an ideal setting for his new and fresh ideas, and when, in 1936, the band made its first records, Lester's innovative solos made a lasting impact on other musicians.

He also collaborated with Billie Holiday, with whom he became very close personally, on a series of masterpieces that rank with the greatest jazz on record. Though critics and Hawkins-followers were slow to accept his innovations, which to some deviated too far from the accepted norm, some young musicians, among them Charlie Parker and later Stan Getz, were profoundly touched. Along with Charlie Christian, the equally creative guitarist, Young had begun to lay the foundations with their harmonic explorations of what would become bebop.

Personal rather than musical disagreements with Basie, who demanded more discipline than Young wanted to live by, led to Lester's leaving the band in 1940. He formed his own group, worked for the USO, then returned to Basie

Pres

for a short time before being drafted into the Army, a career for which he was particularly unsuited. Trusting, and perhaps too naïve, he answered "yes" to an army questionnaire concerning the use of marijuana, whereupon a "cracker" officer railroaded him into a five-year jail sentence. This was commuted, but Lester was scarred for life.

Always an introvert, he began to retreat further into himself, becoming more and more eccentric. Although his music had helped to make bop possible, he began, upon his return to civilian life, to feel eclipsed by the new style and its players. His dependency on liquor and his blue moods increased. His health declined and his playing suffered, though at times he was still capable of those great bursts of creativity that had inspired and set the standards for many future jazz musicians. When the "Pres" died in his fiftieth year, there just was no "Vice-Pres" to succeed him—he was that much of an original.

(1909–1959)

Frank Zappa

The cult hero of weirdo theater-jazz-rock.

"I've always wanted to have an eighty-piece rock and roll band with at least twenty guitars, eight percussion, eight brass, six keyboards, three basses, and a raft of singers," Frank Zappa insisted in the mid-1970s. Was he serious, or was this just another put-on by the musician/singer/conductor/composer/arranger/actor whom the New York *Times*'s John Rockwell has called "the cult hero of weirdo theater-jazz-rock"?

Who knows? Zappa admits he loves to put people on. "It makes them listen, and, besides, I have fun doing it." And so, in addition to his music, which at times has been startlingly impressive, he has concentrated on numerous gimmicks like weird costumes, loony props, sometimes scandalous lyrics, and often ear-splitting sound levels. The contrast between Zappa, the sensitive musician, and Zappa, the diabolical showman, was never more evident than at a late-1960s Grammy awards dinner. During rehearsal, his group, the Mothers of Invention, delivered fifteen minutes of charming, very musical sounds—just what the producers had requested. But for the actual performance before an audience filled with musical celebrities, Zappa and Co. pulled their "put-on" act, relentlessly pounding out a half hour of such distressingly ugly, often infantile, undisciplined nonsense that some guests walked out while others simply wondered what sort of drugs the group was on.

Zappa claims that he never uses drugs, though he admits that the title of his first big album, *Freak Out*, describes many of his fans. He himself has been turned on by music since he began playing drums at the age of twelve and guitar at eighteen. Unusually bright and self-reliant, he holed up in libraries, studying various forms of music while avoiding music schools because "they teach you technique, but they don't tell you how to use it."

His breadth of musical activity is impressive. He is a first-rate guitarist, has written an original ballet, *Lumpy Gravy*, conducted members of the London Symphony in Royal Albert Hall, and composed what he calls "a ponderous orchestral absurdity" that was debuted by the Los Angeles Philharmonic conducted by Zubin Mehta and became the basis of a Zappa-produced film, *200 Motels*, featuring the London Philharmonic and Ringo Starr!

In assessing Zappa's involved musical scores, former symphony percussionist Terry Bozio has noted, "The hardest of classical music I'd been playing was comparable to Frank's easier works."

Does Zappa compose especially difficult music just to "put on" musicians?

Nobody knows for sure. However, he does enjoy their respect, while he, in turn, responds to good musicianship, notably that of the better jazz artists. And yet the total effect of his music can sometimes be diminished by his obsession with irreverence. To some it reflects the antisocial mood of the 1960s, when Zappa's Mothers of Invention first gained recognition. Perhaps it mirrors more accurately his repudiation of what he considers the music business' preoccupation with "merchandising images that must be taken seriously rather than with the music itself."

Zappa recently confessed to the *Times*'s Rockwell how much he hated to try to conform to the demands of recording companies and AM radio stations in order to achieve success. "I love to write music, to record it, to play guitar," he insisted, "and to make people laugh and jump up and down at a concert."

Is that all?

Only Zappa knows.

(1940–   )

Zappa